Facsimile [illegible] Thomas [illegible] [illegible] [illegible] p 37

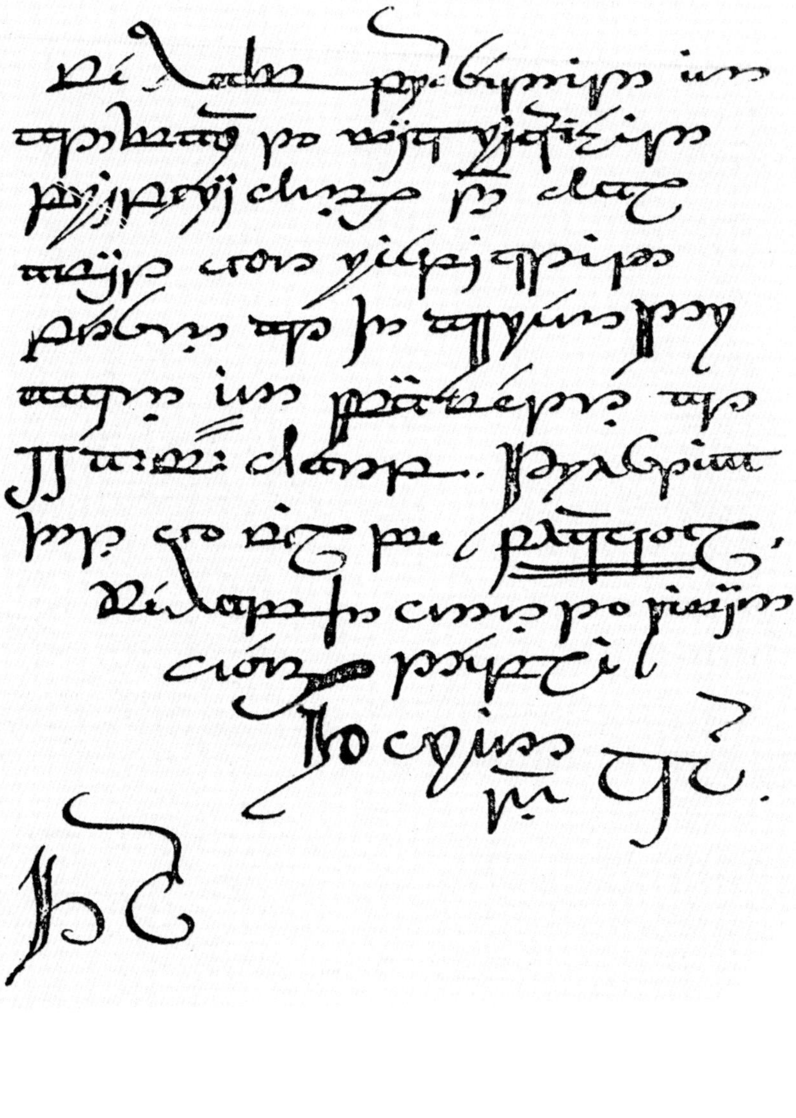

THE HISTORY OF THE HOBBIT

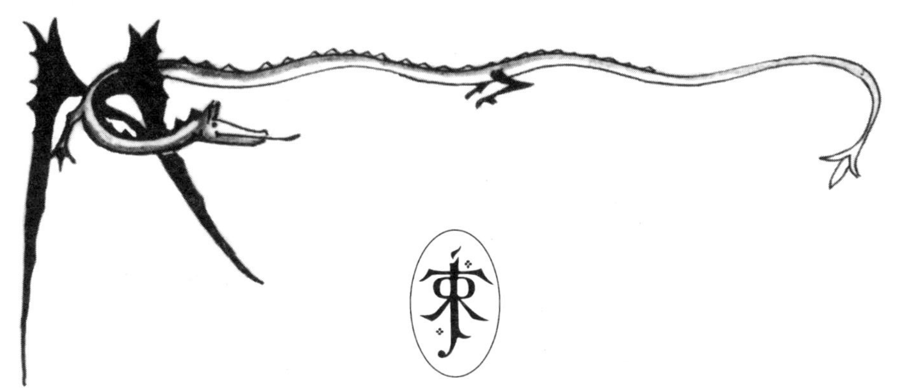

The History of The Hobbit

Part Two: Return to Bag-End

John D. Rateliff

HarperCollins*Publishers*

HarperCollinsPublishers
77–85 Fulham Palace Road,
Hammersmith, London W6 8JB
www.tolkien.co.uk

Published by HarperCollins*Publishers* 2007
1

ISBN-10 0-00-725066-5
ISBN-13 978-0-00-725066-0

Set in PostScript Monotype Plantin by
Rowland Phototypesetting Ltd, Bury St Edmunds, Suffolk

Printed and bound by Clays Ltd, St Ives plc

CONTENTS

THE SECOND PHASE
[continued]

Chapter XI
THE LONELY MOUNTAIN

As before, the story continues without chapter break, in this case near the bottom of manuscript page 136 (1/1/12:1). This brief chapter is written quickly, with many abbreviations ('R. Running') and minor errors or omissions, which I have for the most part silently expanded or corrected. Perhaps significantly, it is a fairly clean text, with relatively few changes made in the course of composition; thanks to the brief sketch of these events in Plot Notes B (see pp. 362–3), Tolkien knew what he wanted to happen in this part of the story and seems to have simply concentrated on getting it down in full without for the moment worrying about details of phrasing.

They rowed right up it in two days' <journey> and passed out into the River Running, and saw now the Mountain towering grim and tall before them. The stream was strong and their going slow. At the end of the third day some miles up the River Running they halted on the bank to their left, the West bank, and disembarked. Here a store of provisions and other necessarys was made, but no men would stay there so near the shadow of the Mountain.[TN1]

'Not at any [rate] until the songs had come true' said they. Still there was no need for any guard. The lands were wide and empty. Here they joined the horses that had been sent for them; and bade farewell to their escort. The next day packing what they could carry on horseback they set out, Bilbo riding with Balin on one horse, leading another heavily laden beside them; the others were ahead in single file, picking [*added*: out] a slow road. They made due North, slanting away from the River Running and drawing nearer & nearer to a great spur of the Mountain that was flung out Southward towards them.

It was a weary journey, and a quiet and stealthy one. There was no laughter or song, and the pride and hopes which had stirred in all their hearts (esp. Thorin's) at the singing of the old songs by the lake had died away to a plodding gloom. They knew they were drawing near to the end of their journey – and that it might be a very horrible end. The land grew barren, though once, as Thorin said, it had been green and fair. There was little grass. Soon there were neither bush nor tree, and only broken stumps to speak of ones long vanished.

They were come to the desolation of the Dragon, and they were come at the waning of the year.

They reached the skirts of the mountain without meeting serious danger, all the same. There was no sign of the dragon. The mountain lay dark and silent before them, and ever more above them. They made their first settled camp on the lowest slopes of the great southern spur – I have marked it on the copy of Thror's map; as he did himself, though of course it was not there when Bladorthin had it.[TN2] Before setting out to search the western slopes for the hidden door, on which all their hopes rested, Thorin sent out a scouting expedition to spy out the land to the east by the Front Gate. Bilbo went with them – and Balin and Fili and Kili. After a couple of days of silent journey they came back to the Running River, which here took a [?sudden >] great western turn and flowed towards the mountain, which stretched out great arms to meet it. The bank was rocky, tall, and steep here, and gazing out from the brink, over the narrow river, foaming and splashing over boulders, they could see in a wide valley shadowed by the mountain's arms, the grey ruins far-off of ancient [?towers >] houses, towers, and walls.

'There lies all that is left of Dale' said Balin. 'The mountain's sides were green with woods then, and all this valley rich and sheltered.' He looked both sad and grim as he said this: he had been one of Thorin's companions on the day the Dragon came.[TN3] They did not dare to follow the river much further towards the gate; but they went on until lying hidden behind a rock they could look out, and see the dark cavernous opening in a great wall between the mountain's arms, out of which the water ran. And out of which too there was coming steam and a dark smoke. Nothing else moved in the waste, save the vapour and the river [> water], and every now and again a dark and ominous raven. The only sound was the sound of stony water, and every now and again a raven's croak. Balin shuddered. 'Let us return' he said. 'We can do no good here! And I do not like those dark birds; they look like spies of evil'.[TN4]

'The dragon is still alive and in the halls under the Mountain then?' said the hobbit. 'Or I imagine so from the smoke'.

'That doesn't prove it' said Balin; 'though I don't doubt you are right. But he might be gone [*added*: away] some time, and [> or] he might be lying on the mountain's-side watching us [> keeping watch], and still I expect smokes and steams would come out of the gates because of the heat he leaves behind'.

With such gloomy thoughts, followed ever by croaking ravens, they made their weary way back to the others and the camp. A year and more had passed since they had been guests at the fair house of

Elrond, in June; and now the summer of the year after was drawing to a bleak end, and they were alone in the perilous waste.[TN5] They were at the end of their journey, but as far as ever it seemed from the end of their quest. None of them had much spirit left.

Now strange to say Bilbo had more than any of them. He would often borrowed Thorin's map and gaze at it, pondering the runes, and the message of the moon-letters Elrond had read.[TN6] It was he who made them begin the dangerous search upon the western slopes for the secret door.[TN7] They moved their camp to a long valley deeper and narrower than that one where stood the great gates of the River, but hemmed in with lower spurs. Two of these here [sprouted >] thrust forward West from the main mass of the mountain, great long ridges with steep sides, [that] fell ever downwards towards the plain. Here there was less sign of the dragon's marauding feet, and there was grass for their ponies.[TN8] From their second camp, shadowed all day by cliff and wall until the sun began to sink west towards the forest, day by day they toiled in parties seeking for paths up the mountain side. If the map was true somewhere high above the cliff at the valley head must stand the secret door, now their only hope. Day by day they came back weary to the camp without success.

But at last they found what they were seeking. Fili and Kili and the hobbit went back one day near to the [end of the >] Southern corner of the valley, and here scrambling up some loose rocks they came suddenly on what looked like rough steps. Following these excitedly they came upon traces of a narrow track, often lost, often found again, that wandered onto the top of the sunken ridge and brought them at last to a narrow ledge. This turned north and looking down they saw they were at the top of the [valley >] cliff at the valley head, looking down on their own camp below.[TN9] Silently, clinging to the rocky wall on their right they went in single file along the ledge till the wall opened and they turned into a little steep walled bay, grassy floored, still and quiet. At its end a flat wall rose up at its lower part close to the ground as smooth and upright as man's work, but without a joint or crack. No sign was there of post nor lintel nor threshold; no sign of bar or bolt or key. Yet they did not doubt they had found the door at last. They beat on it, and they pushed, they implored it to open, they spoke fragments of broken magic, and nothing stirred. At last tired out they rested before their long climb down.[TN10]

There was excitement in the camp that night. In the morning they prepared to move. Bofur and Bombur were left behind to guard the ponies and the stores. The others went down the valley, and up the newly found path, and so to the narrow ledge, along which they cd. have carried no bundles or packs, so narrow and breathless was it, with a fall of a hundred and fifty feet beside them. But each of them carried a coil of rope tight about his waist. And so they reached the little grassy bay.[TN11]

There they made their third camp, hauling up what they needed by <knotted> ropes. Down the same way one or two of the most active, such as Fili, would go back from time to time to the valley, [and tell the others > Bofur and Bombur > of what was >] and bring such news as there was, or take a share in the guard, while Bofur climbed to the higher camp. Bombur would not go. 'I am too fat for such fly-paths' he said. 'I should [tread on a >] turn dizzy and tread on my beard and then you would be thirteen again!' Some of them explored the ledge beyond the opening and found a way leading higher onto the mountain; but that way they did not dare to go far.[TN12] Nor was there much use in it. All the while a silence reigned, broken by no bird or voice, nothing except the wind. They spoke low, and never shouted nor sang, for danger brooded in every rock.

Nor did they succeed in discovering the secret of the door, or where exactly it was in the flat face of rock. [*added in margin*: They had brought picks and tools of many sorts from Lake Town. But they soon gave up trying these on this part of the rock. Their handles splintered and jarred their arms with <illegible>, or the steel heads bent like lead. Mining work was no good at all.] Bilbo found that sitting on the doorstep [*added*: wearisome] – there wasn't one of course, really, but they used to call the little grassy space between the door and the opening onto the cliff edge 'the doorstep' in fun, remembering Bilbo's words long ago at the party in the hobbit-hole, that [they] could sit on the doorstep till they thought of something. And sit and think they did, or wandered aimlessly about, and glummer and glummer they became. Their spirits had risen a little, at the discovery of the path; but now they sank into their boots, and yet they wd. not give up and go away. The hobbit was no longer much brighter than the dwarves. He would do nothing but sit with his back to the rock face staring away West through the opening over the cliff over the wide lands to the black wall of Mirkwood and the blue distances beyond in which he sometimes thought he cd. catch glimpses of the Misty Mountains.

'You said sitting on the doorstep [*added*: & thinking] would be my job, not to mention getting inside the door', said he, 'so I am sitting and thinking'. But I am afraid he was not often thinking of the job, but of what lay beyond the blue distances, the western land and The Hill and his hobbit-hole under it. A large grey stone lay in the centre of the grass, and he stared moodily at it; or watched the great snails that seemed to love this little shut in bay with its rocky wall [> sides] crawl slow and stickily along the sides.

'Autumn will be in tomorrow' said Thorin one day.

'And winter comes after autumn' said Bifur.

'And next year after that' said Dwalin. 'And our beards will grow till they hang down the cliff to the ground, before anything happens here.[TN13]

What is our Burglar doing for us! Seeing he has got an invisible ring and so ought to be a specially excellent performer, I am beginning to think he ought to go through the Front Gate, and spy things out a bit.'

Bilbo heard this – he was on the rocks up above the enclosure. 'Good gracious!' thought he '– So that's what they are beginning to think are they? What ever am I going to do. I might have known something dreadful would happen to me in the end. I don't think I could bear to see the ruined valley of Dale again, and as for that steam<ing> gate –.'

That night he was very miserable and hardly slept. Next day the dwarves went wandering off in various directions. Some were exercising the ponies down below; some were on the mountain side. All day Bilbo sat gloomily in the grassy bay gazing at the stone or out West through the opening.[TN14] He had a queer feeling that he was waiting for something. 'Perhaps the wizard will suddenly come back to day' he thought.[TN15]

He could see then a glimpse of the forest. As the sun turned west there was a gleam of yellow light upon its distant roof, going brown towards autumn. Suddenly [> At last] he saw the orange sun sinking towards the level of his eyes. He went to the opening and there pale and faint was a thin new moon above the rim of the earth. At that very moment he heard a sharp crack behind him. There on the [*added*: grey] stone in the grass was a large thrush, nearly coal black its pale yellow breast freckled with dark spots. Crack. it had caught a snail and was knocking it on the stone. Crack, crack!

Suddenly Bilbo understood. Forgetting all caution he stood on the ledge and hailed the dwarves, shouting and waving. Those that were nearest came tumbling over the rocks to him, wondering what on earth was happening, the others made for the path from the valley as fast as ever they could. You can just picture Bilbo standing now beside the thrushes' stone, and the dwarves with wagging beards watching excitedly by the walls. The sun sank lower and lower. Then their hopes fell. It sank into a belt of red-stained clouds and disappeared. The dwarves groaned, but still Bilbo stood almost without moving. The little moon was dipping to the [river >] horizon. Evening was coming on. Then suddenly when their hope was lowest, a red ray of the sun escaped like a finger through a rent in the bars of cloud. A gleam of light came straight through the opening in the bay, and fell on the smooth rock face. [There was a loud crack >] The old thrush which had been watching from a high perch with beady eyes [& head] cocked on one side gave a sudden trill. There was a loud crack. A flake of rock split from the face and fell. A hole appeared suddenly about three feet from the ground.

Quickly trembling lest the chance shd fade [Thorin fitted >] the dwarves rushed to the rock and pushed. 'A key a key' said Bilbo 'we need a key'.

'But we have no keys' said the desperate dwarves.

'Gandalf[TN16] gave me my father's map not keys of his' said Thorin. 'Gandalf – '

'Gandalf!' said Bilbo. 'He gave us [> you] the troll-keys.[TN17] Try them quick. You never know'.

Thorin stepped up and fitted [> put] in the only key that was small enough. It fitted it turned. Snap! and the sun gleam went out, the sun sank, and evening sprang into the sky. The moon was gone.

Now they all pushed together, and slowly a part of the rock-wall gave way. Long straight cracks appeared and widened. A door five feet high and three broad was outlined,[TN18] and slowly without a noise swung inwards. It almost seemed as if darkness flowed out like a vapour from the mountain side; deep darkness in which nothing could be seen lay before their eyes, a mouth leading in and down.

The manuscript continues on the same page (manuscript page 142; 1/1/13:1), but after the next sentence (see page 504) the ink becomes noticeably darker, indicating at least a brief pause in composition.

TEXT NOTES

1 This store of provisions would later become important; see Plot Notes E ('Little Bird'), a hasty half-page of notes describing Tolkien's original conception of the Siege of the Mountain, page 626.

2 This 'camp' can be seen, in exactly the position described here, on Fimbulfambi's Map (see the Frontispiece to Part One: *Mr Baggins*). It also appears on Thror's Map I (Plate I [top]), which follows the earliest map very closely. However, it is probable that this and other details were added to Fimbulfambi's Map long after the Pryftan Fragment was originally drafted, as part of the drafting for Thror's Map I, and thus dates from the time the latter was created. The location of the camp does not appear on the final map (Thror's Map II, DAA.97) that appeared in the published book.

Note that *Bladorthin* is still the name of the wizard here – that is, although 'Gandalf' had been dropped as the name of the chief dwarf before Chapter X was written, it was not immediately transferred to the wizard, although that would in fact occur later in this same 'chapter'; see Text Note 16 below.

3 This is our first indication that Balin, like Thorin, is a survivor of 'the day the Dragon came'. Taken altogether, his is perhaps the most eventful life of any dwarf on record, rivaled only by the great Dain Ironfoot. He was not only one of the few† who survived Smaug's attack upon the Lonely Mountain and the destruction of the dwarven Kingdom there but almost certainly also fought in the Battle of Azanulbizar to avenge Thror's murder, where the death rate among the dwarven combatants approached 50% (a casualty rate exceeding that of the Battle of the Somme) – not only did his father die there but Balin is mentioned as being among Thrain's and Thorin's company immediately after the battle (cf. *LotR*.1113). He accompanied Thrain on his ill-fated quest that ended with Durin's heir imprisoned in the dungeons of the Necromancer (*LotR*.1114), fought alongside Thorin in the Battle of Five Armies (see page 672), and finally reconquered Moria for a time and reclaimed the crown of Durin himself (*LotR*.258 & 338–41).

All this is all the more remarkable because according to the family tree presented in 'Durin's Folk' (*LotR* Appendix A part iii), Balin would have been only seven years old at the time of Smaug's attack and thus an unlikely candidate to be a companion of the twenty-four-year-old Thorin. This is obviously too young to match the information given in *The Hobbit* by at least a decade and probably more; while it is implied that Balin must be younger than Thorin from a remark in Chapter IX ('"What have we done, O king?" said Balin, the oldest left now that Gandalf [Thorin] was gone' – cf. page 380 and Text Note 4 to Chapter IX), there's no indication that they're separated by more than a few years, nor any descriptions of Thorin to indicate that he is or looks old (unlike Balin, who from the first description of him on Bilbo's doorstep is 'a very old-looking dwarf' with a white beard, and whose age is reinforced by the many references to him throughout the story as 'old Balin'). By the official reckoning of *The Lord of the Rings*, Balin was thirty-six at the time of the Battle before Moria (when Dain, described as 'only a stripling', was himself thirty-two). He and his brother Dwalin – the latter not even born at the time of Smaug's attack – must therefore have been among the youngest members of Thrain's expedition, being at that time seventy-eight and sixty-nine respectively; compare Fili and Kili from Thorin's group, constantly referred to as youngsters, who are eighty-two and seventy-seven respectively, and Gimli, who at sixty-two was considered too young to accompany his father Glóin on Bilbo's adventure ('The Quest of Erebor', *Unfinished Tales* page 336 and DAA.376). At the time of his death in Moria, King Balin is officially two hundred and thirty-one, a respectable age considering that Thror, who is described as 'old' and 'crazed perhaps with age' (*LotR*.1110) is not that much older at the time of his murder (two hundred and forty-eight), nor is the 'old' and 'venerable' Dain (*LotR*.245), whom Gandalf describes as being of a 'great age' (two hundred and fifty-one;

LotR.1116). In fact, given the unlikelihood that he was only seven when the Kingdom under the Mountain fell or merely a dignified one hundred and seventy-eight at the time of Thorin's quest (when Thorin, who is never described as old, is himself one hundred and ninety-five), Balin was probably at least two hundred and forty at the time of his death and possibly, if we discount the reference in Chapter IX, much older; Thorin, had he lived, would then have been two hundred and forty-eight, the same age as old Thror at the time of his murder. See also *The Peoples of Middle-earth*, HME XII.284–5 & 288 for more on dwarven longevity.

†In the original conception as described in *The Hobbit*, it is clear that very few indeed escaped Smaug's attack, only Thror and Thrain (through the secret door) and 'the few' who like Thorin and Balin were outside at the time. When Tolkien revisited the history of the dwarves while constructing Appendix A of *LotR*, he greatly increased the number of survivors, stating (in contradiction to the account in *The Hobbit*) that 'many' of Thrór's kin escaped, including not just his son Thráin and grandson Thorin but Thorin's younger brother Frerin (later killed at the Mines of Moria) and his sister Dís (then only a child of ten, later the mother of Fíli and Kíli); furthermore, they were joined with 'a small company of their kinsmen and faithful followers' – the former including presumably Balin and his parents (Dwalin's having not yet been born until two years later indicates that their unnamed mother survived the disaster, and his father Fundin being among Thrain's company at the disastrous battle of Moria). A footnote adds that 'It was afterwards learned that more of the Folk under the Mountain had escaped than was at first hoped; but most of these went to the Iron Hills.' – *LotR*.1110.

4 Balin's distaste and distrust for the ravens shows that the idea of the ancient friendship between the dwarves and the ravens of the mountain had not yet arisen – there being no reference to conversations with either ravens or crows in Plot Notes B, nor in Plot Notes C (which followed immediately upon the writing of this chapter). There is however a very important reference to a crow in the earliest draft of the moon-runes passage all the way back in the Pryftan Fragment, where the secret writing had read 'Stand by the grey stone when the crow knocks and the rising sun at the moment of dawn on Durin's Day will shine upon the keyhole', but this had quickly been changed to a thrush (see page 22).

Crows do appear in Plot Notes D, but it seems that there the dwarves overhear the carrion fowl speaking rather than meet with them (see page 571). Not until Tolkien comes to write the last few pages of the Second Phase manuscript, the first third or so of what became Chapter XV – the last bit of writing Tolkien completed before breaking off the Second Phase and returning to the beginning of the story to create the First Typescript – do the ravens finally appear, with such suddenness that Bilbo himself comments upon it (see page 618). It is possible that they first appeared in the lost drafting of which the only surviving fragment is the half-page upon the back of which Tolkien jotted down Plot Notes E ('Little Bird'); at any rate, having introduced them as friends and allies of the dwarves, Tolkien initially projected the ravens of the mountain to play a larger part in the Siege; see page 626.

Since ravens appear in that later scene as much more sympathetic figures than those described here, Tolkien recast this passage in several stages to remove the incongruity. Thus 'a dark and ominous raven' becomes in the First Typescript 'a black and ominous crow' (1/1/61:2), while 'every now and again a raven's croak' becomes 'every now and again the harsh croak of a crow', which in turn at some point after the Second Typescript was made is changed to 'croak of a bird' (ibid. & 1/1/42:2). However, just a few paragraphs later 'followed ever by croaking ravens' was changed to 'by croaking crows and ravens', which did not resolve the problem at all. This latter reading survived into the page proofs (Marq. 1/2/2 page 211), where the words 'and ravens' was deleted (and 'above them' inserted so that the following lines would not need to be reset), thereby achieving the wording in the published book.

5 Tolkien originally wrote 'A year or more had passed since they had been guests at the fair house of Elrond, in June. The next . . .' before striking out the last two words and replacing the period with a semicolon and continuing '. . . and now [*added*: the] summer of the year after was drawing to a bleak end'. Once again, we see the more leisurely time-frame of the original draft is still in place; rather than it only being five or six months since their setting out as in the published book, here it is fifteen months or more since Bilbo left his hobbit-hole.

In the First Typescript (1/1/61:2), this passage was replaced with

> . . . made their weary way back to the camp. Only in June they had been guests in the fair house of Elrond, and though autumn was now crawling towards winter that pleasant time now seemed years ago. They were alone in the perilous waste without hope of further help. . . .

See also Text Note 13.

6 In the text of Chapter II (page 116), these had read 'Stand by the grey stone where the thrush knocks. Then the rising [> setting] sun on the last light of Durin's Day will shine upon the key hole'. This is very similar to the revised text that appears on Fimbulfambi's map; see page 22.

7 This sentence was originally followed by an unfinished sentence beginning '[One day they >] Day by day they would toil in small parties up the lower slopes and'; a revised form of this sentence appears later in the paragraph.

8 This is the point at which the 'horses' described in the final paragraph of the preceding chapter and the opening paragraphs of this chapter become instead 'ponies', in keeping with Thorin and Company's two previous sets of mounts (cf. pages 89 & 131, and 241–3). Despite much

equivocation in later chapters, where Tolkien would occasionally write 'horses' and then alter it to 'ponies', they remained ponies henceforth.

9 This passage seems to ignore the idea, stated back in Chapter VI, that Bilbo is afraid of heights; see page 209 and Text Note 32 for Chapter VI. Possibly we are meant to conclude that Bilbo has simply learned how to face his fears better after his experiences in Mirkwood.

10 Later Tolkien created a schematic drawing of the mountain to help clarify the relationship of the first camp, second camp, hidden high path, and grassy bay hiding the secret door; see Plate II [top]. The second camp seems to be displaced in this illustration from the position described in the text; since 'looking down on their own camp below' suggests it was directly below the cliff they were atop – i.e., nestled against the right-hand spur (that is, the more southernly of the mountain's two short western spurs), not off on the other side of the valley below the left-hand (more northernly) spur, especially since they continue on past this point to reach the hidden bay at the head of the valley.

11 In the original (cancelled) drafting of this passage, the sequence of events was slightly more complicated:

> Bofur and Bombur were left below with the ponies. The rest carrying all they could went back by the newly found path, and came to the narrow ledge. But they could not carry bundles nor packs along there – as [they >] they ought to have thought of before. But luckily they had <illegible> brought ropes, a long coil each [slung over their >] about their waists. With these they lowered their packs.
> Bifur and Bomfur <sic>

Aside from the miscalculation of bringing baggage inappropriate to the route and the narrator's unsympathetic comment thereon, and the curious portmanteau combination of Bofur's and Bombur's names, the only significant difference here from the published text is Tolkien's apparent hesitation over whether Bifur or Bofur would be the dwarf who stayed below with Bombur.

12 Since Thorin & Company cannot explore the rest of this path for fear of exposing their presence to the dragon, we never learn anything more about where this path ultimately leads, though given the difficulty of building it, it must have some important purpose. Presumably it terminates in a lookout post at the mountain's peak, also accessible from other paths – cf. the account of the Battle of Five Armies in Chapter XVII, where the goblins scale the Mountain from the north and hence are able to attack the defenders' positions up against the spurs on either side of the river-valley, because '[e]ach of these could be reached by paths that ran down from the main mass of the Mountain in the centre' (DAA.343).

13 The original concept of Durin's Day coming on the first new moon of autumn, not the last, is still in place (see Chapter III, page 116). Accordingly, in the manuscript, this scene is envisioned as taking place just before the equinox, or around 21st–22nd September. By contrast,

in the First Typescript this passage is replaced by '"Tomorrow begins the last month [> week] of Autumn" said Thorin one day. "And winter comes after autumn" said Bifur. "And next year after that" said Dwalin . . .' (1/1/61:4). Similarly, the passage earlier in the chapter '. . . now the summer of the year after was drawing to a bleak end' is replaced in the typescript by '. . . autumn was now crawling towards winter' (1/1/61:2); see Text Note 5.

This revised timeline as it appears in the published book introduces a major difficulty into the chronology by placing this scene in December (around the end of the second week in December, or 14th–15th December to be precise, if we assume the winter solstice occurs on or around December 21st). This hardly seems to allow enough time for the death of the dragon, the siege, and the battle to all occur and yet leave Bilbo time to travel to the far side of Mirkwood (by a more circuitous route) and celebrate Yule with Medwed/Beorn (see page 682, Chapter XVIII). Even if we were to assume 'Yule-tide' here corresponds not to Christmas but to the last day of the year, as in the later Shire-calendar (see Appendix D, *LotR*.1143), still we are told that Bilbo and the wizard on their return journey reached Beorn's house 'by midwinter' – e.g., the solstice† – which cannot easily be reconciled with the statement here that Thorin & Company only gained entrance into the Mountain a week before, in the last week of autumn.

No such difficulty occurred in the original conception, of course, in which Durin's Day fell near the beginning of autumn (e.g., late September), allowing more than three months for the events of the final chapters to take place.

†'Midwinter' traditionally means not halfway between the solstice (circa 21st December) and the vernal equinox (circa 21st March) – that is, around Groundhog's Day/Candlemas – but the day of the winter solstice itself, the shortest and darkest day of the year. Similarly 'midsummer' (cf. page **000** and DAA.95) means not the dog days of late July/early August but the longest day of the year, the day of the summer solstice (circa 21st June). This association is ancient; the OED traces it back for more than a thousand years. Essentially it dates back to a time when the year was divided into two seasons: summer (our spring and summer; the warm months of the year) and winter (our autumn and winter; the cold months of the year).

14 Given all the restless activity depicted in 'The Back Door' (Plate IX [top]), this sketch at first glance seems to be intended as an illustration for this scene, showing what Bilbo and the dwarves (some of whom are 'out of shot') were doing on Durin's Day. But, on closer examination, it is clear that the scene presented is a composite, not a single moment in time. Apparently unseen by any of the characters, the secret door stands open, revealing a dark tunnel going down into the mountain. We see Bilbo sitting between the door and the rock, apparently watching a dwarf at work with a pick-axe on the bay's wall who seems to be looking for the door in the wrong place (note that according to the

text they couldn't tell exactly where it was). In the background, higher up the mountain behind the door, we see two dwarves (no doubt the intrepid Fili and Kili) exploring the path's higher reaches. In the foreground, a dwarf is just arriving up the high path to the right, a coil of rope slung over his shoulder, while to the left another carefully raises or lowers something by rope from the base camp. A third dwarf lies flat between them, looking straight down the cliff, his beard hanging down over the edge. There is no sign of the third 'camp' in the little bay, and more importantly the rock is not 'in the centre of the grass' as described in the text but off-center to the left. Tolkien originally called this drawing 'The Back Gate' to correspond to 'The Front Gate' (DAA.256; H-S#130) but changed the name to the more accurate 'The Back Door'. See Plate IX [middle] for an unfinished companion piece to this drawing that shows the same scene facing west rather than east (that is, looking out from the secret door rather than looking towards it). While the rock outcroppings in these two companion pieces exactly correspond, 'View from Back Door' too omits the central thrush's stone and, while it shows the setting sun, there is no sign of the new moon.

15 Unfortunately for Bilbo, the wizard's return was still several chapters away (cf. the end of Chapter XVI) and in fact would not occur until well into the Third Phase manuscript; see page 663. This is the first reminder of the wizard since Chapter IX (the one in Chapter X having first appeared in the typescript) and reminds the reader of this off-stage character and so anticipates his eventual return.

16 This is the first appearance in text of Gandalf as the wizard's name – appropriately enough, in the mouth of the character who had originally been named 'Gandalf' himself; earlier in this same chapter (see page 472 and Text Note 2 above) it had still been 'Bladorthin'. After this scene the name 'Gandalf' only reappears once before the end of the Second Phase manuscript, near the end of Plot Notes D. When the name 'Bladorthin' next appears it has already been re-assigned to the long-dead King Bladorthin; cf. Chapter XII page 514. The directions set down in Plot Notes A (see page 293) to change several of the major characters' names had now finally been carried out.

17 Cf. the end of Chapter II, where among the items in the troll's lair they found '. . . a bunch of curious keys on a nail' which they almost left behind, until Bladorthin notices them and decides to take them along at the last minute (page 97). Elrond in Chapter III had identified one of these as a 'dwarf-key', not a troll-key, and advised Gandalf (the dwarf) to 'keep it safe and fast', which he does by 'fasten[ing] it to a chain and put[ting] it round his neck under his jacket' (page 115), hence incidentally preserving it from confiscation when he is captured first by goblins and later by elves. Tolkien seems to have forgotten this detail, since he added a rider into the parting scene in Chapter VI where at the last minute Bladorthin remembers the key and gives it to Gandalf (see the additional text on page 244). This rider was prob-

ably added back into the manuscript of Chapter VII as a result of Tolkien's note to himself in Plot Notes A: 'Don't forget the key found in troll's lair.' (see page 293). Here in the present scene it is clear that Gandalf is carrying not a single key on a chain but the whole ring of keys; Bilbo says the wizard 'gave us [> you] the troll-key*s*' (emphasis mine), and this is borne out by the statement that '[he] . . . fitted in *the only key that was small enough*' (ibid.). Had Tolkien retained this plot-thread into the published book, he would have resolved these discrepancies, which are merely an artifact of the difficulty of keeping track of minor details in a complicated story composed in several distinct stages.

The idea that the key to the secret door was found somewhere along the journey survived into the First Typescript (1/1/61:5), where it is replaced by a pasteover ('The key that went with the map'); this revision was done before the Second Typescript was made, since the latter incorporates the pasteover silently into its text (1/1/42:6).

18 Interestingly enough, these dimensions, which have remained in the text of the published book to this day (cf. DAA.266), do not match those set down on Thror's Map: 'Five feet high is the door *and three may walk abreast*', a reading that goes all the way back to the Pryftan Fragment (see page 22 and the Frontispiece to Part One; italics mine) and remained remarkably stable through all iterations of the story. Granted that this 'seems like a great big hole' to Bilbo, and that dwarves are undoubtedly smaller than humans, still it seems unlikely that three dwarves could walk side-by-side in a passage only three feet wide.

(i)
The Desolation of the Dragon

> The land grew barren, though once, as Thorin said, it had been green and fair. There was little grass. Soon there were neither bush nor tree, and only broken stumps to speak of ones long vanished. They were come to the desolation of the Dragon . . .

One of the more interesting bits of Tolkien's dragon-lore, as presented in *The Hobbit* and elsewhere, is the idea that dragons are not only found in desolate places (like the 'Withered Heath' north of the Lonely Mountain),[1] but that they make places desolate simply by dwelling in them. The connection between dragons and wastelands is ancient, going all the way back to the *tannin* (*taninim*) of the Bible, the great dragons who were named in Genesis as the first created beings.[2] In most dragon-legends, however, the countryside surrounding the dragon's lair is not described as desolate or destroyed. This is certainly not the case with Beowulf's dragon, who until disturbed was sleeping peacefully in a barrow among the rich farms and fields of the Geatish lands. We might extrapolate and conclude that, once roused, if left unchecked he would eventually have reduced the kingdom to a wasteland as ruined as the moors surrounding Grendel's mere,[3] but the poem itself does not even hint at such an outcome. Nor does it apply to the most famous retelling of the St. George & the Dragon story, that found in Book I Canto XI of Spenser's *Faerie Queene* [1590], where the dragon lives in paradisial surroundings (in fact, the land that was once Eden) that seem to have escaped his depredations relatively unscathed. Nor, to speak of Tolkien's favorite dragon,[4] do the *Fáfnismál* and the *Reginsmál* in the *Elder Edda* hint that the area around Fafnir's lair is a barren wasteland, unless this is implied in its name, Gnitaheath ('The Glittering Heath'). It seems rather that dragons live in remote and hence wild areas than that they have reduced their surroundings to ruination.

Tolkien, on the other hand, goes beyond this. For him, dragons don't seek out wastelands to live in: areas *become* wastelands *because* dragons live there. This idea almost certainly derives from William Morris's treatment of the Fafnir story, first in his translation (with Eiríkr Magnússon) of the twelfth-century *Volsunga Saga* [1870], then in his long narrative poem *Sigurd the Volsung* (in full *The Story of Sigurd the Volsung and the Fall of the Niblungs* [1877]). Tolkien's first introduction to this work came when he was still a child, through the juvenilized redaction published as the final story in Andrew Lang's *The Red Fairy Book* [1890], 'The Story of Sigurd' (the only story in the volume adapted by Lang himself), which makes no mention of a desolation in its text though the accompanying pictures do suggest a barren, rocky landscape.[5] The actual saga, which derives directly from the Sigurd poems in the *Elder Edda* but greatly expands upon them, with typical saga conciseness does not talk much about the landscape any more than do the highly elliptical poems but does at one point say that Fafnir lies 'on the waste of Gnita-heath' (Morris & Magnússon, page 44). That this 'waste' (i.e., wasteland) is unnatural is established not in the saga itself but by Morris's expansion and adaptation of it into *Sigurd the Volsung*. In Morris's development of the tale, when Fafnir's brother Regin returns to his homeland long after being expelled by the greedy dragon, he finds all fallen into ruin and transformed into desolation:

And once . . .
I wandered away to the country from whence our stem did grow.
There methought the fells[6] *grown greater, but waste did the meadows lie,*
And the house was rent and ragged and open to the sky.
But lo, when I came to the doorway, great silence brooded there,
Nor bat nor owl would haunt it, nor the wood-wolves drew anear.

—*Sigurd the Volsung*, page 98.

Long years, and long years after, the tale of men-folk told
How up on the Glittering Heath was the house and the dwelling of gold,
And within that house was the Serpent . . .
Then I wondered sore of the desert; for I thought of the golden place
My hands of old had builded . . .
This was ages long ago, and yet in that desert[7] *he dwells.*

—*Sigurd the Volsung*, page 99.

In addition to Morris, the idea that dragons are bad for the surrounding countryside and, over time, reduce it to a desolate condition can also be found in various ballads and folktales, most notably 'The Laidly Worm' and 'The Lambton Worm'. In one nineteenth-century version of the former, it is said of the Laidly Worm that

For seven miles east and seven miles west,
And seven miles north and south,
No blade of grass was seen to grow,
So deadly was her mouth.

—Jacqueline Simpson, *British Dragons* [2nd ed., 2001], page 59.

Similarly, the hero of 'The Lambton Worm' returns from a seven years' absence to find 'the broad lands of his ancestors laid waste and desolate' and his aged father 'worn out with sorrow and grief . . . for the dreadful waste inflicted on his fair domain by the devastations of the worm' ('The Wonderful Legend of the Lambton Worm' [circa 1875]; reprinted in Simpson, *British Dragons*, page 138). The same idea also appears in somewhat more whimsical form in the work of another of Tolkien's favorite fantasy writers, Lord Dunsany, who has one of his heroes seek out

a dragon he knew of who if peasants' prayers are heeded deserved to die, not alone because of the number of maidens he cruelly slew, but because he was bad for the crops; he ravaged the very land and was the bane of a dukedom.

—'The Hoard of the Gibbelins',
The Book of Wonder [1912], page 77.

Building then from hints in Morris's work and perhaps also influenced to some degree by ballad and folktale tradition, Tolkien places his great wyrms in 'desolations' or wastelands of their own devising. Dragon-made wastes appear in three of Tolkien's works: in the story of Túrin, in *The Hobbit*, and in *Farmer Giles of Ham*.[8] Of these, 'Turambar and the Foalókë' [circa 1919], the earliest version of the Túrin story, predates *The Hobbit* by more than a decade and probably had the most influence on the depiction of the Desolation of Smaug and the lands around the Lonely Mountain. In *The Hobbit* itself, the effect is rather understated – for example, with the exception of birds (crows, ravens, and the thrush) and some snails there is no mention of Bilbo and the dwarves encountering a single living creature once they leave the Lake-Men behind other than the ponies they brought with them. Instead we have a careful description of a landscape so desolate that the presence of grass in one protected nook (see pp. 473–4 & DAA.285) is cause for comment, a point made more forceful by the contrast between the ruins of Dale and the once-prosperous town of farmers and craftsmen who had lived there in the days before the dragon came; we know this barren valley (depicted in 'The Front Gate', DAA.256) was once fertile enough to grow food for both the town of Men and the entire dwarven community within the Mountain as well (DAA.55). Finally, although it adds little to these two accounts, *Farmer Giles of Ham* (which in its original form is roughly contemporaneous with the composition of *The Hobbit*, either immediately preceding or immediately following it)[9] serves rather to confirm the pattern.

The Túrin story clearly sets a precedent: when Tinwelint [Thingol]'s band of would-be dragon-slayers warily scout out the area the dragon has made his own, they are appalled to discover that what had been 'a fair region' surrounding an underground city, a river-valley 'tree-grown' on one side and 'level and fertile' on the other, has been utterly ruined:

> . . . they saw that the land had become all barren and was blasted for a great distance about the ancient caverns of the Rodothlim [Nargothrond], and the trees were crushed to the earth or snapped. Toward the hills a black heath stretched and the lands were scored with the great slots that that loathy worm made in his creeping . . .
>
> Now was that band aghast as they looked upon that region from afar, yet they prepared them for battle, and drawing lots sent one of their number . . . to that high place upon the confines of the withered land . . .
>
> —'Turambar and the Foalókë', BLT II.96–7.

Indeed, so destructive is Glorund the firedrake that when he later sets forth to seek out Turambar (Túrin), he leaves behind him so great a 'path of desolation' and broken trees that from afar off can be seen 'that region now torn by the passage of the drake' (ibid.103–4). When Túrin and his band seek him out for a final combat they see 'a wide tract[10] where all the trees were broken and the lands were hurt and scorched and the earth black', and this scorched earth aspect of the dragon's passage is so pronounced that it complicates their tactics: 'not by day or by night shall men hope to take a dragon of Melko unawares . . . behold, this one hath made a waste about him, and the earth is beaten flat so that none may creep near and be hidden' (ibid.105).

This is entirely in keeping with the account of the kinds of damage Chrysophylax Dives does as he moves across the Middle Kingdom:

- 'He did a deal of damage in a short while, smashing and burning, and devouring sheep, cattle, and horses' (FGH, page 25)
- 'On the night of New Year's Day people could see a blaze in the distance. The dragon had settled in a wood about ten miles away, and it was burning merrily. He was a hot dragon when he felt in the mood' (page 28)
- '[In] the neighbouring village of Quercetum [Oakley] . . . [h]e ate not only sheep and cows and one or two persons of tender age, but . . . the parson too. Rather rashly the parson had sought to dissuade him from his evil ways . . .' (page 30)
- '[A]ll too soon they . . . came to parts that the dragon had visited. There were broken trees, burned hedges and blackened grass, and a nasty uncanny silence.' (pages 39–40)

Even closer is the description of the area around Chrysophylax's lair:

> . . . dragon-marks were now obvious and numerous.
>
> They had come, indeed, to the places where Chrysophylax often roamed, or alighted after taking his daily exercise in the air. The lower hills, and the slopes on either side of the path, had a scorched and trampled look. There was little grass, and the twisted stumps of heather and gorse stood up black amid wide patches of ash and burned earth. The region had been a dragons' playground for many a year.
>
> —*Farmer Giles of Ham*, page 58.[11]

Finally, we have one dragon-haunted region which is never described directly but which links the dragons of *The Silmarillion* with those of *The Hobbit*. For it seems likely that the Withered Heath,[12] from whence Smaug came, was originally none other than the ruined land known by many names in the various Silmarillion texts, including the Blasted Plain ('The Lay of the Children of Húrin', HME III.49 & 55), Dor-na-Fauglith ('the Land of Thirst'; ibid.), the Black Plain ('The First "Silmarillion" Map'; HME IV.220 and the color plate ff), and ultimately the Anfauglith (translated as 'The Gasping Dust'; cf. 'The Grey Annals' and 'The Wanderings of Húrin', HME XI). Not only does the Withered Heath lie in a similar geographical position, north of the Grey Mountains just as the Land of Thirst had lain north of the highlands of Hithlum and Taur-na-Fuin (which, as we have seen elsewhere, is associated with Mirkwood; see page 20), but Tolkien actually describes Dor-na-Fauglith as 'withered' and 'the heath' ('The Lay of the Children of Húrin', lines 1054 and 1068 respectively; HME III.41 & 42). Close comparison of the respective locations of Taur-na-Fuin and the Thirsty Plain on the earliest Silmarillion map (HME IV) with the Wild Wood and Withered Heath on Fimbulfambi's Map (Frontispiece to Part One) reveals just how close the two were in initial conception. Moreover, whereas in the earliest versions of the tale this seems to be simply an arid volcanic region (cf. the Túrin poem and also the 1926 'Sketch'), starting with the 1930 *Quenta* (written about the same time Tolkien began writing *The Hobbit*) it is definitely depicted as a destroyed land, once fair and green[13] but now scorched bare, blackened and lifeless ('burnt and desolate', 'burned . . . to a desolate waste'; HME IV.101 & 105).

As we have seen, by its very name, the Withered Heath must be a similarly destroyed land – and we have no less an authority than Jacob Grimm for associating heaths with dragons; he notes in *Teutonic Mythology* (Stallybrass translation, vol. II page 689) that one of the old names for a dragon was *lyngormr* (*lyng-ormr*, that is 'ling-worm' or heath-dragon, *ling* being another name for heather). Furthermore, we are told that dragons first arose inside Morgoth's fortress of Angband beneath Thangorodrim in the Iron Mountains just to the north of the burned plain of Bladorion, and Gandalf the dwarf is quite definite that the Withered Heath is where dragons come from: 'Over here is the Wild Wood and far beyond to the North, only the edge of it is on the map, is the Withered Heath where the Great Dragons used to live' (Pryftan Fragment, page 9). In the manuscript continuation of the Bladorthin Typescript (that is, the first few pages of the Second Phase), the link between 'some dwarves [being] driven out of the far north' and coming to the Lonely Mountain and the presence of dragons is already implicit:

> There were lots of dragons in the North in those days, and gold was probably running short there with the dwarves flying south or getting killed, and all the general waste and destruction dragons make going from bad to worse.

Some two decades later Tolkien made it explicit with the story of the cold-drake killing Thror's father and younger brother ('Durin's Folk', *LotR*.1109): 'there were dragons in the waste beyond [the Grey Mountains]; and after many years they became strong again and multiplied, and they made war on the Dwarves, and plundered their works'.

The name 'Withered Heath' dates back to the very earliest stage of the story, appearing on Fimbulfambi's Map in the Pryftan Fragment, immediately to the north of the Wild Wood (Mirkwood); the Grey Mountains seem not to have arisen yet. By contrast, on Thror's Map I (which seems to have accompanied the original submission of the story to Allen & Unwin) it is off the map to the north, as indicated by an arrow next to the words 'To the North lie the Grey Mountains beyond which is the Withered Heath'. In short, it has become one of the four framing features, along with the Iron Hills to the east, Long Lake to the south, and Mirkwood the Great to the west, all surrounding the central area that was once the dwarf-kingdom ('Here of old was the land of Thrain[14] King under the Mountain') but is now the dragon's realm ('Here is the

Desolation of Smaug'). Thror's Map II, the final version published in the book, is even more explicit in its linkage of the dragons and Heath: 'Far to the North are the Grey Mountains & the Withered Heath *whence came the Great Worms*' (italics mine). On the final version of the Wilderland Map used in the published book, the label 'Withered Heath' is inserted into a long narrow valley between the two eastern arms of the Grey Mountains, this vale being marked with similar hatching to that used to indicate the Desolation of Smaug. We should note, however, that this was a late change; on the version of the Wilderland Map that had accompanied Tolkien's original turnover to Allen & Unwin (Plate I [bottom]), 'Withered Heath' is simply the land north of the low line of hills which are the Grey Mountains, with no indication of how far into the distance off the map it might extend – a depiction in keeping with the original conception.

Finally, we should note one curious feature of the Desolation of Smaug which the earlier Wilderland Map calls attention to, also prominent in Tolkien's picture of the Front Gate (DAA.256; H-S#130): the curious fact of Running River arising in the dragon's lair. In one sense this could merely be verisimilitude – most caverns are carved by underground rivers, after all, and its presence suggests that the dwarves expanded upon caves that were already there to create their underground kingdom, just as Gimli later does early in the Fourth Age at Aglarond (*LotR*.1118). However, it is worth noting that throughout world mythology dragons are associated with water – specifically, with springs, wells, and similar spots where streams and rivers begin (cf. Simpson, *British Dragons*, pages 48–50).

(ii)
The Thrush

> There on the grey stone in the grass was a large thrush, nearly coal black, its pale yellow breast freckled with dark spots . . . it had caught a snail and was knocking it on the stone . . . The old thrush, which had been watching from a high perch with beady eyes & head cocked on one side, gave a sudden trill (pp. 475–6).

> . . . The old thrush was sitting on a rock nearby with his head cocked on one side . . . (page 513).

> . . . [T]here was the old thrush, perched on a stone; and as soon as they looked towards him he flapped his wings and sang; then he cocked his head on one side as if to listen, and again he sang, and again he listened.
>
> 'I believe he is trying to tell us something' said Thorin . . . (page 618).

It is entirely characteristic of Tolkien that, even though he nowhere identifies the specific type of thrush that Bilbo, Bard, and the dwarves encounter, nonetheless he provides enough details of its appearance and behavior to make that identification certain. Out of the many thrush species native to England, the Lonely Mountain thrush is clearly a song thrush (*T. philomelos*),[15] a species particularly noted for its diet of snails and its habit of crushing their shells on a rock. Many song thrushes in fact choose a favorite rock as their 'snail anvil' and return to it again and again, making the clue on Thror's Map a plausible application of real-world avian behavior to the fantasy story. Song thrushes are also, as the name suggests, noted singers, whose voices can carry a half-mile, and often hold their head to one side as if listening (possibly in fact listening for prey such as earthworms beneath the soil).

The size and coloration (not to mention longevity) of the Lonely Mountain thrush indicates that he is an exceptional individual, but then Thorin does identify him as a member of 'a long lived and magical breed' (page 513). It seems very likely that Thror and Thrain set this particular thrush, one of those who 'came tame to the hands of my father and grandfather', the duty of watching the secret door so that others could use the instructions on the Map to find the secret door, should neither Thror nor Thrain return (as indeed through ill fortune proves to be the case). While there is a widespread tradition of helpful birds in folk and fairy tale, mythology and medieval romance, here Tolkien seems to be drawing on Celtic legendry, particularly the Welsh tale *Culhwch and Olwen* (the oldest surviving Arthurian story, found in *The Mabinogion*, and a tale with which we know Tolkien was familiar; see page 194), which depicts a bird performing the same innocuous action over and over for vast lengths of time – perhaps significantly, an ouzel or blackbird, depending on the translation[16] (each being another member of the thrush family, *T. torquatus* and *T. merula* respectively).

Initially the thrush existed merely to indicate the correct spot from which to find and open the secret door, but Tolkien later expanded his role in two crucial respects, first to bring the all-important information to Bard of Smaug's weak spot (in interpolations to Chapters XII and XIII), and then to introduce the dwarves to Roäc and so bring them news of Smaug's downfall (Chapter XVa). Somewhat curiously, the thrush disappears from the story after this point; presumably he either withdraws from the ensuing chaos of claims and counter-claims or else aligns himself with Bard, just as the ravens align themselves with Thorin and the dwarves, and hence is absent from our point-of-view character's perspective for the remainder of the Lonely Mountain chapters. In any case, he remains an extremely minor character without whom the major events of the story could not occur – a perfect example of the 'small hands turning the wheels of the world', as Tolkien put it.[17]

NOTES

1 A heath is a wilderness of open, uncultivated, treeless, uninhabited land, typically covered by tough dwarf shrubs such as heather (which gets its name from the fact it grows on heaths) and gorse. By contrast, a similar tract of marshy land is called a moor. It may be significant that most heaths are the result of deforestation and, left to themselves, regrow as forests over time – that is, the very word contains a suggestion of a land that was not always so barren as it now appears but was reduced to its current state by an outside agency (in this case, the dragons themselves).

2 Modern translations prefer 'great leviathan' or 'whale' or even 'crocodile' for the Biblical creatures haunting the wilderness and the deeps, but these were understood to be dragons in Medieval tradition – cf. Leslie Kordecki's *Tradition and Development of the Medieval English Dragon* (dissertation, Univ. of Toronto, 1980).

3 A scene which Tolkien twice illustrated; cf. H-S#50 & 51, both titled '*Wudu Wyrtum Faest*', or 'trees firm by the roots' (taken from line 1364a). For the poet's description of the moor, see in particular lines 1357 through 1376a.

4 See OFS, page 40: '. . . best of all the nameless North of Sigurd of the Völsungs, and the prince of all dragons', i.e. Fafnir. For more on the influence of Fafnir on Tolkien's depiction of Smaug, see the commentary following Chapter XII.

5 Although described as a 'heath' where 'no man dared go near', the *Red Fairy Book* version of the area surrounding Fafnir's lair apparently includes trees, since we are told the dying dragon 'lashed with his tail till stones broke and trees crashed about him' (*Red Fairy Book*, page 360). We should probably not put too much weight on this, since Lang seems more concerned with striking images than narrative consistency. Although Lang claimed his version was 'condensed by the Editor [i.e., Lang] from Mr. William Morris's prose version of the "Volsunga Saga"' (Preface, *Red Fairy Book*, page [vi]) – i.e., the Morris/Magnússon translation – in fact Lang draws as much from Morris's narrative poem, *Sigurd the Volsung*, as the saga account; his reticence to admit this may be due to the fact that Morris was still alive at the time (not dying until six years later, in 1896) and might have objected to liberties being taken with his own poem, which fleshed out the sparse saga story in his own inimitable fashion.

Carpenter claims that Tolkien as a child thought 'The Story of Sigurd' 'the best story he had ever read' (*Tolkien: A Biography*, page 22), which seems to be Carpenter's extrapolation from Tolkien's remark in 'On Fairy-Stories' ranking the story (or, more accurately, the *setting* of the story in 'the nameless North') of Sigurd and Fafnir above Lewis Carroll or pirate stories, above tales of 'Red Indians' and their great forests, and *even* above stories about Merlin and Arthur (OFS.39–40, emphasis mine). See also Note 4 above.

6 A fell is any rocky or barren heights or wasteland – in short, a heath or moor at a high elevation.

7 Morris, who loved archaic English and made much use of it in his narrative poems and pseudomedieval fantasy romances, is probably using 'desert' here in its older sense of a deserted or depopulated region, but with echoes of its more modern application of an arid, barren countryside incapable of supporting life no doubt also present.

8 There are of course many other wastelands in Tolkien's works, lands once fertile that have been destroyed by Morgoth's or Sauron's evil – not surprising, perhaps, in a man who had after all witnessed first-hand not just the scourges brought by industrialization and urbanization ('the country in which I lived in childhood was being shabbily destroyed before I was ten' – Foreword to *The Lord of the Rings*, page 12) but also had spent several months living next to the largest man-made desert in Europe, better known as No Man's Land,† parts of which were still treeless and not yet arable more than fifty years later. *The Lord of the Rings* alone has the Brown Lands (once the Gardens of the Entwives), the Dead Marshes, and Mordor itself, not to mention regions depopulated by the forces of evil and turned into wilderness, such as Hollin ('laid waste' more than four thousand years before in S.A. 1697 and still desolate during the time of Frodo's journey; cf. Book II Chapter 3: 'The Ring Goes South' and Appendix B 'The Tale of Years', *LotR*.1120), the Enedwaith, and most of the lands that had once made up the Kingdom of Arnor ('Tale of Years' entry for Third Age year 1636: 'many parts of Eriador become desolate'; *LotR*.1123).

†Tolkien actually included No Man's Land or Nomensland as a label on several of the *Lord of the Rings* maps in the early 1940s (see 'The First Map', HME VII, esp. pages 320–21). While the word vanished off the map after 1943, it appears in the text of the published book to describe the area between the Dead Marshes and the ash-heaps before the Black Gate: 'a dismal waste . . . dead peats and wide flats of dry cracked mud. The land ahead rose in long shallow slopes, barren and pitiless, towards the desert that lay at Sauron's gate . . . the arid moors of the Noman-lands' (*LotR*.656–7).

9 It is not known when Tolkien wrote the earliest of the four versions of *Farmer Giles of Ham*, but since the story originated as an impromptu tale told during a family picnic according to his eldest son, Fr. John Tolkien, it was certainly after 1926 when his family returned from Leeds to Oxford, especially since part of the story's inspiration is to provide the 'real' explanation for Oxfordshire place-names such as Worminghall (and later Thame as well) and, I suspect, the nearby barrow known as Dragon Hoard (see Leslie Grinsell, *Folklore of Prehistoric Sites in Britain* [1976], pages 145 and 70). Since Tolkien was working on *Roverandom* from 1925–27 and *The Hobbit* from 1930–32/33, the most probable

dates for FGH's composition† are 1928–29 or 1933–34. And since the handwriting of the surviving pages of the Pryftan Fragment, the earliest part of *The Hobbit* to be set down, resembles that of the first draft of *Farmer Giles*, this makes it likely that Farmer Giles' story immediately preceded Mr. Baggins'.

†That is, of the first two drafts, in which the narrator is called 'Daddy' and the 'Family Jester', respectively; the third draft, the greatly expanded version known as *The Lord of Thame*, was written in 1936–7 and the final version shortly before the book's publication in 1949.

10 Christopher Tolkien notes that the word might be *track* instead of *tract* and that instead of 'the lands were hurt and scorched' his father might actually have written '. . . burnt and scorched' (BLT II.118). In either case, Tolkien is clearly drawing here on the Fafnir story – in the saga and subsequent versions Fafnir has over the years worn a track or path through the stone between his lair and the spot where he goes to drink, and it is in this slot or groove that Sigurd digs his pit and lies in wait to stab him as he goes by:

Thou shalt find a path in the desert, and a road in the world of stone;
It is smooth and deep and hollow, but the rain hath riven it not,
And the wild wind hath not worn it, for it is Fafnir's slot,
Whereby he wends to the water and the fathomless pool of old . . .

—*Sigurd the Volsung*, page 122.

By contrast, Glorund is so terrible and destructive that he carves such a path simply by moving across the landscape.

11 These parallels were present from the very first draft of *Farmer Giles of Ham*, although the description of the destruction around the dragon's lair was much briefer in the original:

There was no mistaking the dragon's tracks now. They were right in the parts where the dragon often walked or alighted from a little passage in the air. In fact all the smaller hills had a burned look about their brown tops as if these parts had been a dragon's playground for many an age. And so they had.

—FGH, expanded edition, page 94.

12 This name had originally appeared with a different application in *The Book of Lost Tales*, where it was used for a spot near Tavrobel (Great Haywood in central England), site of the disastrous last battle wherein the Elves of Tol Eressëa were utterly defeated; cf. BLT II.284 & 287.

13 This fair green plain received the name *Bladorion* ('the Wide Land') in the '(Earliest) Annals of Valinor', written in 1930 or very shortly thereafter (cf. HME IV.280). This was eventually replaced (circa 1951) in 'The Grey Annals' and other late Silmarillion texts by *Ardgalen* ('the Green Region'); cf. HME XI.113. This latter name is the one used in *The Silmarillion*, in the hyphenated form *Ard-galen*; cf. *Silm.*119. Ardgalen was apparently similar in terrain to Rohan, since an inverted

form of the same name, Calenardhon (Calen+ardhon), was the original Gondorian name for that province (*Silm.*317).

14 For the inversion of Thror's and Thrain's names on the maps ('the map tradition'), see the commentary following Chapter X.

15 For those unfamiliar with birds who wouldn't know a thrush from a warbler, suffice it to say that the song thrush is about the same size as the (American) robin, a fellow thrush (*T. migratorius*),† and has much the same habits, except that it prefers snails to earthworms. Despite their particular association with snails, song thrushes are omnivores and also eat worms, bugs, and berries as available. I am grateful to Yvette Waters and especially Jacki Bricker for help in identifying the particular species of thrush Tolkien based his Lonely Mountain thrush upon.

†not to be confused with the English robin, which is a different bird altogether, and only about the size of a sparrow.

16 In *Culhwch and Olwen*, Arthur sends Gwrhyr Gwastad Ieithoedd ('interpreter of tongues') with Cei (Kay) and Bedwyr (Bedivere), his two most trusted companions, on this quest because Gwrhyr 'know[s] all tongues, and can translate the language of birds and animals':

> They went forth until they came to the Blackbird of Cilgwri.
>
> 'For God's sake,' said Gwrhyr, 'do you know anything about Mabon son of Modron, who was stolen from between his mother and the wall when only three nights old?'
>
> 'When I first came here,' replied the Blackbird, 'a smith's anvil was here, and I was a young bird. No work was done on it except while my beak rested upon it each evening; today there is not so much as a nut-sized piece that isn't worn away, and God's revenge on me if I have heard anything of the man you want. But what is right and just for me to do for Arthur's messengers, I will do: there is a species of animal that God shaped before me, and I will guide you there.'
>
> —tr. Patrick Ford, *The Mabinogi and other Medieval Welsh Tales* [1977], page 147.

This is merely the first of five encounters with progressively older creatures – a stag, an owl, an eagle, and finally a salmon – whom the questers question in turn before finding a clue to the location of the person they seek. Both Jones & Jones [1949] and Gantz [1976] prefer 'Ouzel' (page 124) and 'Ousel' (page 164), respectively, this being an old-fashioned term (along with water ouzel) for the bird also known as the dipper.

17 JRRT to Denys Gueroult, 1965 Radio BBC interview. Tolkien's remark originally applied to the hobbits in *The Lord of the Rings* but is generally applicable throughout many of his works.

PLOT NOTES C

As noted on page 361, these two pages (1/1/10:3–4) form a single sheet which replaced the original third and fourth pages (1/1/25:1–2) of Plot Notes B, which had begun with the same four words (the fifth and final page, describing the end of the story, was left in place; see page 366). Significantly, Bladorthin '(Blad.)' is still the wizard's name, suggesting that this outline was written during the composition of Chapter XI (which had used Bladorthin for the wizard's name early in the chapter but shifted to using Gandalf by the chapter's end). For discussion of significant developments and variations from the Plot Notes it replaced, see the commentary following the transcription.

[page] 3

Bilbo earns his reward: – the dwarves say now he must go in, if he is to fulfil his contract. They won't go with him, only Balin Yellow-beard comes part of the way, in case he calls for help.

Hobbit creeps into dark mountain. Easier than he thought. Absol.[TN1] straight tunnel going gently down for a great way. Begins to see a light at end, getting redder and redder. A bubbling snoring sound. It gets v. warm. Vapours float up.

B. peeps into the great bottomost dungeon at Mountain's root nearly dark, save for glow from Smaug. The great red dragon is fast asleep upon a vast pile of precious things. He is partly on one side: B. can see he is crusted underneath with gems.

B. steals a cup to show he has been there.[TN2] [Describe some of things dimly seen especially swords and spears]

Dwarves pat him on the back. Wrath of Dragon, who comes out to hunt the thief, and settles flaming on the Mount. Then flies all round it roaring.

Terror of dwarves, hiding under rocks. They dig holes.

Bilbo goes back again. The D. is only pretending to be asleep. Bilbo catches glint in his eye and stays at mouth of tunnel. [*added*: slips on his ring. D. asks where he has gone to.] [*added in margin*: B. does not say who he is but says he came over the water in a barrel,

D thinks he is one of LongLake men] (Riddling?).[TN3] D. tries to poison his mind with half-truths ag.[TN4] the dwarves. Says they don't worry about him or paying him. Supposing they could get treasure how cd. they carry it off? They <didn't> tell you <shares won't> work.

B. says they have not only come for treasure but revenge.

D. laughs.

B. flatters him, and says he cert. never imagined Smaug was so tremendous.

D says no warrior could kill him now. He is armoured with gems underneath. B. asks him to show – and sees a patch.[TN5] Then he escapes but D. sends fiery spurts after him.

B goes back and talks to dwarves. Warns them dragon knows of exit. <Asks> them about plans. They are a bit flummoxed. They tell him of the Jem of Girion king of Dale, which he paid for his sons' arming in gold & silver mail made like steel.[TN6]

[page] 4

B. creeps in third time and waits in shadows till Dragon creeps out of hall

He steals a bright gem which fascinates him

The dragon returning finds theft: and is awful rage.[TN7]

He goes to war with the Lake Men. The people sees him coming and cut bridges to lake-dwelling. D. flies over them and set houses alight, but dare not settle right in lake. They quench fire with water and shoot darts at him. Glint of gems in dragon's belly in light of fire. He settles at side of lake and tries to starve them out.

Dwarves see the steam from afar; and are bent on carrying out gold. B. watches them stagger out. But warns them D. will come back to entrance of tunnel? What can they do with gold.

Burglary is no good – a warrior in the end. But no one will go with him. Bilbo puts on ring and creeps into dungeon. and hides. Dragon comes back at last and sleeps exhausted by battle.

Bilbo [takes >] plunges in his little magic knife and it disappears. he cannot wield the swords or spears.

Throes of dragon. Smashes walls and entrance to tunnel. Bilbo floats <away> in a golden bowl on D's blood, till it comes to rest in a deep dark hole. When it is cool he wades out, and becomes hard & brave.

Discovers sources of Running River and floats out through Fro[nt] D[oor]. in a golden bowl.

Found by the scouts of the Lake-Men.

The dwarves dig through the tunnel and take possession of their old homes but the gold is mostly crushed, and they cannot use it because of the dragon's body

The men of <the> Lake and Woodelves come up and besiege the dwarves. Attempt to block F. Door.

Bilbo sorrowful meets Blad. in the <illegible> place of Lake-town.[TN8]

Blad rebukes the besiegers. And makes dwarves pay Bilbo.

A share of his <part> he gives to Lake-men, and to wood-elves (though they may not deserve it).

They escort Blad & B back through Mirkwood.

This entire page, from 'B. creeps in third time' to 'back through Mirkwood', was struck through with a single slash. At the same time that this page was cancelled, Tolkien wrote in the left margin of this page and underlined:

Dragon killed in the battle of the Lake

This change almost certainly dates from the same time as the two new pages that replace the canceled page were written, which was demonstrably after the next chapter (Chapter XII) had already been drafted, and probably most of the following chapter as well. I treat this new material separately as Plot Notes D and have placed it following the next chapter, beginning on page 568.

TEXT NOTES

1 'Absol.': Absolutely (see Plot Notes B, page 363).

2 That is, he steals the cup to prove to the dwarves that he reached the treasure-chamber, not to alert Smaug to his presence.

The following sentence is bracketed by Tolkien in the original, and the word *spears* underlined for emphasis. Compare the parallel passage in Plot Notes B: 'He sees shields and spears', where one of these spears had been projected to play a crucial roll in the climax as the weapon with which Bilbo was to kill the sleeping dragon (see page 364). Interestingly enough, while its significance disappeared after this point, these spears survive as an element in Smaug's horde and actually appear in the painting 'Conversation with Smaug' (Plate XI [top]), made some five years later after the book had been published.

3 'Riddling' here indicates not a riddle-game such as Bilbo had played with Gollum but instead the first indication of the 'riddling talk' whereby Bilbo identifies himself while refusing to tell the dragon his actual name. The 'barrel-rider' motif first emerges here in the interpolated passage (although puzzlingly enough Bilbo claims to have

ridden *in* a barrel, not on one – perhaps Tolkien here is thinking of Bilbo's solitary escape in a barrel from Plot Notes A; see page 296), along with Smaug's mistaken conclusion that the men of Lake Town are behind this intrusion.

4 'ag.': i.e., against.

5 'a patch': i.e., a bare patch.

6 'his sons arming': since the apostrophe is missing in this very lightly punctuated passage, we cannot tell for certain whether the right form is *sons'* or *son's*. I have concluded that the former is more probable, since the manuscript of the next chapter (written from this outline) uses the plural – 'which he paid for the arming of his sons, in coats of dwarf mail the like of which had never before been made' – and is punctuated accordingly.

For the spelling 'Jem', carried over from Plot Notes B, see page 364.

'gold & silver mail made like steel': This passage further develops the mithril coat which later plays such an important part in *The Lord of the Rings*, although that term would not arise for almost another decade (see HME VI.465 & also 458). This remarkable piece of armor is not associated with Bilbo here, although it had been in page 5 of Plot Notes B (see page 366), nor is it a unique item since one was made for each of King Girion's sons. The presence of these suits of mail within Smaug's horde is incidentally proof of the mingling of 'much of the wealth of [Girion's] halls and towns' with the dwarves' goods mentioned by Bard in the parley before the Gate (see page 648).

7 Presumably Tolkien meant to write here either 'is [in an] awful rage' or possibly '[h]is awful rage' but in the haste of getting thoughts down on paper left the sentence compressed.

8 The illegible word is probably 'market', though it might also be 'smashed'.

Into the Lonely Mountain

Since the story sketched out in Plot Notes C represents Tolkien's projection of what would happen in Chapters XII and the chapters to follow, it was obviously written before Chapter XII (from which it notably diverges) was begun, probably while Chapter XI was still in progress – cf. the use of 'Bladorthin' near the beginning of Chapter XI on manuscript page 137 (page 472 in this book) and in these Plot Notes, whereas by manuscript page 141 near the end of Chapter XI (page 476 in this book) 'Gandalf' had finally replaced it as the wizard's name. Interestingly enough, rather than start a new outline Tolkien retained the same pagination and made the new material a replacement for the now-superseded middle section of Plot Notes B (which had been written at the end of Chapter VIII, probably the preceding year).

The new material at first follows the pages it replaced closely, particularly in the first six paragraphs, where many of the same words and phrases recur, although thereafter Plot Notes C develops and reshapes the material. Bilbo is still the dragon-slayer, but the sequence of events inside the Mountain is now somewhat different. Instead of stealing a cup on his first visit, another cup on his second, talking with the dragon on his third visit, and deliberately entering the tunnel a fourth time for the express purpose of killing Smaug in order to earn the Jem of Girion as his reward, as in Plot Notes B, Bilbo now steals a cup on his first visit, has an extended conversation with the dragon on his second visit, steals 'a bright gem' on his third visit when the dragon is (briefly) away, then hides within his lair on his fourth visit and stabs the weary dragon after Smaug returns from his attack on Lake Town – a sequence much closer to that of the published book, where the first three of these visits occur more or less as in this outline.

Instead of a spear found within the hoard (page 364), Bilbo now kills the dragon with his little knife (Sting, although that name has not yet arisen), apparently losing it in the process, driving it in so deeply that it 'disappears' within the dragon. His motivation now seems to be less pure greed, as in the preceding version of the Plot Notes, and more a desperate pragmatism: the dwarves are too busy carting gold up the secret passage to face the urgent question of what to do when Smaug returns, forcing Bilbo to take it upon himself. By contrast, Plot Notes B had stressed how 'Bilbo keeps on looking at his gem' (i.e., the Jem of Girion), which the dwarves tell him he must earn; the very next line describes his going to kill the sleeping dragon (page 364), strongly suggesting cause and effect: he wants the gem so badly he'd take on a dragon to get it. Plot Notes C thus somewhat downplay the theme of possessiveness in Bilbo himself, although we are told that the bright gem (presumably the Jem of Girion, which the dwarves had told him about shortly before) 'fascinates' him; this motif would later return strongly in Plot Notes D (see page 568).

It is interesting to note that the Lake-men fare rather better in their battle with Smaug here and in Plot Notes B than in any other version of the story, making them indeed the only community attacked by a dragon who succeed in driving it off in all of Tolkien's work: the Rodothlim of the early Túrin story and their later analogues the elves of Nargothrond, the dwarves of the Lonely Mountain and the men of Dale at the time of Smaug's advent, the Lake Men of the published tale, even the villagers of Bimble Bay in the poem 'The Dragon's Visit' [1937] all see their peoples decimated and their city or town destroyed.[1] By contrast, the people of Lake Town's spirited defense leaves the dragon temporarily stymied: once the bridges are destroyed he cannot reach his enemies, and any buildings he sets alight they 'quench with water'. Far from cowering or fleeing, they resolutely 'shoot darts[2] at him' whenever he flies over, although these cannot hurt him because of his gemstone armoring. Given that they have an endless supply of fresh water and are presumably skilled as fishermen (which, given their boatcraft and the placement of their town over the water, seems a reasonable assumption), Smaug's attempt to 'starve them out' seems unlikely to succeed. Small wonder that the dragon eventually abandons his siege and returns exhausted to the mountain, no doubt to plot his next move.

Smaug's death-throes, which destroy Lake Town in the published version, here take place within the Mountain and are vividly depicted in terms partially derived from the old saga and partly from the death of Glorund in the Túrin story.[3] In particular, the enormous flood of blood that gushes out, enough to float Bilbo in a golden cup,[4] comes directly from *Volsunga Saga*, where Regin advises Sigurd to dig a pit in Fafnir's path to his favorite watering hole but treacherously plans for his protégé to drown in the dragon's blood, leaving Regin in sole possession of the treasure – a plan Odin foils by advising Sigurd to dig many pits, which drain off the excess blood.[5] In one particular the final book is closer to Tolkien's sources than are these Plot Notes: Morris has his dragon's last words be a lament that he dies 'far off from the Gold' (*Sigurd the Volsung* page 126), and in the published *Hobbit* of course Smaug dies at Lake Town ('he would never again return to his golden bed' – DAA.313) and his bones thereafter lie among its ruins.[6] Here, by contrast, Smaug dies atop his vast sleeping-bed of gold, and the tumult of his death-agonies collapses the secret tunnel[7] in which the dwarves had stored all the gold they had carted away from Smaug's lair during his absence.

One idea about Smaug's death from these Plot Notes did survive into the final book, albeit in a very different form. Here we are told that 'the gold is mostly crushed, and they cannot use it because of the dragon's body', whereas in the published tale the many gems attached to Smaug's underbelly are similarly lost to the dwarves when the dragon plummets into the lake; it is known where the gems lie deep in the water amid the ruins of Lake Town but none dare dive down through 'the shivering water' surrounding the dragon's bones to retrieve them (DAA.313).[8]

The idea that Bilbo becomes 'hard and brave' because he waded in dragonblood comes from yet another version of the Sigurd legend, not the Eddic poems nor the saga but the *Nibelungenlied* [circa 1200], which derives from German rather than Norse tradition:

> When he slew the dragon at the foot of the mountain the gallant knight bathed in its blood, as a result of which no weapon has pierced him in battle ever since . . . When the hot blood flowed from the dragon's wound and the good knight was bathing in it, a broad leaf fell from the linden between his shoulder-blades. It is there that he can be wounded . . .
>
> — *The Nibelungenlied*, tr. A. T. Hatto [rev. ed., 1969], page 121.[9]

Similarly, *Thidreks Saga*, a rambling thirteenth-century romance about Theodoric the Great, includes at one point a somewhat confused version of the Sigurd story (in which Regin is the dragon, rather than the dragon's brother), stating that after killing the dragon Sigurd 'smears his body with dragon's blood, except where he cannot reach between the shoulders, and his skin becomes horny' (ibid., page 375; cf. also *The Saga of Thidrek of Bern*, tr. Edward R. Haymes [1988], pages 107–8 & 210). Since Tolkien did not develop the theme, there's no way to know how Bilbo's becoming a great warrior, one of the few dragon-slayers in Tolkien's legendarium, would have influenced the end of the book, but it seems likely that having become 'hard and brave', 'a warrior in the end', he would play a significant role in the battle gathering in the east described on the last page of the composite Plot Notes B/C ('the Battle of Anduin Vale'; see pp. 366 & 375). The deft drawing-together of so many themes and characters who had appeared earlier in the book – Medwed/Beorn, the goblins, the wood-men, the wargs, and possibly the eagles – on the return journey would therefore in this projection still occur only after Bilbo had parted company with Thorin and the dwarves, forming the great adventure still to come on his homeward journey.

One point Plot Notes C does make clear that had been hazy in the original Plot Notes B material is exactly when Bladorthin re-enters the story. As in the final lines of Plot Notes A (page 296), here the wizard's reappearance is still enough to set things to rights and avoid bloodshed or further unpleasantness: Bladorthin rebukes the besiegers and makes the dwarves pay Bilbo the dragon-slayer his fair share, a portion of which Bilbo then parcels out to the Lake-men and wood-elves though, as Tolkien tartly observes, the latter 'may not deserve it' (a true enough statement based on what he had written about them so far in this book). Even with the major recastings and expansions to come, the linkage between Bilbo's share and the dragon-slayer's share (a large part of which gets turned over to the Men of the Lake and the wood-elves) remains, though after these had become two separate characters the scene of Bilbo giving the Gem of Girion (or Arkenstone, as it came to be called) to the character who had replaced him as dragon-slayer had to be invented.

Finally, the brief passage telling how the dwarves tunnel back through the partially collapsed secret passage 'and take possession of their old homes' seems to be our first glimpse of the re-establishment of the Kingdom under the Mountain. As corroboration of this, we are told that Bladorthin and Bilbo set out on the return journey, yet no mention is made of any of the dwarves accompanying them, suggesting that Thorin & Company remain behind at the Lonely Mountain (contrast Plot Notes B, page 366, where this could be inferred but was not actually stated). The deaths of Thorin, Fili, and Kili that darken the penultimate chapter of the published book had not yet arisen; there it is Thorin's cousin Dain who becomes the new King under the Mountain, but here there is no reason to think that it is anyone other than Thorin himself, finally restored to his full inheritance.

NOTES

1 We might also include Gondolin in this tally, since Elrond says 'dragons it was that destroyed that city many ages ago' (page 115). I am not counting here Túrin's ambush of Glorund, which was achieved en route before the dragon reached the woodmen's settlement, nor Giles' encounter with Chrysophylax on a back-road several miles from Ham; these were essentially heroic or mock-heroic single combats à la Sigurd, not cooperative defenses by beleaguered townsfolk.

2 'darts': that is, arrows. The word was originally not restricted to the small darts thrown in pub games but also applied to javelins, to arrows shot from a bow, and even to projectiles from siege weapons.

3 Compare the three following passages:

- 'Now when that mighty worm was ware that he had his death-wound, then he lashed out head and tail, so that all things soever that were before him were broken to pieces' (*Volsunga Saga*, page 59).
- '[T]he Dragon lashed with his tail till stones broke and trees crashed about him' ('The Story of Sigurd', *The Red Fairy Book*, page 360).
- 'Then did that drake writhe horribly and the huge spires of his contortions were terrible to see, and all the trees he brake that stood nigh to the place of his agony' ('Turambar and the Foalókë', BLT II.107).

4 Although the gruesome, grotesque, and striking episode of Bilbo floating out through the Front Gate in a golden bowl vanished from the narrative, it is interesting to note that a huge cup appears both in the text ('the great cup of Thror'; see page 514 [= DAA.287]) and also in the color painting 'Conversation with Smaug' (Plate XI [top]); these may owe something to the long-since-abandoned plot-thread.

5 In full, the passage in question (from Chapter XVIII: Of the Slaying of the Worm Fafnir) runs thusly:

> Then said Regin, 'Make thee a hole, and sit down therein, and whenas the worm comes to the water, smite him into the heart, and so do him to death, and win for thee great fame thereby.'
>
> But Sigurd said, 'What will betide me if I be before the blood of the worm?'
>
> Says Regin, 'Of what avail to counsel thee if thou art still afeard of everything? Little art thou like thy kin in stoutness of heart.'
>
> Then Sigurd rides right over the heath; but Regin gets him gone, sore afeard.
>
> But Sigurd fell to digging him a pit, and whiles he was at that

work, there came to him an old man with a long beard, and asked what he wrought there, and he told him.

Then answered the old man† and said, 'Thou doest after sorry counsel: rather dig thee many pits, and let the blood run therein; but sit thee down in one thereof, and so thrust the worm's heart through.'

And therewithal he vanished away; but Sigurd made the pits even as it was shown to him.

†[Morris's note:] i.e., Odin in one of his many guises.

— *Volsunga Saga*, pages 58–9.

Morris's *Sigurd the Volsung* omits the detail of the many pits but does describe 'the rushing river of blood' (page 124) that gushes forth when Fafnir receives his death-wound. By contrast, Lang's 'The Story of Sigurd' includes the many pits but with typical carelessness omits any reason for their presence (Lang, *The Red Fairy Book*, page 360).

6 Glorund also died far away from his great bed of gold; cf. BLT II.87–8 & 107–9 ('Turambar and the Foalókë') and HME IV.127 & 129–30 (the 1930 *Quenta*).

7 Or, to be more accurate, part of the secret tunnel, presumably including that section in which the dwarves had stored their gold. The entire tunnel could not have collapsed, because it must have been within this passage that the dwarves hide when Smaug returns and thus escape being killed in the tumult. From the detail of Smaug smashing 'walls [of his lair] and entrance to tunnel', it seems clear that only the lower end of the passage is collapsed, which '[t]he dwarves dig through' to once more gain access to Smaug's great chamber.

8 The odd detail of the water around Smaug's death site 'shivering' perhaps relates to the idea, expressed in the description of Leviathan (the dragon in the sea) in the Book of Job chapter 41 verse 31, that dragons make the water around them boil ('like a pot'); see Text Note 33 following the next chapter (pp. 523–4) for more on this whole passage's possible influence on Tolkien's description of Smaug the Chiefest and Greatest of Calamities.

9 In this version of the story, Sigurd is called 'Siegfried', which led to Wagner's usage of that name in his opera-cycle *The Ring of the Nibelung* [1869–76]; in *Beowulf* (lines 874–898) the dragon-slayer is Sigemund, whom Norse tradition by contrast considered the dragon-slayer's father.

Chapter XII

CONVERSATIONS WITH SMAUG

The text continues on the same page as before (manuscript page 142, Marq. 1/1/13:1), with only a paragraph break to mark what would later become a new chapter. However, there seems to have been a pause in composition, probably quite brief, after the first sentence; with the words 'At last Thorin spoke' a new, darker ink and more deliberate and legible lettering begin.

The dwarves stood before the door and held long council.

At last Thorin spoke: 'Now is the time for our esteemed Mr Baggins, who has proved himself a good companion on our long road, and a hobbit full of courage and resource far exceeding his size, and if I may say so good luck far exceeding the usual allowance; – now is the time for him to perform the service for which he was included in our company: – now is the time for him to earn his Reward'. You are familiar by now with Thorin's style on important occasions. This cert. was one. But Bilbo felt impatient. [He >] By now he was familiar enough with Thorin and knew what he was driving at.

'If you mean you think it is my job to go into the [open tunnel >] secret passage first O Thorin Thrain's son,[TN1] may your beard grow ever longer' he said crossly. 'Say so at once and have done! I might refuse. I have got you ought of two messes already which were hardly in our original bargain,[TN2] and am I think already owed some reward. But somehow, I hardly think I shall refuse. Perhaps I have begun to trust my luck more than I used to in the old days (– he meant the spring before last, before he left his house, but it cert. seemed centuries ago –). But third time pays for all as my father used to say.[TN3] I think I will go and have a peep at once and get it over. Now who's coming in with me?'

He did not expect a chorus of volunteers, so he wasn't disappointed. Fili and Kili looked uncomfortable and stood on one leg. But the others frankly made no pretence about [> of] offering – except old Balin the look-out man, who was rather fond of the hobbit. He said he would come inside at least, and come a bit of the way, ready to call for help if needed. [One >] I can at least say this for the dwarves: they intended to pay Bilbo for his services, they had brought him to do a job, and didn't mind letting the poor little fellow do it; but they would have all done their best at any risk to get him out of trouble if they could [> if he got into it], as they did in the case of the trolls the year before.[TN4]

There it is: dwarves aren't heroes, but commercial-minded; some are [thoroughly bad >] tricky and treacherous and pretty bad lots; some are not, but are decent enough people like Thorin and Co. if not [filled with >] over high-minded.

The stars were coming out behind him in a pale sky barred with black, when the hobbit crept through the enchanted doors,[TN5] and stole into the M[ountain]. It was far easier going than he expected. This was no goblin-entrance, nor rough wood-elf cave. It was a passage made by dwarves at the height of their wealth and skill: straight as a ruler, smooth-floored and smooth-sided, going [direct >] with a gently never-varying slope direct – to some distant goal in the blackness below. After a while Balin bade Bilbo "good luck", and stopped, where he could still see the faint outline of the door, and by a trick of the echoes of the tunnel hear the rustle of the whispering voices of the others just outside.

Then the hobbit slipped on his ring, and warned by the echoes to [be >] take more than hobbit's care to make no noise [> sound], crept noiselessly down down down into the dark. He was trembling with fear, but his little face was set and grim. Already he was a very different hobbit to the one that had run out without a pockethandkerchief from Bag-end long ago. He hadn't had pocket hank. for a year. He loosed his dagger in its sheath, tightened his belt, and went on.

'Now you are in for it at last, Bilbo B.' he said to himself. 'You went and put your foot right in it that night of the party, and now you've got to pay for it.[TN6] Dear me what a fool I was and am' said the least Tookish part 'I have absolutely no use for dragon-guarded treasures, and the whole lot could stay here for ever, if only I could wake up and find this beastly tunnel was my own hall at home!'

He did not wake up, of course, but went on still, and on, till all sign of the door behind had faded away. He was altogether alone. Soon he thought it was beginning to feel warm.

'Is that a kind of glow I see on my right ahead down there?' he thought. It was. As he went forward it grew and grew, and [> till] there was no doubting it. It was a red light, steadily getting redder and redder. Now it was undoubtedly hot. Wisps of vapour floated up and past him, and he began to sweat. A sound began to throb in his ears, a sort of bubbling – like a large cat [*added*: purring],[TN7] or like a big pot galloping on a fire. It grew to a most unmistakable gurgling snore of some great animal asleep somewhere in the red glow ahead.

It was this point that Bilbo stopped. Going on from that point was the bravest thing he ever did. The tremendous things that happened afterwards were as nothing compared to it. [Once he had made himself go on to the tunnel's end nothing else se[emed] >] He fought his real battle in the tunnel alone, before [the d. >] he even really saw this <vast>[TN8] danger that lay in wait.

At last you can picture the tunnel ending in a square opening [> a opening of much the same size as the door above].[TN9] Through it peeps the hobbit's little head. Before him lies the great bottommost [dungeon >] cellar or dungeon-hall of the ancient dwarves right at the Mountain's root. It was nearly dark so that its great size could only be dimly guessed, but rising from the floor there was a great glow. It was the glow of Smaug.

There he lay, a vast red-golden dragon fast asleep. A thrumming came from his jaws and nostrils and wisps of smoke, but his fires were low in slumber. Beneath him under all his limbs and huge-coiled tail and about him on all sides stretching away across the unseen floors, lay countless piles of precious things, gold wrought and unwrought, gems and jewels,[TN10] and silver red-stained in the ruddy light.

Smaug lay with wings folded like an immeasurable bat; he lay partly on one side and Bilbo could see his underparts, and his long belly were crusted with gems and fragments of gold stuck into his slime with his long lying on his costly bed. Behind him where the walls were nearest, could dimly be seen coats of mail and axes swords and spears hung, and great jars filled with wealth only to be guessed at.[TN11]

To say that Bilbo's breath was taken away is to say too little. There are no words to express his staggerment.[TN12] He had heard tell and sing of dragon-hoards before,[TN13] but the splendour the lust the glory of such treasure had never before come home to him. His heart was filled and pierced with the desire of dwarves – and he gazed, almost forgetting the frightful guardian, at the gold, gazed and gazed for what seemed ages, before drawn almost against his will he stole from the shadow of the door, across the floor, to the nearest edge of the mound of treasure. Above him the sleeping dragon lay, a fearful [> dire] menace even in his sleep. He grasped a great two handed cup[TN14] as heavy as he could carry; and cast one fearful eye upwards. The dragon stirred a wing, opened a claw, the rumble of his snoring changed its note. Then B. fled. But the dr. did not wake – yet – but shuffled into other dreams of greed and violence, lying there in his stolen hall, while the little hobbit toiled back up the path. His heart was beating faster, and his hands shaking & a more fevered shaking was in his legs than when he was going down; but still he clutched the cup, and his chief thought was 'Yes I've done it! This will show them. More like a grocer than a burglar indeed[TN15] – well we'll hear no more of that.'

Nor did he. To do Balin justice he was overjoyed, [when he >] to see Bilbo again. Fill[ed] with [great delight > delight greater than >]

delight as great as his surprise, and as great as his fear when he said goodbye. He picked Bilbo up indeed and carried him out to the open air. It was midnight. Clouds had masked the stars, and Bilbo sat gasping, taking pleasure only in the fresh air again, and hardly noticing the excitement of the dwarves, or how they praised him and patted him on the back, and put themselves and all their families for generations to come at his service.

A vast rumbling woke suddenly in the mountain underneath, as if it had been an extinct volcano that was suddenly [> unexpectedly] making up its mind to start eruptions once again.[TN16] The door was pulled nearly to, and blocked with a stone – they had not dared to risk closing it altogether – but up the long tunnel came the deep far echoes of a bellowing and a tramp that made the ground beneath them tremble.

Then the dwarves [stopped >] forgot their joy and their own confident boasts of a moment before, and cowered down in fright. Smaug was still to be reckoned with. It does not do to leave a live dragon out of your count if you live near him. Dragons may not have much real use for all their wealth, but they knew it to an ounce as a rule, especially after long possession: Smaug was no exception. He had passed from an uneasy dream in which a small warrior, altogether insignificant in size, but provided with a bitter sword, and great courage, figured most unpleasantly,[TN17] to a doze, and from a doze to wide waking. There was a breath of strange air in his cave. Cd there be a draught from that little hole? He had never felt quite happy about that hole, yet it was so small, but now he [liked it >][TN18] did not like the look of it at all. He stirred and missed his cup. Thieves fire murder! Such a thing had not happened since he first came there. His rage passes description – the sort of rage that is only seen when folk that have more than they can enjoy, suddenly lose something they have had before but have never before used or wanted. His fire belched forth, the hall smoked, he shook the mountain's roots. He thrust his head in vain at the little hole, and then coiling his length together, roaring like thunder underground he sped from his deep lair out through its great door, out and up towards the Front Gate.

To hunt the whole mountain till he [found >] caught the thief and burned and trampled him was his one thought. He issued from the gate, the water rose in fierce whistling steam, as up he soared into the air and settled on the mountain top in a spurt of flame. The dwarves heard the awful rumour of his flight. They ran and crouched against the rock walls of the grass terrace, <cringing> under the sides of boulders, hoping to escape the frightful eyes of the hunting dragon.[TN19] 'Quick Quick!' whispered Bilbo 'the door the tunnel'.

(So he saved their lives again) They crept inside the tunnel door and closed it as much as they dare. 'Bombur and Bofur!' cried Bifur their brother 'They are down in the valley!' 'They will be slain and all our ponies and all our stores'[TN20] moaned the others. 'You can't let them be' said Bilbo 'without a struggle. Where are the ropes?'

It was a terrible time. The worst they had ever been through. The horrible sound of the dragon's anger [*added*: was] echoing in the stony hollows far above; at any moment he might come down this side or fly whirling round; and there they were near the cliffs edge hauling like mad on the ropes. Up came Bofur and still all was safe; up came Bombur [added in pencil: puffing & blowing while the ropes creaked], and still all was safe; up came their [> some] bundles of tools and stores that had been left below – and danger came upon them. A whirring[TN21] roar was heard. A red light touched the points of standing rocks. The dragon was upon them.

They had barely time to get back in the tunnel. pulling and dragging in their bundles when Smaug came whirling from the North licking the mountain wall with flames,[TN22] beating his great wings with a noise like roaring wind.

His hot breath shrivelled the grass [in the >] before the door, and drove in through the crack and scorched them as they lay hid. Red light leapt up and black rock shadows danced. Then darkness fell as he flew south [> passed]. The [horses >] ponies shrieked with terror and galloped off for they were free. The dragon swooped & turned and hunted them.

'That'll be the end of our poor beasts' said Thorin. 'Nothing can escape him once he sees it.' They crept further down the tunnel, and there they lay and shivered till the dawn, hearing ever and anon the roar of the flying dragon grow and pass and fade as he hunted all the mountain sides. He guessed from the horses and from the tracks of the dwarves and their camps he had seen that men[TN23] had come up from the lake by the river and scaled the mountain side [<by> >] from the valley where the ponies had been, but the door withstood his searching eye, and the little walled bay kept out his fiercest flame; so that he hunted in vain, till dawn chilled his [fire >] wrath and he went back to his golden couch to sleep.

The dwarves even so [did not yet >] were not yet in the mood give up their quest; nor could they fly yet [*added in pencil*: had they wished]. The ponies were lost or killed, and they dare not march standing in the open while the dragon's wrath was still burning. They grumbled as is the nature of folk at Bilbo, of course, blaming him for what they had at first so praised him – for bringing away a cup and stirring up Smaug's wrath.

'What else do you suppose a burglar is to do?' said Bilbo 'I was not engaged to kill dragons, that's warrior's work, but steal treasure. [if you >] Did you expect me to trot back with the whole treasure of Thror on my back!'

The dwarves, of course, saw the sense of this; and begged his pardon. 'What do you propose we shd. do now, Mr Baggins?' said Thorin politely. 'Stay where we are by day and creep in the tunnel by night' said the hobbit '– in the meantime I will creep down and see what the dragon is doing [> Smaug is up to], if you like'.

This was too good an offer to be refused. [So when evening came with as yet >] So Bilbo got ready for another journey in the Mountain. He chose daytime this time, thinking Smaug would not rest for long, nor stay indoors for many a night – if he was to be caught napping (figuratively speaking: Bilbo had no thought of [*added*: really] catching him, of course!) about midday was the most likely time.

All the same it was as dark as night-time in the tunnel. The light from the door – almost closed behind him – soon failed as he went down. So silent was Bilbo's creeping that smoke on a gentle wind could hardly have beaten it, and he was inclined to feel a bit proud of himself as he drew near the lower door. The glow was very faint this time

'Old Smaug is weary and asleep' he thought. '[He'll neither hear nor >] He can't see me, and he won't hear me. Cheer up Bilbo'.

Smaug certainly looked fast asleep, almost dead[TN24] and dark with scarcely a rumble or a snore, as Bilbo peeped from the entrance. He was just about to step out on the floor, when he caught a sudden thin piercing ray of red from under the lids of the dragon's closed eyes [> the closed eyes of Smaug]. He was only pretending to sleep! He was watching the tunnel entrance.

Bilbo stepped back and [<?thanked> >] blessed the luck of his ring.[TN25] Then Smaug spoke.

'Well thief – I smell you, and I feel your air. I hear your breath. Come along! help yourself again. There is plenty and to spare.'

'No thank you O Smaug the tremendous!' said Bilbo. 'I did not come to take anything. I only wished to have a look at you and see if you were truly as great as tales say. I did not believe them.'

'Do you now?' said the dragon somewhat flattered, even though he did not believe a word of it.

'Truly songs and tales fall short of the truth O Smaug chiefest and greatest of calamities' said Bilbo.

'You have nice manners for a [lying >] thief and a liar' said the dragon. 'You seem familiar with my name – but I don't seem to remember smelling you before. Who are you, and where do you come from may I ask?'

'[I am he <that> walks unseen. >] I come from under the hill, and under the hills my paths led. And through the air – I am he that walks unseen.'

'So I can well believe' said Smaug, 'but that is hardly your name.'[TN26]

[*added in left margin*: 'I am the clue-finder the web-cutter the stinging fly, the']

'Lovely titles' sneered Smaug.

'[I am barrel-rider > I am friend >] I am he that buries his friends alive, that drowns them and [fishes them from water >] draws them alive from the water. I am come from the end of a bag, but no bag went over me.' [*added in left margin*: '[Those are not >] These don't sound so creditable' scoffed Smaug.] 'I am [barrel-rider >] the friend of bears and eagles. I am ring winner & luck wearer, and I am Barrel-rider,' went on Bilbo.

[*added, crowded in at end of paragraph*: 'That's better' said Smaug. 'But don't let your imagination run away with you.']

This of course is the way to talk to Dragons if you don't wish to reveal your name (which is wise), and don't want to infuriate them by a flat refusal (which is also wise). No dragon can resist the fascination of riddling talk, and of wasting time trying to understand it. There was a lot here Smaug didn't understand at all,[TN27] but he thought he understood enough and chuckled in his wicked inside – 'Lake-men, some nasty scheme of those nasty pier <handling> lake men' he thought 'I haven't been down there for an age and an age. I will soon put that right.

[Nor >] 'Very well O Barrel-rider' he said. 'Perhaps "barrel" is your pony's name. You may walk unseen, but you did not walk all the way. Let me tell you I ate six ponies last night, and shall [<soon> >] catch and eat the others before long. But I will give you one piece of advice for your good. Don't have more to do with dwarves than you can help.'

'Dwarves!?' said Bilbo in pretend surprise.

'[Yes >] Don't <tell> me' said Smaug. 'I know the smell (and taste) of dwarf extremely w[ell] – no one better. Don't tell me I can eat a dwarf-ridden pony – and not know it! You'll come to a bad end, if you go with such friends Thief Barrel-rider. I don't mind if you go back and tell them so from me.[TN28]

'I suppose you got a fair price for that cup last night – come now did you? Nothing at all! Well that's just like them. And I suppose they are skulking outside, and your job is to do all the dangerous work, and get what you can when I'm not looking – for them? And you will get a fair share? Don't you believe it. If you get off alive you will be lucky.'

Bilbo was beginning to feel really uncomfortable. Whenever Smaug's roving eye, seeking ever for him in the shadows, flashed across him, he trembled; and an unaccountable desire to reveal himself and tell all the truth to Smaug would seize hold of him. He was coming under the dragon-spell;[TN29] but plucking up courage he spoke again.

'You don't know everything O Smaug the mighty' said he. 'Not gold alone brought us hither'.

'Ha ha! you admit the "us" ' said Smaug ' – why not say us fourteen and be done with it. I am very pleased to hear that you had other business in these parts, besides my gold. Perhaps you will then not altogether waste your time. I don't know if it has occurred to you, but if you could steal all the gold bit by bit – a matter of a hundred years or so – you couldn't get it very far. Not much use on the mountain side? Not much use in the forest? Bless me – had you never thought of the catch! A fourteenth share I suppose or something like – that were the term<s> eh. But what about delivery, what about cartage.' And Smaug laughed. He had a wicked and [a] wily heart. He knew his guesses were not far out.

You will hardly believe it but poor Bilbo was really very taken aback. So far all their [> his] thoughts and energies had been concentrated on getting to the Mountain and finding the entrance. He had hardly even thought of how the treasure was to be removed, certainly never of how any part of it was to reach Bag-End Under Hill. Now a nasty suspicion began to cross his mind – had the dwarves forgotten this important point too, or were they, or were they laughing in their sleeves all the time? That is <the> effect dragon talk has on the inexperienced. Bilbo's really ought to have warned him;[TN30] but Smaug had [*added*: rather] an overwhelming personality.

'I tell you' he said in an <effort> to keep his end up 'that money [> gold] was no object or only a secondary one [> part].[TN31] We came over hill and under hill, by water and by wave and wind for revenge. Surely O Smaug the unassessably wealthy you must realize your success has made you some bitter enemies?'

Then Smaug really did laugh – A devastating sound which shook Bilbo to the floor, while far up in the tunnel the dwarves huddled together and imagined the hobbit had come to a sudden end.

'Revenge' he snorted and the red light lit the hall from floor to ceiling like scarlet lightning. 'The King under the Mountain is dead and where are his kin that dare take revenge. Girion lord of Dale is dead and I have eaten his people like a wolf among sheep and where are his sons' sons[TN32] who dare approach me. I kill where I wish and none dares resist. I laid low warriors of old and their like is not in the world today. Then I was young. Now I am old and strong, strong,

strong – thief in the shadows' – he gloated. 'My armour is like tenfold shields, [my feet like >] my teeth are swords my claws spears, the shock of my tail a thunder bolt, my wings a hurricane, and my breath death!'[TN33]

'I have always understood' murmured Bilbo in an astonished squeak 'that dragons were tender underneath, especially in the region of the – er chest; but doubtless one so fortified has thought of that.'

The dragon stopped short in his boasts 'Your information is antiquated' he snapped. 'I am armoured above and below; with iron scales and hard gems. No blade can pierce me.'

'I might have guessed it' said Bilbo '– truly there can be no equal of Smaug the impenetrable. [Nor any waistcoat >] What wealth to possess a waistcoat of fine diamonds!'

'Yes it is rare and wonderful indeed' said Smaug absurdly pleased. He did not know that Bilbo had already had a glimpse of his peculiar adornment & was only itching for a closer view. He rolled over 'look' he said '– what do you say to that.'

'[Absolutely Perfectly dazzling >] Dazzlingly marvellous. Perfect. Flawless. Staggering.' said Bilbo, but what he thought was 'Old fool, and there is great patch in <the> left of his breast [> in a hollow of his left breast], [without >] as bare as snail out of its shell.'

'Well really I must not detain you any longer' he said aloud, 'or hinder your much needed rest. Ponies take some catching, I am told after a long start. And so do burglars' he added as a parting shot. Rather an unfortunate one for the dragon spouted flames after him, and fast as he ran up the tunnel, he had not gone far enough before the ghastly head of Smaug was [pressed >] thrust into the opening – no more would go – and fire and vapour pursued him and nearly overcame him.

He had been feeling rather pleased with his conversation with Smaug, but this [> his] mistake at the end shook him into better sense. 'Don't laugh at live dragons Bilbo my boy' he said, & a sound remark too. 'You aren't through this adventure yet.' That was equally true.

Inserted into the text at this point is a rider (manuscript page '151b'), seven paragraphs written on the back of the same page; the original page thereby changed from being '151' to being broken between '151a' (the two paragraphs before this point) and '151c' (the rest of the page following it) by Tolkien. This full page of additional text must have been added by Tolkien after he had finished the chapter, or else he would not have needed to resort to the unorthodox numeration or have drafted this on the back of a sheet; as noted earlier, all this section of the story, from manuscript page 119 (the capture by wood-elves) to 167 (the scene on Ravenhill), was written only on the front of each sheet, rather than on front and back as had been the case before (with the bulk of the Second Phase, manuscript pages 13–118) and after (the Third Phase manuscript pages with new numeration 1–45 concluding the book). Since it introduces the idea of the thrush learning of the immediate threat Smaug now poses to Lake Town, the information that some of the men of Dale could understand bird-speech, and the essential detail of Smaug's exposed weak spot, it must have been added after Smaug's death scene on manuscript page 155 (1/1/15: 3), where none of these details initially appear, and at the same time as the paragraph added to the bottom of that page incorporating all those details (see page 549).

The afternoon was getting late when he came out again. The dwarves were all sitting on the 'doorstep' and were delighted to see him, and made him sit down and tell them all that had passed.

But Bilbo was worried and uncomfortable – he was regretting some of the things he had said and did not like confessing [> repeating] them. The old thrush was sitting on a rock near by with his head cocked on one side [*added in margin*: listening to all that was said] and Bilbo crossly threw a stone at him; but he only fluttered out of the way and came back.

'Drat the bird!' said Bilbo 'I don't like the look of him.'

'Leave him alone' said Thorin. 'The thrushes are friendly – this is a very old bird, probably one of those that used to live here tame to the hands of my father and grandfather – they were a long lived and magical breed. The dwarves and the men of Dale used to have the trick of understanding their language and use them for messengers to fly to the Lake-town.'[TN34]

'Well he will have news to take there if he likes' now said Bilbo. 'Why what has happened?' cried the dwarves 'Get on with your tale' So B. told them – and he [told them > confessed a fear that <his> >] confessed an uncomfortable foreboding that the Dragon might go hunting back to the Lake, since he must guess from their camps and the ponies how they had come. 'O why did I ever say that about barrel-rider' he groaned.

['Yes and why did you let him find out your way of escape?' said they >] 'Well you found out one useful thing at any rate' Balin comforted him '– the bare patch in old Smaug's diamond waistcoat may come in useful yet.' Then they fell to discussing stabs and jabs and weapons and the various dangers attending prodding a sleeping dragon.[TN35] [*added in margin*: and all the while the thrush listened, and at last as the sun sank towards the forest he flew away.] All the while as [evening drew > the sun went West >] the long shadows lengthened B. became more and more unhappy.

'I am sure we are very unsafe here' he said

The page of new material ('151b') ends here, and the text resumes with what had been the third paragraph on the original manuscript page 151, now marked by Tolkien '151 (c)'.

'You had better look out' said he – '[*added*: let's go on &] close the door and risk being shut in. The dragon [> Smaug] will <begin> going out before long [*added*: now] and I am very mistaken if he doesn't search this side of the mountain and break it bit by bit to find the outer entrance to the tunnel. What he doesn't know about it he guesses.'

The delight of the dwarves at seeing him was overwhelmed in terror [> fear]. 'What have you been saying' they asked him; and though B. gave them as close an account of all his words as he cd. they were far from satisfied.[TN36]

[All was now quiet, and >] [*added in margin*: Still the > The dwarves > The > When evening came on the dwarves took his advice as far as going inside the tunnel went.] But they delayed shutting the door – it seemed a desperate plan, and they were not willing yet to take the risk of cutting themselves off from the outer air with no way of escape except through the dragon's very lair. All was quiet below at any rate.[TN37] So for a while they sat near the tunnel's mouth and talked on.

Bilbo wished he cd. feel quite certain that they were being honest when they swore that they had never had any clear idea of what to do after the recovery of their treasure.

'As for your share Mr Baggins' said Thorin 'I assure you we are more than satisfied with your professional assistance; and you shall choose it yourself, as soon as we have it! I am sorry we were so stupid as to overlook the transport problem – it is many years since the eldest of us were in these lands, and the difficulties have not grown less with the passing of time. But what can be done [*added*: for you] we will do it. For ourselves well that is our affair. We shall see when the time come.'

There they sat and the talk drifted on to things they remembered, that must now be lying in the hall below – the spears that were made for the armies of Bladorthin,[TN38] each with a thrice forged head, each shaft <bound> with cunning gold [; the shields >], but they were never delivered nor paid for; shields for warriors long dead; coats of mail gilded and silvered; [the great cup of Thror two handled gold cold-wrought out of >] the great golden cup of Thror, hewn and carven like birds and flowers <with> eyes and petals made of pearls; and most fair of all the white gem of Girion Lord of Dale,[TN39] which he paid for the arming of his sons, in coats of dwarf mail the like of which had never before been made. [*added*: of silver wrought the power and strength of steel] The white gem of Girion like a globe with myriad facets shining like water in the sun, like snow in starlight [> under stars] like silver in firelight, like rain on the moon. [> Shining like silver in firelight, like water in the sun, like snow under stars, like rain upon the moon (like Sirius upon Earth).]

[Their speech was interrupted by the >] All the while Bilbo was only half-listening. He was near the door with an ear cocked for any sound without, his other was listening to the dwarves, but over and beyond straining for any sound from far below. Evening fell and deepened and became uneasy. 'Shut the door' he begged them. 'I fear that dragon in my bones. I like this silence less than the uproar of last night: Shut the door before it is too late'.

Something in his voice [made > moved >] gave the dwarves an uncomfortable feeling. Grumbling Thorin rose and pulled the door towards him 'How can we close it' he said 'without bar nor handhold this side?' He pushed the door and kicked [*added*: away] the stone that blocked the door. Then he thrust upon it and it closed with a snap and a clang. [They were shut >] No trace of a key hole was there left. They were shut in the Mountain. And not a moment too soon. A blow smote the side of the Mountain like a crash of battering rams made of forest oaks and swung by giants. The rocks boomed; stones fell on their heads. They fled far down the tunnel glad to be [*added*: still] alive, pursued by the roar without where Smaug was breaking the rocks to pieces smashing wall and cliff with his great tail till their little lofty camping ground, the thrush's stone the scorched grass the narrow ledge and all disappeared in a jumble of smashed boulders, and an avalanche of splintered stone fell over the cliff into the valley underneath.

Smaug had left his lair in silent stealth and crept to the west of the mountain [a heavy floating slow >] floating heavy and slow in dark like a crow down the wind, in the hopes of catching somebody or something there, or of spying the outlet to the tunnel which the thief had used. This was his outburst of wrath when he found nobody and could see nothing, even where he knew the outlet must in fact be.

Still he was well pleased; he thought in his heart that he would not be troubled again from that direction; [or he would hear and have ample warning >] or would have ample warning of any hammering or tunnelling.

But in the meanwhile he had revenge of his own to wreak. 'Barrel rider' thought he '– your feet came from the water side, and up the water you came without a doubt. If you are not one of those men of the Lake, you had their help; and now you shall see who is King [> They shall see me and remember who is King under the Mountain].' He rose in fire and went away South towards the Running River.

The text continues with only a line break before starting the account of Smaug's attack on Lake Town, what is now Chapter XIV of the published book but was Chapter XIII of the manuscript version of the tale. Much later, when preparing the First Typescript, Tolkien added in pencil at this point (between the first and second paragraphs of manuscript page 153 [Marq. 1/1/15:1]):

Here insert 'Not at home'

and at the same time added a chapter title – the first to appear in the manuscript:

Ch. Fire and Water

For more on the re-arrangement of the story that reversed the order in which the next two chapters appeared, see page 548.

TEXT NOTES

1 Note that the genealogy of the 'text tradition', with Thrain as Thorin's father rather than his grandfather, is firmly in place; see the section of commentary entitled 'Thorin, son of Thrain, son of Thror' following Chapter X.

2 'two messes already': Bilbo is referring of course to rescuing the dwarves (*sans* Gandalf/Thorin) from the Spiders of Mirkwood and also to freeing all the dwarves from the dungeon of the Elvenking.

3 This, the first of Bungo Baggins' sayings recounted by his adventurous son in the Lonely Mountain chapters, is Tolkien's adaptation of an actual medieval proverb occurring in line 1680 of the Tolkien–Gordon edition of *Sir Gawain & the Green Knight* (published in 1925, with a revised printing in 1930), where the phrase *'þrid tyme þrowe best'* is placed in quotation marks and glossed 'third time turn out best' (SGGK pages 52 & 201). Tolkien's note (page 109) slightly recasts it as an expression of hope rather than a statement of fact, 'third time, turn out best' and comments:

> *Þrid tyme, þrowe best* is a proverbial expression which is quoted also in *Seven Sages* 2062 'Men sais þe þrid time þrowes best.' The modern equivalent is 'third time pays for all'.

The Seven Sages of Rome [fourteenth century] is another Middle English romance, about twice the length of SGGK, preserved in the famous Auchinleck Manuscript; this is an English translation of a French original of seven misogynistic tales within a frame narrative. For Tolkien's own commentary on the proverb as it appears in *The Hobbit* and *The Lord of the Rings*, see his letter of 31st July 1964 to Jared Lobdell, quoted in Anderson's *Annotated Hobbit*, page 267:

> It is an old alliterative saying using the word *throw:* time, period (unrelated to the verb *throw*); sc. this third occasion is the best time – the time for special effort and/or luck. It is used when a third try is needed to rectify two poor efforts, or when a third occurrence may surpass the others and finally prove a man's worth, or a thing's.

Anderson also notes that Tolkien translates *þrid tyme þrowe best* as 'third time pays for all' in his own translation of *Sir Gawain* (*Sir Gawain and the Green Knight, Pearl, Sir Orfeo*, tr. JRRT, ed. Christopher Tolkien [1975; 1978]; stanza 67, page 66).

4 'the year before': As elsewhere throughout the first draft, the extended time-scheme for Bilbo's adventures with a longer journey through Mirkwood and lengthy imprisonment by the elves is still in place. See also, for example, 'He hadn't had [a] pocket hank[erchief] for a year' three paragraphs later or the reference to his journey having begun 'the spring before last' a paragraph earlier.

5 The plural is remarkable, but the manuscript clearly reads *doors* not *door* at this point. I suspect that as usual Tolkien was describing the scene as he happened to envision it, ignoring for the moment possible contradictions until he had committed the scene to paper and trusting to the next draft to iron out any inconsistencies, as in fact it did: the First Typescript (1/1/62:1) reads 'door', along with all subsequent texts.

6 Added in pencil (i.e., at the time of the creation of the First Typescript): 'and now you've got *to pull it out or* pay for it.'

7 The idea that dragons purr is not Tolkien's invention, but derives from Kenneth Grahame's 'The Reluctant Dragon', a short tale originally published as part of *Dream Days* [1898] and later as a separate small book illustrated by Ernest Shepherd [1938], who is most famous for his work on *Winnie-the-Pooh.* Tolkien was conversant with Grahame's work; see the commentary following the Bladorthin Typescript (pp. 45–6) and Note 3 on page 58 for more on Tolkien's familiarity with, and admiration for, Grahame's writings. It is characteristic of Tolkien's eclecticism that he could combine in the figure of Smaug elements from sources as disparate as Grahame's whimsical little tale, the grim *Volsunga Saga*, and the Book of Job (see Text Note 33 below).

8 This word is very difficult to read in the manuscript and might just as well be 'worst'. 'Vast' is the reading of the First Typescript (1/1/62:2) and published book (DAA.270).

9 The sudden brief shift in perspective here to second person and present tense and then back again is anomalous and striking, but it persists through all subsequent versions of the passage (cf. DAA.270). The idea that the tunnel ended in a square opening was rejected at once, probably because he had already described the secret passage as 'straight as a ruler, smooth-floored and smooth-sided, going . . . with a gently never-varying slope direct . . . to some distant goal in the blackness below' and hence the exit should exactly match the entrance. The lower exit is not shown on Tolkien's painting of Smaug's chamber, 'Conversation

with Smaug' (Plate XI [top]), but its size and shape can be guessed by comparison with the upper entrance shown in 'The Back Door' (Plate IX [top]), which is definitely taller than it is wide – i.e., rectangular, not square.

10 Although often used interchangeably, 'gems' here indicate carved precious stones, while 'jewels' are gemstones set in items of jewelry. Thus the 'Gem of Girion' (the later Arkenstone), 'like a globe with myriad facets' is correctly named, while the 'five hundred emeralds green as grass' that make up the 'necklace of Girion' (which makes its first appearance in a pasteover in the First Typescript; Marq. 1/1/62:11) are jewels.

11 This sentence was slightly revised to read 'and *here* great jars *stood* filled with wealth . . .' Compare the painting 'Conversation with Smaug' (Plate XI [top]), where several such jars, one marked with Thror's rune (Þ), do indeed stand in an archway by the far wall. The two great jars in the foreground therefore probably stand against the near wall of the chamber, which would be out of our sight to the left; similar jars are probably hidden from our view behind the mound of Smaug's treasure. See 'The Dwarvenkings' Curse' in part i of the commentary following Chapter XIV (pp. 602–3).

12 See 'The Only Philological Remark', part iii of the commentary following this chapter.

13 Having spent months travelling on the road with dwarves, it would have been surprising if Bilbo had not 'heard tell and sing of dragon-hoards'. For example, the dwarves' first poem, 'Far Over the Misty Mountains Cold' – only 'a fragment' of which is set down in Chapter I – describes 'many a gleaming golden hoard' (page 37) and details of the wonderful things in them. Likewise, at Medwed's house the dwarves tell 'many stories . . . about gold and silver and jewels and the making of them' (page 238), and at Lake Town the townspeople are full of songs and speculation about the King under the Mountain's treasure (pp. 439–40). Also, of course, we know from his very first conversation with Bladorthin that Bilbo was already familiar, before he ever set out on the quest of Erebor, with stories about dragons (see page 31 and DAA.35); cf. his knowledge of their weak spot (' "I have always understood" murmured Bilbo . . . "that dragons were tender underneath, especially in the region of the – er chest" ' [page 512]), which precedes the dwarves' discussion of the best way to attack a dragon by more than a page [page 513].

14 The detail of the stolen cup is a homage to a similar scene in *Beowulf*; see part ii of the commentary following this chapter.

15 'More like a grocer than a burglar': Dwalin's dismissive words (spoken by Gloin in the published book) go all the way back to the Pryftan Fragment (see page 8), as does Bilbo's reaction to them, his desire 'to be thought fierce', even if it meant travelling to a desert far to the east and fighting a dragon. Given that he is currently in the midst of the Desolation of the Dragon and soon to engage Smaug first in a battle of

wits and then, according to Plot Notes C, to kill him, his earlier words have in a sense come true, and would have done so more literally had Tolkien stuck to his original outline.

16 In fact, from its shape, general topography, and isolation from other heights, the Lonely Mountain is almost certainly an extinct volcano; compare its outline with that of such real-world volcanoes as Mt. Rainier or Mt. St. Helens.

17 Note that this description, which is amusingly ironic in the published book, was written when the idea of Bilbo killing the dragon himself with his little sword was still Tolkien's intention (see Plot Notes C). Hence, Smaug is in effect having a prophetic dream of his own approaching death here.

18 Added in left margin in cursive script and marked for insertion at this point: 'of late he had half fancied he had caught the din of echo of a knocking sound from far above.' This is marked for insertion at this point, but more properly goes at the end of the sentence, its corresponding placement in the published story.

19 The manuscript actually has 'frightened' here ('the frightened eyes of the hunting dragon'; 1/1/13:4); I have supplied the reading 'frightful' from the First Typescript (1/1/62:4).

20 This sentence was slightly altered with the addition of the word 'lost' following *ponies*, then replaced by 'They will be slain, and all our ponies *too*, and all our stores *lost*' in the typescript (since the stores could not be 'slain'). Note that in the next sentence in the manuscript it is Bilbo, not Thorin as in the published book, who makes the panic-strickened dwarves rescue their fellows. The paragraphs describing Thorin's coolly taking command to leave no dwarf behind while sending Bilbo, Balin, and Fili and Kili into the tunnel (so that if worse comes to worse 'the dragon shan't have all of us') first appear, without any surviving drafting, in the First Typescript (typescript page 118; 1/1/62:4), in exactly the words used in the final book (cf. DAA.274), except that Bifur at first refers to Bombur and Bofur as 'My brothers!', altered in ink to 'My cousins'. See Text Note 34 following Chapter VIII for more about this change in their family relationships.

21 'whirring': to make a continuous vibrating sound (OED). Note that this word falls within the portion of the OED upon which Tolkien worked during his time on the Dictionary staff in 1919–20, a decade before starting *The Hobbit*, although so far as we know 'whirr' was not one of the words which Tolkien personally researched; see Hammond, *Descriptive Bibliography*, page 278; Winchester, *The Meaning of Everything*, pages 206–8; and Appendix I (particularly pages 229–31) of *Lexicography and the OED: Pioneers in the Untrodden Forest*, ed. Lynda Mugglestone, Appendix I (particularly pages 229–31). The best account of Tolkien's time on the Dictionary, and his contributions to that vast ongoing collaborative project, can be found in *The Ring of Words: Tolkien and the Oxford English Dictionary* by Gilliver, Marshall, and Weiner [2006].

22 A new ink begins at this point, indicating at least a short break in composition. The same ink was also used to touch up some words in the preceding lines and make them easier to read.

23 Tolkien is probably not using the word in the generic sense here (cf. the exchange with Arthur Ransome discussed in Appendix IV); although Smaug knows dwarves are present (see page 510), he also believes that lake-men are with them, of whom the unseen 'thief' is one (ibid.). Had he captured and eaten all fourteen ponies,† no doubt he would have been better informed about the composition of the intruders. Still, Smaug does know that there are fourteen individuals among the group camped on the mountain ('why not say "us fourteen"'? and 'a fourteenth share', both page 511).

†Apparently Thorin & Company have sixteen in the published book; contrast the manuscript account of their approach to the mountain described on page 471, where Bilbo and Balin are on the same pony leading a single pack-pony, with the account in the published book where Bilbo and Balin each lead a pack-pony and appear to be riding separate ponies themselves (DAA.255).

24 'almost dead and dark': That is, his fires seem to have died down, leaving the room almost dark.

25 This line, which survives into the published book, is one more indicator that Tolkien did not, when writing *The Hobbit*, regard Bilbo's ring as anything more than a harmless and useful treasure; the One Ring of the sequel cannot by any means be described as a luck-bringer. Cf. also Bilbo's riddling description of himself, a few paragraphs later, as 'luck-wearer'.

26 Bilbo's conversation with Smaug evolved and expanded in the very act of writing; in the lines originally following this sentence, the dragon immediately confronts the unseen intruder with his knowledge that dwarves were involved:

> Nor did you walk here unless > all the way here; unless you > let me tell you I ate six ponies last night, shall probably catch and eat the others before long. But never mind about your thirteen companions dwarves of course, don't tell me! I know the smell and taste of dwarf; and they had left tokens enough on the ponies for me. But

All this was struck through and the dialogue expanded in the telling in order to allow Bilbo to spin out his riddles and pseudo-names alluding to his adventures so far. Similarly, the only significant *nom de guerre* is 'barrel-rider', since it sparks Smaug's next remark (and determines the course of action that leads to his death); Tolkien twice wrote it and each time crossed it out, deferring it to the end of the passage.

Note that, like Odysseus (*The Odyssey*, Book IX), Bilbo refuses to tell his foe his real name (which, as Tolkien notes, is wise; cf. 'Turambar and the Foalókë', where knowledge of Túrin's true identity enabled Glorund to beguile the headstrong human into abandoning those who depended upon him and instead rushing off onto a fool's errand). Sigurd also at first refuses to tell the mortally wounded Fafnir his name in both *Fáfnismál* (stanzas 1–3) and *Volsunga Saga* (Morris, page 59); the compiler of the Edda interrupts the poem to prosaically state that 'Sigurd concealed his name because it was believed in ancient times that the words of a man about to die had great power if he cursed his enemy by name'. Odysseus eventually does tell the Cyclops his true name, which brings down the curse of his long-delayed homecoming upon him; Sigurd likewise, after some hesitation ('A wanderer named for a noble beast,/the son of no mother,/I had no father as other men do;/always I go alone'), tells the dragon his true name but seems to escape any death-curse from the dragon; it is the treasure itself, Fafnir warns him, that dooms the man who claims it (*Fáfnismál*, stanzas 9 & 20). Bilbo, wiser than both, never does tell Smaug his name† but nonetheless reveals a little too much about himself ('barrel-rider'), thus bringing doom down upon the Lake-men – although, given the dragon's suspicions (page 508), he would sooner or later have attacked the town anyway.

†Note, however, that his having identified himself to Gollum (see page 155) led to much trouble in the sequel; see *The Lord of the Rings* Chapter II ('The Shadow of the Past') and Appendix B: 'The Tale of Years', as well as 'The Hunt for the Ring' in *Unfinished Tales*.

27 The typescript (1/1/62:7) adds, parenthetically, '(though I expect you do, since you know all about Bilbo's adventures to which he was referring)'. In fact each self-assumed epithet alludes to one specific episode earlier in the book:

- *I am he that walks unseen* – because of his magic ring (Chapters V & ff). Note that the shadow which had given Bilbo such trouble in the early days of his possessing the ring – cf. the episode with the goblin guards at the end of Chapter V, or the care needed to keep the sharp-eyed elves of Mirkwood from spotting it (page 381) – is no longer mentioned in the scene with Smaug, probably because the lighting here is dim enough (apparently coming entirely from Smaug himself)† that no shadows can be seen among the mirk, as had presumably been the case during his battle with the Mirkwood spiders.
- *I come from under the hill* – an allusion to the address of Bilbo's home, given in the first surviving paragraph of the Pryftan Fragment as 'Bag-end, Under-Hill' (page 7); see also Tolkien's drawing of the outside of Bilbo's home, labelled 'Bag-End, Underhill' (DAA.46).
- *and under the hills my paths led* – the goblin-caves (Chapter IV). The typescript adds '*and over the hills*' – i.e., the mountain-path (also Chapter IV, which in the First Typescript is given its now-familiar title, 'Over hill and Under hill' [1/1/54:1]).
- *And through the air* – when carried by Eagles (Chapters VI & VII).
- *I am the clue-finder* – this could refer to any of several episodes. It might mean Bilbo finding the key to open the trolls' lair (page **000**, Chapter II) but more likely refers to his discovering the exact application of the moon-runes on Thror's Map and thus enabling Thorin &

Company to find the keyhole at the exact moment on Durin's Day (Chapter XI).

- *the web-cutter* – in his battle with the Spiders of Mirkwood (Chapter VIII).
- *the stinging fly* – Bilbo attacking the Spiders with his little sword; he calls himself a 'naughty little fly' in his spontaneous song 'Lazy lob and crazy Cob' (page 311) and the spiders refer to his little sword in terms they understand as 'a sting' (Chapter VIII). Later, of course, the sword would be given *Sting* as its proper name by Bilbo (DAA.208), but this would not occur until the First Typescript (see Text Note 23 for Chapter VIII).
- *I am he that buries his friends alive* – this might refer to Bilbo's getting all the dwarves safely underground inside the secret tunnel just before Smaug's attack the night before (Chapter XIII).
- *that drowns them* – i.e., Bilbo's hiding the thirteen dwarves in the barrels thrown into the Forest River to escape the dungeons of the Elvenking (Chapter IX).
- *and draws them alive from the water* – by opening the aforesaid barrels upon the arrival at the Long Lake (Chapter X).
- *I am come from the end of a bag* – e.g., the name of Bilbo's home, Bag-End (Chapter I).
- *but no bag went over me* – Bilbo and Bladorthin were the only members of the expedition not to have bags thrown over their heads by the three trolls (Chapter II).
- *I am the friend of bears* – the visit with Medwed/Beorn (Chapter VII).
- *and eagles* – the rescue by Eagles, and brief sojourn in their eyries (Chapters VI & VII).
- *I am ring winner* – the riddle-contest with Gollum (Chapter V).
- *& luck wearer* – see the comment in Text Note 25 above about 'the luck of his ring', though we should also note that Bilbo was chosen as the lucky number (Chapter I) and that in the typescript version of Chapter VIII the dwarves come to recognize 'that he had some wits, as well as luck, and a magic ring' after he rescues them from the spiders (1/1/58:15; cf. DAA.217).
- *and I am Barrel-rider* – during the long, dark, cold ride down the Forest River in the first hours after escaping from the Elvenking's halls (Chapter IX). It is ironic that Smaug quips 'maybe "Barrel" is your pony's name', since at the time the narrator had likened Bilbo's attempt to stay atop the barrel 'like trying to ride without bridle or stirrups a roundbellied pony that was always thinking of rolling on the grass' (page 387).

†E.g., the chamber's being completely dark the third time Bilbo enters it, in Smaug's absence (see page 578).

Note that, unlike the actual riddles he had exchanged with Gollum, which rather resemble the riddle-contest in *Heidrek's Saga* (see page 168), these here are all tests of knowledge, like the final, fatal 'riddle' Odin asks the giant in *Vafþrùðnismál* (see page 169), where the speaker deliberately refers to events about which his listener is ignorant. It may be significant that in *Fáfnismál* Sigurd questions the dying dragon, very much as Odin questions the giant in *Vafþrùðnismál.*

28 The typescript (1/1/62:7) adds the following sentence at the end of this paragraph, which enables us to know that Bilbo's pony was one of the ones Smaug had eaten: 'But he did not tell Bilbo that there was one smell he could not make out at all, hobbit-smell; it was quite outside his experience and puzzled him mightily.'

29 This sentence was altered to read 'He was *in grievous danger of* coming under the dragon-spell'. Compare the Tale of Turambar, where the dragon's eye held the hero motionless: 'with the magic of his eyes he bound him hand and foot . . . and he turned the sinews of Túrin as it were to stone' (BLT II.85–6), while the dragon's voice beguiled him: 'for the lies of that worm were barbed with truth, and for the spell of his eyes he believed all that was said' (ibid., page 87).

30 Presumably the missing word should be something like 'friends': e.g., 'Bilbo's *friends* really ought to have warned him.' The words 'warned him' were canceled in pencil and replaced by 'put him on his guard', a reading similar to that in the First Typescript and published book ('Bilbo of course ought to have been on his guard'; 1/1/62:8 and DAA.281).

31 Added in top margin: 'gold was only an afterthought with us.'

32 The apostrophe marking the possessive is absent in the lightly punctuated original; I have chosen *sons'* over *son's* here because two pages later in the manuscript Tolkien unambiguously refers to King Girion's sons in the plural; see page 514 and also Text Note 6 for Plot Notes C.

33 Compare Smaug's boasts (manuscript page 150), and also the description of Smaug's attack on Lake Town that follows a few pages later (manuscript pages 154–155), with the description of the great dragon in the deeps in the Book of Job, chapter 41:

Can you draw out Leviathan . . . ?
Will he speak to you soft words? . . .
No one is so fierce that he dares to stir him up . . .
Who can penetrate his double coat of mail?

. . . Round about his teeth is terror.
His back is made of rows of shields,
shut up closely as with a seal.
One is so near to another
that no air can come between them.

. . . [H]is eyes are like the eyelids of the dawn.
Out of his mouth go flaming torches;
sparks of fire leap forth.
Out of his nostrils comes forth smoke,
as from a boiling pot and burning rushes.

His breath kindles coals,
and a flame comes forth from his mouth.
In his neck abides strength,
and terror dances before him . . .
His heart is hard as a stone . . .

When he raises himself up the mighty are afraid;
at the crashing they are beside themselves.
. . . [T]he sword . . . does not avail,
nor the spear, the dart, or the javelin.
He counts iron as straw,
and bronze as rotten wood.
The arrow cannot make him flee;
for him slingstones are turned to stubble.
. . . he laughs at the rattle of javelins.

His underparts are like sharp potsherds . . .
He makes the deep boil like a pot . . .
Behind him he leaves a shining wake . . .
Upon earth there is not his like,
a creature without fear . . .
[H]e is king over all the sons of pride.

Tolkien is reported by some sources to have worked on the translation of Job found in *The Jerusalem Bible* [first edition, 1966], in addition to his recognized role in translating Jonah; cf. Carpenter's checklist of Tolkien's publications (*Tolkien: A Biography*, page 274) and Tolkien's letter to Charlotte and Denis Plimmer (letter of 8th February 1967; *Letters*, p. 378). Hammond cites a letter from the bible's publisher stating that Tolkien 'also worked on the Book of Job, providing its initial draft and playing an important part in establishing its final text' (*Descriptive Bibliography*, page 279), but his role on that book seems to have been limited to reviewing an early draft by another translator. I am indebted to Wayne Hammond for this clarification. According to the *Reader's Guide*, vol. two of Christine Scull & Wayne G. Hammond's *The J.R.R. Tolkien Companion and Guide* [2006], Tolkien also did some work on Isaiah and probably Job as well, and was offered the Pentateuch or Books of Moses (Genesis, Exodus, Leviticus, Numbers, & Deuteronomy) as well as the historical books (Joshua, Judges, and 1st & 2nd Samuel), but ultimately had to decline because of the press of other work (*Reader's Guide* pages 437–9).† In any case, that work came many years after he had completed work on *The Hobbit*.

†Tolkien was of course also familiar with the Jonah story professionally through its vivid and amusing fourteenth-century Middle English retelling in the same manuscript as (and universally believed to be by the same author as) *Sir Gawain & the Green Knight* and *Pearl*: the Gawain-poet's adaptation is known as *Patience*.

34 'The dwarves and the men of Dale' was changed in the manuscript to simply 'The men of Dale'; otherwise, of course, some member of Thorin's company might be expected to be able to talk to the bird. The motif of the dwarves' special friendship with the Ravens of the Mountain may have originated by the displacement of this motif from the original thrushes to another breed of bird.

35 This sentence is replaced in the First Typescript by the passage essentially as it appears in the published book: '. . . they all began discussing dragonslayings historical, dubious, and mythical, and the various sorts of stabs and jabs and undercuts, and the different arts devices and stratagems by which they had been accomplished. The general opinion was that catching a dragon napping was not as easy as it sounded; and the attempt to stick one or prod one asleep was more likely to end in disaster than a bold frontal attack' (1/1/62:10; cf. DAA.285). The latter sentence, of course, postdates the abandonment of the Bilbo-as-dragon-slayer plot from Plot Notes B & C which had probably still been in place when this chapter was written: originally, the discussion of how to kill a sleeping dragon would have been immediately relevant to the upcoming chapters.

36 This paragraph was bracketed by Tolkien and marked for deletion, probably when the vast expansion represented by 151b replaced it.

37 As written, this sentence reads 'All was no quiet below at any rate'; this might be a slip for 'All was *now* quiet below . . .'

38 Only fourteen manuscript pages after it had been used as the wizard's name for the last time (see page 472), 'Bladorthin' has here been reassigned to an elusive figure who appears only in this single sentence. The First Typescript (1/1/62:11) makes this 'the great King Bladorthin (long since dead)', about whom nothing is otherwise told; a sad relic for what had been the name of one of the story's major characters.

39 The 'Gem of Girion' here makes its first appearance in the story, having been long anticipated in the Plot Notes (see page 364). Later this would be replaced by the Arkenstone, which would be given its own earlier history; see commentary following Chapter XIV. Similarly, the coats of mithril mail (although that term had not yet arisen and is in fact never used in *The Hobbit*), foreseen in Plot Notes C, also now appear in the narrative.

(i)
Tolkien's Dragons

I first tried to write a story when I was about seven. It was about a dragon. I remember nothing about it except a philological fact. My mother said nothing about the dragon, but pointed out that one could not say 'a green great dragon', but had to say 'a great green dragon'. I wondered why, and still do. The fact that I remember this is possibly significant, as I do not think I ever tried to write a story again for many years, and was taken up with language.

—JRRT to W. H. Auden, 7 June 1955 (*Letters* p. 214).[1]

Few elements in Tolkien's work have had as much influence on modern fantasy, the genre he himself essentially created, as his depiction of dragons. When Tolkien began writing, dragons had dwindled to whimsical fairy-tale creatures in the popular mind, treated more as figures of fun than the deadly menaces they had been in old legend. Even among scholars of those old legends, the feeling ran that dragons were pedestrian, unimaginative, and trivial, 'the merest commonplace of heroic legend' (W. P. Ker, *The Dark Ages* [1904]; quoted more in sorrow than in anger in Tolkien's 'Beowulf: The Monsters and the Critics' [1936], page 7). The great R. W. Chambers (*Widsith* [1912]) even lamented that the Beowulf-poet had given us a story about Grendel and the fire-drake when he and his fellow critics would have much preferred a melodrama of tangled loyalties at the Danish court above 'a wilderness of dragons' (quoted in 'Beowulf: The Monsters and the Critics', page 8).

There were, of course, notable exceptions to the general neglect; writers who fully appreciated the appeal and impact of what we may call dragons of the old school, such as Lord Dunsany ('The Fortress Unvanquishable Save For Sacnoth' [1907], 'The Hoard of the Gibbelins' [1912], 'Miss Cubbidge and the Dragon of Romance' [1912]) and Kenneth Morris (*The Book of Three Dragons* [1930]), but by and large the whimsical dragons of E. Nesbit (e.g., *The Book of Dragons* [1899] and 'The Last Dragon' [1925]) and above all Kenneth Grahame ('The Reluctant Dragon' [1898 and 1938]) had won the day. Tolkien, who considered dragons the quintessential fantasy creature ('The dragon had the trade-mark *Of Faërie* written plain upon him. In whatever world he had his being it was an Other-world' – OFS.40), presented them so dramatically and successfully in his own work that he single-handedly reversed the trend of the preceding half-century and more, both in fantasy and in scholarship.[2]

Tolkien's interest in dragons was life-long: he recalled in his Andrew Lang lecture that his favorite fictional world when growing up had been 'the nameless North of Sigurd of the Völsungs, and the prince of all dragons . . . I desired dragons with a profound desire . . . [T]he world that contained even the imagination of Fáfnir was richer and more beautiful, at whatever cost of peril' (OFS.40).[3] In his 1965 radio interview with Denys Gueroult, he admitted to a fondness for these 'intelligent lizards':

> [D]ragons always attracted me as a mythological element. They seem to be able to comprise human malice and bestiality together . . . a sort of malicious wisdom and shrewdness. Terrifying creatures.

Writing to Christopher Bretherton a few months earlier [1964], he described how in his youth he had been 'interested in traditional tales (especially those concerning dragons)' in addition to philology and metrics, before '[t]hese things began to flow together when I was an undergraduate' (i.e., between 1911 and 1915; *Letters*, page 345). Indeed, so steeped in thinking about dragons was he that when as a child he found a fossil on the beach at Lyme Regis, he believed he had found a piece of petrified dragon.[4] It is no wonder, then, that when he came to write his mythology he filled it with dragons.

Dragons are one of the most persistent features in Tolkien's work, appearing in the Silmarillion tradition (Glorund the Golden, the 'dragons of the north' who destroy Gondolin, Ancalagon the Black), in both of his children's tales that preceded *The Hobbit* (*Roverandom*'s Great White Dragon of the Moon and *Farmer Giles of Ham*'s Chrysophylax Dives) as well as in the Father Christmas Letters (cf. the 1927 letter, the full version of which appears in *Letters from Father Christmas* pages 32–4), in several of his poems ('The Hoard', 'The Dragon's Visit'), in his scholarly essays ('On Fairy-Stories' and particularly 'Beowulf: The Monsters and the Critics'), and of course in his art: in addition to his illustrations for *The Hobbit*, *Roverandom*, and the Silmarillion tales, all of which have some featuring dragons, see the dragon-drawings reproduced in *Artist & Illustrator* (H-S#48 & 49), only two out of a number of uncollected pieces. A dragon (almost certainly Smaug himself) can even be seen in one of the Father Christmas Letters, painted on the cave walls along with prehistoric beasts in the letter for 1932 (see Plate VI [detail] and *Letters from Father Christmas*, page 75), and a tiny toy dragon belonging to a monster child appears in one untitled miscellaneous sketch (H-S#77). A recognized authority on the subject who even lectured on dragons at Oxford's Natural History Museum,[5] Tolkien argued that, far from being a worn-out folktale cliché, dragons were eminently fitted to serve as the supreme challenge for any hero. Like the elves, whom he rescued from being treated as dainty flower fairies, Tolkien also redeemed the dragon and re-established it as the greatest of all fantasy monsters. There is a reason that the world's pre-eminent role-playing game, which borrows liberally from folklore, mythology, legendry, and modern fantasy, is named *Dungeons & Dragons* rather than featuring any other monster in the title.

Turning from Tolkien's theory to his practice, we can divide the dragons appearing in his work into essentially three groups. The first, and least important, are those who remain undifferentiated from one another in the background of the stories, although their deeds *en masse* may be of importance: the dragons of the north who destroy the dwarves' settlements in the Grey Mountains (*LotR*.1124, 1109), the host of dragons who destroyed Gondolin ('for dragons it was that destroyed that city many ages ago' – cf. page 115), those dragons in *Farmer Giles of Ham* who consider 'knights merely mythical' but nonetheless remain in their lairs far from Giles' land, the various lesser moon-dragons mentioned in *Roverandom* who wreak such havoc in the *Father Christmas Letters* when the Man in the Moon is temporarily absent (*Letters from Father Christmas*, 1927 letter), and of course the great host of winged dragons who nearly defeat the Army of the Valar in the final battle that once and for all ends the First Age. Although only described in general terms, these background dragons are important mainly because they provide a context, evidence that the few individual dragons with whom we meet are not the only ones of their kind but typical of the species.[6]

Secondly, there are those dragons who are merely a name (Ancalagon the Black, Scatha the Worm) or deed (the nameless cold-drake – that is, a flameless dragon – that forced Durin's Folk to flee the Grey Mountains) but who are given no line of dialogue or any characteristic that would mark them as individual personalities. While we would naturally like to know more about all of these, even in their abbreviated state they too serve an important purpose in the legendarium. Every collection of real-world myths is of necessity incomplete; there is always some story that has been lost, some figure who is reduced to a bare name or fact (e.g., the Old English 'Earendel', the 'recovery' of whose myth sparked Tolkien's creation of his legendarium). The inclusion of such figures, of obvious significance but shorn of all detail, helps make Tolkien's created myth seem much more like those surviving mythologies painstakingly compiled by generations of scholars. For example, we are fortunate that the story of Wayland the Smith has survived (e.g., in the poem 'The Lay of Völund' [*Völundarqviða*], part of the *Elder Edda*), so that we do not have to puzzle it out from such allusive evidence as the illustration of one scene from the legend on the Franks Casket (cf. the frontispiece to Dronke, *The Poetic Edda*, volume II [1997]), but the once-popular story of his father Wade the Giant has been lost (cf. R. M. Wilson, *The Lost Literature of Medieval England* [1952], pages 19–22). Similarly, we have lost the stories that once explained geographical features such as the chalk-figures now known as the White Horse of Uffington (which may in fact be intended to represent a dragon; cf. Paul Newman, *Lost Gods of Albion* [1997]), the Cerne Giant, or the Long Man of Wilmington, while image and story alike have vanished in the case of other hill-figures such as the Red Horse of Tysoe [destroyed 1800] or the pair of giants known as Gogmagog [destroyed in the 1660s] that once overlooked Plymouth harbour. In a chronicle or condensed account such as those represented by the appendices of *The Lord of the Rings* or the later parts of the 1977 *Silmarillion* there may be room for only the barest facts, but even here Tolkien makes sure that dragons are represented, including some that would be wholly unknown if we had only the major Silmarillion stories (e.g., the stories of Beren & Lúthien, Túrin, and Tuor) to go by or indeed the main story of *The Lord of the Rings* shorn of its Appendices.

Thirdly and most importantly, we have those dragons who are presented with fully developed personalities, true characters in their respective works: Smaug, Glorund, Chrysophylax Dives (whose name simply means 'Rich Treasure-Guardian'), and, to a lesser extent, the unnamed dragons appearing in 'The Dragon's Visit', 'The Hoard', and *Roverandom*. Of these, Glorund (also known at various times and in various texts as Glórung [1926 'Sketch'], Glómund [1930 *Quenta*], and finally Glaurung ['Grey Annals', published *Silmarillion*]), the Father of Dragons, is the most purely malicious; devious in preferring to inflict misery rather than indulge in straightforward destruction, as when he enspells Túrin and Nienor rather than simply killing them. He is also the most powerful of all Tolkien's dragons, save only Ancalagon the Black (of whom more later), and the one who has the most impact on the mythology, being not only deeply enmeshed in the Túrin story but fighting in two of the six great battles of Beleriand: the Fourth Battle, Dagor Bragollach ('the Battle of Sudden Flame'; *Silm.* Chapter XVIII) and the Fifth Battle, Nirnaeth Arnoediad ('[the Battle of] Unnumbered Tears'; *Silm.* Chapter XX) – incidentally, the only two in this sequence of battles which Morgoth won – as well as an earlier sally when he was 'yet young and scarce half-grown' (*Silm.*116; cf. also Smaug's having been 'young and tender' at the time of his descent upon Dale, DAA.282). Smaug can destroy a dwarf-kingdom and powerful human city at the same time, while Chrysophylax, though not overbold (FGH 25 & 58), twice routs the knights of the Middle Kingdom ('all the King's horses and all the King's men'; FGH 59 & 72) and the green dragon of 'The Dragon's Visit' handily destroys the entire village of Bimble Bay when provoked, despite the best efforts of its fire brigade.[7] But Glorund is in a different league entirely: he leads balrogs into battle (*Silm.*151), destroys whole armies ('Elves and Men withered before him'; *Silm.*192), lays waste one of the great elven cities of old ('Glaurung came in full fire against the Doors of [Nargothrond], and overthrew them, and passed within'; *Silm.*213), and even commands orc armies and sets himself up as lord over his own realm under Morgoth's overlordship ('he gathered Orcs to him and ruled as a dragon-king'; 1930 *Quenta*, HME IV.129), rather like the much earlier Tevildo in 'The Tale of Tinúviel' and as Thû the Necromancer (i.e., Sauron) does from Wizard's Isle (Tol Sirion) in 'The Lay of Leithian'. And we should remember that these elven armies he opposed were not made up of wood-elves or wild-elves but Eldar; it takes Prince Fingon and a host of elven archers to repel him when he is still young and not yet at his full strength, and at his height he plays a devastating role in the Fourth and Fifth Battles and destroys the mighty Noldor of Nargothrond, a hidden city full of elven warriors, Finrod's men, who are probably the peers of those three Elrond sends out much later against the Nazgûl (Glorfindel and two others; cf. *LotR*.226). In his 'malicious wisdom', piercing eye and hypnotic voice, nigh-unstoppable might, gloating possessiveness over treasure, and vulnerable underbelly, Glorund obviously served as Tolkien's model for all the dragons who came after him, most especially Smaug, the greatest dragon of latter days (*LotR*.1109).

(ii)
Smaug the Magnificent

It is entirely in keeping with the 'Children of Morgoth' theme running throughout *The Hobbit* that, while Tolkien had established in the Silmarillion writings that dragons were created by Morgoth,[8] Smaug by contrast is solitary and independent. Unlike Glorund, he comes alone when he descends upon the Mountain, much as do Chrysophylax Dives in *Farmer Giles of Ham* and the green dragon in 'The Dragon's Visit'. And although like his progenitor Smaug too sets himself up as a king over his usurped halls – cf. 'They shall see me and remember who is King under the Mountain' (page 515; cf. DAA.288) and '"Which king?" said [Bard] . . . "As like as not it is . . . the dragon, the only King under the Mountain we have ever known"' (pages 547–8; cf. DAA.302–3) – his is a kingship in name only. Smaug is never seen commanding armies of orcs or following anybody's command; he has no connection with the other scattered survivors of Morgoth's minions who appear elsewhere in the book, such as the Necromancer, the goblins of the Misty Mountains, or the great bats of Mirkwood who later appear in the Battle of Five Armies (cf. Morgoth's messenger-bats in 'The Lay of Leithian' Canto XI lines 3402–3408a [HME III.278–9] and *Silm*.178).

This represents a different conception not just from the earlier Silmarillion stories, in which all evil things were united under Morgoth's command (although they also sought to advance their own interests, as when Glorund first serves Morgoth's bidding by destroying Nargothrond and then indulges himself by claiming all its treasures), but also from the *Lord of the Rings* era that followed, where once again the various evil races and beings of Middle-earth are falling under the command of (or at least into allegiance with) a Dark Lord: as Gandalf says of Gollum, 'Mordor draws all wicked things, and the Dark Power was bending all its will to gather them there' (*LotR*.72). In short, at the time *The Hobbit* was written (1930–32), Tolkien seems to have conceived of Middle-earth as no longer having a Dark Lord since Morgoth's fall. Morgoth's taint remained, but the evil creatures that once served him no longer had any unified purpose. Not until the creation of the Númenórean material (*The Lost Road* [circa 1936] and 'The Fall of Númenor' [ibid.]; cf. HME V and see also *The Notion Club Papers* [circa 1944–6] in HME IX), shortly before *The Hobbit*'s publication, does the idea of Sauron (whom Tolkien in his 1965 radio interview described as Morgoth's 'petty lieutenant') assuming Morgoth's mantle as a second Dark Lord seem to have arisen. This latter concept obviously underlies *The Lord of the Rings* (as reflected in that work's title), and later as part of his work to reconcile Bilbo's world to Middle-earth as it had developed in the sequel Tolkien deftly re-envisioned *The Hobbit* by presenting Bilbo's adventure as taking place during a lull in Sauron's activities, just before the long-banished Dark Lord (quiescent or incognito since the loss of the One Ring at the beginning of the Age) reasserted himself, dropping his guise as 'the Necromancer' and reclaiming his title as Lord of Mordor (cf. 'The Tale of Years', Appendix B to *The Lord of the Rings*).

In the post-*Lord of the Rings* period Tolkien would even speculate on how Sauron might have made use of Smaug, had the dragon survived to the time of the War of the Ring. Gandalf believed him fully capable of destroying Rivendell and ravaging Eriador, including the Shire ('The Quest of Erebor', *Unfinished Tales* pp. 322 & 326). In fact, Bilbo's sudden mental image while listening to the dwarves' song during the unexpected party –

> . . . in the wood beyond the Water a flame leapt up . . . and he thought of plundering dragons lighting on his quiet hill and setting it all in flames. Then he shuddered . . . (Pryftan Fragment, page 7)

– which almost dissuades him from going on the quest, becomes oddly prophetic when, a quarter-century after writing this passage, Tolkien decided that this is what *would* have come to pass had the hobbit *not* joined Thorin & Company and thus set in motion the chain of events that brought about the dragon's demise before the War of the Ring.[9] This is not to say that Smaug would have been under Sauron's command as Glorund had been under Morgoth's, any more than Shelob or Caradhras or the Watcher in the Water were, merely that Sauron would have been able to stir him up to new villainy that would surpass any destruction he wrought in his youth.

Thus, while clearly greatly influenced by Tolkien's earlier portrayal of Glorund – who in turn had been inspired by what was for Tolkien the quintessential dragon, Fafnir the great, guardian of the Nibelung treasure, a foe killable only by the greatest of all saga-heroes, Sigurd Fáfnirsbane – Smaug is also quite distinct from the great *foalókë* of the First Age.[10] One major cause of this divergence is that with Smaug Tolkien is drawing not just on his own legendry but also on another outside literary source, one which dominated his professional scholarship during the 1930s: *Beowulf*. Tolkien said in his Beowulf essay that there were only three great dragons in Old Norse and Old English literature: the Midgard Serpent (*Miðgarðsormr* or the Middle-earth Wyrm), Fafnir, and Beowulf's dragon ('Beowulf: The Monsters and the Critics', page 9). Fafnir, as we have already seen, became the primary model or inspiration for Glorund. The Midgard Serpent, whom Tolkien described as the fit adversary for the gods themselves rather than merely human heroes (it is foretold in *Völuspá* and the *Prose Edda* that in the battle after the destruction of the sun and moon, Ragnarök, he will slay and be slain by Thor, the greatest warrior of all the gods of Valhalla and most popular of all the Old English and Norse gods in pre-Christian times), found his analogue in Tolkien's legendarium in Ancalagon the Black, the greatest of all the winged dragons, who almost won the day for the Dark Lord in the apocalyptic battle that ended the Elder Days (the Great Battle or War of Wrath; cf. *Silm*.251–2). Dragons play an important role in this 'Battle of Battles' from its very first appearance in the 1926 'Sketch of the Mythology' (HME IV.39); Ancalagon makes his first appearance in the revised (Q II) version of the 1930 *Quenta* (contrast HME IV.160 with IV.157) and also features in such later works as the '(Earliest) Annals of Beleriand' ([circa 1930]; HME IV.309), the '(Later) Annals of Beleriand' ([circa 1937]; HME V.144) and the 'Conclusion' of the 1937 *Quenta Silmarillion* (HME V.329). Ancalagon's mythological significance within the legendarium, and his parallelism to the Midgard Serpent, were both significantly enhanced near the very end of Tolkien's life through a few late [post-1968] references in Tolkien's linguistic writings to 'the prophecy of Andreth' (a wise woman, one of the two main characters in *Athrabeth Finrod ah Andreth*, or 'The Debate of Finrod and Andreth', HME X.301–66), which foretells that 'the Great Dragon, Ancalagon the Black' was to return to fight in the Last Battle (*Dagor Dagorath*) when Morgoth returns from Outside to destroy the world at the end of time, where he was fated to be slain by Túrin, who would return from the dead for that final deed (HME XII.374–5).

The third of these great dragons, Beowulf's bane, dominates the final third of the Old English poem just as Grendel dominates the first third (and just as Smaug dominates the final third of *The Hobbit*, even after his demise). *Beowulf* was a major source for both *The Hobbit* and the Rohan sections of *The Lord of the Rings*, and we need not explore all the parallels here – indeed, a book-length study has been devoted to just the influence of *Beowulf* on *The Hobbit* (Bonniejean Christensen's *Beowulf and The Hobbit: Elegy into Fantasy in J. R. R. Tolkien's Creative Technique* [dissertation, Univ. of S. Calif., 1969]), a whole chapter of which is devoted to elements of Beowulf's dragon adapted to the Smaug chapters.[11] But the way in which Tolkien selected elements that fit what he needed for his story is instructive of his complex relationship with all his outside sources: he was neither a naive reader nor a passive borrower but transformed and remade what he chose to take (consciously or otherwise) from earlier authors.[12] For example, in both *Beowulf* and *The Hobbit* the dragon lairs in a hill or barrow where he guards ancient treasure for centuries, unmolested by any outsider, until stirred up by the theft of a cup from his hoard he embarks on an orgy of destruction which leads to the destruction of a nearby town and shortly thereafter his own death. But the Beowulf-dragon had discovered a hidden hoard and claimed it for his own, while Smaug, like the unnamed dragon in Tolkien's poem 'The Hoard',[13] steals his treasure and kills its previous owner(s); the Beowulf-dragon has as much right to the treasure as anybody, while Smaug's ownership is tainted with blood from the start. So too the dragon's arousal leads to the death of an old king (King Beowulf after half a century leading the Geats, old Thorin after a century as leading Durin's folk in exile and soon after his becoming King under the Mountain) and the emergence of a young warrior who suddenly steps forward to become hero and then king (Wiglaf the Wægmunding, Bard the Bowman). But again the differences are many: Beowulf proudly orders his honor-guard to hold back and not interfere in the fight and is only saved from throwing his life away when one young warrior disobeys his command and rushes to his aid, helping him to kill the dragon; Thorin is surrounded by his closest companions when mortally wounded in one last desperate heroic sally. Beowulf's dying thoughts are of the treasure he has won, but after his death his people bury it with him in his barrow; Thorin's death-speech renounces greed and gold in favor of the virtues Bilbo embodies (see page 679 & DAA.348), and his treasure (*sans* Orcrist and the Arkenstone) is distributed among his people and their neighbors, enriching the land.

Tolkien's debt to *Beowulf*, and the way he drew on (and played off of) the older work when making something new, are best revealed in three specific details. First, the cup which Bilbo steals from Smaug's lair (page 506) is a precise match for the cup (Old English *wæge*) which a thief steals from the dragon's lair in *Beowulf* (line 2216). Just as in *The Hobbit*, the thief in *Beowulf* manages to enter the dragon's lair stealthily, steal the jeweled cup, and escape. Second, whereas Bilbo is 'Mr. Lucky Number', included in the quest specifically so that Thorin and Company will not number thirteen (page 9), Beowulf chooses to confront the dragon with eleven picked warriors, forcing the nameless thief who had stolen the *maðþum-fæt* ('treasure-cup') to guide them to the spot as the thirteenth of their company. Third and perhaps most significantly, Tolkien felt that dragons in medieval literature suffered from being too abstract and not individual enough: '*draconitas* rather than *draco*', as he put it in his Beowulf essay (page 15) – i.e., representing 'dragon-ness' in an allegorical sense rather than just being a 'plain pure fairy-story dragon' (ibid., page 14).

Leslie Kordecki, in *Tradition and Development of the Medieval English Dragon* [dissertation, 1980], notes that early medieval stories concerning dragons tend to portray them as living, breathing creatures, whereas later stories often reduce them to mere symbols vanquished by the sign of the cross, and Tolkien himself distinguished in his dragon lecture between 'the symbolic dragon', such as the one fought by St. George, and 'the legendary dragon', which he greatly preferred. Tolkien's allegiance and approval are wholly reserved for 'dragon [as] real worm, with a bestial life and thought of his own' (Beowulf essay, pages 14–15), albeit being willing to allow him to be invested with a certain amount of symbolism as an embodiment of 'malice, greed, destruction' (ibid., page 15). His most significant change that transforms Beowulf's bane into Smaug is granting the latter individuality, indeed a 'rather overwhelming personality'. Unlike the *Beowulf* dragon but like Fafnir, Smaug speaks; indeed, he has a highly individualistic turn of phrase that combines sarcasm with arrogance ('You have nice manners, for a thief and a liar'); his manner of speaking establishes him as an even more striking character than Glorund, one of the most vivid in *The Hobbit* despite the fact that he only appears in two chapters out of nineteen. It's hard to disagree with Christensen's judgment, made nearly four decades ago, that in Smaug Tolkien creates 'a "real" dragon unsurpassed in medieval or modern literature' (Christensen, page 121).

For the present, I defer discussion of Smaug's death until the commentary following Chapter XIII and a look at his hoard until Chapter XIV.

(iii)
'The Only Philological Remark'

In his comments on the proposed blurbs for the dust-jacket of *The Hobbit* that accompanied his 31st August 1937 letter to Allen & Unwin, Tolkien remarked that

> The only philological remark (I think) in *The Hobbit* is on p. 221 (lines 6–7 from end): an odd mythological way of referring to linguistic philosophy, and a point that will (happily) be missed by any who have not read Barfield (few have) and probably by those who have.
>
> —*Letters* p. 22.[14]

In the original manuscript, the specific passage in question reads

> To say that Bilbo's breath was taken away is to say too little. There are no words to express his staggerment. (page 506)

However, in the First Typescript this has been expanded:

> To say that Bilbo's breath was taken away is *no description at all*. There are no words to express his staggerment, *not even in the language of the pithecanthropes which consisted (we are told) largely of exclamations*.
>
> —typescript page 117, Marq. 1/1/62:3; italics mine.

This reading was preserved in the Second Typescript and represents the text as it was originally submitted to Allen & Unwin. However, the passage changed again in the page proofs, when 'left' was added to the first part of the second sentence to fill up a shortfall in the typeset line and the rest of that sentence cancelled and replaced:

> . . . no words *left* to express his staggerment, *since Men changed the language that they learned of elves in the days when all the world was wonderful*.
>
> — 1/2/2: page 221; italics mine.

This achieves the reading of the first edition (page 221), which has remained unaltered ever since (cf. DAA.271).

Tolkien nowhere elucidates just what the underlying 'point' to which he refers might be, nor why only those familiar with Barfield's thought might grasp it, but his use of the nonstandard 'staggerment' does draw attention to the passage and suggests the essential point: that Bilbo cannot put what he feels at that moment into words. Quite literally, words fail him, falling short of the reality of the experience.[15] Barfield's theory (perhaps best expressed in his books *Poetic Diction* [1928] and *Unancestral Voice* [1965]),[16] that the history of language serves as a record of the evolution of human consciousness, is complex and subtle, and its application to Bilbo's experience here is not immediately obvious. An essential element of Barfield's theory, however, lies in his belief that nineteenth-century philologists such as Max Müller were entirely in error when they supposed that early humans had simple languages with small vocabularies in which all the words represented simple, concrete things, although they could be applied metaphorically to abstract concepts – for example, that the same word might be used for 'wind' and 'breath' (cf. Latin *spiritus*), and by extension figuratively to 'soul' or 'life-force' (modern 'spirit'). Barfield completely disagreed, arguing instead that in such languages a single word expressed a concept which we in later days cannot conceive of as a whole: hence in the more modern form of that language the 'breath of life' becomes *respiration*, the feeling of an outside force entering you becomes *inspiration*, the life-force within becomes *spirit*, and so forth, all thought of as distinct and separate things, whereas in the earlier language the ancestor-word had meant all these and more. Or, to pick another example, the O.E. word *mōd* (the direct ancestor of our modern word *mood*) puzzles most students who try to learn Old English, because it seems to mean so many different things: heart, mind, spirit, temper, courage, arrogance, pride (cf. Clark Hall, *A Concise Anglo-Saxon Dictionary* [4th ed., 1962], page 239). Thus in his translation of a passage from 'The Battle of Maldon' in *The Homecoming of Beorhtnoth Beorhthelm's Son*, Tolkien translates *mōd* as 'spirit', while in the essay 'Ofermod' which accompanies his verse-play he translated the compound *ofer-mōd* not as 'too much spirit' but as 'overmastering pride' or 'overboldness' (the latter a fair approximation of the original meaning of Tolkien's own surname, we might note, i.e. *tollkühn* = 'foolhardy' [*Letters* p. 218] or 'rashbold' [*The Notion Club Papers*, HME IX.151]).

While the 'ancient semantic unity' Barfield postulates may never have existed – after all, anyone learning a foreign language soon discovers that a similar phenomenon exists whenever we try to translate one language into another; we find some word which can be approximated by a cluster of words in one language but not exactly matched to any one word, since the concept it reflects doesn't exist as a whole in the other language (hence the popularity of the modern American word 'okay', which has been adopted into daily use in a number of unrelated languages around the world, such as Japanese) – Tolkien was wholly sympathetic at any rate to the idea that ancient languages could express more, in fewer words compact with meaning, than modern-day tongues. Such a concept fit in perfectly with his legendarium, where the Elven languages of Sindarin and Quenya are semantically rich despite having a relatively small recorded vocabulary (something already true of them in their earliest forms, as Gnomish and Qenya respectively). Tolkien's respect and admiration for the past meant he was wholly free of what Lewis called 'chronological snobbery';[17] he takes pains, for example, in 'On Fairy-Stories' to defend so-called 'primitive' peoples (footnote to OFS.27; see also OFS.39) and revolutionized *Beowulf* criticism by preferring and defending the aesthetic choices and literary judgments of the author, who had lived a thousand years or more before, above those of the critics of his own day ('Beowulf: The Monsters and the Critics'). Furthermore, from a very early stage of the legendarium the idea was already ensconced that humans were originally without language and learned how to speak from the elves:

> At the rising of the first Sun the younger children of earth [= humans] awoke in the far East . . . They meet Ilkorindi [Dark-Elves] and learn speech and other things of them, and become great friends of the Eldaliё.
>
> — 1926 'Sketch of the Mythology' (HME IV.20).

Similar statements appear in the 1930 *Quenta* (HME IV.99) and 1937 *Quenta Silmarillion* (HME V.246), and there seems little doubt that this is the 'mythological way' to which Tolkien refers in his letter to Allen & Unwin: like his later conception of the ents (*LotR*.489 & 494),[18] Tolkien initially conceived of humans as being without speech until they learned language from the elves (whose own name for themselves, Quendi, means simply 'the Speakers' – *LotR*.1171). And that language, once they acquired it, was not halting or primitive but full of meaning, subtlety, and beauty.

Finally, there is Tolkien's rather surprising use, in the typescript version of this passage, of the precise scientific technical name *pithecanthropus*. The term was first proposed by Ernst Haeckel, a disciple of Darwin, in 1866, just seven years after the publication of *On the Origin of Species* [1859]. Haeckel theorized that, if humans and apes truly shared a common ancestor, then there must once have existed an ancestral form which would combine human and ape characteristics, a 'missing link' which he called *pithecanthropus alulus*: 'speechless ape-man'. Several decades later, when Eugène Dubois discovered fossils of early humans that seemed to match Haeckel's prediction, he named his discovery *pithecanthropus erectus* ('upright ape-man' [1894]) – more popularly known as 'Java Man'. Today, Dubois' discovery is classified with 'Peking Man' [discovered in 1928ff] as *homo erectus*, along with the recently discovered hobbit-sized *homo floresiensis*. Significantly, not only is Tolkien's terminology correct in the contemporary usage of the time, but the skepticism expressed by his parenthetical '*which consisted (we are told) largely of exclamations*' makes it clear that he is well aware of the second part of Haeckel's proposed name, *alulus* or without language. Rather than enter into the paleoanthropological debate on just when humans acquired language (cf. for example Johanson & Edgar, *From Lucy to Language* [1996], page 106), Tolkien provided a mythological answer within his subcreated world, of mankind born mute (*alulus*) but then acquiring full-fledged language from our forerunners and sibling-race, the Elder Children or elves.

NOTES

1 This would have been about 1899, the year before Tolkien began his formal education at King Edward's School; by this time he had already been able to read and write for about three years, or since the age of four (Carpenter, page 21). Tolkien gave another account of this story a decade later in his piece 'Tolkien on Tolkien' printed in the October 1966 Tolkien issue of the magazine *Diplomat*: 'Somewhere about six years old I tried to write some verses on a *dragon* about which I now remember nothing except that it contained the expression a *green great dragon* and that I remained puzzled for a very long time at being told that this should be *great green*' (*Diplomat*, page 39; reprinted in *Letters* p. 221).

The next story we know of that Tolkien wrote after this piece of lost juvenilia, about fifteen years later [circa 1914], was 'The Story of Kullervo',† a William Morris-style adaptation from the *Kalevala*, which strongly influenced his slightly later Túrin story [circa 1919] written for

The Book of Lost Tales. While the original Finnish story has no dragon, Túrin's story featured one so prominently that it shared the title with the hero: 'Turambar and the Foalókë' (that is, Túrin and the Dragon).

In any case, by drawing his attention to the phenomenon known as the hierarchy of adjectives, the chance phrase 'green great dragon' seems to have played a role in Tolkien's becoming aware of the deep structure of his own language and helped him discover his vocation as a philologist. For more on hierarchy of adjectives, and why for example an adjective of color (like 'green') idiomatically follows an adjective of size (like 'great') in English, see Jose A. Carillo's article 'The hierarchy of adjectives', available online at http://www.manilatimes.net/national/2003/may/21/top_stories/20030521top16.htm.

†It is unclear whether 'The Story of Kullervo' predates or postdates the Eärendel poems; the two seem to have been essentially contemporaneous, two different expressions of the same creative impulse (see Carpenter pages 71–3, BLT II.267, and John Garth's *Tolkien and the Great War* [2003] page 45).

2 For more on dragons in modern fantasy, and Tolkien's influence on the way they are depicted, see my article 'Dragons of Legend' in the June 1996 issue of *Dragon* magazine (*Dragon* #230), available online at http://www3.sympatico.ca/ci.kerr/dragons.html. For more on dragons in children's literature from the 1890s to the 1950s, see Christina Scull's 'Dragons from Andrew Lang's retelling of Sigurd to Tolkien's Chrysophylax' in *Leaves from the Tree: J.R.R. Tolkien's Shorter Fiction* [1991]. For more on Tolkien's borrowing from, and transformation of, dragons in Old Norse and Old English literature and lore, see Jonathan Evans' 'The Dragon-Lore of Middle-earth: Tolkien and Old English and Old Norse Tradition', in *J.R.R. Tolkien and His Literary Resonances*, ed. George Clark & Daniel Timmons [2000]. Of particular note is Evans' observation that

> In Tolkien's Middle-earth the dragon-lore of our own Middle Ages is analyzed into its elementary components, rationalized and reconstituted, and then reassembled to fit the larger thematic purposes of Tolkien's grand narrative design. Tolkien treated the disjointed inferences and disparate motifs found in medieval literature as if they were the *disjecta membra* [i.e., scattered fragments] of a once-unified whole – that is, as if there really were a coherent underlying medieval conception of the dragon from which all scattered references drew information. This is in fact a fiction . . . an example of what Shippey has described as the reconstruction of a hypothetical . . . 'asterisk reality' that characterizes Tolkien's vision and method. It is analogous to, and for Tolkien part and parcel of, comparative historical linguistic reconstruction . . . of lost . . . languages and thus lost worlds . . . The dragon-lore embedded in the medieval literature of . . . our world . . . is *not* coherent: it springs from sources as diverse as medieval European geography, ancient Semitic and Hellenistic cosmology and cosmogony, Roman myth-

ology and popular legend, Latin hagiography, and Germanic legend and folklore.

—Evans, in Clark & Timmons, pages 27–8.

3 Tolkien seems to have had *The Hobbit* in mind when drafting this discussion of dragons in 'On Fairy-Stories', since part of what he says in the essay strongly parallels a passage in *The Hobbit* that goes all the way back to the Pryftan Fragment. Compare Tolkien's words in OFS

> I desired dragons with a profound desire. Of course, I in my timid body did not wish to have them in the neighbourhood, intruding into my relatively safe world, in which it was, for instance, possible to read stories in peace of mind, free from fear. But the world that contained even the imagination of Fáfnir was richer and more beautiful, at whatever cost of peril. The dweller in the quiet and fertile plains may hear of the tormented hills and the unharvested sea and long for them in his heart. For the heart is hard though the body be soft. (OFS.40)

with Bilbo's thoughts in the Pryftan Fragment:

> . . . something Tookish awoke within him, and he wished to go and see the great mountains and the seas, the pine trees and the waterfalls, and explore the caves and wear a sword instead of a walking stick. He looked out of the window. The stars were out in a dark sky above the trees. He thought of the jewels of the dwarves shining in dark caves. Then in the wood beyond the Water a flame leapt up – somebody lighting a wood fire probably – and he thought of plundering dragons lighting on his quiet hill and setting it all in flames. Then he shuddered, and quite suddenly he was plain Mr. Baggins of Bag-end Under-Hill again (page 7; cf. DAA.45–6 for the final published text).

4 Carpenter, page 38. Carpenter's source seems to have been Tolkien's 1938 Christmas Dragon lecture (see Note 5 below), in which as an aside Tolkien says:

> I [*added*: once as a boy] found a saurian jaw myself with nasty teeth at Lyme Regis – and thought I had stumbled on a bit of petrified dragon.†
>
> —Ms. Tolk. A 61. fols. 98–125.

Carpenter dates this as having occurred on a summer holiday with Father Francis after Mabel Tolkien's death, so probably in the summer of 1905, summer 1906, or summer 1907, when Tolkien was between thirteen and fifteen years old. However, this seems rather old for literal belief in dragons, especially given Tolkien's stated annoyance at the attempts during his childhood of condescending adults to conflate prehistoric animals with dragons (Note D, OFS.69). It seems likely, therefore, that the episode Tolkien recalls dates from an earlier unrecorded visit during his mother's lifetime – Hammond & Scull, for example, reproduce a seaside watercolour by Tolkien which they tentatively date to 1902, when Tolkien was only ten (*Artist & Illustrator*, pages 11 & 13), and Judith Priestman, in the centenary Bodleian catalogue, reproduces a two-page spread from the same sketchbook entitled 'Sea Weeds and Star Fishes' (*Life and Legend*, pages 12–13). Priestman does not date the piece, but places it between items from 1896 and 1900; in any case it was clearly painted by a child, not a teen. Hammond & Scull suggest the watercolour they reproduce might have been painted at Bournemouth or Poole, which are about forty miles east of Lyme Regis; all three are on the south English coast, a little over 200 miles south of Birmingham, where Tolkien was living at the time. At any rate, Tolkien's recollection about finding the fossil and the early watercolours taken together show that a visit to Lyme Regis during his mother's lifetime is certainly possible.

Lyme Regis is, incidentally, famous for its fossil finds, especially ichthyosaurs (which is probably what young JRRT found), plesiosaurs, and pterodactyls, many of which were discovered by amateur fossil-hunters in the early 1800s. For the role which actual fossils may have played in the rise of dragon-myths and legends of 'giants in the earth', see Simpson, *British Dragons*, pages 20–22.

†A faint echo of this 'bit of petrified dragon' might perhaps be found in the comment, added in the First Typescript of this chapter, that Smaug 'went back to his golden couch to sleep – and to gather new strength. He would not forget or forgive the theft, *not if a thousand years turned him to smouldering stone,* but he could afford to wait. Slow and silent he crept back to his lair and half closed his eyes' (typescript page 119, Marq. 1/1/62:5; compare page 508).

5 See Tolkien's 16th December 1937 letter to Stanley Unwin (*Letters* pp. 27 & 435). Rather than a learned disquisition, this was a light-hearted slide-show for children, where Tolkien showed slides of dinosaurs† and of dragons, including his own dragon-paintings such as 'Conversation with Smaug' (Plate XI [top]), of which he said 'This picture was made by my friend Mr Baggins or from his description . . . it shows a powerful lot of treasure'. Nonetheless, in the course of his lecture he makes a number of interesting points highly revealing of his personal dragon-lore. He describes the dragon as 'a very special creature: draco fabulosus europaeus, the "European fabulous dragon"', which he further divides into two kinds, 'repus or creeping' and 'alatus or winged'; clearly, Glorund and Fafnir would belong to the former category, while Smaug is most definitely in the latter.†† In addition to alluding to several famous dragon stories, such as Thora's dragon (from the legend of Ragnarr Shaggybreeks)††† and Thor's encounter with the *Miðgarðsormr* ('the Dragon of the Island-earth'), he observes of the dragon that 'he is largely man-made, and therefore very dangerous' and gives the admonition 'If you ever come across a dragon's egg, don't encourage it.' He describes dragons as 'legendary creatures founded on serpent and lizard', unlike the dinosaurs ('No one I suppose can tell . . . how long strange obsolete creatures may have survived lurking in odd corners. But even such accidents cannot affect the fact that the Dinosaurs passed away infinitely long before the adventures of Men began'). Of Smaug in particular he says 'A dragon made a desert. He

rejoiced in destruction' (see 'The Desolation of the Dragon' following Chapter XI).

Regarding encounters with dragons, Tolkien warns that a dragon will first try to catch your eye and then get your name in order to curse you before he dies with 'evil magic'; Smaug of course tries to do both, and Glorund succeeds on both counts, with disastrous results for the would-be dragon-slayer. Tolkien gives as a maxim that the right place to look for a dragon is in a burial mound, no doubt basing this rule upon Beowulf's dragon, but Chrysophylax Dives is the only dragon of his known to me who actually follows this rule. He is emphatic that dragon-slaying is a solitary art, observing that 'It was the function of dragons to tax the skill of heroes, and still more to tax other things, especially courage [*added*: and fortune].' Armies, he maintains, are no use at all, nor would modern weaponry avail: '. . . machine-gun bullets are usually no more troublesome to them than a cloud of gnats; armies cannot overcome them; poison gas is a sweet breath to them (they invented it); bombs are their amusement'. Instead, 'Dragons can only be defeated by brave men – usually alone. Sometimes a faithful friend may help, but it is rare: friends have a way of deserting you when [you are faced >] a dragon comes'; this is certainly the experience of Beowulf and of Túrin. Finally, 'Dragons are the final test of heroes', requiring 'luck (or grace) . . . a blessing on your hand and heart'.

—Ms. Tolkien A61 e., fols. 98–125.

†Stegosaur, brontosaurus ('only recently named'), pteranodon, triceratops ('a good name for a terrible creature'), and iguanodon, among others, including one slide he called 'two jolly dinosaurs at play'.

††Tolkien elsewhere notes that he is deliberately leaving out Chinese dragons, who are quite distinct from the European tradition, and symbolic dragons, such as St. George's dragon, although he notes that the latter appears on the English money of the time (the gold sovereign).

†††This is the same Ragnar Lodbrok one of whose sons was named Beorn (see page 282) and whose son Ivarr the Boneless led the viking invasion of England. In brief, Thora was given a dragon's egg or hatchling which grew up to be so fiercely protective of her that it endangered the whole area; Ragnar was the brave and clever hero who devised a scheme for challenging and defeating the dragon, thus winning her hand.

6 Two of these cases – e.g., in the attacks on Gondolin and on the host of the Valar – have additional significance because they depict dragons acting in groups. Tolkien is almost unique among fantasy authors in showing dragons working in unison towards some goal; the great legends always depicted them as solitary beasts, and most later authors have followed suit. The only post-Tolkien modern fantasy of note to deal with dragons *en masse* are the 'Dragonriders of Pern' series by Anne McCaffrey [1968ff] and the 'Dragonlance' novels by Margaret Weis & Tracy Hickman, et al. [1984ff]. Even here, the McCaffrey novels are not true fantasy but romance novels given fantasy trappings

and a science-fiction rationale: later books in the series reveal that the 'dragons' are in fact creatures genetically engineered by space colonists to fulfill a specific role in that planetary ecosystem. By contrast, the Dragonlance novels, although describing considerable numbers of dragons over the course of the series, only very rarely depict more than one dragon at a time; scenes in which dragons interact with each other are extremely rare. As a result, in modern fantasy dragons remain pre-eminently solitary creatures.

7 In the original [1937] version of this poem, the destruction is complete; in the version Tolkien re-wrote [circa 1961] for possible inclusion in *The Adventures of Tom Bombadil* the village's sole survivor (Miss Biggins) ambushes and slays the dragon. Even this modern-day dragon is not the last of his kind, however; the final lines of the original poem describe how, having destroyed the town, he flies back to his own land of Finis-Terre (or, as Dunsany liked to call it, the World's End):

Far over the sea he saw the peaks
round his own land ranging . . .
And the moon shone through his green wings
the night winds beating,
And he flew back over the dappled sea
to a green dragons' meeting.

It may be that in this poem Tolkien finally told the story of the 'green great dragon' he had begun circa 1899.

Note that Tolkien is explicit that dragons survived the Third Age (*Letters* p. 177); in the account of the Last Battle that overthrew Morgoth in the 1926 'Sketch of the Mythology', he is careful to include the detail that two (presumably one male and the other female, with this latter being the only female dragon to appear anywhere in Tolkien's work) escaped the slaughter to propagate their kind (HME IV.39). In the Father Christmas Letters, he describes the modern-day dragons on the moon who cause eclipses (*Letters from Father Christmas*, 1927 letter), and in his 1937 Dragon Lecture he calls the moon 'a refuge of dragons' and showed a slide of one of the Roverandom pictures (also from 1927), describing his own white dragon (called the Great White Dragon of the Moon in *Roverandom*) as 'a Saxon White Dragon that escaped from the Welsh borders† a long while ago.' Tolkien is here probably drawing on the old tradition, most notably embodied in Ariosto's *Orlando Furioso* [1516], that the moon is the home of lost things and hence an appropriate retreat for mythological monsters lost from the world before modern times, such as dragons.

†Chrysophylax's home in *Farmer Giles*, we should note – cf. *Letters* page 130.

8 Probably, as Paul Kocher speculated long ago (*A Reader's Guide to The Silmarillion* [1980], page 271), Morgoth created dragons from balrogs – who are, after all, fire demons – by a process similar to that which created the orcs; see page 138 and the section of *Morgoth's Ring* entitled 'Myths Transformed' (HME X). Particularly significant in this context

is the description in 'The Fall of Gondolin' of dragon-forms 'given hearts and spirits of blazing fire' (BLT II.170).

9 For another 'prophecy' in *The Hobbit* that does not come to pass, see Smaug's dreams of being slain by Bilbo (page 507 & Text Note 17 on page 519). This example is the exact obverse of Bilbo's sudden vision while sitting safely at home in the Shire, since at the time it was written it foretold what Tolkien expected to happen in the next chapters. When he actually came to write them the story shifted in unexpected directions, leaving the dragon's prophetic dream symbolically significant but no longer literally true.

10 Tolkien himself acknowledges both Smaug's affinities to Fafnir and his distinctiveness in his 1965 radio interview with Denys Gueroult:

> DG: I suppose Smaug might be interpreted as being a sort of Fafnir, is he?
>
> JRRT: Oh yes, very much so. Except no, Fafnir was a human or humanoid being who took this form, whereas Smaug is just pure intelligent lizard.

It should be noted that, unlike Sigurd's dragon, there is never any hint in *Beowulf* that its nameless dragon has ever been anything other than a 'real worm, with a bestial life and thought of his own . . . a foe more evil than any human enemy' (Beowulf essay, pages 14–15).

11 Christensen's dissertation is mainly important because one section from it was revised and published separately as the article 'Gollum's Character Transformation in *The Hobbit*', which appeared in *A Tolkien Compass*, ed. Jared Lobdell [1975], pages 9–28. A careful analysis of the changes Tolkien made between the first and second editions of *The Hobbit* (also covered in Part Four of this book), it gives the variant texts in parallel passages and remains one of the dozen or so best essays ever written on Tolkien's work.

For another detailed study of *Beowulf*'s influence on *The Hobbit*, see Roberta Albrecht Adams' *Gollum and Grendel as Cain's Kinsmen* (M.A. thesis, Stetson Univ., 1978).

12 A good example of this is the phrase 'the lord of the rings', which appears in William Morris's *The Tale of Beowulf* (tr. Wm Morris & A. J. Wyatt, Kelmscott Press [1895], page 82) as a translation of '*hringa fengel*' (*Beowulf*, line 2345b), a phrase usually translated as 'the prince of rings' – that is, King Beowulf himself as 'ring-giver' or distributor of treasure to his followers. We know Tolkien read, and disliked, Morris's translation (cf. his slighting reference to it in passing in the draft of his Beowulf essay given in Drout, *Beowulf and the Critics* [2002], page 97) – not surprising, given that Tolkien had probably already read *Beowulf* in the original before coming to Morris's deliberately archaic, not to say idiosyncratic, translation – and it is certainly possible that this phrase popped back into Tolkien's mind a quarter-century later when he was casting about for a suitable title to 'The New Hobbit'.

13 This poem was in existence by at least 1923, when it was published in the *Gryphon*, a Leeds University literary magazine. A revised version appeared in *The Oxford Magazine* in 1937 (only a month after 'The Dragon's Visit' had appeared in the same journal) and, further revised, was collected in *The Adventures of Tom Bombadil* [1962] as 'The Hoard' (poem #14); the original version can be found in *The Annotated Hobbit* (DAA.335–7). The original title, 'Iúmonna Gold Galdre Bewunden' (loosely 'The gold of men of old time was wound about with enchantment'), comes from line 3052 in *Beowulf* near the poem's end. The poem's links with *Beowulf* are strengthened by the fact that Tolkien included the entire poem in early drafts of his Beowulf essay (cf. Drout, *Beowulf and the Critics*, pages 56–8 and 199–205), along with C. S. Lewis's 'The Northern Dragon',† which had obviously been inspired by Tolkien's poem. Lewis's poem is given the title 'Atol inwit gæst' ['The Terrible Unwanted Guest'; *Beowulf* line 2670a] in the second draft of Tolkien's essay (see Drout pages 110–14), but it is unclear whether this title is assigned by Tolkien or Lewis's own. A slightly revised version is reprinted under the title 'The Dragon Speaks' in *Poems*, ed. Walter Hooper [1964], pages 92–3, but again it is unclear whether this title is Lewis's or provided by the editor.

†This title appears to be Drout's, taken from the chapter of Lewis's book in which the poem first appeared (*The Pilgrim's Regress* [1933], Book Ten, Chapter VIII).

14 Tolkien here was objecting to two sentences in the proposed blurb that compared his work to that of Lewis Carroll ('The birth of *The Hobbit* recalls very strongly that of *Alice in Wonderland*. Here again a professor of an abstruse subject is at play'), pointing out among other things that Rev. Charles Dodgson, the mathematics lecturer who wrote under the pen name of Carroll, never reached his own rank of professor. More importantly, Tolkien maintained that 'I do not profess an "abstruse" subject [e.g., Old English] . . . Some folk may think so, but I do not like encouraging them'. He did however concede that philology, which he called 'my real professional bag of tricks', might perhaps be 'more comparable to Dodgson's maths.' If so, then any parallel would lie in 'the fact that both these technical subjects in any overt form are absent' (*Letters* pp. 21–2). See Note 30, pp. 64–5.

15 Although the text of the rest of this paragraph gives a fair idea of how deeply Bilbo is moved by the sight, and hints at the enchantment that almost falls upon him (especially when compared with the dwarves' similar but even stronger reaction to the same sight a few chapters later; cf. page 580 & DAA.295–6). Note the lack of punctuation in the original text ('the spendour the lust the glory') where Tolkien piles on words to suggest aspects of the irreproducible experience:

> He had heard tell and sing of dragon-hoards before, but the splendour the lust the glory of such treasure had never before come home to him. His heart was filled and pierced with the desire of dwarves – and he gazed, almost forgetting the frightful guardian, at the gold,

gazed and gazed for what seemed ages, before drawn almost against his will he stole from the shadow of the door, across the floor, to the nearest edge of the mound of treasure.

16 At the time Tolkien wrote *The Hobbit*, Barfield had published three books: *The Silver Trumpet* [1925], *History in English Words* [1926], and *Poetic Diction: A Study in Meaning* [1928]. We know that Tolkien read, and was deeply impressed by, *Poetic Diction*, since Lewis reported to Barfield:

> You might like to know that when Tolkien dined with me the other night he said *à propos* of something quite different that your conception of the ancient semantic unity had modified his whole outlook and that he was always just going to say something in a lecture when your conception stopped him in time. 'It is one of those things,' he said 'that when you've once seen it there are all sorts of things you can never say again.'
>
> — CSL to OB [date unknown], quoted in Carpenter, *The Inklings* [1978], page 42.

Based on this, Verlyn Flieger has eloquently argued that Barfield was a greater influence on Tolkien than any other writer excepting perhaps the Beowulf poet (*Splintered Light: Logos and Language in Tolkien's World* [1983, rev. ed. 2002], page xxi). This is probably overstating the case, since there seems to be no great break or change in the late 1920s in the ongoing evolution of either Tolkien's invented languages nor in the myths expressed in the Silmarillion tradition of his legendarium (i.e., between the 1926 'Sketch of the Mythology' and the alliterative lays on the one hand and the 1930 *Quenta*, the Annals, and the 1937 *Quenta Silmarillion* on the other). It might be better to say that, like many other readers of Barfield, Tolkien found Barfield's ideas challenged his preconceptions and forced him to rethink the grounds upon which he based his ideas. As a result, Tolkien's work did not become Barfieldian but even more Tolkienesque, a process that was already a constant feature (indeed a hallmark) of the legendarium.

As for the other two books, we know that shortly before Tolkien submitted *The Hobbit* to Allen & Unwin, Lewis loaned him Barfield's little children's story *The Silver Trumpet*, which Tolkien read to his children to an enthusiastic reception – so much so that, when he had finished, the younger Tolkiens are said to have protested: 'You're not going to give it back to Mr. Lewis, are you?' (CSL to OB, June 28th 1936; *The Collected Letters of C. S. Lewis*, vol. II [2004], page 198).

By contrast, *History in English Words* lays out the groundwork and provides a good deal of the proofs for the ideas expressed in *Poetic Diction*. There is no direct evidence that Tolkien read this book, but it seems very likely; it may even have inspired the abortive Tolkien–Lewis collaboration *Language and Human Nature*, which Tolkien described as being 'on "Language" (Nature, Origins, Functions)' (*Letters* pp. 105 & 440); this project was first mooted in 1944 and abandoned circa 1949–50 (cf. *Letters of C. S. Lewis*, revised edition [1988], page 399). In any case, *History in English Words* certainly served as the model of Lewis's *Studies in Words* [1960], a book which Tolkien greatly disliked.

Finally, we must not forget that Tolkien actually knew Barfield, although not well. The two men had first met through their mutual friend Lewis sometime in the late 1920s, when the Barfields were living in the village of Long Crendon a few miles from Lewis's home at the Kilns (in fact, near Thame and Worminghall, the sites where Tolkien set his Oxfordshire story, *Farmer Giles of Ham*), and both were founding members of the Inklings (circa 1933–34), although having by that time joined his family firm of solicitors (Barfield & Barfield) in London, Barfield could only rarely attend meetings. Tolkien particularly admired Barfield's knack of puncturing Lewis at his most dogmatic (cf. *Letters* p. 103), and felt that of all the memoirs of their joint friend in *Light on C. S. Lewis* [1965] that 'Barfield who knew him longest . . . gets nearest to the central point' (*Letters* p. 363).

17 One side effect of Barfield's theory is that it counters the assumption, implicit in almost all discussions of the past, that people who lived a long time ago were somehow stupider than those of us fortunate enough to live in the present day. The phrase 'chronological snobbery' represents C. S. Lewis's coinage to express this attitude and neatly encapsulates the concept he took from Barfield (cf. *Surprised by Joy: The Shape of My Early Life* [1955], page 208).

18 Barfield may also have contributed to the inspiration for Entish with his description in *Poetic Diction* of 'the "holophrase", or long, rambling conglomeration of sound and meaning, which is found among primitive and otherwise almost wordless peoples.' In the same context, he also mentions 'languages in which there are words for "gum-tree", "wattle-tree", etc., but none for "tree"' (*Poetic Diction*, 3rd ed. [1973], page 83). In its love of specificity over common nouns and its additive, repetitive word-building and syntax, Entish sounds very like a language of the type Barfield describes, except that Tolkien removes any pejorative sense of the language's being 'primitive' (it has, after all, been preserved and presumably developed over more than seven thousand years by the time Merry and Pippin hear Treebeard and the other ents use it).

Chapter XIII

THE DEATH OF SMAUG

As before, this chapter break was added at the time Tolkien created the First Typescript and divided the text of the original continuous manuscript into the familiar chapters of the published book. In this particular case, the new chapter began with what had been the third paragraph on Ms. page 153 (Marq. 1/1/15:1); between this and the preceding paragraph Tolkien inserted, in pencil, the directions:

Here insert 'Not at home' Ch. Fire and Water

Thus, the decision to flip what are now chapters XIV ('Fire and Water') and XIII ('Not at Home') – or XIII ('Death of Smaug') and XIV ('While the Dragon's Away'), respectively, in the original draft and this edition – was made at the same time that Tolkien determined where the chapter breaks would fall.

This chapter also marks the spot where, later, the First Typescript broke off and the point to which Tolkien returned when he began the Third Phase drafting that completed the work; see page 638.

The men of the Lake-town were [sitting on the quays >] mostly indoors for the wind was from the North and chill, but some were walking on the quays, and watching as they were fond of doing the stars shine forth from the smooth patches of Lake as they opened in the sky.

From their town the Lonely Mountain was screened by the low hills at the far end of the lake, through a gap in which the R. Running came down from the North. Only its highest peak could they see and they looked seldom at it, for it was ominous and drear even in the morning light. Now it was lost and gone, blotted in the dark.[TN1]

Suddenly it flickered back to view, a brief glow touched it and faded. 'Look!' said one 'the lights again. Last night [they > I >] the watchmen saw them start and fade from midnight till dawn.[TN2] Something is happening up there.'

'Perhaps the King under the Mountain is forging gold' said another. 'It is long since he went North. It is time the songs began to prove themselves again.'

'Which king?' said another with a surly voice.[TN3] 'As like as not it is the marauding fire of the dragon – the only K. under the Mountain we have ever known.'

'You are always foreboding gloomy things' said the others 'from floods[TN4] to poisoned fish' they said. 'Think of something cheerful.'

Then suddenly a great light appeared red and golden in the low place in the hills [> the northern end of the lake turned golden]. 'The king beneath the Mountain' they shouted. '"[The rivers golden run >] His wealth is like the sun, his silver like a fountain. [his gold like rivers run >] his rivers golden run."[TN5] The river is running gold from the mountain' they cried, and everywhere windows opened and feet were hurrying. There was tremendous excitement and enthusiasm. But the surly fellow ran hot foot to the master. 'The dragon is coming or I am a fool' he cried: 'cut the bridges; to arms to arms!'

[So it was that >] The warning trumpets were sounded and the enthusiasm died away. So it was that the dragon did not find them quite unprepared. Before long they could see him as a spark of fire speeding towards them, and not the most foolish doubted that the prophecies had gone somewhat wrong. Still they had a little time. Every vessel in the town was filled with water; every warrior armed, every arrow ready and the bridges[TN6] to the land were cast down and destroyed before the roar of Smaug's terrible approach grew loud, [and the trees by the shore were >] and the lake rippled [red as] fire beneath his coming.

Amid the shrieks and wailing and the shouts of men he came over them, swept towards the bridges, and was foiled. The bridges were gone and his enemies were on an island in deep water – too deep and dark and cool for his liking: If he plunged therein a vapour and a steam wd rise enough to cover all the land with a mist for days, but the lake was mightier than he, it would quench him before he could pass through.

Roaring he swept by on the town. A hail of dark arrows swept up and snapped and rattled on his scales and jewels and their shafts fell back burning and hissing in the lake. No fireworks you ever imagined equalled the sight that night. Now the dragon's wrath blazed to its height till he was blind and mad with it. He circled high in the air lighting all the lake; and the trees by the shore shone like copper and like blood with many [*added*: <dancing>] black shadows at the feet. Now he swooped through the arrow storm taking no heed [for >] to turn his scales towards his foes, seeking only to set their town a blaze. Fire leapt from thatched roofs and wooden beams [But being <hurriedly> >] drenched though they had been with water. Water was flung by hundreds of hands wherever a spark appeared. Back swooped the dragon. A swirl of his tail and the roof of the Great House crumbled; fire unquenchable leapt up. Another swoop and more house[s] [leapt in >] sprang afire or fell. [Men were taking to boats or leaping into the water >] Men were leaping into the water on every side; women and children were being huddled into <?crowded> boats in the market-pool. [Soon all >] Weapons were flung down. The Master himself was <?brung> to his gilded boat. Soon all the town would b<e> burned down to the lake. That was the dragon's hope. They could stay in the boats till they starved, let them try to get to land and he would see. Soon he would set all the shoreland woods ablaze and wither every field and pasture. Just now he was enjoying such sport in town-baiting as he had not had for years.

Still a company of archers held their ground. Their captain was the surly man whose friends accused him of prophesying floods and poisoned fish. But [his >] Bard was his real name, a descendent as tales said of Girion lord of Dale. He shot with a great bow till all but one arrow was spent. The flames were near him, his companions were fleeing. He bent the bow for the last time.

'Arrow' he said '– black arrow I have saved you to the last. I <ha>d you [from] my father and he from old. If ever you came from the forges of the true king of the Mountain go now and speed well.'[TN7] The dragon swooped once more lower than ever.[TN8] The great bow twanged. The black arrow sped [straight >] straight for the hollow by the left breast where his foreleg was flung wide. In it smote and vanished. barb shaft and feather. With a shriek that [cracked >] deafened men, felled stars and split stone[TN9] the Dragon [> Smaug] shot into the air, turned over, and crashed down from a height in ruin. Full upon the town he fell. His last throes splintered it to gledes[TN10] and sparks. The lake roared in. A vast steam leapt up white into the sudden dark. And that was the end of Smaug and Esgaroth[TN11] and Bard.

The text breaks off here, about three-quarters of the way down the page (manuscript page 155; Marq. 1/1/15:3), indicating a pause in the composition. The last two words of this paragraph ('and Bard') were cancelled and replaced by 'but not of Bard'. Probably at the same time, the rest of the manuscript page was filled with the following paragraph, which was marked for insertion before the preceding paragraph (that is, between 'He bent his bow for the last time' and '"Arrow" he said'):

Suddenly out of the dark something fluttered to his shoulder – he started, but it was an old thrush and it perched by his shoulder and it brought him news. Marvelling he found he could understand its tongue – for he was of the Dale race. 'Wait wait' it said 'the moon is rising. Look for the hollow of the left breast as he flies and turns above you.' The[n] Bard drew his last arrow from his quiver. The dragon was circling back, and the moon rose above the eastern shore and silvered his great wings.

This addition clearly dates from the same time as the extended rider (manuscript page 151b) given on page 513, inserted into the end of the preceding chapter, where the old thrush is given a larger role in the story than simply being a passive signifier that they have found the right snail-stone marking the Secret Door.

The next page following the death of Smaug (manuscript page 156; Marq. 1/1/14:4) is marked by somewhat neater writing and also slightly more yellowed paper, indicating that the next thirteen pages probably came from a similar but slightly different batch of unused students' papers. Tolkien also starts further down the page than usual on this new sheet, leaving roughly enough room blank to have written another paragraph there, though in the end all he wrote were the words 'A great fog', which seem to have been partially erased. In both typescripts and the published book a blank line is skipped here to mark the break in the action.

A great fog

The moon [rises >] rose higher and higher, and the North wind grew loud and cold. It twisted the white fog upon the lake into bending pillars and hurrying clouds, and drove it off to the West to scatter in tattered wisps over the marshes before Mirkwood. Then the many boats could be seen dotted on the surface of the lake, and down the wind came the sound of the voices of the people of Esgaroth lamenting their lost town and goods and ruined homes. But they had really much to be thankful for, had they thought of it – which perhaps it was asking too much to expect them to do: [the dragon's was at end, >] three quarters of the people of the town had escaped at least alive, and their woods, fields, pastures and cattle, and most of their boats remained undamaged; and the Dragon was dead, and at an end. What that meant they had not yet realized.

They gathered in sorry crowds upon the western shores, shivering in the cold wind. The first grumbles were for the Master who had left the town so soon, while still [defenders were >] some were willing to defend it.

'He may have a good head for business – especially his own business –' some murmured, 'but he is no good in a crisis!' And th<ey> praised and lamented Bard and his courage.

'If only he were not slain we would make him a king' they said 'Bard, [<King> >] the Dragon-shooter, of the line of Girion. Alas that he is lost!'

And in the very midst of their talk a tall figure stepped from the shadows. He was drenched[TN12] with water, his black hair hung wet over his face and shoulders; a fierce light was in his eyes.

'Bard is not lost' he cried. 'I am Bard the dragon-piercer of the race of Girion. I dived from Esgaroth only when none else was left, only when the enemy was slain. I will be your king!'

'King Bard, King Bard' they shouted, and the master ground his chattering teeth, as he sat upon the ground.

'Girion was Lord of Dale not King of Esgaroth' he said. 'In this lake town we have ever had masters elected from the old and the wise, and not endured the rough rule of mere fighting men. Let King Bard win [> take] back his own Kingdom – Dale is free, nor is more ruined now than Esgaroth. He has slain the slayer of his fathers and nothing hinders him. And those that like may go with him, though wise men will stay here and rebuild our town, and enjoy its richness and peace'.

'We will have king Bard' the people shouted. 'We have had enough of the old men & money-counters'.

'I am the last one to underpraise [> undervalue] Bard the Bowman' said the Master warily, for Bard was standing near him fierce and grim, 'and indeed his bravery tonight has made him the greatest benefactor the men of the Lake have known since the coming of the Smaug the unceasing Threat. But I don't quite see why I get all the blame. Who stirred up the dragon, I might ask? Who got rich gifts of us and ample help, and led us to believe that old songs would come true? What sort of gold have they sent down the river? To whom should we send a claim for the repair of all our damages and the help [*added*: & comfort] of widows and widowers and orphans?'

Cunning words. For the moment people forgot the idea of a new king and [were >] turned their thoughts and anger to Thorin and his company. Their hate flowed up against them, and their words grew ever more wild and bitter. Some of those who had sung the old songs loudest were now [singing parodies of them >] heard loudly to suggest that the dwarves had deliberately sent the Dragon down upon them.

Added later in the bottom and left margin and intended for insertion at this point: 'Fools' said Bard. 'And why waste hate on those unhappy creatures. They have doubtless perished in fire before Smaug came to us.' But even as he spoke, the thought of the treasure of the Mountain came into his heart, and he fell silent, thinking of the Master's words, and dr<eam>ing of Dale rebuilt, if he could find the men.

It was fortunate they [> that the lakemen] had something to discuss and to occupy their thoughts, for their night under the trees and in such rough shelter as could be contrived was miserable. Many [who >] took ill that night and afterwards died. Even Bard would have had a hard task in the following days to order them, and begin upon the rebuilding of the town, with such tools as were left in the huts upon the shore, if other help had not been at hand.

The spies of the woodelves had sent tidings of the dragon's rousing [> dwarves' north<ern> journey and of] to their King, and he was as astonished as the Master had been; but he too expected only a bad end for the dwarves [> yet he did not expect any other ending of their venture than their death in the jaws of Smaug]. When news of the rousing of the Dragon reached him, and of the fire upon the mountain tops, he thought that he had heard the last of Thorin Oakenshield.

Then came messengers telling him of the fall of Esgaroth and the death of Smaug. He knew then the time had come to move. 'It is an ill wind that blows no man any good' he said,[TN13] for he too had not forgotten the legend of the hoard of Thror.

So he led forth all the host he could muster, a great army of [woode<lves> >] the bowmen and spearmen of the woodelves. Some he sent North towards the Mountain; some he bid bring all the supplies they could gather down the river to the lake. It was a long march, for he had not rafts enough for all his folk, but in seven days he came upon the shores, and the unhappy men were glad indeed to see him, and ready to make any bargain for his help.

That is how it happened that while many were left behind with the women and the children, busily felling trees and making huts along the shore, and beginning under the direction of the Master (and with the help of woodelves) the replanning and building of their <restore>d town, [all the bravest warriors but those of the king, >] many gathered under Bard and marched away North with the Elven king.

The chapter comes to an end at the bottom of manuscript page 158 (Marq. 1/1/15:6), as the scene shifts back the activities of Bilbo and the dwarves at the Mountain; see page 577.

TEXT NOTES

1 This paragraph was preceded on the page by a paragraph of drafting. I transcribe this cancelled passage just as it appears in the manuscript, since it offers a good example of Tolkien's seeking to visualize and properly describe a specific image – in this case, exactly what the people of Lake Town could see of Smaug's distant attack on the Mountain when he destroyed the Secret Door (cf. page 515).

> Suddenly a great light shone in the North and filled the low place in the hills which screened all but the top [> highest peak] of the lonely M. from the view. Though The highest peak of the Lonely Mountain was lost in dark – that was all they could see of it above the hills at

> the North end of the lake. Suddenly the low place in those hills through which came the R. Running from the North was filled with a great light, the Northern end
>
> The Mountain flickered with a glow of light such as

The gap between the hills at the northernmost point on the Long Lake at the inflow of the River Running out of the Lonely Mountain past Dale mentioned here can just be seen in 'Esgaroth' (Plate VIII [bottom]), on the horizon in a direct line above the dwarf popping his head up out of the barrel; it is slightly more evident in the finished version of this drawing ('Lake Town'; cf. DAA.244 & H-S#127).

2 'from midnight until dawn': this corresponds exactly with the account in Chapter XII, where it is midnight when Bilbo emerges from the tunnel with the stolen cup (page 507) and Smaug immediately thereafter discovers the theft and flies out '[t]o hunt the whole mountain till he caught the thief and burned and trampled him' (ibid.), scorching the mountain-side with his fiery breath 'till dawn chilled his wrath and he went back to his golden couch to sleep' (page 508).

3 This unpromising characterization marks the first appearance of Bard,† who will soon emerge as the hero of the coming battle. The description of his voice as 'surly' is distinctly unheroic; elsewhere the word is used of Ted Sandyman ('The Scouring of the Shire', *LotR*.1054) and Snaga the orc ('The Tower of Cirith Ungol', *LotR*.940). Within the published *Hobbit* itself, it appears only to describe the starving dwarves' attitude when questioned by their elven captors in Mirkwood (page 380) – the same elves who had the night before ignored their pleas for food and left them to the spiders' tender mercies.

There is certainly nothing in these paragraphs preceding the battle foretelling the heroic figure this as-yet-unnamed guardsman is about to become. In the First Typescript, *surly* has been replaced with *grim* (typescript page 127; Marq. 1/1/64:1), which conveys the same pessimism but leaves open heroic possibilities. Whereas 'surly' (which derives from Old French) usually means churlishly ill-humored, 'grim' (which comes from Old English) can mean not just fierce, cruel, or harsh but also determined or bold: in *Beowulf* it is used not just of Grendel (e.g., line 121) but of Wiglaf when he addresses his fellow guardsmen who deserted King Beowulf in his time of need (line 2860b); see commentary pp. 557–8.

†Unless this guard is the same character as the nameless guard captain who kept such a poor watch back in Chapter X; see Text Note 10 on page 444.

4 Tolkien originally wrote 'from a fi<re>' here but immediately changed it to 'from floods', perhaps in order to avoid anticipating the conflagration that erupts a few paragraphs later.

5 I have added the quotation marks here, since these lines would seem at first to be quoted from the poem in Chapter X (see pp. 439–40 and Text Note 14 on pp. 445–6), but not all of them actually occur there, nor in this sequence, either in the rough draft nor the final poem. We

must either imagine that the Lake-men are garbling their own song a few weeks later or, more probably, that this is a part of the song not recorded earlier, where we are told 'there was a great deal more of it'.

6 Note that Lake Town still has multiple bridges connecting it to the shore here and also in the accompanying First Typescript (1/1/64:1); cf. Text Notes to Chapter X, page 444.

7 An additional sentence appears in this passage in the First Typescript:

> *You have never failed me and always I have recovered you.*

This addition, along with some polishing, thus achieves in the First Typescript the text that appears in the published book. For more on the rather curious motif of an arrow that is always recovered until one final shot when it fulfills its destiny, see the commentary on page 558.

8 Added in the left margin and marked for insertion at this point:

> As he turned [*added*: and dived down] his belly glittered [with >] white with sparkling fire in the moon – but not in one spot.

For the role of moonlight in this scene, see the commentary on the picture 'The Death of Smaug', page 561.

9 The detail about Smaug's death cry causing stars to fall from the sky, while striking, disappeared by the time the First Typescript was made, where this passage reads '. . . a shriek that deafened men, *felled trees,* and split stone' (1/1/64:3). For a precedent elsewhere in Tolkien's work of falling stars being caused by dramatic earthly events, see the *Father Christmas Letters*, where in the 1925 letter two stars 'shot' (i.e., became shooting stars) when North Polar Bear broke the North Pole, and a third 'went red when [the] Pole snapped' (*Letters from Father Christmas*, 1925 Letter, page 23).

10 'Glede': a rare (dialectical) word more commonly spelled 'gleed' (Middle English *glede*, Old English *glēd*), meaning a glowing coal or ember. Douglas Anderson notes (DAA.308) that the word occurs both in *Beowulf* and in *Sir Gawain & the Green Knight*, as well as in Tolkien's translation of the latter (where it is once translated 'coals' and once left untranslated as 'gledes'; cf. SGGK line 891 [Tolkien translation page 47] and line 1609 [Tolkien translation page 65]).

11 This is the first appearance of the name *Esgaroth*. For the probable meaning of this elven name for Lake Town, see pp. 561–2. Several letters at the beginning and end of the word have been re-written in a darker ink, and it is possible that the original reading here was *Esgaron*, the form of the name found in Plot Notes D; see page 569 and Text Note 7 on page 571.

12 This marks the point at which the First Typescript broke off in the 'home manuscript' that Tolkien circulated among his friends; the next page which followed in that composite text was the first page of the Third Phase handwritten manuscript. For an explanation of how these texts fit together, see the headnote at the beginning of Chapter XVb: King Bard on pp. 637–8. Note that when Carpenter says that 'shortly

after he had described the death of the dragon' Tolkien broke off the story (*Tolkien: A Biography*, page 179), he is referring to the typescript. In fact, as the next two chapters show, Tolkien continued the story on past Smaug's death for the rest of that chapter, all the following chapter (which now precedes it in the re-arranged published sequence), and well into the chapter that followed – or, in the published book, for twenty-one out of the remaining sixty-five pages of the story (in the pagination of the first edition, not counting illustrations).

13 This proverb, while undoubtedly venerable, hardly dates back to the Third Age of Middle-earth. The earliest recorded usage, *an yll wynde that blowth no man to good, men saie*, appears in Henry VIII's time in John Heywood's *Proverbs* [1546], along with such still-familiar phrases as *no fire without some smoke*, *cart before the horse*, *more the merrier*, *penny for your thoughts*, and *hitteth the nail on the head*. Shakespeare uses slightly different forms of it twice (*Henry IV, Part II*, Act V, scene iii, line 87; *Henry VI, Part III*, Act II, scene v, line 55), and it has remained in use down to the present day. The most familiar form today is the eighteenth-century one, *'tis an ill wind which blows nobody any good* (cf. Laurence Sterne's *A Sentimental Journey* [1768]).

(i)
Bard the Dragon-Slayer

As we have seen in Plot Notes C, the idea that Smaug would die during the attack on Lake Town rather than be stabbed by Bilbo while he slept on his bed of gold emerged suddenly. Since Bilbo was no longer to be the dragon-slayer, Tolkien had to either re-assign the role to an already existing character within the book, such as Thorin or Gandalf, or create a new one with very little preamble.[1] Designating any other character already present as Smaug's bane would simply shift the problem without solving it, since all the dwarves were at the mountain with Bilbo and no other character who had appeared so far on their journey could be re-introduced to fill the role without usurping too large a part in the story and taking attention away from the main characters.[2]

Tolkien's solution was to introduce a new character to fill the necessary narrative role. Initially he planned to kill off this character as soon as his role of dragon-slayer was achieved: only two pages of manuscript separate his first appearance (manuscript page 153)[3] and his death in the ruin of Esgaroth (manuscript page 155), crushed beneath the dragon's fall. Before proceeding any further, however, Tolkien thought better of it and changed the line 'And that was the end of Smaug and Esgaroth and Bard' to '. . . the end of Smaug and Esgaroth *but not of Bard*' (italics mine) – as significant a change within such a small space of words as he achieved anywhere within the book.

Having decided to keep Bard alive was a crucial decision that greatly affected the concluding section of the book. The chapters immediately following the death of Smaug (Chapters XIV–XVIII in this edition, XIII and XV–XVIII in the published book) have long been noted as strikingly different in tone from all that had come before.[4] Initially, as we shall see, Tolkien's sympathies in the next several chapters were to remain with Thorin and the dwarves and no rift between Bilbo and his companions had been contemplated (see especially the 'little bird' outline, i.e. Plot Notes E), with the elves and their allies being cast in a much more hostile light (capturing and wounding Fili, pursing Kili, shooting arrows at the friendly ravens bringing food to enable the besieged dwarves and hobbit to hold out, etc.). Before the introduction of Bard, none of the outsiders described in the Plot Notes who descend upon the mountain after Smaug's death have any legitimate claim on the treasure there: certainly not the Elvenking who imprisoned the dwarves for months in solitary confinement merely for trespassing. Nor are the men of Lake Town, although certainly due generous recompense for all their aid in the dwarves' time of need (much of their sorry state having been due to the elves' mistreatment, it must be said), entitled thereby to any significant portion of Thorin's inheritance. That the elves and Lake-men were in the wrong in their attempts to steal or extort Thror's treasure and besiege his heir when he finally comes back into his own is shown by Bladorthin's words and actions when the wizard finally reappears:

> Blad[orthin] rebukes the besiegers . . .
> A share of his part [Bilbo] gives to Lake-men, and to wood-elves *(though they may not deserve it)*.
>
> —Plot Notes C (page 497, italics mine).

But the introduction of survivors from Dale changes this: it gives those who like Bard are descended from the Dale-folk a rightful claim to at least part of the hoard – albeit probably a relatively small part: it is after all the gold of the King under the Mountain that has lived on in Lake-folk song and legend and likewise 'the legend of the hoard of Thror' that brings the Elvenking marching at top speed, not any legacy of Girion. Now Thorin faces a rightful claimant to any wealth of Girion's mixed into Smaug's treasure, and one who furthermore also legitimately serves as spokesman for the Lake-folk's claim for aid in time of need to reciprocate their own earlier generosity, plus a hero who by preventing Smaug's return has done the new King under the Mountain a great service and deserves his own reward as the dragon-slayer (cf. Bilbo's recognition of the essential fairness of Bard's presentation of his three-part claim in the latter part of Chapter XV, the first new text in the Third Phase drafting, on page 648 & DAA.323). Significantly enough, it was just at the point where Tolkien would either have to reject some of these new elements, particularly Bard, because of the complications they introduced into his projected conclusion, or else have to find a way to incorporate them by changing that conclusion, that he broke off the Second Phase of composition, just as Bilbo and the dwarves learn of the approaching elven and human armies (see page 620).

Bard is an important figure for another reason: he represents a turning point in Tolkien's legendarium. He is not the first of Tolkien's human heroes, having been preceded a decade and a half before by Beren, Húrin, Túrin, and Tuor, but unlike these tragic and rather remote figures, his is a fortunate fate. A dispossessed heir, he lives to achieve unexpected victory over the surpassingly strong hereditary foe who had destroyed his homeland, re-establishes the kingship, and founds a dynasty that renews alliances with nonhuman neighbors and helps bring renewed prosperity to the region.[5] In short, he is a precursor of Strider (Aragorn), who through his own efforts and the great deeds of others claims his ancestor's throne and re-establishes his kingdom; all that is lacking is the love story (a relatively late element of Aragorn's story; cf. HME VIII–IX). Bard is thus a pivotal figure, a turning point between the tragic figures of the First Age and the triumphant returning king of Volume III of *The Lord of the Rings*.

The sudden emergence of the unlikely hero, the one who dares to undertake some task or challenge which his apparent 'betters' shirk – as in, for example, the farmer who (twice) goes dragon-hunting in *Farmer Giles of Ham* or indeed Bilbo's exploration of Smaug's lair when Durin's heir dares not enter – is of course a traditional fairy-tale motif, frequently matched with the subsequent discovery that the new hero is in fact a lost prince or noble heir. However, the primary external influence for Bard's sudden emergence, aside from sheer narrative necessity, probably lies not in fairy tales but (as so often the case in the Smaug chapters) in *Beowulf*. When King Beowulf sets forth to fight the dragon that has burned down his royal hall, he brings along as companions eleven picked warriors but forbids them to take part in the battle, ordering them to stand back at a safe distance and serve as witnesses. But when it becomes clear that Beowulf is losing the fight, one of his companions springs into action. Heretofore merely one of eleven unnamed warriors, Wiglaf disobeys his king's orders and rushes to the old man's side; with his help, Beowulf is able to kill the dragon but is mortally wounded in turn. The dying king names Wiglaf as his heir, and it is he who takes charge of the disposition of the treasure and directs the construction of Beowulf's barrow. The differences from *The Hobbit* are considerable, but the essential points are the same: (1) an anonymous guard is first named when he shows the courage to fight a dragon, (2) all his fellows lack the courage to do likewise and abandon their duty (either by deserting their posts in *The Hobbit* or in *Beowulf* by failing to fulfill their oaths to defend the king, as Wiglaf angrily upbraids his fellows), (3) the newly named hero turns out to be of royal lineage (Bard being the descendant of Girion king of Dale and Wiglaf the last of the Wægmundings, Beowulf's kin; cf. *Beowulf* lines 2813–2816), and lastly (4) each becomes king as a direct result of his role in the dragon-slaying.

(ii)
The Black Arrow

The motif of the Black Arrow both harkens back to the alliterative poems of the 1920s and ahead to the Númenórean blades in *The Lord of the Rings*. In 'The Lay of the Children of Húrin', Beleg the Bowman carries a special arrow named *Dailir*,[6] of which we are told

> *. . . Dailir he drew, his dart beloved;*
> *howso far fared it, or fell unnoted,*
> *unsought he found it with sound feathers*
> *and barbs unbroken*
>
> —lines 1080–1083a (Canto II: 'Beleg') HME III.42.

When Beleg stumbles in the dark while rescuing Túrin and breaks this lucky arrow, injuring his hand in the process, the narrator makes clear this is an omen of disaster (ibid., lines 1187–1192; HME III.45), and indeed Túrin murders Beleg only minutes later in a tragic case of mistaken identity.

Bard is more fortunate, in that although his arrow too is ultimately lost, its final act is to exceed all hope by slaying his people's greatest foe, with a sense that it perishes in the act of fulfilling its destiny. This is hinted at by Bard's final words before that fateful shot: '*If ever you came from the forges of the true king of the Mountain go now and speed well*'; compare the narrator's comment when Merry's blade burns away after helping to slay the Witch-King of Angmar (that is, the Lord of the Nazgûl):

> So passed the sword of the Barrow-downs, work of Westernesse [Númenor]. But glad would he have been to know its fate who wrought it slowly long ages ago in the North-kingdom when the Dúnedain were young, and chief among their foes was the dread realm of Angmar and its sorcerer king. No other blade, not though mightier hands had wielded it, would have dealt that foe a wound so bitter, cleaving the undead flesh, breaking the spell that knit his unseen sinews to his will.
>
> —*LotR*.877–8.

Once again *Beowulf* may have contributed something to the idea of a weapon that achieves its goal but then perishes: in the battle with Grendel's dam, Beowulf finds that the sword he has brought cannot harm the monster, but he is able to slay her and to cut off Grendel's head with an ancient sword he finds within her lair. This *ealdsweord eotenisc* (*Beowulf* line 1558a; literally, 'old entish sword') then melts away (lines 1606b–1609), leaving only the hilt behind (1614b–1617). In any case, like Bard himself in the original draft, the Black Arrow is no sooner introduced than it fulfills its role in slaying the seemingly invulnerable dragon and leaves the story.

(iii)
The Death of Smaug

The great moment that would at first seem to be the climax of the entire book and the fulfillment of Thorin & Company's quest is remarkable because when it comes it not only occurs 'off-stage' so far as the main point-of-view characters are concerned[7] but it comes five-sixths of the way through the book, not in the last or even penultimate chapter, and what follows is far from dénouement. Indeed Smaug's sudden and permanent removal, while essential to any 'happy ending' for the story, immediately complicates the situation and leads to the tangle that takes another six chapters to resolve.

Unlike the traditional methods of dragon-slaying proposed in the Plot Notes but ultimately rejected, which derive primarily from the Sigurd legend and his own Glorund story, so far as I have been able to discover the method Tolkien chose for slaying The Dragon is unprecedented in fairy-tale, English folktale, or Old English/Old Norse lore. The closest parallel seems to be classical: the Eleventh Labour of Hercules, where in some forms of the story the demigod slays Ladon, the Dragon of the Hesperides, with an arrow or arrows in order to gain the Golden Apples it guards. Most stories seem to hold with the author of Job that arrows or darts are no good against a dragon's armor (Job 41.26–29; see Text Note 33 following Chapter XII), and, a few humorous folktales aside, traditionally only hand-to-hand combat has seemed sufficiently heroic for such an epic encounter. Simpson notes that while many dragons are described or depicted as winged, most storytellers and artists ignore this capacity for flight once battle is actually joined:

> . . . it is indeed only in literature, in Spenser's *Faerie Queene*, that one can find a fully thought-out, detailed, visualized, blow-by-blow account of how a duel between an armed knight on horseback and a flying, fire-breathing dragon with claws and a spiked tail might be expected to unfold. In particular, Spenser makes good use of the dragon's power of flight.[8]
>
> —*British Dragons*, page 75.

Tolkien's account does not involve an armored knight, but it is complex, combining as it does the traditional motif of a dragon's weak spot (specifically the soft underbelly of the Sigurd/Fafnir legend, already seen in Glorund) with the Beowulf dragon's fiery breath none can withstand (also present in Glorund; cf. BLT II.85, 'with the power of his breath he drove Túrin from those doors') and a tactically wily wyrm who uses his power of flight to attack foes on what is essentially a manmade island surrounded by deep water. Furthermore, Smaug has learned from his ancestor's mistake and armored himself so that a lurking assassin cannot ambush him (as Sigurd did Fafnir and Túrin Glorund). He does not know that there is a fatal weak spot in his 'jeweled waistcoat', but even so had he not lost his head to pride (allowing Bilbo to inspect his armaments) and to anger in the heat of battle he could have guarded against even that possibility.[9] The description of Smaug's attack – 'the dragon's wrath blazed . . . till he was blind and mad with it . . . *taking no heed to turn his scales towards his foes*' (italics mine) – implies he is so sinuous and serpentine (as indeed the illustrations bear out) that he could with care have kept his vulnerable belly turned away from his foes on each strafing pass. After all, he must have done so in his initial assault on Dale and Thror's halls, since at that time he lacked the embedded gemstones against which presumably even the Black Arrow was of no avail ('then I was young *and tender*' – DAA.282; italics mine).

We are fortunate that Tolkien illustrated this dramatic scene;[10] even though he left the picture unfinished it is full of interesting details (see Plate XII [top]), from an alternate view of Lake Town (viewed more from the south rather than in the westerly published view [DAA.244] or in the slightly earlier variant thereof ['Esgaroth', Plate VIII bottom]) and the Lonely Mountain looming ominously on the horizon like an erupting volcano (cf. Tolkien's [earlier] Thangorodrim and [later] Mount Doom in the backgrounds of his pictures of the vale of Sirion [H-S#55] and the Barad-dûr [H-S#145], respectively) to the dragon himself in his death agonies. Smaug is much yellower here than in the companion picture 'Conversation with Smaug' (Plate XI [top]) – in the text he is always described as 'red-golden' (cf. page 506) – but this may simply be an accident of the picture's having been left incomplete. Most notably of all, Tolkien annotated this picture, suggesting that he at one point thought of offering it as a guide to another artist, perhaps at the time Houghton Mifflin suggested hiring an American artist to illustrate their edition (cf. Hammond's *Descriptive Bibliography* page 18).[11] These annotations show that Tolkien drew a scene as he visualized it and only then worried about reconciling it to what he written and also his extreme precision in getting those details right during the revision stage:

left margin: The moon should be a crescent: it was only a few nights after the New Moon on 'Durin's Day'.[12]

lower left corner: Dragon should have a white naked spot where the arrow enters.

bottom margin: Bard the Bowman shd be standing after release of arrow at extreme left point of the piles.

Ultimately this picture did not appear in the first edition of *The Hobbit*, either redrawn by Tolkien or adapted by another hand, but it was published in Tolkien's lifetime as the cover of the second British paperback edition of *The Hobbit* (Unwin Books, trade paperback [1966]). In this publication the bottom of the illustration was trimmed slightly, cutting off those annotations, but the scrawled title 'Death of Smaug' did appear in the center of the drawing, along with the annotation concerning the moon to the far left (wrapped around on the back cover); the sharp-eyed could even catch the arrow on the bottom spine indicating where Bard stood, although there's no way they could have known its significance.[13] Tolkien himself was diffident about using this unfinished piece: with typical humility,[14] he wrote to Rayner Unwin: 'I am in your hands, but I am still not very happy about the use of this scrawl as a cover. It seems too much in the modern mode in which those who can draw try to conceal it. But perhaps there is a distinction between their productions and one by a man who obviously cannot draw *what he sees*' (JRRT to RU, 15th December 1965, *Letters* p. 365; italics mine). The final phrase is significant: Tolkien's chief concern is to capture the inner vision and convey to us in image as well as in words a scene from his story and his subcreated world.

(iv)
The Name 'Esgaroth'

This name is clearly Elvish, either Sindarin (Noldorin) or a dialect thereof; cf. *Esgal*duin (originally *Esga*duin),[15] the river that flowed past the door of Mene*groth* ('the Thousand Caves'), King Thingol's halls in Doriath. The simplest explanation is to assume that 'Esgaroth' and 'Lake Town' essentially say the same thing in different languages, and there is some support for this if we take the *–roth* element,[16] whose primary meaning is 'cave' (generally in the context of fortified cave-dwelling or underground city), as also having the more general meaning of 'dwelling' and could thus plausibly be extended to mean 'town'. Unfortunately, no such simple equivalence can be found for *esga-*. The river-name is not translated within the alliterative poems, and the only gloss I can find that Tolkien ever offered for it comes in 'The Etymologies' [1937–8, written to accompany the 1937 *Quenta Silmarillion*]. Under the root ESEK- comes the following entry:

> Ilk. *esg* sedge,[17] *esgar* reed-bed. Cf. *Esgaroth* Reedlake, because of reed-banks in west.
>
> —HME V, page 356.

This gloss is straightforward and clear, but unfortunately it is also certainly an afterthought. For one thing, Esgaroth is clearly *not* the name of the Lake, as this entry would indicate, but of the town itself: cf. the label on the published version of Thror's Map: '*In* Esgaroth *upon* the Long Lake dwell Men' (DAA.97; emphasis mine); perhaps Tolkien might have been misled by glancing at the final Wilderland Map (DAA.[399]), where the name 'Esgaroth' appears directly below the name 'Long Lake', and momentarily become confused and taken this to be another name for the same feature. Furthermore, this translation offers no explanation at all relating *–roth* to 'lake'. Finally, the *Esga-* element is clearly the same element that had appeared long before [circa 1918] in the river Esga(l)duin. In the Noldorin Word-lists, the oldest of which is contemporary with the name's first appearance (*Parma Eldalamberon* XIII [2001] page 133), *esk, esg* appears (ibid., page 143) and is glossed 'sharp upstanding rock in water' (e.g., a carrock – see page 265), apparently deriving from the *esc*/*aisc* (meaning 'sharp point, sharp edge') of the still earlier *Gnomish Lexicon* [circa 1917]; *Parma Eldalamberon* XI page 31. Combined with our earlier hypothesis that *–roth* could mean city, this provides a hypothetical but satisfactory gloss for 'Esgaroth': city standing in or rising up out of the water, perhaps with a suggestion of pilings like reeds.[18]

Finally, as already noted during our discussion of the name 'Dorwinion' (see page 418), years later Tolkien wrote regarding Elven names in *The Hobbit* that 'Esgaroth . . . [is] not Sindarin (though perhaps "Sindarized" in shape) or . . . not recorded in Sindarin'. Given its obvious affinities to Gnomish and Noldorin (the earlier forms of Sindarin within the real-world sequence of Tolkien's invented languages), I take this to mean that the name no longer fit Sindarin as he saw it at this late date and hence had to be relegated to a dialectical or aberrant form. But just as he clearly changed his mind several times regarding the name's meaning (see above), there seems little doubt that *Esgaroth* was Sindarin (i.e., Noldorin) when the name was created, like all the other Elven names in *The Hobbit*, although some were later disowned or orphaned, like *Esgaroth* and *Girion*. Unfortunately, Tolkien does not translate the name in this passage, in the end leaving us with no acceptable authorized gloss.

NOTES

1 That Smaug had to be slain by a single character rather than simply perish in a hail of arrows or smash into the lake in a misjudged dive or be crushed beneath the rockfalls that Tolkien intended would partially collapse the chamber within the Lonely Mountain (cf. Plot Notes C) goes without saying. To repeat what Tolkien said in his unpublished lecture on dragons (see Note 5 following the commentary to Chapter XII), Tolkien felt that

> Dragons can only be defeated by brave men – usually alone. Sometimes a faithful friend may help, but it is rare: friends have a way of deserting you when [you are faced >] a dragon comes. Dragons are the final test of heroes . . .

It follows that, if a dragon is the supreme challenge for a hero, it is only fitting that a dragon face a hero as his nemesis in turn, dying in single combat in the traditionally approved manner.

2 For example, if Gandalf re-appeared suddenly and struck the dragon dead in mid-flight, the reader would wonder why the wizard had bothered to involve the hobbit in Thorin's quest at all, and it would make hay of all Gandalf's earlier assertions that this is not *his* adventure after all (e.g., page 230).

3 I am assuming here that the surly-voiced watchman looking at the lights to the north is not the same character as the watch-captain who kept such poor look-out over the main bridge to Lake Town (cf. page 438 and Text Note 10 to Chapter X), who might have been expected to show a little more interest in the return of Thror's Heir if he himself were a descendant of Girion Lord of Dale. It seems likely that Tolkien would have clarified this point and introduced Bard into the earlier scenes in Lake Town (Chapter X) in the 1960 Hobbit, had his revisionary work reached this far into the story, paralleling his work in *The Lord of the Rings* drafts to insert brief appearances by or mentions of Arwen back into the earlier parts of the story before her first actual entry quite late in the story (see HME VIII.370, 386, & 425; HME IX.52, 58–9 & 66).

Even if we were to assume that the two characters are the same, then the point still applies, though then we should say that only two pages separate the character's sudden assumption of significance from his death.

4 See, for example, C. S. Lewis's comment in his review of *The Hobbit*, where he remarks upon 'the curious shift' between the earlier parts of the story and 'the saga-like tone of the later chapters' (*TLS* 2nd October 1937; reprinted in C. S. Lewis, *On Stories*, ed. Walter Hooper [1982], page 81). For more on Lewis's critique, see Note 3 following the commentary on the Bladorthin Typescript.

5 It is important that from the very first we are told that Bard is a descendant

of Girion (a fact that enters in with the same sentence as his name; see page 549); this gives a new application to Bilbo's words to Smaug about revenge and his reminder that 'your success has made you some bitter enemies' and a direct answer to Smaug's rhetorical question 'Girion lord of Dale is dead . . . and where are his sons' sons who dare approach me?' (page 511). Bard's heritage as Girion's heir gives him just as much right to revenge the Fall of Dale as Thorin would have for the destruction of Thror's kingdom; it keeps the scales of poetic justice balanced.

Dynasty: We know nothing about Bard's queen and little about his son Bain, who apparently ruled after him, but we do know that his grandson Brand is the king of Dale at the time of the War of the Ring some eighty years later and dies fighting alongside King Dain Ironfoot defending the Kingdom under the Mountain against Sauron's forces in the Battle of Dale (*LotR*.1116 & 1130). By King Brand's time, the Men of Dale are known as the Bardings (*LotR*.245; cf. the Beornings and Eorlings and *Beowulf*'s Scyldings) and the Kingdom of Dale extends down to include the lands surrounding the Long Lake: 'his realm now reaches far south and east of Esgaroth' (ibid.). Despite Glóin's description of him as 'a strong king', Brand seems to have been a less forceful personality than his progenitor, since Glóin reports at the Council of Elrond that messengers from Mordor seeking news of hobbits have come not just to Dain but 'also to King Brand in Dale, and he is afraid. We fear that he may yield. Already war is gathering on his eastern borders' (*LotR*.259) – that is, that Brand might try to appease the Dark Lord and buy peace by giving Sauron's emissaries news of Bilbo. After Brand's death fighting in battle alongside King Dain Ironfoot, his son Bard II becomes 'King in Dale', extending the dynasty into the Fourth Age (*LotR*.1131), partnered with Dain's son Thorin III Stonehelm as King under the Mountain.

6 *Dailir*: The word is Noldorin, Tolkien's more developed form of 'Gnomish' (i.e., what during the *Lord of the Rings* period would be renamed 'Sindarin'), and means 'cleaver' ('Noldorin Word-lists', *Parma Eldalamberon* XIII [2001], page 141). The *–ir* suffix here indicates a verb (*daila*, 'to cleave') transformed into an 'agent noun' (cf. Salo, *A Gateway to Sindarin* page 165), as in English pierce > Piercer, or the goblins' names for Orcrist and Glamdring ('Biter' and 'Beater', respectively).† If we accept Dailir as parallel to the contemporary names Dairon and Daideloth, then the *dai-* element would probably have become *dae-* in later Elvish (cf. Dairon > Daeron and Daideloth > Dor Daedeloth). In any case, while Beleg's arrow itself clearly served as a model for Bard's arrow, its name is not an Elvish parallel to 'Black Arrow', which in the Noldorin of *The Hobbit* would have been something like *Morlin* or *Morhlin* (*mor-* 'black', as in *Mor*ia and *Mor*dor, + *lhinn* 'arrow'; cf. *Parma Eldalamberon* XIII page 163).

†Note that Tolkien believed that the unknown god Nodens' name was also of this type, derived from a verbal form and thus meaning something like The Hunter or The Catcher ('The Name "Nodens"' [1932], pages 135–7).

7 This is not the only such passage in the book – cf. the Lord of the Eagles scene in Chapter VI or Gandalf/Thorin's capture by the wood-elves – but it is by far the longest, and the only one which complicates the narrative, forcing Tolkien to choose which of the two series of events to tell first: the story of what happened to Smaug or the adventures of Bilbo and the dwarves at the Mountain in his absence. Here we see Tolkien employing the interlace narrative technique which will come to be such a feature of *The Lord of the Rings*, especially in Book III and the early parts of Book V of that work (cf. Richard West's masterly article 'The Interlace Structure of *The Lord of the Rings*' in *A Tolkien Compass*, ed. Jared Lobdell [1975], pages 77–94). Initially Tolkien chose to follow the epic storyline, describing the dragon's death and its effect on Bard, the wood-elves, and the folk of Lake Town and only then turning back to the Lonely Mountain; in the published book he reversed this and transposed the two respective chapters.

8 Glorund, the only dragon described in detail in the older Silmarillion material, is of course wingless. Ancalagon the Black is the first great winged dragon, and his combination of flight, fiery breath, and draconic strength prove almost too much for the host the Valar send against Morgoth, so that he is only defeated by a similarly airborne foe, Eärendel in the flying ship Wingelot. Unfortunately, Ancalagon's battle is only described in remote and general terms. Spenser's archetypical dragon provides a better example, but like Chrysophylax his wing is injured early in the fight and thereafter his ability to fly plays no part in his combat. The Green Dragon in 'The Dragon's Visit', Chrysophylax in his battle against the Middle Kingdom's knights, and especially the White Dragon of the Moon in his pursuit of Roverandom all make full use of their wings; along with Smaug's devastating attacks on the Secret Door and Lake Town, these make it clear that flying combat is very much a feature of Tolkien's dragons.

9 That pride is the cardinal sin in Tolkien's ethos has been universally acknowledged among Tolkien scholars since Paul Kocher pointed it out more than thirty years ago (*Master of Middle-Earth* [1972]). It is perhaps less apprcciated how often wrath accompanies it; the first sign of someone giving in to pride in Tolkien's work is usually his losing his temper – cf. the scenes between Gandalf and Saruman (*LotR*.605–6), Sam and Sméagol (*LotR*.742), Frodo and Boromir (*LotR*.419–20), etc.

10 This is unusual in itself, since Tolkien rarely did action shots; almost all of his illustrations to his Middle-earth works are landscapes or mood pieces, designed to help the reader more vividly visualize the places in the books. The three exceptions to this rule among his art for *The Hobbit* are 'The Three Trolls are turned to Stone' (Plate V [top]), 'Death of Smaug' (Plate XII [top]), and 'The Coming of the Eagles' (Plate XII [bottom]), of which the burning of Lake Town and the smiting of the dragon is by far the most dramatic.

11 This unfinished painting may have been created in July 1937, when Tolkien was working to make several colour illustrations of *The Hobbit*

for the American edition (see Note 10 following Chapter XIV on pp. 613–14). In addition to the five watercolours he submitted to Houghton Mifflin, illustrating The Hill (Hobbiton), Rivendell, the eagles' eyrie, the barrel-ride down the Forest River, and Bilbo's meeting with Smaug – all of which have appeared in many editions since – he also made or began colour pictures of Gandalf's approach to and arrival at Bag-End, the trolls' hill, four alternate depictions of Rivendell, Beorn's Hall, the elf-hill in Mirkwood, two alternate versions of the barrel-riding scene, Smaug flying around the Lonely Mountain, the Battle of Five Armies, and Smaug's death over Lake Town. Some of these were essentially black and white drawings enhanced with a very effective bit of color, such as the firelight in 'Troll's Hill' (Plate IV [bottom]) and 'Firelight in Beorn's house' (Plate VI [bottom]).

12 In fact, it was the very next night, so even the crescent shown here should be far more slender.

13 The best reproduction of this picture appears in *Pictures by J. R. R. Tolkien*, plate 19.

14 Similarly, he had denigrated his own art in public during his 1937 dragon lecture, when he included slides of several of his own dragon-pictures among the images he showed, saying of his charming little drawing 'The White Dragon Pursues Roverandom & the Moondog' (reprinted in *Roverandom* on plate 3, facing page 27) that 'though a poor drawing' it clearly showed a Saxon White Dragon, and drawing attention to 'the world up in the sky' (i.e., the image of Earth as seen from the moon in the upper left corner). Similarly, he said of the magnificent 'Conversation with Smaug' (Plate XI [top]) that 'It is not very good – but it shows a powerful lot of treasure'. That is, in both cases the pictures included details he wanted to convey about dragons, whatever their merits (in his too-self-critical eyes) as art.

15 For the original spelling of this river-name as *Esgaduin*, rather than the later *Esgalduin*, see Christopher Tolkien's notes to 'The Lay of the Children of Húrin' (the A text and pre-revision B text, HME III.81) and 'The Lay of Leithian' (rough workings, ibid.158). 'Esgaduin' is also the form of the name that appears on the First Silmarillion Map [circa 1926], reproduced in HME IV between pages 220 and 221.

Esgaroth itself first appears in the text on manuscript page 155 (see page 549); an alternate spelling, *Esgaron*, appears in Plot Notes D. See Text Note 11 above and Text Note 7 following Plot Notes D (page 571).

16 The element *-roth* corresponds to *-(th)rond* '(fortified) cave', the same element that we have already seen in the personal name *Thrand*uil and the place-name Nargo*thrond*; see page 417. 'The Etymologies', HME V page 384, under the root ROD- (cave), gives *rondo* as the Quendian (Quenya) form, *rhond/rhonn* as the Noldorin (Sindarin) form, and *roth* as the Doriathrin equivalent – that is, the form the word would take in the dialect of Ilkorin or native Middle-earth Elvish spoken in Thingol's kingdom.

17 'Ilk.' here means Ilkorin, the language of the elves of Middle-earth who never made the Great Journey to Valinor; cf. 'The Three Kindreds of the Elves' on page 406.

18 By contrast, in 'The Etymologies' Tolkien glossed this same word-element twice in contradictory ways, neither of which agrees with the earlier 'Noldorin' nor with the ESKE-/reed entry given elsewhere within 'The Etymologies', which certainly suggests uncertainty on his part as to the word's meaning. First he gives it under the root EZGE- ('rustle, noise of leaves'): 'Q *eske*; Ilk. *esg*; cf. *Esgalduin*' (HME V.357) but then this is cancelled and the word given yet a third alternate explanation under the root SKAL- ('screen, hide [from light]'): 'Ilk. *esgal* screen, hiding, roof of leaves' with the derivative name 'Ilk. *Esgalduin* "River under Veil (of leaves)"'. The Quendian form includes the meanings 'veiled, hidden, shadowed, shady' (HME V.386), and accordingly Salo glosses it as 'the river of the veil' (e.g., the Veiled River), '"veiled" or screened by the trees that overhung it' (Salo, *A Gateway to Sindarin*, page 377). None of these meanings yields a satisfactory gloss for Lake Town, which is certainly not hidden nor overshadowed by trees and does not stand in the reedy part of the lake, as may plainly be seen by Tolkien's various illustrations of the scene.

Luckily, the *–duin* element of *Esgalduin* is relatively straightforward, meaning 'river', likewise described as an Ilkorin term in 'The Etymologies' (HME V.355). Its most familiar appearance is as part of the Sindarin name An*duin* ('the Great River') in *The Lord of the Rings*.

PLOT NOTES D

The following sheet (Marq. 1/1/10: 5–6) replaced the fourth page or latter half of Plot Notes C (1/1/10:4; see page 497). It is difficult to date exactly when this occurred, but it seems to have been written immediately following the death of the dragon on manuscript page 155 (see page 549) and before the rider on manuscript page 151b and marginal addition on manuscript page 155 (see pages 512–13 & 549–50). A few elements from the cancelled page of Plot Notes C, particularly the last few lines (from 'The men of the lake and Woodelves come up and besiege the dwarves' through '[the wood-elves] escort Blad[orthin] & B[ilbo] back through Mirkwood'; see page 497), were incorporated into the new outline but expanded and developed in the process.

[page] 4

The Dwarves and Bilbo sit and <?quake>. Unable to tell passage of time. The silence goes on and on. and still they dare not move. They doze and wake and still the silence. The next day and next night and no sign of the dragon. They try to open the door – no good of course.

We are trapped they said and grumble at Bilbo.

[Only >] In desperation they go down the tunnel.

Bilbo slips on his ring. Absolute dark in the hall. no sign or <sound> of Smaug. The stillness is uncanny.

<Illegible> he gets [Oin to light >] Gloin to light him a little torch. He climbs the mound of gold – the dwarves see him from afar like a little spark. They see him stoop but don't know why. The gem of Girion & its fascination for him.

He explores all the hall. Peeps through its door into the vast passages above. The dwarves prepare to creep through the old halls.

Thorin is their guide

Dreading at every step to hear Smaug's return they climb the long stairs and passages <through> dark deserted halls <illegible>.[TN1]

At last <?they> reach the outer gate. <A whirl> of bats. A smooth and slimy passage worn by the dragon by the river-side.[TN2] They stand in the blessed light of day and see it is early morning in the east.

Crows are fly[ing] South in flocks

<Thorin> <?interprets> their speech.[TN3] There is great feasting <?&> a <slaughter> <?there>

[They <wonder> if <Smaug> <had> <?truly> has been <?destroy[ed]> >]

And armies are on the march. North.

In the evening [the crows >] a raven brings word. Bows to Thorin (now Smaug is dead)[TN4] and they learn of the Battle & Smaug's <overthrow>. The <illegible> of the Lake men & wood elves are coming to take the gold. The dwarves block the entrance <working> mightily ?

The thrush reappears[TN5]

[page] 5 (verso and continuation of preceding)

Put this in on p 155? before the part about dwarves?[TN6]

What happened [<?when> >] at Esgaron ((Lake-town)).[TN7] <How> Bard escaped. The anguish of the Lake-men & <wrath> of the Master. They now hate the dwarves as source of the <trouble>: some even suggest the <?driving forth> of the dragon against them was deliberate.

<Messengers> go to the wood-elves; and the king's spies bring him news. He leads forth the soldiers and they join with the lake men <under> Bard. They go north to capture <the> dwarves and the gold.

Tolkien drew a line under this sentence, struck through the top part of the page, and put a check mark in the right margin next to the seven cancelled lines, indicating that this part of his instructions to himself had been carried out. As noted above this suggests that Plot Notes D were written during the pause that followed the destruction of Lake Town, and specifically immediately after the writing of the line 'the end of Smaug and Esgaroth and Bard [> but not of Bard]' on manuscript page 155 (page 549 of this edition).

The siege of the mountain.

Bilbo <sneaks> forth at night and comes to the camps. He calls <for> Bard and sits <amid> the counsellors. He says the Gem of Girion is his own since he <is> <illegible> <illegible> share. If it were all – and the dwarves prize it more dearly than all else – he would give it to Bard the heir of Girion to let his friends go in peace. The woodelves and other counsellors speak ag[ainst] him.

An old man rises from the floor. It is Gandalf!

He speaks to Bard. Prophecies often come true in diff. <guise>. Be not a greater fool than the fools who <illegible> the dragon <from> his wealth. Believe not prophecies less because you yourself have <aided> in their fulfilment. The gold is not yours. Prosperity shall reign if the real King under the M. comes back. Be not outdone in generosity by <plain> Mr. Baggins who has <?bargained> all his reward for his friends. [Girion >] Dale & Lake Town are to be rebuilt[TN8]

'Who are you?' says the king of the wood elves.

'I am Gandalf!'

Then he believed at last that Thorin is indeed Thorin son of Thrain son Thror. why did he not say so? [A >] Your own acts <?condemn> you. – because dwarves understood better than all others the <power> of the greed of gold. and fear therefore more <certainly> to <?extend> it. You owe <them> aid not <?enmity>.

Thus came the peace and pact of the Ruined <City>

Woodelves rich presents

<Huge> <?sums> of <money> for rebuilding of Esgaron.

Messengers are sent many dwarves from N S E W

<Thorin> has <?decided>[TN9] never more <forsaken the> western lands.

In the left margin:

<Since the> dragon was slain beyond hope. <Thorin> <?grieves> at first when he learns of Bilbo's dealing with the Gem of Girion – but after a while he says 'There is indeed more <in> you than you know yourself. We <have> <illegible> as seemed unlikely to be thankful to Gandalf. And yet perhaps you have more to thank him for than all – even though you went hence empty-handed.' They bid Bilbo take his share over & above the gem. He says he is sick of the sight of gold – yet in the end he accepts <illegible>[TN10] <dwarves> a set of golden dinner service and a silver kettle. With these he sets out home with Gandalf. An escort of wood-elves is found <through> Mirkwood. How Gandalf came here?

TEXT NOTES

1 The illegible phrase following 'dark deserted halls' may be '?followed his torch'.

2 This detail of a smooth slot worn in the rock derives from the Fafnir

story, in which Sigurd knows where to dig his pit-trap because of the groove worn in the stone where the dragon goes to drink; cf. page 493.

3 This line is very difficult to make out, and may actually read 'Their ?whispered <illegible> speech.' In either case, whatever the exact wording the situation is the same, that they overhear conversation among the passing crows that warns them of the coming crisis.

4 The interesting detail of the raven bowing to Thorin 'now [that] Smaug is dead' suggests that the birds recognized Smaug's suzerainty while he lived and only acknowledge Thorin as the new King under the Mountain when the all-powerful usurper is dead. This might account for Smaug's tolerance of their presence; aside from the furtive creatures who have crept Gollum-like into the outer reaches of his lair (see page 581), the crows and ravens are almost the only living things found within the Desolation of Smaug, a fact that becomes more explicable if he views them as subjects instead of interlopers – fellow birds of prey, as it were, yet posing no threat to his authority.

5 This phrase is scrawled in large letters across the lower right-hand portion of this page, the writing having otherwise stopped some five or six lines short of the bottom of the page.

6 This line, added in the top margin, seems to refer to the Thrush mentioned at the bottom of the preceding page. The manuscript page specified gives the account of Smaug's death, and in fact Tolkien added to the bottom of that page an account of the thrush appearing and bringing word to Bard of Smaug's weak point. The 'part about dwarves' would seem to be the Master's turning the townsfolk against the dwarves and blaming them for all their woes; either that or the section where the focus shifts back to the Mountain and what happened to Bilbo and the dwarves there (e.g., Chapter XIV).

7 *Esgaron*: Both here and again below Tolkien gives this earlier, alternate spelling of the Elven name for Lake Town, which is always Esgaro*th* in the main text (cf. page 549). The two names clearly have the same meaning (see commentary following Chapter XIII and especially Text Note 11 on page 554), with Esgaro*n* being the Noldorian form (as opposed to Esgaro*th*, which is Doriathian; see Note 16 following Chapter XIII on page 566). See below for the probable point Tolkien had reached in the text when he wrote these Plot Notes.

8 This sentence is crammed in at the end of the line and may have been added slightly later.

9 These three words are very difficult to make out, and may instead read 'Then his ?descendents . . .'

10 The illegible passage may read 'a bag &' – that is, a single bag filled with treasure; cf. the small chest of gold and another of silver he winds up accepting in the published book (DAA.351).

The Pact of the Ruined City

These two replacement pages, which form part of the Plot Notes B/C/D sequence,[1] are closely tied with changes Tolkien made to Chapters XII (the rider on page 513) and XIII (particularly to the important marginal additions given on pp. 549–50), and clearly preceded Chapter XIV, for which it provided the framework. While by its very nature sketchy and tentative, it is also, with Plot Notes E, the closest we can now come to recovering the details of the Siege of the Mountain as Tolkien originally intended them, before the decisions to retain Bard and introduce the Dragon-sickness complicated the plot and diverted his plans.

It is remarkable that, having come so far, Tolkien still at this stage seems to have kept to his original plan in which there was to be no battle at the Lonely Mountain; the Battle of Five Armies had not yet arisen, its place being filled by 'the Battle of Anduin Vale', a quite distinct conflict in which the dwarves were to play no part. Hence there is no need even now for the invention of Dain and his company of dwarven reinforcements: the Siege of the Mountain (elves and lake-men against Thorin & Company) is present, but Tolkien still expected Gandalf to be able to resolve the conflict by diplomacy. The only battle taking place in the east is that of Lake Town, which is already past by this point, and there is still no need to bring goblins, wolves, bears, or eagles out of the west to join the conflict. Tolkien did not yet know that Thorin or any of his companions were to die; instead, the story ended with him restored to his rightful place as King under the Mountain. Whereas in Plot Notes C Bilbo gives 'A part of his share' to the Lake-men and wood-elves, he now gives away his entire stake to save his friends. It is important to note that in the published tale Bilbo's attempt to buy peace fails,[2] and the battle between dwarves, wood-elves, and lake-men is averted only by the unexpected arrival of the goblin-warg army on the scene. By contrast, in Plot Notes D Bilbo's goodwill gesture provides Gandalf the opportunity he needs to reveal himself and talk sense to the dragon-slayer and his treasure-greedy allies, thus avoiding battle entirely.

This War for Gold

The anger of the lake-men is understandable enough, although their eagerness to fix blame and demand reparations smacks more of post-Great War politics than *wergild*. The recalcitrance of the wood-elf king, however, is especially notable; his reluctance in the published book to shed blood over something as trivial as dragon-gold[3] represents a complete reversal of his role in these events as Tolkien originally foresaw them in the Plot Notes. With no legitimate claim to the treasure himself, he tries to convince Bard to reject Bilbo's offer ('The woodelves and other counsellors speak ag[ainst] him'), probably motivated by the knowledge that if his human allies recover the whole treasure his own share will of course be all the greater. Indeed, as far back as Chapter X, he had decided to seize any treasure the dwarves might gain from Smaug as it passed west through Mirkwood ('no treasure will come back through Mirkwood without my having to say in the matter', page 441). His behavior prompts Gandalf to remark 'Your own acts condemn you,' a judgment in keeping with Tolkien's earlier observation that although the wood-elves share in the treasure Bilbo gives to the Lake Men, they 'may not deserve it' (Plot Notes C, page 497).[4] However, since the woodelves and woodmen were to fight at Bilbo's side in the Battle of the Anduin Vale outlined in the final page of Plot Notes B/C/D/B, clearly the elvenking was to be given a chance to redeem himself before the story was over, as of course he does in the published book. Indeed, this projected final battle that Tolkien never came to write out would, in its alliance of elves and men against goblins, have been rather like one of the battles described in the early versions of the Silmarillion story (i.e., the wars against Melkor the Morgoth); in the more circumscribed world of *The Lord of the Rings* such battles are ascribed to the distant past, the last such being in the days of 'the Last Alliance' three thousand years before.[5]

During the Third Phase of composition on *The Hobbit* that brought the book to its conclusion, Tolkien was to shift this greed from the elvenking to the dwarves, which makes all the more fascinating the idea that can just be glimpsed here that, since dwarves 'understood better than all others the power of the greed of gold', for that very reason they try not to expose others to that temptation. This seems to suggest that long association with treasure has to some degree inoculated the dwarven people against dragon-sickness: certainly in the chapter that follows the dwarves are far less giddy and obsessive about the vast treasure, the very sight of which had moved Bilbo beyond words (and to the very uncharacteristic pocketing of the Gem of Girion when he has the chance), than in the published book – and far more practical about pocketing what they can of their temporarily recovered possessions while the opportunity lasts. In support of this, there is also the matter of Thorin's urging Bilbo to take a full share of the treasure 'over & above the gem'.[6]

Under the Mountain

Unfortunately, neither the relevant section of Plot Notes C nor this expansion and replacement of it tells us what the dwarves are doing between their blocking off the Front Gate in preparation of the siege and their deliverance when Bilbo and Gandalf between them break the deadlock. There is a hint of disagreement between Bilbo and the dwarves in the line 'Bladorthin . . . makes dwarves pay Bilbo' (Plot Notes C), the fact that Bilbo *sneaks* out to find Bard, and Thorin's later grief when he learns that Bilbo has bartered away the Gem of Girion, but this latter may simply be regret that Bilbo has lost the treasure Thorin intended him to take home with him as his reward for all he has done (see Plot Notes B and C for the Gem as Bilbo's portable payment). Given the lakemen's stated hatred for the dwarves (page 551) and the wood-elves' intention to 'capture' them and seize the gold (ibid.), Thorin & Company's failure to negotiate a satisfactory resolution with the besiegers may be due less to dwarvish stubbornness and more to a prudent desire not to surrender themselves to what might be a lynch mob accompanied by traditional enemies who would gladly take all Thror's treasure and condemn the dwarves to indefinite if not interminable imprisonment. If this is the case, then Bilbo's attempt to strike a deal may not be going against Thorin's wishes to circumvent an intractable dwarven king so much as the hobbit's simply taking the initiative when the dwarves are fearful to, the established pattern of all the hobbit's dealings with the dwarves from the time they send him off down the newly-opened secret tunnel alone at the beginning of Chapter XII to the end of the Second Phase text. In any case, we have Gandalf's word for it that their motivation is not unreasoning greed, but a salutary fear of what effect the dragon-sickness might have on the already aroused Lake-men and treasure-hungry elves.

The Gem of Girion

As in the earlier stages in this sequence of Plot Notes, the Gem of Girion continues to play a significant role in the events of these final chapters. Earlier it had served as a motivator for Bilbo to kill the dragon, his promised reward for delivering the treasure into Thorin & Company's hands. Now that the role of dragon-slayer has been split off and assigned to a new character, Bard, the Gem becomes a bargaining chip with which Bilbo hopes to satisfy Bard's claim for his rightful share of the treasure (what better way than with Girion's own Gem to Girion's heir?). Thus it has moved into the role it will play in the final story, although the events which followed in the Third Phase text (Bard's attempt to ransom it back to Thorin for a one-fourteenth share of the treasure, a transaction eventually completed by Dain) have not yet emerged. Instead of Bilbo bringing it home with him as his chief memento of his eventful journey, it has now become the peace-price he is willing to pay to save his friends, and the idea that Bilbo comes home with only a few token treasures to show for all his troubles, present since the earliest layer of Plot Notes B, nears its final form.

True, After a Fashion

In keeping with the general interest in dreams and prophecies in the latter section of the book, for the first time the 'pleasant fable' mentioned casually in an addition to Chapter X – 'Thror and Thrain would come back one day and gold would flow in rivers through the northern falls, and all that land would be filled with new song and new laughter' – has now been elevated to the dignity of a prophecy. But unlike in the final book here it is Bard, not Bilbo, who is surprised to find himself its fulfiller, and Gandalf's pointing out of this fact comes much earlier ('Believe not prophecies less because you yourself have aided in their fulfilment'), as part of the negotiations to resolve the conflict (the pact we might call 'the Peace of the Ruined City').

In any case, primed by the writing of these Plot Notes, Tolkien soon resumed the story and brought it within what he must have thought a chapter or two of the ending, not foreseeing the tangle that would require him to break off and reconsider the events of the climax.

NOTES

1 Actually, more accurately the B/C/D/B sequence, since the original final page of the earliest layer was renumbered 5 > 6 when Plot Notes D was inserted into the composite document, indicating that this page was still intended to outline the conclusion.

2 In this he is like Frodo, who in Tolkien's opinion actually fails in his mission to destroy the Ring (cf. JRRT 1965 BBC radio interview with Denys Gueroult), but who is a hero nevertheless for having made its destruction possible. Similarly, Bilbo in the published book fails to establish an accord between King Thorin and the besieging forces, loses for a time the friendship (or at least the trust) of the dwarves, and actually finds himself joining forces with the men and elves who are there to kill his travelling companions and take Smaug's gold by force; disaster is averted only through the unforeseen intrusion of the goblins.

3 'Long will I tarry, ere I begin this war for gold . . . Let us hope still for something that will bring reconciliation' (DAA.338).

4 One must, however, sympathize with his outburst that, if Thorin was indeed the heir of Thrain and Thror, 'why did he not say so?' The comment that 'then he believed at last', which presents the wood-elf king in a slightly more favorable light, however contradicts his having already accepted Thorin's identity back near the end of Chapter XIII ('When news of the rousing of the Dragon reached him, and of the fire upon the mountain tops, he thought that he had heard the last of Thorin Oakenshield', and he certainly knew exactly who Thorin was since 'he . . . had not forgotten the legend of the hoard of Thror').

5 In *The Lord of the Rings*, Elrond makes clear that the Last Alliance is so called because 'Never again shall there be any such league of Elves and Men; for Men multiply and the Firstborn decrease, and the two kindreds are estranged' ('The Council of Elrond', *LotR*.261). It is unclear on the surface why the alliance here in *The Hobbit* of men and elves fighting side-by-side against first dwarves and then wargs and goblins does not count, unless by 'such league' Elrond meant something grander than the relatively small armies and localized battles of the Anduin Vale or Lonely Mountain projected here. In any case, his statement reflects a later conception than that described in *The Hobbit*, especially so far as the projected 'Battle of Anduin Vale' is concerned, and can only be accepted as true if we reserve the grand title of 'alliance' for massive struggles between great hosts (e.g., the surviving Númenóreans and Noldor against all Sauron's armies) resulting in the end of an Age of the world. Here again we see *The Hobbit* closer in conception to similar battles described in the early Silmarillion material than either is to *The Lord of the Rings* and the later Silmarillion material.

6 Although, strictly speaking, Thorin may just have been wanting to honor the letter as well as the spirit of the contract: 'one fourteenth share of total *profits* (if any)' and been willing to count the sacrifice of the Gem of Girion as a necessary 'expense' in achieving their goal. Even so, this re-enforces the point that he shows no signs of contracting the dragon-sickness anywhere in these Plot Notes or in the few remaining pages of the Second Phase text that follow.

Chapter XIV

WHILE THE DRAGON'S AWAY . . .

This chapter start is one of the very few marked as such in the original manuscript, with 'Chapter XIV.' written in ink at the top of manuscript page 159 (Marq. 1/1/15:7). This forms the verso of manuscript page 158: for the few remaining pages of the Second Phase manuscript (manuscript pages 158–167), Tolkien writes on both the front and back of each sheet, as he had done in the original Pryftan Fragment and the earlier parts of the Second Phase but unlike his practice from manuscript page 119 (the capture by wood-elves) onward, where he had written only on the front of each sheet.

This chapter underwent considerable revision and expansion when it was recast (as new Chapter XIII: Not at Home) to better fit its new place preceding the chapter describing Smaug's death (original Chapter XIII, which now swapped places with it to become the new Chapter XIV: Fire and Water). Remarkably enough, a fair copy in manuscript exists of this chapter, titled '(Smaug is) Not at home' (manuscript pages 'a'–'m'; Marq. 1/1/14:1–14), which serves as an intermediate text between the original Second Phase manuscript draft of this chapter (manuscript pages 159–65; Marq. 1/1/15) and the First Typescript version of the chapter (typescript pages 127–34; Marq. 1/1/63). I have not reproduced this fair copy manuscript, which belongs to the early part of Tolkien's work on the Third Phase, because for most of its length it closely resembles the text of the First Typescript and thus of the published book, but in the Text Notes that follow I have noted the most significant changes between the manuscript and the fair copy, between the fair copy and the First Typescript, or between the typescript and the published book.

Their great foe was dead, and the hoard no longer had a keeper, but the dwarves did not know it. [Another danger was gathering about them, an army come > armies coming for the ransacking and plundering of the mountain palace. >] Nor would they have rejoiced had they known that the last great danger, the danger Thorin had dreaded all along, and which their silence before the Elvenking had not averted, was gathering about them – a host was marching up to ransack and plunder the halls of Thror. But they knew nothing of all this. They sat in the dark, and eventually silence fell round them. Little they ate and little they spoke. The passage of time they could not count, they scarcely dared to move, the whispers of their voices echoed and rustled in the tunnel. If they dozed they woke still to darkness and the silence going on unbroken.

At last after days [*added*: & days] <of waiting> as it seemed, when they were choked and dazed for want of air – it was but two [days >] nights and the day between in reality – they could bear it no longer. Almost they would have welcomed some sound of the dragon's return below. In the silence they feared his cunning devilry, not knowing that he would never again return to his golden bed, but was lying cold as stone [upon the twisted >] twisted upon the floor of the shallows of the lake, where forever after his great <bones> could be seen in calm weather, [and >] amid the ruined pile of the old town, [but no >] if any one dared to cross the accursed spot.

At last heedless of noise they went back to the door only to find by their groping that all the outer end of the tunnel was shattered. Neither they nor the magic which it had once obeyed – even if they had known it – would open it again.

'We are trapped!' they say. 'This is the end; we shall die here when our food is gone, or [choke >] stifle before that'.[TN1]

And yet somehow Bilbo felt a lightening of the heart. The gloom and foreboding that had settled on him on the night of the dragon's last assault was lifted. He felt as if a menace had departed [and] his courage returned (and trust in his proven and astonishing luck).

'Come come!' he said. ' "While there's life there's hope," as my father used to say, and "third time pays for all".[TN2] I am going down the tunnel once more. I have been down twice when I knew there was a dragon at the other end, and I think I will risk a third visit, when I am no longer at all sure – and anyway <there> is no other way out of this.

'If you will take my advice you will all come with me this time; but do be careful and as quiet as you can be. There may be no dragon, but then again there may be. I am not going to take unnecessary risks with Smaug any more'.

[Something >] In desperation they agreed, and Thorin was the first to creep forward by Bilbo's side. Down down they went – but dwarves are not as good as hobbits when it comes to real stealth, and it was fortunate there was no listening ears at the far end of the echoing passage: the very puffing of their breath magnified in that place would have been enough for Smaug.[TN3] But no sound stirred below.

Near the bottom (as well as he could judge) Bilbo slipped on his ring again. But he scarcely needed it; the darkness was complete, and they were all invisible, with rings and without. So dark was it that Bilbo came to the opening unexpectedly put his hand on nothing, and stumbled forward and rolled headlong into the hall. There he lay still not daring to get up or even breathe. But nothing moved. There was not a gleam of light – unless far off, as his eyes [got >] stared fearfully into the blackness, he caught a pale white gleam. But certainly it was no spark of dragon-fire though the stench of the worm was still in the place, and it was hot and the taste of his vapour was on the tongue.[TN4]

At length B. could bear it no more. 'Confound you Smaug, you villain' he said aloud. 'Stop playing hide and seek. Give us a little light and eat me after if you must!'

Faint echoes ran about the unseen hall, but there was no answer. Bilbo got up, but he did not know in which direction to turn.

'Something seems to have happened to Smaug, I do believe' he said.[TN5] 'Now I hope Oin or Gloin has got a tinderbox, or can make a light. Let's have a look round before the luck turns!'

The dwarves were very alarmed when B. fell forward with a noise and were still frightened when they heard his voice, but Oin [> Gloin] was sent back as Bilbo asked to find some materials for light, if he could, among their goods near the upper end <of the> tunnel. Before long a little twinkle of light showed that he was returning with a small pine-torch alight and a bundle of others under his arm.[TN6]

Bilbo took the little lighted torch, but the Dwarves would not yet use the others, but preferred to stop inside the tunnel and see what would happen first. As Thorin explained [he > B >] Mr Baggins was still officially their expert burglar and investigator. If he liked to risk a light that was his affair: they would wait for his report.

So they sat near the opening and watched. They saw him steal[TN7] across the floor holding aloft his tiny light – a little flickering patch of red in the blackness. Every now and again there was a glint at his feet as he stumbled upon some golden thing. The light [<rose?> >] grew smaller as he wandered away into the huge hall, then it began to rise dancing into the air. Bilbo was climbing the great mound of treasure. Soon he stood near the top, and from afar they saw him stoop but they did not know the reason.

It was the Gem of Girion,[TN8] for such Bilbo guessed it to be from the description of the dwarves. Ever as he climbed forward the same [pale >] white gleam had shone before him like a small globe of pallid light; now as he approached it was tinged with [a] flickering sparkle of red [> splintering beams] reflected from his torch. At last he looked down upon it, and caught his breath. It held his eyes and he gazed in wonder. It was a great white gem, that shone of its own light within, and yet cut and fashioned by the dwarves to whom Girion had given it,[TN9] it caught and splintered all light that it received into a thousand sparkles of dazzling white. It was a large gem and heavy, larger than the hobbit's small hand – that was stretched out to it, drawn by its enchantment. Suddenly he stooped, lifted it and put it in his pocket.[TN10]

'Now I am Burglar indeed' thought B. '– but I suppose I must tell the dwarves what I have done. Yet they said I could take my share as I could [> pick and choose my own share] – and I think I would choose this, if they took all the rest. But it remains to be seen, if I have won my share at all yet'.[TN11]

With that thought he went on. Down the mound he climbed, [and all round the walls he wandered >] and his spark was hidden from the watching dwarves. All round the walls he wandered, and they saw it dimly again in the distance, and then coming back [> Then they saw it red and far in the distance again].

On he went till he came to the great doors of the hall at the far side, and a draught of air nearly blew out his torch. He peeped through, shielding the flame with his hand, and caught a glimpse of vast passages, and stairs going up into the gloom.

Then a black shape flew [> swooped] <in the air> [> at him], brushed his hair; the flame flickered as he started, stumbled back, and fell. The torch dropped head downward & went out. 'Only a bat I suppose and hope' he said ruefully, 'but now what am I to do.'[TN12]

'Thorin Balin!' he cried out. 'The light's gone out. Some one come and help me!' He didn't like being lost in the dark so far away from the tunnel at all and for the moment his courage failed altogether.

Faintly from far off the dwarves heard 'Thorin Balin!' echoing and 'help!' 'Now what on earth or under it has happened?' said Thorin. They waited a minute, but no dragon-like noises came. 'Come on one of you' said Th. 'strike another light. We must go and help Mr Baggins I suppose'.

'It does seem our turn' said Balin.

So when Gloin had lit a couple of torches they crept out[TN13] and went along the wall as hurriedly as they could; and before long they met Bilbo trying to feel his way round. They were very relieved to hear his account of what had happened, though what they would have said if he had told them at that moment about the gem of Girion I don't know. The mere fleeting glimpses of the treasure which they had caught had rekindled all the fire of their hearts; and when the fire of the heart of a dwarf is kindled by jewel and gold his courage grows.[TN14] They no longer needed any urging of Bilbo's. Both Balin and Thorin were eager now to explore, and willing to believe that at any rate for the present Smaug was not at home. Soon they had all the torches alight and all the party stole out of the tunnel and entered the hall which the dwarves had never [*cancelled*: again] entered since the days long ago [of] the dragon's coming.

Once they had started the exploration they forgot fear and

<caution>. They lifted old treasures from the mound and held them up in the light and felt them and fingered them. They took down mail and weapons from the walls and armed themselves.[TN15] Royal and princely Thorin looked in a coat of gold with a silver-hafted axe in his belt.

'Mr Baggins!' he said 'Here is the first payment of your reward! Cast off your old coat and put on this!' Then he put upon Bilbo a small coat of mail, <wr>ought for some elf-prince long ago.[TN16] It was of silvered steel,[TN17] [and pearls were <clustered> >] adorned with pearls, and a belt of pearls and crystals went with it. A light helm of figured leather strengthened within with hoops of steel, and studden about the rim with gems they set upon his head. An absurd desire to look at himself in a glass took hold of him: [He began to >] but he still kept his head more than the dwarves.[TN18]

[He grew >] 'Come!' he said 'we are armed, but what has any such armour availed against Smaug the Dreadful? The treasure is not yet regained. We are seeking not for gold but a way of escape. Let us get on.'

'True, true' said Thorin '– and I will be your guide. Not in a thousand years shall I forget the ways of this palace.' So now the dwarves covered their glittering mail with their old[TN19] cloaks and the helms with <their> hoods, and followed behind Thorin, a line of little torches in the Dark.

Out [into the >] through the wide doors they went in single file. Dreading at every step to hear the rumour of Smaug's return, for Bilbo's words had recalled them only too well to their danger, they crept in single file into the passages <outside>. Though all was befouled [*added*: & <blackened>] with the dragon and all the old adornments rotten or torn away, Thorin knew every road and turn. They climbed long stairs, turned and went down <hollow> echoing ways, turned again and climbed yet more stairs, smooth carved and even in the long rock; and yet more stairs again, [Till Bilbo could go on no more. >] Up and up they went and met no sign or <word> of anything, save wild and fierce animal shapes,[TN20] and suchlike forms that slipped off into the shadows. At last Bilbo felt he could go on no more – the stairs were steep and high for him, although he alone was not carrying any <other> treasure than his armour.[TN21] The dwarves' pockets were stuffed with gold & gems (for fear this shd be their only chance of gaining anything); and besides they had all the bundles of such foods as they had got into the tunnel to carry on their backs.

'A little further still' said Thorin. 'We shall see the Day ere long. Cannot you feel the <sniff> of [> beginnings of] a new air?'

'Come on [> along] Bilbo' said Balin, taking his arm '– if we get out safe and alive it will be due to you many times over; we cannot leave you here, nor can we wait.' So as they had done in the goblins cavern they picked him up and carried him[TN22] forward, until suddenly the roof sprang high far above the waning light of their torches. Light came in from an opening in the roof. Pale and white, and more light from great doors at the far end, one of which was fallen on the ground, the other was hanging on one broken hinge.

'This is the Great Hall of Thror, his hall of feasting and of council. And from the Gate it is not far off' said Thorin.

They passed out again[TN23] and soon [*cancelled*: before them the great arch of the Front Gate shone – blackened and ruined but still <?standing> <?firm> at the <illegible> and <splendid> at the <illegible> >] a sound of water fell upon their ears. Out of a dark tunnel issued, a boiling water and flowed in a built channel beside their road. 'There is the birth of the Running River' said Thorin, 'and it is hasting to the Gate. Let us follow!'

Round a wide turn they went and before them stood the [*added*: broad] light of day. A rising sun sent its light from the East between the arms of the mountain, and beams of gold came in and fell upon the floor. Before them was a great arch, still showing cunning work within, blackened and ruined & splintered as it was. They were come to Front Gate, and were looking forth to the East. A whirl of bats went up affrighted by their smoking torches which they had not put out. Their feet slipped upon the floors that were smooth and slimy with the passing of the great Dragon that had lived there long. The water rushed noisily past them [> below them] in its bed. They were dazzled by the morning light.

This paragraph and those that followed in the Second Phase manuscript were rearranged, rephrased, and expanded in the 'fair copy' (page 'i'; I/I/14:9), which has so many changes and crossouts in the course of writing that it here becomes essentially another draft, although still unusually legible by Tolkien's standards. The First Typescript here represents a polished and slightly revised version of the fair copy text. Parts of this section were also revised again at the page proofs stage (Marq. 1/2/2: pages 248–50 plus rider to page 249), with Tolkien (an experienced proofreader) taking care that each revision took exactly the same amount of space as the line(s) it replaced so that necessary changes would only affect those specific lines and not force the resetting of subsequent pages.

I do not reproduce the details of these three intermediate stages here, since the fair copy revision essentially achieves the familiar text of the published book except for geographical details regarding the orientation of the Front Gate with the rising sun and the path to the outlying watch-post; the most significant of these revisions are covered in the Text Notes.

Fair indeed was the morning <clear> with a cold North wind upon the threshold of winter when they looked out blinded with the light after the days and nights of dark; and sweet was the feel of the air on Bilbo's face. Far off he saw the ruins of Dale in the valley below, to which a long road wound down [*added*: <below> the stones], ruinous but still to be seen. On his right the clifflike bank of the Running River rose in the distance from which he and Balin had gazed. It was <only then> that he realized how hot the dragon's lair had been;[TN24] and that smokes and vapours were drifting out of the Gate <water>head and up into the morning air – which struck him now keen and piercing chilly.

'What are all those birds doing I wonder?' he said to Thorin, pointing up to great clouds of them that were circling in the sky southward over the river, while ever more seemed to be gathering <beyond> them, flying up dark from the South.

'There is something strange happening' said Thorin. 'The crows are all gathering as if after a battle, or as if a battle was afoot. I would give a good deal to know where Smaug is and what he is doing.'

'One thing we must do at any rate' said Bilbo '& that is get away from his Front Gate [as soon >] while we have a chance'.

'My Front Gate' corrected Thorin '– still your advice is good. There is a place just beyond the Gate where [we can >] there used to be a bridge, and doubtless the river can anyway still be crossed, and there are steps beyond up the high South bank – and onto the long <Southern> Spur where [> under which] our first camp was made. [From there we may be able to find >] From there we can see far to South and West & East'.[TN25]

'More climbing!' groaned Bilbo.

'Your own advice!' said Thorin. 'We can have some food at the top.'[TN26]

The bridge was broken of course but they easily forded it. When they reached at last the top of the steps, and the winding upward path beyond, they found they were on an old flat look-out post with a wide view. There was a rocky opening there – 'steps lead down back into the mountain'[TN27] said Thorin 'or used to [> once did]. We used to keep watchmen here ever in the old days. If only it had had a northern view we might have [*added*: been ready in time to] kept [> keep] out Smaug & all this adventure wd never have been necessary! Still here we can lay hid and see without being seen.'[TN28]

They look [South >] West & there was nothing, nor East, and in the South there was no sign of man or dragon; but ever the birds were gathering.

The Second Phase text continues for another two manuscript pages, into what is now Chapter XV, but I halt here at the bottom of manuscript page 165, the spot Tolkien would later choose for his chapter-break.

TEXT NOTES

1 The opening paragraphs of this chapter were recast once the decision was made to make it precede, rather than follow, the account of Smaug's death. Accordingly, these paragraphs were replaced by the following in the intermediate fair copy manuscript:

> In the meantime the Dwarves sat in darkness and utter silence fell about them. Little they ate and little they spoke. They could not count the passing of time; and they scarcely dared to move, for the whisper of their voices echoed and rustled in the tunnel. If they dozed they woke still to darkness and to silence still unbroken.
>
> At last after days and days of waiting, as it seemed, when they were becoming choked and dazed for want of air, they could bear it no longer. Almost they would have welcomed some sound from below of the dragon's return. In the silence they feared some cunning devilry of his, but they could [not] sit still in hunger there for ever.
>
> Thorin spoke: 'Let us try the door' he said. 'I must feel the wind on my face soon or die. I think I would rather be smashed by Smaug in the open than suffocate in here'. So several of the dwarves got up and groped back to where the door had been. But they found that the upper end of the tunnel had been shattered, and blocked with broken rock. Neither key nor the magic it had once obeyed would ever open that door again.
>
> 'We are trapped' they groaned. 'This is the end. We shall all die here!'

This passage was slightly revised, both in contemporary ink and later pencil, bringing it more into line with the typescript (which is here identical with the published text; cf. DAA.289), but I have given it here as it was originally written.

2 For 'third time pays for all', Tolkien's (or, rather, Bungo Baggins') variant on a traditional but now unfamiliar maxim, see Text Note 3 following Chapter XII on page 516. We now learn a second saying of Bilbo's father, 'While there's life there's hope', a familiar proverb credited to the Roman orator Cicero [died 43 BC]. In its original form, appearing in a letter to his friend Atticus (*Epistolarum ad Atticum*, ix.10), the saying went 'While the sick man has life, there is hope'.

From these two proverbs, we can conclude a few things about the elusive Bungo, about whom very little indeed appears in the legendarium. First, he shared either his son's fondness for apt quotation or knack of coining proverbial sayings – cf. Bilbo's 'escaping goblins to be caught by wolves', which Tolkien equates to the later 'out of the frying pan into the fire' (Chapter VI page 203), and 'don't laugh at live dragons' (Chapter XII page 512), which in typescript became 'never laugh at live dragons' and 'passed into a proverb' (typescript page 128, Marq. 1/1/62:9; DAA.283). Furthermore, those sayings of his which Bilbo remembers reveal a sunny disposition; they are words of encouragement, the very opposite of the gloomy sayings 'Sunny Sam' the blacksmith is fond of airing in *Farmer Giles of Ham* (e.g., FGH expanded edition page 55). Secondly, he had the daring to court and marry Belladonna Took, who is not only 'famous' in her own right but 'one of the three remarkable daughters' of The Old Took, who himself seems merely a notable personality in *The Hobbit* but who we learn in *The Lord of the Rings* was in fact the ruler of his country at the time (i.e., the Took and Thain, a position held successively by Bilbo's grandfather, uncle, and, at the time of the Unexpected Party, his first cousin, according to the genealogical tables in Appendix C of *The Lord of the Rings*) – an example of solid upper middle-class stock marrying old nobility. Finally, Bungo had a gift for satisfying creature comforts (Bag-End, which he planned and built, is an exceptional hobbit-hole, enviously desired by Bilbo's and Frodo's relations) and the foresight to plan for future comforts, having laid down wine of such excellence (Old Winyards) that was fully mature seventy-five years after his death (*LotR*.50 & [1136]).

3 This sentence was replaced in the fair copy by

> . . . to real stealth, *and they made a deal of puffing and shuffling which the echoes magnified alarmingly. Every now and again in fear Bilbo would stop and listen,* but no sound stirred below.

This revision removes the reassurance that 'no listening ears' waited below and increases the suspense for readers who did not yet know Smaug was dead, which of course would now only be revealed in the following chapter.

4 At this point, there is a change in the handwriting, which becomes distinctly neater and more legible for the next three paragraphs (the last on manuscript page 160). The ink is also darker, and this same ink has been used to touch up some of the less legible words in the preceding paragraph. Clearly, this represents a pause in composition, but probably only a brief one, possibly no one than from one night's writing session to the next.

5 This sentence was replaced in the fair copy with ' "Now I wonder what on earth Smaug is playing at" he said. "He is not at home to day (or tonight, or whatever it is) I do believe . . ." ' (fair copy page 'c'; 1/1/14:3), once again increasing uncertainty about Smaug's inexplicable absence for the reader as well as the characters.

6 This paragraph serves as a good example of the sort of development parts of this chapter underwent, where the essential points change very little but their expression was expanded and polished. In both of the examples below I have indicated changes from the previous text in italics:

> The dwarves, *of course,* were very alarmed when Bilbo fell forward with a *bump into the dragon's hall,* and *they* were *both* frightened *&* *surprised* when they heard his voice. *At first they did not like the idea of striking a light at all; but Bilbo kept on squeaking out for light, so* [*added: that at last*] *Thorin* sent Oin *and* Gloin back *to the* goods *they had saved at the top* of the tunnel. Before long a little twinkle showed *them* returning, *Oin* with a small pine-torch [*added*: alight] *in his hand, and Gloin with* a bundle under his arm.
>
> *Then Bilbo knew again in what direction the tunnel was. Quickly he trotted back and took the* torch . . . (fair copy page 'c'; I/I/14:3).

This passage was revised in both contemporary ink and later pencil, and developed further in the first typescript:

> The dwarves, of course, were very alarmed when Bilbo fell forward *down the step* with a bump into the hall, and they *sat* [*added*: *huddled*] *just where he had left them at the end of the tunnel.*
>
> *'Sh! sh!' they hissed,* when they heard his voice; *and though that helped the hobbit to find out where they were, it was some time before he could get anything else out of them.* But *in the end, when* Bilbo *actually began to stamp on the floor, and screamed out* 'light!' *at the top of his shrill voice,* Thorin *gave way, and* Oin and Gloin *were sent* back to *their bundles* at the top of the tunnel.
>
> *After a while* a twinkl*ing gleam* showed them returning, Oin with a small pine-torch alight in his hand, and Gloin with a bundle *of others* under his arm. Quickly Bilbo trotted *to the door* and took the torch . . . (typescript page 128; I/I/63:2).

For all the additional detail and fleshing out of the scene, the most significant change here is the addition of the idea that a step down separated the secret tunnel from the vast chamber that Smaug had made his lair; no such step had been mentioned in the earlier descriptions of Bilbo's two previous trips down the tunnel.

7 This highly suggestive word choice, coming as it does in the paragraph before he pockets the Gem of Girion and becomes 'a burglar indeed', survived into the intermediate fair copy text – 'They saw the little dark shape of the hobbit steal across the floor . . .' (page 'c') – but vanished thereafter; the First Typescript reads instead '. . . *start* across the floor'.

8 Here the manuscript reading, 'the Gem of Girion' (manuscript page 161; I/I/15), survives into the fair copy as 'the gem of Girion' (fair copy page 'd'; I/I/14), which is then changed in ink to 'the Arkenstone'. At some later time, probably at the time of the creation of the First Typescript, 'Heart of the Mountain' was added in pencil to the fair copy page alongside 'Arkenstone'. The typescript reading (I/I/63:2) is the same as that of the published book: 'the Arkenstone, the Heart of the Mountain'.

9 The original story, that Girion had given Thror the Gem in payment for the arming of his sons (see Plot Notes C), is reflected in the wording of the Second Phase manuscript here. Although this paragraph is developed and recast in the fair copy (so that it resembles the typescript

and published texts), the phrase 'the dwarves to whom Girion had given it' remained, until it was struck out and replaced in faint pencil which seems to read 'the dwarves who dug it from the mountain's heart' (fair copy page 'd'; 1/1/14:4). In the First Typescript this has become 'the dwarves, who had dug it from the heart of the mountain long ago' (typescript page 129; 1/1/63:3), the reading of the published book (DAA.293).

10 This passage was carefully revised to establish the qualities of the Gem or Arkenstone, both physical (that is, its size and weight) and magical, carefully balancing hints of Bilbo's being under the power of the wondrous stone versus his acting on his own volition when he takes and hides it. First, an addition to the original manuscript made the Gem somewhat smaller, so that 'larger than the hobbit's small hand' became 'larger than the hobbit's small hand *could close upon*' (manuscript page 161; 1/1/15). The passive tense of the Second Phase manuscript ('the hobbit's small hand . . . was stretched out to it') was initially retained into the fair copy, which devotes its own paragraph to Bilbo's taking the gem and becomes, for the moment, a new draft (albeit an unusually neat one) as Tolkien experiments with the phrasing:

> [Suddenly Bilbo's hand was drawn towards it. He >] Suddenly Bilbo's arm went towards it, drawn by its enchantment. [He could scarcely lift it, for it was large and heavy. >] His small hand would not close over it, for it was a large and heavy gem; but he lifted it, shut his eyes, and put it in his largest pocket.

The typescript stays very close to this, only dropping one comma and substituting *deepest* for *largest*, apparently over an erasure. The phrasing of this final version – where Bilbo's arm is 'drawn by its enchantment', but the actual passive tense has been removed, and ending in a string of simple active tenses (lifted, shut, put) – nicely captures the ambivalence of the passage.

11 For Thorin's assurance that Bilbo could choose his own share, see their discussion near the end of Chapter XII (page 514), from manuscript page 151c:

> 'As for your share Mr Baggins' said Thorin 'I assure you we are more than satisfied with your professional assistance; and you shall choose it yourself, as soon as we have it! I am sorry we were so stupid as to overlook the transport problem . . .'

The line about Bilbo's uneasy feeling over what he has just done first appears in the fair copy text, replacing the final sentence of the paragraph:

> '. . . I would choose this, if they took all the rest!' All the same, he had an uncomfortable feeling that the picking and choosing had not been really meant to include this marvellous gem, and that trouble would still come of it.

12 Here and throughout the original Second Phase manuscript depiction of the scene in Smaug's empty lair, Bilbo is much less panic-strickened than in the published account. We are told that 'his courage failed

altogether', but the actual description of his actions, both here and in his earlier stumble in the dark on page 578–9, does not really bear this out – for example, Bilbo is already feeling his way along the walls when the dwarves finally strike a light in the original draft, whereas in the fair copy 'his wits had returned as soon as he saw the twinkle of their lights' (fair copy page 'e'; 1/1/14:5). Many details added at the fair copy and First Typescript stages – e.g., the description of Bilbo's shouts after the loss of his torch as 'squeaking', his peeping *timidly* through the great doors, 'ruefully' being replaced by 'miserably', et al. – all have the cumulative effect of diminishing Bilbo's stature and courage throughout this scene, from the time he enters the dragon's lair for a third time until the dwarves rejoin him there.

13 The fair copy text (fair copy page 'e'; 1/1/14:5) adds 'crept out, *one by one,*' which marks a final appearance in the book of the Unexpected Party motif, which we have also seen in the troll scene, the arrival at Medwed and the Mirkwood bonfires scene along the way.

14 The effect that the sight of treasure has on dwarves shifts from positive ('his courage grows') in the Second Phase manuscript to ambivalent (not just 'bold' but 'fierce', no longer 'kindled' but 'wakened')† in the fair copy:

> . . . when the fire of the heart of a dwarf is wakened by jewels and gold [> by gold and by jewels] he grows suddenly [fierce >] bold, and he may become fierce.

The typescript rearranges this slightly, and makes one significant addition:

> . . . when the heart of a dwarf, *even the most respectable,* is wakened by gold and by jewels, he grows suddenly bold, and he may become fierce.

These changes were obviously made to match the evolving conception and introduction of the idea of dragon-sickness taking hold on Bilbo's companions, which had been absent in the Second Phase story – cf. the mention of 'respectable' dwarves, a term specifically applied to Thorin & Company by Medwed (see page 234).

†Implying it was already there, though dormant.

15 Added in hasty script in the bottom margin, and marked for insertion first following 'in the light' in the preceding sentence and then at this point:

> They gathered gems in their hands & let them fall <with a sigh>. – and always Thorin sought from side to side for something he could not see. It was the gem of Girion <Thror's> chief treasure, but he did not speak of it <again>.

This passage accords well with the conception of the dragon-sickness taking hold on the dwarves and especially Thorin, a plot-point not present when this chapter was first drafted (that is, in the Second Phase story). Accordingly, although there is no appreciable difference in ink, this marginal addition probably dates from the Third Phase and represents drafting for the intermediate fair copy manuscript, a transition between the original story and the familiar one that appears in the typescript and subsequently the published book.

The passage about Fili and Kili playing the harps (cf. DAA. 295) entered as a hasty pencilled addition onto the fair copy (page 'f'), appearing in more polished form in the First Typescript. Fili and Kili were obviously musical; back in the first chapter they had played fiddles (page 36) while it had been Gandalf (= Thorin) who played the harp; here they prove skilled at the harp as well.

16 Added in pencil, and thus appearing in the fair copy and typescript: 'for some *young* elf-prince long ago'. This is possibly of significance, because it suggests that Tolkien might have conceived of the elves as somewhat smaller than human size when he originally wrote this passage. Initially, in his early 'fairy poetry' such as 'Goblin Feet' and 'Tinfang Warble' and in *The Book of Lost Tales*, Tolkien had thought of the elves as much smaller than human, but by the mid-1920s came to reject this and envisioned them instead as of similar stature to humans (as in the feys of medieval romance, legends of the Tuatha dé Danaan, and Spenser's *Faerie Queene*).

17 This is of course the same suit of armor which will become Frodo's mithril coat in *The Lord of the Rings*, but the idea of 'mithril' had not yet arisen. In Plot Notes C, this had been 'gold & silver mail made like steel' – that is, soft precious metals somehow hardened by dwarven craft to serve as protection. Tolkien may have changed this upon realizing that such armor would be so heavy that its wearer could hardly move (gold being almost as heavy as lead, and silver roughly twice the weight of iron) – cf. the similar change of Thorin's armor from 'a coat of gold' (Second Phase manuscript and fair copy) to 'a coat of gold-plated rings' (First Typescript and published book).

Although it's tempting to view *The Hobbit*'s 'silvered steel' as simply mithril under another name, the only thing that indicates that Bilbo's armor is anything more than silver-plated steel here is the fact that it has not tarnished or disintegrated, as real silver does over time,† and the same is obviously true of the many other silver objects in the legendarium – e.g. the Sceptre of Annúminas (already more than five thousand years old when Elrond surrendered it to King Aragorn; cf. *LotR*.1009 & 1080), the Elendilmir (that is, the silver circlet bearing the Star of Elendil, some three thousand years old), the horn from Scatha's hoard presented to Meriadoc ('wrought all of fair silver' and at least a thousand years old; cf. *LotR*.1014, 1102, & 1123), and indeed the silver harpstrings Fili and Kili play (which we are specifically told are 'magical') – forcing us to conclude that Tolkien simply chose to ignore this detail of physics for aesthetic effect, since he preferred perishable silver to immutable gold.

†Hence we have many more items of gold than of silver from ancient Egypt not just because silver was rarer than gold in the Nile valley but because gold does not oxidize and thus can survive for millennia unharmed, while silver

tarnishes within a few years and eventually oxidizes away entirely over the course of centuries.

18 This simple statement is invested with ominous overtones in the fair copy version, which reads '*All the same Mr Baggins* kept his head more *clear of the bewitchment of the hoard* than the dwarves *did*' (fair copy pages 'f'–'g'). Similarly, the reference to Thorin's 'recovering his wits' when he replies, which enters in with the First Typescript, emphasizes the dweomer the dragon-gold casts upon the unwary.

The reference to Beorn's refreshments (see DAA.296) also enters in at the fair copy stage; like Bilbo's thoughts of Gandalf in Chapter XI, this allusion helps remind the reader of this character (who has not appeared since Chapter VII) and helps set up his return a few chapters later.

19 The word *old* is cancelled in the manuscript but restored in the fair copy, so I have retained it here.

20 We never gain any more information about what wild animals might be warily sharing the outer regions of Smaug's lair than this brief reference. These 'animal shapes' became, in the fair copy, 'furtive shadows':

> . . . no sign of any living thing, save furtive shadows that fled from the approach of their fluttering torches [> torches fluttering in the draughts].

(fair copy page 'g'; 1/1/14:7). With the exception of one word changed in the typescript ('save furtive shadows' > '*only* furtive shadows'), this is the reading in the published book (DAA.296), so we never learn any more about these Gollum-like lurkers in Thror's deserted halls.

21 This statement of course ignores the fact that Bilbo is carrying the Gem of Girion in his pocket; even though it had not yet gained the status it later reached of being worth 'a river of gold in itself' (DAA.326), it was nonetheless already the pre-eminent item of treasure within the hoard; cf. Chapter XII page 514 and Text Note 39 following that chapter. Compare the dwarves' reasonable behavior here of taking as much of the treasure as they can manage on what may be their only chance before the dragon returns (and only after arming themselves and as a last action before leaving the treasure-chamber), not forgetting the more practical business of preserving their supplies and remaining food (another practical detail that vanished after the Second Phase manuscript), with their more greedful behavior in the published account, where they caress the treasure longingly – e.g. the inserted passage cited in Text Note 15 above and its fair copy analogue:

> . . . they lifted old treasures from the mound and held them in the light, caressing and fingering them. They gathered gems and stuffed their pockets, and let what they could not carry fall back through their fingers with a sigh.
>
> —fair copy page 'f' (1/1/14:6); cf. DAA.295.

22 This rather touching scene of Balin's solicitude for the exhausted hobbit and the dwarves taking turns to carry him disappeared from the story, although it survived into the fair copy, which adds the detail 'as in the

goblin-caves, *but now more willingly*' (fair copy page 'h'; 1/1/14:8). The fair copy text also makes clear that one element of Bilbo's exhaustion was the mail-coat: 'he felt dragged down by the unaccustomed weight of his mail coat, and his head swam. He sat down and panted on a step.' To this was added a hasty pencilled addition which seems to read '. . . of his mail coat, *and the stone weighing heavy in his pocket.*' – that is, the idea that the Arkenstone itself was a heavy burden was still present. The typescript omits this entire passage.

For the weight of the gem, see Text Note 10 above; for the weight of the 'silver-steel' armor, see Text Note 17.

23 The grisly detail of this chamber being littered with the skulls and bones of Thorin's people first appears in the fair copy (page 'h'; 1/1/14:8):

> They passed through the ruined chamber. Tables were rotting here and chairs overturned and decaying. Skulls and bones were upon the floor among flagones and bowls and broken drinking-horns [*added*: and dust].

Oddly enough, neither in the fair copy nor in any later text is there any mention of distress among the dwarves at the sight of their murdered and unburied kinsmen, or of their afterwards seeing to the remains. Perhaps, given the dwarven tradition of entombment (cf. Chapter XVIII and *LotR*.1113) and the pressing circumstances (with, so far as they knew, the murderer still on the prowl), Thorin & Company felt that being in stone chambers underground was burial enough until more formal arrangements could be made – compare, in *The Lord of the Rings*, Gimli's grief at finding Balin's tomb with his apparent unconcern about the bones of Ori and his companions lying scattered about the chamber (*LotR*.338–44).

24 In comparing how hot and stuffy it was inside Smaug's lair with the chill outside, the fair copy text (page 'i'; 1/1/14:9) specifies that it is not just cool but almost winter:

> 'Well' said Bilbo. 'I never expected to be looking out of this door. And I never expected to be so pleased to see the first sun on a cold wintry morning as I am now. [Ugh! >] But the wind is cold!'
>
> It was. A cold breeze from the North [> East], from the threshold of winter, [> A cold North-easterly breeze coming from the gates of winter] was slanting into the valley and sighing in the rocks. They shivered in the sun, after their long time in the stewing depths of the caves, yet the feel of the air was sweet upon their faces.

The change here from North first to East and then to North-easterly comes in order for the text to match the evolving map of the Lonely Mountain. In Fimbulfambi's Map (see Frontispiece to Part One), the eastern spur of the mountain already had its slight southward curl at the end but this would not have blocked direct line of sight between the Front Gate and the rising sun in the east, especially since in winter the sun rises somewhat to the south of East. In the redrawn version, Thror's Map I (Plate I [bottom]), the curl is less pronounced but the mountain's arm is longer, so that it would have blocked the view directly to the east but still has a clear south-east view.

This is not the case with the third and final map, Thror's Map II, which is printed in all copies of *The Hobbit* (for example, DAA.97). The map's orientation has changed, so that East rather than North now appears at the top (in keeping with the tradition of medieval and renaissance maps, rather than our modern practice of putting north at the top). Here that arm of the mountain has shifted from just south of east (ESE) to stretch just east of south (SES), completely blocking the view to the east. Similarly, the newly lengthened matching arm with the watch-post by this point known as Ravenhill on its southernmost tip (and which forms the other wall of the little valley that gives Dale its name) blocks off everything to the west, so that the Front Gate now has a clear view only to the south. Hence in the final text written onto the page proofs the relevant passage reads:

> . . . wind is cold!'
>
> It was. A bitter easterly breeze blew with a threat of oncoming winter. It swirled over and round the arms of the Mountain into the valley and sighed among the rocks. After their long time in the stewing depths of the dragon-haunted caverns, they shivered in the sun.

Accordingly, since they could no longer see the sunrise, in another set of last-minute page proof corrections the *rising* sun became the *misty* sun, its light changed from *red* to *pale*, the sunbeams changed from *ruddy gold* to simply *gold*, and it has now become *late* morning (I/2/2: page 248) rather than dawn.

The changes from 'wintry' and 'threshold of winter' are interesting, since they seem to reflect the revised time-scheme of the published book, in which Durin's Day fell on the *last* new moon before the onset of winter – i.e., no more than twenty-eight days before the solstice on or around December 21st, several days of which have already passed between the opening of the secret door and the dwarves' arrival at the Front Gate. Bilbo and company thus reach the Front Gate in early to mid December, just a few days before midwinter, whereas in the original time-scheme where Durin's Day falls on the *first* new moon of autumn it would be early autumn, sometime between the very end of September through mid-October. See page 481 for more on the unresolved difficulties created by the shift in timing.

25 This paragraph describing the lay-out of the valley was replaced by the following in the fair copy (page 'j'), with Balin as the speaker:

> 'Five hours' march or so. But we can have a rest on the way. Do you see there on the right? There is the high cliff-like bank of the river that we looked out from when we first came here, Bilbo.† Between that and this gate there used to be a bridge, and beyond it steps cut in the rock-wall that led to a path winding up on to the southern mountain-spur, above where our first camp was made.'

†See page 472 in Chapter XI.

Aside from the usual polishing of phrasing and the changing of the first sentence to 'Five hours march, I should think, as we are tired and it is mostly uphill', this is essentially the text of the First Typescript and the original page proof. It was replaced by Tolkien's emendations of the page proofs to:

> 'Five hours march, I should think. It will be rough going. The road from the Gate along the left edge of the stream seems all broken up. But look down there! The river loops suddenly east across the Dale in front of the ruined town. At that point there was once a bridge, leading to steep stairs that climbed up the right bank, and so to a road running towards Ravenhill.† There is (or was) a path that left the road and climbed up to the post. A hard climb, too, even if the old steps are still there.'

†See page 618 and Text Note 4 for Chapter XV(a) for the first mention of Ravenhill in the manuscript.

26 The eight paragraphs of dialogue that replaced this simple two-line exchange first appear in the fair copy (from the middle of page 'j' to the top of page 'k'). The fair copy is similar to the final text (see DAA.299–300), with the most interesting variant being a cancelled passage in Thorin's reply:

> 'Come come,' said Thorin, laughing his spirits rising *as he <thought> of his golden armor and his fists full of gems, and all the treasure yet to <?come>* [> with the hope of treasure].

This passage comes at the bottom of an unnumbered cancelled page (replaced by fair copy page 'j') which forms the verso of fair copy page 'k'.

27 This suggests that there might once have been a tunnel from the guardpost to the dwarven city in the mountain's heart, as was the case with the secret tunnel on the western side. No such implication survives into the published text, but see Plot Notes E (pp. 626 & 627) for a stronger indication of this possibility.

28 This paragraph's brief description of the journey from the Front Gate to Ravenhill, and their initial exploration of the old guard post, was greatly expanded in the fair copy (pages 'k'–'l'). In general the fair copy account closely resembles the typescript that followed aside from the usual small variations in phrasing and some reassignments of speeches: in the typescript Thorin's speech regarding the watchpost is reassigned to Balin, while Balin's reply is split between Dori and Thorin – although Balin's original reply (' "Small protection, if Smaug spots us, I fear" said Balin; "but we must take our chance of that. Anyway we can go no further to-day".') lacks Dori's apprehensions – and a brief rejoinder from Bilbo is inserted to close the conversation.

Aside from one addition regarding *cram* (see part iii of the commentary to this chapter), the typescript carried over almost verbatim into the page proofs, but the paragraphs describing their journey to the outpost were carefully revised at the proofs stage to better match the geography of the valley containing the Front Gate and ruins of Dale as they emerged in the final version of Thror's Map and also the various illustrations of the Lonely Mountain Tolkien made near the end of his work on the book. In particular, the altered course of the river results in shifting the ruins of Dale from the river's right (eastern) bank in Thror's Map I (Plate I [top]) and the painting 'Smaug flies round the Mountain' (Plate X [bottom]), to the river's left (west) bank in several other drawings such as 'The Lonely Mountain' (DAA.273, H-S#136; see also H-S#134 & 135) and the final map (DAA.50 & 97); note also the contrast between the boulder-strewn eastern bank of the Running River and the floodplain bordered by cliffs on the western bank in 'The Front Gate' (DAA.256; H-S#130). I here give the changes made to this section of the proofs (corresponding to DAA.300) in tabular form:

- So on again they trudged along the northern bank of the river – to the south the rocky wall above the water was sheer and pathless > So on they trudged *among the stones on the left side* of the river – to the *right* the rocky wall above the water was sheer and pathless (the reading of the first edition; Douglas Anderson notes that Tolkien revised this line again in the 1966 Ballantine paperback edition; cf. DAA.300).
- After going for a short distance eastward along the cliff top they came on a nook sheltered among rocks and there they rested for a while > After going a short *way they struck the old road, and before long* came *to* a *deep dell* sheltered among *the* rocks; there they rested . . .
- After that they went on again; and now the path struck southwards and left the river, and the great shoulder of the south-pointing mountain-spur drew ever nearer. Soon the narrow road wound and scrambled steeply up > 'After that they went on again; and now the *road* struck *west*wards and left the river, and the great shoulder of the south-pointing mountain-spur drew ever nearer. *At length they reached the hill-path. It* scrambled steeply up'.

One interesting detail that should be mentioned here is that the Second Phase manuscript describes the southern arm of the mountain as 'the long Southern Spur'. However, on Thror's Map I (Plate I [top]), the arm of the mountain pointing directly south is rather short, certainly shorter than the two eastern arms extending towards the Iron Hills. By contrast, on the published map (DAA.50) the southern arm is much longer. It is certain that the published map (Thror's Map II) did not exist at the point when Tolkien drafted this chapter, so the description here of the southern spur being 'long' could mean that this draft served as an intermediate stage in its extension.

Finally, the last page of the fair copy (page 'm'; 1/1/14:14) includes a single short paragraph that was moved to the start of the next chapter when the First Typescript was created, bridging the time-difference between these two chapters now that their original sequence had been reversed and the new Chapter XIV made into essentially one long flashback:

> Now you will be wondering as much as the dwarves about Smaug and it is time to tell you. You must go back to the evening when the Smaug had burst forth in rage, two days before [*cancelled*: the end of].

(i)
Dragon-sickness ('The Hoard')

> [T]he last great danger, the danger Thorin had dreaded all along, and which their silence before the Elvenking had not averted, was gathering about them – a host was marching up to ransack and plunder the halls of Thror.

While greed over the dragon's treasure was to play an important part in the climax of the story from the earliest draft, as we see from the preceding text and also Plot Notes C & D, Tolkien's original intent was to portray this as essentially an external force acting upon Thorin & Company from outside. Bilbo's uncharacteristic behavior of pocketing the Gem of Girion for himself and hints of disagreement between the hobbit and the dwarves about how best to handle the crisis of being besieged by angry lake-men and greedy, calculating elves aside, there are no indications whatsoever in the Second Phase materials that Thorin or any of the other dwarves succumb to the dragon-sickness of lusting after 'gold upon which a dragon has long brooded' (page 648). In fact, a passage from Plot Notes D suggests the opposite, and that their silence before the Elvenking had not been anxiety over splitting the treasure but

> . . . because dwarves understood better than all others the power of the greed of gold and fear therefore more certainly to <?extend> it.

The wisdom of this reticence is shown by the unedifying scramble for the treasure that ensues immediately following Smaug's death among the lake-men, enraged by their losses and deliberately stirred up into a blood frenzy by the Master (to deflect attention from his own inglorious behavior during the defense of their city), and by the wood-elves' king's plan to coolly seize the treasure with no better claim to it than the goblins of the Third Phase text have, namely because he shows up with an army large enough to take it.

Thus although the idea of the dragon-sickness bringing together rival claimants for the treasure was already the motivating factor for the projected climax in the final pages of the Second Phase text, resolving that crisis in the unwritten chapters, had Tolkien proceeded according to his original plan, would have been a relatively straightforward matter of dealing with a wholly external threat (the besieging armies). All this was to change when the second of the two great complications that derailed the

Second Phase narrative entered the text:[1] the idea that Bilbo's companions would themselves succumb to the 'dragon-sickness' more strongly than any other group present, whereas he himself would be able to throw off the 'bewitchment' and 'enchantment' of the dragon-hoard and thus take actions that would estrange him from his trusted companions of the last year and more,[2] and even ultimately place him on the opposite side of the coming battle, which could no longer be averted. The great moral complexity of the published book's final chapters and its bittersweet resolution were thus an innovation of the Third Phase; the original Second Phase ending would have been much more of a piece with the bulk of the book that preceded it – full of incident but morally unambiguous.

Given the heavy influence of the Túrin and Sigurd stories throughout the 'Lonely Mountain' section of *The Hobbit*, it is no surprise that they played an important role here as well. But as is usual with Tolkien, he was careful and creative in his borrowings, and here the Fafnir legend exerts much less influence over *The Hobbit* than it does over the earlier Túrin's story and Tolkien's borrowings are mainly from his own earlier unpublished work (as would henceforth be the case with all his subsequent work, from *The Lord of the Rings* onward). The theme of cursed treasure had been a powerful narrative thread in *The Book of Lost Tales* (especially in the tale of 'The Nauglafring' or Necklace of the Dwarves) and no doubt owed much to the story of Fafnir's and Sigurd's treasure (also known as Andvari's Hoard after its original owner, or the Gold of the Nibelungs, or Das Rheingold, depending on which version of the legend one consults). The Völsungs' treasure on the one hand (in Germanic and Norse myth) and the gold of the Rodothlim, the Silmarils, and indeed the One Ring on the other (within Tolkien's legendarium) indiscriminately bring doom to all their owners one by one, although a few (like Bilbo, Beren, and Eärendel) escape the curse's full effects.

So strongly did this theme appeal to Tolkien that it inspired one of his finest poems, 'The Hoard' (ATB poem #14), earlier known as 'Iúmonna Gold Galdre Bewunden' – a title ('ancient gold, entangled with enchantment') which itself laid equal emphasis, in two metrically balanced Old English half-lines, on the gold and on the spell or curse it was under (see Note 13 following Chapter XII). The poem tells of a wonderful treasure of gold and silver and jewels owned successively by elves, a lone dwarf, a dragon, and a hero who becomes a king, all of whom perish miserably, leaving the hoard in the end lost forever, buried in a grassy mound. Furthermore, the poem makes clear that all but the original owners are chained to the hoard, possessed by their own possession. Tolkien explicitly drew a connection between 'The Hoard' and the Túrin/Nauglafring legend in his Preface to *The Adventures of Tom Bombadil* [1962], where he assigned the poem's authorship to Bilbo (who after all knew a thing or two about possessive possessions – cf. the first chapter in both Book I and

Book II of *The Lord of the Rings* ['A Long-Expected Party' and 'Many Meetings', respectively] – but who had not been created as a character until at least seven years after this poem had first appeared in print!) during his years at Rivendell and said 'it seems to contain echoes of the Númenorean tale of Túrin and Mim the Dwarf' (ATB page 8). This tale is told in its fullest form in *The Book of Lost Tales* in the two stories 'Turambar and the Foalókë' (BLT II.69–143) and even more in 'The Nauglafring' (BLT II.221–51). We have already briefly touched on the Nauglafring story in Chapter IX (see 'The King of Wood and Stone', pp. 412–13), but the extraordinary degree to which the Rodothlim's treasure blights all who come into contact with it, a fate narrowly averted by most of the various claimants in *The Hobbit*, deserves revisiting, since the earlier story seems to have acted as a template underlying our tale.

The treasure's original owners, the Rodothlim elves (who in later forms of the legend became the Noldor of Nargothrond, Finrod Felagund's people), were destroyed by Glorund and his goblin [Orc] army, largely because of the arrogance and *ofermod* of Túrin before the battle. After his victory, Glorund claims all the treasure for himself and uses it for his bed, just as Smaug will later do with the wealth of Girion's and Thror's people:[3]

> all the mighty treasure that [the Orcs] had brought from the rocky halls and heaped glistering in the sun before the doors he coveted for himself and forbade them set finger on it, and they durst not withstand him, nor could they have done so an they would . . . (BLT II.85).

> . . . the dragon gloated upon the hoard and lay coiled upon it, and the fame of that great treasure of golden vessels and of unwrought gold that lay by the caves above the stream fared far and wide about; yet the great worm slept before it . . . and fumes of smoke went up from his nostrils as he slept (BLT II.87–8).[4]

As in *The Hobbit*, a small group later dares to venture into the dragon's territory to see if they can gain the treasure, but in the earlier tale these are not any survivors of the dragon's attack but an outside group, a picked band of wood-elves[5] sent by Tinwelint the elvenking, who is frank about his motivations:

> Now the folk of Tinwelint were of the woodlands and had scant wealth, yet did they love fair and beauteous things, gold and silver and gems . . . nor was the king of other mind in this, and his riches were small . . .
>
> Therefore did Tinwelint answer: '. . . it is a truth that I have need and desire of treasury, and it may be that such shall come to me by this venture . . .' (BLT II.95).

In the event, the expedition ends in disaster and achieves nothing besides stirring up the dragon and exposing Nienóri, Túrin's sister, directly to the dragon's curse.[6] Some time later, after Glorund's death at Túrin's hands far to the north (see commentary following Chapter XIII), the treasure passes into the keeping of Mîm the dwarf, who is here a figure of much greater stature than the petty-dwarf of the same name in the published *Silmarillion* (*Silm.*202–6 & 230). Indeed in the early tale Mîm is almost a Durin figure, called 'Mîm the fatherless', whose slaying is one of the factors that cause the dwarves of Nogrod (the Nauglath) and those of Belegost (the Indrafangs, a name later applied to Thorin's kin) to unite in a war of vengeance 'vow[ing] to rest not ere Mîm was thrice avenged' – a situation strongly reminiscent of the seven kindreds of the dwarves uniting to avenge the death of Thror, Durin's heir; cf. pp. 73 & 782 and *LotR.*1111. Mîm's warnings to Úrin of the Woods (the later Húrin, Túrin's father, who comes with a band of elven outlaws to carry off the treasure), are very much in keeping with the ideas expressed more than a decade later in Plot Notes D:

> . . . one only dwelt there [in the caves of the Rodothlim] still, an old misshapen dwarf who sat ever on the pile of gold singing black songs of enchantment to himself . . . when those Elves approached the dwarf stood before the doors of the cave . . . and he cried: '. . . Hearken now to the words of Mîm the fatherless, and depart, touching not this gold no more than were it venomous fires. *For has not Glorund lain long years upon it, and the evil of the drakes of Melko is on it, and no good can it bring to Man or Elf,* but I, only I, can ward it, Mîm the dwarf, and by many a dark spell have I bound it to myself' (BLT II.113–14; italics mine).[7]

Thus the twin motifs of dragon-haunted gold bringing bad luck and a dwarven claim to immunity from the dragon-sickness were established very early on in the legendarium (although in the end both would be almost entirely reversed; see below). Glorund's hoard, doubly cursed by the dragon-sickness and Mîm's dying curse upon it – the one attracting people irresistibly to the gold and the other striking down those who give in to its allure and claim it – brings disaster to all its subsequent owners: the outlaws who carry it away (slain by the wood-elves), the wood-elves and Tinwelint himself (slain and their realm overthrown by angry dwarven smiths cheated of their payment for recasting the gold into treasures), the victorious dwarves (who fall to fighting among themselves over the treasure and are ultimately ambushed and killed by Beren's green elves), and even Tinúviel (i.e., Lúthien, whose second, human, life is cut short by the Nauglafring Beren gives her, the only piece of treasure he retained).[8] And although 'The Nauglafring' stresses Mîm's curse as the chief agent at work in the betrayals and murders that follow (cf. Christopher Tolkien's comment on BLT II.246), the dragon-sickness is also definitely at work:

> Now came Gwenniel [Melian] to Tinwelint [Thingol] and said: 'Touch not this gold, for my heart tells me it is trebly cursed. Cursed indeed by the dragon's breath, and cursed by thy lieges' blood that moistens it, and the death of those they slew; but some more bitter and more binding ill methinks hangs over it that I may not see' (BLT II.223).[9]

Over and over again the tale stresses the unnatural power that sight of this gold has over the actions of those who come into contact with it: 'he [Tinwelint] might not shake off its spell' (BLT II.223), 'the spell of the gold had pierced [Ufedhin's] heart' (ibid., page 224), 'by reason of the glamour of the gold the king repented his agreement' (ibid., page 225), 'he [Narthseg] was bitten by the gold-lust of Glorund's hoard' (ibid., page 231). Late in the Tale, Gwendelin [Melian] reaffirms the complex nature of the curse, including 'the dragon's ban upon the gold' (BLT II.239), while it is explicitly stated that the elf-on-elf battle wherein the Sons of Fëanor kill Dior, Beren's son, and destroy the green-elves' kingdom is not only because of their remorseless pursuit of the Silmaril but also 'nor indeed was the spell of Mîm and of the dragon wanting' (BLT II.241).

Perhaps this long and complicated story offers a salutary lesson into what might have happened had Bilbo and the wizard not intervened: the dwarves in possession of the dragon-treasure slain by the men of Lake Town, who in turn might soon have found themselves at odds with the wood-elves over its distribution, if the earlier story is any guide. Dragon-treasure has a way of arousing treachery and setting allies at each other's throats. Even within the Sigurd story, the hero's first act after slaying the dragon is to murder his foster-father, Regin, who had taught him how to kill Fafnir but was now expressing remorse over the deed (Fafnir having been his own brother before his transformation into a dragon after killing their father and stealing the entire treasure for himself). In words that sound remarkably like internal paranoia, the birds warn Sigurd that 'Regin [is] minded to beguile the man who trusts him' (i.e., young Sigurd himself): 'Let him [Sigurd] smite the head from off him then, and be only lord of all that gold . . . not so wise is he if he spareth him, whose brother he hath slain already . . . Handy and good rede to slay him, and be lord of the treasure!' (Morris & Magnússon, pages 64–5).

Luckily, Smaug's hoard is not cursed to the same degree: the dragon-sickness is there, but not the additional death-curse. It's true that the dwarves cursed Smaug himself ('[we] sat and wept in hiding and cursed Smaug' and '. . . we still mean to get it back, and bring our curses home to Smaug' – Chapter I (c), pp. 72–3), but it is specifically the dragon that they curse, not the treasure itself (which was, after all, their own). Then too there is the curse inscribed on the treasure-jar in the painting 'Conversation with Smaug' (see Plate XI [detail] and commentary below), but this would not apply to Thorin & Company, who are Thror and Thrain's rightful heirs, nor Bilbo, who is their contracted representative. Despite the later development of the 'dragon-sickness' theme in the Third Phase and published book, relatively few succumb to it: Bilbo (very briefly), Thorin himself (who heroically throws off its influence during the Battle of Five Armies and dies free of it), most of Thorin's fellow dwarves to a lesser degree, and the Master of Lake Town at some later date. Ultimately, in fact, Thror's recovered treasure brings prosperity and peace to the region in the hands of those who can resist the dragon-sickness: Dain (who renews the Kingdom under the Mountain) and Bard (who re-establishes and rebuilds Dale and eventually extends his realm all the way down to include the rebuilt Lake Town); those who cannot resist meet with personal disaster but their fate has little effect on others (e.g., the Master of Lake Town's death from starvation does not harm Esgaroth's thriving recovery). This forms a stark contrast with Tolkien's models: the Völsung hoard is lost (knowledge of its location perishing with the execution of Sigurd's murderers), as is the gold of the Rodothlim (which Beren casts into the river, since it is tainted with all the injustices and murders committed over its possession), and also the treasure guarded by Beowulf's dragon (which is promptly buried once again, this time in Beowulf's barrow, and does his people no good whatsoever). Tolkien here creates a near-catastrophe followed by a happy ending appropriate to a fairy-story, in keeping with his ideas of eucatastrophe (cf. OFS): our hero may himself not wind up with a river of gold, but that gold is used instead of hoarded and makes his world a better place, so that in the end 'prophecies do come true, after a fashion'.

Such Mighty Heaps of Gold

Curiously enough, for all the mentions of the vastness and splendour of Smaug's hoard, relatively little space is devoted to describing it, and most of that is added in the expanded account of the dwarves reveling in their recovered treasure in the fair copy and First Typescript. Bilbo's awe at first seeing it robs him of all descriptive power, while the account of his later climbing the treasure-mound is almost casual, and the manuscript's description of the dwarves' exploration is more practical than sensuous, describing their choice of arms and armor and only then loading up on the most portable precious items (jewels and gemstones). To find a verbal portrait of such a hoard, a true Scrooge McDuck moment, we must go all the way back to *The Book of Lost Tales* and its description of the hoard of the Rodothlim:

> . . . such mighty heaps of gold have never since been gathered in one place; and some thereof was wrought to cups, to basons, and to dishes,

> and hilts there were for swords, and scabbards, and sheaths for daggers; but for the most part was of red gold unwrought lying in masses and in bars. The value of that hoard no man could count, for amid the gold lay many gems, and these were very beautiful to look upon . . . (BLT II.223).

After the great dwarven craftsmen have laboured for months at it, the hoard's beauty and splendor are exponentially increased:

> . . . in silken cloths, and boxes of rare woods carven cunningly . . . Cups and goblets did the king behold, and some had double bowls or curious handles interlaced, and horns there were of strange shape, dishes and trenchers, flagons and ewers, and all appurtenances of a kingly feast. Candlesticks there were and sconces for the torches, and none might count the rings and armlets, the bracelets and collars, and the coronets of gold; and all . . . subtly made and . . . cunningly adorned . . .
>
> A golden crown they made . . . and a helm too most glorious . . . and a sword of dwarven steel brought from afar that was hilted with bright gold and damascened in gold and silver with strange figurings . . . a coat of linked mail of steel and gold . . . and a belt of gold . . . a silver crown . . . [and] slippers of silver crusted with diamonds, and the silver thereof was fashioned in delicate scales, so that it yielded as soft leather to the foot, and a girdle . . . too of silver blended with pale gold. Yet were these things but a tithe of their works, and no tale tells a full count of them (BLT II.226–7).

The gem of the collection, quite literally, is the Nauglafring itself:

> Gems uncounted were there in that carcanet of gold, yet only as a setting that did prepare for its great central glory, and led the eye thereto, for amidmost hung like a little lamp of limpid fire the Silmaril of Fëanor, jewel of the Gods. (BLT II.228).

This imbalance was more than rectified with the inclusion, beginning with the first American edition of 1938, of Tolkien's painting 'Conversation with Smaug' (Plate XI [top]), which not only shows the treasure-hoard in all its glory but is full of specific detail from the text.[10] First and foremost there is Smaug himself – clearly a favorite of Tolkien's, whom he illustrated more times than any other character in the entire legendarium – red-gold and resplendent, looking very sly and self-satisfied in a smiling crocodilian way, the very picture of 'malicious wisdom'. The Arkenstone also draws the eye, shining brightly from the very peak of the treasure-mound. The emerald necklace, the Necklace of Girion (which arose in the Third Phase text when the Arkenstone became too precious for the old story of Girion's having given it to Thror in exchange for his sons' armour to remain credible – see page **000**), stretches between Smaug's head and tail. Directly below the Arkenstone can be seen a two-handled cup, no doubt just like the one Bilbo made off with on his first venture into the dragon-lair;

horns, swords, shields, helmets and at least one crown, bowls, goblets, chests, many, many gems, and of course a mort of gold and silver coins, along with a few less identifiable objects,[11] make up the rest of Smaug's bed. Bilbo's mail coat and accompanying cap can be seen on the far wall, above Smaug's folded wings, along with a pair of spears that might be a relic of the spear with which Bilbo was to kill the dragon in Plot Notes B (page 364) but which along with the shields and spears seen to the right is more probably the 'mail and weapons' with which the dwarves arm themselves. The 'great jars' standing along the walls 'filled with wealth only to be guessed at' are here as well (see commentary below). Even the bats who later extinguish Bilbo's torch (not to be confused with the more bloodthirsty bats who accompany the goblin army) and the passage up are included, as is of course Bilbo himself (who, Tolkien noted, was much too large in proportion – *Letters* p. 35). The one element remarkable for its presence here when nothing in the text so much as mentions it are the dwarven bones that lie scattered about, many of them alongside the sword, axe, shield, or helm that all too obviously failed to avail them against the dragon. The only feature of the hoard specifically mentioned in the text which this picture fails to include are the golden harps with silver strings that so delight Fili and Kili; doubtless these were hung on the walls to the left or right outside our field of view.

The Dwarvenkings' Curse

Among the most interesting details of this painting is the inscription on the massive treasure-cup in the lower left (see Plate XI [detail]). The words are English but the alphabet used is Tolkien's Tengwar except for the initials at the bottom, which use the same Old English runes employed for Fimbulfambi's Map (Frontispiece to Part One) and Thror's Map I (Plate I [top]). It is unusual for Tolkien to combine both writing systems in a single illustration but not absolutely unprecedented; see the title page for *The Lord of the Rings* itself, with runes at the top (this time in Tolkien's own runic arrangement, which he called the *cirth*) and continuing in Tengwar at the bottom. Tolkien nowhere translates the writing on the cup and the inscription is partially obscured by the ladder, but the missing ligatures can be restored with confidence:

A literal transcription, with vowels indicated by diacritical marks in the original enclosed in parentheses and restored letters obscured by the ladder given in italics, reads as follows:

G (O) L D TH R (O) *R* TH R A (I) N
A K (E) R S T *B* (E) *TH (E)* TH (E) F
TH [ror] TH [rain]

– that is, '. . . gold [of] Thror [and] Thrain . . . accursed be the thief', signed with the initials of THror and THrain. Note that this is only half of the full inscription, since the writing encircles the jar and we cannot know what appeared on the far side.

(ii)

The Arkenstone as Silmaril

The evolution of the Gem of Girion into the Arkenstone of Thrain, the Heart of the Mountain and supreme treasure of Durin's line,[12] was a gradual process throughout the latter parts of Tolkien's work on the Second Phase story from Plot Notes B on, until it finally reached its now-familiar form in the Third Phase texts. Initially invented to serve as a portable one-fourteenth share of the hoard to give the lie to Smaug's insinuation that the dwarves knew all along that Bilbo could never carry away his fair share, its value and allure were greatly increased with each iteration, until instead of Bilbo's designated portion it became the one item from the hoard Thorin most wanted to reclaim (DAA.326) and, in an ironic reversal, the one item he would have forbidden Bilbo to take.

In the original conception, the Gem of Girion is so named because it was given by Girion, King of Dale, to the dwarves of the Lonely Mountain in payment for the arming of his sons; we are never told how it came into Girion's possession. And just as a new character had to be introduced to fill the role of dragon-slayer once Tolkien decided it strained credulity to have little Bilbo in that role (Bard, whom Tolkien economically made the heir of Girion, thus opening up new plot-threads and possibilities even as he resolved one issue), so too the elevation of the 'Gem of Girion' into the Arkenstone led to the introduction of the Necklace of Girion to assume some of the plot-elements no longer suitable for the original item as it had evolved. For example, it is no more plausible that a human king would surrender a wonder like the Arkenstone for his son and heir's armor, however finely wrought, than that Gollum's grandmother gave away Rings of Power as birthday-presents (*LotR*.70), and the stories had to be changed to match the later conceptions. It is interesting, given the other echoes of the old 'Nauglafring' story in this cluster of chapters, that having split the Gem of Girion into two items, Tolkien chose to make this new item a necklace, since the Nauglafring itself had combined a wondrous necklace with a fabulous gem.

In the new conception, as represented by the First Typescript and associated Third Phase manuscript(s), the Arkenstone was found by dwarves and had never been owned by men. The account of its discovery in fact appears in the same piece of text that introduces the Necklace of Girion:

> . . . the necklace of Girion, Lord of Dale, made of five hundred emeralds green as glass, which he gave for the arming of his eldest son in a coat of dwarf-linked rings the like of which had never been made before, for it was wrought of pure silver to the power and strength of triple steel. But fairest of all was the great white gem, which the dwarves had found beneath the roots of the Mountain, the Heart of the Mountain, the Arkenstone of Thrain.[13]

Obviously, since in the revised story this gem had never been owned by Girion, the old name 'Gem of Girion' had to be replaced. The choice of *Arkenstone* is significant, since in other writings Tolkien was making at the same time he was using a variant of this same name as a term for the Silmarils themselves, forging a link between the Jewels of Fëanor and the Arkenstone of Thrain in the legendarium.

Thus, in the '(Earliest) Annals of Valinor', the entry for the Valian Year 2500 (that is, the equivalent of 25,000 solar years from the time the Valar entered Arda), reads:

> About **2500** the Noldoli [Noldor] invented and began the fashioning of gems; and after a while Fëanor the smith, eldest son of Finwë chief of the Noldoli, devised the thrice-renowned Silmarils, concerning the fates of which these tales tell. They shone of their own light, being filled with the radiance of the Two Trees, the holy light of Valinor, blended to a marvellous fire (HME IV.265).

This work is associated with the 1930 *Quenta* and only very slightly later in date – that is, contemporaneous with Tolkien's work on *The Hobbit* (HME IV.262). And among the very earliest work Tolkien did on the Annals (ibid., page 281) was an Old English version by Ælfwine/Eriol, the frame narrator of *The Book of Lost Tales*, in which the entry given above is translated thusly:

> **MMD** Hér þurh searucræftas aþóhton and beworhton þá Nold-ielfe gimmas missenlice, 7 Féanor Noldena hláford worhte þá Silmarillas, þæt wǽron Eorclanstánas (ibid. 282).

Literally translated, this remarkable passage reads:

> [The Year] 2500. Here through cunning craft/artistic skill the Noldor elves devised ('a-thought') and created ('be-worked') many gems, &

> Fëanor the Noldor lord wrought the Silmarils, that were precious/holy stones [*Eorclanstánas* or 'Arkenstones'].

Furthermore, in a later draft of the same work in Mercian dialect, the fictional translator 'Ælfwine of Ongulcynne' (Elf-friend of England) lists the three parts that make up 'The Silmarillion' – The Annals of Valinor, the Annals of Beleriand, and the Quenta – noting 'and þes þridda dǽl man éac nemneð *Silmarillion* þæt is Eorclanstána gewyrd', which translates as 'and this third part is also named "Silmarillion"; that is '[the] history/fate [of the] Precious/Holy Stones' (HME IV.291). The equivalent Eorclanstána = Silmarils also appears in Ælfwine's Old English translation of part of the 'Annals of Beleriand', which date from about the same time as the complementary 'Annals of Valinor':

> Morgoþ . . . genóm þá eorclanstánas Féanóres . . . ond þá eorclanstánas sette he on his isernan helme ['Morgoth . . . stole the silmarils of Fëanor . . . and the silmarils he set in his iron crown'].
>
> —HME IV.338.

The idea that the Arkenstone could be a Silmaril, or was at least somehow linked to the Silmarils in Tolkien's mind, has additional support from the philological roots of the word. As Jacob Grimm pointed out back in 1844, there was little stone-lore in Teutonic mythology, but foremost among what he discovered he cites the 'time-honoured myth' of the holy *iarkna-steinn* of the Elder Edda, listing the Old English equivalent (*eorcan-stân*) and postulating Gothic (*áirkna-stáins*), and Old High German (*erchan-stein*) forms (Jacob Grimm, *Teutonic Mythology*, tr. Stallybrass [1883]; vol. III page 1217).[14] Furthermore, within the Edda, the term is at one point applied to gems made by craft, not natural stones.[15] In Old English, the most famous usage of *eorcanstan* occurs in *Beowulf* (line 1208a), where it appears under the variant spelling *eorclanstānas*; interestingly enough, it is used there to describe a wonderful jeweled necklace of gold and gems given to Beowulf by Queen Wealhtheow (Hrothgar's consort).[16] Tolkien's source, however, may have lain not in *Beowulf* but in Cynewulf's *Christ* – the same work from which he took the name 'earendel' (line 104) some twenty years earlier – where *earcnanstān* ('precious/holy stone') appears in line 1194 as a metaphor for Christ [cf. Gollancz's edition, pages 100–101, and Cook's edition, pages 45 & 200]. This is made somewhat more likely by the spelling found in Cynewulf's poem, and the fact that words in Old English which began with *eor-* (eorl, eorth, eornoste) generally became *ear-* in modern English (earl, earth, earnest), whereas words beginning *ear-* typically became *ar-* (e.g., earc > ark [= Noah's Ark]). Alternately, rather than modernization of the Old English, 'Arkenstone' as it appears in *The Hobbit* could represent an anglicization from the Old Norse. It is, after all, a dwarven stone and hence should have a dwarven name, and all the names Tolkien gives the dwarves in *The Hobbit* (this being several years before the creation of a distinctive Dwarven language, e.g. Khuzdul), from Fimbulfambi to Dain, are Old Norse.

One element worth stressing that would link the Arkenstone even more closely with the Silmarils is the implication of the *eorcan* element in its name. Although usually translated simply as 'precious' (that is, highly valuable) and generally applied to any gemstone (e.g. at various times to topaz, opal, and pearl), Grimm stressed that the Gothic equivalent *airkna* meant rather 'holy', and was so used in the Gothic translation of the New Testament (the oldest surviving document in any Germanic language). G. H. Balg (*A Comparative Glossary of the Gothic Language*, 1887)[17] goes further, linking *aírkns* to the Greek *argos* or *'apyós* ('bright') and Sanskrit *arjuna* ('bright, pure').[18] The Silmarils are referred to over and over again in the legendarium as the 'holy jewels', who burn evil-doers (such as Melkor the Morgoth, Karkaras/Carcharoth, Maidros/Maedhros and Maglor) at the touch. We have no way of knowing if the Arkenstone shares this same power, since within our story it never comes into direct contact with any evil-doer (or, if we do assume it shares this characteristic with the other Silmarils, then its failure to scorch Bilbo is a testament to the integrity of his intentions and the rightness of his action in purloining it, concealing it from Thorin, and giving it to Bard as a hostage for the dragon-slayer's due portion of the treasure). Certainly, although like Beren's Silmaril the Arkenstone inspires fierce possessiveness in all who behold it, so that not even Bilbo can give it up without a pang, it seems nonetheless pure and innocent (again, like the Silmarils); no pejorative or sinister terms are ever employed in describing it (not even the obvious one within Tolkien's moral lexicography, 'precious', a word never applied to the Arkenstone within *The Hobbit*). Like the Silmarils in the main branch of the legendarium, and unlike the One Ring in the sequel, the Arkenstone inspires greed but is not itself malicious in any way:

> 'The Arkenstone! The Arkenstone!' murmured Thorin in the dark, half dreaming with his chin upon his knees. 'It was like a globe with a thousand facets; it shone like silver in the fire-light, like water in the sun, like snow under the stars, like rain upon the Moon!'
>
> —First Typescript, pasteover on typescript page 125 (I/I/62:11).

The original description of the Gem of Girion as a bright, shining jewel, a globe with many facets (pp. 514–15), which shone of its own light yet catches and magnifies all light that falls on it (page 579), sounds remarkably like Tolkien's descriptions of the Silmarils. Unfortunately we cannot compare them in detail, because for all their importance to the story Tolkien only rarely describes the Silmarils themselves, and then more in terms of their effect on the viewer than in appearance. For example, the earliest account of their creation (BLT I.128) lists the materials Fëanor assembled – the sheen of pearls, phosphorescence, lamp- and candle-light reflected through other gems, the half-colours of opals, and the all-important Light of the Two Trees – but aside from their radiance the only specific detail about their appearance is that '[he gave] all those magic lights a body to dwell in of such perfect glass as he alone could make', implying that they were clear.[19] Although we are told Fëanor started by acquiring 'a great pearl' we could not even tell from this account whether the Silmarils were smooth or faceted (the pearl cannot have provided the actual body for the first Silmaril, since he has only one such pearl yet makes three Silmarils before he runs out of materials). References in the alliterative poems to 'fair enchanted globes of crystal' ('The Flight of the Noldor from Valinor', lines 139b–140a; HME III.135) and 'thrice-enchanted globes of light' ('The Lay of Leithian', line 1642; HME III.212) imply a smooth sphere, but the descriptions of them in the 1926 'Sketch' (HME IV.14) and 1930 *Quenta* (e.g., HME IV.88) are too cursory to provide any details beyond that they shine with their own inner light. Not until the 1937 *Quenta Silmarillion*, which of course postdates *The Hobbit* and hence the Arkenstone, do we learn that 'all lights that fell upon them . . . they took and reflected in marvellous hues to which their own inner fire gave a surpassing loveliness' (HME V.227), implying that they had facets that refracted incoming light. Compare Bilbo's first sight of the Arkenstone as 'a small globe . . . that shone of its own light within . . . *cut and fashioned by the dwarves* . . . it caught and splintered all light that it received' (page 579; emphasis mine). It thus seems that some of the most characteristic features of a Silmaril's appearance familiar to us from the published *Silmarillion*[20] – that it magnifies incoming light and that it splinters this light like a magnificent prism – derive not from the direct line of descent (BLT > 'Sketch' + alliterative poems > 1930 *Quenta* + earliest Annals > 1937 *QS* + later Annals > later *QS* + final Annals) but first appeared in the description of the Arkenstone in *The Hobbit* and from there were imported back into what had been the 'main line' of the legendarium. This does not prove, of course, that the Arkenstone is a Silmaril, but it does show that not only was the description of the Gem of Girion based upon the Silmarils but that it in turn influenced the way the Silmarils were described henceforth.

If however the Arkenstone is indeed a Silmaril, the question arises: which one? Is there any way to reconcile the presence of a Silmaril within the fabled Hoard of Thror with what is said of the Jewels of Fëanor elsewhere in the legendarium? It is out of the question that it might be a 'fourth Silmaril', since all accounts from *The Book of Lost Tales* onwards are unanimous that Fëanor made only three and could never repeat his achievement, but might one of the Three have found its way hence?

The answer, just as with the identification of the Elvenking with Thingol Greycloak, is both 'yes' and 'no'.

The fate of the Silmarils is not addressed in *The Book of Lost Tales*, aside from the one rescued by Beren and Tinúviel and later incorporated within the Nauglafring, which according to Tolkien's outlines for the unwritten 'Tale of Eärendel' was lost in the sea when Elwing drowned.[21] Tolkien himself left the fate of the other two an open question, jotting 'What became of the Silmarils after the capture of Melko?' in his notebook, and Christopher Tolkien observes: '. . . the question is itself a testimony to the relatively minor importance of the jewels of Fëanor' at the time (BLT II.259; see also BLT I.156). The matter was not addressed until Tolkien came to write the 1926 'Sketch of the Mythology', where Elwing's Silmaril is still lost at sea, while of the two recovered from Morgoth's crown one is stolen by Fëanor's son Maglor the minstrel who, finding that the holy jewel burns him, 'casts himself into a pit' – presumably with the Silmaril, since the next sentence states 'One Silmaril is now in the sea [i.e., Elwing's], and one in the earth [i.e., Maglor's]' (HME IV.39). The third is claimed by Maidros the maimed, Fëanor's last surviving son, but the Valar deny his right to it because of the Fëanoreans' many evil deeds and grant it instead to Eärendel, who with Maidros's aid finds Elwing and transforms her from a seabird back into her own form again: 'thus it was that the last Silmaril came into the air' (HME IV.41). As Christopher Tolkien observes (HME IV.201–2), this was shuffled about in the 1930 *Quenta*: first (QI) Elwing's is still lost in the sea 'whence it shall not return until the End' (HME IV.150), while Maidros and Maglor seize the other two (IV.158). Both are scorched by the holy jewels: Maglor throws himself and his jewel 'into a yawning gap filled with fire . . . and the jewel vanished into the bosom of the Earth' (IV.159), while Maidros throws his to the ground and kills himself (IV.158) and his Silmaril is reclaimed by Fionwë the Valar's herald; this text breaks off just before the jewel was presumably given to Eärendel (IV.164). The revised version of the 1930 *Quenta* (QII) has Elwing surviving and bringing her Silmaril to Eärendel (IV.153), who sails the night sky with the Silmaril on his brow (IV.164), while Maidros 'cast himself into a gaping chasm filled with fire', taking his Silmaril 'into the bosom of the Earth', and Maglor 'cast [his] . . . into the sea' (IV.162); this idea was retained, in much the same words, in the Conclusion to the 1937 *Quenta Silmarillion* (HME V.331) except that here instead of simply stating that the three Silmarils came to rest in 'sea and earth and air' (HME IV.40 & 165),[22] as had been the case in the three earlier versions (1926 'Sketch', 1930 *Quenta*, and revised 1930 *Quenta*), they now 'found their long homes: one in the airs of heaven, and one in the fires of the heart of the world, and one in the deep waters' (HME V.331), words that would be carried over verbatim into the published *Silmarillion* four decades later (*Silm.*254).

Thus while to us, thirty years after the posthumous publication of *The Silmarillion*, it seems inevitable that the three jewels would be lost beyond recovery – in fact, an addition to the revised 1930 *Quenta* is explicit on this point, stating that 'the Silmarils . . . could not be again found, unless the world was broken and re-made anew' (HME IV.163) – in 1931–2 when Tolkien created the 'Gem of Girion' or in late 1932 when he was writing about the Arkenstone in the Third Phase text of *The Hobbit*, this was most definitely not the case. Despite the sense of finality in the passage just quoted, Tolkien had in fact at that point changed his mind four times in the previous fifteen years about the holy jewels' fate, all in a series of unpublished works that remained in flux and were each to be replaced by a new version of the story. There is no way any observer at that time could have told that this one point would henceforward remain relatively fixed within the Silmarillion texts; the one constant had been that the story ended with all three of the jewels remote and inaccessible. Just as the sword of Turgon King of Gondolin had somehow survived the fall of his city and found its way through the ages into that troll-lair and hence Bladorthin/Gandalf's hands, it is thus more than possible that Tolkien was playing in *The Hobbit* with the idea of having one of Fëanor's wondrous Jewels re-appear, no doubt the one that had been thrown into a fiery chasm and lost deep within the earth – which is, after all, exactly where the dwarves find the Arkenstone, buried at the roots of an extinct volcano. As with his borrowings regarding Tinwelint's quarrel with the dwarves in 'The Nauglafring' for the chapter about the wood-elves and their king's 'old quarrel' with the dwarves, Tolkien drew on his legendarium without committing himself: it was a one-way borrowing in which elements from the 1930 *Quenta* and Early Annals found their way into *The Hobbit* but that 'unofficial' usage did not in turn force changes in what Tolkien was still thinking of as the main line of the legendarium. By avoiding the use of the word *silmaril* and instead using the ingenious and agreeable synonym Arkenstone (*Eorcanstán*), Tolkien got to draw on his rich homebrew mythology, which by the early 1930s had developed a remarkable depth and sophistication, without worrying what the effect of his new story would be on that mythology (and hence could blithely include such statements as 'indeed there could not be two such gems, even in so marvellous a hoard, even in all the world'). It was probably this idea of one-way borrowing to which Tolkien referred when, on occasion, he denied that *The Hobbit* was part of his mythology (e.g., *Letters* pp. 215 & 346). Not until the publication, and success, of *The Hobbit* called for a sequel did the new side-line of Middle-earth's story displace the old legend of the war against Morgoth as the main story of the legendarium and the events of *The Hobbit* and *The Lord of the Rings* require the older stories to be rewritten and revised with the published chronicles in mind.

(iii)
A Note on Cram

The first mention of *cram* appears in the First Typescript (typescript page 133; 1/1/63:7); the line about its being made by the Lake-men is added there in ink at some point before the corresponding passage in the Second Typescript (1/1/44:8) was created, and it was taken up into the page proofs and published book. Douglas Anderson notes (DAA.300) that Tolkien gave 'cram' an Elvish derivation in 'The Etymologies' (which seems to have been mostly written in late 1937 and early 1938, or at least five years after this part of the First Typescript):

> **KRAB-** press. N[oldorin] *cramb*, *cram* cake of compressed flour or meal (often containing honey and milk) used on long journey.
>
> —HME V.365.

This is however almost certainly an afterthought on Tolkien's part, like the entry there regarding 'Esgaroth' (see the commentary following Chapter XIII on page 562). Not only would it be extraordinary for the Noldorin (Sindarin) and English words to be so similar in both form and meaning – the elvish meaning being due to the ingredients being pressed together and the Old English ancestor (*crammian*) of the modern-day familiar word 'cram' meaning to squeeze in or stuff, itself in turn deriving from an Indo-European root (**grem-*) meaning 'to press or compress' – but Tolkien explicitly states in a draft passage for *The Lord of the Rings* that

> *Cram* was, as you may remember, *a word in the language of the men of Dale* and the Long-lake . . . Bilbo Baggins brought back the recipe – he used *cram* after he got home on some of his long and mysterious walks. Gandalf also took to using it on his perpetual journeys . . . (HME VI.177; emphasis mine).

Furthermore, the entry regarding the Elvish root KRAB- and its derivation *cram* is a later addition to 'The Etymologies' (HME V.365), and neither appears in the earlier Noldorin, Qenya, or Gnomish material (cf. *Parma Eldalamberon* volumes XIII, XII, and XI), whereas the *Lord of the Rings* passage just cited was written before the summer of 1938 (cf. HME VI.214) and may predate it. Indeed, the passage in *The Lord of the Rings* Book III Chapter VIII: Farewell to Lórien (written sometime after August 1940 – cf. HME VII.271 & 267) makes it clear that this hardtack is called 'cram' by the men of Dale and dwarves (i.e., in the human language of the North) whereas the elves of Lórien have no direct knowledge of *cram* and call their trail rations by the Sindarin name *lembas* (= literally 'journey-bread'; HME XII.404):

> 'I thought it was only a kind of *cram*, such as the Dale-men make for journeys in the wild,' said [Gimli].
>
> 'So it is,' [the elves] answered. 'But we call it *lembas* or waybread, and it is more strengthening than any food made by Men, and it is more pleasant than *cram*, by all accounts.'
>
> —*LotR*.389.

Thus it seems certain that Tolkien's final decision was to have *cram* be a 'Mannish' word, just as it had been in its original appearance, and the proposed Elvish etymology was simply a mooted alternative that was quickly abandoned.

NOTES

1 The other being the introduction of Bard, the legitimate heir of Girion.

2 That is, according to the original time-scheme, in which Bilbo with Thorin & Company spent more than a year on the road.

3 So ancient is the idea of dragons sleeping on gold that Jacob Grimm noted *ormbeðr* or 'worm's bed' as a standard kenning (traditional metaphor) for gold in Old Norse poetry; *Teutonic Mythology* (tr. James Stallybrass [1883], vol. II, page 689).

4 The later developments of this passage in subsequent Silmarillion texts brings it much closer into line with Smaug's situation. Thus, in the 1926 'Sketch of the Mythology', the rather odd detail of the dragon's gold-bed being outside the caves out in the open is dropped:

> Glórung lies in the caves of Narog and gathers beneath him all the gold and silver and gems there hoarded (HME IV.30).

This brings the Glorund story back into accord with the Sigurd story, in which Fafnir's 'abiding place' is 'dug down deep into the earth: there found Sigurd gold exceeding plenteous . . .' (*Völsunga Saga*, tr. Morris & Magnússon, page 67). The 1930 *Quenta* refines this still further, until it becomes a very close approximation of Smaug's practice:

> Glómund . . . gathered unto himself the greater part of its wealth of gold and gems, and he lay thereon in its deepest hall, and desolation was about him (HME IV.127).

It would have been on the basis of a line such as this that Gandalf the dwarf can say with such confidence that '. . . all their wealth he took for himself. Probably, for that is the dragon's way, he has piled it all up in [a] great heap in some hall far inside, and sleeps on it for a bed' (page 72). Like Glorund, Smaug chooses the deepest chamber within the Lonely Mountain for his lair: every stair Thorin & Company take after leaving it leads up (cf. page 581).

5 It is true that the elves are accompanied by Túrin's mother and sister, who might be thought to serve as a parallel for the presence in *The*

Hobbit of Thorin, Fili, and Kili, since Mavwin and Nienóri were close kin of the man who had been acting as the Rodothlim's champion while the three dwarves are all descendants (grandchild and great-great-grandchildren, respectively) of Thror, whose people had been destroyed or dispossessed by Smaug. It might also be noted that disaster comes about in every iteration of the Túrin story because of the presence of the two women in the group, just as it is Thorin's behavior under the dragon-sickness that almost brings disaster in the Third Phase *Hobbit* story, but this might be pressing the point too far. Finally, Tinwelint's sending a group whose brief is not just to take the treasure but also slay the dragon (a point made explicit on BLT II.96, where they are described as 'that band of dragon-slayers') could be taken as a parallel for the projected Bilbo-as-dragon-slayer theme of Plot Notes B & C.

6 This curse, the dragon's ability to directly manipulate the minds of those who look into his eyes and to individually curse any whose name he knows, is distinct from the more general dragon-sickness attached to treasure that has come into contact with a dragon. Both Túrin and Nienóri make the mistake of making eye contact with the wyrm and are beguiled, and his knowledge of who they are enables Glorund to craft specific curses that set both on the road to incest and suicide. There is no mention of whether Sigurd looks into Fafnir's eyes while the dragon is still alive, but the *Fáfnismál* and *Völsunga Saga* both agree that he initially gives a false name to avoid Fafnir's dying curse; Bilbo wisely both avoids meeting Smaug's gaze and giving him his real name. Both motifs are lacking in *Beowulf*, whose dragon is more animalistic and less of a personality, but note that even in *Farmer Giles of Ham* Chrysophylax wants to know the farmer's name at their first meeting and the farmer refuses to tell him until he has gained the upper hand (FGH.41 & 43). See also Tolkien's dragon lecture summarized in Note 5 following the commentary to Chapter XII.

7 Later Tolkien inserted a reference earlier in the text to Glorund having 'set a guard that he might trust to watch his dwelling and his treasury, and the captain of these was Mîm the dwarf' before he set forth on his final fatal mission to seek Túrin (BLT II.103 & 118).

8 The curse might be so relentlessly effective in part because, as Tinwelint concedes, none of the initial claimants have any real right to this treasure: 'the Rodothlim who won it from the earth long time ago are no more, and no one has especial claim to so much as a handful save only Úrin by reason of his son Túrin, who slew the Worm, the robber of the Elves' (BLT II.222). He advances his own claim on the fact that (a) 'this gold belongs to the kindred of the Elves in common' (a particularly specious argument, given that he is using it to deny Úrin's elven companions more than a token share†) and (b) 'Túrin is dead and Úrin will have none of it; and Túrin was my man' (who had murdered a kinsman of the king and fled Tinwelint's halls, abandoning his allegiance). The latter suggests additional complications that could have arisen in the scramble over Smaug's gold had Bard not survived, as had been

Tolkien's original intent (see page 549), and the Master of Lake Town and Elvenking been left to settle matters between them.

†These outlaws had been human in the original draft of this tale but became elves in the revision, from which this sentence is taken; see BLT II.242.

9 I.e., Mîm's curse: 'Now Elves and Men shall rue this deed, and because of the death of Mîm the dwarf shall death follow this gold so long as it remain on Earth, and a like fate shall every part and portion share with the whole' (BLT II.114). Mîm's dying curse in 'Turambar and the Foalókë' pointedly excludes his own people, the dwarves, but a later passage in 'The Nauglafring' implies that whatever immunity they might have to the dragon-sickness does not protect them from Mîm's all-encompassing curse: 'Indeed all that folk love gold and silver more dearly than aught else on Earth, while that treasury was haunted by a spell and by no means were they armed against it' (BLT II.229).

To this might be added yet a third curse, that laid upon the Nauglafring itself by the dwarven-smiths held in prison by Tinwelint and forced to expend their craft in slave-labor on his behalf: 'even had that gold of the Rodothlim held no evil spell still had that carcanet been a thing of little luck, for the Dwarves were full of bitterness, and all its links were twined with baleful thoughts' (BLT II.228) – not to mention that they incorporate into the necklace the Silmaril Beren and Tinúviel took from Morgoth's crown, with the additional perils that gem (and its proximity to the original Dark Lord) might bring.

10 This piece was painted between 8th and 24th July 1937, too late for inclusion in the first printing but late enough that the text had already been typeset and thus finalized. The idea that Tolkien might himself provide additional illustrations, in colour, for the American edition was first mooted in May in a brief exchange between Charles Furth of Allen & Unwin and Tolkien (Furth to JRRT 11th May 1937, JRRT to Furth 13th May, Furth to JRRT 14th May), at which point Tolkien dispatched several Silmarillion illustrations as examples of his colour artwork. Unfortunately Houghton Mifflin mistook these for the actual pieces to be used, resulting in several months of confusion. In a letter written on or soon after 8th July, Tolkien says 'I have done nothing about the new ones. I will now set about them, if they are still required, or it is not too late' (JRRT to Furth, undated reply to Furth's letters of 1st June & 8th July). In another undated letter, probably written on 24th or 23rd July, Tolkien asks for an update ('I do not want to labour in vain') and arranges to call on Stanley Unwin in London 'on Wednesday next, 28th July' to 'submit what I have done' and see if A&U's production department thinks them 'passable, & . . . suitable for reproduction'. Although HM had still not replied by 24th July (SU to JRRT), Tolkien seems by this point to have finished the four paintings,† since in his reply of 25th July (JRRT to SU) discussing their upcoming meeting he says '. . . I shall not take much of your time, as it will not take long to tell me if what I have done is suitable, & if unsuitable what is wrong', suggesting that he was going to bring the paintings along for Unwin to

vet them. Apparently the pieces were deemed acceptable, since the next mention of them is in Tolkien's letter to Furth of 13th August, written while on vacation at Sidmouth in Devon, stating that 'You are very welcome to use the coloured drawings at any time' (that is, in any future reprint), suggesting the originals be stored at A&U's offices once they are returned by the Americans, and concluding 'I have completed the coloured version of the frontispiece.†† Would you care to have it to lay by (hopefully)?' (JRRT to Furth, August 13th) – an offer which Furth, in his reply, gratefully accepts (Furth to JRRT, 16th August).

†These four were 'Bilbo Comes to the Huts of the Raft-elves', 'Bilbo Woke Up with the Early Sun in His Eyes', 'Conversation with Smaug', and 'Rivendell' (H-S#124, 113, 133, & 108 ; DAA plates 2B, 2A, 3A, and 1B)

††This fifth painting is 'The Hill: Hobbiton-across-the Water' (H-S#98; DAA plate 1A).

11 For example, the glowing cone-shaped object directly above the bowing hobbit, or the three glowing low mounds to the left behind Smaug's elbow.

12 Supreme, that is, within the context of *The Hobbit*; in *The Lord of the Rings* it is eclipsed by the Ring of Power belonging to Durin's house, one of the Seven. After all, while they left the Arkenstone behind when they fled the Lonely Mountain Thror and Thrain managed to save their house's Ring, just as their ancestors had done even from the Balrog's rampage that drove them from Khazad-dûm (Moria); it later passed from Thror to Thrain and was not lost until the Necromancer captured Thorin's father, a hundred years before the time of Bilbo's journey (*LotR*.286, 1110, & 1113–14). But this is a *Lord of the Rings*-era innovation, not present at the time *The Hobbit* was written. For more on the emergence of Durin's Ring, see the draft of Gloin's speech at Rivendell in HME VI.398.

13 This passage appears on a piece of typescript pasted over the original text of the First Typescript (typescript page 125; 1/1/62:11); the underlying text cannot now be read even when the page is held up to the light, due to the darkening of the glue or paste Tolkien used. This replacement occurred before the Second Typescript was made, since the latter faithfully reproduces the pasteover text; presumably the obscured text closely resembled the manuscript version on page 515 of this book describing 'the white gem of Girion Lord of Dale'.

Even though less is made of the Necklace of Girion than of the Arkenstone, it must be stressed that this was a rare and wonderful treasure in its own right: emeralds are far rarer and more valuable than diamonds or even rubies.

The description here of silver with a strength three times that of steel sounds very like the later *mithril*, but Tolkien never made this connection in later editions of *The Hobbit* after the introduction of mithril in *The Lord of the Rings*, although he did insert a single mention of mithril into the earlier book in his 1966 revision for the Ballantine paperback with regard to Bilbo's 'silvered steel' mail-coat (DAA.295). It might be expected that the wondrous suit of mithril-mail, whose value is revealed in *The Lord of the Rings* to be greater than the Shire and everything in it (*LotR*.335), would turn out to be the very suit of armor King Girion surrendered his wondrous necklace for, but the connection is never made (perhaps because then the conscientious Bilbo would feel obliged to give Bard his mail-coat as well in the end).

The 'Thrain' here, by the way, is Thorin's grandfather, the King under the Mountain; the reversed genealogy was in place when Tolkien made this addendum to the typescript (see page 458). In later years rather than simply making it the 'Arkenstone of Thror' he instead resolved the inconsistency by ascribing it to a distant ancestor, Thrain I, Thorin's great-great-great-great-great-great-grandfather. In the later story, it was this Thrain I who led the exodus from Moria after his father and grandfather had been killed by the Balrog and the ancestral kingdom overthrown, founding the realm-in-exile at the Lonely Mountain, and discovered the Arkenstone there deep beneath the mountain (*LotR*.1117 & 1109).

14 For more on Eorcanstan and the cognate names in other Germanic languages, see Christopher Tolkien's discussion in *The Shaping of Middle-earth* (HME IV.283) and Douglas Anderson's note in *The Annotated Hobbit* (DAA.293–4). I am grateful to Doug's entry for drawing my attention to Grimm.

15 In the rather gruesome story of Wayland the Smith's captivity, crippling, revenge, and escape, he murders the sons of his captor and makes goblets of their skulls, brooches of their teeth, and 'pure gems' (Old Norse *iarknasteina*) of their eyes (*Vǫlundarkviða*, stanzas 25 & 35; cf. Dronke, vol II. pages 250 & 252).

16 So beautiful is this piece of jewelry that the poet compares it to the legendary *Brosinga mene* ('necklace of the Brosings', line 1199b), familiar in Old Norse legend as the Brisingamen, the goddess Freya's most valued treasure (cf. 'The Deluding of Gylfi' [*Gylfaginning*] in Snorri's *Prose Edda*, 'The Lay of Thrym' [*Þrymsqviða*] in the *Elder Edda*, and the tale of Loki's theft of the necklace hinted at in the surviving fragments of the *Húsdrapa* ['House Song'] of Ulf Uggason). Like the *Book of Lost Tales*' Nauglafring ('Necklace of the Dwarves'), which it no doubt inspired, the Brisingamen was made by great dwarven craftsmen working at the behest of others. Interestingly enough, Tinwelint's captive dwarven jewelsmiths demand an elven maiden apiece as payment (which the elvenking refuses, having them beaten instead); Freya had to promise to sleep with each of the four dwarves who make her necklace and honors her agreement.

17 Christopher Wiseman told me (interview, August 1981) that Tolkien used to come to Rugby practice with a great big Gothic book under his arm, which he would apparently read in snatches when not engrossed in the game or actually on the field. This could not have been either Joseph Wright's *Gothic Grammar* or *Gothic Primer*, both of which are smallish (octavo) volumes. I suspect Balg's massive quarto (more than

ten inches tall, seven inches wide, and over six hundred pages thick), simultaneously published in New York, London, Germany, and Mayville Wisconsin, to have been the book Wiseman remembered.

18 The Greek word is best known as the name of the hundred-eyed monster Argos (more commonly spelt *Argus*), who was so-named because of the clarity and sharpness of his vision. The Greek, Sanskrit, and Gothic words all probably go back to the same Indo-European root **ar(e)g-* meaning 'shining' or 'bright' – the same root, in fact, which seems to underlie the word *elf* (Germanic **alba-* or **albinjo*, which seem to have meant 'white' and 'shining' – cf. 'the White People' as one of the euphemisms of the Fair Folk and the discussion of an uncanny whiteness as a defining elven characteristic in the commentary following Chapter IX). The Latin word for silver, *argenta*, also derives from the same root, and it may underlie the names for the Alps ('the Whites', so called for their snow-cover; cf. the White Mountains of Gondor) and Albion, a traditional name for Britain in old legends ('The White Land', from the White Cliffs of Dover, the first part of the island seen by someone approaching from mainland Europe).

19 By 'glass' Tolkien here probably means some sort of clear crystal, since the Silmarils survive many encounters that would have shattered mere glass. Cf. also the reference in the alliterative poems to the Silmarils as crystal, such as the allusion to Beren's Silmaril as 'the Gnome-crystal' in *The Lay of the Children of Húrin* (line 379; HME III.107).

The appearance of pearls and opals here may owe something to Jacob Grimm's guess, in *Teutonic Mythology*, that *eorcanstan* probably originally was applied either to 'the oval milk-white opal' and/or to the pearl (Grimm/Stallybrass, vol. III pages 1217–18).

20 The passage from the 1977 *Silmarillion* derives primarily not from the *Later Quenta* (X.187), which closely resembles the passage in the 1937 *Quenta Silmarillion*, but from the 'Annals of Aman' (the final version of the 'Annals of Valinor', supplemented by a few details taken from the *Later Quenta*):

> . . . As three great jewels they were in form . . . Like the crystal of diamonds it appeared and yet was more strong than adamant, so that no violence within the walls of this world could mar it or break it. Yet that crystal was to the Silmarils but as is the body to the Children of Ilúvatar: the house of its inner fire, that is within it and yet in all parts of it, and is its life. And the inner fire of the Silmarils Fëanor made of the blended Light of the Trees of Valinor . . . Therefore even in the uttermost darkness the Silmarils of their own radiance shone like the stars of Varda; and yet, as were they indeed living things, they rejoiced in light and received it, and gave it back in hues more lovely than before.
>
> —HME X.94–5.

21 The *Gnomish Lexicon*'s entry for 'Nauglafring' agrees, stating plainly that the Necklace of the Dwarves was '[m]ade for *Ellu* [= Tinwelint/

Thingol] by the dwarves from the gold of *Glorund*, that Mîm, the fatherless, cursed and that brought ruin on *Beren Ermabwed* [the One-Handed], and *Damrod* [Dior], his son, and was not appeased till it sank with *Elwing*, beloved of *Earendel*, to the bottom of the seas' (*Parma Eldalamberon* XI.59).

22 Note that the Three Rings of the Elves were originally to have been 'of earth, sea, and sky' (e.g., in the draft of the Ring-verse [HME VI.269] and also the 'third phase' text of 'Ancient History' [VI.319]: 'the Three Rings of Earth, Sea, and Sky'). In the original draft of the Lothlórien chapter(s), it is plainly stated that Galadriel's ring is the Ring of Earth (HME VII.252) and an associated page of drafting speculates that Fëanor himself made the three elven rings, 'the Rings of Earth, Sea and Sky' (ibid., page 255).

In the published book, of course, *Kemen* the Ring of Earth is replaced by *Narya* the Ring of Fire, Galadriel holds *Nenya*, the Ring of Water, and Elrond *Vilya* the Ring of Air, so that Earth, Sea and Sky have been replaced by Air, Water, and Fire. This later arrangement better matches the later (1937) *Quenta Silmarillion*, in which the three Silmarils are lost in the sky (Air), the fires in the depth of the earth (Earth > Fire), and the sea (Water).

Chapter XVa

THE KINDNESS OF RAVENS

As before, the text continues onward without anything more than a page break, with the section that later became Chapter XV starting at the top of manuscript page 166 (Marq. 1/1/15). This last sheet of the Second Phase manuscript, along with the associated Plot Notes that follow, represents the point the story had reached when Tolkien broke off to go back to the beginning and create the First Typescript.

Suddenly Bilbo said: 'There is that old thrush again – he seems to have escaped when the dragon smashed the terrace, though I don't suppose his beloved snails have!'[TN1]

Sure enough, there was the old thrush, perched on a stone; and as soon as they looked towards him he flapped his wings and sang; then he cocked his head on one side as if to listen, and again he sang, and again he listened.

'I believe he is trying to tell us something' said Thorin 'but I do not understand the tongue of small-birds – it is very quick and difficult. Do you Mr Baggins?'

'Not very well' said Bilbo, 'and I can't make this old fellow out at all, except that he is very excited.'[TN2]

'I only wish he was a raven!' said Balin.

'I thought you did not like the ravens of these parts, when we came this way before' said Bilbo to him.

'Those were crows!' said Balin, 'and nasty suspicious-looking ones at that, and rude as well. You must have heard the ugly things they were calling after us – there was one old raven, you remember how he flew after us a long way home [> towards camp],[TN3] but he never said anything beyond a croak. But there are some ravens still about here, though, for I have seen them in my wanderings about, that remember the old friendship between us in Thror's day. They used to live on many many years, and their memories are long, and they hand their wisdom on to their children. I had many a friend among the Ravens of the Mountain when I was a boy – this very ridge we stand on was called Ravenhill[TN4] by many, for it was a favourite place of theirs close to the watchmen's seat. There's never a sign of them now: I suppose they are off to see what all this gathering forebodes, though they are not birds for company, unless great things are brewing. If we had one here now we shd soon have news'.

Loud shrilled the Old Thrush and off it flew.

'That old bird understood all you said, at any rate' said Thorin. 'Keep watch now and see what happens!'

Before long there was a flutter of wings and back came the thrush. With it came another most decrepit old bird: it was getting blind, it could hardly fly and the top of its head was almost bald. It was a very aged raven of great size. It alighted stiffly on the ground, flapped its wings slowly & bobbed towards Thorin and Balin, and began to croak. – 'O Thorin Thrain's son Thror's son [and Balin son of Fundin]' it began [> said], & Bilbo to his surprise could understand all it said. 'I am Roäc son of Carc.[TN5] Carc is dead, but once he was well known to you. It is one hundred years and three and fifty since I came out of the egg, but I do not forget what my father told me. I am the chief of the old [> great] Ravens of the Mountain, who remember still the king that was of old. I bring tidings of joy to you and yet other tidings not so good. Behold the birds are gathering back again to the Mountain from South and East and West, for word has gone forth that Smaug is dead! The Thrush, may his feathers never fall, has seen it and we trust his words. He saw him fall in battle with the men of Esgaroth on Tuesday night, that is the night before the night before last [> eight nights ago at the rising of the moon]. So much for joy O Thorin Oakenshield! You may go back to your palace in safety, all the treasure of your fathers is yours once more – for the moment. But there is more to tell. Among the flocking birds are many crows and birds of carrion – indeed ravens are among them though they fly by themselves – for they espy a gathering of arms, and to our minds an army and a hoard means dead men ere long. The Lake-town of Esgaroth is destroyed, but the men of the lake, most of whom have escaped, and the Elven king have joined together, and their warriors are marching north to plunder the mountain, and it is said that they trouble not whether the dwarves of Durin are alive or dead.

'I have spoken. I and the Thrush have looked for you in the West and we feared you dead.[TN6] We rejoice to see you safe, but a hard strife looms ahead. Thirteen is [not >] but a small remnant of the great folk of Durin that [was wont >] once was here. The <thrush> says that he who shot the Dragon, one Bard of the race of Dale and of the line of Girion is among the host, and he is a grim man yet true. Fear him not so much as the Elven king and the Master that remains behind. We would see peace once more between dwarves and men after the long desolation. But it may cost you dear in gold.'

Then Thorin's wrath blazed forth 'Our thanks Roäc Carcson' he said. 'You and your people shall not be forgotten. But none of our gold shall the thieves of [the] Lake and the Wood get from us alive. If you would earn [*added*: our thanks] still more bring us tidings at once of their approach. Now we have work to do. Back to the Mountain' he cried to the dwarves 'For we must stand a siege'.

'But we have no food' cried Bilbo always practical on such <points>.

At this point, at the bottom of manuscript page 167, the Second Phase text ends.

However, associated with this material is a half-page fragment of rough drafting (Marq. 1/1/24b) that preceded manuscript pages 166–7; this survives only because Tolkien tore the sheet in two, turned it over, rotated it 90 degrees counterclockwise, and used the blank space on what had been the bottom half of its verso to hastily sketch out events that were to occur during the Siege of the Mountain (Marq. 1/1/24a, or Plot Notes E). We do not know how much such rough drafting preceded the 'first draft' of the Second Phase manuscript, but by good fortune this small surviving fragment offers us a rare chance for comparison, suggesting that it strongly resembled what followed in storyline but only generally corresponded in word choice and expression.

The line just above the tear has vanished almost completely, but a large descending ligature at the beginning of the line indicates that it began with a capital 'L' and from the context it almost certainly read 'Loud trilled the Thrush' or something very like it. Similarly, since the lines slant slightly upward across the page the last two or three words at the end of the first line below the tear are lost but probably read 'we said'.

L<oud> . . .

'[If that >] That old bird understood all that <we> . . .' Thorin. 'Keep watch now and see what happens!'

Before long there was a flutter of wings, and back came the Thrush. With it came a most decrepit old bird, nearly blind. It could hardly fly and the top of its head was almost bald. It was a very aged raven. It lighted stiffly on the ground, flapped its wings and bobbed towards Thorin and Balin; then it began to croak. Bilbo did not know what it was saying, but Balin seemed to. Afterward he told them all that he had learned.

'O Thorin Thrain's Son, Thror's son' he said 'this is a most Venerable Raven, Roäk [> Roäc] by name, the son of Carc. Carc I knew in the old days when I was young, but alas he is now dead. Röac his son must be 180 years old if he is a day – he is the last raven of the Mountain left who [we can understand the language >] who can understand our language, being taught by his father, or make himself understood by me. He brings tidings truly tremendous and <astonishing> and bewildering: joy and sorrow.

The birds are gathering back again to the mountain from S. E and W. for word has gone forth that the Dragon is dead!

This brings the text to the bottom of 1/1/24b. The top half of the back of this sheet (1/1/24a) is missing, having been discarded by Tolkien himself, but two lines below the tear remain:

Loud the Thrush trilled again. Roac croaked.
'It seems that the Thrush

At this point, the draft breaks off in mid-sentence half-way through a line of dialogue. The rest of this page is devoted to the 'little bird' outline (Plot Notes E); see page 626.

Besides seeing the emergence of the raven's name – the exact form of which, Roäk/Roäc/Röac, remained unfixed for the present[TN7] – and having the venerable bird being even older than in the published book,[TN8] the most significant difference between the draft and the text that replaced it is that originally only Balin could understand the raven's speech, and translates it for the benefit of his friends. While reminiscent of their meeting with Medwed/Beorn and his horses, this was replaced in the main draft with the simpler and more direct route of allowing the raven to speak directly to Thorin & Company without an interpreter.[TN9] Tolkien may have felt that having two tiers of interpreters – the Thrush speaking to the Raven, the Raven to Balin, and Balin to the rest – was too cumbersome and so simplified it, especially since ravens, like parrots, are famous for their ability to speak (in the words of Edgar Poe, 'quoth the raven: "Nevermore" ').

TEXT NOTES

1 Crowded into the left margin, and presumably meant for insertion preceding this paragraph, is the following:

> For several days they remained there on the Mountain, keeping watch by day and guard at night. Nothing happened, and they became sorely puzzled. At last their supplies began to run low, and [in] the morning they began to discuss whether they should send some of their number down to the riverside store, or whether all should go, or whether they should again seek the aid of the men of Lake-town. [Thorin > Bilbo >] The hobbit was looking about him taking no part in the discussion. Already he was wondering what had happened to [> in] Lake-town, for he had not forgotten his fear that Smaug would go <thither>. He was looking about him idly when suddenly he saw a fluttering on his right.

This additional text not only stresses Thorin & Company's bafflement about the dragon's continued absence but expands the time-frame, no doubt to allow the elven and human host time to gather and begin its march north; before its addition the story moves directly from the dwarves' arrival at Ravenhill to their encounters with the thrush and raven. The published text compromises between these two, having them arrive at the watch-post at sunset (DAA.301) and encountering the birds early the next morning (DAA.314). See the added reference a few paragraphs later about it now having been eight days since Smaug's death, whereas in the original texts only three nights had passed (the Battle of Lake Town taking place on Tuesday night and the conversation with Roäc on Friday morning). The original timeline thus ran like this:

- Monday, Durin's Day: Bilbo enters the secret tunnel just after sunset, emerging again at midnight. (pp. 505 & 507–8)
- Tuesday: Smaug destroys the secret door almost exactly twenty-four hours later, flies south, and dies in the attack on Esgaroth. (pp. 513 & 515, 549)
- Wednesday: Bilbo and the dwarves spend all the previous night, all this day, and this night huddled in the tunnel. (page 578)
- Thursday: Bilbo and the dwarves explore Smaug's lair and traverse the dwarven city. (page 578ff)
- Friday: Thorin & Company reach the Front Gate at sunrise; Balin leads them to Ravenhill, where they soon encounter the thrush and raven, who tells them Smaug died 'the night before the night before last'. (pages 582, 619).

The expanded time-scheme of eight days better matches the statement in Chapter XIII that the Elvenking's army reached Lake Town seven days after Smaug's fall (page 552), presumably setting forth for the Mountain the next day.

For the 'riverside store' (that is, storage site or supplies depot beside the river-bank), this lay three days' journey north of Lake Town where they disembarked from the boats; see the first paragraph of Chapter XI on page 471.

2 Note that the implication here is that Bilbo can understand bird-talk; in the Third Phase and subsequent texts he merely diplomatically pretends to; see page 642.

3 No such incident in fact occurred during the earlier chapter. Had he retained this passage, Tolkien would no doubt have inserted this event back in Chapter XI on or about the section represented by page 472 in the Second Phase text. By contrast, Balin's claim to have already made contact with the ravens of the mountain during their earlier explorations, while significant, would simply have served to set up the encounter which follows and could have been retained as is.

4 This is the first appearance of the name 'Ravenhill', one of those names that like Bag-End and Rivendell and Lake Town remained unchanged from its first recorded appearance onward.

5 As Douglas Anderson notes, both these names are 'marvelously onomatopoeic' (DAA.316), being approximations of the croaks these birds themselves might make (roughly *rroahkk* and *kahrrkk*, respectively). This is all the more appropriate since the very word 'raven' itself

(OE *hræfn*, ON *hrafn*) is believed to derive from an Indo-European root imitating the bird's cry (**kor-*, **ker-*), just as the modern English 'crow' represents the sound now more usually spelled *caw* (i.e., *kraw! kraw!*).

6 'I and the Thrush have looked for you in the West' – that is, on the western side of the Lonely Mountain, where they had last been seen before Smaug destroyed the Secret Door. As with the mention of Balin's earlier contact with the ravens, this suggests a more active role for the Ravens of the Mountain somewhat earlier than in the final text.

7 The dieresis (¨) indicates that both vowels are to be pronounced, not blended into a diphthong – for example, as in *cooperate* (formerly spelled 'coöperate'), rather than *coop*. The name's final appearance in the penultimate line of this rough draft also has a dieresis, but from its placement it is not possible to tell which vowel it is meant to cover and thus whether Roäc or Röac is intended.

8 In fact, according to the chronology in 'The Tale of Years' (*LotR*.1125–6), old enough to remember the days of King Thror and to have known Balin personally before the dragon came one hundred and seventy years earlier. This chronology of course post-dates *The Hobbit* and it is clear that Roäc was taught dwarf-speech after those days were past, so it simply indicates that Tolkien initially had an even greater span of time in mind between the fall of the Kingdom under the Mountain and its restoration under Thorin.

9 For all the linguistic richness of his work and the many (mutually incomprehensible) invented languages included in its narratives, scenes where an interpreter must mediate between two groups who do not share a common tongue are rare in Tolkien, the chief example being Legolas speaking with the border-guards of Lórien on behalf of the Fellowship (*LotR*.360 & 362).

(i)
The Ravens of the Mountain

Helpful birds had played an important part in Tolkien's writing from the earliest days: the Eagles of Manwë (cf. Chapter VI), the swans of Ulmo, the birds of Melian, even Mew the seagull in *Roverandom*, so it is no surprise to see the wise Thrush and old Raven figure prominently in the Lonely Mountain chapters, from the discovery of the Secret Door to the revealing of Smaug's weak spot and setting in motion preparations for the Siege of the Mountain. In particular there had long been a traditional association of talking birds with the aftermath of a dragon-slaying: by accidentally tasting Fafnir's heart Sigurd was able to understand the language of birds and discovered that the woodpeckers in the nearby trees were actually discussing him and how his foster-father planned to kill him and, after he kills Regin on their advice, tell him how to find Brynhild the valkyrie (*Fáfnismál* stanzas 32–44; *Völsunga Saga* Chapter XIX, esp. pages 64–6). Tolkien had referred to this motif as far back as the tale of Túrin, where it is said that eating the heart of a dragon grants knowledge of 'all tongues of Gods or Men, of birds or beasts' (BLT II.85), a philologist's dream which Christopher Tolkien in his commentary explicitly credits to the story of Sigurd Fafnisbane (BLT II.125). But here in Tolkien's story it is *because* the dragon-slayer has the ability to speak with birds (Bard and the Thrush) that he is able to kill the dragon, and Thorin & Company's only encountering the raven after Smaug's fall seems more a matter of chance than necessity, the result of not having earlier visited the part of the mountain frequented by ravens (i.e., Ravenhill).

Tolkien's specific choice of ravens combines both elements of traditional myth and real-world fact. Not only are ravens and crows traditionally associated with battles, but they are the smartest of all birds, exceptionally long-lived (one of the ravens at the Tower of London lived to be forty-four years old, and a less-well-attested individual is said to have reached eighty), and capable of speech, at least to the extent of being able to learn and intelligibly repeat several words or phrases. Tolkien has exaggerated or rather enhanced their intelligence, longevity, and loquaciousness or linguistic ability for the purposes of his story, but his fantasy builds on a solid factual basis here. He combines their rather sinister reputation as harbingers of battle (they are, after all, carrion birds, as Roäc admits) with their legendary exploits as messengers: Odin's two ravens, Hugin and Munin ('Thought' and 'Memory'), fly forth every day and report back to him all that passes in the world (*Prose Edda* pages 63–4). He also rather surprisingly in the Plot Notes which follow (Plot Notes E) draws on the Biblical account of ravens feeding the prophet Elijah 'bread and meat' in the Wilderness (1st Kings, Chapter 17, verses 1–7) and has the Ravens of the Mountain bring 'meat and bread' to the besieged dwarves until (even more surprisingly) they are driven away by elven archers.[1]

Once present in the story, the ravens may also have inspired Tolkien's re-introduction of the eagles in the final chapters as the Siege of the Mountain evolved into the Battle of Five Armies, but since this development belongs rather to the Third Phase I postpone discussion of it for now; see page 715.

NOTES

1 It might seem unlikely that birds could carry enough food to make any appreciable difference, but ravens are quite large, typically about two feet in length and with a wingspan of some four feet. They are not only

quite capable of killing and carrying off small animals but also sometimes carry off small items that attract their curiosity (a habit for which their smaller cousins the jackdaws are notorious).

THE SIEGE OF THE MOUNTAIN

I now give the 'little bird' outline, or Plot Notes E, the final piece of text unambiguously associated with the Second Phase storyline. In these hasty jottings we see how the events of the next chapter would have unfurled had the Second Phase text not been abandoned.

Plot Notes E

'Little Bird'

Raven tells of 2 or 3 ponies still alive. Offers also to <assemble> <their> folk[TN1] and bring food from far and wide.

Fili and Kili go off to catch ponies: Others go into Mountain. Great <labours> day and night at the great door. Bilbo keeps watch on Ravenhill.

The birds bring news of approach of the men of lake and the Elvenking and the <joining> of the host with that of <?men> host of the Elves. Fili and Kili have not come back they are pursued by warriors

The dwarves gather weapons and a store of arrows to the G.D.[TN2] which is now blocked with stones <with crevices> for shooting from. The opening on Ravenhill is guarded by Dori & Nori.[TN3]

Three days later Kili [rides up >] comes to the G.D. & begs for admitance. Their horses were shot under them but they have laid all the stores they could carry near the foot of the great spur, but as they climbed the hillside Fili was wounded & captured.[TN4] The host is already at the foot of the mountain.

Each of the ravens fly bringing meat and bread. But that night the dwarves steal out and recover the <bags>. The camp fires start up in the <ruins> of Dale.

The parley at the Gates. Thorin's scornful words. He will give nothing to demand. What got they out of the last K.u.M?[TN5] The Elvenking on behalf of the Lake men demands payment <for/from> <illegible> of Smaug, the destruction of the town, all <?slain>. Thorin says first remove your menace from my <?palace>. Stores run low for the elves shoot at the ravens.

There seems little doubt that these hastily scribbled words comprise Tolkien's final work on the Second Phase, differing greatly as they do from the events as they would appear in the actual written texts of the chapters that followed. At this point, he probably thought that no more than two or three chapters would be needed to complete the story: one to resolve events at the Mountain, a second to cover the Battle of Anduin Vale (see page 713) on the return journey, and a third to see Bilbo safely home afterwards. And it must be stressed that in one sense he was right. Even with the folding together of the projected 'Battle of the Anduin Vale' with the Siege of the Mountain and the greater complexity and added complications that Bard's legitimate claim on the treasure and Thorin's succumbing to dragon-sickness would bring in the Third Phase text, Tolkien here has come within forty-five pages of the end,[TN6] and nearly half of the book's earlier chapters had reached twenty pages or more.[TN7] In the final book the remaining material would be divided into five chapters (out of the book's total of nineteen), making it seem at first glance that Tolkien abandoned the book less than three-quarters of the way through. But this does not take into account the extreme brevity of these closing chapters, three of which are among the shortest in the book. If we go by page count, then, Tolkien was more than five-sixths of the way through the story when he broke off, not abandoning the book as Carpenter claimed but instead going back to the beginning and embarking on the creation of the First Typescript.

TEXT NOTES

1 By offering to assemble their folk, Roäc does not mean the dwarves but ravens; neither Plot Notes B/C/D nor E contain any reference to Dain, who had not yet been invented, and no dwarven army was to march to their relief.

2 That is, the Great Door, usually referred to as the 'Front Gate'.

3 Since it seems unlikely that any dwarves would be posted where they would be cut off from their fellows once the valley was occupied, the idea of a tunnel leading from within the guard-post back into the dwarven city behind the Front Gate, suggested in Chapter XIV, must still be present.

4 The first seven words of this sentence were cancelled.

5 Here Thorin seems to be referring to Smaug, not Thror; cf. the surly watchman's words in Chapter XIII (pp 547–8). This is surprising, both for the threat implied and for its recognition of Smaug's suzerainty – not to mention unwise, since he is speaking to survivors of Smaug's attack who have all too much reason to blame him for their sufferings. Thorin's refusal to hand over his family treasures to an angry mob or

to negotiate at swords-point is in itself an admirable display of courage. Even though with hindsight provided by Third Phase developments we might see his 'scornful' reply to the massed army outside his gate as the first signs of dragon-sickness, within the context of the Second Phase story it is entirely in keeping with the heroic saga tradition.

6 That is, near the bottom of page 265 of the first edition, which had 310 pages.

7 In order to better see just how variable the chapter lengths are in the book, and how the longer chapters tend to cluster in the earlier half, the following chart lists all the chapters in order from longest to shortest, given the pagination of the first edition. I have used a copy of the third (wartime) printing from 1942 [cf. Hammond, *Descriptive Bibliography*, page 16] to determine these figures, which lacks the 'Mirkwood' half-tone and color plates (none of which were included in the original pagination in any case).

i. Chapter VIII. Flies and Spiders (30 pages)
ii. Chapter VII. Queer Lodgings (27 pages plus one illustration)
iii. Chapter I. An Unexpected Party (27 pages)

iv. Chapter XII. Inside Information (22 pages)
v. Chapter VI. Out of the Frying-Pan into the Fire (21 pages)
vi. Chapter IX. Barrels Out of Bond (18 pages plus one illustration)
vii. Chapter V. Riddles in the Dark (17 pages)
viii. Chapter II. Roast Mutton (17 pages plus one illustration)

ix. Chapter IV. Over Hill and Under Hill (13 pages plus one illustration)
x. Chapter XVII. The Clouds Burst (12 pages plus one illustration)
xi. Chapter XIII. Not at Home (12 pages) [= manuscript chapter XIV]
xii. Chapter X. A Warm Welcome (12 pages plus one illustration)
xiii. Chapter XV. The Gathering of the Clouds (11 pages)

xiv. Chapter XIV. Fire and Water (10 pages) [= manuscript chapter XIII]
xv. Chapter III. A Short Rest (10 pages)
xvi. Chapter XI. On the Doorstep (9 pages plus one illustration)
xvii. Chapter XVIII. The Return Journey (9 pages)
xviii. Chapter XIX. The Last Stage (9 pages plus one illustration)
xix. Chapter XVI. A Thief in the Night (7 pages)

Plot Notes F

This brief outline (Marq. 1/1/23:3), scribbled on a torn sheet of good paper (in fact, the back of an unsent letter[TN1]), is little more than a collection of notes in now-faint pencil on miscellaneous points that

Tolkien jotted down as a reminder to himself of loose plot-points that would need to be addressed in the wrapping-up. Unlike Plot Notes E, which represent the final work on the Second Phase, these notes seem to belong to the beginning of the Third Phase.

Bilbo's treasure all lost on the way home – except his kettle & a pair of studs.

And were the dwarves forever at his service?

Send message back by Thrush to Lake Town – it arrives too late but reaches Bard before his last shot.

Bring him <?word> in last <moment>.

Wood-elf king gives back orcrist
How troll-key fitted – Gandalf explains.
Trolls had <?even> <illegible>[TN2] Moria, where Thrain son of Thror <was> prisoner

Bilbo hangs his sword over mantlepiece & has his mail put on a stand

Prophecy came true for the Dale became rich, and the Dwarves of Thror for long were good till their race faded, and gold flowed down the river & <fountains> were made.

Battle of Five armies and disenchantment of Beorn

Written in the left margin:

1	2	3	4	5			
woodelves,	dwarves,[TN3]	eagles,	men,	bears	–	goblins	wolves
						6	7

But <illegible> Bilbo got out of it was a set of useful proverbs

Written in the right margin:

Lost his <reputation> & found another.
Digs up <?trolls'> treasure, <distributes> it.

The most notable feature of Plot Notes F is that the inclusion of dwarves among the participants in 'The Battle of Five Armies' (which is finally and for the first time given that name) suggests this event might have now shifted from taking place not far to the west as part of Bilbo's return journey, but as the culmination of the events at the Lonely Mountain. Even so, Tolkien remained in difficulties deciding just which of the forces present counted as one of the 'Five'; cf. the commentary on page 714 following the Third Phase text. Beorn's bear army is still present, as in the final page of Plot Notes B. One significant and intriguing new element here is the brief mention of the 'disenchantment of Beorn'; see the commentary on Bothvar Bjarki following Chapter VII for more on this unrealized motif. Otherwise, these notes closely correspond to what Tolkien actually came to set down once he began writing the Third Phase text; the two significant departures are the absence of Beorn's bear-army (his prowess being upgraded until followers would have been superfluous),[TN4] and of the loss of Bilbo's treasure (a scene which Tolkien began to write but then crossed out; see page 690 & Text Note 11 on page 698).

TEXT NOTES

1 The unsent letter (1/1/23:4), written in Tolkien's neatest script, is undated; Tolkien tore the page in half and only the top half survives (because of its blank verso's reuse for plot-notes). It represents Tolkien's reader's report for some unidentified publisher on a book he had been sent to evaluate for possible publication. Despite the letter's lack of context, Tolkien's opinion is clear, as he definitely advises against publication: '. . . published without a competent revision it would receive ungentle handling from any reviewer in this country who knew anything about Old English. I hardly like to think of what I should say about it, if I was a reviewer myself, and not your adviser.' Possibly this letter was not sent because it was superseded by a more circumspect replacement.

2 This illegible word seems to begin with *p-* and end with *-d*, but it is clearly not *plundered*, the reading of the Third Phase text (see page 688), because it lacks the ascender for the *-l-* and has an ascender immediately followed by a descender in the middle; possibly it is two short words run together, the first of which ends in *-ly*. The doubtful word preceding this word or phrase might be *been* rather than *even*.

3 This word is circled, but the significance of this is unclear: possibly Tolkien hesitated between the old idea of the Battle of Anduin Vale (without the dwarves' presence) and the new idea that seems to be emerging of bringing the battle to the Lonely Mountain (where he could segue between the Siege of the Mountain directly into the battle). For more on the Battle of Five Armies, see the commentary on page 713ff following the Third Phase text.

4 See the North Polar Bear's similar immunity to goblins ('for of course goblins can't hurt *him*') and similar tactic of wading into battle with a sea ('more like 1000') of goblins in the Father Christmas Letters for 1932 and 1933: 'squeezing, squashing, trampling, boxing, and kicking Goblins sky-high'; see *Letters from Father Christmas* pages 74 and 87 and the commentary following Chapter VII.

THE THIRD PHASE

'A THIEF INDEED'

Perhaps the most important misconception about the writing of *The Hobbit*, even more significant than its alleged lack of connection to the earlier legendarium (which is self-evidently false from the various allusions within the original manuscript, not to mention explicitly refuted by Tolkien himself in his first statement in print about the book after *The Hobbit* was published),[1] is the claim that Tolkien abandoned the story unfinished in the early 1930s, only resuming work on it sometime in the summer or fall of 1936 at the prodding of a publisher. This claim was first advanced by Humphrey Carpenter in his authorized biography, and since all subsequent accounts derive from Carpenter's, it seems best to examine his argument and assertions in some detail:

> The writing of the story progressed fluently until the passage not far from the end where the dragon Smaug is about to die. Here Tolkien hesitated, and tried out the narrative in rough notes – something he was often to do in *The Lord of the Rings* but seems to have done only rarely in *The Hobbit*. These notes suggest that Bilbo Baggins might creep into the dragon's lair and stab him . . . But this idea, which scarcely suited the character of the hobbit or provided a grand enough death for Smaug, was rejected in favour of the published version where the dragon is slain by the archer Bard. And then, shortly after he had described the death of the dragon, Tolkien abandoned the story.
>
> Or to be more accurate, he did not write any more of it down. For the benefit of his children he had narrated an impromptu conclusion to the story, but, as Christopher Tolkien expressed it, 'the ending chapters were rather roughly done, and not typed out at all'. Indeed they were not even written in manuscript. The typescript of the nearly finished story . . . was occasionally shown to favoured friends, together with its accompanying maps (and perhaps already a few illustrations). But it did not often leave Tolkien's study, where it sat, incomplete and now likely to remain so. The boys were growing up and no longer asked for 'Winter Reads', so there was no reason why *The Hobbit* should ever be finished.
>
> —Humphrey Carpenter, *Tolkien: A Biography*, pages 179–80.

In addition to a great deal of information conveyed succinctly and clearly, this account unfortunately also includes a good deal of misinformation, details that Carpenter, who has to cover a great deal of territory in very little space, all of it without any prior scholarship on the point to guide him, got wrong, misinterpreted, or oversimplified. For example, while he clearly alludes to Plot Notes B & C, he takes no account of the first outline (page 229), the extensive Plot Notes A, the 'little bird' outline (Plot Notes E), Plot Notes F, nor the complicated evolution that produced the composite, multilayered document that is Plot Notes B/C/D/B. His account ignores one of the three major breaks in the book's composition, discussing the ones at the end of Chapter I (that is, at the end of the First Phase) and early in Chapter XV (although failing to convey exactly where this break takes place) but not the break at the beginning of Chapter IX (at their capture by wood-elves, which like the other two is marked by a change of paper). Carpenter's account is also unintentionally misleading to readers who do not know that Chapters XIII and XIV were later switched, so that in the manuscript the story continued for about another chapter and a half beyond Smaug's death.

Similarly, there is no evidence known to me of these impromptu oral conclusions; certainly Tolkien never mentions them in any of his later recollections, nor are they alluded to in any of the memoirs by his sons that I have seen. Carpenter may be relying here on information he received directly from John and Michael Tolkien (whose evidence, while valuable, is demonstrably wrong on some points). It is more probable that, given his stage background[2] and not having the benefit of the *History of Middle-earth* series before him with its many examples of Tolkien working out difficulties foreseen in upcoming sections through plot-notes before undertaking the actual writing of those chapters, Carpenter mistook the plot-notes as cues for an oral performance.

More importantly, there is no evidence to support Carpenter's assertion that the concluding chapters 'were not even written in manuscript'; indeed, such evidence as there is, is to the contrary. For my argument that we should take young Christopher's words literally as an accurate description of the Third Phase text (129 pages of typescript completed by a 13-page 'fair copy' interpolation and the 45 pages of Third Phase manuscript) as it stood between January 1933 and summer 1936 (see page xviii). As a refutation of the claim that the story was abandoned because the 'Winter Reads' ceased, see Note 16 to the commentary following Chapter XII for evidence that Tolkien's sessions of reading aloud to his children were still ongoing at the time Tolkien was preparing *The Hobbit* for publication in the summer of 1936.

Tolkien himself contradicts Carpenter's claim that the manuscript 'did not often leave Tolkien's study' when he noted that 'the MS. certainly wandered about' (*Letters* p. 21); over the course of some three and a half years he loaned it not only to C. S. Lewis but at least three other people that we know of: Rev. Mother St. Teresa Gale (the Mother Superior at Cherwell Edge), his graduate student Elaine Griffiths, and a twelve-to-thirteen-year-old girl (possibly Aileen Jennings, daughter of a family friend who attended the same church; Aileen and her younger sister Elizabeth [later a moderately well-known poet] both received presentation copies from Tolkien as soon as the book was published),[3] and there might of course have been others. The Inklings might count among their number: Tolkien noted that the story had been read to the group but did not specify when this occurred;[4] certainly before publication, and it seems likely that it would have been during the period when Tolkien was preparing the book for publication in 1936 – that is, after Dagnall had returned the 'home manuscript' to him but before he sent the completed typescript to Allen & Unwin for official submission in early October 1936. And of course he proved quite willing to loan it to Dagnall herself, who clearly borrowed it in an informal capacity, whatever hope she might have been able to hold out to him of putting in a good word regarding the book with her employers.

In short, we should view the Third Phase text, and the final chapters of the book, as still part of the original two-to-three-year impetus of composition, written after a gap of no more than a year from where he left off, not as the return to an abandoned work that had languished untouched for three years or more. The very fact that Tolkien had in the meantime decided to go back to the beginning of the story and create the First Typescript – at 129 single-spaced pages a significant investment of time and energy for a ten-fingered typist like himself who carefully revised as he typed – is a testament to his faith in the story. Far from lying abandoned between the breaking off of the Second Phase and the drafting of the Third Phase, during that period all he had so far achieved of the story was in fact laboriously being put into legible form where it could be shared with others. The great differences between these final chapters and the early parts of the book are the result of internal development within the story, the working out of the twin complications Tolkien introduced late in the Second Phase. Tolkien's decision to cut the Gordian knot of Bard's legitimate claim to an indeterminate portion of the treasure versus Thorin's inability to accept any negotiation or compromise that meant parting with any of the treasure because of his succumbing to dragon-sickness, and his decision to raise the stakes by re-introducing virtually all the creatures encountered earlier in the book into one grand melee, avoids the anticlimax of a long dénouement following the dragon's death and creates a climax even more comprehensive and, ultimately, more satisfactory than the dragon-quest Bilbo had originally set out on.

NOTES

1 'My tale is not consciously based on any other book – save one . . . the b"Silmarillion", a history of the Elves, to which frequent allusion is made' – JRRT, letter to *The Observer*; see Appendix II. Although at times Tolkien sought to distance *The Hobbit* from the pre-existing legendarium, at others he freely admitted or even laid stress upon the connection.

2 Carpenter's first involvement with Tolkien's work was to direct a children's theater adaptation of *The Hobbit*, and he later wrote a radio-play depicting Tolkien as a detached eccentric ('In a Hole in the Ground, There Lived a Tolkien' [1992]); most of my second meeting with him (in Oxford, in 1985) was spent watching him direct a rather odd adaptation of *The Wizard of Oz* for an all-teen cast. For more on Carpenter's interests and background in drama, see the obituary by Charles Noad and Jessica Yates, published in the March 2005 issue of *Amen Hen*; I am grateful to its authors for sharing a pre-publication copy with me. See also Douglas A. Anderson's detailed account of Carpenter's work with Tolkien in Volume II of *Tolkien Studies* (pages 217–24).

3 See the Introduction to Douglas Anderson's *The Annotated Hobbit* for more on the identities of those who read the book before its publication (DAA.12).

4 See Tolkien's 4th June 1938 letter to Stanley Unwin telling him of 'our literary club . . . before whom the *Hobbit*, and other works (such as *The Silent Planet*) have been read' (*Letters* p. 36). Our best evidence suggests that the Inklings did not yet exist in January 1933 when Tolkien completed the story, but came together very shortly thereafter, one of the significant factors that led to the group's formation being the retirement of Major (then Captain) Warnie Lewis in December 1932, his return from Shanghai to live with his brother at the Kilns, and his joining Tolkien and Lewis at some of their regular gatherings. The Inklings seem to have come about from the two men's desire to include Warnie in their meetings while providing a comfortable environment for less exclusively academic discussion; the late Dr. Humphrey Havard told me he was invited to join the group upon returning to Oxford and meeting the Lewis brothers in 1934. The first documentary evidence for the group's existence comes in C. S. Lewis's first letter to Charles Williams (11th March 1936) inviting him to attend a meeting of 'a sort of informal club called the Inklings' (*Collected Letters of C.S.L*, ed. Walter Hooper, vol. II, page 183). The early members of the group included Tolkien, Lewis, Warnie, and Havard (the four who formed the core of the group throughout its existence), as well as Nevill Coghill (a fellow member with Lewis in Tolkien's Kolbítars, and specially mentioned along with Tolkien and Warnie in Lewis's letter to Williams), Hugo Dyson, Owen Barfield (usually *in absentia*, since he lived in London), Adam Fox (who seems to have promptly quit the group after they elected him Professor of Poetry in 1938), and C. L. Wrenn.

Chapter XVb

KING BARD

The Third Phase text began with the creation of the First Typescript, when Tolkien returned to the beginning of the story and produced a legible, polished version of almost all the material he had written so far, incorporating into earlier chapters changes made necessary by developments in later chapters, such as the changes in names of some characters, and inserting the chapter breaks for the first time into the hitherto continuous text. This typescript reached as far as typescript page 129, the page describing the death of Smaug (Marq. 1/1/64:3; the third page in Chapter XIII [> XIV]). Tolkien then created the 'fair copy' version of the chapter describing Bilbo and the dwarves' adventures inside the mountain (Chapter XIV [> XIII]; Marq. 1/1/14), carefully written on good paper, numbering the pages a–m to show that they formed a separate sequence. We can show that this 'fair copy' text of what is now Chapter XIII is *later* than the first few pages of the typescript of what is now Chapter XIV by the pagination of the latter: the First Typescript has sequential page numbers neatly typed in the upper left corner of each page from Chapter I through the third page of Chapter XIII [> XIV]. When Chapter XIII (The Death of Smaug) became Chapter XIV ('Fire and Water') and later a typed version of the new Chapter XIII ('Not at Home'; Marq. 1/1/63) was inserted in place of the 'fair copy' text, the new typed pages lacked any typed page numbers and are instead numbered 127–34 in black ink, while the first three pages of 'Fire and Water' were re-numbered in the same ink: 127 > 135, 128 > 136, and 129 > 137, followed by page 1 of the Third Phase manuscript. Similarly, we know the next typescript page in 'Fire and Water' (Marq.1/1/64:4) is *later* than the new typescript of the transposed chapter because it lacks any typed page number and instead is numbered in ink '138'; close comparison of the text also confirms that it derives from the Third Phase manuscript, not the earlier Second Phase version of this passage. In short, it was here that the 'beautifully typed copy' Elaine Griffiths recalled borrowing (Ann Bonsor radio interview; see also DAA.12) ended and the 'rather roughly done' ending chapters described by thirteen-year-old Christopher (see page xvii) began.

Thus, the circulating copy of Bilbo's adventures which Tolkien loaned to Lewis, Griffiths, the Reverend Mother, the thirteen-year-old girl, and possibly others, which he called the 'home manuscript' in a later letter to Allen & Unwin, was a composite of typescript and fair copy manuscript:

- typescript pages 1 through 126 (Chapters I through XII)
- fair copy pages 'a' through 'm' (Chapter XIV > XIII)
- typescript pages 127 through 129 plus Third Phase manuscript pages 1 through 45 (Chapters XIII > XIV through XIX/end).

The First Typescript carried the story up to the words *'And in the very midst of their talk a tall figure stepped from the shadows. He was drenched'* at the bottom of typescript page 129 (Marq. 1/1/64:3). The Third Phase manuscript begins in mid-sentence with the next word on page 1 *'with water'* (the Second Phase text has a pencilled mark at this exact point indicating where the First Typescript ceased and the Third Phase manuscript took its place; see page 551 and Text Note 12 following Chapter XIII on page 554).

Like the first half of the Second Phase manuscript (manuscript pages 13–117), the Third Phase manuscript is written on good-quality 'foolscap' paper, unlike the larger pages (lined on one side and torn from student exam books) which had supplied the paper for the latter half of the Second Phase (i.e., manuscript pages 118–67 and the 'little bird' fragment).

The first seven pages of this new manuscript present a new draft of material which has already appeared in Chapters XIII and XVa of this book, but I include the overlap and give the entire Third Phase manuscript here for purposes of comparison to show how Tolkien expanded and polished the material in the course of making a fresh draft.

As with so many of Tolkien's manuscripts, the Third Phase text began as fair copy, very neatly and legibly written in Tolkien's best script on good paper. And as is also typical with Tolkien's fair copies, the handwriting begins to deteriorate (in this case, after the first twenty pages or so), but even so this text remains much more legible than most.

Finally, the Third Phase manuscript includes a number of cancelled pages; those that survive after they had been superseded by replacement text do so because after he struck through the rejected text Tolkien re-used the verso for a later page. Thus, for example, what seem to be the original second, third, and fourth pages of the Third Phase were all cancelled but survive because they form the versos of pages 14, 9, and 8, respectively. See Text Notes 3, 4, and 7 for the cancelled texts. There is evidence that other cancelled pages once existed but did not survive.

with water, his black hair hung wet over his face and shoulders, and a fierce light was in his eyes.

'Bard is not lost!' he cried. 'I am Bard, slayer of the dragon. I dived from Esgaroth only when no one else was left, and only when the enemy was slain. I am of the race of Girion, Lord of Dale. I will be your king!'

'King Bard! King Bard!' they shouted; and the Master ground his chattering teeth, as he sat upon the earth.

'Girion was Lord of Dale, not king of Esgaroth', he said. 'In this lake-town we have always elected masters from the old and wise, and have not endured the rule of mere fighting men. Let King Bard go back to his own kingdom; and anyone go with him that wish to. Dale is [*added*: now] free; and he has slain the slayer of his fathers; nothing hinders his return. But the wise will stay here and rebuild our town, and hope to enjoy again in time its riches and its peace, any that prefer the mountain-shadowed valley to this water-side can go with him!'[TN1]

'We will have King Bard!' the people clamoured. 'We have had enough of the old men and money-counters'.

'I am the last man to undervalue Bard the bowman' said the Master warily (for Bard had come & stood now close beside him). 'He has tonight earned a chief place in the list of our benefactors, and is worthy of many imperishable songs. But, why, O people?' – and here the Master rose and spoke very loud and clear – 'why do I get all your blame? Who aroused the dragon from his <illegible> slumber,[TN2] I might ask?[TN3] Who obtained of us rich gifts and ample help, and led us to believe that old songs could come true? Who played on our soft hearts and pleasant fancies? What sort of gold have they sent down the river to reward us? Fire and ruin! From whom shall we claim the recompense of our damage, and aid for our widows and orphans?'

As you see the Master had not earned his position for nothing. For the moment the people quite forgot the idea of a new king, and turned their angry thoughts towards Thorin and his company. Wild and bitter words were shouted from many sides; and some of those who before had sung the old songs loudest, were now heard as loudly crying that the dwarves had stirred the Dragon up against them deliberately!

'Fools!' said Bard. 'Why waste words and wrath on those unhappy creatures? Doubtless they perished first in fire, before Smaug came to us.' Then even as he was speaking, the thought of the fabled treasure of the Mountain came [suddenly >] into his heart, and he fell suddenly silent; and he thought of the Master's words, and of Dale rebuilt, and filled with golden bells, if he could but find the men.

At last he spoke again: 'This is no time Master for angry words, or for considering weighty plans and great changes. There is work to do. I serve you still – though after a while, I may think again of your words, and go North with any that will follow me'.[TN4] Then he strode off to help in the ordering of the camps and in the care of the sick and wounded. But the Master scowled at his back as he went, and remained sitting on the ground. He thought much, but he said little, unless it was to call loudly for men to bring him fire and food.

Now everywhere Bard went he found talk running like fire among the people concerning the vast treasure that was now without a guard. Men spoke of the recompense for all their harm that they would soon get from it, and wealth over and to spare wherewith to buy rich things from the South;[TN5] and it cheered them greatly in their plight. That was fortunate, for their night was bitter and miserable. Shelters could be contrived for few, and there was little food. Many took ill of wet and cold and anguish [> sorrow] that night, and afterwards died, who had escaped uninjured from the town; and in the days that followed there was much sickness and great hunger. Meanwhile Bard took the lead, and ordered things as he wished, though always in the Master's name; but he had a hard task to govern the people, and to arrange [> direct] the preparations for their protection and recovery. Probably most of them would have perished in the winter that now hurried [onwards >] after autumn, if help had not been to hand.[TN6]

But help came swiftly; for Bard had at once had [swift >] speedy messengers sent up the river to the Forest to ask help of the King of the Elves, and these messengers had found a host already on the move, although it was only the second day after the fall of Smaug.[TN7]

The Elven king had received news of what passed from his scouts and from the birds that loved his folk. Very great indeed was the commotion among all things with wings that dwelt on the borders of the desolation of the dragon. The air was filled with circling flocks, and swift-flying messengers sped here and there across the sky. Above the borders of the forest the air was filled with the noise of birds whistling, crying and piping. Far over Mirkwood the tidings spread: [*added*: 'Smaug is dead'] Leaves rustled and startled ears were lifted. Even before the Elvenking rode [from his <?halls> >] forth the news had passed west even to the pinewoods of the Misty Mountains, and the Goblins were at council in their halls.

[But >] 'That will be the last we shall hear of Thorin Oakenshield, [*added*: I fear]' said the king. 'He would have done better to remain my guest. It is an ill wind all the same' he added 'that blows no one good', for he too had not forgotten the legend of the wealth of Thror. So it was that Bard's men found him now riding [> marching] with all the spearmen and bowmen he could muster; and all the crows were gathered above him, for they thought they saw signs of <?battle and> wars awakening again, such as had not been for a long time. [*cancelled*: But some of the woodelves were gone <a route> direct towards the Mountain:]

Now the king when he received the prayers of the Bard because of his old friendship with the men of the lake; and because he was a lord of good and kindly race turned his march[TN8] which had been purposed to go direct toward the mountain, and turned [> went] along the river towards Lake-Town [> the Long lake]. He had not boats or rafts enough for all his host and they had [> were forced] to go the slower road [> way] by foot, but great store of goods he sent ahead by water. Still elves are light-footed, and though [they] were not much used to the marshes and treacherous lands between the Forest and the Lake, their going was swift; and but four days from the fall of Smaug the[y] came upon the shores of the Lake, and looked on the burnt ruins of the town. Their welcome was good, as may be expected, and the men & their Master were ready to make any bargain for the future in return for the Elvenking's aid.

Their [<?dangers> were s[oon] >] plans were soon made. With the women and children, the old and the unfit the Master remained behind, & with him were some men of crafts and many skilled elves; and they busied themselves felling trees and with these and such timber as was sent from the Forest they set about the raising of many huts by the shore against the oncoming winter; also under the Master's direction [farther >] they began the planning of a new town, designed more fairly and more large even than before, but in a place removed somewhat [> a little] northward, for they liked not the water where the body of the dragon lay.

A rider (I/I/15:11), written in pencil on a loose, unnumbered sheet of lined student notepaper, was clearly meant to be inserted at this spot, although there is no indication of its existence or exact placement on the page it supplements:

He would never again to his golden bed, but was lying cold [*added*: as stone, his bones > twisted] upon the floor of the shallows of the Lake – where forever after his great bones could be seen in calm weather amid the ruined pile<s> of the old town if any dared to cross the accursed spot. But [<?men> >] they rebuilt the town in a different place and none ever <dared> afterwards to gather the precious stones that were [<?fallen> >] fell out from his rotting carcass – not even the Master

A second rider (I/I/15:12), more carefully written in ink on a small piece of good paper, replaces this with a more polished form of the same passage:

He would never again return to his golden bed but was lying cold as stone, twisted upon the floor of the shallows of the lake, where for ever after his great bones could be seen in calm weather amid the ruined piles of the old town, if any one dared to cross the accursed spot.[TN9]

At the bottom of this text appear the penciled words 'new p. 4.', indicating that this rider is meant to go with Third Phase page 4 (I/I/16:I), which began with the words 'four days from the fall of Smaug' a paragraph and a half earlier.

But all the men of arms who were still able, and the most of the host of the king, got ready to march north to the Mountain. It was thus that in seven days from the death of Smaug that the head of their host passed the rock-gates at the end of the lake and came to the desolate lands.

At this point, Tolkien later began a new chapter (Chapter XV: 'The Gathering of the Clouds'). On the manuscript page itself, in the middle of Third Phase manuscript page 4 (I/I/16:I), only a double skipped line between the third and fourth paragraphs marks the shift in scene. There is some evidence that Tolkien did not intend a chapter break to come here in the 'home manuscript'; see page 666 below.

Now we will return to Bilbo and the Dwarves. All night one of them in turn had watched, but when morning came no sign of danger had been seen. But still yet more thickly the birds were gathering. Their companies came flying from the south, and the crows that still lived about the mountain were wheeling <&> crying unceasingly [*added*: above].[TN10]

'Something strange is happening' said Thorin. 'The time has gone for the autumn wanderings; and there are birds that dwell ever in the land, starlings and flocks of finches – and there are many crows [> carrion birds far off] as if a battle were afoot.'

Suddenly Bilbo pointed: 'There is that old thrush again' he cried. 'He seems to have escaped when Smaug smashed the mountain-side; but I don't suppose the snails have!'

Sure enough the old thrush was there, and as Bilbo pointed he flew towards them and perched on a stone nearby. Then he fluttered his wings and sang; then he cocked his head as if to listen; and again he sang and again he listened.

'I believe he is trying to tell us something' said Balin; 'but I don't understand the tongue of small [> such] birds, it is very quick and difficult. Do you, Mr Baggins?'

'Not very well' said Bilbo (he did not know anything about it as a matter of fact),[TN11] 'but this old fellow seems very excited.'

'I only wish he was a raven' said Balin.

'I thought you did not like them' said Bilbo. You seemed to be very nervous [> shy] of them when we came this way before.'

'Those were crows! And nasty suspicious-looking creatures at that, & rude as well. You must have heard the ugly names they were calling after us. But the ravens are different. There used to be a [*added*: great] friendship between them and the people of Thror, and they were often our scouts and news-bringers [> bringers of secret news to us]. [There are some that still linger here, I know, for I have seen > But I do not suppose there > any of that wise race that linger here now. >] They live many a year and their memories are long, and they hand [on] their wisdom to their children. I had many friends [> knew many] among the ravens of the rocks when I was a dwarf-lad. This very ridge we are on was once named 'Ravenhill' for there was a wise and famous pair [added: old Kark and his wife] that dwelt here above the guard-chamber. But I do not suppose that any of that ancient race linger here now.'[TN12]

No sooner had he finished speaking than the old thrush gave a loud call, and immediately flew away.

'[That old bird >] We may not understand him, but that old bird understood [> understands] us, I am sure' said Thorin. 'Keep watch now, & see what happens!'

Before long there was a fluttering of wings, and back came the Thrush; but with him came another most decrepit old bird. He was getting blind, he could hardly fly, and the top of his head was bald. He was an aged raven of great size. He alighted stiffly on the ground before them, slowly flapped his wings and bobbed towards Thorin.

'O Thorin, Thrain's son, Thror's son, & Balin son of Fundin' he croaked, and Bilbo found he could understand what he said. 'I am Roäc son of Carc. Carc is dead, but he was well-known to you once. It is a hundred years and three and fifty since I came out of the egg, but I do not forget what my father told me. [Now] I am the chief of the great Ravens of the Mountain. We are few [and we >] but we remember still the King that was of old. The others are mostly gone south, where there are great tidings – some are tidings of joy to you, and some you will not think so good. Behold! the birds are gathering back again to the Mountain from South and East and West, for word has gone forth that Smaug is dead!'

'Dead?' shouted the dwarves. 'Dead! Then we have been in needless fear – and the treasure is ours!' They sprang up and began to caper about for joy.

'Yes, dead' said Roäc. 'The thrush, may his feathers never fail, has seen it [> saw him die], and we may trust his words. He saw him fall in battle with the men of Esgaroth the third night back from now, at the rising of the moon. So much for joy, Thorin Oakenshield. You may go back to your halls in safety; all the treasure is yours – for the moment. But many are gathering hither other than [> besides] the birds. The news of the death of the guardian has gone far and wide, & many are eager for a share of the spoil. Already an army is on the way, and carrion birds are with them, hoping for battle and slaughter. The Elvenking is coming hither; and by the Lake men murmur that their sorrows are due to you; For they are homeless and many are dead, & Smaug has destroyed their town. They purpose too to find amends from your treasure, whether you are alive or dead (as they expect). [I have sp[oken] > I have <nought> >] Your own wisdom must decide your course; but thirteen is small remnant of the great folk of Durin that now is scattered far. If you will hearken to my advice you will trust [rather Bard the bow-man; for he it was that shot >] not the Master of the lake-men, but rather him that shot the dragon with his bow. Bard is he, of the race of Dale, of the line of Girion; he is a grim man but true. We would see peace once more among dwarves and men and elves after the long desolation; but it may cost you dear in gold. I have spoken.'

Then Thorin burst forth in wrath [> anger]: 'our thanks Roäc Carc's son. You and your people shall not be forgotten. But none of our gold shall thieves or the violent have while we are still alive. If you would earn our thanks still more bring us news of any approach [> that draw near]. Also I would beg you, if any of you are yet young and strong of wing, that you would send messengers to our kin in the mountains of the North, both west from here and East, and tell them of our plight. But go specially to my cousin Dain at [> in] the Iron hills, for he has many people well armed and bid him hasten [> and dwells nearest to this place; and bid him hasten].'[TN13]

'I will not say if this plan be good or bad' [said >] croaked Roäc; but I will [*cancelled*: try to] do what can be done,' and off he slowly flew.

'Back now to the mountain' said Thorin. 'We have little time to lose.'

'And little food to use!' cried Bilbo, always practical on such points. In any case he felt that the adventure was properly speaking over with the death of Smaug – in which he was much[TN14] mistaken – and would have given much of his share of the profits for a peaceful winding-up of these affairs.

'Back to the mountain' cried the dwarves, as if they had not heard; so back with them he had to go.

As you have heard some of the events that were going on about already you will see that the dwarves still had some days before them. They laboured hard, for tools were still to be found in plenty in their old halls [*added*: and at such work they were greatly skilled] and [*added*: as they worked] the ravens brought them constant tidings.

This last sentence was cancelled and replaced by an expanded passage crowded into the left margin:

> They explored the halls once more, & found as they had expected that, but the main Gate remained open. All the others save the more [> smaller] secret door, had long ago been broken and blocked by smaug. So now they laboured hard in fortifying the Eastern Gate. Tools were to still be had in plenty that the miners and quarriers and builders of old had used, and at such work they were greatly skilled. As they worked the Ravens brought them constant tidings.

Thus they learned [after four days' toil that the joined host of the elves >] that the Elvenking had turned aside to [the] Lake, and they still had breathing space. Better still they heard that three of their ponies were wandering wild far down upon the river banks, not far from where their stores had been left. So while the others went on with their chief task of fortifying the gate, Fili and Kili were sent guided by a raven to [bring in such suppl[ies] >] find the ponies and bring back all they could.

[It was four days >] They were four days gone, and by that time they knew that the joined armies of the lake-men and Elves were hastening towards them. But now their hopes were more high, for they had food for some weeks with care, and the gate was block[ed] with a wall of squared stones laid dry but very thick and high across the opening. There were holes in it [for see >] from which they could see or shoot, but no entrance. They climbed in and out by ladders, or hauled stuff up with ropes. For the issuing of the river [> stream] they had contrived an arch [> a small arch], [but they so altered its bed near the entrance that >] under the new wall, but near the entrance they so altered its [narrow] bed that a wide pool [stood >] stretched from the mountain wall to the head of the falls over which it went on towards Dale, and approach to the Gate was only by a narrow path that wound close to the high [bank >] cliff southward. [There was no pasture for the ponies, so these they took >] The ponies they had brought only to the head of the steps above the old bridge[TN15] and unloading them had bidden return to their mortal masters,[TN16] and sent them back riderless to the south.

The[re] came an evening [> a night] when suddenly there were many lights as of fires and torches away East [<out> the >] in Dale before them. 'They have come,' called Balin 'and their camp is great. They must have come into the valley under the covering of dusk; and most are on the north side of the River.'

That night they [> the dwarves] slept little. The morning was still pale when they saw a company approaching. From behind their wall they watch[ed] them come up the valley's head and climb [<the rock> >] slowly up. Soon they saw that both men of the lake armed as for war, and elvish bowmen were among them. At last they climbed the rocks and appeared at the fall's head; and great was their surprise to see the pool before them, and the [blocked gate >] gate blocked with a wall of new-hewn stone.

Then Thorin hailed them: 'Who are you' he called in a loud voice 'that come as if to war to the gates of Thorin son of Thrain, king under the Mountain, and what do you desire?'

But they answered nothing; some turned swiftly back and [the] others after gazing long at the gate and its defences soon followed them. That day the camp was moved, and came right between the arms of the mountain. The rocks echoed then with voices and with song, as they had not done for many a day. There was sound [too] of elven-harps and sweet music; and Bilbo longed to escape and go forth and join in the feasting by the fires. Even the dwarves [> Thorin was] moved, & muttered that he would things had fallen out otherwise, and that he might welcome such folk as friends.[TN17] But Thorin scowled.

A pencilled addition, scribbled at the end of the paragraph and in the left margin, introduces the idea of dwarven music as a counter to the elven song outside:

But the dwarves themselves brought forth the[ir] harps and <?instruments> regained from the hoard & made music to heart[en] <him> and they sang again songs as they had done in B's <home>.

There is no indication here that Tolkien intended to include an actual song at this point, but an unnumbered page in pencil on a loose sheet of student paper (1/1/16:12) survives that is clearly the very first rough workings for the poem that was later inserted here (i.e., in the resumed First Typescript). The typescript version of the preceding paragraph notes that 'their song . . . was much like the song they had sung long before in Bilbo's little hobbit-hole' (1/1/65:4), and indeed one stanza of the final poem is identical (the third in the new poem and the second in the old) and another reproduces three lines out of four (the fourth in both poems, differing only in one line and one word), while the other stanzas reuse some of the rhymes and phrasing from the earlier poem (compare DAA.321–2 with DAA.44–5). The two are clearly meant to be companion pieces, depicting the hoped-for goal at the onset of the quest and its apparent achievement at what Bilbo had optimistically hoped would be its end.

Under the Mountain dark and tall
[The King is > returns <to> his ha[ll] >] The King is come
unto his hall
The [<?thane> >] worm of dread
This foe is dead the worm of dread   *<illegible>*
[And so shall his foes >] And ever so his foes shall fall

[The Gate is strong, the >]
The sword is sharp the spear is long
The arrow swift the Gate is strong
The heart is bold that looks on gold[TN18]
That   *wrong.*[TN19]
[It <brooks> . >]
It fears not
The <illegible> is swift the   *[> No more the dwarves]*
The king shall suffer <no>[TN20] *[> shall suffer wrong]*

The Dwarves lift up the hearts afar
Where ever folk of Durin are.
Come haste come haste across the waste
The king has need of friend <&> [> friend and k.][TN21]

[The dwarves >] The mountain throne once more is freed
O folk of Durin O wandering folk the summons heed
The king of kin and friend hast need.
the melody of harp they wrung

Now call their voices over mountains cold
Come back unto the cavern old
*Rejoice where [*added: *hoarded] silver lies and gold*
*Here at the gates the king [*added: *now] awaits*
his hands [are <illegible> >] with silver > with gifts of silver
and of gold

Despite its extreme roughness, this first draft is recognizably the same poem as the final piece in the published book, the main differences being the insertion of two stanzas from the companion poem in Chapter I (one of which was slightly altered in the process), thus expanding it from the five stanzas of the draft to the seven of the final poem, the combination of the draft's third and fourth stanzas into a single stanza (the fifth) in the final, and the addition of a final stanza that recaps the first but with its lines in slightly different order. The poem appears in its final form in the continuation of the First Typescript exactly as in the published book and, like all the other poems in *The Hobbit*, Tolkien left it unaltered from the first printing onwards.

The next morning a company of spearmen came and they bore amid them the green banner of the Elvenking and the blue banner of the Lake; and they came by the narrow path [and >] until the[y] stood right before the wall at the gate.

Again Thorin asked the same question[TN22] as before, and this time it was answered. A tall man stood forward dark of hair and he cried:

'Hail Thorin! [We >] Why do you fence yourself like a robber in his hold. We are not [*added*: yet] foes, and we rejoice that you are alive beyond our hope. [But still > We come hither > we came hither not >] We came expecting to find none living here, yet now that we are met there seems to be much matter for a parley and & a council.'

'Who are you and of what would you parley' answered Thorin.

'I am Bard and by my hand was the Dragon slain and your treasure delivered. Is not that a matter that concerns you? Moreover I am by right descent the heir of Girion of Dale, and in your hoard is mingled much of the wealth of his halls and towers, which of old Smaug stole. Is not that a matter of which we may speak? Further in his last battle Smaug destroyed the town of Esgaroth, and I am yet the servant of its master. I would speak for him and ask whether you have no thought for the sorrow and misery of his people, who aided you in your distress, and on whom you have thus far brought ruin only, if undesigned, in recompense.'

Now these were fair and true words, if [hars[h] >] proudly and grimly spoken, and Bilbo thought that Thorin would admit what justice was in them. But he did not reckon with the power that gold [*added*: has] upon which a dragon has long brooded, nor with dwarvish hearts.[TN23] Long hours in the past days had Thorin spent in the treasury, and the lust of it was heavy upon him. Though he hunted chiefly for the Arkenstone, yet he had an eye for every other thing that here was gathered, and about most were wound old memories of the labours and the sorrows of his race.[TN24]

'You put your worst cause in [last >] the chief place he answered.[TN25] To the treasure of my people you have no claim because Smaug who stole it from us also robbed you of life and home. The treasure is not Smaug's that his heirs should pay for his evil deeds with it![TN26] The price of the goods that we had of the lake-men we will fairly pay [and > in due time > hour] – but <u>nothing</u> will we give, not a loaf's worth, under threat of force. While an armed host lies before our doors, we look on you as thieves and foes.

'It is in my mind to ask what [recompense you >] share of their inheritance you would have paid to our kindred had you found the hoard unguarded and us dead.'[TN27]

'A just question' replied Bard. 'Yet you are not dead, and we have no thought at least of robbing you alive. [And still >] Moreover the wealthy may have pity on the needy [*added*: that helped [> befriended] them when they needed help]. And still my other claims remain unanswered.'[TN28]

'I will not parley, as I have said, with armed men at my gate. Nor at all with the people of the Elvenking, whom I remember with small kindness. In this debate they have no place. Begone now ere our arrows fly. And if you would speak with me again, [*added*: first] dismiss the elvish host [*added*: to the woods where it belongs] and come [hither >] to my gates and lay down [first >] your arms upon the threshold.'

'The Elvenking is my friend, and he has succoured the people of Esgaroth in their need, though we have [> they had] no claim but friendship on him,' answered Bard. 'We will give you time to repent your words. Gather your wisdom ere we return.' Then he departed and went back to the camp.[TN29]

Ere many hours were past, the banner bearers [and trumpeters >] returned and trumpeters stood forth and blew a blast. 'In the name of Esgaroth and the Elvenking' one cried[TN30] 'we bid you [> him] consider the claims that have been urged, or be declared our foes [> foe]. At least shall you deliver one twelfth portion of the treasure unto Bard, as the dragon-slayer, and as the heir of Girion. From that he will himself contribute to the aid of Esgaroth; but if you will have the friendship of the lands about you, as your sires of old, then you will add also somewhat of your own beside.'[TN31]

Then Thorin seized a bow of horn, and shot an arrow at the speaker. It smote in his shield and stuck quivering there.[TN32]

'Since such is your answer' he called in return 'I [can >] declare this Mountain besieged. You shall not depart from it until you call [> ask] on your side for a truce and a parley. We bear no weapons against you, but we leave you to your gold; and you may eat that, if you will.'

With that the messengers departed swiftly, and the dwarves were left to consider their case. So [fie[rce] >] grim had Thorin become that they did not dare to murmur against him.[TN33] Indeed most of them seem to share his mind, except perhaps for old fat Bombur, and Fili and Kili; and of course for Bilbo. He had by now had more than enough of the Mountain, and being besieged in it was not at all to his taste. It still smelt hatefully of dragon anyway; and food was short and poor.

TEXT NOTES

1 The latter half of this paragraph, all the words following 'his own kingdom', was cancelled and replaced at once by 'Dale is now free – but wise men will stay here' which in turn was changed to '– Dale is now free, and nothing hinders his return. And any that wish can go with him, if they prefer the cold stones under the mountain-shadow to this waterside. The wise will stay here and hope to rebuild our town, and enjoy again in time its peace and riches.'

2 I cannot read the cancelled word preceding 'slumber', but it ends in *-dable*, possibly *mendable*.

3 A cancelled page (I/I/17:3) survives that represents an earlier draft of the Third Phase text that originally followed this passage. Undoubtedly once the second page in the Third Phase text, it survives because its blank verso was used shortly thereafter to become new page 14 [= I/I/17:2].

> his slumber, I might ask? Who obtained of us rich gifts and ample help, and led us to believe that our old songs would come true? Who played upon our foolish [*added*: soft hearts] generosity and our pleasant dreams? What sort of gold have they sent down the river to recompense [> reward] us? Dragon-fire and ruin! From whom shall we claim the recompense of our damage, and the help of our widows and orphans?'
>
> [From which >] You can easily see that the Master had not earned his position for nothing. For the moment the people quite forgot their idea of a new king, and turned their angry thoughts towards Thorin and his company. Hate flared up against them, and wild and bitter words were shouted. Some of those who had sung the old songs loudest were now heard as loudly crying that the dwarves had sent the dragon down upon them deliberately!
>
> 'Fools!' said Bard. 'Why waste words or hate on those unhappy creatures. Doubtless they have perished in fire before Smaug came to us.' Yet even as he spoke, the thought of the fabled treasure of the mountain came into his heart, and he fell suddenly silent; and he thought of the Master's words, and of Dale rebuilt and filled with golden bells, if he could but find the men.
>
> At last he spoke again. 'This is no time, Master, he said for [<illegible> >] counsels of change. There is work to do. I serve you yet; though after a while I may think again of your words and go north with such folk

This passage marks the point at which the detail of Dale's 'golden bells' enter the story, although the destroyed city had been linked with bells as far back as the first poem (Bladorthin Typescript, page 37; DAA.45), all accounts of Smaug's attack (page 72; DAA.56), and Balin's sad memories upon seeing the ruins (where the mention of bells first appears in the typescript, contrast page 472 with DAA.258). The contrast between alarm bells and these golden bells recalls Edgar Poe's poem 'The Bells' [1849], which successively contrasts the sounds and associations of silver, golden, brass, and iron bells (delight, happiness, alarm, and melancholy, respectively); the juxtaposition of golden bells ringing on happy occasions immediately followed by brazen alarm bells sounding warning at times of sudden danger/disaster is particularly suggestive.

4 A cancelled page (1/1/16:10) survives that represents an earlier draft of the Third Phase text that originally followed this passage. Originally the third page in the Third Phase text, as with the text given in Text Note 3 above it survives because its blank verso was used shortly thereafter (in this case, to become page 9 [= 1/1/16:6]).

> as will follow me.' Then he strode off to help in the ordering of the camps, and in the helping of the injured; [*added, then cancelled*: but first he sent messengers as swift as <illegible> find to ask for the help of the king of the Elves] But the Master scowled at his back, and sat still upon the ground. If he thought much, he said little save to call loudly for men to bring him fire and food.
>
> But now the talk ran ever among the people of the fabled hoard of the mountain that lay now without a guardian. And men spoke of [the] recompense and to spare for all their harm that they should get from it; and it cheered them much in their plight. And that was fortunate, for their night was bitter and miserable. Shelters could be contrived for few, and there was little food. Many took ill then and afterwards died, who had escaped unhurt from the town. In the days that followed there was much sickness and hunger, and even Bard would have had a hard task to order the people, for now he took the lead [> . . . and hunger. Bard now took the lead] and ordered things as he wished, though always in the Master's name. But he had a hard task to govern the people and direct the preparations for [the] rebuilding of their town. Probably the most of them would have perished in the winter, if other help had not been to hand <in> <this/their> <illegible> the help of the Elves. [*Added, in smaller letters at the end of the paragraph and continued in the bottom margin*: It was not long before the wood-elves came. Swift messengers were sent > But help soon came, for Bard had at once had swift messages sent to the Forest to ask help of the King of the Elves.]
>
> The spies of the wood elves [> Their spies] had sent news of the dwarves' northward journey to their King; and he was as astonished as the Master of the town had been to learn of it, but he expected no other ending than their death in the jaws of the dragon.

5 The image of rich, warm lands to the South, the source of unimagined luxuries, that underlies *The Hobbit* (and to a lesser extent some passages in the early legendarium) is very much in keeping with the Old English,

Gothic, and Scandinavian view of the Mediterranean. Cf. my commentary on the trade in the wine of Dorwinion (Chapter IX) and also the reference in Chapter X to 'the trade that came up the great river from the south'.

6 'the winter that now hurried after autumn': This reference, which survives into the published book (DAA.311), shows that this scene is set in the days immediately before the onset of winter, in keeping with the shift of Durin's Day to the *last* full moon of autumn. For the problems this creates in the story's chronology, see Text Note 13 following Chapter XI.

7 Again the text that follows was preceded by a cancelled page (1/1/16:11), now the verso of new page 8 [= 1/1/16:5]; this earlier draft was once the fourth page of the Third Phase text, following immediately the text given in Text Note 4 above.

> When news reached him of the rousing of the dragon and of fire upon the mountain-top, he became alarmed, and fear for his woods fell on him; but he thought at least he had heard the last of Thorin Oakenshield.
>
> But soon other messengers came in rowing madly up the Forest River, and they told of the fall of Esgaroth and the death of Smaug. Then he thought the time had come to move. 'It is an ill wind that blows no one any good' he said; for he too had not forgotten the legend of the wealth of Thror.
>
> So now he led forth all the host he could muster, or that would follow him beyond the eaves of their beloved forest. It was a great army of bowmen and spearmen, and they were robed in green and brown, and their going was exceedingly swift. Some were sent with speed North towards the Mountain; some he led bearing great store of goods down the river towards the lake. These had a long march for they were not used to the marshes and the lands beyond the forest, and they had not boats or rafts enough to carry them. Yet elves are quick and light-footed, and [in] but four days from the fall of Smaug he reached the lake-shores, and the unhappy men were glad indeed to welcome him; and ready (as he had expected) to make any bargain for the future in return for his help.
>
> [So >] This is how it came about that while many, both men and skilful elves, were left behind upon the [<?lake> >] shores, with the women and children, busily felling trees [and gathering >] for the making of huts against the winter, and beginning under the direction of the Master to re-plan and re-fashion a town like the one destroyed, yet in a place removed further north, and planned [> designed] even more fairly and more large

While this corresponds in general to the more polished text that replaced it, some interesting details are worth noting. The inelegant detail of elves frantically rowing up-river was dropped, replaced by swift-footed messengers and, more significantly, birds 'that loved his folk', a parallel to the ravens and thrush who are shortly thereafter telling Thorin &

Company the same news, and more. The statement that he brings 'all . . . that would follow him beyond the eaves of their beloved forest' suggests for the first and only time that he is not an absolute monarch; there are commands he could give that at least some of his people would not obey. This assumes, of course, that all the elves who march under his banner belong to his kingdom: the description that 'they were robed in green and brown' recalls the 'elfin folk all clad in green and brown' (BLT II.234) that Beren summoned to lead against the dwarven host in 'The Nauglafring', ambushing them and taking away all the treasure those dwarves had just claimed. It seems possible, even likely, that 'the brown Elves and the green', a phrase used three times in 'The Nauglafring' (BLT II.237, 240, & 242), distinguishes between the elves who dwelt in the caves of Artanor (Doriath) with King Tinwelint/ Thingol (= the brown elves or wood-elves) and those wanderers who live in the woods (later in revisions to the 1930 *Quenta* specifically identified as the Green Elves of Ossiriand, wandering the woods in the northeast corner of Beleriand just as the wood-elves of *The Hobbit* live in the northeast corner of the area shown on the Wilderland map). The dichotomy is maintained in the 1926 'Sketch' ('the brown and green Elves of the wood', HME IV.33) but vanishes thereafter. Finally, the mercenary aspect of the elvenking's charity, explicit in this draft, was still present but de-emphasized in the main Third Phase manuscript that replaced it and in the published book (DAA.312–13). Indeed, the replacement text goes out of its way to stress that he diverted his host from marching straight to the mountain to instead helping the lake-men 'because he was a lord of good and kindly race' – a statement not in harmony with his role as projected in the Plot Notes associated with the end of the Second Phase and the first indicator that Tolkien has shifted the book's attitude towards the wood-elves to something much more favorable than their depiction in the Second Phase texts.

8 This passage initially read 'Now the king *divided his forces* because of his old friendship with the men of the lake; *some he sent westward to skirt the marshes and come more direct upon the Mountain* and because he was a lord of good and kindly race turned his march *and went so[uth]*'.

9 Although this more nearly approaches the text of the published book (DAA.313), that familiar text is not achieved until the continuation of the First Typescript (compiled when Tolkien was preparing the book for submission to Allen & Unwin in summer-autumn 1936), where it appears as first typed exactly as in the printed book (1/1/64:6, revised typescript pagination page '140').

10 The following was written neatly in the left margin in black ink, but it was neither completed nor was the specific point at which it was to be inserted indicated; presumably it would have replaced part of the paragraph just given, probably the second sentence: 'Three nights and days they dwelt in the watch-chamber, and did not dare to go far afield. Ever they grew more puzzled, and though they debated ever the matter of'.

11 Compare the equivocation of the Parson in *Farmer Giles of Ham*, when faced with an inscription on a sword he cannot make out: the reader is told 'he could not make head or tail of them', but rather than admit this, 'to gain time' he tells the sword's owner that '[t]he characters are archaic and the language barbaric . . . [a] little closer inspection will be required' (FGH.32). In the Second Phase version of this passage (page 618), there was no hint of Bilbo's deliberate evasiveness on this point.

The idea that different animals all have their own individual languages harkens back to the Dr. Dolittle books, which were favorites of the Tolkien children; see page 266ff.

12 This variant spelling of the more usual *Carc* appears only this once. The first typescript, which also gives this line as a later (ink) addition, has the more usual 'old Carc and his wife' (1/1/65:1). The second typescript (1/1/46:1) includes 'old Carc and his wife' (who never receives a name in any version of the tale) as first typed.

13 This sentence marks the first mention of Dain Ironfoot; for more on this remarkable figure, see page 702ff.

The statement that Thorin has kin in the mountains of the north first appears here, and remains unchanged into the published text (cf. DAA.318). The later account in *The Lord of the Rings*, however, seems to contradict this by stating that after the great cold-drake killed Thror's father and brother 'most of Durin's Folk abandoned the Grey Mountains' for the Lonely Mountain and Iron Hills, an event that the Tale of Years states took place some one hundred and eighty years before Smaug overthrew the Kingdom Under the Mountain, or some three hundred and fifty years before Thorin's return (*LotR*.1124–26).

14 Tolkien inserted an end-bracket in the text at this point; the only significance I can see for this is that this marks the end of later typescript page '142' (1/1/65:2) and was, of course, very near the point at which the Second Phase manuscript had broken off. It thus presumably marks a pause in the creation of the later typescript in summer-autumn 1936.

15 There is no mention of this bridge in their first view of the ruined valley in Chapter XI (page 472), but Thorin mentions it near the end of (original) Chapter XIV and they ford the spot where it once stood on their way to Ravenhill; see page 583. The support-stones for this bridge are also visible in several pictures Tolkien drew of the Lonely Mountain, such as 'The Front Door' (plate X [top]), but not in the black and white drawing 'The Front Gate' which appeared in the published book (this picture's point of view being from the valley floor, where the bridge would be behind the viewer).

16 This phrase, reminiscent of the 'mortal men, doomed to die' in the Ring-verse of the sequel, suggests that the dwarves are not mortal in the same sense. This agrees with what is said of the dwarves in *The Book of Lost Tales* ('. . . a strange race and none know surely whence

they be . . . Old are they, and never comes a child among them' – BLT II.223–4). See 'The Halls of Waiting' starting on page 720.

17 Changed by later ink to '*Some of the younger dwarves also were* moved, & muttered that *they* would things had fallen out otherwise . . .'

18 'The heart is bold that looks on gold': cf. Text Note 14 following Chapter XIV on page 588.

19 Tolkien wrote only the first and last (rhyming) word on this line, leaving the space between them blank. Similarly, the next two lines were left incomplete.

20 These two half-lines were replaced by

No more the dwarves
shall suffer wrong.

21 I.e., 'friend and k[in]'.

In the right margin above this point, Tolkien has jotted down several rhyming words as an aid to composition: bar, car, <?char>, far, jar, shar, scar, tar. He was apparently unable to come up with a suitable third line with this rhyme (to match with *afar* and *are*) and so dropped both of the earlier lines from the final poem.

22 Tolkien underlined the words same question in pencil and wrote 'repeat' above them, indicating that Thorin's actual words were to be given here, as indeed they are in the typescript that followed (1/1/65:5), although not phrased exactly the same as on the previous day; compare DAA.320 and 322.

23 As the reference to 'dwarvish hearts' shows, Tolkien has now reversed his original idea about dwarves and dragon-gold; instead of being at least partially immune to the dragon-sickness, he now sees dwarves as particularly susceptible to it. See the commentary ('Dragon-sickness') following Chapter XIV, starting on page **000**.

24 This passage was slightly revised to read 'he had an eye for *many an*other thing . . . and about *each* were wound . . .'. Tolkien also added at the end of the paragraph 'Also he remembered the Elvenking with small kindness and was little pleased to see the elves among' but cancelled this, no doubt when he incorporated it into the discussion that followed. Finally, Tolkien seems to have originally begun to write 'the sorrows of his *people*' before changing this to 'of his race'.

25 Thorin's rejection of charity, which should be a legitimate concern whatever the legitimacy or otherwise of all the other claims, is a warning sign of just how deeply sunk in dragon-sickness he has fallen. The Elvenking's delaying his expedition to seize the treasure in order to help the victims of the disaster at Lake-town gives him the high moral ground in the Third Phase text over Thorin, who will not even repay the charity he received a few weeks earlier when he was similarly cold, hungry, destitute, and homeless. Note also that in contrast to the final Second Phase Plot Notes, here the Elvenking makes no claim but merely supports the claims of Bard and the lake-men.

26 This sentence was revised several times, probably to eliminate the problematic concept of 'Smaug's heirs':

> To the treasure of my people *no one has a* claim because Smaug who stole it from us also robbed *him of* life *or* home. The treasure is not Smaug's that *from it his* evil deeds *should be paid for*

This second sentence was then cancelled in its entirety and replaced with the following in the left margin:

> The treasure [is not >] was never [Smaug's >] his that his evil deeds should be amended with [> his evil deeds should be atoned for with] a share of it.

27 Tolkien later answered this question for us with the story of Scatha the Worm, which can be found in Appendix A of *The Lord of the Rings*. After Fram of the Éothéod [Horse-folk], one of the ancestors of Eorl the Young, kills 'the great dragon of Ered Mithrin' [Grey Mountains], the dwarves claim his hoard, which had been stolen from them by the dragon (as evidence of which, note that Merry's horn, which came from that hoard, 'was made by the Dwarves'; *LotR*.1014). Fram 'would not yield them a penny, and sent to them instead the teeth of Scatha made into a necklace, saying "Jewels such as these you will not match in your treasuries, for they are hard to come by." Some say that the Dwarves slew Fram for this insult. There was no great love between Éothéod and the Dwarves' – *LotR*.1102. Note that this incident probably did not involve Durin's folk, since these events took place more than a century before Thorin I removed from Erebor to the Grey Mountains.

28 Thorin's rejection of the appeal to pity, especially on those in desperate need who had aided him when his folk were in similar straits, is a second warning sign of his moral corruption.

29 This paragraph replaced Bard's original, much simpler, response:

> 'We will give you time to repent your words' said Bard and then he departed.

This type of expansion in the course of writing is typical of the Third Phase manuscript.

30 Added in the bottom margin, and marked for insertion at this point: 'We speak unto Thorin Thrain's son calling himself King under the Mountain.'

31 Changed to 'but if you *would* have friendship *and honour in* the lands about you, as your sires *had* of old, then you will *give* also somewhat of your own beside.' The detail that Bard and his allies requested one-twelfth of the treasure remained constant through the typescripts and various editions of the published book, but there is no indication how they determined that this figure would represent the proportion of Girion's wealth to Thror's hoard.

32 Attacking a herald, even symbolically like this, was of course a gross violation of the heroic code and hence significant. It shows that even if Thorin is within his rights to withhold charity and not to negotiate

under threat, and quite justified in his resentment of the Elvenking, he is still, in Gandalf's words, 'not making a very splendid figure as King under the Mountain' (see page 668).

This point also marks a slight pause in composition; the next paragraph is more neatly written and in darker ink.

33 This sentence was changed several times in the course of writing it: 'murmur against him > offer him other counsel, and indeed > that had they wished they would not have dared to grumble at > find fault with him.' That Thorin's most trusted companions dare not speak their mind is of course another sign that Thorin is no longer the person he was, and sets the stage for his threats against them in the next chapter and his assault on Bilbo in the chapter after that. It is rather surprising that Balin, the most reasonable of all the dwarves, is not listed as having mental reservations à la Bilbo, Bombur, Fili, and Kili; perhaps his disdain for the Elvenking (made plain in his bluntness before him back in Chapter IX) affected his judgment here.

Chapter XVI

DIVIDED LOYALTIES

As before, there was initially no chapter division in the manuscript, merely a paragraph break between the third and fourth paragraphs (of five) on this page (Third Phase manuscript page 14; 1/1/17:1). However, at some later date, probably during the continuation and completion of the First Typescript in summer–autumn 1936, Tolkien wrote 'Ch' (i.e., 'Ch[apter]') in the left margin in pencil and marked it for insertion at this point, indicating where he had decided the chapter break should occur. There is some evidence that Tolkien initially considered this the fifteenth chapter, not having yet inserted the chapter-break on page 642; see page 666 below.

Now the days passed slowly and wearily. Many of the dwarves spent their time piling and ordering the treasure, and Thorin [asked >] bade them eagerly to look for the Arkenstone of Thrain. 'For that' he said 'is worth more than a river of gold in itself and to me yet more.'

Added in pencil at the bottom of the page and marked for insertion here:

> That of all the treasure I name unto myself and I will slay any one that [added: finds it > takes it <&>] withholds it.[TN1]

Bilbo heard these words and he grew afraid wondering what would happen if the stone was found – wrapped in an old bundle of tattered oddments that he used as a pillow. Yet he did not yet speak of it, and as the weariness of the days grew heavier [he thought of >] a plan came into his little head.

Things had gone on thus for some while, when the Ravens brought news that Dain and five hundred dwarves were hurrying from the Iron Hills in the N.E. and in a few days' time would be coming to Dale.

'But [I >] they cannot [come >] reach the Mountain unmarked' said Roäc. 'And I fear lest there be battle in Dale. Nor do I call this counsel good. Though they are a grim folk they are not likely to overcome the host that besets you, and even should they do so what will you gain? [*added*: Winter and snow is hastening behind them.][TN2] [Without >] How shall you be fed without the friendship and good will of the lands about you?[TN3] The treasure is likely to be your death though Smaug is dead!'

But Thorin would not listen [> was not moved]. 'Winter and snow will bite [the >] both men and elves' he said, 'and they may find their dwelling in the vale too grievous to bear. With my friends [upon their >] behind them and winter upon them they will perchance be in better mood [for >] to parley with.'

That night B. made up his mind. Bofur & Bombur were the watchmen about the middle of the night. The sky was dark and moonless. As soon as it was full dark he slipped on his ring and going to a <illegible>[TN4] corner he drew from his bundle a rope and the Arkenstone. Then he climbed to the top of the wall. Bifur & Bombur were there, for the dwarves kept but tw[o] watchmen. Bilbo sat beside him and after a while he sneezed 'It is mighty cold' said Bombur. 'I wish we could have a fire as they have in the camp.'

'It's warm enough inside' said Bilbo.

The paragraph describing his preparations for departure was re-written even while it was being set down, eventually becoming as follows:

That night B. made up his mind. The sky was dark [> black] and moonless. As soon as it was full dark he went to a corner of an inner chamber and drew from his bundle a rope and the Arkenstone [*added*: <wrapped in a rag>]. Then he climbed to the top of the wall. Bombur was there, for the dwarves kept but one watchman [*added*: and it <was> his turn]. 'It is mighty cold' said Bombur. 'I wish we could have a fire as they have in the camp.'

It is warm enough inside' said Bilbo.

Originally Bilbo's exit from the group was both more whimsical and more dramatic, as the following cancelled draft (1/1/17:6), which survives as the verso of new page 17 (=1/1/17:7), demonstrates:

'But I am bound here until midnight' grumbled Bombur 'A sorry business altogether. Not that I say a word against Thorin may his beard grow ever longer; yet he was ever a dwarf stiff in the neck!'

'My eyes are sharp' said Bilbo '[and I have >] it is long since I did watch. [Lend me your >] Let us sing songs to cheer us up.' said Bilbo.

'Singing is thirsty work and calls for more than water.'

'I will sing to you' said Bilbo.

And he began to sing in his small voice an absurd song one that used to be sung to him long ago in the green of the world when he was a small hobbit in a little bed in his father's hole.

Birds are

[For which we have >]

At this point, all but the first paragraph on this page was cancelled, after which the drafting continued:

'Not as stiff as my legs' said Bilbo. 'I am tired of stairs and stone-passages. I will be going to bed, I think.'

Bombur gave a shiver and a sneeze. 'Stay here a moment' he begged. 'I will fetch <us> another cloak and some wraps, against the Eastwind. There is no need to freeze at one's post.'

No sooner had B. gone than Bilbo [fastened >] slipped [> put] on his ring secured his rope slipped over the wall and was gone.

'Confound that hobbit!' said Bombur when he returned. '[I should be >] What Thorin would say if he knew the watch were broken I don't know.' But in the dark he did not see the rope & it was not until morning

At this point the drafting breaks off, well shy of the bottom of the page. Clearly, Bilbo absconds in the night without meaning to come back, taking the Arkenstone with him. His further movements would probably have been along the lines of those outlined in Plot Notes D (see pp. 569–70).

The drafting actually gives two variants of the scene with Bombur (Bifur/Bofur having already been eliminated), shifting focus in the middle; the writing is somewhat neater in the second half, perhaps indicating a brief pause in composition. Initially the idea seems to be that Bilbo sings a lullaby that sends Bombur to sleep, perhaps with the aid of strong drink; cf. Bombur's reference to the need for something 'more than water' (i.e., alcohol). It is regrettable that only the first two words of Bungo's lullaby were written down, since this is our only opportunity to hear what sort of bedtime songs Bilbo's father sang his son; from the subject matter (a lullaby) and the tiny scrap preserved here, I suspect it would have resembled the choruses (e.g., 'little birds are sleeping') from Lewis Carroll's poem 'The Pig Tale' in *Sylvie and Bruno Concluded*, from which Arry Lowdham quotes in *The Notion Club Papers* (HME IX.179 & x–xi).

All this is changed in the latter half, so that instead of singing Bilbo now slips off while Bombur's back is turned, much to the latter's chagrin. However, the guileless dwarf does not suspect that Bilbo has crept out toward the enemy and simply assumes Bilbo has gone off to sleep, as had been his stated intention ('I will be going to bed, I think'); his concern is merely for the watchpost's having been left unmanned for a brief interval. When Tolkien decided that Bilbo would be able to conclude his business that same night and rejoin the dwarves before his disappearance had become known, he recast the scene on the replacement page (Third Phase manuscript page 15; I/1/17:4) into a very close approximation of its familiar final form:

'But I am bound here till midnight' grumbled Bombur. 'A sorry business altogether. Not that I venture to disagree with Thorin, may his beard grow ever longer; yet he was ever a dwarf [with a stiff neck >] stiff in the neck!'

'Not as stiff as my legs' said Bilbo. 'I am tired of stairs and stone-passages. I would give a good deal for the feel of grass at my toes.'

'I would give a good deal for [*added*: the feel of] a strong drink in my throat and a soft bed after good supper' said Bombur.

'I can't give you those' said Bilbo; 'but it is long since I watched, and I will [watch for >] take your turn for you, if you wish. I have no sleep in me tonight.'

'You are a good fellow Mr Baggins. I will take your offer kindly. [I will >] If there should be anything to note, rouse me first, mind you . I [sha[ll] >] will lie in the inner chamber to the left not far away.'

'Off you go' said Bilbo. 'I will wake you at midnight, and you can wake the next watchman.'

As soon as Bombur had gone Bilbo put on his ring secured the rope, slipped over the wall and was gone. He had [*added in pencil*: nearly] six hours before him.[TN5] It was very dark and the road after a while when he left the narrow path and climbed down towards the [riv[er] >] stream in its lower course below the falls was strange to him. Fording the river narrow and shallow as it was was not easy for the little hobbit. He missed his footing on a boulder & fell into the cold water with a splash; and he had barely scrambled out on the northern bank, shivering and spluttering, when up came elves in the gloom and seized him.

> To this was added in bottom margin: '. . . up came elves in the gloom *with lanterns* and *searched for* him.' This sentence was recast as:
>
> 'That was no fish' one said. 'There is a spy abroad. Hide your lights they will help him more than us.'
>
> Suddenly Bilbo sneezed and they gathered towards the sound. 'Let's have a light' he said. 'I am here if you want me' and he slipped off his ring.
>
> Quickly they seized him. 'How have you got so far past our sentinels' they asked.

'Who are you' they asked 'and what are you doing?'

'I am Bilbo Baggins' he answered, 'companion of Thorin. I know your king well by sight though he does not know me; but Bard perhaps will remember me, and it's he that I wish to see.'

'[O ho >] Indeed' said they 'and what may be your business?'

'That's my own affair, my good elves' he answered. 'But if you wish ever to get back to your woods from this cold cheerless place,' he answered shivering, 'you will take me along quickly to a fire where I can get dry – and let me speak with your chiefs as quick as may be. I have only a hour or two to spare.'

So it came about that about 2 hours from his escape B. was sitting beside a large [> warm] fire before a large tent, and there sat gazing curiously at him both the Elvenking and Bard. An [>A] hobbit in elvish armour (covered with the tatters of a coat and waistcoat) was something new to them.

'Really you know' Bilbo was saying [*added*: in his best business-manner] 'Things are impossible. Personally I am tired of the whole affair. I wish I was back in [my >] the West in my own home, where folk are more reasonable. But I have an interest in this matter – a fourteenth share to be precise according to a letter which I think I have kept.'[TN6] He drew out from a pocket the [> a] crumpled and much folded Thorin's letter that had been put under his clock on the mantelpiece in May! 'A share of <u>profits</u>, mind you.' he went on. 'I am aware of that. Personally I am only too ready to consider all your claims, and deduct them from the total before putting in my own claim. However you probably don't know Mr Thorin O. as well as I do now.

'I assure you he is quite ready [to starve sitting >] to sit on a heap of gold and starve as long as you sit here.'

'Well let him' said Bard. 'Such a fool deserves to starve'.

'Quite so' said Bilbo. 'I see your point of view. At the same time winter is coming on fast. Before long you will be having snow [and all sorts >] and what not, and supplies will be difficult. Also there will be other difficulties. I think you may not know quite all I do. You have not heard of Dain and the dwarves of the Iron Hills?'

'No we have not, and what has he to do with us' The king asked.[TN7]

'I thought not. Well here is now but a few [> less than 2] days' march off and has at least five hundred grim dwarves with him, not a few that have [> had] experience in the dreadful dwarf and goblin wars of which you may have heard.[TN8] When he arrives there may be serious trouble.'

'What do you tell us this for? [> Why do you tell us this?] Are you betraying your friends or are you threatening us?' asked Bard grimly.

'My dear Bard' squeaked Bilbo 'don't be so hasty. I merely wish to [avoid all trouble >] stop trouble for all concerned. Now I will make you an offer –'

'What offer' said they.

'This!' said he and he drew forth the Arken stone. The Elvenking himself whose eyes were not unused to things of wonder and of beauty stood up in amaze. Even Bard gazed a while in silent wonder. It was as if the moon lit water had caught the sharp glitter [*added*: netted all the glinting] of all the frosty stars and risen radiant in the <illegible> before [them].[TN9]

'This is the Arkenstone of Thrain' said Bilbo, 'and it is the heart of Thorin. He will value it above a river of gold.[TN10] I give it to you. It will aid you in your bargaining.'

Then Bilbo not without a shudder, not without a longing glance handed the marvellous stone to Bard, and he <held> it [in] his hand as though dazed.

'But how is it yours to give' he asked at last with an effort.

'O well' said the hobbit uncomfortably. 'It isn't exactly, but, well I am willing to let it stand against all my claim, don't you know. I may be a burglar (or so they say: [I never >] personally I never really felt like one) but I am a honest one, I hope, more or less. Anyway I am going back now, and the dwarves can do what they like to me.'[TN11]

Then the Elvenking looked on B. in a new wonder. 'Bilbo Baggins' he said. 'You are more worthy to wear the armour of elf princes than many who have looked more comely in it. But I wonder if Thorin Oakenshield will see it so. I have perhaps more knowledge of dwarves in general than have you. I counsel you to remain with us, and here you shall be honoured & twice welcome.'

'Thank you very much' said Bilbo 'I am sure. But I don't think I could leave my friends [*added*: like that] after [such a lot we >] all we have gone through together. And I promised to wake old Bombur by midnight too. Really I must be going, and quickly.'

And nothing they could say would stop him. [So h[e] >] So an escort was provided for him, and as he went both the Elvenking & Bard saluted him with honour. Guided to a safe ford and set safely across Bilbo soon scrambled back to the Gate, and it was well before midnight when he climbed his rope again, untied it and hid it, and sat down upon the wall.

This last sentence detailing Bilbo's return to the lookout post was cancelled and a new scene inserted:

As they passed through the camp, an old man sitting by a tent door rose and came towards them.

'Well done Mr Baggins!' he said clapping B. on the back. 'There is always more about you than any one expects![TN12] [*cancelled*: There is a]'

It was Gandalf!

For the first time for many a day B. was really delighted; but there was no time for all the questions that he wished suddenly to ask.

'All in good time' said Gandalf. 'Things are drawing towards an end, now. There is an unpleasant time just before you, but [be of >] keep your heart up. There is news brewing that even the ravens have not yet heard. Good night.'

Puzzled but cheered Bilbo hurried on. Guided to a safe ford and set across dry he said farewell to the elves, & climbed back towards the Gate. Great weariness began to come over him; but it was well before midnight when he climbed his rope again, untied [it >] and hid it, and sat down on the wall to wonder what would happen now.

At midnight he woke up Bombur, and then in turn rolled himself up in his corner, without listening to the old dwarf's thanks (which he felt he had hardly earned); and soon he was fast asleep, forgetting all his worries till the morning.

TEXT NOTES

1 This hastily pencilled addition is significant, since it shows that Thorin is slipping into madness and can no longer be trusted. That he would threaten capital punishment over a piece of treasure to one of the loyal companions he has led for a year and more is completely out of character (cf. his courage in the face of Smaug's attack in Chapter XII, sending others to safety while risking his life to save Bofur and Bombur from danger) and foreshadows his attack on Bilbo in the next chapter.

2 This sentence is added at the bottom of the paragraph and marked for insertion here; it recasts the unfinished and cancelled sentence that originally began this paragraph:

> 'But winter and snow is hastening behind them' said Roäc and their food is

3 By Thorin's own account in Chapter I, the Kingdom under the Mountain depended upon the nearby human communities for food, trading worked goods in order to gain all the produce and other foodstuffs they needed. Remarkably enough, here we have a carrion bird advising against a battle, something which we have just been told (through a later interpolation) none of Thorin's fellow dwarves dared to do.

4 This cancelled unfinished word seems to be either *stor[eroom]* or *stai[r]*.

5 It is one indication of just how late in the year it is that it is already full dark shortly after six in the evening – again a detail more in keeping with the revised timing of Durin's Day (the last new moon before winter) rather than the original version (the first new moon of autumn).

6 Tolkien later created a facsimile of this very letter that Bilbo had carried with him on his trip; see Frontispiece for a reproduction of Bilbo's contract, and page 107 for a transcription.

7 This sentence was preceded by a fragment of another, cancelled paragraph in which Bilbo continued speaking:

> 'Quite so. I thought not' he

When Tolkien decided to include the others' reply, it is originally 'B' (i.e., B[ard]) not the Elvenking who asks this question. The First Typescript changes this to the familiar

> 'We have, a long time ago; but what has he got to do with us?' asked the king.
>
> —new typescript page 150; 1/1/66:3.

8 See Chapter I (c) for an earlier reference to the dwarf-goblin war and the battle of the mines of Moria.

9 The illegible word might be *heart*, but this is doubtful. This sentence was revised, then cancelled and replaced:

> It was as if the moon lit water had *netted all the glinting* of all the frosty stars . . . > It was [as] if a globe had been filled with moonlight and hung in a net woven of the glint of all the frosty stars before them.

10 Here Bilbo echoes Thorin's words from the beginning of this chapter; cf. page 658.

11 Written in the left margin alongside this paragraph is an additional sentence: 'I only wish to save trouble and foolishness all round, and this seemed to me a possible way'. There is no indication of its exact placement, but it is probably intended to follow the words 'don't you know'. This sentence was not picked up on in the typescripts and thus does not appear in the published book.

12 Bladorthin here is more or less repeating his words to Bilbo the last time they were unexpectedly reunited (at which time the wizard's name was of course still Bladorthin) – 'Mr Baggins has more about him than you'd guess'; cf. page 200.

Chapter XVII

THE BATTLE OF FIVE ARMIES

As before, there is no chapter break in the original Third Phase manuscript, merely a gap of one skipped line between the first and second paragraphs on new manuscript page 20 (1/1/18:1). Later Tolkien wrote, in pencil, 'Ch. XVI' in this gap. That he wrote *XVI* rather than *XVII* might be inadvertence, but that would be very uncharacteristic. It seems more likely that the break between what are now chapters XIV and XV had not yet been inserted (see page 642); no such break having existed in the Third Phase ms., either as originally written or in later markings as had been the case for the starts for what are now chapters XVI (page 658), XVII (this page), or XIX (page 687).

Next day the trumpets rang early in the camp. Soon a single runner was seen hurrying along the narrow path. At a distance he stood and hailed them, asking whether Thorin would hearken [*added*: now] to [an embassy as new tiding had occurred, which >] another embassy since new [things >] tiding had occurred & matters were changed.

'That will be Dain' said Thorin when he heard. 'They will have got wind of his coming. I thought that would soften their mood. Bid them come few in number and weaponless and I will hear.'

About mid morning the banners of the Wood and Lake were seen to be borne forth again. [Behold > As they drew > <As the entire> >] A company of twenty was approaching. At the beginning of the narrow path they laid aside sword & spear, and [behold among them >] drew near. <Wondering> the Dwarves saw that among them was [*added*: both] Bard & the Elvenking, and before them one carried a strong casket of iron bound wood.

'Hail Thorin' said [> cried] Bard. 'Are you still of the same mind?'

'[A>] My mind changes not with the rising & setting of a few suns' said Thorin 'And [<did> > see >] not yet has the elfhost departed as I [sai[d] >] bade. Till then no bargaining will you have of me.'

'Is there nothing for which you would yield any of your gold?'

'Nothing that you or your friends have to offer?'

'What of the Arkenstone of Thrain' said he and he bade open [> opened] the box and held aloft the jewel in his opened hand. The light leapt from his palm bright even in the morning.[TN1]

Then Thorin was stricken dumb with amazement & confusion. No one spoke for a long while.

[That stone >] At length Thorin spoke and his voice was thick with wrath. 'That stone was my father's and is mine'[TN2] he said. 'Why should I purchase mine own? [*cancelled*: Yet I knew you were thieves.]' But wonder got the better of his anger [> him] and he added. 'And how came you by the heirloom of my house – if there is need to ask such a question of robbers.'

'We are not robbers' Bard said. 'Your own we will yield in return for our own.'

'How came you by it' shouted Thorin in gathering rage.

'I gave it them!' squeaked Bilbo, who was peeping over the wall, by now in a dreadful fright.

'You, you' cried Thorin turning upon him and grasping him with both hands. 'You miserable hobbit, you you burglar' he shouted at a loss for words, and he shook poor B. like a rabbit.[TN3] 'By the beard of Durinn[TN4] I wish I had Gandalf here. But I will wring your neck first' he said.[TN5]

'Your wish is granted' said a voice and Thorin paused. From the company a man stood forth, and cast aside his hood & cloak.[TN6] 'Here is Gandalf – and not too soon it seems! If you don't like my burglar please don't damage him.[TN7] Put him down and listen first to what he has to say.'

'You all seem in league' said Thorin putting Bilbo down. 'Never again will I have dealing with a wizard or his friends. What have you to say you descendant of rats.'

'Dear me dear me!' said Bilbo. 'I am sure this is all very [unfor[tunate] >] uncomfortable: [If >] You may remember saying that I might choose my own fourteenth [*added in pencil*: share]. Perhaps I took it too literally though the time was when you seemed to think I was of some service. Descendant of rats indeed. Is this all the service of you and your family that I was promised, Thorin. Take it that I have disposed of my share as I wished, and let it go at that.'

'I will' said Thorin grimly. 'And I will let you go.'[TN8] Then he turned and spoke over the wall. 'I am betrayed' he said. 'It was rightly guessed that I could not forbear to redeem the Arkenstone the treasure of my house. For it I will render one fourteenth of the hoard in silver and gold, but that shall be for the share of this cre[ature] – hobbit, and with that reward he shall depart. [But to you I will >] I will give him to you and [> but] no friendship of mine goes with him.'[TN9]

'Get down now to your friends' he said [*added in pencil*: to B.] 'or I will throw you down.'

'What about the gold' said Bilbo.

'That shall follow after' said he. [*added in different ink*: as can be arranged.]

'Until it does [> then] we keep the stone' said Bard.

'You are not making a very splendid figure as King under the Mountain' said Gandalf. 'Still matters may change yet.'

'They may indeed' said Thorin – and already so strong was the bewilderment of the treasure upon him, that he was pondering whether by the help of Dain he could not recapture the Arkenstone and withhold the share of the hoard.

And so Bilbo was swung down from the wall and departed without any reward for all his trouble, except for the armour which [he >] Thorin had given him before. Many of the hearts of the dwarves felt >] More than one of the dwarves in the[ir] hearts felt shame and pity at his going.

'Farewell' he cried to them. 'We may [meet] again, as friends'

'Be off' cried Thorin. '[If you had not mail upon you. >] You have mail on you which was made by my folk and is not to be pierced with arrows. But if you do not hasten I will sting your miserable feet. So be swift.'

In the bottom margin of this page (Third Phase manuscript page 23; Marq. 1/1/18:4) is a pencilled note 'see 23b' and an arrow, indicating that a new paragraph numbered '23b' on the verso (= Marq. 1/1/18:5) should be inserted at this point:

> 'Not so hasty' said Gandalf [> Bard] '[in three days >] we will give you until the day after tomorrow. At noon on that day we will return, and see if you have brought from the hoard the gold and silver that is to be set against the stone. If that is done without deceit, then we'll depart, and the elfhost shall go back to the Forest. In the meantime, farewell.'[TN10]

With that they departed to the camp, but Thorin sent messages by Roäc[TN11] telling Dain of what had passed, and bidding him come [with > warily and >] with wary speed.

That day passed, and the night. The next day [came a bitter >] the wind shifted west and it was a dark morning [> and the air was dark and gloomy]. The morning was still early when a cry was heard in the camp. Messengers ran in to tell that a host of dwarves [were marching >] had suddenly appeared round the east spur of the Mountain, and were hastening into Dale!

Dain was come. [The > At dusk he had reached the first >] He had hurried through the night and came thus suddenly upon them. His five hundred were [armed >] clad in steel-mail and wielded heavy mattocks [with >] two-handed in battle; yet each had also a short sword at his side and a round shield slung at his back. Their beards were [plaited >]

forked and plaited and thrust into their belts. Their caps were of steel and their shoes were of iron,[TN12] and their faces were grim.

Trumpets called men and elves to arms, and before long the dwarves could be seen from the camp coming [down >] up the valley till they halted about a mile to the East. Some [> A few] still went on their way until they drew near the camp, and there they laid down their arms [> weapons] and lifted up their hands, in sign of peace.

Bard went out to meet them and with him went Bilbo. 'We are sent from Dain son of Nain'[TN13] they said when questioned. 'We are hastening to our kinsmen in the Mountain, since we learn that the kingdom of old is renewed. But who are ye that sit in the plain as foes before defended walls?'

By now you will know well enough the sort of things that are said at such parleyings; and I will not recount all that was said on either side.[TN14]

On Bard's side the dwarves were refused passage to the Mountain until Thorin had paid for the Arkenstone; but the dwarves muttered angrily and retired. Later they moved their camp yet nearer.[TN15]

But when messengers were sent to the Gate they found no gold or payment; and arrows came forth as soon as they drew within shot. Returning they found all astir, as if for battle; for the dwarves of Dain had advanced almost to within hail of their camp.

'Fools!' said Bard '– to come thus within the mountain's arms. They do not understand war above ground! There are many of our archers [*added*: & spearmen hid] now in the rocks upon both their flanks. Dwarf-mail may be good, yet they will [> <?would>] soon be in [<illegible> >] hard put to it. Let us at them now from the front, ere they be fully rested.'

But the Elvenking said: 'Long will I tarry [even though the advantage slip from us, save what we have in numbers which is very > and that is sufficient >] ere I begin this war for gold. The dwarves cannot pass us unless we will, and our advantage of numbers will be sufficient [> enough] if it must come to unhappy blows.'

But he reckoned without the dwarves. The knowledge that the Arkenstone was in the hands of the besiegers burned in their minds; and they guessed the hesitation of Bard and his allies.

Suddenly without a signal they began to advance and sprang silently forward to attack. [Arrows >] Bows twanged and arrows whistled, and well-nigh battle had begun.

Suddenly a darkness came on with dreadful swiftness. A dark cloud hurried over the sky. Thunder rolled in the mountain and lightning lit its peaks. Beneath it another cloud could be seen whirling forward; but like a cloud of birds so dense that [it could >] light cd. not be seen [beneath their >] between their wings.[TN16]

'Halt!' cried Gandalf and he ran and stood suddenly [before >] between the advancing dwarves and the ranks awaiting them. 'Halt!' he cried and his staff blazed with a sudden flash. '[The dread >] Dread has come upon you all more swiftly than I guessed. The Goblins are upon you. Bolg of the North is coming, whose father you slew in Moria.[TN17] Behold the bats are above his army like a sea of locusts[TN18] [and the wargs & wolves of >] They ride upon wargs [> wolves] and wolves [> wargs] are in their train.'

Amazement and confusion fell upon them all; and even as [they >] he spoke the darkness grew. 'Come' shouted Gandalf 'there is yet time for counsel. Let Dain son of Nain come swiftly to us.'

So began the battle in a fashion none had expected. And it was called after the Battle of Five Armies, and it was very terrible. For upon one side were the Goblins and the Wolves and upon the other were men elves and dwarves.[TN19]

This is how it fell out. [The Goblins <had> >] ever since the fall of the Great goblin of the M. Mountains the hatred of their race for the dwarves had been aroused [> rekindled] to fury. Tidings in secret ways they had gathered; and in all the Northern Mountains there was forging and an arming. [When they learned of the fall of Smaug their plan was soon made. >] They marched and gathered by hill and mountain [and till in the great >] going ever by tunnel or under dark until [<under> >] around and beneath the great mountain Gondobad of the North[TN20] a vast host was assembled, ready to sweep down upon the South. Then they learned of the death of Smaug and joy was in their hearts; and they hastened night after night through the mountains, and came thus at last on a sudden from the North East, and not even the Ravens knew of their coming until [the broken >] they issued in the broken lands which divided the Lonely M. from the [lands >] hills behind.[TN21]

This was the plan of Gandalf and of Bard and the Elvenking and of Dain who now joined them, for the Goblins were the foes of all and at their coming all other quarrels were forgotten.[TN22] Their only hope was to lure the goblins into the valley between the mountain's arms; and themselves to man the great spurs that stuck [> struck] S. and East. Yet this would be perilous if the goblins were in sufficient numbers to overrun the mountain itself and so attack them also from above. But there was no time to devise anything else. Soon the thunder passed rolling away to the SE, but the bats cloud came [down >] flying over the mountain and whirled above them. 'To the mountain' said Bard 'Let us take our places while there is time.'

On the Southern spur [were arranged the Elves >] in its lower slopes and in the rocks at its feet the Elves [took >] were set, on the

Eastern were men and dwarves (since there was less <cover>). But Bard and some of the nimblest of men and elves climbed [higher >] to the height of the E. shoulder to look out [> forward] to the North.

Soon they could see all the lands to the north and the M. foot black with the hurrying hosts. Ere long they swirled round <illegible> and came into Dale – the swifter wolfriders and their howls rent the air. A few brave men were there to make feint of resistance, [but >] and many there fell ere the rest drew off to either side. As G. had hoped the goblins' army [enraged >] had gathered behind the resisted vanguard, and poured now in rage into the valley, seeking for the foe. Their banners were countless black and red and <they> came on like a tide, but their order was wild.

This was a terrible battle: the most dreadful of all B's experiences & the one he hated most (& which is also to say the one he was after most proud of, & most fond of recalling).[TN23] Yet actually I may say he put on his ring early in the business and vanished from sight if not from danger. A magic ring of that sort is no complete protection in a goblin charge, nor does it stop flying arrows and wild spears; but it does help in getting out of the way, and prevents your head from being chosen [by a goblin swordsman for >] for a sweep stroke by a goblin swordsman.

The Elves were the first to charge. As soon as the g. host was dense in the valley they sent into it a shower of arrows [*added in pencil*: set afire by magic]. And behind [*added*: five hundred > a thousand spearmen] they leapt down and charged the enemy. The yells were deafening, and the rocks [were] stained black with goblin blood. But just as the goblins were recovering and the elf-charge halted; there rose from across the valley a deep throated roar. With a cry [> cries] of 'Moria' [and] 'Dain Dain' the dwarves of the Iron Hills plunged in wielding great Mattocks upon the other side. And beside them came the lake men with long swords.

Panic came on the goblins and even as they turned to meet this new foe the elves charged again. Already some of the goblins were turning back down the river to escape from the valley, and victory seemed at hand, when a cry was raised above.

The Goblins had scaled the mountain and were on the heights above the Gate and many were streaming down to attack the spurs from above. They had only stemmed the first attack. [Now the bats flew down >] Now darkness was coming early in a stormy sky, and the bats wheeled darkly over the field [&] heedless of arrows they swirled about the heads and ears of elves and men. Behind in the valley a host of wargs came running [> ravening] and with them a new host of goblins of huge size. Already [their >] Bard was fighting on the Eastern slopes and the Elves were withdrawing to stand about the king upon the <southern> arm near the watch-place of Ravenhill. Suddenly there was a shout and from the Gate came a trumpet call. Part of the wall moved by levers from within fell outward with a crash into the pool. Down leapt Thorin and his companions no longer in hood and cloak but all in royal armour, and in the gloom Thorin shone like gold in a dying fire. Rocks were hurled down from on high by the goblins above, but they held on, leapt down the fall's foot and rushed forward against their foes. Wolf and rider fell before them. Thorin wielded an axe with <huge> strokes and nothing seemed to harm him. 'To me to me elves and men to me O my kinsfolk' he cried and his voice shook like a horn [between the >] in the valley.

Down rushed all the dwarves of Dain heedless to his help and down came such men as Bard would spare with him; down upon the other side came elvish spearmen. Once again the goblins were stricken in the valley and they were slaughtered in heaps till Dale was dark with them; but among them lay many men, many men and dwarves, and many a fair elf that should have lived yet many an age merrily in the <borders> of the woods.

But as the valley widened they made slower progress and soon the attackers were attacked, and slowly they were forced into [a ring >] a mighty ring all hemmed about with goblins and with wolves. But their friends could not succour them for they were fighting bitterly on the hillsides and slowly they were being beaten down.

'It will not be long' thought Bilbo 'before they win the gate; and then goodness knows what will happen. I would rather old Smaug had all the [gold >] treasure tha[n] these <hateful> Goblins. I have heard songs of many battles, and I have always understood defeat may be glorious. It seems very very uncomfortable. I wish I was well out of it.'

[*cancelled*: Suddenly high and far off he saw]

The clouds were torn by the wind and a red sunset slashed the west. Suddenly high and far off B saw a sight that made his heart leap: dark shapes small yet majestic against the distant glow.[TN24] 'The Eagles the Eagles' he cried – he was among elves up Ravenhill '– the Eagles the Eagles are coming.' And happily his eyes were seldom wrong. The Eagles were coming.

The Very rumour of them changed the day. The Goblins on the mountain wavered and hesitated.[TN25]

'The Eagles are coming' he cried again [> shouted] and the elves took up the cry and it echoed across the valley. [Even the Goblins looked up, but it >] and <many> eyes [were >] looked up. [But only >] 'The Eagles' cried Bilbo once more, but at that moment a rock [> stone] hurled from above smote heavily on his helm and he fell with a crash & knew no more.[TN26]

TEXT NOTES

1 That is, the Arkenstone casts enough light that even in the full daylight it can be seen to shine brightly. This passage was emended to read 'bright *&* *white* in the morning'.

2 The apostrophe indicating singular possessive (*father's* rather than *fathers'*) is clear here (Third Phase manuscript page 21; Marq. 1/1/18:2), and also in both typescripts (1/1/67:1 and 1/1/48:1). See the discussion of Thrain and Thror following Chapter X.

3 See Text Note 1 following Chapter VII (page 245) for Shippey's claim that this line and others like it show that Tolkien associated hobbits with rabbits. While Shippey's argument is intriguing, it does not take into account the fact that the majority of references to rabbits in the final book (eleven out of sixteen) do not refer to Bilbo, or that Bilbo is also compared to other animals (e.g., 'descendant of rats!').

4 The alternative spelling here of *Durinn* rather than the more usual *Durin* is perhaps in order to more closely reproduce the Old Norse original. Dronke, for example, gives *Durinn* in her edition of *Vǫluspá* (*The Poetic Edda*, Vol II: Mythological Poems [1997], page 9), while Young gives *Durin* in her edition of Snorri's *The Prose Edda* (page 41), for reasons given in her foreword (ibid., page 19). The typescript (1/1/67:1) reverts to the familiar *Durin*.

5 This sentence was cancelled and replaced by the following:

> 'I wish I had Gandalf here. I will [> would] have words for him and his choice. But I will throw you on the rocks first [> But now I will throw you on the rocks],' he said, and lifted B. in his arms.

The idea that Thorin might actually attempt to murder Bilbo in a fit of rage, which would have been unthinkable in the Second Phase text, has been carefully prepared for over the last two chapters; cf. Text Notes 1 & 3 for Chapter XVI and Text Notes 23, 25, 28, 32, & 33 for Chapter XVb, as well as Text Notes 14 & 18 for the fair copy and typescript revisions to Chapter XIV.

6 Added in pencil: '. . . his *tall* hood & *long* cloak'.

7 Tolkien initially wrote 'please don't h[arm] . . .'; shifting the word choice to *damage* casts Bilbo in the role of Gandalf's property ('*my* burglar'), thus subtly enhancing his value in the treasure-smitten dwarf's eyes. Perhaps the implication is that Thorin might have killed a traitor, but in the grip of the dragon-sickness he would be unable to destroy anything of (monetary) value.

8 This sentence was altered slightly so that Thorin's words became parallel with Bilbo's: 'And I will let you go *at that*.' The added clause ' – and may we never meet again!' first appears in the extended typescript (1/1/67:2).

9 The last two sentences of this paragraph were cancelled and the words 'What will you have for it > What price will you have for it? > What

price will you set upon for it?' written below them. This was then cancelled in turn and the word 'stet.' written next to the paragraph to indicate that the cancellation of those sentences was rescinded. Later, in pencil, Tolkien added '. . . he shall depart; *and you can divide it as you wish.* I will give him to you . . .'

10 An earlier draft of both this paragraph and the first paragraph on the following page (Third Phase ms. page 24; Marq.1/1/18:6) can also be found on this page's unnumbered verso (1/1/18:5):

> 'Not so hasty' said Gandalf. 'Tomorrow the elf-host will prepare to depart as you desire. But at noon we will return with the stone, and by that time you must have ready [within >] outside the wall or near within all the gold and silver that is its price.'
>
> That day passed. Evening was come [> approaching], when sudden there was a cry in the camp. Messengers ran in. 'A host is marching with speed into Dale' [he >] they cried. It was the dwarves of Dain, and they were armed with steel. From afar the men of Bard and the elves watched them until they halted about a mile [fr[om] >] to the east. Dusk was deepening, when three dwarves came

11 This is the last mention of Roäc in the book, but we can assume that he survived the upcoming battle, since Tolkien would have told us otherwise.

12 Changed to 'Their caps and their shoes were of iron'. Hence, no doubt, Dain's later *encomium* or epithet 'Dain Ironfoot'. This name does not however arise within *The Hobbit* and is never used in the earlier book (or indeed until Tolkien was at work on the Appendices of *The Lord of the Rings* – cf. HME XII.281 where it first occurs, in a passage apparently not written until 1948–9 or shortly thereafter).

13 Dain's ancestry, unlike Thorin's (with the two competing Thror-Thrain-Thorin and Thrain-Thror-Thorin genealogies) or later Balin's (who briefly went from 'son of Fundin' to 'son of Burin' and then back again; cf. HME VI.443–4 & 460), never varied: he remained 'Dain son of Nain' from this first mention through to the final references in Appendix A of *The Lord of the Rings*. As with Dain, Thorin, and all the other dwarf-names in *The Hobbit* except Fimbulfambi (and possibly Balin), *Nain* comes from the *Dvergatal* or dwarven name-list in the *Vǫluspá*, although it does not appear in all manuscripts (cf. Dronke page 90); Snorri also includes it in the *Prose Edda* (page 41). The pattern of giving brothers rhyming names (Fili/Kili, Balin/Dwalin, Oin/Gloin) is also evident here; since Dain is Thorin's cousin (page 644), then Thror's sons were *Thrain* and *Nain*. Like 'Dain', 'Nain' is unusual in that it has a wider meaning and circulation beyond the *Dvergatal*; see the commentary on 'Dain son of Nain' beginning on page 702.

14 This simple statement is replaced in the typescript (1/1/67:3) by a greatly expanded account of what was said at the parley and also of the dwarves' plans; cf. DAA.337–8.

15 Tolkien originally followed the semicolon with 'on' (i.e., on [the dwarves' side] . . .). This paragraph was recast to read:

> Bard refused the Dwarves' passage to the Mountain until Thorin had exchanged gold for the Arkenstone; but the dwarves muttered angrily and retired.

16 This paragraph was revised, in several layers, to eventually read:

> *Then still more* suddenly a darkness came on with dreadful swiftness. A dark cloud hurried over the sky. *[A winter > Winter >]* Thunder *& a wild wind rolled up and rumbled in the* mountain and lightning lit its peaks. Beneath it another *blackness* could be seen whirling forward; *from the North* like a cloud of birds so dense that light cd. not be seen between their wings.

17 This is the first appearance of Bolg, whose name remained unchanged thereafter; see the commentary starting on page 708.

18 For bats as yet another of the 'Children of Morgoth', see commentary on pp. 716–8.

19 See Plot Notes F for Tolkien's earlier hesitation about just who did and did not count as one of the 'five armies'.

20 The spelling was later changed to *Gundobad* in pencil (Third Phase manuscript page 27; I/1/18:9) and this form appears in both typescripts (I/1/67:4 & I/1/48:5); the published book has *Gundabad.* This is the only mention of Gondobad in *The Hobbit*, although 'Gundobad' does appear on the draft Mirkwood map [Plate I (bottom)] and 'Gundabad' on the final Wilderland map (DAA.[399]), in both cases at the juncture of the north-south Misty Mountains and the east-west Grey Mountains. The name is Gnomish-Noldorin (i.e., early Sindarin); cf. *Gondobar* ('City of Stone'), one of the alternate names for Gondolin in *The Book of Lost Tales* ([1917–20]; BLT II.158), the unfinished 'Lay of the Fall of Gondolin' ([early 1920s]; HME III.145), and the poem 'The Nameless Land' ([written 1924, published 1927]; HME V.100 & 104). I can find no place where Tolkien defines Gondobad, but GON-/GOND-/GONDO- means 'stone' or 'of stone' (*Gondo-lin*, 'Song of Stone'; *Gondor*, 'Stone-land') and the -BAD element may relate to the Gnomish word *bad* meaning 'way, path' (*Gnomish Lexicon, Parma Eldalamberon* vol.XI.21; 'Noldorin Dictionary' and 'Noldorin Word-lists', *Parma Eldalamberon* vol.XIII.160 & 137). If so, 'Gondobad' might mean something like 'the crossroads of stone', which would suit its position at the meeting of these two great mountain ranges riddled with dwarven and goblin mines and tunnels, but this is only a guess. Much later [1969 or after] Tolkien decided that *Gundabad* was a dwarven (Khuzdul) name (HME XII.301), but this clearly could not have been the case at the time *The Hobbit* was written, since the idea of a dwarven language and nomenclature distinct from Old Norse seems to have first arisen several years after *The Hobbit* was finished, in the 1937 *Quenta Silmarillion* (HME V.273–4) and the *Lhammas*, which dates from about the same period (HME V.178–9). Tolkien also in this late essay created a new

backstory for Mount Gundabad, deciding that this was the spot where Durin had woken from sleep and that it was thus, like Moria, originally a revered dwarven stronghold now fallen into orcish hands (HME XII.301). Of all this later development there is of course no trace in *The Hobbit*, unless its seeds lie in Gandalf/Thorin's remark that his ancestors first came to the Lonely Mountain when they were 'driven out of the far north' (page 71); *The Lord of the Rings* suggests that Khazad-dûm (Moria), if anywhere, was the stronghold revered for its associations with Durin the Deathless.

21 Fimbulfambi's Map [see Frontispiece of Part One], the original Mirkwood map (Plate I [bottom]), and the pictorial view of the Lonely Mountain on the Long Lake map (Plate II [top]) – the latter two of which accompanied the 'home manuscript' (i.e., the composite First Typescript/Third Phase manuscript) when it was loaned out to Tolkien's friends – all agree in showing the foothills to the northeast as coming within a short distance of the mountain; these hills can also be seen in the background to the right of the drawing 'The Lonely Mountain' (H-S#136).

The typescript alters the account of their approach slightly:

> . . . came thus at last on a sudden from the North hard on the heels of Dain. Not even the ravens knew of their coming until they came out in the broken lands which divided the Lonely Mountain from the hills behind. How much Gandalf knew cannot be said, but it is plain that he had not expected this sudden assault. (1/1/67:4)

This account made it into the published book (cf. DAA.340) but unfortunately does not match the final version of the Wilderland Map (DAA.[399]), where the line of hills is to the east, not north-east as in the earlier map. Here the goblins would have been entirely in the open from the time they left the Grey Mountains, a distance much too far to have marched in a single night (it is some four times the distance between the Lonely Mountain and the Long Lake), and their north-to-south march would not have overlapped Dain's east-to-west march from the Iron Hills.

22 This idea of enemies uniting when faced with a threat from true evil resurfaced a decade later when Tolkien was drafting the early parts of what became Book V of *The Lord of the Rings*; when King Théoden arrives at Dunharrow to muster his troops for the ride to Minas Tirith, he finds among the forces gathered some of the Dunlendings he has just defeated at Helm's Deep a few days earlier, men willing to set aside a five-hundred-year feud in the face of the threat of Sauron (HME VIII.249 & 247).

23 The closing parenthesis is lacking in the manuscript; I have supplied it editorially in what seems the appropriate place.

24 For Tolkien's own depiction of this scene from Bilbo's point of view, see the unfinished drawing labelled 'The Coming of the Eagles' in tengwar (Plate XII [bottom]).

25 This sentence was left unfinished, ending in a semicolon, and the paragraph cancelled.

26 It will be seen that this earliest account of the Battle of Five Armies, while following the same lines as the published version, leaves out many details, especially as relate to the role that Bolg of the North and his bodyguard play in the fight – indeed, there is no indication that Bolg's forces differ from any other goblins. A few such details are added in pencil to this Third Phase manuscript, but most appear for the first time in the typescript (1/1/67:4–7) with no intermediate drafting (or at least none which survives), and except in typographical details and the spelling of the name 'Gundobad' the typescript exactly achieves the text of the published book in its description of the actual battle (although some of the preliminary scenes, such as that describing the parley with Dain's dwarves, were revised considerably in the page proofs). Of particular note is the fact that Thorin's charge, which is ambiguously depicted as glorious but perhaps unwise in the published text (cf. DAA.343, where Bard is unable to restrain his men from abandoning their positions to join it), is here unambiguously heroic. For more on this climactic scene, see my commentary beginning on page 713.

Chapter XVIII

'AND BACK AGAIN'

As usual with the Third Phase manuscript (or indeed with *The Hobbit* manuscripts as a whole), the text originally continued with no chapter break. In fact, Tolkien at first simply indented and began a new paragraph, but had not even completed the first word ('Wh[en]') when he stopped, crossed it out, and drew a squiggle in the middle of the (blank) line that followed, and skipped the line after that. Thus he clearly intended a section break to come at this point. The text for what became the new chapter begins matter-of-factly with its description of the battle's aftermath, about one-third of the way down the manuscript page (Third Phase manuscript page 31; Marq. 1/1/19:1).

When he came to himself he was lying on the flat rock [> stones] of Ravenhill, and no one was near. Night was fading from the sky. [Dawn >] A cloudless dawn but cold was pale in the East.[TN1] He was shaking with cold [> & chilled as stone], but his head burned like fire.

'Now I wonder what has happened' he said to himself 'At any rate I am glad to find that I am not yet one of the glorious dead – but I may be soon enough yet.'

He sat up painfully. Looking into the valley he saw no goblins. After a while as the light grew he thought he saw elves moving in the rocks below; and suddenly he was aware of a great eagle perched upon a mountain just above.

'Hullo there!' he called 'Hail O Eagle, may your wings be ever blessed. I am hurt'.

'[Who is it that speaks >] What voice is it that speaks unseen among the stones' said the Eagle, <tak>ing to his wings and circling above Bilbo. Suddenly Bilbo remembered his ring. 'Well I am blessed' said he. 'This invisibility has its drawbacks after all! I suppose otherwise [> Otherwise I suppose] I should [> might] have spent a warm and comfortable night in bed!'

'It's me Bilbo Baggins companion of Thorin' he said, hurriedly taking off the ring.

'It is well that I have found you; you are needed and long sought' said the Eagle: and it was that [> the] very selfsame eagle, as it proved that had borne him from the [> to the] Carrock long before. 'I will bear you.'[TN2]

In this way Bilbo was borne swiftly down into the valley, and set down before a tent. Gandalf greeted him [*added*: at the door].[TN3] 'Baggins!' he said. 'Well I never alive after all. [Who >] But come' he said more gravely. 'tidings may wait: you are called for;' and leading the hobbit he took him within.

'Hail Thorin' said Gandalf 'I have brought him.'

There lay Thorin wounded with many wounds, and his rent armour and notched axe were cast upon the floor.

'Farewell o gracious thief' said Thorin. 'I go now to the halls of waiting to sit beside my fathers until the world is renewed. The goblins have slain me.[TN4] Since I leave now all gold and silver and go where it is of little worth, I wish to part in friendship with [> from] you, and would take back my words and deeds at the Gate.'

Bilbo knelt on one knee filled with sorrow. 'Farewell O king [> my king]' he said. 'This is a bitter adventure if it must end so; and not a mountain of gold can amend it. Yet I am glad that I have been of your servants & your company [> shared in your perils] – and that has been more than any Baggins deserves [> might hope for].'

'Nay' said Thorin. 'There is more <to> you than you know descendent of [> son of] the <kindly> West – [sure and >] valour & wisdom and little greed. [> wisdom in good & blended measure]. If more valued food and cheer above hoarded gold [that >] it wd be a merrier world. But sad or merry I must leave it now. Farewell.'

Then Bilbo turned away and he went by himself and sat alone in a tent, and whether you believe it or not he wept until his eyes were red and his voice hoarse. He was a kindly little soul. Indeed it was very long before he had the heart to make a joke again.[TN5]

'Thank go[odness] > M[ercy] > A mercy it was' he said to himself at last 'that I awoke when I did. I [wish] Thorin were living, but I am glad that we parted in kindness'.

All that happened Bilbo learned of course bit by bit, though he was no longer as interested as I hope you are. He was aching in his bones for his homeward journey.

The Eagles [had > in great number >] had had suspicion of the Goblins gathering [> mustering] and they had gathered in great numbers and come down upon the wind in the nick of time. They it was that dislodged the Goblins from the Mountain and cast them over precipices or drove them shrieking down among their foes; [Soon the Elves and men could turn and go to the help of the battle in the valley. >] so that soon all those on the mountain were overcome or in flight. Then Elves and Men turned to [> came at last to] the help of the battle in the valley. But they were still outnumbered. In that hour Beorn had himself appeared – no one knew how or whence,

[<saved> >] and he seemed to have grown to half-giant size in his wrath. The roar of his voice was like thunder and he tossed goblin and wolf from his path like straws and feathers.[TN6] He fell upon their rear and broke into the ring and there he lifted Thorin who had fallen pierced with spears and bore him out of the fray. Then he returned and none could withstand his onslaught.[TN7] Thus enheartened the weary companies had fallen on and soon the goblins <?they were> [scattered >] broken. The <most> were driven into the river and such as escaped across were hunted into [> right to] the marshes about the Forest River and there most perished, or coming into the wood-elves' realm were slain or driven to die deep in the trackless dark of Mirkwood.

[All this had befallen ere full >] The victory had been assured before night fall, but the pursuit was still on foot when B. returned to the camp, and not many were there save the wounded.[TN8]

'Where are the eagles?' he said to Gandalf that evening as he lay rolled in many warm blankets. 'They are gone' said G. 'for they [do not love >] will not tarry here, [But they are >] now that they have hunted the last fugitives from the mountain.'

'[Good >] I am sorry: I should have liked to see them again,' said B. sleepily. '[When d[o] >] I suppose I shall be going home soon?'

'As soon as you like' said Gandalf.

[But >] Actually it was some days [before Bilbo was strong again on his legs. He left the Mountain >] before Bilbo left the place. They buried Thorin deep beneath the Mountain, and Bard laid the Arkenstone upon his heart.[TN9] 'There let it lie with the last of the kings' he said, 'and may it guard [bring good fortune to >] all his folk that dwell here after.'

Two more sentences are squeezed in at the end of the paragraph, running over into the bottom margin:

And by him [*added*: upon his tomb.] the Elven king laid Orcrist the <illegible> sword that had been taken from Thorin in captivity. It is said it gleamed ever in the dark if foes approached.[TN10]

But Dain son of Nain took up his abode there, and all his dwarves; and [many >] he became king under the Mountain and <?many> dwarves of the race of Durin [were >] came back to <illegible> old halls. The twelve dwarves[TN11] chose also to remain there; and [> for] Dain dealt his treasure well. [Yet >] There was, of course, no longer any question of dividing it in shares among Balin Dwalin, Bifur Bofur & Bombur [(or Bilbo) >] and the rest or Bilbo.

Yet a fourteenth share [> part] of all the gold and silver made &

unmade was given up to Bard; for Dain said 'we will honour the agreement of the dead, and he has now the Arkenstone in his keeping.' [*Added*: And even a fourteenth share was wealth exceeding rich.]

And of that Bilbo was given a chest full of silver and a chest full of gold by Bard himself – he would take no more. 'And it will be difficult enough to get that home as it is' he said; which proved true enough.[TN12] To the Elven king for his aid many jewels such as he loved were given, and <?among them> the emeralds of Girion that Dain gave to Bard.[TN13]

<Now> the hour came to say farewell to his friends. 'Farewell Dwalin' he said 'and Farewell Fili & Kili, and Farewell Dori and Nori, and Oin and Gloin, and Bifur & Bofur and Bombur' he said. And turning towards the mountain 'Fairwell king Thorin Oakenshield.'[TN14]

And the Dwarves bowed low and their words stuck in <their throats> '[Farewell >] Goodbye and good luck' they said '– if ever you visit us again when these halls are made fair again, the feast shall indeed be splendid' said Balin.[TN15]

'If ever you pass my way' said Bilbo 'don't wait to knock. Tea is at four, but any time [is time for >] will do for you! Goodbye'.

And he rode [> turned] away.

The Elfhost was on the march and if it was sadly lessened yet many were glad, for now the world would be merrier for many a day. [T]he dragon was dead and the goblins would [be >] have small power in the North for many ages of m.[TN16] and their hearts look forward [to a >] over winter to a spring of joy.

Gandalf and Bilbo rode behind the Elvenking.[TN17] But when they drew within sight of Mirkwood they halted; for the wizard and hobbit were going [to str >] north <along> the Forest and towards the Hills. Now that the Goblins were overcome it was a safer road if long[er] than the dark & dreadful pathways under the trees.

'Farewell O Elvenking' said Gandalf, 'Merry be the greenwood while the world is yet young; and merry be all your folk.'

'Farewell Gandalf. May you ever turn up [> appear] where you are [wanted >] most needed; and the oftener you appear in my halls the better shall I be pleased' said the king.

'I beg you' said Bilbo stammering 'to accept a gift,' and he brought out a silver necklace [> necklace of silver and pearls].

'In what way have I earned gifts of you [> such a gift] O hobbit' said the king.

'Well er' said Bilbo 'I thought don't you know that some little return for your hospitality should be made. I mean even a burglar has his feelings, and I drank a deal of your wine and eat much of your bread [– though >] without by your leave.'

'I will take it O Bilbo the magnificent' said the king gravely. 'And I name you elf-friend[TN18] and blessed: may your shadow never grow less (or we should [> might] all be ruined). Farewell.'

Then the Elves [wen[t] >] turned toward the Forest and
Bilbo <went> home.

Indeed yes! He had many adventures ere [> before] he got there. The wild was still the wild, and the Battle had not changed it much, but he was never in any great danger again. The wizard was with him and for long Beorn too.

The following two paragraphs (and the first sentence of the third paragraph) were later bracketed and then cancelled, and the words 'Put in Later' written beside them in the margin, no doubt when the passage was moved to its present position near the end of the next chapter.

If you would have all things settled I will tell you this: Bard brought Men back to Dale and rebuilt a town there and all the valley became in time rich and tilled, and many boats were on the running river which [fell >] ran less swift below [> after] its sudden Southern turn. and much folk gathered there And Lake Town was rebuilt in time and became prosperous once more; but the Master came to a bad end.

He stole what treasure he could lay ha[nds on] > Bard sent much treasure to him for the help of the town; and being of the sort that is easily <illegible> he fell under the spell of it, and took it and fled with it; and those who went with him, murdered him for it, and threw him in to > left him > and he died of starvation in the waste.

But that was long after Bilbo went away . . .

. . . Christmas [> Yule-time] he spent in Beorn's house – <with> Gandalf and it was warm and merry, and men came from far and wide for the Misty Mountains were now freed.[TN19] And Beorn became a great chief [*added*: afterward] and ruled the [> a] wide land between the mountains & the wood; and it is said that for many a generation the men of his line had the power of taking bear's shape; and some were grim men [*added*: and bad], but [some were of rough >] most were just such as Beorn, if less in size and strength. [As long as they ruled >] In their day the last goblins were hunted from the Misty Mountains, and new peace came over the edge of the wild.[TN20]

[And after that Bilbo crossed the mountai[ns] > When Yule was over Beorn invited them to stay here >] It was spring and a fair one with mild weather and bright sun before Bilbo and Gandalf left; and

B. left then with regret for the flowers of the gardens of Beorn were in spring [mo[re] >] no less marvelous than in high summer.

At last they came [over the >] up the long road and to the very pass where the goblins had captured them before; but they came there at morning, and looking back a white sun was shining over the distant [> outstretched] lands, and mirkwood, darkly green even in spring, stretched across the lands laid out below away from left to right and blue. [> There behind lay Mirkwood blue in the distance and darkly green even in spring at the nearer edge.] There far away was [a glint of s[now] >] the Lonely Mountain on the edge of eyesight. On its highest peak snow yet unmelted glinted pale.

'So comes snow after fire, and even dragons have an ending' said Bilbo and he turned his back on his adventure. The tookish part was getting very tired and Baggins was daily coming forward. 'I now wish only to be in my home' he said.

TEXT NOTES

1 This is changed to 'A cloudless day [*added*: but cold] was broad above.' That is, the amount of time Bilbo spends unconscious on the battlefield is increased; originally he is wounded and passes out at sunset, waking with the next day's dawn. In the final version, it is already well into the next day when he recovers consciousness.

2 These five paragraphs were re-written to remove the eagle and replace him with one of the lake-men:

> . . . suddenly he was aware of a man standing at the door of the watch-chamber nearby.
>
> 'Hullo there!' he called '[How goes >] hullo! what news?'
>
> 'What voice is it that speaks unseen among the stones' said the man peering forward. Suddenly Bilbo remembered his ring. 'Well I am blessed' said he. 'This invisibility has its drawbacks after all! Otherwise I suppose I might have spent a warm and comfortable night in bed!'
>
> 'It's me Bilbo Baggins companion of Thorin' he said, hurriedly taking off the ring.
>
> 'It is well that I have found you; you are needed and long sought' said the man: 'Are you hurt?' 'A knock on the head' said Bilbo, 'but I have a helm and a hard skull. All the same I feel sick. My legs are weak.' 'Then I will carry you,' said the man, 'to the camp in the valley' (Third Phase manuscript pages 31–32; 1/1/19:1–2).

This change was no doubt made because Tolkien remembered that earlier he had written of the eagles that 'Bilbo never saw them again. But he didn't forget them' (see page **000** and Text Note 5 following Chapter VII).

3 The idea that Gandalf was wounded in the battle, which seems so out of keeping with the character as he was later developed in *The Lord of the Rings*, did not appear in the original manuscript but entered in with the typescript: '. . . set down before a tent in Dale; and there stood Gandalf, with his arm in a sling. Even the wizard had not escaped all hurt; and there was scarcely one unharmed in some way in all the host [> and there were few unharmed in all the host].' (I/I/68:1).

4 This line was cancelled. For more on 'the halls of waiting' and the dwarven afterlife, see part four of the commentary (iv. 'The Halls of Waiting') following the Third Phase manuscript, beginning on page 720.

5 The ink of the following lines is darker, again indicating a slight pause in composition.

6 It took Tolkien several tries to find the right simile. He tried first 'like a dog amo[ng]', then broke off and replaced this with 'as if they were but yapping pupp[ies]', before settling on 'like straws and feathers'.

7 Bolg's fate is not mentioned here, instead first entering in with the typescript: 'Swiftly he [Beorn] returned and his wrath was redoubled, so that nothing could withstand him, and no weapon seemed to bite upon him. He scattered the bodyguard, and pulled down Bolg himself and crushed him. Then dismay fell on the Goblins and they fled in all directions. . . .' (I/I/68:2–3); see Text Note 26 to Ch. XVII and also the commentary starting on page 708.

8 This sentence was originally followed with 'The eagles were all off on the mountain hunt > Bilbo > Among these Bilbo found himself counted' – i.e., among the wounded.

9 This word looks like *heart* in the manuscript (Third Phase manuscript page 34; I/I/19:4) but might instead be *breast*, the reading of the typescript (I/I/68:3).

10 The word preceding 'sword' is difficult to make out but may be *Elfin*.

11 In the original story neither Fili nor Kili died fighting alongside their great-uncle but survived to the end of the tale. The idea that the two most likeable of all Bilbo's companions should also die in the battle – one of the saddest moments in the whole story, even though it occurs offstage while our narrator is *hors de combat* – first appears in the continuation of the typescript that eventually (autumn 1936) replaced the Third Phase manuscript: 'Of the twelve companions of Thorin ten remained. Fili and Kili had fallen defending him with shield and body, for he was their mother's elder brother' (I/I/68:3). This change thus postdates the completion of the book by some three and a half years. Thorin had still been their great-uncle when the First Typescript reached Chapter X (cf. I/I/60:4), where at some point after the page was typed 'sons of my father's daughter's son' was changed to 'sons of my father's daughter'. The phrase 'their mother's *elder* brother' perhaps suggested the presence of another brother as well, as would indeed eventually be the case, although the unfortunate Frerin was not invented until late in Tolkien's

work on *The Lord of the Rings* (*LotR*.1110–11 & 1117 and HME XII.276, 281, & 287); note his absence from the family tree given on HME XII.277. For more on issues of dwarven inheritance and the kingship, see the section of commentary entitled 'Dain son of Nain' beginning on page 702.

12 Several cancelled words originally came between 'full of gold' and 'by Bard himself', but I cannot make any of them out. That Bilbo would return home with little or no treasure had long been foreseen in the Plot Notes – cf. the last page of Plot Notes B, as well as Plot Notes D & F, particularly the last, where he loses most of his treasure on the return journey. Ironically, setting off with two chests full of treasure (here a sign of modest restraint) may derive from *Fáfnismál*, where Sigurd finds so much gold in Fafnir's hoard that it fills two chests, with which he loads down Grani, his faithful horse (Terry, *Poems of the Elder Edda* page 159). This becomes 'two great chests' in Morris & Magnússon's translation of the *Völsunga Saga* (page 67), and Snorri Sturluson tells us that 'Grani's burden' became a kenning for 'gold' from this incident (*Prose Edda*, page 113), while Bilbo's chests became 'two *small* chests . . . *such as one strong pony could carry*' in the typescript (I/I/68:4). Of course Bilbo also kept his little sword, his mail coat, and the Ring, and it seems a parallel beyond coincidence that the three additional treasures Sigurd took with him from Fafnir's hoard were a famous sword, a gold byrnie (mail-coat), and the *ægishjálmr* or 'Helm of Awe' – an item famed for its power to make the wearer invisible.†

†Also known as the Helm of Terror, the *ægishjálmr* is better known today by the name Wagner used in *Das Rheingold*, the *Tarnhelm*.

13 This sentence was preceded by the line ' "I beg of you" said Bilbo to the Elvenking', which was cancelled and the replacement text squeezed into place, with many hesitations. Originally the insertion seems to have read 'To the Elven king for his aid many jewels such as he loved were given, but the emeralds of Girion were given to Bard, and by him <illegible> that B. were' before this broke off and was altered rather illegibly to read as I have given it in the main text. The typescript clarifies the sequence of events: 'To the Elvenking he [Bard] gave the emeralds of Girion, such jewels as he most loved, which Dain had restored to him' (I/I/68:3).

14 Aside from the inadvertent omission of Balin and Ori, Bilbo here takes his leave of the dwarves in exactly the same order in which he was first introduced to them back in the first chapter. Fili and Kili are of course alive and present (see Text Note 11 above). The line where he bids farewell to their memory (cf. DAA.352) first appears in the typescript (I/I/68:4), where both Balin and Ori are included in their proper order, except that Balin precedes his brother Dwalin in this listing (no doubt as Bilbo's special friend among all the remaining dwarves, and the Company's leader now that Thorin is gone), whereas he had been the second to arrive at the 'unexpected party'.

15 *The Lord of the Rings* records that Bilbo did indeed take them up on this invitation and pay them a visit many years later, after he had vanished from the Shire and before settling down to his retirement at Rivendell (*LotR*.247).

16 That is, 'many ages of m*en*'; the elision is an example of the speed with which Tolkien set down the latter half of the Third Phase manuscript in his hurry to reach the end of the story. Cf. young Christopher Tolkien's description of this material as 'rather roughly done' in his 1937 letter to Father Christmas (reprinted in the Foreword to the Fiftieth Anniversary *Hobbit*, page vii).

17 Added above the line, but not marked specifically where it should be inserted: 'and Beorn strode beside'.

18 This seemingly casual remark gains great significance in the sequel, where both Bilbo and Frodo enjoy special privileges because they are known to be 'elf-friends' (cf. *LotR*.94). More significantly, it ties Bilbo into a long tradition of Tolkien's elf-friends, a line of figures stretching back to Eriol in *The Book of Lost Tales* [1917–20] and his slightly later counterpart Ælfwine in 'Ælfwine of England' [circa 1920 & afterwards], through the elf-friends of the Silmarillion tales such as Tuor, Húrin, and Beren, and onward to those time-travellers Oswin and Alboin Errol of *The Lost Road* [1936] and Arry Lowdham and Young Jeremy in *The Notion Club Papers* [1944–6], and ultimately Smith Smithson in *Smith of Wootton Major*, Tolkien's last completed story [1964].

19 These sentences were revised to read:

> But that was long after Bilbo went away. Anyway By Mid winter Bilbo & Gandalf had reached Beorn's house – And there they stayed. Yule tide was warm and merry there, and men came from far and wide to feast for the goblins of the Misty Mountains were now few and <terrified>, &nd men went abroad without fear.

20 Unlike Gandalf's prediction a few pages later (see Text Note 4 for Chapter XIX), this statement does come true, since the goblins suffer catastrophic losses upon Sauron's downfall at the climax of *The Lord of the Rings* which seem to leave them near extinction (cf. *LotR*.985: 'the creatures of Sauron . . . ran hither and thither mindless; and some slew themselves, or cast themselves in pits, or fled wailing back to hide in holes and dark lightless places far from hope'), although we have the testimony of the *Father Christmas Letters* that a few still linger in remote spots even in our time (see in particular the 1932 letter).

PLATE IX

Left 'The Back Door': A flurry of dwarven activity in the hidden bay on the western side of the Mountain.

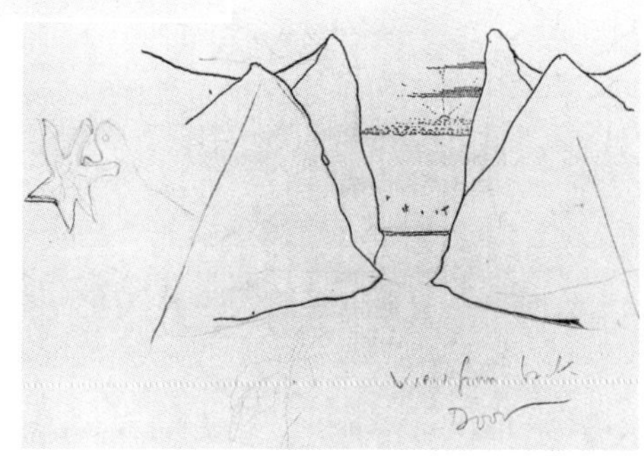

Right 'View from Back Door': companion piece to the preceding, showing the view from inside the secret tunnel looking out towards the setting sun.

Left Dwarves marching, with sketch of Smaug flying overhead.

PLATE X

Above 'The Front Door': the Lonely Mountain by daylight. Note the smoke-rings above the Mountain, the river looping around the ruins of Dale, and the opening on Ravenhill.

Above 'Smaug flies round the Mountain': a night-time scene in muted colour. Note placement of Dale and aberrant phase of the moon.

Above 'Conversation with Smaug': Bilbo's meeting with the Dragon in a picture full of significant detail. Note the dwarven curse on the jar to the lower left.

Left 'The wrong way to do it': even before he began writing *The Hobbit*, Tolkien was thinking about dragons, and this drawing from 1928 shows one of the 'creeping' kind being attacked in 'the wrong way'.

Above 'Death of Smaug': Tolkien's annotated sketch showing the destruction of Lake Town.

Above 'Not competent produce drawings required. Can send rough sketch and directions [to] artist': previously unpublished sketch of Bilbo.

Above 'The Coming of the Eagles': this rough sketch shows the only known depiction of the Battle of the Five Armies, with the figure in the foreground possibly that of Bilbo.

Chapter XIX

THE END OF THE JOURNEY

As before, no break separated the paragraphs in the original manuscript (Third Phase manuscript page 38; Marq. 1/1/19:8), but Tolkien later inserted 'Ch' in pencil here to mark where he had decided that the final chapter should begin.

[So homesick was he that even the House of Elrond could not long delay him. He called there of course and spoke with the elves > It was already May and >] It was on May the 1st that he came back to that valley of the last homely house. Again it was evening and as he rode down beside the wizard the elves were still singing in the trees. As soon as Bilbo and Gandalf [came >] appeared they burst into song very much as before

Put in a song like the one on p 28.[TN1]

The page which follows, providing a very neat handwritten copy of the poem that ultimately appeared here, was interpolated later, since all the remaining pages of the Third Phase manuscript that follow (Third Phase manuscript pages 39–45; Marq. 1/1/20:2–8) were later renumbered to accommodate the addition of a new page '39' bearing the poem (1/1/20:1).

O where are you going,
so late in returning?
The river is flowing,
the stars are all burning!
O whither so laden
so sad and so dreary?
Here elf and elf-maiden[TN2]
Now welcome the weary

Come, tra-la-la lally,
Come back to the valley

The stars are far brighter
than gems without measure,
The moon is far whiter
than silver in treasure;

The fire is more shining
on hearth in the gloaming
Than gold won in mining!
So cease from your roaming!

Come tra-la-lalley
come back to the valley!

The dragon is withered
His bones are now crumbled,
His armour is shivered,
his splendour is humbled.
Though swords shall be rusted,
and crown and throne perish,
with strength that men trusted
and wealth that they cherish
Here [grass] is yet growing
And leaves are yet swinging,
the white water flowing
and elves are all singing

Come tra la lally
come back to the valley[TN3]

A warm welcome was made there in the house of Elrond. and [*added*: <there> were many] eager ears to hear the tale of all their adventures. Gandalf it was who spoke, for Bilbo was fallen quiet and drowsy; but every now and again he would open an eye and listen when some part of the story he did not know came in.

Written following the next paragraph but marked for insertion here, following 'quiet and drowsy':

Most of the tale he knew, for he told much of it to the wizard himself on the homeward way. But

So he learned that Gandalf had been to a council of good wizards; and that the Necromancer had been driven from his hold in the south of Mirkwood, and had fled to other lands. 'The North is freed from that horror for many an age' said G. 'yet I wish he were banished from the world'. [*cancelled*: Also one thing that had often puzzled him was explained – the trolls had been traced by Elrond. They had plundered > been <buried>][TN4]

'It would be well indeed' he said [> said Elrond] 'but I fear that will not be [> come about] in this age of the world, or for many after.'

After the tale of their journeys there were other tales, and yet more tales, tales of long ago, and tales of new things, and tales of no time at all: till Bilbo's head fell on his chest, and he <snored> comfortably in a corner.[TN5]

He woke to find himself in bed, and the moon shining through an open window. Below the elves were still singing.[TN6]

[Song]

This instruction is written in pencil in the top margin of Third Phase manuscript page 40 [> 41] (=I/I/20:3); the actual text of the poem appears on a separate sheet later inserted into the manuscript, as may be seen from its being given a sequence of page numbers (39 > 40 > 41):

Sing all ye joyful, now sing all together!
The wind's in the tree-top the wind's in the heather;
The stars are in blossom, the moon is in flower,
Bright are the windows of night in her tower!

Dance all ye joyful, now dance all together!
Soft is the grass, and let foot be like feather!
The river is silver, the shadows are fleeting,
Merry is Maytime and merry our meeting.

Sing we now softly, and dreams let us weave him,
Wind him in slumber and there let us leave him!
The wanderer sleepeth, now soft be his pillow!
Lullaby, lullaby, alder and willow!

Hush, hush, oak ash and thorn!
Sigh no more pine till the wind [that >] of the morn;
Fall Moon, dark be the land,
Hushed be all water, till dawn is at hand![TN7]

The original manuscript continued with Bilbo's reaction to the elven singing:

'Well merry people' said Bilbo looking out. 'What time under [> by] the moon is this? Your lullaby would wake a drunken goblin. Yet I thank you.'

'And your snores would wake a stone dragon' [they answered. 'Yet for your >] 'Yet we thank you' they answered with laughter. 'It is but midnight; and you have slept now since early evening. Tomorrow perhaps you will be cured of weariness.'

'Maybe. A little sleep [goes >] does a great cure in the house of Elrond' said he. 'But I will take all I can get. Good night fair friends.' And he went back to bed, and slept till late morning.

Weariness fell from him soon in that house and he had many a merry jest and dance[TN8] with the elves of the valley. Yet even that place could not long delay him now. He thought ever of his home.[TN9]

In but [> After but] three days therefore he said farewell to Elrond and giving him many gifts of gold and receiving much he rode away on a fine morning with Gandalf.[TN10] But even as they left the valley the sky darkened behind them [> in the west] and wind and rain came up to meet them.

'Merry is may time' said Bilbo as the rain beat on his face 'but <?our> back is to legends and we are coming home. I suppose this is a first taste of home coming.'

'There is a long road yet' said Gandalf.

'[But >] Yet it is the last road' said Bilbo.

Soon they reached the ford in the river with the steep bank and down this they slithered.

Gandalf did not like the look of the river.

The river was somewhat swollen, and as they plunged in soon came above their feet as they sat their ponies. They were but halfway across when Bilbo's pony slipped on a stone and floundered into the water.[TN11]

Soon they were over the ford and had left the wild behind. At each stage in the road Bilbo recalled the happenings of a year ago (which now seemed so [far >] long ago).[TN12] It was not long before they came to where they had laid the troll-gold [*added*: they had hidden]. 'I have enough to last me my time' said Bilbo. '[This had better be >] You had better take this Gandalf.'

'Share and share alike' said Gandalf 'You may have more needs than you expect.' So they slung the bags [> gold in bags] upon the ponies and after that their going was slow, for most of the time they walked.

But the weather soon mended & as it drew near to June became warm and hot. The land was green and fair about them.

And as all things come at last to an end even this story a day came when they came to the mill by the river and passed the bridge and came right back to Bilbo's own door.[TN13]

'Bless me what is going on' said he! For there was a great commotion and people were thick round the door and many were coming and going in & out – not even wiping their feet as Bilbo noticed with disgust.

If he was surprized they were more surprized still. He had arrived back in the middle of an auction! Nearly all his things had [*added*:

already] been sold for little money or old songs and his cousins the Allibone Baggins[TN14] were busy measuring the rooms to see if their furniture would fit.

Bilbo in fact was 'Presumed Dead' and not everybody that said so was sorry to find the presumption wrong.

The return of Bilbo in fact created quite a [comm[otion] >] disturbance both under hill and across the water and was a great deal more than a nine days wonder.[TN15] The legal bother indeed lasted for months [> years]. It was a long time indeed before Mr Baggins was admitted to be alive, and even then, to save time, he had to buy back a lot of his own furniture. The Allibone Baggins never fully admitted it [added in pencil: that he was genuine], and at any rate they were never on speaking terms with him again.

Indeed Bilbo found he had lost <one> thing altogether – and that was his reputation.

[Nothing he > He was no longer res[pectable] >] It is true that for ever after he remained an elf-friend and had the honour of dwarves wizards and all such folk as ever passed his way; but he was no longer respectable.[TN16]

Indeed he was held by all the hobbits to be 'queer' – except his nephews & nieces[TN17] on the Took-side and even they were not encouraged in the friendship by their elders.

I am sorry to say he did not mind very much. [His sw[ord] >] He was perfectly happy [> quite content]; and the sound of his own kettle on the hearth was ever after more musical than it had been in the quiet days before the unexpected party.[TN18] His sword he hung on the mantlepiece. His armour was arranged on a stand in the hall [*added in pencil in left margin*: till he lent it to a museum]. His gold and silver was large[ly] [> mostly] spent in presents both useful and extravagant and his [*added*: invisible] ring was chiefly employed when unpleasant callers came.[TN19]

He took to writing poetry and visiting the elves and [<if> >] though many shook their heads and said 'poor old Baggins', and only few believed any of his tales, he remained perfectly happy to the end of his days and those were extraordinarily long.

At this point a line was drawn across the page and the rest of this manuscript page (Third Phase manuscript page 43 [> 44]; Marq. 1/1/20:6) cancelled. I give the original text here:

> One day [when >] long long after
>
> put in visit of Gandalf <here> news of dwarves
>
> So the prophecy came true?
>
> Yes of course – don't disbelieve in them because you helped to bring them about.

To this is added in hasty pencil:

> After all you don't really suppose [that you contrived all your adventures and all your escape[s] >] that all your adventures and all your escapes were <contrived> by you do you [> by you yourself]. You are a very [*added*: fine] person Mr Baggins & I am very fond of you, but you are only quite a little fellow in a wide world after all.
>
> Thank goodness said Bilbo.

All this material, forming as it does the rough draft for the brief epilogue was cancelled, and replaced by an additional sheet (Marq. 1/1/20:7–8) of fair copy text (Third Phase manuscript pages 45 and 45 [> 46]) written in a very neat hand:

One day [> autumn evening] long afterwards Bilbo was sitting in his study writing his memoirs – he thought of calling them 'There and Back Again'[TN20] – when there was a ring at the door.

It was Gandalf and a dwarf; and the dwarf was actually Balin.

'Come in, come in!' said Bilbo, and soon they were settled in chairs by his fire. If Balin noticed that Mr Baggins' waistcoat was more extensive (and had real gold buttons) he [> Bilbo] also noticed that Balin's beard was several inches longer, and his jewelled clothes [> belt] of great magnificence. They fell to talking of their times together of course, and Bilbo asked how things were going in the Lands of the Mountain. It seemed they were going very well.

Bard had rebuilt a town in Dale and men had gathered to him from the Lake and from South and West, and all the valley had become tilled again and rich, and the desolation was now filled with birds and blossom in spring and fruit and feasting in autumn. And Lake-town had been refounded more prosperous than ever, and much wealth went up and down the Running River; and there was friendship in those parts between elves and dwarves and men. The Master had come to a bad end; for Bard had sent much gold for the help of the lake-people, and being of the kind that [is >] easily catches such disease he fell under the dragon-sickness and took it [> the gold] and fled with it, and died of starvation in the waste. 'The new Master was [> is] of [more >] wiser kind,' said Balin 'and very popular; for of course he gets most of the credit of the present prosperity. They say that in his day the river runs with gold.'

'Then the prophecies of the old songs have [accidentally >] come all right by [*added*: happy] accident,' said Bilbo.

'Of course!' said Gandalf. 'How else would they come true? Surely you don't disbelieve the prophecies because you had a share in bringing them about yourself? After all you don't really suppose, do you, that all your adventures and all your wonderful escapes were managed by you yourself, do you? You are a very fine person, Mr Baggins, and I am very fond of you; but you are only quite a little fellow in a wide world, after all.'

'Thank goodness!' said Bilbo and pushed over the tobacco-jar.[TN21]

END

Roads go ever ever on
under [> over] rock and under tree
by caves where never sun has shone
by streams that never find the sea.

[R >] over grass and over stone
and under mountains in the moon
over snow by winter sown
and through the merry flowers of June[TN22]

Roads go ever ever on
under cloud and under sun [> star],
But [never >] <foot> <?hath> never never gone
Beyond the seas to <?Gondobar>[TN23]
[Yet feet that wandering have gone]
[turn at last to home afar.]

Eyes that [have >] fire and sword have seen
and terror walking in the wild[TN24]
Look at last on meadows green
and trees and hills they long have known.[TN25]

* * * * *

This represents the end of the composite typescript/manuscript of the completed story (i.e., the Third Phase) which Tolkien reached in December 1932 or, more likely, January 1933, loaning it to C. S. Lewis by February. For more on its 'wander[ing] about' over the next three and a half years, see page 635. For the well-known story of how the book came to Allen & Unwin's attention and the subsequent stages that led to its acceptance and publication, see Carpenter (*Tolkien: A Biography*, pages 180–1), Anderson (DAA.12–13, including a facsimile of ten-year-old Rayner Unwin's reader's report on DAA.14), Hammond (*Descriptive Bibliography*, pages 7–8), and especially Elaine Griffith's account.[TN26]

It is probable, however, that this had not been Allen & Unwin's first contact with Tolkien. The project which Dagnall travelled to Oxford to pick up from Griffiths on the day that she was persuaded by Griffiths, who had not actually yet done the promised work, to ask to borrow Professor Tolkien's 'frightfully good' story rather than return to London empty-handed, was probably the Clark Hall *Beowulf*. This prose translation[TN27] had originally been published in 1901 by Swan Sonnenschein, a firm that had later [1911] merged with George Allen & Sons, which in turn had been acquired [1914] by young Stanley Unwin and renamed George Allen & Unwin. Although reprinted in 1911 and popular among students who wanted to avoid actually reading *Beowulf* in the original (an attitude Tolkien deplored), it now badly needed updating, and Stanley Unwin or one of his staff (e.g., Charles Furth) seems to have approached Tolkien to see if he would undertake the job (see Hammond, *Descriptive Bibliography*, page 296, who dates this contact to 'probably in early or mid-1936).[TN28] Tolkien, who expresses a low opinion of Clark Hall's translation in his own Prefatory Remarks to the eventual reprint (Clark Hall, page xv), declined the job (possibly because he had already translated *Beowulf* himself into both verse and prose) but with typical generosity seems to have recommended his former graduate student, Elaine Griffiths, for the job. Griffiths eventually proved unequal to the task (throughout her long career she published very little, concentrating her energies instead on teaching) and two years later the project reverted back to Tolkien, who passed it along to fellow Inkling Charles Wrenn; Wrenn completed the work within a year and the revised edition, with Tolkien's essay on Old English prosody, appeared in 1940. An updated version followed in 1950 that was still being reprinted thirty years later (Hammond, page 299), though its longevity owes far more to the presence of Tolkien's essay than the quality of Clark Hall's translation or Wrenn's notes.

The acceptance, publication, and success of *The Hobbit* quickly led to Allen & Unwin's decision to publish more Tolkien: *Mr. Bliss* (with the proviso that he needed to redraw the pictures into a more easily, and cheaply, reproducible format), *Farmer Giles of Ham* (as soon as he could flesh out the volume with the addition of similar stories), and most of all a sequel to *The Hobbit* (as soon as he could write it). They probably envisioned the latter either as stories about Bilbo's further adventures, rather like Lofting's Dr. Dolittle books – to which Tolkien objected that 'he remained very happy to the end of his days, and those were extraordinarily long' (DAA.361) left very little wiggle room for further exploits (cf. *Letters* p. 38) – or else as a series of stories each about a different hobbit, which is in fact what they eventually got. In the event all these projects were delayed in their publication for many years, but within three months of *The Hobbit*'s publication in September 1937 Tolkien had begun work on 'The New Hobbit', which at one point he thought of calling *The Magic Ring* (a handwritten title-page bearing this title survives among the papers at Marquette, Marq. 3/1/2:2). Eventually the sequel, far from being the thinner repetition of Bilbo's adventure he had feared ('For nearly all the "motives" [i.e., motifs] that I can use were packed into the original book' – *Letters* p. 38) was such an engrossing project that it took him fourteen years to complete, and picked up on all the unanswered questions from the earlier book – Gollum, the ring, the Necromancer, Moria, et al. (the chief exception being no mention of Beorn's earlier history), as well as elements from *The Lost Road*, the 1937 *Quenta Silmarillion*, Tolkien's 'fairy poetry', his scholarly work, &c., until it became the definitive masterpiece of his subcreated world.

More importantly from the point of view of *The Hobbit*, *The Lord of the Rings* turned out to be quite different from its predecessor, although clearly linked to it in story, style, and characters. And as his ideas developed Tolkien came to reject some of what was said in the original book, particularly in the crucial encounter with Gollum. Once he had established that Bilbo's ring inspired possessiveness even beyond what the Arkenstone (and, earlier yet, the Silmarils) evoked, the idea that Gollum honestly intended to give Bilbo his ring when he lost the riddle-game became untenable. At first Tolkien decided to reveal in *The Lord of the Rings* that the account that appeared in *The Hobbit* was not what actually happened, and he had Gandalf recount the true story in the new book. Eventually, however, he realized that it would be a simpler solution if he could actually alter what was said in the first book, which would have the added benefit of not casting his earlier book into the status of unreliable narrative. Accordingly, in 1944 he drafted replacement text for a large portion of Chapter V: Riddles in the Dark, and in 1947 sent it off to Allen & Unwin to see if they thought inserting it into the next printing would be feasible. Due to a miscommunication (see Hammond, *Descriptive Bibliography*, pages 22–3, and *Letters* p. 120–4) Tolkien thought the publisher had decided not to make the change and so was taken by surprise when three years later in 1950 he was sent proofs for the next printing which incorporated his replacement text (*Letters* p. 141). This of course became the second edition of 1951, the form of the story that has been familiar to readers ever since. For the complete text of this new material Tolkien sent Allen & Unwin in 1947, the Fourth Phase of his work on the book, see the section beginning on page 729.

TEXT NOTES

1 Tolkien's note to himself here refers to page 28 of the First Typescript (Marq.1/1/53:3), corresponding to page 113 in Chapter III of this book. This is yet another piece of evidence that the First Typescript for chapters I through XII and part of XIV, replacing the bulk of the Second Phase text, already existed before the Third Phase manuscript was written.

2 Elf-maiden: This is the only reference to female elves within *The Hobbit*, aside from the (cancelled) mention of (Lúthien) Tinúviel.

3 The poem as we have it here is a fair copy obviously preceded by drafting that does not survive. It strongly resembles the version published in the book, the main variance being, as any comparison soon shows, that the three stanzas appear in reverse order in the manuscript from how they appear in the typescript and published book (the typescript text – 1/1/69:1–2 – being exactly that which saw print). Tolkien later numbered the stanzas from top to bottom '3', '2', and '1' respectively in pencil in the left margin, indicating that the decision to reverse their sequence belongs not to the Third Phase but a somewhat later stage of work on the book, the period of the completion of the typescript (summer-autumn 1936).

Aside from the re-sequencing of the stanzas, Tolkien also made a few other changes. The line 'Here is yet growing' near the end I have treated as a miscopying from the lost draft for an intended 'Here *grass* is yet growing', since the line is otherwise short one syllable; in any case, Tolkien altered it in contemporary ink to read 'Here *grass* is *still* growing'. In the final line (sans chorus) of the poem, 'and elves are all singing', he underlined the words are singing and wrote 'are yet/ at their' in the right margin. This I take as offering two variant revisions, so that instead of 'and elves *are yet at their* singing', which is euphonious but metrically irregular, he was weighing the respective merits of 'and elves *are yet* singing' versus 'and elves *at their* singing'; comparison with the typescript and published book (DAA.[355]) show he decided upon the former.

In addition to these changes on the manuscript itself, between the fair copy manuscript and the typescript 'So cease from your roaming' (line 8 in the middle stanza) became 'So why go a-roaming?'. The slight indentation of every other line was abandoned, and the chorus elaborated somewhat, especially in the final refrain. So that instead of 'Come' being repeated three times we instead get 'Come! . . .', 'O! . . .', and 'With . . .', followed in the last case with an additional flourish of fa-la-las.

4 These last two sentences were cancelled, leaving the second one (an attempt to pick up a loose thread from Plot Notes F) unfinished. The rest of the paragraph was extensively revised and supplemented with marginal additions until it read as follows:

> So he learned that Gandalf had been to a council of *many magicians and wise and learned men masters of lore and beneficial wizardry [> white wizardry]*; and that the Necromancer had *at last* been driven from his hold in the south of Mirkwood, and had fled to other lands. 'The North is freed from that horror for many an age' said G. 'yet I wish he were banished from the world'.

It is remarkable to find Tolkien using the word 'magician' in a favorable context; cf. his more usual negative associations with the term in *On Fairy-Stories* (OFS.15 & 49) and *Letters* (page 200), and indeed the phrase 'magicians and' was cancelled in ink. The presence of enough wizards and magicians to form a council is less surprising: Tolkien's early work was filled with wizards, from *The Book of Lost Tales*' Tû the wizard ('Gilfanon's Tale', BLT I.232–3) to the *Father Christmas Letters*' Man in the Moon, Father Christmas himself, and presumably Fr. Christmas's Green Brother as well, to *Roverandom*'s same Man in the Moon, Psamathos Psamathides the sand-sorcerer, and Artaxerxes the wandering wizard. The idea that Middle-earth in the Third Age had only five wizards (Saruman, Gandalf, Radagast, and the two Blue Wizards of the east), none of whom are human, was like the concept of the Third Age itself a much later development; cf. HME VIII.64 & 67, the essay 'The Istari' in *Unfinished Tales* (UT.388–402), and 'The Five Wizards' (HME XII.384–5). Tolkien's final thoughts on this 'council of good wizards' transformed it in *The Lord of the Rings* into the White Council, composed of three wizards (Saruman the White, Gandalf the Grey, and Radagast the Brown) and the most powerful of the Elves (Galadriel of Lothlórien, Elrond of Rivendell, Círdan of the Havens, and a few others who are not identified but probably included Glorfindel; cf. *LotR*.61, 267–8, & 376 and 'Of the Rings of Power and the Third Age'; *Silm*.299–300).

Thus, while it is clear from the various Plot Notes that mere dramatic necessity required the wizard to leave Thorin and Company to their own devices for most of the second half of the story and that Tolkien had no particular idea of what the wizard was doing in the meantime (cf. Plot Notes A, page 296),† Tolkien's ultimate decision regarding what Gandalf had been up to evolved from a neat tying up of loose ends in the original *Hobbit* to have significant ramifications in the sequel. Ultimately, of course, it proved untrue (or at least premature) that 'the North [was] freed from that horror for many an age', since during the War of the Ring there was war in Mirkwood ('long battle under the trees and great ruin of fire' – *LotR*.1131), an invasion that occupied Dale (and presumably Esgaroth), and a second deadlier Siege of the Lonely Mountain that ended in the deaths of both the Lord of Dale and the King under the Mountain (ibid.), so it was not until the beginning of the Fourth Age some eighty years later, at the very end of Bilbo's extraordinarily long life, that Gandalf's prediction comes true.

†He never does provide any explanation of the means by which Gandalf reaches the far side of Mirkwood; presumably, given his aversion to entering the forest itself (see page 243), he rode not through but around the great forest by the south once Sauron had been defeated.

5 Compare the account of the Cottage of Lost Play, wherein Eriol hears all the stories that were to make up *The Book of Lost Tales* (BLT I.13ff).

6 Changed in pencil to 'Many elves were singing clear beside the river below his window'.

7 This earliest surviving text of the poem ('Sing All Ye Joyful') is a careful fair copy, clearly preceded by drafting that does not survive. Aside from changes in capitalization, punctuation, and indentation, all its lines are

identical to the published version, but the sequence of the last four was shifted:

Sigh no more Pine, till the wind of the morn!
Fall Moon! Dark be the land!
Hush! Hush! Oak, Ash, and Thorn!
Hushed be all water, till dawn is at hand!

Their re-arrangement was a late change, since the original sequence occurs in both the continuation of the First Typescript (1/1/69:2–3) and the corresponding page from the Second Typescript (1/1/50:3), both made in 1936.

The only other notable feature of this poem is its reference to the moon being 'in flower'. Rather than a poetical conceit of a piece with the flowering stars, this may be an allusion back to 'The Tale of the Sun and Moon', where the Moon was formed from the last blossom of Silpion the Silver Tree (BLT I.191).

8 It is perhaps an indicator of the change in Bilbo brought about by his adventures that whereas at the end of Chapter III he goes 'to see the elves dance and sing' (page 116), now he joins in with their dancing.

9 Added here in pencil are the words 'B.'s first poem'. This refers of course to 'Roads Go Ever Ever On', which Tolkien apparently considered inserting at this point. For more on this, the third interpolated poem in this final chapter, see Text Note 13 below.

10 Added at this point, mostly in the left margin:

> Each was on a pony and they led also a third [> another] laden with many things – including Bilbo's little treasure chests.

This was apparently added to set up a scene a few paragraphs later wherein Bilbo's treasure would be swept away during a river-crossing; see Text Note 11.

11 The three preceding paragraphs, which would have culminated in Bilbo's pack pony losing the treasure in the rushing water (see the first line of Plot Notes F: 'Bilbo's treasure all lost on the way home'), were all cancelled in the manuscript (Third Phase manuscript page 41 [> 42]; 1/1/20:4). The word 'pony' is changed to 'pack-pony' in the last line, and there is a cancelled partial word, 'wh', after 'the steep bank'; I suspect that Tolkien began to write 'wh*ere*' – that is, where they had trouble with the ponies just before meeting the trolls on the outward journey. At any rate, this is clearly the same river described in Chapter II, as Tolkien makes explicit in the typescript: 'They came to the river that marked the very edge of the borderland of the Wild, and to the ford beneath the steep bank, which you may remember' (Marq.1/1/69:3; cf. DAA.358). It may be significant that when Tolkien returned to re-envision *The Hobbit* in 1960, the first new scene he inserted into the story dealt with Bilbo's troubles at a river-crossing; perhaps the idea of this abandoned scene stayed in his mind for the almost thirty years that intervened.

12 The one-year's journey of the published book is finally unambiguously in effect, as opposed to the longer time-frame of the original (Second Phase) draft; cf. Bilbo's remark about may-time a few lines earlier. '. . . so long ago' was later altered to 'ten <illegible> at least'; the illegible word does not look like *years* but might possibly be *may*[s] – i.e., that ten Mays rather than just one have passed since he was last here.

13 At the bottom of this page (Third Phase manuscript page 41 [> 42]; Marq. 1/1/20:4), immediately below this paragraph, Tolkien has added in hasty pencil

> and could see the woods upon the Hill. The[n] Bilbo
> stopped & said suddenly – the poem
> 'Something is the matter with you Bilbo' said G.
> 'You are not the hobbit you were.'
> And so they passed

– i.e., 'passed *the bridge and came right back to Bilbo's own door*'. The poem alluded to here (see also Text Note 9 above) is 'Roads Go Ever Ever On'; see part five of the commentary following this chapter, beginning on page 723.

Note that it is still the Mill (clearly to be seen in the foreground of all Tolkien's versions of the Hobbiton illustration; cf. Plate IV [top]), which is the landmark here and not the Green Man or the Green Dragon Inn.

14 The original name of Bilbo's cousins, the Allibone Baggins, was altered to *Sackville* Baggins in pencil here and *Sackville*-Baggins (that is, with the hyphen) two paragraphs later; this change probably dates to the period of the book's preparation for publication in 1936, and the latter form appears in the typescript (1/1/69:5). I am unable to explain the exact significance of 'Allibone', which probably originated not as part of their surname but in reference to a place (i.e., to distinguish between the *Allibone* Bagginses and the *Bag-End* Bagginses). Certainly it seems unlikely that Tolkien here was alluding to any real person with this name, such as Samuel Austin Allibone (a leading figure in the Sunday School movement and compiler of the *Critical Dictionary of English Literature and British and American Authors* [1854 & 1871]), journalist and travel/nature writer Thomas Allibone Janvier [d.1913], or physicist T. E. Allibone (a much younger colleague of Rutherford), just as *Sackville* almost certainly derives not from the Elizabethan poet Thomas Sackville (*A Mirror for Magistrates*, *Gorboduc*) nor literary personality V. Sackville-West (a friend of Virginia Woolf's) but rather is simply as T. A. Shippey points out a comic variant between *sack* and *bag*: *Sack*ville vs. *Bag*gins (*The Road to Middle-earth*, expanded edition [2003], page 72). Rather, I would argue that 'Allibone' is a variant of *Alboin*, the name Tolkien gave one of the two main characters in his time-travel story *The Lost Road* [circa 1936] in which one of the main characters states 'at school . . . they call me All-bone' (HME V.37). If so, its application to Bilbo's stay-at-home relatives is deeply ironic, for *Alboin* is the sixth-century Lombardic equivalent of the Old English *Ælfwine*

or 'Elf-friend',† and it is Bilbo rather than his cousins who has earned such a title.

†For more on Alboin the Lombard, a Germanic prince whose people gave their name to Italy's Lombardy region, see Christopher Tolkien's commentary on *The Lost Road*, HME V.53–5.

15 The very first page of the earliest draft of the sequel puts the matter nicely: '[Bilbo] had disappeared after breakfast one April 30th and not reappeared until lunchtime on June 22nd in the following year' (HME VI.13). As an encapsulation of his hobbit neighbors' point of view, this can hardly be bettered. According to the typescript of this final chapter (1/1/69:5) Bilbo returned home on June 2nd; this was changed to June 22nd in the page proofs (1/2/2: page 306).

16 The statement that among Bilbo's visitors in later years were *wizards* (note the plural) remains even in the most recent texts of the published book although the later conception makes it extremely unlikely that Radagast or Saruman, not to mention either of the long-missing Blue Wizards, dropped by during the years following Bilbo's return.

17 Just as with the 'lads *and lasses*' whom Bladorthin/Gandalf encouraged to go off and have their own adventures, we hear very little about Bilbo's nieces in the sequel; a few who would probably qualify for the title in the looser sense used in *The Lord of the Rings* appear or are referred to briefly (Caramella Took,† Angelica Baggins, Melilot Brandybuck, Pearl Took††) but play no role in the main story.

†HME VI.15. ††Cf. *Letters* page 295.

18 This is the first usage in the manuscript of the phrase that would give its name to the first chapter of the book, but it had already occurred in the First Typescript for Chapter XI:

> they used to call the little grassy space between the wall and the opening the 'doorstep' in fun, remembering Bilbo's words long ago at the unexpected party in his hobbit-hole
>
> —typescript page 113; Marq. 1/1/61:4.

19 At this point Tolkien started a new paragraph and wrote 'It was one of his jokes to put it on and open the door and if' but left the sentence unfinished and cancelled it. Cf. Bingo's tricks with Farmer Maggot in early drafts of 'A Short Cut to Mushrooms' (HME VI.96–7 & 292–3).

20 This marks the first appearance of the phrase that later became the book's subtitle.

21 In this final line 'pushed over' remained the reading in both typescripts (1/1/69:6 and 1/1/50:7), not being changed to 'handed him' until the page proofs (1/2/2: page 310), probably to avoid readers thinking that Bilbo had accidentally knocked the jar over.

22 These four lines were re-sequenced by Tolkien, who wrote the numbers 3, 4, 1, and 2, respectively, in the left margin alongside them, shifting the lines to the order they have in the typescript version of this poem and the published book (DAA.359).

23 These last two lines, which seem to have formed the original conclusion of the poem, were cancelled in ink. The two lines that follow ('Yet feet . . . to home afar'), which I have bracketed and slightly indented here to set them apart, are written in ink over pencil underwriting, indicating a pause in composition before these replacements were drafted. The final four lines that follow the replacement lines have no such underwriting.

Unfortunately, the two highly interesting cancelled lines – with their parallel of 'never never gone' for journeys not taken with the 'ever ever on' of those that are now coming to an end – are in parts nearly illegible; the final *-h* of <?hath> is particularly dubious. Similarly, the word or words that end the next line could also be read '*find the bar*', which might be an allusion to the old notion of 'crossing the bar', made famous by Tennyson's poem of the same name ('Crossing the Bar', [1889]), with its imagery of sailing beyond the world into eternity; Tolkien had already used similar phrasing in the final stanza of his poem 'The Nameless Land' [written 1924, published 1927]; cf. Text Note 20 following Chapter XVII (page 675) and HME V.100.

On the other hand, if I am correct in reading this final, nearly illegible series of ligatures as 'Gondobar', then we have here another reference to the city more commonly known as *Gondolin*, one of the great elven kingdoms of the legendarium, which had already been mentioned by Elrond in Chapter III. At first glance its reappearance here might seem rather unlikely, but this variant of the name was particularly associated with Tolkien's poetry about voyaging to the Undying Land and glimpsing Tol Eressëa, as in the revised version of 'The Nameless Land' retitled 'The Song of Ælfwine', the two texts of which seem to date from circa 1936 and circa 1945, respectively:

> *O! Haven where my heart would be!*
> the waves that beat upon thy bar
> *For ever echo endlessly,*
> *when longing leads my thoughts afar,*
> *And rising west of West I see*
> *beyond the world the wayward Star,*
> Than beacons bright in Gondobar
> *more clear and keen, more fair and high . . .*
>
> —'The Song of Ælfwine', 1936 version, lines 51–58; emphasis mine†

and the later version of 'The Happy Mariners' [circa 1940]:

> *O happy mariners upon a journey far,*
> *beyond the grey islands and past Gondobar,*
> *to those great portals on the final shores . . .*
>
> —lines 23–25; HME II.275.††

†See HME.V.100–104.

††See also Christopher Tolkien's commentary HME II.274 and HME.V.104.

24 This line was partially cancelled and replaced by 'And [terror >] horror in the halls of stone', written at the end of the poem and marked for insertion at this point.

25 The text of this poem, which is given the pencilled title 'Bilbo's first poem', appears on a separate piece of paper (I/I/3I) meant to be inserted into the final chapter somewhere around page 690; Tolkien wrote '41' in pencil in the upper right corner, making this the third 'page 41' in the Third Phase manuscript.† Its actual placement wavered; first Tolkien thought to insert it just before Bilbo's departure from Rivendell (see Text Note 9), then instead to give it on Bilbo's doorstep (see Text Note 13). Ultimately it is given its final placement, just as Bilbo glimpses 'his own Hill in the distance', in the first typescript (I/I/69:4); cf. DAA.359. Given his uncertainty, I have thought it best to offer it here as an appropriate coda for the story as a whole.

†The others being in the main Third Phase text just before the middle of the final chapter (numbered '40 > 41'; I/I/20:3) and also the page bearing the inserted poem 'Sing All Ye Joyful' (numbered '<?top> 39 > 40 > 41').

26 Griffiths' (oral) account was initially broadcast as part of Ann Bonsor's 1974 Radio BBC Oxford tribute to Tolkien (produced by Humphrey Carpenter), along with other memoirs of Tolkien by friends (e.g., Nevill Coghill) and family; a transcription of Griffiths' contribution is reprinted in *The Annotated Hobbit* (DAA.12) and the original audiotrack was incorporated into Brian Sibley's *J.R.R. Tolkien: An Audio Portrait* (BBC [2001]) as part of CD 1, track 12.

27 Not to be confused with Clark Hall's 'Metrical' (verse) translation, published in 1914 and again in 1926 by Cambridge University Press.

28 That Allen & Unwin would contact an author they had never worked with before out of the blue like this to see if he was interested in undertaking a project for them was not unprecedented; coming across E. R. Eddison's translation of *Egil's Saga* (Cambridge University Press, [1930]), Stanley Unwin wrote to him asking if he would be interested in translating more sagas for Allen & Unwin. Engrossed in his own creative work, Eddison declined, but the episode shows Unwin's willingness to seek out potential authors and scholars rather than wait for them to come to him. This correspondence is now in the Bodleian (Ms. Eng. Misc. e 456/1, fol. 123 & 124).

(i)
Dain son of Nain

One of the most appealing of all Tolkien's dwarven characters, Dain of the Iron Hills plays a small but crucial role in *The Hobbit*, essentially stepping in to fulfill Thorin's role after Thorin is no longer capable of doing so himself, first because he succumbed to dragon-sickness and then because of his death. That Thorin was to die was a late development, not present at all in the Second Phase: there is no hint of it in any of the Plot Notes, and clear indication to the contrary as late as Bilbo's discussion with Thorin after the battle in Plot Notes D. Even when Tolkien concluded that Bilbo would be unable to resolve the crisis and lift the siege without a battle (Plot Notes F), the idea of bringing a dwarven army to the scene was one of the last plot-points to emerge: no such army is described as playing a part in the Plot Notes B/C/D sequence or Plot Notes E, and their listing among the seven forces present in Plot Notes F could mean just the thirteen members of Thorin & Company; in any case the word 'dwarves' on that list is circled in pencil, as if for removal or further development: Dain himself nowhere appears until the Third Phase. Like Bard (or, later, Arwen in *The Lord of the Rings*), Dain is a character Tolkien introduces abruptly to fill a specific plot-function – in this case, to bring a dwarven army to the fight at the Mountain – but with his usual keen eye to potentialities, once the character is present Tolkien makes good use of him. Nothing in fact anticipates Thorin's death scene in the original manuscript until Gandalf actually ushers Bilbo into the dying dwarvenking's tent, but once Tolkien had made the surprising decision to drive home the cost of victory with the tragic but heroic death of the second most important character in the book,[1] he needed someone else to fill Thorin's role as the new King under the Mountain, dealing out treasure and restoring the lost realm so that the prophecies could come true.

In a sense, Dain is to Thorin as Faramir is to Boromir in *The Lord of the Rings*: the close kinsman who avoids the fall from grace of his elder. Even Gandalf at one point describes himself after his return as Gandalf the White as being Saruman as he was supposed to be ('The White Rider', *LotR*.516). It is easy, in retrospect, to forget Thorin's or Boromir's virtues even after their heroic deaths and dying renunciations of their misdeeds, but an unprejudiced reading of the First Phase and Second Phase *Hobbit* (and indeed the bulk of the published book, right up to the dwarves' discussion of the treasure at the end of Chapter XII) shows Thorin as a capable leader, fair in his judgments, determined to leave none behind, and courageous (although not to the point of being willing to beard the dragon who destroyed his people in its lair). Dain is all this and more: Thorin as he is meant to be, who either because of the example of Thorin's fall before him or more likely because of an unshakable bedrock of good sense and a lack of *ofermod* (again, cf. Faramir's ability to avoid repeating Boromir's mistakes) is able to resist the dragon-sickness. Dain deals out the treasure fairly, keeps his bargains, and establishes good relations with his neighbors – all the things Thorin should have done and that we like Bilbo expected him to do based on our experience of him prior to his glimpsing the dragon-gold. The good effects of King Dain's reign are already apparent by the time of the Epilogue – a brief glance ahead ten years that enables us to see the fulfillment of Thorin's dream to re-establish the Kingdom under the Mountain as a thriving dwarven haven for Durin's Folk at peace with its neighbors and no longer surrounded by desolation – and Glóin in 'Many Meetings' (*LotR* Bk II Ch. I) gives a glowing report of their progress in the decades since.

That Thorin's heir proves to be a new character, Dain, and not one of Thorin's companions – say, his second-in-command Balin or perhaps Fili and Kili, already established as his great-nephews – might have surprised some readers among whom Tolkien circulated the original version of the story (e.g., C. S. Lewis), especially since *Beowulf*, which had a marked influence on the closing chapters, provided the parallel of an old king dying and being succeeded by a relatively unknown much younger kinsman. But the two young dwarves' descent is through the female line, being the grandsons of Thorin's sister (the sons of his sister in the published text and later family trees), whereas the patriarchal dwarves obviously trace the kingship through the male line; it is indeed possible that the deaths of Fili and Kili were added to the story during the typescript stage precisely to avoid such confusion. Then too whereas strict patrilineal descent became the norm during feudalism (with sometimes disastrous results when a small child inherited the throne and left a country with a decade or two of regencies while he grew up), in the 'heroic' cultures that preceded feudalism a closely-related capable adult male (brother, uncle, nephew) often succeeded instead of a son.[2] As Thorin's first cousin,[3] the battle-hardened Dain, who proved himself a loyal kinsman by coming at once to Thorin's aid and who had already accomplished heroic deeds in killing Bolg's father in the goblin war, is obviously an eminently suitable candidate to re-establish the Kingdom under the Mountain.

For all his importance to the resolution of the story, however, Dain remains almost entirely in the background, his words and deeds reported at second hand. Despite this, like so many of Tolkien's 'minor' characters his personality and character come across clearly, revealing him as the most sensible and ultimately quite possibly the most fortunate of all Tolkien's dwarves (with the exception of the legendary Durin and possibly also of Gimli Glóinson in his later career as described in the Appendices of *The Lord of the Rings*). We know he proves to be an excellent king and have already noted his fairness in sharing out treasure (the *sine qua non* for being a great king or 'ring-giver' according to the Anglo-Saxon heroic code – at least according to the surviving poetry);[4] that his generosity and sense of fair-play go beyond merely keeping his word or fulfilling Thorin's bargains is shown by his giving Bard the Necklace of Girion, clearly a fabulous treasure, above and beyond the one-fourteenth share that was supposed to settle Bard's claim on the treasure. His chief defining characteristics seem to have been an unshakable practicality, a keen appreciation of his own limits, and willingness to aggressively defend a good cause. In the later story ('Durin's Folk', *LotR* Appendix A part iii) he answers Thrain's call to avenge Thror's murder and fights heroically at Moria, killing Bolg's father (clearly a great feat, even within the context of the original *Hobbit*, since Gandalf has heard of it) but stops short of over-reaching and prevents Thrain from re-claiming Moria since the peril that originally drove them from Durin's halls remains (i.e., the Balrog). Similarly, within *The Hobbit* he comes at once to aid Thorin but does not hesitate to ally with the Elvenking and Bard when the goblins arrive, nor to drop old grudges and negotiate a fair peace after the battle. Later (*LotR*.257–8) he allows Balin to found his own dwarf-colony, despite his personal misgivings, which prove to have been fully justified. At one point Tolkien even considered making him the keeper of one of the dwarven Rings of Power (HME VI.398); although this proved to be only a passing thought it shows his high regard for the character. And Dain is wise enough to resist temptation when Sauron sends messengers with promises of Rings of Power and, unlike his ally King Brand, to realize that attempts to appease the Dark Lord are useless; instead he sends warnings to Bilbo and representatives to the Council of Elrond. One could argue that Gimli goes with the Fellowship not just as a representative of dwarves in general but as one of Dain's folk, the people of Durin, in particular.

As Tolkien eventually developed him, Dain thus plays a large role in the history of his people throughout the last two and a half centuries of the Third Age, contributing in no small part to their survival into the Fourth Age through a remarkable career on a par with those of Thorin and Balin: fighting heroically at Moria when young and killing the leader of the goblin army, thus personally avenging Thror's murder ('held a great feat, for Dáin was then only a stripling in the reckoning of the Dwarves' – *LotR*.1112), leading one of the namesake armies in The Battle of Five Armies (where victory enables him to re-establish the Kingdom under the Mountain with the survivors), and finally dying heroically in War of the Ring fighting over the body of his fallen friend defending the Front Gate from Sauron's armies (*LotR*.1116; 'The Quest of Erebor', *Unfinished Tales*, page 326). Even more important was his maintenance of a safe haven for Durin's Folk first in the Iron Hills and then later in the Lonely Mountain, since we are told 'It is because of the fewness of women among them that the kind of the Dwarves increases slowly, and is in peril when they have no secure dwellings' (*LotR*.1116), especially when we juxtapose this with Thrain and Thorin's group in the Blue Hills whose numbers were apparently few and increased only very slowly, a fact directly linked to the statement that 'They had very few women-folk' (ibid. 1113), Thorin's sister Dís being a rare exception.

Since we do not know how old Dain was supposed to be in the original story, we cannot say whether he like Thror, Thrain, Thorin, and Balin was a survivor of Smaug's attack or whether he was born in the Iron Hills after the event; from the lack of any statement to the contrary it seems probable that in the original conception the Iron Hills settlement was founded by refugees from Erebor, whereas in the later story the colony in the Iron Hills had been founded by Thror's brother (Grór) at the time the dwarves were driven out of the far North (i.e., the Grey Mountains) long before Dain's birth (*LotR*.1109 & 1117), meaning that Dain was certainly born there and was still a small child (only three years old) when Smaug destroyed Thror's nearby kingdom. In this later story, most of the survivors of the catastrophe join Grór in the Iron Hills ('It was afterwards learned that more of the Folk under the Mountain had escaped than was at first hoped; but most of these went to the Iron Hills' – *LotR*.1110), and it is clear that the Iron Hills settlement was the largest and most thriving community of the Longbeards, much larger than Thorin's smaller halls in the distant Blue Hills. For example, Thorin dreams in 'The Quest of Erebor' (*Unfinished Tales*, page 322) of raising a dwarven army to reclaim his lost kingdom but is advised by Gandalf to take only a small trustworthy group, whereas in the original story there is nothing to contradict the conclusion that the Heir of Durin can only manage to gather a band of a dozen followers; by contrast Dain at short notice can bring five hundred warriors to the spot.[5]

Finally, there is the matter of Dain's name, nomenclature always being important in Tolkien's stories. Like the rest of *The Hobbit*'s dwarves (with the possible exception of Balin, already noted), Dain and his father both take their names from the *Dvergatal*; although they do not appear in all manuscripts of the *Voluspá* (see Dronke, pages 10 & 90) they are both in Snorri's list (*Prose Edda* page 41). However, unlike most of these dwarf-names, Dain's name also appears elsewhere, in a variety of different contexts and applications, some rather puzzling. Thus while we are told in *Heidreks Saga*[6] that Tyrfing, a cursed sword which must kill somebody every time it is unsheathed, was made by the dwarfs *Durin* and *Dvalin* (i.e., Tolkien's 'Dwalin'), Snorri in the *Skáldskaparmál* tells a very similar story of a sword called *Dainslaf* ('Dain's heirloom'), used in the Endless Battle between Hedin and Högni (*Prose Edda* page 121);[7] the sword's title implies that 'Dain' was recognized in Norse lore as a famous dwarven maker of weapons. Oddly enough, another of the *Elder Edda*'s poems, the *Hávamál*,[8] tells of another Dain who is the king of elves:

> *Odin for the Æsir [gods], Dain for the elves,*
> *Dvalin for the dwarfs,*
> *Asvid for the giants . . .*
>
> —*Hávamál*, stanza 143; Terry, *Poems of the Elder Edda*, page 31.

We are also told, in the *Gylfaginning*, that the World-Tree Yggdrasil has four harts living in its branches, named Dáin, Dvalin, Duneyr, and

Durathrór (*Prose Edda*, page 45). By contrast, I have found no other references to *Nain*, a name which neither Dronke nor Young translates but which probably means 'near' (cf. E. V. Gordon, *An Introduction to Old Norse*, page 371), although it is certainly a remarkable coincidence that *nain* is actually the French word for 'dwarf' (e.g., cf. Madame D'Aulnoy's 1698 fairy tale *Le Nain Jaune*, translated into English as 'The Yellow Dwarf'). While the scattered references to Dain in the Old Norse sources do not seem to cohere into a single figure, someone who like Tolkien was creating a new mythology out of the incoherent fragments of lost myth[9] might well have concluded that the original Dain had once been a figure of some significance, associated in some way with kingship and with those famous dwarves Durin and Dvalin, but whose story had been wholly lost.

NOTES

1 As the leader of the expedition, Thorin has more lines of dialogue than any other character except Bilbo, and he is present through far more chapters than, say, Gandalf. At first Thorin's sudden death – shocking within the traditions of classic British children's fantasy (e.g., Carroll, Grahame, Milne, Lofting, Nesbit)† – would seem to reverse Tolkien's theory of eucatastrophe, the sudden unexpected happy ending to the tale, but in fact the eagles' arrival that turns the tide serves as the eucatastrophe that makes *The Hobbit* a successful fairy-story within Tolkien's own conception of the genre. Thorin's death, and the later addition of those of Fili and Kili, serve rather to ground the eucatastrophe and prevent the book from being 'escapist' in a negative sense: in Tolkien's terms they confirm 'the existence of *dyscatastrophe*, of sorrow and failure: the possibility of these is necessary to the joy of deliverance; [eucatastrophe] denies (in the face of much evidence, if you will) universal final defeat' (OFS.62).

†MacDonald, who shared the late Victorian sentimentality over early death, is the chief and notable exception to this rule, but Thorin's death is quite unlike anything in MacDonald except perhaps the death-in-combat of the narrator of *Phantastes* [1858], and even there the author's interest is primarily in the character's first-person description of what happens to him immediately following his death.

2 See for instance in *Beowulf*, where Beowulf is offered the throne after his uncle Hygelac's death but insists it go to his young cousin, Hygelac's son, instead. Similar non-direct successions can be found in sources as widely ranged as *Hamlet* (based on Saxo Grammaticus's twelfth-century *Geste Danorum*), where Prince Hamlet is passed over for his father's throne in favor of his uncle Claudius, the early history of Islam (where Mohammad is succeeded as the first caliph by his father-in-law, not by his closest male relative, his cousin and son-in-law), and English history, which especially in early Norman times provides all too many examples.

3 That is, if I am right in my guess that Thrain and Nain were brothers in Tolkien's original conception; see Text Note 13 following chapter XVII. Already by the time of the earliest family tree in the late 1940s Thorin and Dain had become the children of cousins – that is, third cousins or as hobbits would no doubt say each was the other's 'second cousin once removed', descendants of a common great-grandfather – which they remained thereafter; see HME XII.277 and *LotR*.1117. For the idea of Thorin having close kin somewhere in the area that he could call upon in extremity, see his remark to the Great Goblin in Chapter IV: 'We [are] on a journey to our relatives, our nephews and nieces and first, second, and third cousins and other descendents of our grandfathers who live on the East side of these truly hospitable mountains' (page 132); this passage contains the first germ that eventually led to Dain and his band of five hundred hardened warriors marching from the Iron Hills.

4 See for example in *Beowulf* the elaborate comparison between Sigemund the dragon-slayer (= Sigurd) and bad King Heremod (lines 875–915), of whom it is said *nallas beagas geaf Denum aefter dome* – translated by Howell Chickering as 'never a ring did he give, for glory, to the Danish men', adding 'Joyless he lived and unhappy he died' (*Beowulf: A Dual-Language Edition*, lines 1719b-1721, tr. Howell D. Chickering Jr. [1977]).

5 Thus the question arises: why did Thror, Thrain, and Thorin not themselves settle in the Iron Hills and merge their group with the larger settlement of their kin already established there? Tolkien nowhere addresses this issue, but one suspects that King Thror wished neither to usurp his brother's halls nor dwell in them as a guest and that his son and grandson were similarly proud and independent.

6 *The Saga of King Heidrek the Wise*, ed. & tr. Christopher Tolkien [1960], page 68.

7 Tolkien explicitly refers to the story of Högni and Hedin's endless battle in his essay 'The Name "Nodens"' (*Report on the Excavation . . . in Lydney Park* [1932], page 133).

8 This is the same source from which Tolkien had two or three years earlier taken the name 'Fimbulfambi' as the last King under the Mountain; see page 15.

9 Cf. Jonathan Evans on Tolkien's dragon-lore; see Note 2 to the commentary on 'Tolkien's Dragons' following Chapter XII (page 538).

(ii)
Bolg of the North

Bolg of the North plays a far less dramatic part in the Third Phase manuscript than will eventually develop in the typescript (see below) and final book. Nonetheless he is remarkable as one of only two goblins to gain the distinction of a name in the original edition of *The Hobbit* (if we exempt 'The Great Goblin' as a title).[1] The parallelism between 'Bolg of the North' and 'Gondobad of the North', when laid alongside Bladorthin's earlier admonition that the North End of the Misty Mountains was 'stiff with goblins, hobgoblins, and orcs of the worst description' (page 244), suggests that Mount Gundabad might have been Bolg's capital. In any case, like Morgoth's forces in the earlier tales in the legendarium, the goblins of Bilbo's time seem clustered in the north; only after their devastating defeat in the Battle of Five Armies do Bilbo and Gandalf, accompanied by Beorn, dare to take the northern route around Mirkwood.

Also in the Third Phase, we learn more about the famed goblin-dwarf war, although the full story has to wait until 'Durin's Folk' (specifically *LotR*.1110–13). That it was fought to avenge the death of Thror was already clear from Thorin's comment in Chapter I that the 'goblins of Moria have been repaid' as he considers going after the Necromancer to exact similar vengeance for Thrain (page 73). It is not yet revealed that Moria is an ancestral dwarven city overrun by goblins, and on the whole it seems likely that this idea had not yet arisen when Tolkien was working on *The Hobbit*; he may have conceived of Moria at this time as simply a goblin stronghold, probably mines worked by those unfortunates who have been captured and made slaves by the goblins (a fate Bilbo and the others narrowly escaped thanks to Bladorthin's timely intervention). Certainly similar mines were an omnipresent threat to the elves of Beleriand in early versions of the legendarium: Flinding bo-Dhuilin (known in the published *Silmarillion* as Gwindor of Nargothrond) is one example of the terrible changes wrought by long captivity in 'the mines of the north' (cf. 'Turambar and the Foalókë' [BLT II.78–79], 'The Lay of the Children of Húrin' [HME III.36], the 1926 'Sketch' [HME.IV.29], the 1930 *Quenta* [HME.IV.124], *Silm*.207, et al.). All we know for certain is that the goblin-dwarf war took place more than a century ago (page 73), was famous (Bilbo expects Bard and the Elvenking to have heard of it – page 662) and that the Battle of the Mines of Moria was a significant encounter in that campaign, since it was there that Dain killed Bolg's father (page 670) – although we could probably also have guessed this from the fact that 'Moria! Moria!' is one of the battle-cries of Dain's dwarves when they attack Bolg's goblins.[2] Finally, we can reasonably conclude that the dwarves must have won the war, since Thrain, Thorin, and Dain all survived and Bolg's father did not; more significantly, Thorin considers that it settled the score over his grandfather's death (which would not have been the case with a dwarven defeat or even stalemate). In the later development of the Moria story, the battle was made more devastating for both sides (Thorin's brother, Dain's father, and Balin's father all died there, and Thrain was permanently disfigured – *LotR*.1117 & 1112), and the mortality so high as to make it unlikely that a significant portion of the forces Dain brings with him a century and more later in answer to Thorin's call could be survivors of that battle (or that many, if any, of the goblins now facing them were veterans of the same combat).

Magol

One of the most interesting things about Bolg is of course his name, which is neither Norse (like the dwarves') nor Sindarin/Noldorin (like most of the other personal and place names within *The Hobbit*). Instead, it comes from one of Tolkien's minor invented languages, called *Mago* or *Magol*, about which little is known other than that at one point Tolkien considered making it the Orkish language, only to reject this idea. In that tongue, *bolg* is an adjective meaning 'strong' (Magol document, page 3) – an eminently suitable name for a great goblin-chief.[3]

However, it may be significant that another similar name, later identified as Noldorin, is given to an Orc leader in 'The Lay of Leithian' and the 1930 *Quenta*. This *Boldog*[4] was a captain whom Morgoth sent to raid Doriath to capture Lúthien; his importance may be guessed not just from the fact that he is one of only two orcs (the other being Bolg) named in the legendarium before *The Lord of the Rings*. Even more significantly, originally Morgoth had ordered Thû (the Necromancer; the later Sauron) to undertake that mission ('The Lay of the Children of Húrin', HME III.16 [lines 391–394] & 117 [lines 763–766]), which in slightly later parts of the legendarium was reassigned to Boldog instead:

A captain dire,
Boldog, he sent with sword and fire
to Doriath's march; but battle fell
sudden upon him: news to tell
never one returned of Boldog's host,
and Thingol humbled Morgoth's boast.

—'*The Lay of Leithian*', lines 3670b–3675 – HME.III.288.

In fact, Beren and his elven companions, trying to enter the Dark Lord's land disguised as orcs, claim to be part of Boldog's host when captured and questioned by Thû (ibid., lines 2121–2136; HME III.229). That Boldog's raid was no minor skirmish but a major battle is indicated by the account in the 1930 *Quenta*:

> Assaults . . . there were on Doriath's borders, for rumours that Lúthien was astray had reached Angband. Boldog captain of the Orcs was there slain in battle by Thingol, and his great warriors Beleg the Bowman and Mablung Heavyhand were with Thingol in that battle.
>
> —HME.IV.113.

A synopsis for the unwritten cantos of 'The Lay of Leithian' adds still more details:

> Thingol's army meets with the host of Boldog on the borders of Doriath. Morgoth has heard of the beauty of Lúthien, and the rumour of her wandering. He has ordered Thû and the Orcs to capture her. A battle is fought and Thingol is victorious. The Orcs are driven into Taur-na-Fuin† or slain. Thingol himself slays Boldog. Mablung Heavyhand was Thingol's chief warrior and fought at his side; Beleg was the chief of his scouts. Though victorious Thingol is filled with still more disquiet at Morgoth's hunt for Lúthien.
>
> †Mirkwood; cf. page 20.
>
> —HME.III.311.

Obviously, Bolg in *The Hobbit* cannot be the same character as Boldog in the Silmarillion stories contemporary with its drafting (since the latter is killed by Thingol), but the parallel is interesting. Perhaps significant in this context is a late note [circa 1960] Tolkien wrote on the name 'Boldog' in which he stated that 'it is possible that *Boldog* was not a personal name, and either a title, or else the name of a kind of creature: the Orc-formed Maiar, only less formidable than the Balrogs' (X.418). That is, according to this line of thought, evil Maiar in Morgoth's service sometimes incarnated themselves into orcish form in order to command orc troops, and 'boldog' was the generic term for these, no more individualized than, say, *Nazgûl*. For more on Maiar incarnating themselves as super-orcs ('orcs of the worst description', perhaps?), see commentary on page 138.

Orcs

Finally, there is the question of whether Bolg was a normal goblin, despite his rank as leader of the goblin-horde, or something more. The original Third Phase text offers no clues on this point, but the account of the Battle of Five Armies as developed in the typescript that followed does, and suggests that he was in fact an Orc, not merely a goblin (cf. in a later account the contrast between the rather puny goblins of the Misty Mountains against the much more dangerous Orcs of Mordor – not to mention Saruman's Uruk-hai – in *LotR*.467–8, 472, 473–4). Thus in the typescript and published book, the core of the goblin army around which it rallies after the elf-dwarf-human alliance stems the first onslaught is 'the bodyguard of Bolg, goblins of huge size with scimitars of steel' (typescript 1/1/67:6, DAA.343; contrast page 671 of this book). Similarly, Thorin's charge fails when he comes up against Bolg's honour guard: 'Thorin drove right against the bodyguard of Bolg. But he could not pierce their ranks . . . The bodyguard of Bolg came howling against them, and drove in upon their ranks like waves upon cliffs of sand' (DAA.344). Later Bilbo learns that after Thorin fell, presumably because of injuries inflicted by Bolg's guard if not Bolg himself, Beorn arrives and attacks like an unstoppable force: 'He scattered the bodyguard, and pulled down Bolg himself and crushed him. Then dismay fell on the Goblins and they fled in all directions' (typescript 1/1/68:2–3, DAA.349–50; contrast pp. 679–80 in this book).

The clear distinction between Bolg and his guard on the one hand and the average goblin of the horde on the other certainly carries over into the description of the Battle of Moria in Appendix A of *The Lord of the Rings*, where it is said of his father that Azog 'was a great Orc with a huge iron-clad head, and yet agile and strong. With him came many like him, the fighters of his guard' (*LotR*.1112). Thus the preponderance of evidence, though indirect, shows that Bolg in *The Hobbit* is far more than a mere goblin – in fact an Orc in all but name.

NOTES

1 The other, of course, being *Golfimbul* (or, in the First Phase text, *Fingolfin*) of Mount Gram, killed by Bullroarer Took in the Battle of the Green Fields. Mount Gram appears only in this context, but this may merely be another name for Gondobad/Gundabad, not least because 'Gram' is a Norse name (famous as the name of Sigurd's sword forged or reforged by Regin) and thus would seem to belong to the area north and east of Bilbo's home and because the Misty Mountains, which are particularly associated with the goblins throughout *The Hobbit*, also seem to be the mountains closest to Bilbo's home (cf. Bilbo's never having seen a mountain before, page III.

As for *Azog*, while we are told in the manuscript that Dain killed Bolg's father at Moria, Azog's name does not enter the story until the 1960 Hobbit (see page 781), nor see print within *The Hobbit* until the third edition of 1966 (cf. DAA.56 and 339), having arisen during the creation of the Appendices for *The Lord of the Rings* (contrast HME XII.276, where in early drafts of this material old Thror is 'slain in the dark by an Orc' in Moria, with the specific references to Azog in HME XII.284 and *LotR*.1110–12).

2 Note that Nain's forces chant 'Azog! Azog!', the name of their hated enemy, when they join the attack at the Battle of Moria (*LotR*.1112); hence, Dain's dwarves in *The Hobbit* chant 'Moria! Moria!' as a reminder of the atrocity they wish to avenge on Bolg's goblins (that is, the death of Thror). There is of course a long tradition of battle-cries that evoke famous defeats ('Remember the Maine!' 'The Alamo!') as well as victories.

3 A probable real-world source for the name comes from the *Fir Bolg*, one of the mythical races of Ireland whose deeds are retold in the

twelfth-century *Lebor Gabála Érenn* (or Book of Invasions) along with those of the *Fomorians* and the *Tuatha dé Danaan*. Tolkien was well-versed in this mythic material (see page 427), and his attention might have been drawn to the name by John Rhys's claim in *Celtic Britain* [1884] that *Bolg* was probably an Ivernian name – that is, that it came from the pre-Indo-European language of the British Isles (Rhys, pp. 268 & 281).† Since this is the same book from which Tolkien took the word *ond* (Ivernian for 'stone') and adapted it into Sindarin, it is entirely plausible that it may have influenced him in other borrowings as well.

†Rhys's theory has since been rejected, and scholars now believe that Ivernian, like Pictish, was a Celtic language closely related to British (the ancestor of Welsh), superseded by Gaelic (Irish).

4 David Salo glosses the name 'soldier of torment' (*A Gateway to Sindarin*, page 344) and points out that *The Etymologies*, written circa 1937–8, contain two entries on *Boldog*. The first (HME.V.375, under the root **NDAK-**) identifies the *-dog* element as a variant of *daug*, meaning 'warrior' ('chiefly used of Orcs'), and suggests that Boldog might simply be a generic term for orc-warrior, although this last point seems rather doubtful. The second (HME.V.377, under the root **ÑGWAL-**) gives *bol-* as a variant of *baul*, 'torment', as in the more familiar *bal*rog and states flatly that 'Orc-name *Boldog* = Orc-warrior "Torment-slayer"'.

(iii)
The Battle of Five Armies

As we have seen in the various Plot Notes, Tolkien's original idea was to have the Lonely Mountain chapters end with the Siege of the Mountain, where Thorin & Company (aided by the ravens) would be besieged by the wood-elves and lake-men until Bilbo and Gandalf could negotiate a peaceful ending to the impasse. This would then have been followed on Bilbo's return journey by the unnamed battle I have dubbed for ease of reference 'the Battle of Anduin Vale', which did not involve the dwarves but 'goblins of the Misty Mountains' and their allies the wargs, versus the wood-elves (with whom Bilbo goes to battle, armed in his elven mail), 'the men of the woods' (e.g., the wood-men dwelling on the western side of Mirkwood, described back in Chapter VI), 'men . . . from the south' (presumably the kin of the wood-men, who are said to have moved into the area from the south – page 205), and 'Beorn Medwed' leading 'a troop of bears'.[1] Conspicuous by their absence are the Eagles; more startling to readers familiar with the published story is the absence of any mention of the dwarves, Thorin and Company having remained in the east and Dain not yet having entered the story. Since this battle is said to take place 'in the west', it is no surprise that most of the participants are those associated with what later came to be known as the Vale of the Anduin: goblins, wargs, wood-men, and Beorn-Medwed (from Chapters IV, VI, & VII), plus the wood-elves from deeper in Mirkwood (Chapters VIII–IX). Hence the great climactic battle in the original conception (maintained throughout the Second Phase manuscript)[2] did not take place at the Lonely Mountain at all but somewhere between the Misty Mountains and Mirkwood; only with the advent of the Third Phase did Tolkien reach the decision to transform the stand-off at the Mountain into a dramatic all-out battle, which in turn necessitated the addition of Dain's five hundred dwarves.

Having ultimately decided upon a battle at the Lonely Mountain, initially Tolkien was in great uncertainty as to just who its participants would be. The name 'Battle of Five Armies' first appears in Plot Notes F, along with a marginal addition that seems to represent Tolkien's attempt to decide on which of the forces present counted as an 'army':

1	2	3	4	5			
woodelves,	dwarves,	eagles,	men,	bears	—	goblins	wolves
						6	7

From this, it seems rather that seven armies actually took part and the battle took its name from the five allies who oppose the forces of darkness (perhaps a distant precursor of the later Five Free Peoples who oppose Sauron in *The Lord of the Rings*: ents, elves, dwarves, men, and hobbits). We do not know for sure that 'men' here means only the Lake-men nor that 'dwarves' means Dain's army and not just Thorin & Company's heroic charge, but both seem likely. The plural in 'bears' implies that the idea of Beorn-Medwed's troop of bears is still present, but by the time Tolkien came to write the Third Phase text describing Beorn's role in the battle (which is then expanded upon in the typescript) the great were-bear had become solitary, as he remained in the published text. Neither the bats nor the sole hobbit are taken into account, apparently having negligible effect on the outcome; rather more surprisingly, the wizard is also omitted, while the ravens of the mountain (whom we might expect to battle the bats) make no appearance in any account of the battle, whether draft or outline.

Eventually Tolkien would determine that *the* five armies who gave the battle its name were the elves, the dwarves, the men, the goblins, and the wargs; the eagles and Beorn, while significant, did not really qualify as an 'army' *per se*.[3] Still, it is interesting that between the forces listed in the last page of Plot Notes B, in Plot Notes F, and in the Third Phase draft, almost all those Bilbo had encountered on his journey out were projected to be caught up in the grand climactic battle: only the trolls (who had been turned to stone), the storm-giants (who luckily for all concerned – cf. *Farmer Giles of Ham* – seem to have few dealings with others or to come down from their mountains), Gollum (who, according to the sequel, actually belatedly did make the journey seeking 'Baggins' in hopes of recovering his Ring; cf. *LotR*.70–71), and the spiders of Mirkwood (who clearly never range far from their own territory) are absent.

Herefugolas & Wælceasega

The idea of re-introducing some of the races and creatures who had appeared earlier in the story into the battle at the end (whether that battle took place at Erebor or west of Mirkwood), specifically the wolves and the eagles, may have a philological inspiration; if so it would be just another example of elements in *The Hobbit* arising out of Tolkien's professional work as an Anglo-Saxon scholar (he was, after all, at the time holder of the Rawlinson and Bosworth chair as Professor of Anglo-Saxon at Oxford, one of the most prestigious academic posts in Old English in the world). In his edition of the Old English *Exodus*, a spirited retelling in heroic alliterative verse of the Biblical story, Tolkien includes notes on the words *herefugolas* (literally, 'battle-birds') and *wælceasega* ('chooser of the slain' i.e. carrion-picker).[4] He notes the ancient and pervasive association in Old English heroic verse of wolves, ravens, and eagles (*The Old English* Exodus [1981], page 49), all eaters of carrion who are attracted to battlefields and all of whom he believed to be present in the scene thus described.[5] In the latter, he is careful to distinguish the carrion-pickers (*wælceasega* – a kenning for ravens) from the closely related *wælcyrige*, a word better known in its Old Norse form, *valkyrie*, 'derived partly from the actual carrion-birds of battle, transformed in mythological imagination; partly from the necromantic practices of female followers of Odinic magicians' (ibid., page 50). There are certainly no such followers at the Battle of Five Armies (but see below), but the association of ravens with wolves and with eagles may have turned Tolkien's mind back to earlier parts of the story and made him decide that rather than defusing one conflict only to follow it up with another, he could bring that traditional cluster of creatures together, along with others Bilbo had faced on his journey as enemies or allies to the Mountain itself, elevating the Siege into the great climactic battle of the book and expanding its scope beyond a merely local squabble into a great regional conflict that will decide the fate of that part of the world for years to come.

Bats as 'Children of Morgoth'

Finally, there are the bats, whose presence adds a note of horror to the proceedings. Indeed, the verbal image of them darkening the sky 'like a sea of locusts' was so vivid that Tolkien began a black, white, and red drawing of the scene (Plate XII [bottom]), although he did not complete it. That these are no ordinary bats is clear – for one thing, real-world bats are shy around people and only bite when grabbed and panic-strickened (in fact, they act exactly like the bats inside Smaug's lair, seen in Plate XI [top], who rather than swarming the solitary hobbit only bother him by accidentally making him drop his torch when he startles one). And of course blood-drinking 'vampire' bats are a very small sub-group (only three out of the eleven hundred known species of bats drink blood; two of those prey on birds, not mammals, and all three lap blood oozing from wounds rather than suck it) found only in Central and South America, certainly not part of the fauna of England (past and present) upon which Tolkien based almost all the other animals appearing in *The Hobbit*. Like the spiders of Mirkwood, the other conspicuous exception to Tolkien's general practice, these are clearly not natural animals but evil creatures in animal form, corresponding to real-world bats as wargs do to wolves. They are in fact yet another of the Children of Morgoth, who nowhere else take center stage but had lurked around the edges of the legendarium from 'The Lay of Leithian' onward.[6] For example, when Lúthien casts down Thû's tower,

> *bats unclean*
> *went skimming dark through the cold airs*
> *shrieking thinly to find new lairs*
> *in Deadly Nightshade's branches dread.*
>
> —lines 2805b–2807; HME III.254

and Thû himself flees in bat-form:

> *A vampire shape with pinions vast*
> *screeching leaped from the ground, and passed,*
> *its dark blood dripping on the trees;*
> *. . . for Thû had flown*
> *to Taur-na-Fuin, a new throne*
> *and darker stronghold there to build.*[7]
>
> —lines 2816–2818, 2820b–2822; HME III.254–5.

Not long afterwards Lúthien herself assumes bat-form in order to sneak into Thangorodrim in disguise:

a batlike garb
with mighty fingered wings, a barb
like iron nail at each joint's end –
such wings as their dark cloud extend
against the moon, when in the sky
from Deadly Nightshade screeching fly
Thû's messengers.

—lines 3402–3408a; HME III.278–9.

These references to Thû's taking bat-form and Lúthien adopting the disguise of a great bat (specifically alluded to as an 'evil fay') also appear in the 1930 *Quenta* (HME IV.111–12), the form of the legendarium most closely associated with the original *Hobbit*, and were retained into the published *Silmarillion* (*Silm.*175, 178–9), in a text largely derived from the 1937 *Quenta Silmarillion* (HME.V.295).

Within *The Hobbit* itself, the unnatural behavior of the bats (who although they do sometimes flock in great numbers are not carrion-eaters and thus would not follow an army as crows or ravens often did) was accentuated. Not only do they blot out the sun when they descend into the valley but 'swirled about the heads and ears of elves and men', adding to the chaos and confusion of the scene. Tolkien later (in the typescript, 1/1/67:5–6) added details that make the bats much more sinister, such as the bat-cloud's 'filling them with dread' as it whirls above the defenders, or most notably later in the battle when the bats 'fastened vampire-like on the stricken'.

One other example of bats allying with goblins to stage an attack very slightly postdates *The Hobbit*, having been written in December 1933, but is so nearly contemporaneous and so striking that it deserves special mention here. In the 1933 Father Christmas Letter, Fr. Christmas awakes to see a goblin looking in his window, despite the fact that that window faces out above a cliff several hundred feet high. He realizes that this 'meant there were bat-riding Goblins about – which we haven't seen since the goblin-war in 1453'. The goblins of the *Father Christmas Letters* are smaller than human-size (as are the elves whom we see in combat with them in this same letter's illustrations), but still these must have been extremely large bats, larger than any existing in the real world. The bat-messengers of Morgoth in the legendarium, such as Thuringwethil ('the messenger of Sauron', whose name means 'Woman of Secret Shadow'; *Silm.*178), were clearly of more or less human size, but these might have been were-bats rather than actual animals however enhanced since Lúthien can assume Thuringwethil's form and flying ability by putting on her 'bat-fell' (literally a bat-skin or bat-hide). We cannot tell exactly how large the bats accompanying Bolg's army were, but between the manuscript and the published book Tolkien did change the description of the bats in western Mirkwood from 'big' to 'huge' (Chapter VIII) and those fastening on the fallen became not merely bats but 'great' bats (Chapter XVII). At any rate, they were certainly not large enough for goblins to ride or to combat eagles (in either of which cases they would have counted as an 'army' in themselves), and mainly served to darken the sky (thus providing cover for the sun-shy goblins), to prevent effective arrow-fire from the elves (who are, after all, legendary archers), and disconcert and dismay the defenders – at all of which they succeeded all too well.

NOTES

1 See the last page of the original Plot Notes B and the associated commentary (pp. 366 & 375–6) for more on 'the Battle of Anduin Vale' and its projected participants. The evidence that Beorn-Medwed associated with a large number of other bears, whom he could call upon at need, goes all the way back to the Second Phase text of Chapter VII, where Bladorthin describes following their host in secret and finds

> 'There must have been a regular bear-meeting outside here last night. I soon saw that Medwed could not have made them all – there were far too many of them, and they were of various sizes too: I should say little bears, big bears, ordinary bears, and gigantic big bears must have been dancing outside from dark to nearly dawn. They came from almost all directions except West from over the river, from the Misty Mountains.'

That night Bilbo sees this bear-moot in his dreams when he

> dreamed a dream of hundreds of black bears dancing slow heavy dances round and round in the moonlight in the courtyard.

For Tolkien's original audience's enthusiasm for bears, see the commentary following Chapter VII, page 253ff.

2 It is possible that this idea first arose in Plot Notes F, which represents a transitional stage between the Second and Third Phases. Here there is no hint that the battle might take place elsewhere, but that detail might simply not have been set down in these very sketchy notes; neither is it specifically stated that the battle described takes place at the Mountain, although that is the implication.

3 'So began the battle . . . And it was called after [i.e., afterwards] the Battle of Five Armies . . . For upon one side were the Goblins and the Wolves and upon the other were men, elves, and dwarves' (page 670; cf. DAA.339). This is remarkable, since the text is clear that the eagles played a decisive role in depriving the goblins of the devastating advantage they had claimed by seizing the high ground and that Beorn's intervention turned the tide; the typescript and published book differ from the Third Phase manuscript in denying the eagles a full share of credit for the victory, ascribing it chiefly to Beorn's assault.

4 This edition was not published in Tolkien's lifetime but appeared in 1981, edited by Joan Turville-Petre. Its exact dating is unknown; Turville-Petre simply says it was 'based on full notes for a series of lectures delivered to a specialist class in the 1930s and 1940s' (*The Old English* Exodus*: Text, Translation, and Commentary* by J. R. R. Tolkien, ed. Joan Turville-Petre [1981], page v). However, Tolkien had already given some of the poem's vocabulary a very close look during the period when he was drafting *The Hobbit* (i.e., the very early 1930s): he begins his detailed study of the unusual phrase *Sigelwara land* with a quote from *Exodus* in an article that appeared in the December 1932 issue of *Medium Ævum* (that is, published during the weeks when Tolkien was writing the Third Phase text) and had been announced in the journal's first issue back in May 1932.† It thus seems quite possible that Tolkien's notes on *herefugolas* and *wælceasega*, or at least the thinking that underlies them, dates from the very early thirties.

†The second part of Tolkien's article did not appear until the June 1934 issue (Vol.III No.2).

5 In real life, ravens and wolves often form a symbiotic relationship: the ravens help spot the prey, the wolves make the kill, and the ravens get to feast on the carrion after the wolves have eaten their fill. See Bernd Heinrich's *Mind of the Raven* [1999], particularly the chapters describing ravens as 'wolf-birds' because of the close association between the two in the wild ('Ravens and Wolves in Yellowstone' and 'From Wolf-Birds to Human-Birds'). Bernd also includes a number of accounts of eagles feasting alongside ravens from the same corpses despite the generally hostile relations between the two types of bird (the predator-scavenger eagles and the scavenger-predator ravens).

6 Bats had of course already appeared in 'Goblin Feet', arguably the first piece of what became Tolkien's 'legendarium' to see print (*Oxford Poetry 1915*, pages 64–5; cf. DAA.113). But here they are not threatening ('pretty little flittermice'); like the 'goblins' themselves they are simply one more element of the elusive, gone-before-it-can-be-grasped little people. Hammond & Scull also see 'bat-like faces' on the curtains in Tolkien's early drawing 'Wickedness' [H-S#32], one of the pieces in *The Book of Ishness* [1911–13], but given these images' similarity to the Siamese cat that can just be glimpsed between the parted curtains of this image I suspect they are actually cats' heads instead (cf. *Artist & Illustrator*, pages 37 and 36).

7 'Deadly Nightshade' and Taur-na-Fuin are both alternative names for the same place, the dark forest elsewhere called Mirkwood. The tower Thû the Necromancer builds there after the escape described here is clearly the same Necromancer's tower in southern Mirkwood in *The Hobbit*, where Thrain died and which Bladorthin advises Bilbo to avoid; see page 244.

(iv)
'The Halls of Waiting'

'Farewell o gracious thief' said Thorin. 'I go now to the halls of waiting to sit beside my fathers until the world is renewed. The goblins have slain me. Since I leave now all gold and silver and go where it is of little worth, I wish to part in friendship with you, and would take back my words and deeds at the Gate.'

—page 679; cf. DAA.348.

This passage, with its interesting glimpse into the dwarven afterlife (or at least the dwarves' beliefs about what would happen to them after death), was completely without parallel in the legendarium when it was first written. Nothing marks the distance between Tolkien's initial conception of the dwarves as set down in *The Book of Lost Tales*[1] and dwarves as presented in *The Hobbit* and *The Lord of the Rings* as this disagreement over their fate. From very early on in the legendarium the divergent fates of Men and Elves were a key part in the story: humans who die depart from the world and do not return; their souls leave Arda (Creation) altogether, whereas elves travel to the Halls of Mandos in Valinor to wait until they can be re-incarnated. Dwarves initially fit into neither of these categories – the occasional references in *The Hobbit* to 'Mortal Men' and the extremely long lifespans indicated for dwarves (Thrain having gone away a hundred years ago, many of Dain's band being hale and hearty veterans of a war that took place well before that, Thorin and Balin remembering events that the 153-year-old raven is too young to have experienced first-hand, the elvenking's threat to imprison Gandalf/Thorin for a hundred years before questioning him again) show they are not exactly mortal, or at least have a lifespan far, far beyond human years. As all readers of *The Lord of the Rings* know, Tolkien had his own definitions of mortal and immortal: 'Mortal Men' are 'doomed to die' (*LotR* ring-verse) because they have a finite lifespan and eventually die of sheer old age, unlike dragons (who 'live . . . practically for ever, unless they are killed' – DAA.55; cf. page 72) and elves (on the battlefield 'lay . . . many a fair elf that should have lived yet long ages merrily in the wood' – DAA.344; cf. page 672). Tolkien's elves are 'immortal' in that they do not die of age, disease, or natural causes, although they can be killed; as Tolkien says in his 1965 radio interview with Denys Gueroult, their lifespans extend to the habitability of this planet and 'longeval' might have been a better choice than 'immortal' as most understand the term.[2] And even if killed, elves are re-incarnated with the same memories, personalities, and (apparently) appearance, so that death is for them a temporary state, an interruption of their 'serial longevity' (*Letters* p. 267).

With the dwarves, in *The Hobbit* and subsequent works Tolkien created a third alternative. The early legendarium texts, in which dwarves play a relatively minor part, do not address the question of what happens after dwarves die, making Thorin's dying words (written in December 1932 or January 1933) the first time this issue had been addressed. Oddly enough, several years later (circa 1937), when Tolkien inserted several references to the dwarves' fate in various component texts that he hoped would go together to make up *The Silmarillion* (cf. HME V.167 & 202 and HME IV.284), his comments flatly contradict what had already been stated in *The Hobbit* and instead harken back to the *Book of Lost Tales* and 1930 *Quenta*. These new legendarium texts, written from an elvish point of view, suggest that dwarves are soulless and simply cease to exist upon death:

> Dwarves have no spirit indwelling, as have the Children of the Creator [i.e., elves and men], and they have skill but not art; and they go back into the stone of the mountains of which they were made.
>
> —'(Later) Annals of Beleriand', HME V.129.

Similar comments are made in the *Lhammas* (HME V.178), and the 1937 *Quenta Silmarillion* agrees that dwarves 'return unto the earth and the stone of the hills of which they were fashioned' (HME V.273). This is clearly an allusion back to Old Norse lore which we have already touched on back in the commentary following Chapter II (see Note 9 on page 109), particularly the fate of the dwarf Alvis in the *Elder Edda*, who is turned to stone at the end of the *Alvíssmál*. It also clearly cannot be reconciled with Thorin's dying words, and it was not long before the *Quenta Silmarillion* text was altered to bring it into accord with the concept alluded to in *The Hobbit*. The revised *QS* text reads

> *the Noldor believed* that the Dwarves have no spirit indwelling . . . and that they go back into the stone of the mountains of which they were made. *Yet others say that Aulë cares for them, and that Ilúvatar will accept from him the work of his desire, so that the Dwarves shall not perish.*
>
> —HME V.146; emphasis mine.

This is remarkable as the first instance[3] of the older legendarium being altered to match Bilbo's story; the newly published book clearly has gained an authority over as-yet unpublished material within what had till then been the more venerable main lineage, just as *The Lord of the Rings* would later gain authority over both, requiring further work on *The Hobbit* that became the Fourth Phase and Fifth Phase (the 1947 Hobbit and 1960 Hobbit, respectively). Further development of the ideas suggested in Thorin's dying speech appear in *The Lord of the Rings*' Appendix A ('Durin's Folk'), where it is noted that 'strange tales' of the dwarves' origins are told 'both by the Eldar and by the Dwarves themselves' (*LotR*.1108), one of which is the idea 'that there are no dwarf-women, and that the Dwarves "grow out of stone"' (*LotR*.1116) – so that what was once an authoritative statement is now dismissed as a 'foolish opinion' (ibid.). We also now meet with the story of Durin the Deathless (Durin I), who has been reincarnated five times (Durin II–VI) and has one remaining incarnation yet to come ('Durin VII & Last'; *LotR*.1108 & 1117); although each body dies, his time between lives is referred to as 'sleep' ('Till Durin wakes again from sleep' – *LotR*.334).

A full explication of Thorin's words, if any was needed, had to wait until the *Later Quenta* [circa 1951], which magisterially embraces and places into harmony all the previous discordant thoughts on the subject:

> [The Dwarves] live long, far beyond the span of Men, and yet not for ever. Aforetime the Noldor held that dying they returned unto the earth and the stone of which they were made; yet that is not their own belief. For they say that Aulë cares for them and gathers them in Mandos in halls set apart for them, and there they wait, not in idleness but in the practice of crafts and the learning of yet deeper lore. And Aulë, they say, declared to their Fathers of old that Ilúvatar . . . will . . . give them a place among the Children in the End. Then their part shall be to serve Aulë and to aid him in the re-making of Arda after the Last Battle.
>
> —HME.XI.204.

With the exception of the passage about the dwarven spirits' activity during the period after their deaths – which seems to me to harken back to glimpses of the busy *swart-álfar* in some Norse sources, such as Snorri's *Prose Edda* – this corresponds exactly with Thorin's words, and provides the final clue of what he and the others will be waiting for: a challenge truly worthy of their skill, the chance to rebuild the world (Arda Marred) the way it should have been.[4]

NOTES

1 See the passage quoted on page 78 in the commentary following Chapter I (c). This is echoed in the 1930 *Quenta*, written about the time Tolkien wrote the First Phase of *The Hobbit* (i.e., the bulk of the opening chapter): 'the sons of Fëanor . . . made war upon the Dwarves of Nogrod and Belegost; but they did not discover whence that strange race came, nor have any since' (HME IV.103–4). The story of Aulë's creation of the dwarves (cf. *Silm*.43–4) did not arise until about the time of *The Hobbit*'s publication (i.e., a year or so after the completed typescript had been submitted to Allen & Unwin) in the '(Later) Annals of Beleriand'; see HME V.129 and 149. For the brief later development of the original negative, elven-centric view of the dwarves, see the passages cited on page 721 from the '(Later) Annals of Beleriand', the *Lhammas*, and the 1937 *Quenta Silmarillion*.

2 Note that Tolkien's friend C. S. Lewis, in what is perhaps his best book, *The Discarded Image* [posthumously published in 1964], names the chapter devoted to elves, nymphs, fauns, and fairies 'The Longaevi', i.e. 'long-livers'.

3 That is, the first if we except the Arkenstone affecting the description of the Silmarils; cf. page 607.

4 For Tolkien, the chance for an artist to take part in actual Creation was the highest reward; cf. 'Leaf by Niggle'. For Tolkien's opinion that our own world was itself a sub-creation and that a writer might be able to contribute through his imaginative works in enriching the post-apocalyptic world that would succeed it, see my essay '"And All the Days of Her Life Are Forgotten": *The Lord of the Rings* as Mythic Prehistory', especially part v: '"We Make Because We Are Made": Tolkien's Sub-creative Theology', in *The Lord of the Rings 1954–2004: Scholarship in Honor of Richard E. Blackwelder*, ed. Wayne G. Hammond & Christina Scull [Marquette University Press, 2006].

(v)
Bilbo's First Poem

The decision to incorporate not one, not two, but *three* poems into the final pages of the story not only fleshed out the brevity of this part of the book (even with three poems inserted into the text, the final chapter is still one of the shortest) but marked a return to the lighter mood of the early chapters after the sadness of Thorin's death. We are told that 'it was very long before [Bilbo] had the heart to make a joke again' (page 679), and although we are told in passing that Yuletide was 'warm and merry' at Beorn's house (page 682), not until after the elves' second song are we shown that Bilbo has fully recovered, making 'many a merry jest and dance' (page 690). The inclusion of these songs also re-asserts a stylistic feature of the first half of the book: prose interrupted at unpredictable but frequent intervals by verse – a highly characteristic feature of both *The Hobbit* and *The Lord of the Rings* that sets them apart from all Tolkien's other work. Of the twenty-three poems in the published book, all but four occur in the first ten chapters, and only one of those chapters is altogether without a song (Chapter II).[1] The addition of the poems thus helps create a sense of 'back again' by paralleling a stylistic reversion with Bilbo's return to familiar regions.

Of these three poems, the first is more or less a continuation in much the same spirit of the elves' song in the trees back in Chapter III. The sense that the song has gone on all the time Bilbo has been away juxtaposed with its now incorporating details from Bilbo's adventures highlights the mix of timelessness and time's passing that is characteristic of Rivendell throughout *The Hobbit* and *The Lord of the Rings*; it also reinforces the message that life goes on. The next poem is notable chiefly for the exuberance of its opening stanzas (particularly the striking image of the lights in the night sky as 'windows of Night in her tower'), which segue into the lullaby of the second half. But it is the third poem, 'Roads Go Ever Ever On', which is most notable: a celebration of both the allure of possibilities of unending travel and the joy of homecoming by someone whose journeys are now ending.

Roads go ever ever on,
Over rock and under tree,
By caves where never sun has shone,
By streams that never find the sea;
Over snow by winter sown,
And through the merry flowers of June,
over grass and over stone,
And under mountains in the moon.

Roads go ever ever on
Under cloud and under star,
Yet feet that wandering have gone
Turn at last to home afar.
Eyes that fire and sword have seen
And horror in the halls of stone
Look at last on meadows green
and trees and hills they long have known.[2]

Poems about roads and wanderlust and homecoming ('there and back again', as it were) are of course not uncommon: the very first line of the very first published poem of the legendarium began 'I am off down the road', and the same poem's second half with 'I must follow' ('Goblin Feet', in *Oxford Poetry 1915*, page 64); the same volume contained fellow T.C.B.S. member G. B. Smith's poem about a Roman road, probably Smith's best poem and his most Tolkienesque piece:

This is the road the Romans made,
    This track half lost in the green hills,
Or fading in a forest-glade
    'Mid violets and daffodils.

The years have fallen like dead leaves,
    Unwept, uncounted, and unstayed
(Such as the autumn tempest thieves)
    Since first this road the Romans made.[3]

A much closer parallel, however, to Bilbo's poem is E. F. A. Geach's 'Romance', which appeared in the same book as a reprint of 'Goblin Feet' (in fact, on the very next page following Tolkien's poem):

Round the next corner and in the next street
Adventure lies in wait for you.
Oh, who can tell what you may meet
Round the next corner and in the next street!
Could life be anything but sweet
When all is hazardous and new
Round the next corner and in the next street?
Adventure lies in wait for you.[4]

Geach's poem, while different in expression from Bilbo's, nonetheless nicely anticipates its spirit and also that of two similar poems in the sequel, 'The Road Goes Ever On' (see below) and the hobbits' walking song:

Still round the corner there may wait
A new road or a secret gate,
And though we pass them by today,
Tomorrow we may come this way
And take the hidden paths that run
Towards the Moon or to the Sun.

— *The Lord of the Rings*, page 91.

Similarly, Martin Simonson has pointed out how another of Tolkien's fellow Georgian poets, Edward Thomas (sometimes known as 'the English Frost' from his friendship and affinities with his American contemporary, poet Robert Frost, who outlived him by almost half a century) seems to anticipate Tolkien's poems in his own aptly-titled 'Roads':

Roads go on
While we forget, and are
Forgotten like a star
That shoots and is gone

The next turn may reveal
Heaven: upon the crest
The close pine clump, at rest
And black, may Hell conceal

Often footsore, never
Yet of the road I weary
Though long and steep and dreary
As it winds on forever[5]

In the end, whatever his inspirations for 'Roads Go Ever Ever On', once it was in existence it offered a prime example of Tolkien once again being his own most important source through creative recycling of earlier material. For the most significant poem that resembles 'Roads Go Ever Ever On' is of course Tolkien's own 'The Road Goes Ever On', which essentially provides a third and final stanza to the earlier poem, recited by Bilbo when he finally takes to the road again (*LotR*.48) and also by Frodo when he at length sets off on his own adventure (*LotR*.86–7):

The Road goes ever on and on
Down from the door where it began.
Now far ahead the Road has gone,
And I must follow, if I can,
Pursuing it with eager feet,
Until it joins some larger way,
Where many paths and errands meet.
And whither then? I cannot say.[6]

NOTES

1 The poems in *The Hobbit* are distributed thusly: two in Chapter I ('Chip the Glasses' and 'Far Over the Misty Mountains Cold', plus a refrain from the latter), 'O Where Are You Going' in Chapter III, the goblin song in Chapter IV ('Ho Ho My Lad'), the riddles (eight in all) in Chapter V, the second goblin song in Chapter VI ('Fifteen Birds'), the dwarf song in Chapter VII ('The Wind was on the Withered Heath'), Bilbo's spider songs ('Attercop' and 'Lazy Lob') in Chapter VIII, two river songs in Chapter IX ('Heave Ho Splash-plump' and 'Down the Swift Dark Stream You Go'), the Lake-men's song in Chapter X ('At the Mountain-king's Return'), then a gap before the dwarven song in Chapter XV ('The King is Come Unto His Hall', a reworked version of the second song from Chapter I), and then a second gap before the three songs in Chapter XIX ('Tra-la-la-lally Come Back to the Valley', 'Sing All Ye Joyful', and 'Roads Go Ever Ever On').

Thus Chapter II is the only one of the first ten to lack a poem, while Chapter XV is the only one of the next eight to have one, followed by a sudden burst of three poems in the final chapter.

2 I give here the typescript text (1/1/69:4) for ease of reference; see page 693 above for the initial rough drafting of this poem. The only changes between the First Typescript version and the published text are the latter's capitalization of the first words in the two lines not capitalized here (both are capitalized in the Second Typescript [1/1/50:4–5], a rare case where Michael's typescript more closely resembles the published text than the main typescript) and the indenting of every other line in the published text (cf. DAA.359–60). The third line of the

poem has been erased and retyped in the original, but I think this was simply to correct a carriage return error or some similar typing mistake.

Note that by referring to it as 'Bilbo's first poem' Tolkien has either forgotten about the two spider-songs Bilbo spontaneously composed in Mirkwood ('Attercop' and 'Lazy Lob') or does not consider them 'poems' *per se* so much as rhyming nonsense to annoy his foes.

3 This is the first of the two 'Songs on the Downs' (*Oxford Poetry 1915*, page 60). Smith was one of Tolkien's closest friends, and the poem is included in *A Spring Harvest* [1918], the book of Smith's poems edited by Tolkien after GBS's death in the Battle of the Somme.

4 Both Tolkien's and Geach's poems appear in *Fifty New Poems for Children: An Anthology*, Selected from Books Recently Published by Basil Blackwell (Basil Blackwell, Oxford [1922]). 'Goblin Feet' appears on pages 26–27 and 'Romance' on page 28; a bibliographic note on page 62 notes that Geach's poem first appeared in *Oxford Poetry 1918*. For more on Geach, see *The Annotated Hobbit* (DAA.360–1).

5 These are stanzas two, twelve, and thirteen from Thomas's poem, which continues with an all-too-timely application:

Now all roads lead to France
And heavy is the tread
Of the living; but the dead
Returning lightly dance;

Whatever the road bring
To me or take from me
They keep me company
With their pattering . . .

Simonson's piece, '*The Lord of the Rings* in the Wake of the Great War', appears in *Reconsidering Tolkien*, edited by Thomas Honegger (Walking Tree Press [2005]); see in particular pages 161–163. So far as I have been able to discover, no substantial comparison has yet been written of Tolkien with Thomas, who like Tolkien celebrated the quiet English countryside in his work, wrote fairy-tales, and fought on the Western Front, where he died in 1917.

6 The only difference between the two versions in *The Lord of the Rings* is that when Frodo repeats the poem two chapters later, he changes the word *eager* in line five to *weary*; Christopher Tolkien reveals in *The Return of the Shadow* that 'weary' is in fact the wording of the original draft (HME VI.47).

THE FOURTH PHASE

THE 1947 HOBBIT

The 1947 Hobbit – that is, the material Tolkien created around 1944 while working on *The Lord of the Rings* and sent to Allen & Unwin in 1947 as a way to bring the earlier book into harmony with its sequel – marks the first of a sequence of revisionings that led first to the second edition of *The Hobbit* [1951], then to 'The Quest of Erebor' [1954], and then finally to the 1960 Hobbit (the never-before published Fifth Phase). The first of these made adjustments within the original book to make it better match the sequel, the second retold a small portion of Bilbo's story within the new book (or would have, had it been published as part of Appendix A as Tolkien originally intended), while the third re-envisioned a complete recasting of the old book to agree with the new in minute detail. Unlike these three, the 'third edition' Hobbit of 1966 was imposed upon him by outside circumstance (that is, the need to quickly produce an 'authorized' edition to belatedly assert the American copyright); by contrast, the others had all arisen from Tolkien's internal compulsion to bring the old story of Bilbo's adventure more strongly into accord with the new one of Frodo's quest.

The Fourth Phase material exists in three states: ten sheets of fair copy manuscript numbered 1 to 10 in the upper right corner (Ad.Ms.H.34–53),[TN1] followed by six pages of single-spaced typescript numbered 1 through 6 in the upper right corner (Ad.Ms.H.78–82), followed by eight typeset sheets (sixteen pages) from Allen & Unwin showing how the new material looked when typeset and allowing Tolkien to proofread the changes (Ad.Ms.H.54–61). The first of these dates from 1944; the second either from 1944 or 1947; the third from 1950. They represent, respectively, Tolkien's manuscript of the rewritten passages; his 'home copy' of the typescript of this material that he sent to Allen & Unwin; and Allen & Unwin's page proofs of the changed sections returned to Tolkien for proofing.

Aside from a few ink-over-pencil additions, no drafting survives for these changes, though the fair copy text is far too neatly written to have been spontaneously generated without careful preparation – for one thing, as was his usual practice when revising material already set in type, Tolkien has taken great pains to keep many of his changes as localized as possible, so that only that specific line or lines would have to be re-set without affecting the rest of the page (and thus upsetting the layout of every subsequent page). Although the greatly expanded encounter with Gollum did add five extra pages to the book's length, it added *exactly* five pages, so that for instance where page 99 in the first edition began with the words '"You would have dropped him," said Dori', page 104 in the second edition now began with those exact words; everything from the beginning of Chapter VI on has simply shifted five pages.

All Tolkien's substitutions are preceded by a page and line number indicating exactly where each correction should be inserted into the existing (first edition) text. I have retained these, since even for those without access to a copy of the first or second edition they give a proportional sense of where a passage may be found. In any case, it should be easy for anyone familiar with Tolkien's book in any of its permutations to locate these passages. Since this material transforms what was already an impressive chapter into one of the most moving and memorable scenes Tolkien ever wrote, I have provided unusually full annotation for this section, giving variations between the fair copy and the typescript (and proof pages) in the Text Notes, aside from changes in punctuation or paragraph breaks.

The fair copy page has no title, but in the left margin of the first page (Ad.Ms.H.34) Tolkien has hastily written in pencil:

(i)

Proposed correction of Hobbit to simplify Sequel (Gollum does not give ring).

The typescript (Ad.Ms.H.77) has the following header instead:

Corrections required in THE HOBBIT in order to bring the story into line with the sequel, THE LORD OF THE RINGS.

Above this is written in ink:

or rather if The Hobbit ran so the Sequel would be a little easier to <conduct> as a narrative (in Ch II), though not necessarily 'truer'.

– that is, Chapter II in *The Lord of the Rings*, i.e. 'The Shadow of the Past' (or, as to give it its original title, 'Ancient History'). I now give the fair copy manuscript, beginning on page Ad.Ms.H.34.

p. 85 l. 9. Before he lost all his friends and was driven away, alone, and crept down, down into the dark under the mountains.[TN2]

l. 25–26. We does what it wants, eh? We shows it the way out, yes[TN3]

p. 91 l. [14>]15ff.[TN4] He knew, of course, that the riddle-game was sacred and of immense antiquity, and even wicked creatures were afraid to cheat when they played at it. But he felt [*cancelled*: that] he could not trust this slimy thing to keep any promise at a pinch. Any excuse would do for him to slide out of it. And after all that last question had not been a genuine riddle according to the ancient rules.[TN5]

But at any rate Gollum did not at once attack him. He could see the sword in Bilbo's hand. He sat still, shivering and whispering. At last Bilbo could wait no longer.

'Well?' he said. 'What about your promise? I want to go. You must show me the way'.

'Did we say so, precious? Show the nasty little [noser >] baggins[TN6] the way out, yes, yes. But what has it got in its pocketses, eh? Not string, precious, but not nothing. Oh no! gollum'.

'Never you mind', said Bilbo. 'A promise is a promise'.

'Cross it is, precious, impatient',[TN7] hissed Gollum. 'But it must wait, yes it must. We can't go up the tunnels so hasty. We must go and get some things first, yes, things to help us'.

'Well, hurry up!' said Bilbo, relieved to think of Gollum going away. He thought he was just making an excuse, and did not mean to come back. What was Gollum talking about? What useful thing could he keep out on the dark lake? But he was wrong. Gollum did meant to come back. He was angry now and hungry. And he was a miserable wicked creature, and already he had a plan.[TN8]

Not far away was his island, of which Bilbo knew nothing, and there in his hiding-place he kept a few wretched oddments, and one very beautiful thing, very beautiful, very wonderful. He had a ring, a golden ring, a precious ring.

'My birthday-present!' he whispered to himself, as he had often done in the endless dark day.[TN9] 'That's what we wants now, yes; we wants it!'

He wanted it because it was a ring of power, and if you slipped [it >] that ring on your finger, you were invisible; only in the full sunlight could you be seen, and then only by your shadow, and that would be faint and shaky.[TN10]

[Who knows >] 'My birthday-present' he whispered;[TN11] but who knows how Gollum came by that present, ages ago in the old days when such rings were still at large in the world. Perhaps even the Necromancer [> Master][TN12] who made them could not have said. Gollum used to wear it at first, till it tired him; and then he kept it in a pouch next his skin, till it galled him; and now usually he hid it in a hole in the rock on his island, and went back [> was always going back] to look at it. And still sometimes he put it on, when he could not bear to be parted from it any longer, or when he was very, very, hungry, and tired of fish. Then he would creep along dark passages, looking for stray goblins. He might even venture into places where the torches were lit and made his eyes blink and smart; for he would be safe, oh yes, quite safe. No one would see him, no one would notice him, till he had his fingers on their throat. Only yesterday [> a few hours before][TN13] he had worn it, and caught a small goblin-imp. How it squeaked! He still had a bone or two left to gnaw, but he wanted something softer.

'Quite safe, yes', he whispered [*added*: to himself]. 'It won't see us, will it my precious? No! It won't see us, and its nassty little sword will be useless, yes quite'[TN14]

That is what was in his wicked little mind, as he slipped suddenly from Bilbo's side, and flapped back to his boat, and went off into the dark.

Bilbo thought he had heard the last of him, and he <felt in his bones ?that> Gollum did not meant to keep his promise.[TN15] Still he waited [*added*: a while;] for he had no idea how to find his way out alone. Suddenly he heard a screech. It sent a shiver down his back. Gollum was cursing and wailing away in the gloom, not very far off by the sound of it. He was on his island, scrabbling here and there, searching and seeking in vain.

'Where iss it? Where iss it?'[TN16] Bilbo heard him crying. 'Lost it is, my precious, lost, lost! Curse us, and crush us, my precious is lost!'

'What's the matter', Bilbo called. 'What have you lost?'

'It mustn't ask us', [screech >] shrieked Gollum. 'Not its business, no, gollum. It's lost,[TN17] gollum, gollum, gollum'.

'Well, so am I', said [> cried] Bilbo, 'and I want to get unlost. And I won the game, and you promised. So come along! Come and let me out, and then go on with your looking!' Utterly miserable as Gollum sounded, Bilbo could not find much pity in his heart, and he had a feeling that anything Gollum wanted so much [*cancelled*: and missed so badly] could hardly be something good [*cancelled*: – for Gollum at any rate].[TN18] 'Come along!' he shouted.

'No, not yet, precious!' said Gollum [> Gollum answered]. 'We must search for it, it's lost, gollum'.

'But you [promised >] never guessed my last question, and you promised', said Bilbo.

'Never guessed!' said Gollum. Then suddenly out of the gloom came a sharp hiss. 'What has it got in its pocketses? Tell us that. It must tell us first'.[TN19]

As far as Bilbo knew, there was no particular reason why he should not tell – Gollum's mind had jumped to a guess quicker than his:

naturally, for Gollum had brooded on one thing for ages, and he was always afraid of it being stolen.[TN20] But Bilbo was annoyed at the delay; after all he had won the game, pretty fairly, and among awkward circumstances [> at a horrible risk]. 'Answers were to be guessed not given', he said.

'But it wasn't a fair question', said Gollum. 'Not a riddle, precious, no!'

'Oh well, if it's a matter of ordinary questions' Bilbo replied, 'then I asked one first. What have you lost? Tell me that!'

'What has it got in its pocketses?' The sound came hissing loud and sharp [> louder and sharper], and as he looked towards it, to his alarm Bilbo saw now [> now saw] two small points of light peering at him. As suspicion grew in Gollum's mind, the light of his eyes burned with a pale flame.

'What have you lost?' Bilbo persisted.

But now the light in Gollum's eyes had become a green fire, and it was coming swiftly nearer. Gollum was in his boat again, paddling wildly back to the dark shore; and such a rage [in his heart that >] of fear and suspicion in his heart[TN21] that no sword held any more terror for him.

Bilbo could not guess what had excited the wretched creature <so madly>, but he saw that all was up, and that Gollum had forgotten all promises.[TN22] Just in time he turned and ran blindly back up the [added: dark] passage down which he had come, keeping close to the wall and feeling it with his left hand.

'What has it got in its pocketses?' he heard the hiss loud behind him, and the splash as Gollum leaped from his boat.[TN23]

'What have I, I wonder?' he said to himself, as he panted and stumbled along. He put his [*added*: left] hand in his pocket. The ring felt very cold as it [*added*: quietly] slipped on to his groping forefinger.[TN24]

The hiss was close behind him. He turned and saw Gollum's eyes like small green lamps coming up the slope. Terrified he tried to run faster, but suddenly he struck his toes on a snag in the floor and fell flat, with his little sword under him.

At that moment Gollum came up. But before Bilbo could do anything shout, pick himself up, wave his sword, Gollum passed on, taking no notice of him, cursing and whispering in the dark.[TN25]

What could it mean? Gollum could see in the dark. Bilbo could see the light of eyes palely shining even from behind. Painfully he got up,[TN26] and very cautiously he followed. There seemed nothing else to do. It was no good crawling back down to Gollum's water. Perhaps, if he followed him, Gollum might lead him to some way of escape without meaning to.

'Curse it, curse it, curse it!' hissed Gollum. 'Curse it [> the Baggins]! It's gone! What has it got in its pocketses? Oh we guess[es], we guess, my precious.[TN27] He's found it, yes he must have, my birthday-present.

Bilbo pricked up his ears. [This was so interesting >] He was [*added*: at last] beginning to guess himself. He hurried a little, getting as close as he dared behind Gollum, who was still going quickly, not looking back, but turning his head from side to side, as Bilbo could see from the faint glimmer on the walls.

'My birthday-present! Curse it! How did we lose it, my precious? Yes, that's it, when we came this way yesterday[TN28] catching that nassty little squeaker. That's it. Curse it. It slipped from us, after all these ages and ages. It's gone, gollum!

Suddenly Gollum sat down and began to weep, a <horrible> wheezing and gurgling sound [> a whistling and gurgling sound horrible to listen to]. Bilbo halted, and flattened himself against the tunnel-wall; and hid his sword, which was now glowing faintly again.[TN29] [Then Gollum began to curse >] After a while Gollum stopped weeping and began to talk. He seemed to be having an argument with himself.

'It's no good going back there to search, no. We can't [> doesn't] remember all the places we've visited. And it's no use. It's [> The baggins has] got it in its pocketses; the nassty noser has, we says [> the nassty noser has found it].'

'We guesses, precious, only guesses. We can't know till we finds the nasty creature and squeezes it.'

'But if it's got in its <?pocketses>, we shan't find it, we shan't see it. It'll escape us, gollum! It'll go away, away with our present, gollum!'

'Perhaps, precious. But it doesn't know about the present.[TN30] It doesn't know what the present can do, does it! It'll just leave[TN31] it in its pocketses. It doesn't know; and it can't go far – it's losst itself, the nassty nosey thing. It doesn't know the way out. It said so.'

'It said so, yes; but it's tricksy. It doesn't say what it means. It won't say what it's got in its pocketses. It knows. It's off now, we guess, to the back-door, yes to the back door.'[TN32]

'The goblins[es] will catch it then. It can't get out that way, precious.'

'Sss, sss, gollum! [*added in pencil*: Goblinses!] Yes, but if it's got the present, our precious present, then goblins[es] will get it, gollum! They'll find it, they'll find out what it does. We shan't ever be safe again, never, gollum. One of the goblins[es] will put it on, and [then] no one will see him. He'll be there but not seen. Not even our clever eyeses will notice him; and he'll [creep >] come creepsy and tricksy and catch us: Gollum, gollum!'

'Then let's stop talking, precious, and make haste. If <illegible> [> the baggins has] gone that way we must go quick and see. Go! Not far now. Make haste!'

With a spring Gollum got up and started shambling off at a great pace. Bilbo hurried after him, still as cautiously as he could [> cautiously], though his chief fear now was of tripping on another snag and falling with a noise. His head was in a whirl of hope and wonder. It seemed that the ring he had was a magic ring: it made you invisible! He had heard of such things, of course, in old old tales; but he found it hard to believe [> it was hard to believe] that he really had found one, by accident. Still, there it was: Gollum with his bright eyes had passed him by, only a yard to one side.

On they went, Gollum flip-flapping ahead, wailing [> hissing] and cursing; Bilbo behind going as softly as a hobbit can. Soon they came to places where, as Bilbo had noticed on the way down, [*added*: side-] passages opened, this way and that. Gollum began at once to count them.

'One left, yes! One right, yes! Two left, yes, yes! Two right, yes, yes';[TN33] and so on and on. As the count grew, [he began before <looking> to get slow >] he slowed down, and he began to get shaky and weepy. For they were [> he was] leaving the water further and further behind, and he was getting afraid. Goblins were [> might be] about, and he had lost his ring.

At last he stopped by a low opening, on their left as they went up. 'Six [> Seven] right, yes; four [> six] left, yes!'[TN34] he whispered. '[That's it >] This is it. This is the way to the back door, yes. Here's the passage. [*added*: He peered in *and shrank back*] But we dursn't go in, precious; no we dursn't. Goblins[es] down there, lots of goblins [> Goblinses]! We smells them – sss!'

'What shall we do, curse them and crush them? We must wait here precious, wait a bit and see!'[TN35]

So they came to a dead stop. Gollum had brought Bilbo to the way out after all, but he [> Bilbo] could not get in! There was Gollum sitting humped up right in the opening, and his eyes gleamed cold in his head, as he swayed it from side to side between his knees.

Bilbo crept out from the wall more quietly than a mouse; but Gollum stiffened at once, and he sniffed; and his eyes went green. He hissed softly but menacingly. He could not see the hobbit, but other senses he had, sharpened too by the darkness: hearing and smell. Now he seemed to be crouched right down with his flat hands splayed on the floor [*added*: and his head thrust out, nose almost to the stone]. Though he was only a black shadow in the gleam of his own eyes, Bilbo could see or feel that he was tense as a bow string, gathered for a spring.[TN36]

Bilbo stopped breathing and went stiff himself. He was desperate. He must get away, out of this horrible darkness, while he had any strength left. Thoughts flashed through his mind. He must fight. He must stab Gollum, kill the foul orc-<illegible>,[TN37] put his eyes out, kill him. It meant to kill him. But no, not a fair fight. He was invisible now. Gollum had no sword. Gollum had not actually tried to kill him yet. And he was miserable, alone, lost. A sudden understanding, a pity mixed with horror, welled up in Bilbo's heart; a glimpse of endless unmarked days [of >] without light, hard stone, cold fish, sneaking and whispering. He trembled. All this passed in his mind in a flash of a second. And then quite suddenly in another flash, as if lifted by a sudden strength and resolve, he leaped.[TN38]

No great leap perhaps for a man, but a leap in the dark. Straight over Gollum's head he sprang [> jumped], about seven feet forward and three in the air: indeed he only just missed cracking his skull, had he known it, on the low arch of the passage.[TN39]

Gollum threw himself backwards and <grabbed> as the hobbit fled[TN40] over, but too late: his hands snapped on thin air, and Bilbo falling fair on his sturdy feet sped off down the new passage [> tunnel]. He did not turn to see what Gollum was doing. There was a hissing and a cursing almost at his heels at first, then it stopped. Suddenly [> All at once] there was [> came] a bloodcurdling shriek, filled with hatred and despair. Gollum was beaten [> defeated]. He dared go no further. He had lost: lost his prey, and lost too the only thing he had ever cared for: his precious. The cry brought Bilbo's heart to his mouth, but still he held on. Now faint like [> as] an echo, but menacing the voice came behind:

'Thief, thief, thief! [*added*: baggins!] We hates it, we hates it, we hates it for ever.'[TN41]

Then there was a silence. But that too seemed menacing to Bilbo. 'If Goblins are so near that he smelt them' he thought, 'then they'll have heard his shrieking and cursing. Careful now, or this will [> this way will] lead you to worse things'. The passage was low and roughly made. It was not too difficult for the hobbit, except when in spite of all care he stubbed his poor toes [once again >] again, several times, on nasty jagged stones [*cancelled*: in the floor, but it must have been a bit too low for goblins.] 'A bit low for goblins, at least for the big ones', thought Bilbo, not knowing that even the big ones, the orcs of the mountains, are used to that sort of thing [> go along at great speed stooping low with their hands almost on the floor].[TN42]

Soon the passage, that had been sloping down, began to go up again, and after a while it climbed steeply. That slowed Bilbo down. But at last the slope stopped, the passage turned a corner, and dipped down again, and there at the bottom of a short incline he saw, filtering round another corner – a glimmer of light. Not red light as of fire or lantern, but [a] pale ordinary out-of-doors sort of light. Then he began to run. Scuttling along as fast as his legs would carry him he turned the last corner and came suddenly right into an open place, where the light, after all that time in the dark, seemed dazzlingly bright. Really it was only a leak of sunshine in through a doorway, where a great door, a stone door, was left standing a little open.[TN43]

Bilbo blinked, and then suddenly he saw the goblins: goblins in full armour with drawn swords sitting just inside the door, and watching it with wide eyes, and watching the passage that led to it. They were aroused, alert, ready for anything.

They saw him sooner than he saw them. Yes they saw him. Whether it was an accident or a last trick of the ring before it took a new master, it was not on his finger! With yells of delight the goblins rushed upon him.[TN44]

A pang of fear and loss, like an echo of Gollum's,[TN45] smote Bilbo, and forgetting even to draw his sword he stuck his hand[s] in his pocket[s], And there was the ring still, in his left pocket, and it slipped on his finger. The goblins stopped short. They could not see a sign of him. [The >] He had vanished! They yelled twice as loud as before, but not so delightedly.

p.100 l.14 in three goes.] So I said what about your promise? Show me the way out! But he came at me to kill me, and I ran [*added*: & fell over] and he missed me in the dark. Then I followed him, because I heard him talking to himself. He thought I really knew the way out, and so he was making for it. And then he sat down in the entrance and I couldn't get by. So I jumped over him and escaped, and ran on down to the gate.[TN46]

l.26 respect, when he talked] about jumping over Gollum, [dodging guards ..[TN47]

p.101 l.6 from bottom Gandalf knew all about] the back-door as the goblins called the lower gate [where Bilbo

This marks the end of the new Gollum-story Tolkien drafted in 1944 and sent to Allen & Unwin in 1947. Accompanying the typescript pages of new text was a sheet (Ad.Ms.H.76–7) listing errata Tolkien had discovered and wished for them to fix in the next printing, as was their usual practice. To distinguish it from the 'Proposed correction of Hobbit' (see page 732) of the next six sheets, this sheet is given its own title, 'Errors in "The Hobbit" '; see page 749 below.

Note that close comparison of this fair copy and typescript with Tolkien's spirited reading of the entire encounter with Gollum, recorded in July 1952 at George Sayer's home, reveals that Tolkien used a copy of the newly published book as his text on that occasion.

TEXT NOTES

1 These pages are neatly written with a minimum of cancellations and revisions (at least until the last three paragraphs, which are ink over pencil drafting and seem to have been added slightly later; see Text Note 46 below). They are written on the back of torn half-pages that were once mimeographs detailing the language of the C-scribe of *The Owl and the Nightingale*; Christopher Tolkien notes that this paper was 'extensively used in the later chapters of *The Two Towers*' [annotation to Ad.Ms.H.34]. He also points out, in his introduction to *The Notion Club Papers*, that his father borrowed the name 'Nicholas Guildford' for one of the prominent members of the pseudo-Inklings 'Notion Club' from a character in this early Middle English dialogue [circa 1200] (HME IX.150).

2 This replaced 'before the goblins came, and he was cut off from his friends far under under the mountains' <sic>, the reading of the first edition.

3 In the typescript, 'If it asks us, and we doesn't answer, then we does what it wants, eh? We shows it the way out, yes!' replaces 'If it asks us, and we doesn't answer, we gives it a present, gollum!' from the first edition.

4 The typescript introduces this extended passage with 'For the passage from page 91, l. 15 beginning But funnily enough and ending with not so delightedly on page 95, l. 8 substitute the following account'. For the text thus replaced, see page 160 & ff of this book, the parallel-text presentation in Bonniejean Christensen's 'Gollum's Character Transformation in *The Hobbit*' in *A Tolkien Compass*, ed. Jared Lobdell [1975, abridged edition 2003], and the textual marginalia in Douglas Anderson's *The Annotated Hobbit* (rev. ed.) pages 128–31.

5 The typescript replaces 'the ancient rules' with 'the ancient laws'.

6 Here and on all but one subsequent occurrences the word 'baggins' was written in lowercase in the manuscript but was carefully hand-corrected to 'Baggins' in ink in the typescript; only in Gollum's parting curse was it typed 'Baggins' from the start.

7 The words 'cross' and 'impatient' were reversed in the typescript.

8 This passage originally read

> 'Well, hurry up!' said Bilbo, relieved to think of Gollum going away at least. He thought this was just an excuse, and did not mean to come back, but <he wondered what> things Gollum talking about. What useful thing could he keep out on the dark lake? He guessed but he did <not> <illegible> He was out in his guesses, for Gollum did meant to come back. He was angry and hungry. And he was a miserable wicked creature, and already he had a plan.

9 The typescript reads 'endless dark days'; the original image perhaps more strongly captured the horrific eternal present in which the unaging Gollum has become trapped by the Ring.

10 Here 'faint and shaky' was changed to 'shaky and faint'. The idea that the ring-wearer's shadow can be seen in strong light is still present in the second and subsequent editions of *The Hobbit*, although this feature of the Ring came to be altogether ignored in *The Lord of the Rings*.

11 The opening of this paragraph was recast and supplemented by ink over pencil drafting in the margin to read

> 'My birthday-present! It came to me on my birthday, my precious!' So he had always said to himself, but who knows . . .

12 Although heavily cancelled the word 'Necromancer' is clear here, but was struck out at once and replaced with 'Master'. The typescript includes a second significant change, where *made* is erased and replaced in ink with *ruled*. So that instead of 'the Necromancer [> Master] who made them' we get 'the Master who ruled them'. Had the original name survived it would have been the only time in *The Hobbit* that a specific connection would have been drawn between the sinister Necromancer in his tower and Gollum's ring. Even the replacement offers a subtle link between the two books, since 'the Master who ruled them' is a close synonym of the second book's title, 'the lord of the rings'.

13 This is further changed in ink on the typescript to 'a few hours *ago*'. The removal of 'yesterday' was necessitated by the fact that there was no way of keeping track of the passage of days in the dark beneath the mountains; cf. the 'endless unmarked days' on page 738. See also Text Note 28 below.

The 'small goblin-imp' captured, throttled, and eaten by Gollum is probably our only encounter in the legendarium with an orc-child. Again, see Text Note 28 for Tolkien's description of it as not just 'little' but 'young'.

14 There are no skipped lines, such as the one following this paragraph, in the manuscript; all the ones in this chapter I have taken from the typescript, none of which carry over into Allen & Unwin's page proofs.

15 The last half of this sentence, everything after 'the last of him,' was bracketed and then cancelled.

16 In the typescript, the extra sibilant is absent from the first 'iss' but an

additional one appears in the first 'Lost', so that the line now reads 'Where *is* it? Where iss it? . . . *Losst* it is, my precious . . .' (emphasis mine).

17 Again, the typescript changes 'lost' to '*losst*'.

18 This sentence was revised to read 'anything Gollum wanted so much could hardly be something good.'

19 This last sentence was slightly simplified in the typescript, to 'It must tell first'.

20 This sentence was only achieved after three attempts. Originally Tolkien wrote:

> . . . should not tell – naturally his [<?guessing> >] suspicion awoke slower than Gollum's, who had brooded on this one thing for ages and ages – Gollum's mind had jumped to a guess quicker

Then he stopped, cancelled everything between the dashes, and continued:

> . . . should not tell – Gollum's mind had jumped to a guess quicker than Bilbo's naturally – Gollum had brooded on this one thing for ages and ages

Then again everything after 'quicker than' was cancelled, and text given on page 735 written in the left margin. The typescript, along with some adjustments in punctuation and capitalization, changes the wording and arrangement slightly:

> . . . for Gollum had brooded *for ages* on *this* one thing, and he was always afraid of *its* being stolen.

21 This sentence was later altered to read '. . . such a rage of *loss* and suspicion *was* in his heart . . .'. The replacement of Gollum's first instinctive response of *fear* by the more covetous *loss* is in ink over pencil.

22 This sentence was changed to read 'Bilbo could not guess *what had maddened the wretched creature*, but he saw that all was up, and that Gollum *meant to murder him after all.*'

23 The typescript changes *leaped* to *leapt* here, but 'leaped' was retained on Ad.Ms.H.48 (Ms) and Ad.Ms.H.81 (Ts). See page 738: 'as if lifted by a new strength and resolve, he leaped', and contrast DAA.130 ('Gollum leapt from his boat') with DAA.133 ('[Bilbo] leaped. No great leap for a man . . .').

24 Both of these changes are made in ink over pencil. The phrasing of this sentence is thematically significant: Bilbo does not put on the ring (subject-active verb-object) nor is a passive construction used but rather *it* slips on his finger (again subject-active verb-object, but with the Ring being the actor and Bilbo the acted upon). See Text Note 44 below.

25 This paragraph was revised in pencil, some of which was overwritten in ink:

> *In a* moment Gollum *reached him*. But before Bilbo could do anything *recover his breath*, pick himself up, *or* wave his sword,

> Gollum passed on, taking no notice of him, cursing and whispering *as he ran*.

The typescript refines the phrasing slightly:

> In a moment Gollum *was on him* . . . Gollum passed *by*, taking no notice . . .

26 Later Tolkien added in the margin 'and sheathed his sword <which>', then canceled it. This is clearly drafting for the passage that appears in pencil in the left margin of the corresponding page of typescript, which changes the passage to read 'Painfully he got up, *and sheathed his sword, which was now glowing faintly again. Then* very cautiously he followed . . .'

Originally this action had occurred several paragraphs later; see page 736 and Text Note 29.

27 The change from 'guess' to 'guesses' was not taken up in the typescript and does not appear in the published second edition. The change from 'Curse it!' to 'Curse the Baggins' is added above the line in ink over pencil.

28 This 'yesterday' escaped Tolkien's attention (see Text Note 13 above) and thus made its way into the typescript and then the page proofs, where it was corrected to read 'When we came this way *last, when we twisted* that nassty *young* squeaker' (Ad.Ms.H.56). On the bottom of this page Tolkien explained:

> yesterday won't do. G. knew no days
> cf. unmarked days p. 98

This last is a reference to 'endless unmarked days without light'; see page 738 above.

29 The typescript has '*sheathed* his sword' rather than the manuscript's 'hid his sword', then all of the sentence after 'the tunnel wall' is cancelled (in ink) and the passage entered (in pencil) several paragraphs earlier; see Text Note 26. The original idea that Bilbo kept his sword in hand while following the person who is trying to kill him presents the hobbit as wary in a desperate situation; the revision lays more stress on his wishing to move silently and undetected in dangerous circumstances.

30 These sentences were altered to read

> 'But if *the baggins has found the present*, we shan't see it. It'll escape us, gollum! It'll go away, away with our present, gollum!
>
> '*But* it doesn't know about the present [> precious > present].'

These lines were then bracketed and the word 'omit' written beside them; these sentences are indeed absent from the typescript, which merges the rest of this paragraph with the one preceding it ('. . . and squeezes it. But it doesn't know what the present can do . . .').

31 The word I read as 'leave' here might also be 'have' ('It'll just *have* it in its pocketses'); at any rate, over it Tolkien pencilled '*keep*', and this became the reading in the typescript.

In a rare case of a dropped sibilant, the typescript and proof read 'lost' for the 'losst' in the following sentence.

32 Changed to 'It knows. *It knows a way in, it must know a way out, yes.* It's *off to* the back-door, yes to the back door, *that's it.*'

33 The typescript reverses this: 'Two *right*, yes, yes. Two *left*, yet', probably to avoid the impression that the tunnels fall into a neat unvarying pattern of right, left, right, left, &c.

34 This sentence was changed to read '*Seven* right, yes; *six* left, yes!'

35 On the typescript, Tolkien marked for these two sentences to be transposed. This direction was not carried out for some reason, for they appear in the original order in the page proofs. He seems to have begun to mark the proof page in pencil requesting this change and then erased his directions.

36 This paragraph was revised, both in ink and pencil, to read

> Bilbo crept *away* from the wall more quietly than a mouse; but Gollum stiffened at once, *and sniffed*; and his eyes went green. He hissed softly but menacingly. He could not see the hobbit, but *now he was on the alert and he had* other senses *that* the darkness *had sharpened*: hearing and smell. *He* seemed to be crouched right down with his flat hands splayed on the floor and his head thrust out, nose almost to the stone. Though he was only a black shadow in the gleam of his own eyes, Bilbo could see or feel that he was tense as a bow string, gathered for a spring.

37 I cannot read this cancelled word, but it lacks a descender at the end and thus is not orc-*thing*; orc-*hun*[ter] is more probable. The typescript (Ad.Ms.H.81) replaces this with the familiar '. . . He must stab *the foul thing*, put its eyes out'.

38 This paragraph was carefully revised, and since it is perhaps the most important in the book from the point of view of the sequel – certainly, at least, the key passage in the second edition revisions – I reproduce the whole paragraph as revised here for comparison with the original in the text.

> Bilbo stopped breathing and went stiff himself. He was desperate. He must get away, out of this horrible darkness, while he had any strength left. He must fight. He must stab *the foul thing*, put *its* eyes out, kill *it*. It meant to kill him. But no, not a fair fight. He was invisible now. Gollum had no sword. Gollum had not actually tried to kill him yet. And he was miserable, alone, lost. A sudden understanding, a pity mixed with horror, welled up in Bilbo's heart; a glimpse of endless unmarked days without light, hard stone, cold fish, sneaking and whispering. All *these thoughts* passed *in* a flash of a second. *He trembled.* And then quite suddenly in another flash, as if lifted by a *new* strength and resolve, he leaped.

The typescript again revises this slightly but significantly ('. . . *almost* stopped breathing . . . *No*, not a fair fight . . . had not actually *threatened* to kill him, *or tried to* yet . . . without light *or hope of betterment* . . .'), achieving the text of the published second edition (see DAA.133).

Bilbo's sudden insight into Gollum's inner life here is on par with the unwitnessed moment outside Shelob's lair when Gollum briefly appears as 'an old weary hobbit, shrunken by the years that had carried him far beyond his time, beyond friends and kin, and the fields and streams of youth, an old starved pitiable thing' (*LotR*.742) – not surprisingly, because both were written at about the same time (cf. HME.VIII.183–184, when Christopher dates this chapter in *The Lord of the Rings* to May 1944).† Most significant here is the change in the original of *his, he* to *its, it* when Bilbo is preparing to kill 'It', literally depersonalizing his intended victim, and the shift preserved in the final text back to his using *he* to describe Gollum, along with once again using his name, once Bilbo begins to treat Gollum as a fellow creature again and therefore is unable to murder him, even in self-defense.

†Assuming, of course, that this scene was in the original manuscript of that chapter, which is now lacking that section – cf. HME.VIII.192

39 Several small abridgments and some re-arrangement produced the familiar final version of this paragraph (cf. DAA.133).

40 The manuscript here (page 8, Ad.Ms.H.48) clearly reads 'fled over', while the typescript (page 5, Ad.Ms.H.81) has 'fled over him'. The proofs (page 98, Ad.Ms.H.58) give instead '*flew* over *him*'. Tolkien marked for this to be changed to *fled*, but for some reason the change was not made and the printer's reading persisted into published book (second edition page 98; DAA.133).

The typescript of this paragraph as includes one very minor departure from the fair copy: the replacement of 'a hissing and a cursing' with 'a hissing and cursing'.

41 This marks the spot at which Tolkien's 1952 audio recording of the Gollum chapter ends.

42 Once again the paragraph underwent minor changes for the typescript: 'Goblins' became 'goblins' (lower-cased), part of the cancelled passage was restored so that it was once more 'nasty jagged stones *in the floor*' that Bilbo stubbed his toes on, and the goblins are said to run 'at *a* great speed'. More significantly, the use of the word *orcs* in the fair copy to describe 'the big ones' doubles the number of times this *Silmarillion* and *Lord of the Rings* term appears in the published *Hobbit*,† its only appearance in the original edition or manuscript being Bladorthin/Gandalf's warnings about trying to travel northward around Mirkwood (see page 244 and DAA.188); it also confirms our guesses about Bolg and his bodyguard (see page 711).

†The third mention, discussed in Text Note 37 above, not having survived into the typescript.

43 Only four minor changes differentiate the typescript for the fair copy in this paragraph: the replacement of *glimmer* by *glimpse*, the omission of *ordinary* ('a pale out-of-doors sort of light'), the substitution of a proper

noun for the pronoun ('Then *Bilbo* began to run'), and the omission of *along* ('Scuttling as fast as'). See the commentary on 'The Vanishing People' for connotations of 'glimmer' Tolkien may have wished to avoid here.

A single page (Marq. 1/1/21:1) survives among the *Lord of the Rings* papers that corresponds almost exactly to the last page (page 6) of the typescript, beginning at the exact same point ('a stone door') and also stopping at the identical spot ('. . . the lower gate [where Bilbo'). Comparison reveals that this neat pencil text is an intermediary stage between the manuscript (Ad.Ms.H.52) and typescript (Ad.Ms.H.82), probably drawn up by Tolkien as a guide to the creation of the latter. This page became separated from the rest of the *Hobbit* revision material, probably because the back of this sheet (1/1/21:2) bears some nearly illegible notes and rough drafting for a passage from *The Lord of the Rings*, dealing with calculations regarding the time needed for Boromir and the Nazgûl to travel from Gondor or Minas Tirith to Rivendell.

These notes are written on a page bearing the letterhead of the Oxford Circle of The Catenian Association, listing 'Prof. J.R.R. Tolkien' as the group's Vice-President and giving his address as 20 Northmoor Road (a house the Tolkiens occupied from 1930 to 1947). According to a history of this brotherhood for Catholic laymen, Tolkien was one of the founders of the group's Oxford Circle in 1944 and served as that branch's first Vice-President. Accordingly, it seems likely that these notes date from 1944, although of course they could have been written later, anytime up to 1947 when he sent the typescript version of this material to Allen & Unwin.

44 This paragraph ends with a cancelled incomplete sentence: 'With a sudden <illegible> of fear or loss,' which was plainly cancelled when Tolkien decided to begin a new paragraph instead with a more poignant form of the same sentiment.

In the original (first edition) version of this scene, Bilbo was not wearing the ring when he parted on neutral if not friendly terms from Gollum and so naturally it was not on his finger when he stumbled upon the goblins. The new version of the scene has to account for the facts that (a) Bilbo had to have had the ring on when he escaped from Gollum, and (b) he could not be wearing it when he encountered the goblins (or else they would not have seen him and the encounter would have been far less dramatic), yet (c) he had no reason to take it off in the meantime. Tolkien's solution, to have the ring simply vanish from Bilbo's finger, is the only time it seems to vanish from one place under its own power and reappear in another, unless we assume that it forced Bilbo to unconsciously slip it in his pocket without being aware of the act. It could not have come off accidentally, since someone feeling his way in total darkness with one hand on the wall would hold the other hand out in front, not put it in his pocket.

In any case, its attempt to get Bilbo killed by the goblins and itself into the hands of an orc (cf. Frodo's glib words, 'What . . . Wouldn't an Orc have suited it better?' – *LotR*.69), and hence eventually to the

Necromancer (Sauron), is foiled by Bilbo's luck (he is, after all, Mr. Lucky Number, has just been saved three times by luck during the riddle-game, and later admits 'I have begun to trust my luck' – cf. page 504) or presence of mind. The episode does, no doubt deliberately, call up echoes of its betrayal of Isildur (*LotR*.66 & *UT*.275) and, of course, its purposeful abandonment of Gollum: cf. Gandalf's words to Frodo in 'The Shadow of the Past': 'A Ring of Power looks after itself . . . *It* may slip off treacherously, but its keeper never abandons it . . . The Ring was trying to get back to its master.† It had slipped from Isildur's hand and betrayed him . . . it caught poor Déagol . . . it had devoured [Gollum] . . . So now, when its master was awake once more . . . it abandoned Gollum' (*LotR*.68–69).

†Note here Gandalf's use of the term *master*, the same as that used within *The Hobbit* for Sauron as the Ring-lord: 'even the Master who ruled them'. See also Text Note 12 above.

45 The typescript elaborates this slightly: 'like an echo of Gollum's *misery*'. This is the only time within *The Hobbit*, even the second edition text, where Bilbo's being in danger of succumbing to the 'Ring-sickness', if we may so call it, is hinted at; everywhere else within the story it remains just a magic ring with no sinister connotations.

46 The text being replaced here read, in the first edition, 'And he couldn't guess in three goes. *So I asked for my present, and he went to look for it, and couldn't find it. So I said, "very well, help me to get out of this nasty place!" and he showed me the passage to the door. "Good-bye" I said, and I went on down.*'

This entry and the two that follow it are crowded on the bottom of the last manuscript page (page 10, Ad.Ms.H.51); all are ink over pencil underwriting and probably slightly later than the fair copy text of the rest of the manuscript. The pencil has not been erased, and enough of it can be read under or around the ink to make it clear that it was simply drafting for the text that overwrote it, somewhat different in phrasing but close to it:

> . . . me the way out. But he came at me . . . in the dark . . . it. And he sat down in the passage, and I could not get by so I jumped over him and escaped, and ran on down to the doorway . . . the goblins called the lower <gate> – where

The first of these three entries seems to have given Tolkien a good deal of trouble – not so much in finding what he wanted to say but in getting it to fit in as small a space as possible (even so, its inclusion wound up adding lines to this page; see Text Note 47 below). In addition to the ink-over-pencil text at the end of the last of these ten manuscript pages, two pencilled versions take up the bottom half of the last typescript sheet as well, along with pencilled notations as Tolkien added up letters, adjusting his totals with each change or deletion.

The first of the pencilled drafts reads

> [what's in my pocket >] So I [asked >] said "what about your

> promise?" But he came at me [and I ran >] to kill me and I [*cancelled*: ran. But he missed me and I] dodged him. Then I followed him to the passage to the back-gate. and I jumped over . . .

Before trailing off into illegibility. The next pencil draft, written below it, reads

> So I said "what about your promise?" But he came at me, to kill me, and [I ran >] I dodged him. Then I followed him [*cancelled*: to the passage] till he came [*cancelled*: to the passage] the way out, and I jumped over him, and ran down to the back-gate.

By contrast, although the typed final version in the typescript above this drafting has an 'X' beside it in the margin, it represents the second edition text exactly as it appears in the page proof and subsequently published book. The only difference between the ink-over-pencil text (page 739) and the typescript is the latter's omission of 'on' from the last sentence, so that 'jumped over him and escaped, and ran on down to the gate' becomes '. . . and ran down to the gate'.

47 The usually vigilant typesetters at Unwin Brothers dropped the phrase 'dodging guards' when they inserted 'jumping over Gollum'. Tolkien wrote in the missing words on the proof page but, although the printers did subsequently enter it, they did so in the wrong place, reversing the order of the phrases from what Tolkien intended, and this transposition persists into the published book, so that instead of 'when he talked about jumping over Gollum, dodging guards, and squeezing through' – that is, the events in their chronological sequence – we get 'when he talked about dodging guards, jumping over Gollum, and squeezing through' (second edition page 105; cf. DAA.140). The original first edition text had simply read 'when he talked about dodging guards, and squeezing through' (first edition page 100; cf. page 200).

It should be noted that the changes discussed in Text Notes 46 & 47 were the only ones that created an overrun, since the first expanded its paragraph from seven lines to ten and the second from three lines to four. Once they finally implemented both changes, the typesetters compensated for the expanded page 100/105 by moving one line to the bottom of the preceding page (new page 104, corresponding to old page 99) and two lines to the top of the following page (new page 106, corresponding to old page 101); by the time the second edition text reaches page 107, the second edition text once again corresponds page-by-page to the first edition text (in this case, to old page 102).

(ii)

Errors in 'The Hobbit'. Misprints, or uncorrected verbal errors in the Ms.

[added in pencil: previously sent in]

In addition to a list of purely typographical errors (e.g., then > than, nay > any, find > fine, above stream > above the stream), most of which are noted by Hammond (*Descriptive Bibliography*, pages 4, 7, 16, & 22), Tolkien also wanted to take advantage of the opportunity offered by a new printing to address some issues arising from problems within *The Hobbit* itself. After listing seventeen misprints, Tolkien himself notes:

These are not important, except for precision. Though back p.104 for black is unfortunate; while when [p.64] is required to match the runes on the map.[TN1]

Most of the various corrections Tolkien requests are included in short excerpts on the proofs sent back to him (Ad.Ms.H.59–61) so that the author could check them in context. This list of typos is then followed on the same sheet by the more significant category, with a new header written in ink:

(iii)

Other corrections.

On page 30, ll. 26,27 by inadvertence (that has annoyed some of the 'fans' who have solved all the runes) the text: five feet high is the door and three abreast may enter it does not correspond with the actual runes, and should read: five feet high the door and three may walk abreast. I think the map-maker did not read his text properly,[TN2] but since his map cannot be altered, and his version is better, I hope the text can be adjusted.

The Map-maker has also placed on his map the words HERE OF OLD WAS THRAIN KING UNDER THE MOUNTAIN, in defiance of the fact that his father [> Thrain's father] Thror was still alive and dwarf-kings do not abdicate. I am afraid that nothing can here be done, except to point out in the Sequel that the Thrain referred to was a yet more ancient king.[TN3]

On pages 27 (l. 28) man; and 294 (l. 11) men. Arthur Ransome[TN4] and others pointed out the desirability of not using man, men as 'person, people' in a story in which other rational creatures than Men appear. On p. 27 read 'fellow'; and on p. 294 read 'of us'.[TN5]

More annoying to me is the carelessness on p. 35 And your father went away on the third of March, a hundred years ago last Thursday. Now the Unexpected Party occurred on a Wednesday (as is stated). If this remark is true, then the Party must have occurred on March 9th. But that is impossible. Not only does it make the time far too long before the travellers reach the trolls on the night of May 31st (p. 41); but also they are supposed to start off the next morning, and that is 'just before May'. For 'third of March' we must read 'twenty-first of April' – or regretfully abandon the comic precision of 'last Thursday'. For since Bilbo's birthday was the 22nd of September and fell that year on a Thursday, a party held on a Wednesday near the end of April must have occurred on the 20th [> 27th]. Read therefore either 'on the third of March, a hundred years ago last month' or 'on the twenty first of April, a hundred years ago last Thursday'. [*added in ?pencil*: The latter is better.]

In the event, the printers adopted 'the twenty-first of April, a hundred years ago last Thursday' (Ad.Ms.H.60), although this did not end Tolkien's attempts to reconcile the dates and moons of Bilbo's story to the twin constraints imposed by the reduction of the original journey to a single year and also new complications introduced in *The Lord of the Rings* (e.g., the specific date of Bilbo's birthday, which occurred while they were in Lake Town, and the time required to journey from Bilbo's home to Rivendell). To this was later added the additional constraint of trying to adjust events written by the modern Gregorian calendar to fit the Shire-calendar instead; see 'Timeline and Itinerary' in the 1960 Hobbit, starting on page 815.

TEXT NOTES

1 That is, the text that currently read 'Already the shadows were deepening about them, though far away through the trees and over *the back tops* of those growing lower down' (first edition page 104 line 16) should instead have read '. . . over the *black* tops . . .' Similarly, in Rivendell Elrond states that the moon-letters read 'Stand by the grey stone *where* the thrush knocks', whereas the runes on the actual map provided with the book say instead '. . . *when* the thrush knocks'. Since he could not change the printed map without great trouble and expense and did not wish to have a loremaster like Master Elrond appear careless or in error, the latter error was more significant than the former (which at worst would merely puzzle some readers). Both of these corrections appear in the proofs Tolkien was sent in 1950 (Ad.Ms.H.61) and in subsequent editions of the book from the fifth printing onward.

2 The 'map-maker' whose work Tolkien disparages here is, of course, himself, not the production departments at Unwin Brothers and Allen & Unwin. Compare his similar humorous self-deprecatory remarks in lectures at Oxford about his definitive edition of *Sir Gawain & the Green Knight*, still in print more than eighty years after its first publication: 'Tolkien and Gordon were quite wrong, quite wrong when they said that! Can't imagine what they were thinking of!' (Carpenter, *Tolkien: A Biography*, page 105).

The correction requested was indeed made, bringing the story's text into agreement with the map's runes: *five feet high the door and three may walk abreast* (Ad.Ms.H.60; DAA.52).

3 This paragraph was bracketed, usually a sign that the material so treated needs further attention, either cancellation or replacement. In this case, the point was addressed in the brief prefatory note Tolkien added to the book, starting with the second edition; see part (iv) below.

The matter was further developed in *The Lord of the Rings*, where 'Thráin I' became the dwarf-king who led his people away from Moria after the Balrog killed his father (Náin I) and grandfather (Durin VI), founding the Kingdom under the Mountain at the Lonely Mountain, and discovering the Arkenstone (thus explaining its hitherto puzzling title as 'the Arkenstone of Thrain' and explaining away the remnants in the text of the Thror-Thrain-Thorin/Thrain-Thror-Thorin confusion); see *LotR*.1109 & 1117. For the original drafts of this material, see HME XII.275–7 and Note 5 on HME XII.286.

4 For Ransome's letter, and Tolkien's reply, see Appendix IV.

5 The specific passages in question are Gandalf's description of Bilbo as an 'Excitable little man' (changed in the page proofs to 'Excitable little *fellow*'; Ad.Ms.H.60) and Thorin's dying words 'If more men valued food and cheer and song above hoarded gold' (changed to 'If more *of us* valued . . .'; Ad.Ms.H.59).

Tolkien had suggested these two changes as far back as December 1937 (see *Letters*, p. 28), only three months after the book was first published; they finally appeared in the fifth printing (i.e., the second edition) of 1951.

(iv)
Prefatory Note

One additional significant piece of new writing associated with the second edition is the prefatory note Tolkien wrote to explain why this printing differed from those that had gone before. This note, which first appeared in the fifth printing (i.e., the second edition) of 1951, exists in two states, a long and a short version, each of which is preserved in fair copy manuscript and single-spaced typescript. I give first the fair-copy manuscript text of the long version (A) [Ad.Ms.H.87–8]. The typescript (B)

[Ad.Ms.H.89] based upon this has a number of variations in phrasing, the more significant of which are given in the Text Notes that follow.

This reprint has been revised. Some small inaccuracies have been corrected: such as the failure of the text on pages 30 and 64 to translate precisely the runes on Thror's Map; and the date twenty first of April, previously on page 35 given wrongly as the third of March. The last error was due to a misreading of the difficult hand and language of the original diary [*cancelled*: or memoir].[TN1]

More important is the matter of Chapter Five. I have thought it desirable to give now the true story of the ending of the Riddle Game, in place of the somewhat 'altered' account of it that Bilbo gave to his friends (and put down in his diary). This weighed on his conscience, as notes in his private papers show, and he was uneasily aware that Gandalf did not believe it.[TN2] His story – that Gollum had promised to give the Ring to him as a gift, if he won the game – seemed of course to the wizard most unlikely from the first, and in the light of later developments [*cancelled*: was] simply incredible. But it was not until many years after Bilbo's journey that he pressed the old hobbit to tell him the truth; for the truth about the Ring had become desperately important.

If ever it proves possible to arrange extracts from the Red Book and present them in English to students of hobbit-lore,[TN3] it will be made clear how it was that Bilbo, as honest a hobbit by nature as could be found, came to put out a false tale; and how by that game at the dark roots of the Misty Mountains the history of the Western world and the end of the Third Age was changed. For the Red Book of Westmarch, not long ago rediscovered and deciphered, contains a chronicle (of great length and by many hands) of that perilous time,[TN4] as it was seen by hobbits; and its earlier parts are largely made up of extracts from Bilbo's writings, including the various secret or private papers that he [handed >] gave to his heir.

However, in the meanwhile none of this need trouble those who in this edition make their first acquaintance with hobbit-lore.[TN5] It has little bearing on the tale of the dragon-hoard. Yet I felt that some immediate explanation was due to those who may possess older copies, and might suspect me of wilfully [rewriting >] altering the story, in one version or the other. I have not. The older version is the account in Bilbo's diary;[TN6] the later is the truth as told to Gandalf and revealed in the Red Book. And there for the present I will leave the matter.

I will end with one further note, on a point that several readers have raised. Thorin Oakenshield was the son of Thráin, and Thráin was son of Thrór King under the Mountain. But upon the Map is written here of old was Thrain King under the Mountain Yet dwarf-kings do not abdicate, and Thror was still alive when Smaug put an end to the kingdom for that time. Nonetheless the Map is not at fault. Names [*added*: often] repeat themselves in dwarvish dynasties, and the genealogies of the Red Book show that the Thráin referred to was Thráin I, a distant ancestor of Thrór, who had long before ruled the same realm, before his people passed on to the remoter mountains of the North. Thrór and his son were thus in fact re-entering old [*cancelled*: incomplete] delvings of their kin when, driven out of the North again, they returned to the Lonely Mountain of Erebor.[TN7] Dwarves had been long in the world and known much troublous history before the days of Thrór,[TN8] and when he wrote of old he meant it: in the ancient past remembered still in those deep throated[TN9] songs of lore that the dwarf-kin sang in their secret tongue at feasts to which none but dwarves were bidden. Some say that they sing still.

The 'long version' was followed by another typescript (C) [Ad.Ms.H.86], a 'short version', derived primarily from (B) but incorporating some elements from (A). This in turn was followed by a fair copy (D) [Ad.Ms.H.85], which became the version actually printed (cf. DAA.28). I here conflate (C) and (D) together, with passages present in the typescript but omitted in the manuscript that followed given in italics; the title given here appears only on the fair copy.

Note on corrections and alterations in reprint 1950

In this reprint several minor inaccuracies, most of them noted by readers, have been corrected. For example, the text on pages 30 and 64 now corresponds exactly with the runes on Thror's Map. *On page 35 the third of March, a misreading of the difficult hand and language of the original, is replaced by the correct reading the twenty first of April, a date borne out by the fact that the expedition started on a fine morning 'just before May'.*[TN10] More important is the matter of Chapter Five. There the true story of the ending of the Riddle Game, as it was eventually revealed (under pressure) by Bilbo to Gandalf, is now given according to the Red Book, in place of the version Bilbo first gave to his friends, and actually set down in his diary. This *strange* departure from truth on the part of a most honest hobbit was a portent of great significance. It does not, however, concern the present story, and those who in this edition make their first acquaintance with hobbit-lore need not trouble about it. Its explanation lies in the history of the Ring, as it is set out in the chronicles of the Red Book of Westmarch, and it must await their publication.

A final note may be added, on a point raised by several students of the lore of the period. On Thror's Map is written Here of old was Thrain King under the Mountain; Thrain was the son of Thror, the last King under the Mountain before the coming of the dragon. The Map, however, is not in error. Names are often repeated in dynasties, and the genealogies show that a distant ancestor of Thror was referred to, Thrain I, a fugitive from Moria, who first discovered the Lonely Mountain, Erebor, and ruled there for a while, before his people moved on to the remoter mountains of the North – *Dwarves had already known a long and troublous history in the world before the days of Thror, and when he wrote of old he meant it: in the ancient past, remembered still in the songs of lore that the dwarf-kin sang in their secret tongue at feasts to which none but dwarves were bidden. Some say that they sing them still, and with the lengthening of the years the songs have become very long indeed.*[TN11]

JRRT
9/9/50

At the bottom of the typescript page, Tolkien added the notation in pencil:

Suggested specimen of a prefatory note
to a revised edition of The Hobbit

The fair copy page (D) is stamped '18 SEP 1950' by the printer, showing that this and not the typescript is actually the text sent to be typeset. By the omission of the passages I have italicized, the Note was shortened to the point where it could fit on a single page (in fact, on the hitherto-blank back of the table of contents) and thus not disrupt the pagination; had Tolkien known earlier that such a note would be needed, the pagination could no doubt have been adjusted as it was for the Gollum chapter (see page 732 above).

The Prefatory Notes as published did establish a rationale for changing one of the key chapters in the book, the encounter with Gollum, in a way that served the purposes of the sequel without harm to the coherence and independence of the original book: the replaced passage is revealed to be authentic but inaccurate. And for its part, the passage on Thrain I at last resolves the inconsistency created by the earlier confusion between the two competing Thror-Thrain-Thorin/Thrain-Thror-Thorin genealogies. In a masterly demonstration of his preferred method, Tolkien leaves intact both pieces of information – that Thror was the last King under the Mountain (text) and that 'Here of old was Thrain King . . .' (map) – by adding a third new piece of information alongside them that places them into harmony as part of a larger picture.

The abbreviated published version of this Prefatory Note provides the necessary information to place the new edition in context, but the more extended versions that had to be trimmed down had done more. For example, the closing sentences ('when he wrote of old he meant it') conjure up a vast sense of time only remembered in songs which we, not being dwarves, can never be privileged to hear. More remarkably, like some of the remarks about hobbits in the Prologue to *The Lord of the Rings*, they bring the story down to the present day (e.g., '[Hobbits] *now* avoid us with dismay', 'the regions in which Hobbits then lived were doubtless the same as those *in which they still linger*' – *LotR*.13 & 14, italics mine): 'Some say *they sing them still* . . .' Also, the idea that Thror returned to incomplete delvings from long ago enhances his stature as the founder (rather than merely re-occupier) of the Kingdom under the Mountain.

Significant in another sense, as a road not taken, is Tolkien's proffered explanation that a change here is simply a correction of an 'error due to a misreading of the difficult hand and language of the original'. Had he adopted this simple expedient, which was entirely in keeping with his authorial pose as editor and translator of Bilbo's story (cf. the runic border on the dust jacket, where Tolkien referred to himself as the translator of Bilbo's memoir), it would have served him well when he tried to resolve the conundrum of recalcitrant phases of the moon in the 1960 Hobbit.

TEXT NOTES

1 In the typescript, the example and explanation are both dropped and the paragraphs run together: '. . . have been corrected, *many of them long noted by readers and students of hobbit-lore*. More important *than these details* is the matter . . .'

2 'Gandalf did not believe it' > 'Gandalf *had never* believed it'.

3 The opening of this paragraph was replaced by '*When, if ever, a selection from the matter of the Red Book is presented to students of the period*'.

4 The typescript reads '. . . how by that game at the dark roots of the *mountains* the *fortunes* of the Western *W*orld . . . of Westmarch, *a hobbit-heirloom* not long ago re-discovered and deciphered, contains *chronicles* [*cancelled*: *and commentaries*] of that perilous time . . .'

5 Changed to 'with *hobbitry*'.

6 The typescript reads '. . . the account in Bilbo's *memoirs, my primary source*'. This distinction is significant because there is no mention in *The Hobbit* of Bilbo's jotting down what happened to him each day, while we are told in the Epilogue that Gandalf and Balin visit him while he is writing 'his memoirs'.

7 This sentence was bracketed in the manuscript.

The typescript expands slightly upon the career of Thráin I: 'a distant ancestor of Thrór, *a fugitive from Moria, and the first discoverer of the Lonely Mountain, Erebor, who ruled that land for a while,* before his people . . .'; the sentence about Thror and his son re-entering old delvings upon their return is absent in the typescript. The inclusion of 'and his son' shows how closely Thror and Thrain are linked in Tolkien's mind; the genealogy in *The Lord of the Rings*, which probably postdates this prefatory note, gives the date of Thrain's birth as fifty-four years after Thror's re-establishment of the Kingdom under the Mountain (*LotR*.1117).

8 For the details of this 'troublous history', see Appendix A part iii: 'Durin's Folk' in *The Lord of the Rings*. Even within the context of the original *Hobbit*, note Thorin's thoughts during the Siege of the Mountain: how each piece of treasure had associations for him with 'old memories of the labours and sorrows of his race' (page 648).

9 The words 'deep throated', bracketed in the fair copy, do not appear in the typescript.

10 This passage is bracketed in the typescript and absent in the fair copy. The next sentence began a new paragraph in the typescript but becomes part of the first paragraph in the fair copy.

11 The fair copy might well have once included these sentences, since it ends rather abruptly at the bottom of a page. If so, although bracketed in the typescript they were probably curtailed for reasons of space rather than any dissatisfaction with their content.

(v)
Thrym Thistlebeard

Finally, the following unpublished letter casts an interesting light on Tolkien's thinking about *The Hobbit* at the time he sent the corrections and proposed re-casting of Chapter V in to Allen & Unwin, offering slightly different solutions to some of the problems than the ones he sent to the publisher. Written on 26th September 1947 to Jennifer Paxman, whose father had been one of Tolkien's companions in that memorable 1911 visit to Switzerland from which Tolkien drew memories many years later when writing the Misty Mountain sequences in Chapters IV and VI, the letter first addresses her question about applying to various Oxford colleges, then turns to *The Hobbit*:

As for 'the Hobbit'. There are a fair number of errors in it; and though I keep on sending corrections in to Allen & Unwin they don't seem to get put right . . .

But the author also made errors. On p. 30 the text to agree with red runes should read '<u>five feet high the door and three may walk abreast</u>'

The chief error otherwise is on p. 25: the third of March a hundred years ago last Thursday. The party was on a Wednesday (p. 17, 20). If this was true, therefore, the party must have been on March 9 and the expedition must have set out on March 10. But that was not so: it was just before May (p. 40), and also it would only have taken about a month's slow going to reach the Trolls on 31st May (p. 41). As Bilbo's birthday was Sept. 22nd and a Thursday that year, the party must actually have occurred on Wednesday April 27th. The text should read twenty-first of April /or/ a hundred years [*added*: ago] last month. The latter is correct. . . .

Runes. The whole linguistic situation of 'The Hobbit' has become rather complicated owing to the necessity for translation. The language of the time, or the Common Speech of the West, is represented by English. This particular variety of Dwarf came from the North where a more northerly language was locally spoken. Now Dwarves have their own secret language, but like Jews and Gypsies use the language of the country. So all these Dwarves have Norse dwarf-names to represent the relations of the country and people of Dale (Bard the Bowman) etc. to the Common Language. The Dwarves used a more inscriptional alphabet – and I am now rather sorry that I used instead the Anglo-Saxon Runes (on the translation principle). The dwarf-alphabet was much better. The Elvish Alphabets do not come into the Hobbit – unless you have the full English edn. with coloured pictures, in which case you will see a bit of an inscription in an Elvish alphabet (the Alphabet of Fëanor) on the great jars in the left-foreground. This alphabet plays a considerable part in the sequel 'The Lord of the Rings'. I can let you have all these things, if you want them. They were not, of course, invented for the Hobbit or its sequel, since these things are only fragments torn out of 'the Silmarillion' or The History of the Elves, which no one will publish.

As for the actual runes in the book and your question. Þ·Þ stands for Thror son of Thrain. But that is an error that besides myself you alone have spotted. On p. 202–3, the order is given as Thorin – Thrain – Thror. The map-maker was confused and had the order Thorin – Thror – Thrain. But even that was erroneous as dwarf-kings don't abdicate, and the 'grandfather' was still alive when the map was made. In the sequel it will appear that the grandfather Thror was son of an older King Thrym (Thistlebeard). So that Þ·Þ stands for Thrór Thrym's son. All these dwarf-names (except Thrym and Thistilbarði (Thistlebeard), which is in another list) come out of the list of dwarf-names inserted into the Völuspá or 'Prophecy of the Sibyl' that is the first poem of the Elder Edda.[TN1]

After this, he continues with a discussion on the actual Anglo Saxon runes, his recent visit to Lincolnshire on college business, a dubious reliquary of 'Little Saint Hugh (the supposed martyr)', Chaucer's 'Prologue', and the various editions available of *The Hobbit.*

The logic underlying the problem with 'the third of March' is the same as in part (iii) above, although interestingly enough here, only five days after sending off (i), (ii), and (iii) to Stanley Unwin, Tolkien now prefers a different phrasing in the replacement text. The reference to dwarves adopting the language of the country they live in 'like Jews and Gypsies' shows that this idea was already present long before Tolkien compared his dwarves with the Jews in his 1965 radio interview with Denys Gueroult (see page 86, Note 9 and also page 859), although so far as I am aware the comparison to the Gypsies (an apt parallel to the wandering dwarves mentioned in early parts of *The Lord of the Rings*) occurs nowhere else.

The most interesting passage, of course, is that dealing with Thrym Thistlebeard, a hitherto unknown king of Durin's line. Although like Fimbulfambi he was destined never to appear in canonical form, having already been replaced by Dain (I) in the earliest surviving dwarven family-trees (see Marq. 3/9/1 and also HME XII.277), in this case he was probably not rejected so much as simply forgotten. I have already noted, on pp. 602–3, that the runic initials Þ·Þ on the inscribed jar in the foreground of the painting 'Conversation with Smaug' (Plate XI [top]) must refer to Þror and Þrain (or possibly Þrain and Þror), and that the presence of both's initials here presents some problems. This unpublished letter is proof first that the Thrain-Thror-Thorin genealogy was simply an error ('the map-maker was confused') and that Tolkien himself came to be well aware of the problem inherent in the initials on the inscribed jar. In this paragraph he offers a satisfactory and ingenious solution to their meaning, once again solving a problem in the received text by addition, not contradiction or replacement.

Why then was it never implemented? My guess is that Tolkien had not yet thought of this solution when he sent the errata off to Allen & Unwin on 21st September and that he generated the character on the spot in response to Paxman's question five days later. But he neglected to keep a copy of this letter for his files,[TN2] so that when he came to create the dwarven family tree, he had by that point forgotten about Thrym Thistlebeard.[TN3]

TEXT NOTES

1 Thrym ('Uproar') comes from the *Þrymskviða*, part of the *Elder Edda*, while Thistilbarði ('Thistlebeard') is part of a *þulur* (thulur) or name-list, one of many sometimes appended to Snorri's *Prose Edda*. However, in the original each is the name of a giant, not a dwarf.

Thrym is indeed the famous King Thrym of Jötunheim ('giant-land'), lord of the frost-giants; *Þrymskviða* is the story of how he stole Mjöllnir (Thor's hammer, the bane of all giants) and demanded Freya's hand for its return. Loki convinced Thor to disguise himself as the bride-to-be, enabling the angry storm god to get close enough to reclaim his weapon, whereupon he killed most of the wedding party. This story has an unusual personal connection to Tolkien, for it was retold by his friend Rob Gilson as a short Christmas play in 1903, when the future fellow T.C.B.S. member was about ten years old. Called 'Thor's Journey to Fetch His Hammer', something of its precocious nature can be conveyed through its list of characters, scenes, and the mock-Shakespearian diction of its closing lines:

Characters
Loki: The God of evil
Thor: The God of thunder
Thrym: A wicked giant

Scenes
Scene I: Thor's bedroom
Scene II: Jötunheim
Scene III: The Hall of Valhalla
Scene IV: Dining-Hall in Thrym's castle

Thrym. And now I will fetch the hammer from its hiding-place.
(Exit Thrym)
Thor. Ha, ha, Thrym will soon lie prostrate on the ground.
(Enter Thrym)
(He places Miölnir in Thor's lap)
Thrym. Here is Miölnir.
(Thor rises from his seat and throws off his veil)
Thor. Now giant thou shalt die.
(He kills Thrym)
(curtain)

I am grateful to David Bratman for drawing my attention to R. Q. Gilson's early interest in Eddic myths and providing me with a copy of both this mini-play and 'The Wooing of Gerda', a similar retelling of *Skírnismál* from the year before (Christmas 1902).

As for *Thistilbardi*, Dronke (*The Poetic Edda*, vol. II, page 183) cites it as part of a list of giant names: Þistilbarði, Hrímnir, and Ganglati (Thistlebeard, Sootface, and Slowcoach) all being among the names for giants and Hengikepta, Loþinfingra, and Grottintanna (Hangjaw, Hairyfingers, and Grittingteeth) those for giantesses. The full list, one of a number of verse name-lists or *thulur* appearing in some manuscripts of Snorri's Edda – including lists of names for Odin, Thor, Freya, dwarves (deriving mainly from the *Dvergatal*), valkyrie, giants, giantesses, and the like – is printed in the massive collection *Corpvs Poeticvm Boreale: The Poetry of the Old Northern Tongue*, ed. Gudbrand Vigfusson & F. York Powell [2 vols., 1883], which attempts to bring together virtually all Old Norse heroic and mythological verse still in existence. The 'Thulor' appear in Bk X, §6: 'Rhymed Glossaries' (Vol. II, pages 422–39), and Thistilbardi's name in line 64 on page 425, in the same line with Thrym himself:

Þrymr, Þrúð-gelmir, Þistil-barði.

2 In his letter of 10th September 1950 to Stanley Unwin, announcing his decision to accept the 'second edition' Hobbit as the true and authentic version of the story and sending him the new Prefatory Note, Tolkien mentioned that 'as I have no secretary I rarely keep copies of my own letters, and I do not suppose that my recollections of them at long remove are necessarily accurate' (Ad.Ms.H.83; a portion of this letter, but not this passage, appears in *Letters* p. 142).

3 The absence of any mention of Thrym Thistlebeard from the 1950 Prefatory Note probably indicates that Tolkien had forgotten about him at this point, but in any case it would have been awkward to bring up a point hinging on a detail in an illustration in the introduction to a printing of the book that did not contain that picture.

The Fortunate Misunderstanding

In the end, Allen & Unwin's failure to recognize that although the two batches of material Tolkien sent them on 21st September 1947 were similar in appearance they were different in kind, each having its own title or subtitle, proved to be a fortunate misunderstanding. Eager to please one of their authors when they could, especially at a time when Tolkien was becoming increasingly distressed over the length of the as-yet-unpublished *Lord of the Rings* in a time of paper shortages and by their lack of interest in *The Silmarillion*, they scrupulously incorporated all his changes into the next printing, even to the extent of replacing a five-page section of the old edition with a ten-page section in the new. As Christopher Tolkien points out (letter to Taum Santoski, 3rd March 1989), when Tolkien wrote in his cover letter of 21st September 1947 that he was sending Allen & Unwin '. . . some notes on The Hobbit; *and* (for the possible amusement of yourself and Rayner) a specimen of re-writing of Chapter V . . .' (*Letters* p. 124; emphasis mine),[1] the publisher failed to grasp that the 'and' linked two entirely distinct categories of material. When Stanley Unwin informed Tolkien on 27th September that he was 'passing on The Hobbit corrections to our Production Department', Tolkien naturally assumed he meant the first sheet – that is, parts (ii) and (iii) above and further assumed, since Unwin said nothing further about the 'specimen of re-writing', that its inclusion had proved impossible. Not until Unwin sent him the proofs of the revised sections the next time the book was up for reprint on 26th July 1950 did Tolkien discover that (i), (ii), and

(iii) had all been accepted and, although surprised, he quickly decided to make any necessary changes in *The Lord of the Rings* manuscript to match this change:

. . . I have now made up my mind to accept the change and its consequences. The thing is now old enough for me to take a fairly impartial view, and it seems to me that the revised version is in itself better, in motive and narrative – and certainly would make the sequel (if ever published) much more natural.

—JRRT to SU, 1st August 1950; *Letters* p. 141.

He further noted that

Such people as I have consulted think that the alteration is in itself an improvement . . .

—ibid., 10th September 1950; *Letters* p. 142.

He had now begun work on the prefatory note requested by Allen & Unwin to explain the difference between the first and second editions, sending them one version of it with his 10th September letter – being careful to specify that this was

. . . a *specimen* of the kind of thing that I should want to insert . . . *This is not intended as copy*; but if you would return it, with any comment you like, it would be helpful.

—ibid., italics mine.

This was probably the 'long version' – i.e., (A) or (B) – which was replaced by the 'short version' a few days later:

I enclose . . . a copy of the briefest form of the prefatory note: which is intended as copy, if you should think it well to use it in the reprint.

—JRRT to SU, 14th September 1950; *Letters* p. 142.

Thus, the original first edition text was replaced by a new and improved text which so overwhelmed its predecessor in sales that the existence of the earlier version of the Gollum chapter soon came to be known only through references to it in the editions that supplanted it. The experience also showed Tolkien that he could revisit the book more than a decade later (1944 vs. 1930–33) and improve it while also binding it more closely to what had become his masterwork: *The Lord of the Rings*. This discovery would in turn lead first to 'The Quest of Erebor' in 1954 and ultimately to the Fifth Phase, the abortive third edition now known as the 1960 Hobbit.

NOTES

1 Tolkien had earlier described this material to Unwin in a letter written on 31st July 1947 but not sent until 21st September along with the Fourth Phase Hobbit material:

> . . . when I revise chapter II [of *LotR*] for press: I intend, in any case, to shorten it. The proper way to negotiate the difficulty would be slightly to remodel the former story [*The Hobbit*] in its chapter V. That is not a practical question; though I certainly hope to leave behind me the whole thing revised and in final form . . .
>
> —*Letters*, page 121.

THE FIFTH PHASE

THE 1960 HOBBIT

The second edition Hobbit showed Tolkien that he could revisit Bilbo's story, even after a gap of years, and improve upon the original, while at the same time binding the story and its sequel more closely together. Roughly a decade after drafting that material, and several years after its publication, he returned to the story of the Unexpected Party and wrote 'The Quest of Erebor' [1954] – not a replacement for the opening chapter but in effect a complement to (and commentary on) it, retelling the story from Gandalf's and the dwarves' point of view. Focusing on the events that led Gandalf with Thorin & Company to Bilbo's doorstep, it places Bilbo's adventure in a larger – what we may call 'strategic' – context, as Gandalf considers how to counter the threat of Smaug in a war against Sauron, which he already foresees as impending some eighty years before the event. Fascinating though it is, 'The Quest of Erebor' does set one unfortunate precedent: it diminishes Bilbo in the reader's eyes, casting him very much as a silly fellow puffing and bobbing on the mat. Gandalf, after describing Bilbo as 'rather greedy and fat', says the hobbit 'made a complete fool of himself' and 'did not realize . . . how fatuous the Dwarves thought him . . . Thorin was much more . . . contemptuous than he perceived' (UT.323–4).

Ultimately, only a few paragraphs of 'The Quest of Erebor' made their way into the published *Lord of the Rings* (*LotR*.1115 & 1116), but clearly Tolkien did not so much reject this material as merely find himself forced to cut it for reasons of space. When, around 1960, he decided to undertake a detailed revision of *The Hobbit* and fully reconcile it to the later story in chronology, geography, and style, he drew upon this unpublished material when recasting *The Hobbit* into *The Lord of the Rings*' image. This is not to say that he inserted passages from the alternative opener into the earlier book, or even that he had the 1954 material before him as he worked, but rather that he approached Bilbo's story from the point of view of the rejected Appendix material, very much to Bilbo's disadvantage.

It has long been known that the last work Tolkien did on *The Hobbit*, the third edition of 1966, came about at his publisher's request, since the appearance of the unauthorized Ace paperbacks of *The Lord of the Rings* in the summer of 1965 meant that Houghton Mifflin and now Ballantine Books needed him to produce a revised authorized text in order to belatedly assert the American copyright. Humphrey Carpenter describes how Tolkien began, and

> spent many hours searching for some revision notes that he had already made, but he could not find them . . . When the next day he did get down to *The Hobbit* he found a good deal of it 'very poor' and had to restrain himself from rewriting the entire book.
>
> — *Tolkien: A Biography*, pages 227–8.

These 'revision notes', the Fifth Phase or 1960 Hobbit, are far more extensive than Carpenter's account indicates, in fact nothing less than a wholesale recasting of the book into the mold of its sequel. Aside from this passing mention in Carpenter's book, this material remained wholly unknown until Christopher Tolkien read a substantial section from it as his Guest of Honor presentation at the 1987 Marquette Tolkien Conference (Mythcon XVIII). It is here published, in its entirety, for the first time.

The 1960 Hobbit does not form a continuous text, but rather a series of passages, some brief and some extensive, intended to replace their second edition equivalents – very much as the Fourth Phase replaced superseded passages from the first edition. As with that material (see page 732), I have retained Tolkien's page and line numbers, on the theory that these chapters of *The Hobbit* are so familiar, and the range of pages so short, that it is easy for readers with any edition to locate the specific passage Tolkien means for comparison. Like the 1947 Hobbit, the Fifth Phase greatly expands upon the original in some places. Most of the material exists only in a single typescript, and it seems to have been composed on the typewriter. Although there are extensive plot-notes associated with the timeline and phases of the moon, very little rough drafting of the actual chapters survives; I give the few exceptions at the end of this chapter. I have divided the typescript and associated material into three groups:

- **New Chapter I**, which consists of fourteen pages of typescript [Ad.Ms.H.62–75], numbered 1 through 14 in the center at the top of each page; the first eight pages are double-spaced, the last six single-spaced. Appended to this I give excerpts from the two isolated sheets [Ad.Ms.H.12 & Ad.Ms.H.18] which contain very rough drafting for a few individual lines.
- **New Chapter II**, eight crowded single-spaced pages of typescript [Ad.Ms.H.25–32], numbered 'II 1', 'II 2', and the like in the upper right corner. This is immediately followed by about a single page's worth of text (single-spaced typescript) for New Chapter III, starting in the middle of the last page of New Chapter II and halting about a third of the way down the next page [Ad.Ms.H.32–3] but given its own pagination ('III 1' and 'III 2', respectively). I follow this with the text of a single sheet of notes [Ad.Ms.H.11] which contains a few

queries or reminders of points that need addressing in the preceding New Chapters.

- **Timelines and Itinerary**, which consists of four pages of single-spaced typescript [Ad.Ms.H.21–4] giving a detailed, day-by-day summary of Thorin & Company's trip from Bag-End to Rivendell; four pages of manuscript notes [Ad.Ms.H.19, 20, 13] covering the same ground in rougher form; and six pages of rough notes [Ad.Ms.H.15–18], not wholly legible, dealing with problems in the tale's chronology, particularly focusing on the phases of the moon.

Since this text is wholly unknown, aside from those fortunate enough to have been present at Christopher Tolkien's reading at Marquette in 1987, I have here reversed my normal procedure. In all the earlier sections of this book I give the earliest recoverable version of a text, striving to record the first glimpses as Tolkien puts words down on the page, since the final polished form of that text is familiar to all his readers from the published book. Here by contrast I give the *final* text in all cases, with all significant earlier readings given in Text Notes. A number of ellipses or rows of dots are in the original; these are given in closed format as Tolkien typed them (...), to distinguish them from omissions made in the notes or transcriptions by myself as editor (. . .).

New Chapter I

A WELL-PLANNED PARTY

In a hole in the ground there lived a hobbit. Not a nasty wet hole, filled with worms and an oozy smell, nor a dry hole, bare and sandy, with nothing in it to sit down on or to eat: it was a hobbit-hole, and that means comfort.

It had a round door like a porthole, painted green, with a yellow brass knob in the exact middle. The door opened into a long hall, shaped like a tunnel, airy, but dark when the lamps were not lit. Its floor was tiled and carpeted, there were polished chairs against the walls, and rows of pegs for hats and coats – the hobbit was fond of visitors. The tunnel went on a good way into the side of the hill, the Hill of Hobbiton, near the top of which the hobbit lived; and many little round doors opened out of it, first on one side and then on the other. No going upstairs for the hobbit: bedrooms, bathrooms, cellars, pantries, wardrobes (rooms full of clothes), kitchens, breakfast-room, dining-room, drawing room, all were on the same floor. The best rooms were all on the lefthand side as you went in, for only these had windows, deep-set round windows looking over the garden to meadows beyond, sloping down to the river.

The hobbit was very well-to-do, it was said, and his name was Baggins. The Bagginses had lived in the neighbourhood of Hobbiton for time out of mind, and people considered them very respectable, not only because most of them were rich, but also because they never had any adventures nor did anything unexpected: you could tell what a Baggins would say on any question without the trouble of asking him. But this story tells how a Baggins had an adventure, and found himself saying and doing things altogether unexpected. He got caught up in great events, which he never understood; and he became enormously important, though he never realized it.

How astonishing this was will be better understood by those who know something about hobbits; and some account of them is really needed nowadays for they are becoming rare, and they avoid the Big People, as they call us. They were a small people, about half our height or less, often smaller than the Dwarves of those days, to whom they were quite unrelated: hobbits never have beards. They loved peace and the quiet of a well-ordered and well-farmed countryside; most of them were in fact farmers in a small way, though many were clever with tools. They had long and skilful fingers and made many useful and well-shaped things, mostly of wood or clay or leather [> glass]. But there were very few shoemakers among them, for they seldom wore either shoes or boots. They did not need them, for their feet had tough leathery soles, and were covered as high as the ankles in thick curling hair, warm and brown like the hair on their heads. They had good-natured faces, broad, bright-eyed and red-cheeked, and mouths shaped for laughter. And laugh they did, and eat, and drink, often and heartily; for they were fond of jests at all times, and liked six meals a day (when they could get them).

They dressed in bright colours, especially yellow and green, for they delighted in fields and trees. Though they were inclined to grow rather fat, and did not hurry unnecessarily,[TN1] they were nimble; and quick of hearing too, and sharp-eyed. They had from the first the art of moving swiftly and silently, disappearing when large folk or beasts that they did not wish to meet came blundering by. To us that might seem magical; but Hobbits have never in fact studied magic of any kind, their skill is a gift improved by long practice and helped by their friendship with the earth and all growing things.

More could be said, but for the present that is a good enough description of Hobbits, or at least of that kind that in those days lived, as they had done for hundreds of years, in the little land that they called the Shire, away in the North-west of the world.

The chief family in the Shire were the Tooks, whose lands lay across The Water, the small river that ran at the foot of the Hill. Now that is important, for[TN2] the mother of the hobbit of this tale, Bilbo Baggins, was Belladonna Took, eldest of the three remarkable daughters of the Old Took, head of all the Tooks, and famous for having lived to the age of one hundred and thirty. It was often said (in other families) that the Tooks must have some elvish blood in them: which was of course absurd, but there was undoubtedly some thing queer about them, something not quite hobbitlike, according to the manners of the Shire: an outlandish strain maybe from long ago.[TN3] Every now and again Tooks would go off on adventures. They disappeared, and the family hushed it up.

Not that Belladonna Took ever had any adventures after she married Bungo Baggins. Bungo, that was Bilbo's father, built for her the most commodious hobbit-hole that was to be found in that part of the Shire, always excepting the vast and many-tunneled dwelling of the Tooks. It was meant, of course, to house a large family. But Bilbo was their only son, and they both died young – for hobbits – being still in their early eighties. And there now was Bilbo, in the commodious hole, looking and behaving like a second edition of his solid and comfortable father. But maybe there was something a little peculiar in his make-up coming from the Took side, hidden, but waiting for a chance to come out. The chance never arrived, until Bilbo Baggins was grown up, indeed about fifty years old, and had apparently settled down immovably.

One morning long ago in the quiet of the world, when the hobbits were still numerous and prosperous, and their green corner of the great lands was still enjoying its long peace,[TN4] Bilbo Baggins was standing at his door after breakfast, smoking a long wooden pipe.[TN5] At that moment Gandalf appeared. Gandalf![TN6] Those who go in for Ancient History will prick up their ears, though few know all there is to tell about him. Wherever he went strange things happened, and he left behind him marvellous tales. All the same he seemed fond of hobbits, and at one time he had often visited the Shire. But it was now many years since he had appeared there, except for a brief visit when his friend the Old Took died, and that was now at least twenty years ago. So most even of the older folk in Hobbiton had almost forgotten what he looked like. He had been far away, 'over the Hill and across the Water' as they said, on business of his own,[TN7] since they were young. To little hobbits he was just a character in fireside tales.

All that Bilbo saw that morning was an old man with a tall pointed blue hat, a long grey cloak, and a silver scarf, over which his white beard hung down below his waist. He had tall black boots, and leaned on a staff.

'Good morning!' said Bilbo cheerily. The sun was shining and the grass was very green. But Gandalf looked at him from under his bushy eyebrows that bristled beneath the brim of his hat.

'What do you mean?' he said. 'That it is a fine morning, and you feel pleased with yourself? Perhaps you wish me to feel pleased too. I may. We'll see'.

'Indeed I hope you will', said Bilbo. 'Why not? It is a fine morning anyway for a pipe of tobacco out of doors.[TN8] If you have a pipe with you, pray take a seat and try some of my weed: it is "Old Toby". There is no hurry. All the day's before us'. Then Bilbo sat down on the bench by his door, crossed his legs, and blew out a beautiful grey ring of smoke that sailed up into the air without breaking and floated away over the Hill.

'Very pretty!' said Gandalf. 'But I have no time to blow smoke-rings today. I am looking for someone to share in an adventure that I am arranging, and it is very difficult to find anyone suitable'.

'I should think so – in these parts. We are plain quiet folk and have no use for adventures. Nasty disturbing things! Make you late for dinner! I can't think why anybody has them'. With that Mr. Baggins stuck a thumb behind his braces, and blew out another even bigger smoke-ring. Then he took out his morning letters, and began to read, pretending to take no more notice of the old man. He was not the kind of visitor he liked; he made him feel uncomfortable. He wished he would go away. But the old man did not move. He stood leaning on his staff and gazing at the hobbit without saying a word, till Bilbo began to feel annoyed.

'Good morning!' he said at last. 'We don't want any adventures here, thank you! You might try over the Hill or across the Water. Good morning!'

'Now I understand what you mean by *Good morning*', said Gandalf. 'You mean that you want to get rid of me, and that it won't be good till I move off'.

'Not at all, not at all, my dear sir! Let me see, I don't think I know your name?'

'Yes, yes, my dear sir! But I do know your name, Mr. Bilbo Baggins. And you knew my name once, when you were younger and brighter. It is Gandalf, in this part of the world.[TN9] Gandalf! Do you hear? To think that I should live to be good-morninged by Belladonna Took's son, as if I was selling buttons at the door!'

'Gandalf, Gandalf! Not the old wizard who used to visit the Tooks? Good gracious me! He used to make marvellous fireworks for the Old Took's parties on Midsummer's Eve. I remember them! Splendid! They used to go up like great roses and lilies and snapdragons of fire, and hang in the sky like flowers of golden-rain in the twilight!' Mr. Baggins was not quite so prosy as he liked to believe, and any way he delighted in flowers. 'Bless me!' he went on. 'Not the Gandalf who used to tell such wonderful tales about dragons, and goblins, and giants, and mountains in far countries – and the Sea. They used to send many quiet lads, and lasses, off on *adventures*, it is said: any mad thing from climbing tall trees to visiting Elves, and even trying to sail in ships'.[TN10] Bilbo's voice fell almost to a whisper. 'To sail, sail away to the Other Shore. Dear me!' he sighed. 'Life used to be quite interest— I mean, you used to upset things badly in the Shire, once upon a time. I beg your pardon, but I had no idea you were still in business'.

'Where else should I be?' said the wizard. 'But you have my pardon. Indeed I am pleased, and it *is* a good morning.[TN11] You do remember something about me; and what you say is very promising. For your old grandfather Took's sake, and for poor Belladonna's, I will do something for you'.

'You are very kind; but I have not asked for anything, thank you all the same!'

'That doesn't matter. I have made up *my* mind. Yes, I think you will do. Yes, I will send *you* on this adventure. You may be useful; and anyway it will do you good, if you come through'.

'No, no! I am sorry. I don't want any adventures. Not today, thank you! Good morning!' Bilbo backed towards his doorstep. 'But please come to tea, any time you like', he stammered.[TN12] 'Why not tomorrow? Come tomorrow! Good bye!' With that he scuttled inside his round green door, and shut it as quickly as he dared, not to seem too rude. Wizards are after all wizards.

Bilbo had only just had breakfast, but he felt that a cake or two and a drink would do him good after his fright. 'What on earth did I ask him to tea for!' he said to himself in the pantry. 'But perhaps he won't come. I am sure wizards don't like hobbit-tea'.

Gandalf in the meantime was still standing deep in thought outside the door. At last he laughed softly, and stepping up with the spike on his staff he scratched a curious sign on the hobbit's beautiful green door. Then he strode away, just about the time when Bilbo was finishing his second cake and was beginning to think he had escaped adventures very well.

The next day he had almost forgotten about Gandalf. His letters had brought him much news of his many relations, and some of them were troublesome. And anyway yesterday he had been too upset to mark his invitation on his Engagement Tablet: today, Wednesday, was blank.

Just before his tea-time there came a tremendous ring of the front-door bell; and then he remembered! He rushed and put on the kettle, and put out another cup and saucer, and an extra cake or two, and ran to the door.

'I am so sorry to keep you waiting!' he was going to say, when he saw that it was not Gandalf at all. It was a dwarf, with a blue beard tucked into a golden belt and very bright eyes under his dark green hood. As soon as the door was opened, he pushed inside, just as if he had been expected. He hung his hooded cloak on the nearest peg, and 'Dwalin at your service!' he said with a low bow.

'Bilbo Baggins at yours!' said the hobbit, too surprised to ask any questions for the moment. When the silence that followed had become uncomfortable, he added: 'I am just about to take tea; pray come and join me'. He was a little stiff, perhaps; but he was not used to having uninvited dwarves come and hang up their things in his hall. Without a word of explanation. That would follow, he hoped.

They had not been long at the table, in fact they had hardly reached the third cake, when there came another even louder ring at the bell.

'Excuse me!' said the hobbit, and off he went to the door.

'So you have got here at last!' he meant to say to Gandalf this time. But it was not Gandalf. Instead there was a very old-looking dwarf on the step, with a white beard and a scarlet hood; and he too hopped inside as soon as the door was open, just as if he had been invited.

'I see they have begun to arrive already', he said when he caught sight of Dwalin's green hood. He hung his red one next to it, and 'Balin at your service!' he said with his hand on his breast.

'Thank you!' said Bilbo with a gasp. It was not the correct thing to say, but they have begun to arrive had flustered him badly. He liked visitors, but he liked to know them before they arrived, and he preferred to invite them himself. He had a horrible thought that the cakes might run short, and then he – as the host: he knew his duty and stuck to it, however painful – he might have to go without.

'Come along in, and have some tea!' he managed to say after taking a deep breath.

'A little beer would suit me better, if it is all the same to you, my good sir', said Balin with the white beard. 'But I don't mind some cake – seed-cake, if you have any'.

'Lots!' Bilbo found himself answering, to his own surprise; and he found himself scuttling off, too, to the cellar to fill a beer-mug, and to the small pantry to fetch two beautiful round seed-cakes that he had meant to have last thing, before he went to bed.

When he got back Balin and Dwalin were talking at the table like old friends (as a matter of fact they were brothers). Bilbo plumped down the beer and the cakes in front of them, when loud came a ring at the bell again, and then another ring.

'Gandalf for certain this time', he thought as he puffed along the passage. But it was not. It was two more dwarves, both with blue hoods, silver belts, and yellow beards; and each of them carried a bag of tools and a spade. In they hopped, as soon as the door began to open. Bilbo was hardly surprised at all.

'What can I do for you, my dwarves?' he said.

'Kili at your service!' said the one. 'And Fili!' added the other; and they both swept off their blue hoods and bowed.

'At yours and your family's' replied Bilbo with a bow, remembering his manners this time.

'Dwalin and Balin here already, I see', said Kili. 'Let us join the throng!'

'Throng!' thought Mr. Baggins. 'I don't like the sound of that. I really must sit down for a minute and collect my wits. It's my turn for a drink!' He had only just had a sip – by the fire, while the dwarves sat round the table, and talked about mines and gold and troubles with the goblins, and the depredations of dragons, and many other things which he did not understand, and did not wish to, for they sounded much too adventurous – when ding-dong-a-ling-dang, his bell rang again, as if some naughty little hobbit-boy was trying to pull the handle off.

'Someone at the door!' he said, blinking.

'Some four, I should say by the sound', said Fili. 'Besides, we saw them in the distance, coming along behind us'.

The poor little hobbit sat down in the hall and put his head in his hands, and wondered what had happened, and what was going to happen, and whether they would all stay to supper. Then the bell rang again louder than ever, and he had to run to the door. It was not four after all, it was FIVE. Another dwarf had come up while he was wondering in the hall. He had hardly turned the knob before they were all inside, bowing and saying 'at your service' one after another. Dori, Nori, Ori, Oin and Gloin were their names; and very soon two purple hoods, a grey hood, a brown hood, and a white hood were hanging on the pegs, and off they marched, with their broad hands stuck in their gold and silver belts, to join the others. Already it had almost become a throng.

Two called for cider, and two called for beer; and Gloin called for old ale. 'Bring some honey and spices!' he said. 'I like mine mulled by the fire'. And all the nine called for more cakes, and for butter as well;[TN13] so the poor hobbit was kept very busy for a while.

Great jugs of beer and cider had been set on the table, Gloin's ale was in a pan on the fire, the seed-cakes had gone, and the dwarves were busy toasting buttered cake,[TN14] when there came – a loud knock. Not a ring, but a hard rat-tat on Bilbo's beautiful green door. Somebody was banging with a stick!

Bilbo rushed along the passage, very angry, and altogether bothered and bewildered – this was the most awkward Wednesday he ever remembered. He pulled open the door with a jerk, and they all fell in, one on top of the other. More dwarves, four more! And there was Gandalf behind, leaning on his staff and laughing. He had made quite a dent on the beautiful door, but he had also, by the way, knocked out the secret mark that he had put there the morning before.

'Carefully! Carefully!' he said. 'It is not like you, Bilbo, to keep friends waiting on the mat and then open the door like a trap! Let me introduce Bifur, Bofur, and Bombur, and especially Thorin!'

'At your service!' said Bifur, Bofur, and Bombur, a little coolly, standing in a row. [*added*: They brought in a large bag, and what looked like sticks wrapped in cloths, which they put in the hall-stand.][TN15] Then they hung up two yellow hoods and a pale green one; and also a sky-blue hood with a long liripipe[TN16] ending in a silver tassel. This belonged to Thorin, a dwarf of immense dignity, in fact no other than the great Thorin Oakenshield himself, renowned in history. He was not at all pleased at falling flat on Bilbo's mat with his attendants, Bifur, Bofur, and Bombur, on top of him. For one thing Bombur was enormously fat and heavy. Thorin indeed was very haughty, and he said nothing about <u>service</u>; but poor Mr. Baggins bowed so low and said he was sorry so many times that at last he grunted 'pray do not mention it', and stopped frowning.

'Now we are all here!' said Gandalf, looking at the row of thirteen hoods, and his own hat and cloak, hanging on the pegs. 'Quite a merry gathering! I hope there is something left for the late-comers to eat and drink! What's that? Tea! No thank you! A little red wine, I think, for me'.

'And for me', said Thorin.

'And raspberry jam and pastry', said Bifur.

'And mince-pie and cheese', said Bofur.

'And pork-pie and onions', said Bombur.

'And more cakes, and ale, and cider, if you don't mind', called the other dwarves from the parlour.[TN17]

'Put on a few eggs, there's a good fellow!' Gandalf called after him, as the hobbit stumped off to the pantries. 'And just bring out the cold chicken and pickles!'[TN18]

'He seems to know as much about the inside of my larders[TN19] as I do myself!' thought Mr. Baggins, who was altogether flummoxed, and was beginning to feel alarmed: he wondered whether a most wretched adventure had not come right into his house. By the time he had got all the bottles and dishes and knives and forks and glasses and plates and spoons, not to mention the food, piled up on big trays, he was getting very hot, and red in the face, and annoyed.

'Confound and bother these dwarves!' he said aloud. 'Why don't they come and lend a hand?' Lo and behold! there stood Balin and Dwalin at the door of the kitchen, and Fili and Kili behind them; and before he could say *knife* they had whisked the trays and a couple of small tables into the parlour and set out everything afresh.

Gandalf sat at the head of the party, with Thorin at his right, and the other twelve dwarves round the joined tables; but Bilbo sat on a stool at the fireside, nibbling at a biscuit (his appetite was quite taken away), and trying to look unconcerned, as if this was all just an everyday affair and not in the least like an adventure. The dwarves ate and ate, and talked and talked, and time got on. At last they pushed their chairs back, and Bilbo made a move to collect the plates and glasses.

'I suppose you will all stay to supper?' he said in his politest unpressing tones.

'Of course!' said Thorin. 'And after. We shall not get through our business till late, and we must have some music first. Now to clear up!'

. . . . . .

At this point, the continuous narrative stops and the text becomes a series of replacement passages, very much like the Phase Four typescript (the

1947 Hobbit material). In each case, Tolkien has provided a page number (using the second edition pagination) and line number as well; a minus sign in front of the line number means lines counted up from the bottom.

p. 22/bottom line to 23/top.[TN20] safe and quick, while the hobbit was turning round like a top in the middle of the kitchen, shouting out directions and trying to see that things were put in the right places.

p. 23/4 He was blowing enormous smoke-rings

p. 23/ 22 from inside their jackets; Bombur produced a drum from his bag in the hall; Bifur and Bofur[TN21] went out too, and came back with the clarinets that they had left...

p. 26/ –2 [2 up] he was so overwhelmed

p. 27/3 us (even our friend...

/10–13. important dwarf, and he thought it an important occasion.[TN22]

/16 it burst out like the whee of a rocket going up in the sky

/19 delete magic

/–7 'Excitable little fellow[TN23]

/–5 one of the best – as brave as Bandobras at a pinch'. No doubt an exaggeration; but Gandalf was doing his best in a difficult situation. For Bandobras had been the Old Took's great-granduncle, and usually called Bullroarer. He was so huge (for a hobbit) that he rode a small horse. At the Battle of the Green Fields, when the hobbits were driven back, he charged the ranks of the Goblins of Mount Gram, and smote their king Golfimbul [> Gulfimbul][TN24] to the earth with his great wooden club. So the battle was won, and there had been none since in the Shire. Even the dwarves had heard of Bullroarer Took.

In the meantime, however, Bullroarer's gentler relative

p. 28/13 being brave

/14 a stone dragon out of an enchanted sleep.[TN25]

/20 He looks more of a fool than a burglar

/23 to be thought brave. As for little fellow puffing on the mat it made his blood hot

/26 you were a fool

p. 29/1 strange faces.[TN26]

/9 And I assure you there is a mark on this door – the sign we were told to look for: Tracker and Treasure-hunter it means to those who know the Dwarf-runes. Burglar we say in these days; it is shorter. The fees are the same. Gandalf said there was a hobbit of the sort, living quietly in these parts, waiting for a job – needing one soon. Only yesterday he told us he had arranged a meeting here for today. 'Four o'clock' he said, 'but don't all arrive at once!'

'Of course there was a mark', said Gandalf. 'I put it there myself. You asked me to find a treasure-hunter for your expedition, and I chose Mr. Baggins

/–7 I have chosen Mr. Baggins, and that must be enough for all of you. If I say he is a Burglar, a Burglar he is, or will be when the time comes. If I say he needs a job soon, I know what I am talking about. There is a lot more in him than you see, and a deal more than he guesses himself.

p. 30/3 This was made by Thror, your grandfather, he said to Thorin. Bilbo and the other dwarves gathered round. 'It is a plan of the Mountain'.

'I don't see that this will help me much' said Thorin, after a glance.

/18 Delete (Look...red). Substitute * and a footnote *See the copy of the plan at the beginning of this book.[TN27]

/–6 devouring so many dwarves and most of the Men of Dale'

p. 30/–4 to 31/ top. 'It seems a great big hole to me' said Bilbo, deeply interested. He loved maps, and in his hall there hung a large one of The Hobbiton Country which he had drawn himself, marking all his favourite walks in red. 'How could such a large door be kept secret from everybody outside, apart from the dragon?' he asked. He had of course no experience of dragons, and very little of dwarves.

'In many ways', said Gandalf........method, I believe'.[TN28]

'It is', said Thorin.

/–14 ...what to do. We must go east, of course, by as straight roads as we can find, quietly, attracting as little notice as possible – until we come to the Long Lake. After that the trouble will begin'.

'A long while before that', interrupted Gandalf. 'Things have not changed for the better since you came to the West. Few roads are straight, and none are safe, and the East is full of danger.'

'From the Long Lake we might go up the Running River', Thorin went on, taking no notice, 'and so to the ruins of Dale...

p. 31/–2 to 32/ top 'That would be no good', said the wizard, 'not even for warriors of the Elder Days, who cannot now be matched.[TN29] But we have discussed all that; and anyway we are not looking for a warrior in the Shire: their little swords are blunt; their axes are used for trees, and their bows for small deer.[TN30] We decided that you must use stealth; and I chose your helper. Here he is, Bilbo Baggins: the "burglar", specially selected. So now let us get on'.

'Very well then', said Thorin, turning to Bilbo with mock-politeness. 'Let the selected expert give us some ideas and suggestions!'......

p. 32/18. 'Bless me!' said Thorin. 'Haven't you looked at the map? And didn't you hear our song? And haven't we been talking about all this for hours?'

'All the same, I should like it plain and clear', said Bilbo obstinately, trying to appear prudent and professional. 'Also I should like to know about....' By which he meant: 'What chance is there of my coming back alive? and what am I going to get out of it, if I do?'

'O very well', said Thorin. 'Many years ago, in my great-grandfather's days, our family was driven out of the far North.[TN31] Some went east to the Iron Hills. But Thror my grandfather returned with most of our kin to this Mountain on the map, where Thrain the Old[TN32] his ancestor had lived for a while, once upon a time. There they mined and they tunnelled, and they made deeper halls and greater workshops;[TN33] and they found a wealth of gold and many gems. They grew rich and famous, and Thror became King under the Mountain, and was treated with great reverence by the Men who lived further south, and were spreading up the Running River. In those days they built the merry town of Dale in the valley overshadowed by the Mountain. Their lords used to send for our smiths, and reward even the least skilful most richly. Fathers would beg us to take their sons as apprentices, and paid us handsomely. It was always for food and wine that we asked, so that we had no need to grow it or get it for ourselves. The land was fat and fruitful in those days [> then]. Those were good years for us, and the least of us had gold to spend and to lend, and leisure to make beautiful things for our delight. The young dwarves made marvellous and cunning toys, the like of which are not to be found in the world today. So the halls of Thror were filled with armour and harps and drinking-horns and cups and things carven and hammered and inlaid, and with jewels like stars; and the toy-market of Dale was one of the wonders of the North.

Alas! that brought the dragon upon us! Greed has long ears.[TN34] Dragons, as no doubt a treasure-hunter will know, steal gold and jewels from elves and dwarves and men, wherever they can find them; and they guard their plunder as long as they live, a thousand years[TN35] maybe, unless they are killed, though they never enjoy one small ring of it. They cannot use it, and they do not know good work from bad; but they remember the least thing that they have ever possessed, and woe to anyone who tries to set a finger on it! Curse them!

There were still many dragons in the North in those days,[TN36] and treasure was becoming so scarce that they fell to fighting among themselves, and the waste and destruction that dragons make was going from bad to worse. There was beyond the Grey Mountains a most greedy, strong, and wicked worm called Smaug. One day he flew up in the air and came south

p. 34/ bottom. After that, when we had set our curse on the dragon, we went away; and we

p. 35/2 as low as coalmining, or even road-mending...[TN37]

/6. 'I still mean to get it back, and to bring my curse home to Smaug – if I can'.

/9, 10. had a secret Side-door

/14 'I did not get hold of it, it was given to me', said the wizard with a flash of his eyes. 'Thror, your grandfather was murdered in the mines of Moria by Azog the Goblin –'[TN38]

'Yes, curse Azog!' said Thorin.

'And Thrain, your father, went away on the twenty-first of April, a hundred years ago last Thursday, and has never been seen by you since –'

'Too true, alas!' said Thorin.

'Well your father gave me this map,[TN39] ninety one years ago, and I have guarded it ever since'.

'Ninety one years!' cried Thorin. 'For ninety one years you have kept my property?'

'Thorin', said Gandalf quietly, 'though your fame had reached me, I first met you only a few weeks ago.[TN40] Until then the use and meaning of this map was quite unknown to me; and I did not know who it belonged to. [*added in margin*: Your father could not remember his own name, nor yours, when he gave me the parchment.] If I have chosen my own time for restoring it, you have no right to be angry: I came by it only at the peril of my life, for which I think you owe me some thanks. I give it to you now', he said, handing the map to Thorin with a bow.

'I thank you' said Thorin. 'I would thank you more, maybe, if your words were not dark. I do not understand them at all!' Bilbo felt that he would like to say the same; but he wisely said nothing.

'You are slow', said Gandalf tartly [> sharply]. 'Until I heard your tale, I did not know how Thror and Thrain escaped from the Mountain. Thrain was dying when I found him. I guess that your grandfather gave this map to him for safety before he himself went to the mines of Moria. Then later Thrain, your father, went away, as you have told, though you did not know why. I think he took the map and went to [spy on >] try his luck in the Mountain. But he had no luck; he was caught in dark perils, and never came in sight of his home. How he came there, I cannot tell; but I found him a prisoner in the dungeons of the Necromancer'.[TN41]

'Whatever were you doing there!' said Thorin with a shudder, going pale, and the dwarves hid their faces.

'Do not ask! Not at night.' said Gandalf. 'I will not speak of it.[TN42] But it was my task to search in the shadows, and a dark and dangerous quest it was. Even I, Gandalf, hardly escaped. I tried to save your father, though he was a nameless dwarf to me, alone, in misery. It was too late. He was witless and wandering, and had forgotten almost all that he had known, except a map, and a key'.

Thorin ground his teeth. 'Thror was avenged: we paid the goblins in Moria long ago. We must give a thought to this Necromancer!'

'Hush!' said Gandalf. 'Grief has robbed you of your wits. He[TN43] is an enemy far beyond the powers of all the dwarves in the world, if they could all be gathered again from the four corners of Earth, even from their tombs. The one thing that your father wished was that you should read the map and use the key. *Give them to my son*[TN44] were his last words, though he did not speak your name. They are burden enough. The Dragon of the Mountain is as big a task as you can manage; too big, maybe'.

'Hear, hear!' said Bilbo to himself, but he said it aloud.

'Hear what?' they all said, turning suddenly towards him; and he was so flustered that he answered: 'hear what I have got to say!'

'What's that?' they asked.

'Well, I should say that you must go east, which will take several days,[TN45] no doubt – '. Gandalf smiled, and Thorin snorted. 'Well, then you must have a quiet look round. After all, there is the Side-door, and dragons must sleep sometimes, I suppose. If you sit on the door-step long enough, I daresay you will think of some plan, or something will turn up. And well, don't you know, I think we have talked long enough for one night, if you see what I mean. What about bed, and an early start, and all that? You can have a good breakfast before you go.'

'Before *we* go, I suppose you mean', said Thorin. 'Aren't you the burglar? And what about *stealth*? Isn't sitting on the door-step your job, not to speak of getting inside? But I agree about bed and breakfast. I like six eggs with my ham, when starting on a journey: fried not poached, and mind you don't break 'em'.

p. 37/14 ..., and he was not at all sure now

As will readily be seen, much of the wording of the original book remains, yet the tone is greatly altered. In particular, the voice of the narrator is muted and editorial asides omitted. Word-play is greatly reduced – for example, 'confusticate and bebother' becomes simply 'confound and bother', and 'bewildered and bewuthered' becomes instead 'bothered and bewildered' – and in general the playfulness of the original gives way to a more stately style. Perhaps more significantly, characterization is also changed: Gandalf, for example, now speaks with more authority. He could no longer be mistaken for 'a little old man' in a pointed hat, but this enhanced dignity does come with a price: he is also more remote, less a figure the reader is likely to sympathize with.

The change in Thorin is greater. In keeping with his portrayal in 'The Quest of Erebor', the dwarven leader has become much more abrupt and brusque, and he shows an unhealthy concern over property that anticipates his later fall in the Lonely Mountain chapters. In the original book his succumbing to the dragon-sickness had been a sudden and surprising departure from his usual self, a distortion of his fundamentally admirable personality and a frightening lesson in the corrupting power of dragon-haunted gold; here an obsession with his property and grievance over his rights has simply become part of his character, an innate flaw. Like the anticipations of Saruman's fall Tolkien inserted into some of his later writings, these have the effect of hinting that the character was corrupt from the beginning, which was very much not the case in the original book.

Finally, Bilbo is made more foolish – someone who 'loved maps' and had his favorite walks all marked out on the neighborhood map (made by himself) would know that the dragon-haunted mountain they speak of is more than a day or two, or even a few days' walk away; maps made in the Shire might tend to end at its borders (*LotR*.56), but he would certainly know that Thror's kingdom and Smaug's lair must lie outside those borders. And this naivety is extended beyond the end of the book. We are told that 'He got caught up in great events, which he never understood; and he became enormously important, though he never realized it', but this contradicts *The Lord of the Rings*, where Bilbo took part in the Council of Elrond and learned (if he did not know already from Gandalf) that his ring was the One Ring, who its maker and master was, and what would happen if He regained it. He even volunteered to undertake the Quest of Mount Doom himself, which is not so quixotic as it sounds, given that the quest was to rely on luck and stealth, not martial prowess. More importantly, it contradicts the closing lines of *The Hobbit* itself, where Gandalf, who serves as Tolkien's spokesman more than any other character, assures Bilbo that he played only a small role in all these events. This diminishment of Bilbo, a central feature of 'The Quest of Erebor', becomes even more pronounced in the next chapter.

TEXT NOTES

1 originally: 'Though inclined to grow rather fat, they did not hurry unnecessarily'.

Several small variants from the published text in the section describing hobbits are interesting to note: most significantly, the shift from present tense (all published editions) to past tense (1960 Hobbit); e.g., 'hobbits are (or were) a small people' becomes simply 'hobbits *were* a small people'. The sentence about how hobbits are half our height, introduced into print in the third edition (cf. DAA.30 & 31), makes its first appearance here, but the 1960 text has 'half our height *or less*'; this is a direct link to *halflings*, the generic name for hobbits among other peoples in *The Lord of the Rings*. Finally, the allusion to their 'seldom' wearing shoes or boots seems to refer back to an idea Tolkien had mentioned in a 1938 letter to Houghton Mifflin but never managed to incorporate into any text:

> There is in the text no mention of [Bilbo's] acquiring of boots. There should be! It has dropped out somehow or other in the various revisions – the bootings occurred at Rivendell; and he was again bootless after leaving Rivendell on the way home. But since leathery soles, and well-brushed furry feet are a feature of essential hobbitness, he ought really to appear unbooted, except in special illustrations of episodes.
>
> —JRRT to HM, March/April 1938; *Letters* p. 35.

This comment seems to have arisen from comparison between the various pictures and drawings of Bilbo in the book: he is clearly barefoot in 'The Hall at Bag-End' (DAA.363; H-S#139) but just as clearly booted in the eagle picture (DAA plate two [top]; H-S#113). He seems barefooted in the Barrel-Rider sketch (plate VIII [top]) but clearly has some sort of footwear in both of the finished versions of that scene (DAA.238–9 & plate two [bottom]; H-S#122 & 124) and in 'Conversation with Smaug' (plate XI [top]).

Tolkien is in error in saying that text mentioning Bilbo's boots 'dropped out'; in fact, what seems to have occurred is that he must have thought of adding such text at some point but failed to write it down (at least in any form that survives) and so forgot to implement the change.

2 The words 'that is important, for' were bracketed but not cancelled.

3 Immediately after the sentence about the Old Took originally came the sentence 'There was something queer about the Tooks, something not quite hobbitlike. It was whispered that they had some fairy blood from long ago'; the replacement sentence that followed originally ran 'It was often said (in other families) that the Tooks must have some elvish blood in them: or some outlandish strain, which was of course absurd;

but there was undoubtedly some thing queer about them, something not quite hobbitlike . . .'

4 The phrase 'its long peace' was changed to 'its peace', possibly to avoid what had presumably been the deliberate reiteration in 'long ago' 'long peace' 'long wooden pipe' all in the same sentence.

5 This was originally followed by 'a long wooden pipe *that reached nearly down to his well-brushed toes*'; the latter phrase was bracketed, apparently for omission as a too-whimsical touch.

6 An entire sentence was cancelled here: 'Gandalf! *If you had heard a quarter of what even the hobbits had heard about him, and that was not a hundredth part of all that there was to hear, you would be prepared for any sort of remarkable tale*'. The sentence that followed originally read 'will prick up their ears *expecting remarkable things to happen* . . .'

7 The phrase 'on business of his own' is bracketed as if for removal, but then the brackets were scratched out and the words retained.

8 'a pipe of tobacco': it is mildly surprising that Tolkien has retained the apparent anachronism of 'tobacco' here, given the circumlocution of the more ambiguous 'pipe-weed'† used in *The Lord of the Rings*. But even there he had specified that this was 'a variety . . . of *Nicotiana* . . . not native to our part of the world, but . . . brought over Sea by the Men of [Númenor]' ('Concerning Pipe-weed', *LotR*.20–21). Since *Nicotiana* is a class of New World plants, including tobacco, its presence in Middle-earth is presented not as an anachronism but a piece of lost history.

†The original Carib word (rendered by Spanish explorers as *tabaca*) is generally thought to have meant the pipe, not the plant smoked in it, but the OED notes that the point is disputed: Tolkien's 'pipe-weed' nicely bridges the ambiguity by embracing both.

9 This is an oblique reference to a passage from *The Two Towers*, where Faramir reports Gandalf as once saying '*Many are my names in many countries . . . Mithrandir among the Elves, Tharkûn to the Dwarves; Olórin I was in my youth in the West that is forgotten, in the South Incánus, in the North Gandalf; to the East I go not*' (*LotR*.697).

10 Added, but then omitted: 'to sail in *their* ships'. The passage in the next sentence about Bilbo's wistfully thinking of sailing 'away to the Other Shore' (here significantly capitalized to make it clear that Elvenhome is meant) is of course a foreshadowing, in this first encounter, of his eventual fate in the final chapter of *The Lord of the Rings*.

11 Originally this sentence read 'Indeed I am pleased, *as you wished* . . .'

12 The words 'he stammered' were bracketed, then removed.

13 Originally they called 'for *bread and* butter'; this cancellation probably was made at the same time as the toast was removed from the following paragraph (see Text Note 14).

14 Originally 'busy *making rounds of buttered toast*'; this pencilled change would have been made at the same time as that noted in Text Note 13.

15 This sentence is typed in the left margin and marked for insertion at this point; the bag contains their musical instruments. See the Draftings section at the end of this chapter.

16 A *liripipe* is a long narrow extension at the point of a hood; the word is of unknown (fourteenth-century) origin but seems to have originally been applied to academic costume (a graduate's hood). In Pauline Baynes' illustrations to Tolkien's *Smith of Wootton Major* [1967], Alf the Master Cook wears a liripipe (SWM, expanded edition, page [42]).

17 Originally the other dwarves are in the sitting room rather than the parlour; this change seems to have been made right away in the course of typing, before Tolkien moved on to the next line (Ad.Ms.H.71).

18 In the first and second editions, Bifur asked for 'raspberry jam and *apple-tart*', Bofur for 'mince-*pies* [plural] and cheese', Bombur for 'pork-pie and *salad*', the other dwarves for 'more cakes, and ale, and *coffee*', and Gandalf reminded Bilbo to 'bring out the cold chicken and *tomatoes*'.

Tolkien incorporated one of the changes that first appeared here into the third edition of 1966 (DAA.41), where *tomatoes* did indeed become *pickles*. This change has been the subject of much debate; see, for example, Shippey's *The Road to Middle-earth* (expanded edition, page 69), Anderson's *Annotated Hobbit* (DAA.41), et al. The general consensus has been that 'tomato' was removed as foreign to the time and place, though this did not prevent Tolkien's including tobacco earlier in this same chapter, or potatoes in Bilbo's garden in *The Lord of the Rings* (*LotR*.34), or, for that matter, *coffee* in the same sentence.† More likely, Tolkien (a keen gardener) thought it too early in the year for tomatoes and simply decided that preserved goods like pickles were more likely to be found in Bilbo's larder that early in the year.

†Although an Old World plant (being native to Africa), coffee as a drink dates from early modern times and was unknown in Europe before the sixteenth century, first appearing in England in 1652, about the same time (circa 1650) that tea arrived in England, having made its way westward from Asia.

19 The replacement of the first and second editions' *larder* by *larders* (plural) is another 1960 Hobbit revision taken up into the third edition of 1966; cf. DAA.41, annotation #27. This change was probably made to match the pantries (plural) of the book's second paragraph.

20 That is, from the bottom line on (second edition) page 22 through the top line on page 23.

21 Tolkien actually wrote 'Bombur produced a drum from the [> his] bag in the hall; Bifur and Bombur went out too', but it is clear that *Bofur*, the reading in all published editions, is meant for the second occurrence (for one thing, 'bombur' means *drum* in Old Norse).

22 This entry is added to the typescript, having been proceeded by rough drafting on a separate sheet of paper; see the Draftings section at the end of this chapter.

23 This change, from the first edition's 'Excitable little *man*', had already been made in the fifth printing of 1951; see page 749. For the changes in the preceding lines, compare the suggested replacement or correction with the published text (e.g., DAA.47). For example, '/19 delete magic' (which is added at the same time as the entries discussed in Text Notes 22 & 25) means that the line 'Gandalf struck a blue light on the end of his magic staff' should now read '. . . the end of his staff'. The replacement of 'the whistle of an engine coming out of a tunnel' (page 27, line 16) by 'the whee of a rocket going up in the sky' was no doubt to remove a perceived anachronism, fireworks being firmly established as part of Middle-earth in a way mechanisms like steam engines were not.

24 Golfimbul is changed to 'Gulfimbul', either because of the further evolution of Tolkien's languages (cf. Mt. Gondobad > Gundabad, page 675) or because Tolkien had now dropped the 'golf' joke and so no longer needed (or wanted) the *-golf-* element to appear in the goblin-king's name.

25 This phrase, added to the typescript at the same time as the entry noted in Text Note 22, is one of the few for which drafting exists; see the Draftings section at the end of this chapter.

26 Written in pencil beside this, apparently as a possible replacement: 'funny beards?'

27 That is, for the reading in the second edition '(Look at the map at the beginning of this book, and you will see there the runes in red.)', Tolkien now proposed that an asterisk be inserted in the text and a footnote added to the bottom of the page which would read '*See the copy of the plan at the beginning of this book.'

28 The extended row of ellipses, here and throughout this chapter, is in Tolkien's original.

29 This was originally followed with 'And anyway there are no more battle', then this unfinished sentence was cancelled.

30 By small deer, Tolkien does not mean hobbit-sized deer, appealing though the image is, but 'small game' – that is, creatures such as rabbits, squirrels, and the like. Cf. Shakespeare's *King Lear*: 'Mice, and Rats, and such small Deare, Haue been Tom's food for seuen long yeare' (Act III, scene iv, lines 144–145).

The conversation to which Gandalf refers ('we have discussed all that . . . we decided . . .') is described in more detail in 'The Quest of Erebor'.

31 Several lines of typed drafting, which gave more information about the dwarven exodus from the Grey Mountains, were deleted following this sentence:

> Many years ago, in [Dain >] my great-grandfather's time, our family was driven out of the far North, and [Dain was slain by a dragon >] returned to this Mountain on the map, where their ancestors had

> lived for a while long ago [> once upon a time]. They brought such wealth as they could save >

This seems to have been replaced with

> . . . driven out of the far North, and return with their goods and their tools to this Mountain on the map where our ancestors had lived for a while once upon a time.

This Dain is of course Dáin I, the figure who replaced Thrym Thistlebeard as Thrór's father in the published dwarven genealogy, said in 'Durin's Folk' to have been killed by 'a great cold-drake' (*LotR*.1109) and in the family tree by 'a dragon' (ibid. 1117). His youngest son, Grór, founded the dwarven colony in the Iron Hills at the same time his heir, Thrór, re-established the Kingdom under the Mountain at Erebor.

See also the Draftings section at the end of this chapter for rough drafts on a separate sheet [Ad.Ms.H.18] of this passage relating to Thrain the Old and Thror's return to the Lonely Mountain.

32 This marks the first appearance in the main text of 'Thrain the Old' by that name (an appellation that arose during the drafting given at the end of this chapter); in 'Durin's Folk' (*LotR*.1109 & 1117) and the 1950 Prefatory Note to the second edition he had been simply 'Thráin I'. This is yet another of the proposed 1960 Hobbit changes that got carried over into the 1966 third edition; cf. DAA.54.

33 This passage originally read

> . . . to this Mountain on the map, where our ancestors had lived for a while, once upon a time. There they mined and they tunnelled, and they made [great halls >] wide halls and great workshops

The changes from 'wide' to *deeper* and 'great' to *greater* emphasize the continuity of the dwarven community building on and expanding what had come before, whereas the original readings convey the impression that the earlier settlement was completely dwarfed (so to speak) by the magnificence of the new establishment.

34 Originally these sentences read 'Alas! *Undoubtedly that was what* brought the dragon upon us! *Their* greed has long ears.'

35 Originally this read 'as long as they live, *five thousand years* maybe'.

36 The addition of *still*, typed in the margin and marked for insertion here, suggests that the battles between dragons mentioned in the next clause seriously reduced their numbers. Compare *Farmer Giles of Ham*, which suggests a number of dragons dwelling close together in the mountains, at least one of whom is killed and eaten (by the returning C. Dives) by the end of the story.

The specific detail a few lines later that Smaug came from *beyond* the Grey Mountains appears here for the first time, but this is merely a confirmation of the legend on Thror's Map: 'Far to the North are the Grey Mountains & the Withered Heath whence came the Great Worms.'

37 'as low as coalmining, or even road-mending' replaces 'as low as blacksmith-work or even coalmining', either because Tolkien wished not to disparage blacksmithing (which he celebrates in passing in *Smith of Wootton Major* only a few years later [circa 1964] as a useful craft that is also an appealing art), or because he wished to allude to the association between dwarves and stone roads that appears elsewhere in the legendarium.

38 Azog's name enters *The Hobbit* at this point, this being one of the 1960 changes that carried over into the published third edition of six years later; cf. DAA.56–7 and 339. The name first appeared in 'Durin's Folk' (*LotR*.1110–12) and was now imported back into *The Hobbit* retroactively, replacing the anonymous goblin of the first and second editions.

I have been unable to locate any authoritative gloss for the meaning of Azog's name; even the language it is in is unknown. It may be Magol, like his son Bolg (see page 710), but given the gap of years between their invention and the linguistic situation as it stood at the time Tolkien was writing the *Lord of the Rings* Appendices, *azog* is more probably a word in Black Speech (cf. *LotR*.1165) – cf. for instance the similarity between *azog* and n*azg*, attested from the Ring-inscription (ibid., 271), which share three out of four letters all in the same sequence.

39 To this Tolkien added, then deleted 'and the key' (i.e., 'this map *and the key*'). For more on his hesitancy over whether the wizard gained one item or two from the dying dwarf, note that when two paragraphs later Gandalf ceremoniously hands Thorin the map there is no mention of the key, although in the paragraphs that follow Gandalf mentions the key twice. See also Text Note 44.

40 'a few weeks ago': their first meeting is described in 'Durin's Folk' (*LotR*.1115). For a different account of that encounter, see 'The Quest of Erebor'; cf. *Unfinished Tales* (UT.322 & 332–5) and *The Annotated Hobbit* (DAA.368–77).

41 Rather surprisingly, Tolkien did not at this point have several of the dwarves present – e.g., Balin and Dwalin, and possibly others – reveal that they had accompanied Thrain on his unfortunate expedition; cf. *LotR*.1114. This is all the more unexpected, because while they did not know what ultimately became of Thrain, they certainly could have revealed to his son the purpose of his final mission rather than leave him completely in the dark for a full century about his missing father.

42 In full, including cancellations, Gandalf's reply reads:

> 'Do not ask! Not at night. *NO, not even at noon!*' said Gandalf. [*Only those whom* >] I will not speak of it.'

It is interesting that Gandalf refers to this remarkable achievement – in which he joins Beren, Lúthien, and Sméagol as the only characters in the whole legendarium known to have escaped from a Dark Lord's lair – as a 'task'; presumably one laid upon him by the White Council.

43 Originally Gandalf's reply began:

'Don't speak as a fool!' said Gandalf. 'Grief has robbed you of your wits. *The one that you name* is an enemy . . .'

44 Tolkien first wrote 'Give *it* to my son', meaning the map; when Tolkien decided that this should include the key mentioned in the previous sentence as well, he changed the pronoun to match, although no account of the wizard presenting Thorin with the key, as in the published book, was added back to the text above.

Interestingly, the four words 'even from their tombs' are typed over pencil drafting, suggesting that the typescript at some point halted in the middle of this page (Ts. page 14; Ad.Ms.H.75) after the words 'four corners of the Earth', which was originally followed by a full stop.

45 Bilbo's remark was originally the even more naive 'which will take *a day or two*'.

Draftings

New Chapter I was composed on the typewriter and, like New Chapter II and the fragment of New Chapter III which follow, is itself the sole text of this new version of the book's opening. However, drafting for three individual passages does survive, on two separate sheets. The first, Ad.Ms.H.12, is the back of a page whose brief text I give at the end of the next chapter under the heading 'Queries and Reminders' (see page 811). Ad.Ms.H.12 has some nearly illegible drafting for two passages that appeared in New Chapter I. The first passage reads:

and he thought it an important occasion. If it had been allowed he might have come at last to the explanation. <But> it would not have been brief.

This is clearly a suggested replacement for 'He was an important dwarf. *If he had been allowed, he would probably have gone on like this until he was out of breath, without telling any one there anything that was not known already.* But he was rudely interrupted . . .' (second edition page 27, lines10ff; DAA.47). See page 778 and Text Note 22 above for the addition to the typescript which seems to be Tolkien's final version of this passage. The second passage reads:

a dragon of nine spells of
a dragon out of [> under] nine spells of sleep
even [the >] a drunken dragon.
would be the end of us: it would wake a stone dragon out of an enchanted sleep

These in turn are clearly an attempt to arrive at a satisfactory replacement for Gloin's 'one shriek like that in a moment of excitement *would be enough to wake the dragon and all his relatives, and kill the lot of us'* (second edition page 28, lines 13ff; DAA.48). See page 778 and Text Note 25 above for Tolkien's actual addition to the typescript for this passage.

The second sheet with drafting, Ad.Ms.H.18, forms the verso of the notes on phases of the moon that I give as section (iv) in the 'Timelines and Itinerary' chapter below (Ad.Ms.H.17; see page 831). Here Tolkien is bringing material from the Prefatory Note to the second edition about Thrain I (see page 753) and working it into harmony with what Thorin says about his family on pages 32 and 242 of the second edition (the passages about long ago being driven out of the far north and about the discovery of the Arkenstone, respectively; cf. DAA.54 & 287). Not all of this drafting, most of it hastily written in faded pencil, is legible; I give what I can make out of it to show how Tolkien worked his way to the final wording, with illegible words or passages replaced by ellipses (. . .) and doubtful words enclosed by french brackets < > as usual. At one point Tolkien himself uses an ellipsis to indicate an omitted passage; this is given below as a closed ellipsis (.....) without spaces between the dots.

p. 242[2] [TN1] Thrain Arkenstone . . .

[*cancelled*: back >] my family was driven out far north . . . came back . . .
. . . Old Thrain my ancestor. Long ago . . .
It was discovered by my far ancestor Thrain the Old [but >] . . . they mined <tunneled> . . . and . . . grandfather Thror

[*added in blue ball-point ink*: 32, 242]

. . . grandfather Thror's time my family were driven out of the North [*added*: back] and.....Map. <It> had been discovered long before by my [> our] far ancestor Thrain the Old, but now they <mined> . . . [*cancelled*: great] <hall> . . . they mined <them> they tunneled <them>. <He became> King under Mountain

[p. 24 >] 32 and 242[2]

Unlike the preceding, which is written in pencil, the final paragraph of drafting on this page is in blue ball-point ink:

Long ago in my grandfather Thror's time my [> his] family were [> was] driven out of the Far North and [they] came back with all their wealth and <their> tools to the Mountain on the Map. It had been discovered by our far ancestor Thrain the Old, but now they <mined> they <tunnelled> and they made deeper halls and greater workshops – and Thror became K u M again and his

This final paragraph of drafting in turn directly underlies those passages given in Text Notes 31, 32, and 33 above. Not only do these draftings, sketchy though they are, mark the emergence of the name 'Thrain the Old' (see pp. 780 & 788) but they resolve one lingering question from Tolkien's earlier confusion of the two competing Thror-Thrain-Thorin/Thrain-Thror-Thorin genealogies: why, if Thror was the last King under the Mountain, did Thorin refer to the Arkenstone as 'the Arkenstone of Thrain' (second edition page 242)? The now-familiar answer appears here for the first time in a typically Tolkienian resolution: Thror was indeed Last King, yet the appellation 'Arkenstone of Thrain' is also correct because it refers to a different Thrain, just as the Prefatory Note established was the case on Thror's Map.

Thus Tolkien finally resolved a contradiction accidentally introduced into the text before its first publication; all that would have been required to remove the last traces of the confusion would have been to substitute *fathers* for *father* in the second paragraph of Chapter XVI ('For the Arkenstone of my father . . . I name unto myself') and *fathers'* for *father's* in Chapter XVII ('That stone was my father's, and is mine . . . how came you by the heirloom of my house . . . ?'). But unfortunately Tolkien either did not realize that these two small changes remained to be made (since the 1960 Hobbit never reached so far) or, as seems more likely, he was well aware of it but made no note to that effect at the time and had forgotten this detail when forced to hastily revisit the book in 1965 for the 1966 third edition.

TEXT NOTES

1 I cannot explain the superscript here, which also occurs again further down the page. It does not refer to the second paragraph on that page, which describes the Arkenstone; it is the first paragraph which alludes to its discovery 'beneath the roots of the Mountain'.

New Chapter II

THE BROKEN BRIDGE

The typescript for New Chapter II starts at the top of a new page [Ad.Ms.H.25] but otherwise strongly resembles the last six pages of New Chapter I and clearly marks a continuation of the same text. As before, rather than a continuous narrative this Fifth Phase material varies between short bits of replacement text and longer extended scenes. The most notable addition is the scene of crossing the river beside the broken bridge, necessitated by discrepancies that arose when Bilbo's adventure, which had taken place 'off the map' (literally, since they had not yet entered the area covered by the Wilderland map at this point),† had to be superimposed upon Frodo's well-mapped journey covering the same terrain. Tolkien's solution was to alter both *The Hobbit* (see below) and the second edition of *The Lord of the Rings* (see HME VI.199–203) to match if possible the final published *LotR* map.

†It is not until they reach the ford early in Chapter III that Gandalf informs them that they 'are come to the very edge of the Wild' (DAA.88), and indeed the 'Edge of the Wild' is helpfully drawn as a double red line on the Wilderland Map published as the back endpaper of the second edition.

p. 40/13. and each pony was slung about with bundles and blankets and saddlebags. Four were without riders: two laden with foodbags and gear for cooking and camping; one more for Balin; and last a very small pony (with no baggage), evidently for Bilbo. The whole expedition had clearly been prepared long before[TN1]

p. 41/2 white horse called Rohald.[TN2] He brought no pocket-handkerchiefs, but he did bring a couple of blankets and Bilbo's pipe and tobacco ...... rode forward all that day and the next. <u>After this substitute for</u> except <u>1.5 to</u> William <u>p 46/5 the following:</u>[TN3]

They were still in the Shire, of course, and went at a leisurely pace, spending the nights in good inns; not until the Saturday afternoon did they cross the great bridge over the Brandywine River and enter what Bilbo called the Outlands, where outlandish things might be expected at any turn. At last he felt that his Adventure had begun.

But beyond the Bridge the road was still good, and there were wide lands looking wholesome enough. They met or came up with a number of folk on lawful business: dwarves for the most part going east or west with packs on their backs. Some belonged to Thorin's people of the western mountains, and they saluted him with a low bow; some were of poorer sort, pedlars of iron-ware, tinkers, or road-menders. There were a few Men, farmers mostly, ambling along on large fat horses; and several hobbits on foot. They stared at Thorin's company, but gave them no more than a grin and a nod.

In a day or two they came to Bree on the Hill. There they spent their last comfortable night for many a day to come, in the great inn of Bree, the Prancing Pony, well-known to the hobbits of the east side of the Shire.[TN4] Bree was as far as Bilbo's knowledge reached, even by hearsay. Beyond it the lands had been desolate for many long years. When in a day's journey more they came to the Last Inn, they found it deserted. They camped in its ruins, and next day they passed into a barren country with great marshes on their left as far as eye could see. They went very slowly now, sparing their laden ponies and often trudging on foot, for the road became very bad, rutted and pitted, and in places almost[TN5] lost in soft bog. The weather remained dry – as far as Bree it had been as fair as May can be, even in legends – but it was grey now and rather sad.

Bilbo's spirits fell, and he said very, little, thinking always of the next stop for food, though meals came much more seldom (and more scanty) than he would have liked. So they went on for many days,[TN6] and each day they became more silent and wary; for there was a stillness all round them – as if the land was listening (so Bilbo thought to himself). After a time the flat lands began to rise before them; still far away there were hills looming up, and as they drew nearer Bilbo saw that they were clad in dark trees, and on some there seemed to be the ruins of grim towers and walls. They had an evil look, as if men of evil days had built them.[TN7]

It was at about this time that things took a bad turn. One morning cold wind from the east met them with a breath of far mountains, bringing low clouds and driving rain. Bilbo shivered. 'Not what I call June!' he grumbled as he splashed along behind all the others in a deep muddy track that was fast becoming a stream. Poor hobbit, he was quite out of his reckoning; it was the nineteenth of May,[TN8] but the three weeks on the road began to seem endless. 'Bother adventures and everything to do with them!' he thought. 'I wish I was at home by the fire with the kettle just beginning to sing!' It was not the last time that he wished that.

The track[TN9] climbed to the top of a ridge, and then went down steeply into a narrow valley. They all halted and looked ahead. Through the valley a strong river flowed from the North, cutting across their road. Beyond it the dark hills frowned, and the road faded from sight under the shadows at their feet.

'Ha!' said Gandalf, peering through the rain. 'The bridge! The bridge is broken!' He turned away snapping his fingers and muttering to himself: 'there is mischief here! Elrond must be told'.

They did not know what he meant. This country was not well known[TN10] to the dwarves, and they could not see far before them. But Bilbo, whose eyes were keen, if not so keen as the wizard's, looked down and he thought he could see a grey stone bridge with a single arch over the river; but the arch was broken in the middle.

'Well, what's to be done?' said Gandalf. 'None are better at bridge-building than dwarves'.

'Maybe', said Thorin. 'But not in the wilds, without the tools or the tackle, nor in a storm of rain!'

'Just so' said Gandalf. 'But there is no other bridge over this river. A hundred miles away north you might jump it, but I should not go that way if I were you: it is troll-country.[TN11] Well, let us go down, and see the worst!'

They came to the bridge-end, and found that the river was not yet very wide. But it was swift: at the point where the bridge had been built it flowed over a rocky shelf, and then slid down long rapids away to their right. Here it foamed and swirled round the broken stones of the arch that were tumbled in the midst of its cold grey stream.

'It might be worse', said Gandalf. 'A dangerous ford, but the only one. It is this way, or go back. Unless you think of turning south, where there are no roads at all, and no way to pass the Misty Mountains,[TN12] which still lie ahead. Except, of course, by the Mines of Moria'.

The dwarves stared at him sullenly, muttering in their beards. 'It was you that advised us to come this way', said Thorin. 'What is your advice now?'

'I also said that no roads are now safe' answered the wizard. 'But I have given my advice: we must try to ford the river'. With that he mounted his horse and rode forward. As Bilbo had already noticed Gandalf used no stirrups, and seldom held the reins: Rohald[TN13] answered his commands, spoken softly in a strange tongue. The white horse tried the water and then walked on, slowly but without fear. The ponies lifted their dejected heads and watched him, like hobbit-children staring at some large lad showing off for their benefit. He skirted the tumbled bridge-stones in midstream, where the water was up to his hocks, and waded carefully to the further side. There he slipped, and recovered, for the far bank was steeper and more slimy: at last he scrambled up, and turned back, and neighed.

The ponies snorted. Plainly he had said as much as: 'There you are. Quite easy. You try it!'; but they were not so sure. Neither were the dwarves.

'Now or never!' Gandalf called across the water. No one moved for a moment. Then Thorin mounted and rode forward, beckoning the others to follow. Fili and Kili at once obeyed, but the rest were more reluctant. One behind the other they passed into the dangerous stream, the dwarves hiding their fear under the eyes of the wizard; the ponies going warily but stoutly watched by the white horse. The water in places swirled under their bellies, and some slipped and were nearly carried away, in the end they all reached the far bank without disaster.[TN14] Last of all came the pony bearing Bombur, and he had a heavier task than any, even the pack-ponies.

Thorin mopped his face, wet with sweat, rain and spray. 'Well, we've managed that', he said. 'On we go! There's no shelter here'.

'Don't you want the hobbit any more?' said Gandalf. 'I think you may need him'.

They had quite forgotten poor Bilbo! There he was still on the other side, sitting and shivering, more frightened than he had yet been in his life.

'Confound your hobbit!' said Thorin, 'When will he learn to look after himself?'

'In time', said Gandalf. 'Sooner than you expect'. 'Mr. Baggins!' he called. 'Don't try the crossing by yourself; your pony is small. I will come and help'.

Then the wizard went back over the stream, and set Bilbo behind him on the horse.[TN15] 'Hold on to your pony's reins' he said, 'and keep him on our right, if you can. He may make it, with Rohald[TN16] to break the force of the current'. 'Steady now', he said to the horse. 'Over once more, and your own land is not so far ahead!'

At last they had all crossed: but now the ponies were restive. They seemed unwilling to go further, turning their noses north towards the hills, the lower slopes of which were now close at hand, as if something there alarmed them. Suddenly one of the pack-ponies wrenched the reins from Bombur's hand, and bolted back towards the river. The other dwarves were busy calming their mounts, and before they could help, the wild pony was floundering in the stream, and struggling to cast off all his burdens. In the confusion that followed Fili and Kili were nearly drowned, and the pony was only saved at the cost of most of its baggage. Of course this proved to be the best part of all their food-supplies: away it went towards the rapids, and donk donk was the last they heard of their best cooking-pot as it was rolled among the boulders.

Gandalf spoke in the ear of the white horse, and he strode on to the road beyond the bridge-end. There he stood facing north, arching his neck and neighing loudly. Whatever that meant, it seemed to calm the ponies, or cow them. They allowed themselves to be led forward to his side. There all the company mounted again.

'Well', said Gandalf, 'now you must go on, much faster than before. And on short commons. Nothing more to eat until evening and a meal less each day!'

Bilbo groaned, but they took no notice of him. At once they started to jog along as fast as they could make the ponies go. The road was now much better; it was indeed a road, not a track, and seemed to be kept in some order.[TN17] But before they halted for midday, having covered several miles, they were skirting the hills,[TN18] and dark thickets overhung the steep bank on their right. Tightening their belts, they went doggedly on again, hungry and ill at ease, speaking hardly at all.

The wind rose, seething in the trees, rain drove in their faces, and the light began to fade. Far behind there was a brief stab of red, as the sun sank westwards;[TN19] shadow loomed before them. Still they went on. And last in the line came Bilbo; his hood was dripping in his eyes, and his cloak was full of water, he was empty and cold; but no one turned to look at him, not even to shout 'keep up!' 'I wonder if they would care, if I vanished?' thought Bilbo [> he thought]. It would not have been difficult in the gloom.

At last when it was night-dark under the trees,[TN20] Thorin called a halt. The wind was still blowing, but the rain-storm was passing. The clouds were breaking, and away in the East before them a waning moon was tilted between the flying rags.

'We must eat a little now', said Thorin; 'but where we shall find a dry patch for a bed, I don't know. At least we will have a fire, if we can. Oin, Gloin, look about for fuel!'

'I don't like the look of the woods' said Balin. 'The shelter may be better, but the thinner trees on the right feel more friendly'.

'What would you advise, Gandalf?' said Thorin, looking round. And only then did they discover that Gandalf was missing. So far he had always been with them, never saying if he was in the adventure, or merely keeping them company as long as his road and theirs went the same way.[TN21] But he had been there, always at hand to help, talking most, laughing most, and eating almost as much as Bombur. He was not there now!

'Just when a wizard would have been most useful!' grumbled Bombur, who seemed to think Gandalf might have conjured up roast mutton all hot, if he had been at hand.

They moved to a clump of trees just off the road; but the mould[TN22] was sodden beneath them, and the wind shook the water off the leaves, everything was dripping all round them. Oin and Gloin had gathered fuel, but the mischief was in it, or in their tinder-boxes.[TN23] Dwarves can make a fire for their needs almost anywhere out of almost anything, wind or no wind; but they could not kindle one that night, not even Oin and Gloin who were specially skilful. The others sat round, glum and wet, muttering at them, as they tried in vain to wake a flame; and they lost their tempers and began to quarrel. Bilbo sat huddled against a tree-trunk, hardly caring: he was reflecting that an adventure may start with pony-rides in May sunshine, but it will soon lead you into the Unknown – if it is really an adventure.

Suddenly Balin, who was always the dwarves' look-out man, called softly: 'There's a light over there!' He pointed across the road to a hill-slope thick with bushes and trees. A good way up, they could all now see a light shining out of the dark mass of the forest: a reddish comfortable light, as it might be a fire or torches twinkling.

When they had stared at it for some time in silence, they fell into an argument. Some said no and some said yes. Some said they might at least go and see, and anything was better than little supper, less breakfast, and wet clothes all the night. Gloin said he could think of many things that were much worse. 'You get on with your fire, then', the others answered.

Balin was the most doubtful. 'These are strange parts and not canny', he muttered. 'They are too near the great mountains, if I reckon right. This is Noman's kingdom, without charts, or guards or watchmen.'[TN24]

'Do you mean they haven't heard of the king here?' asked Bilbo with a sinking of the heart, for in the Shire they said that only of wild and wicked things.[TN25]

'The king is long gone', answered Balin. 'There is no law, and the less inquisitive you are, the less trouble you are likely to find'.

'There are fourteen of us' said Fili. 'We could give some account of ourselves'. 'Where has Gandalf got to?' said Bombur, looking about, as if he expected him to pop out from behind a tree.[TN26] That question they all repeated, Bilbo several times. Then the rain began to pour down again, and Oin and Gloin began to fight one another with the sticks that would not burn.

That settled it. 'After all we have got a burglar with us', they said; 'a little stealth is what we need!' And so they made a move, leading their ponies across the road, and beginning, very cautiously, to climb up the hill. There was no proper path to be seen, such as might lead, say, to a woodman's house, and the trees were thick with much undergrowth about them. Do what they could, they made a deal of rustling and crackling and creaking, with much stumbling and muttering, in the pitch dark.

Suddenly the red light shone out very bright through the tree-trunks not far ahead. They halted, for the ponies who had come very unwillingly took fright again, and tried to bolt back down the hill. The dwarves covered the beasts' eyes with their cloaks and tried to calm them.

'Now it's the burglar's turn to do something' they said, looking towards Bilbo, who was standing shivering in the gleam of the fire. 'You must go and find out all about that light', said Thorin, 'what it is, and if it is all quite safe and canny. Off you go, stealthy mind you! Come back quick, if all is well. If not, come back, if you can. If you can't, give a signal: the cry of a night-hawk, and two hoots like an owl, and we will do what we can'. With that he pushed the hobbit forward.

So off Bilbo had to go, before he could explain that he had never heard a night-hawk. 'I wish I could fly like a bat', he thought. He could not, but he could move on the ground as quietly, if not so quick. Hobbits can walk in woods without any sound at all. They take a pride in it, and Bilbo had sniffed more than once at what he called 'all this dwarvish racket' as they went up the hill, though on a windy night Big People would probably have heard nothing at all.[TN27] As for Bilbo walking primly towards the red light, even a weasel would hardly have stirred a whisker as he passed. So naturally he got right up to the fire – for fire it was – quite unnoticed. And this is what he saw.

Three very large persons were sitting round a very large fire of beech-logs. They were toasting mutton on long spits of wood, and licking the gravy off their fingers. There was a fine toothsome smell. Also there was a barrel of ale at hand, and they were drinking out of large jugs. But they were trolls! Obviously trolls. Even Bilbo, in spite of his sheltered life, could tell that: from the great heavy faces on them, and their huge size, and the shape of their legs – and their language! It was not decent Shire-fashion at all.

'Mutton yesterday, mutton today, and blimey, if it don't look like mutton again tomorrer', said one of the trolls.

'Never a blinking bit of manflesh have we had for long enough' said a second. 'What was the blasted good of knocking down the bridge? It ain't caught nobody. Nobody hasn't passed for days and days'.

'Ah, that was William', said the first troll. 'What the ell he was a thinkin of to bring us down into these parts at all, beats me. And the drink runnin short what's more', he said, jogging the elbow of William, who was taking a pull at his jug.

William choked. 'Shut yer foul mouth!' he said as soon as he could. 'Yer can't expect folk to stop here for ever just to be et by you and Bert. You've et a village and a half each, since we came down from the mountains, and folk have all skedaddled. What d'yer expect? But time's been up our way when yer'd have said "thank yer, Bill" for a nice bit o' fat valley mutton like what this is'. He took a big bite off a sheep's leg he was toasting, and wiped his mouth on his sleeve.

That is the way of trolls of their sort.[TN28] Great greedy slow-witted brutes. There are other kinds, more cunning and dangerous; but Tom and Bert and Bill were quite dangerous enough. As soon as he saw them Bilbo ought to have done something at once. Either he should have gone back quickly and warned his friends that there were three large trolls at hand in a nasty mood, quite likely to eat pony, or even try toasted dwarf for a change; or else he should have done a bit of good quick stealing. In legends a really first-class thief would at this point have picked the trolls' pockets, pinched the mutton off the spits, purloined the beer, and escaped while they were still wondering what had happened. Or better still and more practical, he might have stuck a dagger into each of them before they observed it, and then he and his friends could have spent the night cheerily.

Bilbo knew it. He had read or heard tell of many things that he had never seen or done. He was very much alarmed, as well as disgusted; he wished himself a hundred miles away, and yet – and yet somehow he could not go straight back to Thorin and Company emptyhanded. He stood and hesitated in the shadows on the edge of the clearing. Of the various stealthy proceedings that he had heard of picking the trolls' pockets seemed the least difficult, so at last he crept to a tree just behind William. ...

pp. 46/6 onwards, as in text, except as corrected.

p. 47/13 Delete I told you.

47/–10 He rose with a roar and bashed Bert on the nose; and a rampaging row began. Bilbo had just enough wits left when Bert dropped....[TN29]

p. 48/8 (after owl, they)[TN30] left Bombur to mind the ponies as best he could, and one by one they started to creep towards the light. Deserting their companions was not one of their faults.[TN31] Now Balin stood peering and wondering where in all this commotion Bilbo was; but Tom caught sight of his face in the firelight, and he gave a wild howl. Trolls detest the very sight of dwarves (uncooked). Bert and Bill stopped fighting at once, and 'a sack, Tom, quick' they shouted. Before Balin could slip off, a sack was over his head, and he was down.

p.48/–8 Soon Dwalin lay by Balin, and Bifur and Bofur together, and Dori and Nori and Ori all in a heap, and Oin and Gloin and Fili and Kili piled uncomfortably near the fire. 'That'll teach 'em,' said Tom; for Fili and Kili had given trouble, fighting fiercely as dwarves will when cornered.[TN32]

p. 49 is blank[TN33]

p. 50/15 into the top of a thorn-bush,

/18 and lost one of his fangs. He fell back howling and cursing, but at that moment William

p. 52/3 'The night's getting old. I can smell the dawn coming. Let's get on with it quick!'

'Dawn strike you all, and be stone to you!' said a voice that sounded like William's, but it was not. For at that moment the dawn came, light gleamed pale through the branches, and there was a mighty twitter of birds.

/13 Delete , as you probably know,

/18 a great tree, and helped Bilbo to climb out of the thorn-bush

/–12 for annoyed read angry

/–8 twice over, and still Thorin was not satisfied.

'Silly time to go practising your pocket-picking!' he said. 'What we wanted was fire and food'.

'And you wouldn't have got that from trolls without a struggle, in any case', said Gandalf. 'It might have turned out a great deal worse. Anyhow...

p. 53/14 for grabbed read seized

/19 plunder, of all sorts from buttons and rusty brooches to pots of gold coins standing in a corner. There were lots of clothes, too, hanging on the walls – all that was left of many poor wood-men and shepherds who had still lived here and there in the wild lands near-by. But hidden behind the door they found a number of swords and knives of various sizes and strange shapes. Two caught their eyes, because of their beautiful scabbards and their jewelled hilts that seemed to shine in the shadows.

Gandalf took one, and presented the other to Thorin. To Bilbo he gave a knife with a silver pommel. 'A gift for a good hobbit!' he said with a bow, which pleased Bilbo very much, though he did not himself feel that he had earned any praise. He looked at the knife: it had a sheath of black figured leather, and when he drew it, he saw that the blade was bright and unstained. It was long enough to serve a hobbit as a sword.

'These look like good blades too', said the wizard, half drawing the swords and examining them closely. 'They were not made by any troll, nor by any smith among Men of these days. But there's black blood on them, goblin-blood. When they are cleaned and the runes on them can be read, we shall know more about them'. end of page.

p.54/ after l. 8 insert:

'Now you had better look for Bombur', said Gandalf: 'and we shall need the ponies, if you can find them'.

Bifur and Bofur went off, and soon came back with the old fat dwarf. He looked rather glum. Not that he minded at all having missed the affair of the sacks, but they had found him fast asleep, and no sign of the ponies. Thorin was not pleased.

Gandalf laughed. 'Never mind!' he said. 'Let's have breakfast! You were fools to bring them across the road. I wonder you got them so far. No one could have held them when all the noise started. But they'll be all right: my Rohald is looking after them'.

So they all set to, and had a great breakfast, or a feast as it seemed; and after that they slept (even Bombur), for their night had been disturbed. They did not make a move until the afternoon. Then Gandalf got up and went down the hill, and soon he came back leading his white horse, and all the ponies coming meekly behind.

Then the dwarves packed up all the food that was left fit to eat, and other things that might prove useful, and they carried away the pots of gold. These they buried very secretly in a thicket not far from the road, and set many spells on them, and a stone cut with dwarf-runes to mark the place,[TN34] in case they ever had the chance to come back and recover them. When that was done, they all mounted once more and jogged along again on the road to the East.

'Where did you go to without a word, if I may ask?' said Thorin to Gandalf as they rode along.

'To look ahead', said he.

'And what brought you back in the nick of time?'

'Looking behind', said he.

'No doubt', said Thorin, 'but would you mind saying a little more!'

'Well, I hurried on ahead, to find some friends, if I could. The broken bridge was a bad sign; and there was not enough food to see you through the next few days. As I hoped, before long I met some folk from Rivendell'.

'Where's that?' asked Bilbo, who was keeping as close to the wizard as he could.

'Don't interrupt!' said Gandalf. 'You'll get there in a few days now, if we're lucky, and then you'll find out all about it. As I was saying, Elrond had heard of the trouble. The Rangers were out, and he had sent two of his own people to report. They told me that trolls had come down from the North, and they feared that three had settled in the woods not far above the road. Men had fled away south, and they were waylaying strangers.

' "Back you go then, and quick", I said to myself. Looking behind I saw a fire in the distance, and I came as fast as Rohald could carry me. I found all your ponies huddled on the road with their heads down and their tails to the north. The rest you can guess. But please be more careful, or we shall never get anywhere. My friends had no food to spare, for they are hunting: there are other wicked things abroad.[TN35] The trolls' larder is a piece of luck that you hardly deserve. But for Mr. Baggins you might have been lying among the bones on the floor!'[TN36]

'Pray don't mention it!' said Thorin.

This marks the end of New Chapter II, in the middle of the page [Ad.Ms.H.32]. The brief fragment of New Chapter III follows immediately on the same page after only a gap of a few skipped lines, albeit with a new pagination ('III 1'); see page 811.

New Chapter III

ARRIVAL IN RIVENDELL

p. 56/3 They felt that danger was lurking on both sides of their road. They camped where they could, and set watches; and their[TN37]

/7 trolls. On the fourth day from the Bridge[TN38] they passed the shadow of the dark hills. Gandalf laughed and pointed ahead; and still far off they saw another river before them, gleaming in the morning [> evening] sunshine, but all the lands beyond were shrouded in mist.

In the afternoon of the next day[TN39] they came to the river, and found a great ford over wide shallows, and there was a causeway of huge stepping-stones against which the stream gurgled and foamed; but on the far side the path wound steeply up a high frowning bank. When they had climbed to the top, leading their horses, they saw that the great mountains had marched down to meet them. The day was hot and clear and there was no mist, and it seemed only a day's easy journey now to the feet of the nearest.

p. 57/3 'You must not miss the path, or that will be the end of you',[TN40] he said. 'You need food, for one thing, and rest in safety for a while, and advice. None of you have ever tried the north passes, I think. Their perils are always changing, and you must consult one who knows, if you are to make the right choice. Those who take the wrong way in the Misty Mountains never come back to try again!'

/10 'You have come to the last fences of the Westland. Ahead of us [> Over there] lies hidden the fair valley of Rivendell, of which no doubt some of you have heard tell, though few dwarves have ever seen it.[TN41] There Master Elrond lives in the Last Homely House. I sent a message by my friends, and we are expected'.

That sounded comforting; but they had not got there yet, and it was not easy to find the way to the secret valley and the Last Homely House west of the Mountains

p. 58/ 10 Delete about pretty well.[TN42]

/11 They went on until moonless night [> twilight] overtook them, and they lay that night under the bright stars. The next day was failing, and they were still following Gandalf, whose head and beard wagged this way and that as he searched for the white stones in the dusk. White [> Pale] moths were fluttering in the whins[TN43] and long heather, and twilight deepened like a mist about the horses' feet.

'Supper-time and past it!' thought Bilbo, who had not eaten since midday. His tired pony began to stumble over roots and stones.[TN44] Then just ahead Rohald neighed, and he hurried forward, and came to [a] steep fall in the ground so suddenly that he nearly slipped headlong down it.

'Here it is at last!' cried Gandalf, as the dwarves came up and stared over the edge

At this point, the Fifth Phase typescript comes to an end, leaving about two-thirds of the final page [Ad.Ms.H.33] blank. On the blank space, Tolkien wrote a note regarding the projected contents of the rest of this chapter, had he continued beyond this point:

Ch. III should make clear
Elrond's care for roads etc. from
Greyflood to <Mountains>
Also insert the white horse
Róhald belonged to Rivendell, & had
been lent by Elrond to Gandalf.

This final point should perhaps be taken to indicate that Rohald would be left behind in Rivendell when Thorin & Company set out again to attempt the mountain-passes. Certainly it is disquieting enough to think of all the ponies being eaten by the goblins in Chapter IV, now that they have been given a sort of corporate personality and even pseudo dialogue (cf. page 795), much less an elven horse such as Rohald. See also 'Queries and Reminders' below.

TEXT NOTES

1 This last sentence is bracketed for removal.

2 Gandalf's white horse dates all the way back to the earliest pages of the Second Phase manuscript, but he only now gains a name: Rohald. Again I have found no authorized gloss, but the name is clearly Sindarin, with the *ro-* element meaning 'horse'; cf. Aragorn's horse, Roheryn (*LotR*.809), which means 'horse of the lady' (*roch* + *heru*; so named from being Arwen's gift – cf. *Silm*.363), and Rochallor, High King Fingolfin's great horse (*Silm*.153). Salo's *A Gateway to Sindarin* lists no *hald* in its Sindarin-English Glossary, but it does have *hall*, which can mean either 'exalted, high' or 'veiled, hidden, shadowed, shady' (Salo, page 263).

In any case, the line adding the name of Gandalf's white horse was not part of the original typescript here but was added later; Rohald's name does not appear as originally typed until page 796 (see Text Notes 13 & 16).

3 Originally Tolkien intended the replacement text that follows to take the place of the passage beginning on line 5 of page 41 in the second edition ('. . . rode forward all day, *except of course when they stopped for meals* . . .') and continuing through line 22, ending with '*the weather which had often been as good as May can be, even in tales and legends,* took a nasty turn'. Much of this passage would in fact be replaced by Tolkien in the 1966 Hobbit (see DAA.65–6), although in briefer form than the text given here. When Tolkien came to actually write the replacement text, it flowed so fluently that by the time he stopped rather than sixteen lines later on page 41 he had reached the fifth line on page 46 ('. . . *crept behind a tree just behind* William'). I have added the underlinings here and throughout this chapter, matching Tolkien's own practice in New Chapter I, to help distinguish between Tolkien's instructions and the words to which they apply. As with New Chapter I, ellipses without spaces separating the periods (e.g. ......) are Tolkien's own.

4 A pencilled notation in the left margin along these lines seeks to establish a timeline of their trip. The first few words are too faint to read, but the rest of the note reads '. . . 2 ½ days' journey arriving at evening on May 2.' This corresponds to the entry in the Itinerary, which has them crossing the Brandywine Bridge early on 30th April and arriving at Bree on 2nd May; see page 818.

5 The word *almost* is cancelled in pencil and replaced by a passage in light pencil in the right margin, but I cannot make out any of this marginalia.

6 In the left margin along this line is written '16 days', which is then changed to '15 days'. See entries 7 and 8 in the timeline (page 818), which between them equal fifteen days.

7 In the original story, some of these hills had castles on them, of which 'many looked as if they had not been built for any good purpose'. In the more developed history of *The Lord of the Rings*, this area had now come to be the territory of the fallen evil kingdom of Rhudaur (one of the inheritor-kingdoms of fractured Arnor), which had been destroyed more than a millennium before. Accordingly, the slightly sinister castles become evil-looking ruins in the 1960 Hobbit, a change carried over (though not in the same words) into the 1966 Hobbit (the published third edition); cf. DAA.66.

8 See Itinerary, page 819.

9 Originally 'The *deep* track'.

10 Originally this sentence read 'This country was *unknown* to the dwarves', obviously altered because it has already been established that Thorin's people traded and travelled up and down the Great East Road. In addition, Thorin's people could not have passed through Moria on their flight west after Smaug destroyed the Kingdom under the Mountain, nor is it likely that they came by way of the goblin-haunted Mount Gram, or took the extreme long away around through the Gap of Rohan. Instead, they almost certainly came by way of the Forest Road

to the same passes Thorin and Company will attempt in Chapter IV and hence westward down the same East-West road they are now travelling all the way to the Blue Mountains west of the Shire. Furthermore, it seems extremely unlikely that Thorin's dwarf-colony in Harlindon has no contact at all with Dain's people in the Iron Hills, which would also imply east-west travel along this route.

11 The area in question is marked the 'Ettenmoors' on the *Lord of the Rings* map, *etten* (ettin) being an old word for 'giants' (descended from the Old English *eoten*, ent) that remained in use up until the early 1600s. Strider, in 'Flight to the Ford', glosses the term as 'the troll-fells' (*LotR*.216), *troll* being a mid-nineteenth century borrowing from the Scandinavian which supplemented but did not replace *giant* (itself Anglo-Norman in origin). Also on the *LotR* map, the area in which Bilbo and the dwarves encounter the trolls is called the 'Trollshaws', *shaw* being an archaic word for woods or thicket; cf. the thick woods in all three of Tolkien's pictures of the troll-episode, most notably 'Trolls' Hill' (Plate IV [bottom]) and the black and white drawing 'The Trolls' (DAA.74).

12 Originally this passage read 'no way to pass *the great mountains*, which still lie ahead'. Significantly, not even Balin (who, as *The Lord of the Rings* reveals, did later dare to enter Moria) takes Gandalf up on his taunt about trying the Mines of Moria as an alternate route past the mountains. Nonetheless its mention helps tie the geography of the two books (and the two journeys, of Bilbo and the Ring-bearer) together; like the earlier mention of the Prancing Pony at Bree, it emphasizes to those who have read *The Lord of the Rings* before (this version of) *The Hobbit* that both take place in the same world and, in this passage at least, traverse the same territory.

13 Again 'Rohald' is added later, replacing *his white horse* in the original.

14 This was originally followed by a cancelled line, 'Last of all came the pack ponies'.

15 In this passage, Bilbo becomes the first of three hobbits who at one point or another ride with Gandalf on a great pale horse, the other two being Pippin in the ride from Rohan to Minas Tirith (*The Lord of the Rings*, last chapter of Book III and first chapter of Book V) and Odo, the latter in the rejected storyline from early drafts of *The Lord of the Rings* where Gandalf rescued him from the Black Riders at Crickhollow (HME VI.304) and Odo accompanied the wizard as far as Weathertop (HME VI.352, 355–6); none of the Odo material made it into the published book.

16 This marks the first time that Rohald has appeared in the text as first typed; on previous occasions the name had been added in later as replacement text.

17 This was initially followed by the cancelled line 'The rain too had almost stopped.'

18 Originally this passage read 'But before they halted for midday, having covered several miles, they were *under the shadow of the dark hills*'.

19 Originally this sentence read 'Far behind *in the West* there was a brief stab of red, as the sun *sank*'.

20 Originally this passage read 'when it was *nearly night*', which was altered first to 'the dark' (i.e., 'when *the dark* . . .') and then to 'when *the tree-shadowed road was dark*', before finally reaching the form given in the text.

21 In fact, 'The Quest of Erebor' makes this explicit. When Thorin reluctantly agrees in the wee hours of the morning following the Unexpected Party to take Bilbo, at Gandalf's urging (and threats), Thorin makes it a condition that Gandalf shall then accompany them as well:

> 'Very well,' Thorin said at last after a silence. 'He shall set out with my company, if he dares (which I doubt). But if you insist on burdening me with him, you must come too and look after your darling.'
>
> 'Good!' I answered. 'I will come, and stay with you as long as I can: at least until you have discovered his worth.' It proved well in the end, but at the time I was troubled, for I had the urgent matter of the White Council on my hands.
>
> — *Unfinished Tales*, pp. 325–6.

This account finally makes clear therefore that Gandalf does indeed have 'pressing business' of his own (DAA.187) and must leave Thorin & Company as soon as he decently can to deal with a different crisis elsewhere: marshalling the Wizards and the Wise – that is, Radagast and the Elven-princes – to join him in overruling Saruman and attacking the Necromancer before the latter can destroy Rivendell or Lórien (UT.321–2, 326; see also 350–51).

22 *Mould* here means not 'mold' in the sense of mildew or fungus (its most common usage today) but dirt rich with organic decay (in this case, from generations of fallen leaves).

23 The penultimate paragraph of Chapter VI observes that 'Dwarves have never taken to matches even yet' (DAA.159). Whether this line, and the relatively modern touch of Bilbo's pocket-matches in Chapter V (DAA.116), would have survived in the 1960 Hobbit, had the Fifth Phase reached so far, is an unanswerable question; at any rate, they survived unchanged through the third edition changes of 1966.

24 Originally Balin describes this area as 'Noman's *land*', a phrase Tolkien used several times in *The Lord of the Rings* for the area better known as the Brown Lands (*LotR*.394 & 657). The addition of these lines of dialogue by Balin and Gloin, like Fili and Kili's promptly springing into action after Thorin's decision at the fallen bridge and Bombur's fumbling and grumbling, all help characterize the dwarves – for example, Balin's distrust of the woods north of the road helps establish his good judgment, since it is soon revealed that trolls are lurking there. Had Tolkien continued the 1960 Hobbit all the way to the end he

would no doubt have added similar bits of action or dialogue for the less differentiated members of Thorin & Company; i.e., Nori, Oin, Bofur, Bifur, and Ori.

25 Bilbo originally referred to 'the kings' (plural) here, but this may be no more than a typing error, which in any case was quickly corrected to 'king'. This referent replaced the 'They have seldom even heard of the king round here' of the first and second (and ultimately third) editions. In the Prologue to *The Lord of the Rings*, Tolkien explain that this was an allusion to the fallen Dúnedain kingdoms of Arnor, in words he is clearly echoing here in the 1960 Hobbit:

> there had been no king for nearly a thousand years . . . Yet the Hobbits still said of wild folk and wicked things (such as trolls) that they had not heard of the king. For they attributed to the king of old all their essential laws . . . The Rules (as they said), both ancient and just.
>
> —*LotR*.21–2.

There is an irony in this mention of the king here, when with hindsight from *The Lord of the Rings*' Appendices A and B we realize that within a few days they will be arriving in Rivendell, where ten-year-old Aragorn, the rightful king of Arnor and Gondor, is living under the name of Estel ('Hope') in Elrond's household.

26 Bombur's expectation is amusing, given that Gandalf at his reappearance indeed 'stepped from behind a great tree'; see DAA.80 and Tolkien's correction for page 52 line 18 on page 801.

27 Note that the rephrasing here eliminates the direct address to the reader of all the published editions at this point: 'though I don't suppose you or I would have noticed anything . . . I don't suppose even a weasel would have stirred a whisker' (DAA.70); the formerly intrusive narrator ceases to be a character in the story, which now lacks a storyteller.

28 Originally, 'trolls of *that* sort'. In a 1954 letter, Tolkien described the trolls appearing in *The Hobbit* as 'Stone-trolls' (JRRT to Peter Hastings, *Letters* p.191). The 'other kinds' mentioned in the following sentences include the cave-troll that almost forces its way into Balin's burial chamber in Moria (*LotR*.342–3) and the *Olog-hai* (*LotR*.1166), described in the rumors circulating in the Shire in 'The Shadow of the Past': 'Trolls were abroad, no longer dull-witted, but cunning and armed with dreadful weapons' (*LotR*.57).

29 This entry is a late addition, written in the left margin.

30 That is, in place of the original passage that read '. . . after waiting for some time for Bilbo to come back, or to hoot like an owl, they *started off one by one*', the text should now read '. . . hoot like an owl, they *left Bombur to mind the ponies* . . .'

31 This sentence is bracketed in pencil but not deleted. Presumably what called it into question was the new scene earlier in this same chapter

where they had in fact left behind one of their number (the overlooked hobbit) on the far bank of the swollen river.

32 The sequence in which the dwarves arrived at the troll's campfire is altered from the original, which mimicked the order in which they arrived on Bilbo's doorstep (and included the surprising information that Bifur, Bofur, and Bombur were the Heir of Durin's 'attendants' – i.e. either courtiers or an honor-guard). Now the surprisingly good account the last two captured gave of themselves is transferred from the unlikely Bifur and Bombur (not elsewhere distinguished for their valour) to the more active and effective Fili and Kili.

33 This page is not literally blank but it does lack any text, being devoted to the black-and-white picture 'The Trolls' (cf. DAA.74).

34 Originally 'set *a stone over them with dwarf runes*'.

35 Originally Tolkien typed 'there are *more trolls about*' before changing it to the less specific and more evocative 'other wicked things abroad'.

36 Gandalf's final statement, absent from earlier editions, is curious, since nothing added here indicates that Bilbo played any part in saving them from the cannibal feast.

37 The unchanged skipped text that bridges the gap between these two revisions is 'and their *horses had more to eat than they had; for there was plenty of grass, but there was not much in their bags, even with what they had got from the* trolls.' This actually misses an opportunity to correct an error going all the way back to the first edition, since 'horses' should in fact read *ponies* here. The original book had switched back and forth between 'horse' and 'pony', especially in the Lonely Mountain chapters (see page 479), as if the two were interchangeable, but the dichotomy between the dwarves' ponies and the wizard's horse has been stressed throughout New Chapter II.

38 Written in the left margin alongside this: 'May 22'. See Itinerary, page 819.

39 Written in the left margin alongside this: 'May 23'. See Itinerary, page 819.

40 The shift from first person plural ('We must not . . . we shall be . . . We need') in the published editions (cf. DAA.88) to second person ('You must not . . . the end of you . . . You need') here has the effect of exempting the wizard himself, suggesting that whatever dire peril they may find themselves in he at least will come through unscathed. This is in keeping with his enhanced stature in *The Lord of the Rings*, but again it leaves him detached, not really a part of the group struggling to survive the adventure he arranged.

41 The idea that dwarves were not particularly welcome at Rivendell is a new and somewhat disconcerting idea, apparently imported back into *The Hobbit* to match the initially chilly relations between Gimli's people and the elves of Lórien in *The Lord of the Rings*. The version of this passage Tolkien originally drafted, '*no dwarf has*', was even more

uncompromising (i.e., 'though *no dwarf has* [ever seen it]). It is also out of keeping with their extended stay there, which in the 1960 Hobbit is expanded from the two weeks ('a fortnight') of the published book to at least five (see Itinerary, page 823).

42 The passage being altered reads 'Gandalf, who seemed to know his way about pretty well', which would now become 'Gandalf, who seemed to know his way.'

43 *whin*, like heather, is a tough prickly shrub, more commonly known as *furze*, that grows in European wastelands.

44 This sentence was followed by several lines of drafting:

> Suddenly he came to the brink of a steep fall in the ground, so sharp that [he] nearly slipped headlong down it. 'Steady!' said Gandalf. 'You have better come last.'

Although cancelled, this passage shows us that the 'he' who hurried forward in the next sentence is Bilbo, not Gandalf or his horse.

Queries and Reminders

Nothing in the nature of Plot Notes exists for New Chapters I, II, & III – naturally enough, given that Tolkien had already long since completed the story and instead was now trying to bring it into accord with its sequel, and his own revised opinions about how such a story should be told. However, a single page of notes [Ad.Ms.H.11] does exist, clearly meant to serve as reminders to Tolkien of points he had not yet addressed in this revision, and I give those here:

Hobbit

There is no mention in The Hobbit of Gandalf's horse after Rivendell. What did he ride on?

What happened to the musical instruments used by the Dwarves at Bag-end?

Why did they bring them to B-End?

Since the Fifth Phase was abandoned at this point, ultimately none of these points was resolved. The fate of Rohald is suggested by Tolkien's note at the end of New Chapter III (see page 810 above); since the horse was from Rivendell, Gandalf presumably left him there when Thorin & Company departed and headed up into the mountains. The musical instruments are a thornier issue, since these notes indicate Tolkien's dissatisfaction with the text as it stands but give no hint of how he might have resolved the problem. Given his attempt throughout the 1960 Hobbit to reduce the whimsy and comic touches of the original, however, it seems likely that in the end this bit of dwarven exuberance would have been sacrificed to probability and all but the most portable instruments deleted.

The End of the Fifth Phase

The goal of this chapter's revision was not so much to flesh out the rather sketchy account of Bilbo and the dwarves' journey from Bag-end to Rivendell, although it does do that, as to make it fit with the later, more detailed description of travelling over some of that same territory (between Bree and the Last Homely House) in *The Lord of the Rings*. As the late Karen Wynn Fonstad observed in *The Atlas of Middle-earth* [1981]:

> The Troll's fire was so close to the river that it could be seen 'some way off,' and it probably took the Dwarves no more than an hour to reach; whereas Strider led the Hobbits north of the road, where they lost their way and spent almost six days reaching the clearing where they found the Stone-trolls. Lost or not, it seems almost impossible that the time-pressed ranger would have spent six days reaching a point the Dwarves found in an hour . . . the two stories seemed irreconcilable.
>
> —Fonstad, page 97.

As the 'Timelines and Itinerary' show, Tolkien was well aware of this problem, and Christopher Tolkien discusses in *The Return of the Shadow* (HME VI.203–4) how the 1960 Hobbit revisions would have redressed this dilemma. The fact that the 1966 third edition changes failed to do so is, I think, a persuasive bit of evidence that Carpenter is correct in stating that Tolkien did not have the 1960 material before him when he made those final changes to the text. Instead, he was almost certainly working from his memory of this material: the third edition introduces the stone bridge found in *The Lord of the Rings*, but since it is intact in this final authorized edition of *The Hobbit* (DAA.66) its presence only exacerbates the problem of the discrepancy in the time their respective journeys took.

In addition to more diminishment of Bilbo's character – the hapless hobbit now cannot even keep track of what month it is – the new revisions firmly place Bilbo in Frodo's world: to mentions of the Shire and Hobbiton and Moria in New Chapter I are now added another mention of Moria and references to the Prancing Pony at Bree and to the Rangers operating in the area around Rivendell (in fact, hunting down monsters like the trolls). The bridge across the Mitheithel (Hoarwell) upon which Glorfindel leaves a token for Strider (*LotR*.217) now appears in *The Hobbit*, but broken by trolls; clearly Elrond must have restored it sometime in the intervening years (see Tolkien's note on Elrond's maintenance of the road at the end of the New Chapter III fragment, on page 810).[1]

Small wonder, in the face of such specificity, that statements by the narrator such as 'I don't know what river it was' (second edition page 42) vanish in the 1960 revision. In fact, all first person references by the narrator are excised from the text, along with all direct (second person) addresses by the narrator to the reader; Tolkien had come to feel that these were a stylistic flaw and removed them throughout.

What is surprising is that, even with all these changes, large sections of the story remained intact and indeed unaltered. For example, Tolkien had stated in 1954 that 'I might not (if *The Hobbit* had been more carefully written, and my world so much thought about 20 years ago) have used the expression "poor little blighter",[2] just as I should not have called the troll *William*' (JRRT to Peter Hastings, Sept 1954; *Letters* p. 191), yet aside from some additions at the beginning of the encounter the troll's dialogue survived virtually untouched in this extensive 1960 recasting of the chapter, and the now-inappropriate names William (or Bill), Bert, and Tom were all retained.

One other long-standing point is resolved in this revision: the vexing question of why Elrond could read the writing on the swords but Gandalf could not. Now we are told that the runes are obscured by old dried goblin-blood; not until they are cleaned can the letters be seen. Presumably their hosts perform this task for them during their stay, and the scene of Elrond's viewing the swords in Chapter III would probably have been slightly recast to incorporate a presentation of their newly polished swords.

We cannot know what else Tolkien would have added to the story, had the 1960 Hobbit or Fifth Phase continued beyond this point. Bilbo could not have met Arwen at Rivendell, for we know she was at that time in the middle of a decades-long visit to her grandparents, Galadriel and Celeborn, in Lórien. But did Bilbo's lifelong friendship with Aragorn (then a ten-year-old living in Rivendell with his mother and being raised by Elrond) begin during his visit there, either on the outgoing or the return trip? Did Legolas Greenleaf fight in the Battle of Five Armies? Would more light have been cast upon the storm-giants of the Misty Mountains, or the source of Beorn's enchantment, or would we have learned a little more about the elusive Radagast? Would the Spiders of Mirkwood have been made more horrific, à la Shelob, and the wood-elves absolved of all blame in their treatment of the dwarves? Would Balin's visit in the Epilogue include some mention of his plans for Moria? And most importantly, would the Ring have been presented in more sinister terms throughout, with hints of its corruptive influence even on one such as Bilbo?

We will never know the answers to any of these questions. According to Christopher Tolkien, when his father had reached this point in the recasting he loaned the material to a friend to get an outside opinion on it. We do not know this person's identity, but apparently her response was something along the lines of 'this is wonderful, but it's not *The Hobbit*'. She must have been someone whose judgment Tolkien respected, for he abandoned the work and decided to let *The Hobbit* retain its own autonomy and voice rather than completely incorporate it into *The Lord of the Rings* as a lesser 'prelude' to the greater work. When he briefly returned to it in 1965 for the third edition revisions, he restricted himself in the main to the correction of errors and egregious departures from Middle-earth as it had developed (e.g., the policemen of Chapter II; DAA.69) and left matters of style and tone alone. Thus the work begun in a flash of inspiration thirty-five years before – 'in a hole in the ground lived a hobbit' – saw periodic revisioning through several distinct phases over a period of thirty years (1930 to 1960), until in the last decade of its author's life it reached the final form we know and love today.

NOTES

1 While Elrond's maintenance of the road makes sense and is in keeping with his role as the preserver of the last vestiges of the North Kingdom, it is hard to picture the elves of Rivendell working at road-mending, since throughout the legendarium the elves are never associated with road-making. We might speculate that he hires dwarves to do the work without actually permitting these contractors to know Rivendell's exact location (lying as it does some way off the main road), but that solution runs afoul of this text's statements that dwarves were not welcome here and did not know this part of the world well. No doubt if Tolkien had fully developed this idea we would know the answers to these apparent difficulties.

2 Hastings had argued that this phrase implied that William was capable of feeling pity and thus making a moral judgment. This would of course run counter to the legendarium's presentation of the Creatures of Morgoth as irredeemably wicked. Tolkien however disagreed: 'I do not say William felt *pity* – a word to me of moral and imaginative worth . . . Pity must restrain one from doing something immediately desirable and seemingly advantageous. There is no more "pity" here than in a beast of prey yawning, or lazily patting a creature it could eat, but does not want to, since it is not hungry' (*Letters* p. 191). Thus there was no need to rewrite the scene of William's actions, and Tolkien left his little comic masterpiece of the trolls' dialogue intact, even preserving the mild profanity of 'what the 'ell.'

TIMELINES AND ITINERARY

The final group of texts associated with the 1960 Hobbit are concerned with distances and dates, particularly as they relate to time of travel between various points and to the phases of the moon. Primarily, Tolkien was concerned with four main points: (1) the date of Thorin & Company's departure from Bag-End, (2) the date and place of their encounter with the trolls (with its associated phase of the moon), (3) the time of their stay in Rivendell (with *its* associated moon-phase on the eve of their departure), and (4) the timing of Durin's Day. Through the changes incorporated into New Chapter I and New Chapter II, he had managed to bring some of these points into sufficient harmony to satisfy himself; the itinerary below beautifully lays out the specifics, along with many interesting hitherto unknown details about their journey. However, reconciling all of these points, and others that arose as a result of his revisions, ultimately proved impossible without even more radical alterations than he had already carried out, for reasons that will become evident in the material that follows.

(i)
Distances and Itinerary

These two sheets of single-spaced typescript, or three and a half pages of text [Ad.Ms.H.21–4], lay out with admirable clarity the day-by-day details of Bilbo's first journey, from his rendezvous with the dwarves outside the inn in Bywater to their arrival in Rivendell. This document is later than New Chapter I and New Chapter II as they were originally typed, since the latter text is quoted from within it, but before some of the alterations and revisions to those documents.

The Hobbit.

Distances and itinerary of the journey from Bywater Inn to Rivendell. This has been altered to fit the more precise geography of the 'Lord of the Rings', the first Book of which covers the same ground. Also to make more credible and explicable Gandalf's disappearance before the Troll-episode.

The maps in the L.R.[TN1] have been taken as more or less correct and to scale. The scale of the large map is 1 centimetre to 50 miles. That of the Shire-map is not stated, but is approximately 9 times as large (1 millimetre to 5/9 of a mile). But note ** in this map Bywater and its pool is somewhat too far east. There should be no houses of Hobbiton on the south side of 'The Water'. Or rather none at the time of The Hobbit. At time of L.R. ('Scouring of the Shire') there should be a small block of 'new houses' to the right of the road-junction, 'a mile beyond Bywater'; but none to the left.[TN2] It was not more than a mile and a quarter from the footbridge just south of the Mill to the first houses of Bywater, among which was the 'Green Dragon' Inn.

The episode of the broken bridge (The Bridge of Mitheithel in L.R.) is inserted, to fit geography, which does not allow for any part of the East Road running beside a river. It also suggests, though this is not explained (unless perhaps in Ch. III)[TN3] that Elrond exercised some supervision over the road and the territory between the Grey-flood and the Mountains. This makes it more credible that Gandalf should go in search of help, and should actually meet people from Rivendell. The Rangers are just mentioned, as a link with L.R. but not further explained.

As for the journey, before that point (the troll-meeting), the text of The Hobbit, Ch.II, obviously cannot be equated with the L.R., not even if based on the confused memories of Bilbo (who covered the road twice, to and fro).[TN4] But fair speed of narrative is still needed, and even apart from competing with the L.R., no such detail as is given in the later book should be given. It is however impossible that Bilbo would have forgotten Bree, or that he should not have heard of it before:[TN5] it was well-known in hobbit-history. Though he may not have heard the name of the Inn (which in the L.R. is evidently only known to and visited by people from Buckland and the neighbourhood of the Brandywine Bridge).

Bree is therefore just mentioned as a last stopping place before the real wilds began. The Last Inn (by the time of the L.R. called the Forsaken Inn: L.R. I 200)[TN6] a day's journey east of Bree is brought in to emphasize the growing desolation between Bree and the Grey-flood. But Weathertop is not mentioned; nor are the rivers Greyflood and Loudwater named.

Distances.

1. SHIRE. Junction of the Hill Road in Hobbiton and the main East Road to Brandywine Bridge: about 50 miles.
2. Brandywine Bridge to Bree (by road) 50 miles. +
   + called (L.R. I. 162) 'not much [further] than a day's riding' but that refers to quick <journeys> on <unhampered> mounts.[TN7]
3. Wild. Bree Eastgate to ruined Last Inn about 20 miles
4. Last Inn to Weathertop (by road) 80 miles.
   100 miles Bree to Weathertop.
5. Weathertop to Bridge of Mitheithel (by road) 110 miles
6. Bridge of Mitheithel to Ford of Bruinen about 80 miles
   Bridge to point where Troll-fire seen: 20 miles.
   From that point to Ford 60 miles.
7. Ford of Bruinen to entrance to Rivendell, about 22 miles.

The whole journey from Bywater in the Shire to Rivendell was about 412 miles. Time allowed: from morning of April 28 to evening of May 24th. That is, according to the Shire Calendar (followed but nowhere alluded to in The Hobbit),[TN8] from Astron 28 to Thrimidge 24 inclusive: 27 days. That is an average of 16 miles a day. This is slow, but accounted for by leisurely pace at the beginning, and slow progress in the Wilds, especially before passing the Greyflood. But is clear that it could not be 'June the first tomorrow' (i.e. in Shire reckoning May/Thrimidge 30), as in text, p. 41, on the day of the troll-adventure. This is accounted for by Bilbo's loss of reckoning, without the help of any calendar, during the 22 days of the journey up to that point. Hence new text: 'Not what I call June, etc.'

Itinerary.

1. April 28. Spend night at the All-welcome Inn, at junction of the Northway and East Road (on Hobbiton side of Frogmorton). So-called because much used by travellers through the Shire, especially by dwarves on the way to Thorin's home in exile, which was in the west-side of the Blue mountains (southern part, in Harlindon). None of this is mentioned in text, but The All-welcome Inn should be marked on the needed Shire-map in any new edition of The Hobbit.[TN9] It has to be remembered that the East Road though it ran through the Shire was not the property of the hobbits: it was an ancient 'royal

road', and they maintained the traditional duty of keeping it in repair and providing hospitality for travellers. This was of course profitable. It also provided their chief source of 'outside news'. Dwarves were therefore not a rare sight on the East Road or in its inns (It would also appear that they were sometimes employed as roadmenders and bridge-repairers), but they seldom turned off it, and their appearance in a company in Bywater and Hobbiton must have caused a lot of talk.[TN10] They cared very little about hobbits, and had little to do with them, except as a source of food in exchange for metal, or sometimes forged articles (knives, ploughshares, arrowheads, axe-heads and the like). The poorer sort (or Thorin's folk in their earlier time of poverty) might accept employment, as masons and roadmakers for example. But they had the notion that hobbits were a slow stupid folk, with few artefacts, and simpleminded – because the hobbits were generous, never haggled, and gave what was asked.

2. April 29. Night at Whitfurrows.

3. April 30. Early start. They cross the Brandywine Bridge (about 12 miles from Whitfurrows) in the late afternoon, and camp by the road about 10 miles on from the B. Bridge.

4. May 1. They ride another 20 miles, taking their time, with longish halts and good meals (but only three), since there are still supplies ahead.

5. May 2. They reach Bree (another 20 miles). There they stay the night, and also purchase a good many supplies (including pipe-weed).

6. May 3. Early start. They enter the wild. They reach the Last Inn early in the evening, but are depressed at finding it deserted and go no further. [*added in pencil*: Another 20 miles.]

7. May 4 to May 10: 7 days.

Their progress is now very slow, owing to the badness and dangerousness of the road, esp. in the marshy region. They barely manage 12 miles a day, and by evening of May 10 have only reached Weathertop (80 miles from the Last Inn). They camp on its east side.[TN11] This is not mentioned at all in text.

8. May 11 to May 18: 8 days.

It was about 109 miles (for they started on the far side of Weathertop) to the Bridge of Mitheithel (over the Greyflood). By the evening of May 18 they had covered only 106 miles, and camped beside the road, on drier and rising ground, actually only about 3 miles from the Bridge, which could not be seen as it was in a deep narrow valley. In the night the weather took a bad turn.

9. May 19. Wakened in the early morning by wind and rain, they make a hurried meal. Soon reach the top of the ridge and look down. Episode of the broken bridge. They get across Greyflood about 10.30 a.m. 3 miles. They make two foodless halts, at midday about 5 miles on from Bridge, and another (not mentioned in text) about 4. p.m.; and then go on till darkness. Say about 8.30 p.m. (sun-set about 8 p.m.) but the road was under dark trees.[TN12] Ponies become more and more reluctant to proceed, so that in spite of improved road they are slow. Going from 1 p.m. to 4 and 4.30 to 8. (6 1/2 hours) they only cover about 17 miles.[TN13] Episode of the Trolls occurs night of May 19, at a point about 25 miles from the Bridge. 55 miles to go to Ford of Bruinen.

10. May 20. Do not start until afternoon, say 3.30 p.m. Journey till 8 p.m. with one halt: about 4 hours in which they covered about 12 miles: 43 to Bruinen.[TN14]

11. May 21. They go another [20 >] 18 miles. 25 from Bruinen.

12. May 22. 'Fourth day from the Bridge' (19, 20, 21, 22). The weather is clearing up, and the ponies are willing, but they are tired and short of food. They start late, and make a long midday halt. They have only covered about another 15 miles, when in the evening sunshine they see Bruinen gleaming. It is 10 miles away. They go no further that day, for they have passed out of the shadow of the Trollshaws, and feel safer.

13. May 23. They reach the Ford in the afternoon. Probably halting for midday meal on the west bank of the river, though that is not mentioned in text. Further progress is very slow in the heathland. They did not go on when the light failed, and halted when only about 10 miles further on. 12 miles to entrance to Rivendell.

14. May 24. Progress still slow and difficult. Nightfall was near when, after covering 12 more miles, they reached the head of the path down into Rivendell.

The journey of 27 days is over

The typed text ends here about half-way down the fourth typescript page [Ad.Ms.H.24]. Beneath it is written the following penciled note:

But. It is said p. 62 that they stayed in Rivendell 'at least 14 days'. On their last evening it is Midsummers eve if Shire calendar is used that is the Lithe of June. Next day after June 30th (our calendar July 1) On that day there was a broad crescent moon Sc. at or near FQuarter

The abbreviation 'Sc.', used here and elsewhere in Tolkien's notes on phases of the moon, is short for *scilicet*, meaning 'namely' or 'that is to say'.

As for 'Lithe of June', in the Shire Calendar three days fall between June 30th and July 1st. These 'Summerdays' are known as *Lithe* (the day after June 30th, known as the 'June Lithe' or 'June 30+1' as Tolkien expresses it in some of the notes below), *Midyear's Day* (two days after June 30th, or 'June 30+2'), and *Lithe* (the day before July 1st, three days after June 30th, or the July Lithe). Their presence, and that of the two days of Yule at midwinter (between December 30th and January 1st), enable the Shire Calendar to have twelve months of thirty days each (12 × 30 = 360, +5 midwinter/midsummer days).

TEXT NOTES

1 'L.R.': That is, *The Lord of the Rings*. The 'large map' Tolkien refers to is the fold-out map of Middle-earth pasted in the back of *The Fellowship of the Ring* and also *The Two Towers*. The 'Shire-map' is the map labelled 'A Part of the Shire' appearing just after the Prologue (*LotR*.[30]). By 'Book' in the preceding paragraph Tolkien means of course Book I, the first half of the first volume.

2 This sentence and the one before it ('Or rather none . . . to the left') are bracketed but not deleted; this passage may have been singled out because it relates to features of the locale that did not exist at the time of Bilbo's story. See *LotR*.1041 & 1049. Note, however, that several such houses in fact appear on the Shire map printed in *The Lord of the Rings*, where in fact most of Hobbiton is situated south of The Water, with only a very few buildings (primarily those seen in Tolkien's painting of The Hill: Hobbiton [DAA plate 1 (top), H-S#98]) north of the little river.†

†This feature is much clearer in the first edition, which prints this map in two colours (black for the river and houses, red for the roads).

3 An ink note over the parenthetical seems to read 'no explanation <is> <there>'. See Tolkien's note written on page 'III.2' just after the New Chapter III text broke off (Ad.Ms.H.33; see page 810), which may be Tolkien's reminder to himself to insert such an explanation into the text of Chapter III, no doubt as something Bilbo would have learned at Rivendell had the recasting continued beyond this point.

4 Actually Bilbo covered it a third time after his spectacular departure from Hobbiton at the end of the Long-Expected Party, though by that time he had already written at least the earlier portions of his book; cf. *LotR*.247 for the journey and DAA.361 & *LotR*.119 for the book.

5 This sentence originally read '. . . impossible that Bilbo would have forgotten Bree, *and very improbable* that he *had not heard* of it before'.

6 The reference is to page 200 of volume one (*The Fellowship of the Ring*) of the first edition of *The Lord of the Rings* ['L.R.']; emphasis mine:

> 'How far is Rivendell?' asked Merry . . . The world looked wild and wide from Weathertop.
>
> 'I don't know if the Road has ever been measured in miles beyond the *Forsaken Inn*, a day's journey east of Bree,' answered Strider. 'Some say it is so far, and some say otherwise. It is a strange road, and folk are glad to reach their journey's end, whether the time is long or short. But I know how long it would take me on my own feet, with fair weather and no ill fortune: twelve days from here [Weathertop] to the Ford of Bruinen, where the Road crosses the Loudwater that runs out of Rivendell. We have at least a fortnight's journey before us, for I do not think we shall be able to use the Road.'
>
> —*LotR*.204.†

† = Page 200 of *The Fellowship of the Ring* in the first edition.

7 This passage is added in pencil in the top margin and marked as a note applying to this entry. The full passage cited here can be found on *LotR*.166.

8 Tolkien here introduces a new complication: the idea that all dates given in *The Hobbit* are really according to the Shire Calendar described in Appendix D of *The Lord of the Rings* (see *LotR*.1140–46). *The Hobbit* of course had not been written with the Shire Calendar in mind, as the latter had not yet been created when the story was published, and the decision here to adapt the story from one calendar to another would lead him into insoluble paradoxes: see section (iii) below, esp. Text Note 1 on page 830.

9 Added in left margin in pencil: '<Also> Thorin's Dwelling' – i.e., Thorin's halls in exile in the Blue Mountains south of the Gulf of Lune should also appear. Since these lay well outside the Shire, Tolkien presumably means that they should be added to the large foldout map of Middle-earth.

10 This line harkens back to one of the texts of 'The Quest of Erebor', where Gandalf notes that '[Bilbo] did not know . . . the care . . . that I took so that the coming of a large party of Dwarves to Bywater, off the main road and their usual beat, should not come to his ears too soon' (UT.335).

11 Here 'east side' was typed over an erasure; the phrase originally typed seems to have been 'west side'.

12 The text here originally ran 'and then go on till *nearly night*. Say about *8* p.m. (sun-set about *that time*). Ponies . . .' All these changes are in ink, with 'but the road was under dark trees' in the left margin and marked for insertion at this point.

13 This sentence originally read 'Going from 12.00 to 4 and 4.30 to 8.30 (7 1/2 hours) they only cover about 20 miles.'

14 The original version of the next few entries read:

11. May 21, 22.	2 days. Each day they cover about 16 miles (36) and at night are only 7 from the Ford, which they cannot yet see.
12. May 23.	In the morning after a short ride they see the Bruinen ahead and below them in another (less steep) valley.

These were cancelled and replaced by separate entries for all three days giving a somewhat different account of their progress.

(ii)

Timetable from Rivendell to Lake Town

This single sheet of notes (Ad.Ms.H.13), written in ink on the back of an unused page taken from a 'blue book' (student's exam booklet),[TN1] extends the timeline and itinerary from Rivendell through Mirkwood to Thorin & Company's departure from Lake Town. It thus forms a suitable companion piece to the more formal 'Distances and Itinerary' given as section (i) above, which focuses on the first stage of Bilbo's journey (Bag-End to Rivendell), the part covered by New Chapter II and the fragment of New Chapter III. However, it is probably much earlier: all the page references here are to the first edition (i.e., pre-1951), and dates are given in the Gregorian calendar, not the Shire Calendar developed during work on *The Lord of the Rings*. Christopher Tolkien notes (private communication) that this same kind of paper was used for drafting portions of *The Lord of the Rings* pre-1944. So these notes may date from as early as the Fourth Phase. But since annotations with ball-point pens show that if so he was still carefully considering and updating them long afterwards, in the period of the 1960 Hobbit, and since they deal with the same concerns as all the material in this chapter, here seems the natural place to give them.

Hobbit Time table is not very clear.[TN2]

[Written in top margin in dark ink:]

Mirkwood is too small on map it must be 300 miles across

Adventure with Trolls night of 31 May/1 June. reach R'dell appar. about June 3rd. Leave on Midsummer morning: say June 24.

Long days after still climbing p. 66.
On map R'dell is about 50 miles direct to top of the range or pass. Make it more? going <will be> slow and actual distance possibly twice as far as forward distance. Say 100 at 10 miles per day, 10 days. They therefore reach Cave of Goblins on night of July 4th. Summer is getting on down below – haymaking p. 67.[TN3]
Adventure with Goblins takes 3 days. night before night before last. p. 102. They assemble therefore on July 7th
Adv. with wargs night July 7/8.
Reach Beorn afternoon July 8
Depart 3 days later. July 11th (p. 141)
Take 4 days riding to the Forest Entrance (p. 142)
Enter Forest therefore 15 or 16 July.

Ages and ages p. 148 They reach Enchanted River (which is about 1/2 way to Elvenking's hall). And after they have gone on again about as long leaf falls suggesting autumn is coming on p. 153. The Forest is largely dark and they are laden – later carrying Bombur. But must allow at least an average of 12 miles per day. Say 12 days to Enchanted River. 144 miles. July 28th.
12 days to adventure with Spiders.
144 miles. August 9th[TN4]
[total] 288 [miles]
Weary long time in King's Hall. say 3 weeks.[TN5] Aug 30th.
Reach Lake Town about Sept 2/3.
9 days gap
We know Bilbo's Birthday Sept 22 was at Lake Town. They were there about 24 days. Birthday would come after 10 days. Leaves about October 6th?
Reach Lake town on 8th. Stay 10 days. Sept 18.

Rivendell must be further off.[TN6] Reach Cave about July 9th. Therefore enter Forest 21 July. Forest journey must be 300 miles

(150 each) and take about 25 days. 15 August. [*cancelled*: leave King's Halls 5 Sept.]

[Text continued in left margin:]

Taken prisoner on 16 August. Escape <9th> Sept.[TN7] Reach L.T. 12th Sept. B. <illegible>[TN8] Sep 22. Leave <about> 6th of October.

[Added in margin in green ink:]

Use Hobbit Calendar as in L.R.[TN9]

In this time-table, Tolkien attempts to retroactively apply a scale to the Wilderland map published in *The Hobbit* but is not able to do so consistently. If the distance from Rivendell to the Cave of the Goblins atop the Misty Mountains pass (about an inch and a half on the Wilderland map)[TN10] is 50 miles (as the crow flies, 100 miles of actual travel), then the route Thorin & Company wound up taking through Mirkwood (three and a half inches) cannot equal 300 miles but is more like 175 miles (the last part of it in barrels), meaning the dwarves averaged only about six miles a day before their capture. The large Middle-earth map,[TN11] while different in scale, faithfully reproduces the proportions of the earlier map in their overlapping sections: here their route through the dark forest measures about 3½ cm (roughly 1⅜ inches), which again equals about 175 miles by the scale Tolkien decided on in the 'distances' typescript given as section (i) above. By contrast, Gimli in *The Lord of the Rings* as one of the Three Walkers managed to travel roughly the same distance in only five days (albeit as an epic feat under much better conditions, spurred on by both competition from Man and Elf and the desperate necessity to rescue his friends).

Or to pick a less extreme example, Dain and his company of dwarves from the Iron Hills arrive within a very short time – clearly only a matter of days[TN12] – from the time Thorin sent Roäc to summon them. The Iron Hills are not shown on the Wilderland Map in *The Hobbit*, being off the edge of the map to the east, and thus more than one inch [= about 35 miles] away. We are not told exactly where Dain's halls are within the Hills, but since the Hills themselves are clearly nearby, the Wilderland Map leaves it plausible that Dain is easily within the distance of a rapid forced march. But applying this part of *The Hobbit*'s story to *The Lord of the Rings* immediately creates difficulties. According to the Middle-earth Map in *The Lord of the Rings*, we can see that at their nearest point, the Iron Hills are double the distance from the Lonely Mountain that Rivendell is to the top of the mountain-pass; at their furthest point they are seven times that distance. Since we know the latter distance to be at least fifty miles, then Dain had to travel somewhere between a hundred to three hundred and fifty miles to come to Thorin's aid (the latter if coming from the far eastern side of the Hills), after having first taken at least some time to gather and equip his troops. Furthermore the fact that Thorin & Company are heavy-laden cannot be a significant factor, for we are told within *The Hobbit* itself of Dain's army that

> They had brought with them a great store of supplies; for the dwarves can carry very heavy burdens, and nearly all of Dain's folk, in spite of their rapid march, bore huge packs on their backs in addition to their weapons.
>
> —DAA.337

Fonstad observed that doubling the scale on the Wilderland map found in *The Hobbit* would resolve many difficulties (*Atlas of Middle-earth*, page 97), and it is clear that Tolkien himself had arrived at the same realization long before from the note he added at the top of this manuscript page. That would not however have fixed the problem of the speed of Dain's travel versus the slowness of Thorin's journey; only by redrawing the map to make Mirkwood much, much wider could he have resolved the problem of how long it took Bilbo and his companions to travel though the forest. Here then we come to an example – not the last – of a solution (doubling the map scale to make Thorin & Company's travel time more credible) that would in turn create a new problem (doubling the distance Dain's five hundred dwarves travel in much less time), something that proved endemic in the 1960 Hobbit (see below) and no doubt played a part in the project's abandonment: a story written without a specific timetable simply could not in the end be fitted within a fairly narrow time frame without radical alteration of either the existing maps or the time-references and description of scenes within the published text.

TEXT NOTES

1 Actually, a large (8½ by 5½ inch) fragment of such a page, with 'Prifysgol Cymru' (i.e., University of Wales) in the upper left corner and the header 'DEGREE EXA[mination]'. Tolkien worked for many years as an external examiner for other universities, and one of the side benefits was the opportunity to accumulate a supply of scrap paper from unfilled booklets.

2 This line is written in pencil at the top of the page.

3 Above 'haymaking', Tolkien has written *harvest* in red ball-point pen. This is a reference to Bilbo's gloomy prediction regarding their slow rate of travel: 'down below . . . haymaking is going on and picnics. They will be harvesting and blackberrying, before we even begin to go down the other side at this rate' (first edition, page 66; DAA.101).

4 The original numbers in this passage are overwritten in darker ink, but seem to have originally read

> Say *10* days to Enchanted River. *120* miles. July *26th.*
> 12 days to adventure with Spiders.
> 144 miles. August <*5th*>

The final date is largely obscured by the overwriting but seems to be '5th', where one would have expected to see instead 'August 7th'.

5 Note that here an imprisonment that had once been meant to last for months (from fall to spring – cf. Plot Notes A) has now shrunk to a mere three weeks – just enough time, one would think, for the dwarves and Bilbo to recover from their privations before becoming restless to press on with the next stage of their journey, and the same amount of time he now intended for them to spend in Lake Town.

6 The rule across the bottom of the page preceding this sentence indicates that Tolkien had reached a decision and that what followed stood apart from and would modify what came before (in this case, supplanting their dates).

7 The number for the day of the month has been overwritten in ink, obscuring whatever date originally stood here.

8 The illegible word here might be *presents*; it is certainly not 'birthday'.

9 This final instruction added to the page is written with a green ball point pen and thus dates from relatively late in Tolkien's life (post-*LotR*), probably added when he revisited this material as part of his work on the Fifth Phase/1960 Hobbit. It would also soon involve Tolkien in difficulties over the story's chronology; see section (iii) below, specifically Text Note 1 on page 830.

10 Here I use the map appearing as the back endpaper of the second edition (thirteenth printing, 1961), the earliest printing of the map available to me, since my reference copy of the first edition (3rd printing, wartime edition of 1942) lacks the maps. The proportions, however, hold true to any copy of the book including the map; cf. DAA.[399], which is reduced by about one-third, so that from Rivendell to the Mountain is about one inch, the distance across Mirkwood roughly two inches, and so forth.

11 Here I use the fold-out map in the first edition, first printing *The Fellowship of the Rings* as my standard for reference.

12 We know Dain's trip was very rapid, since less than a month passed between Durin's Day (the beginning of the last moon of autumn) and Bilbo's arrival at Beorn's Hall on the far side of Mirkwood in time for Yule.

(iii)
The Timeline Revisited (moons taken into consideration)

These two sheets [Ad.Ms.H.19–20] contain three pages of text, the second sheet having been rotated ninety degrees and folded in half to divide it into two side-by-side half-pages: .20a (left) and .20b (right); the writing comes to an end about halfway through the last half-page. The text is written in ink and legible for the most part but a few lines have faded into illegibility; I indicate illegible words and passages with ellipses (. . .). Several sentences in this text are bracketed by Tolkien, but here I think it was not because of dissatisfaction with the bracketed material but rather for emphasis, to highlight those passages and make those points stand out for when he came back to put this material to use in the intended continuation of the Fifth Phase Hobbit. In order to avoid confusion with brackets added editorially, I have substituted double parentheses ((thus)) for authorial brackets in this section. Also, to improve readability, I have replaced some marks Tolkien used as shorthand: thus ∴ has been replaced by 'therefore', > by 'to' and in some places a slash (/) separating two numbers by 'to' where I thought the results might otherwise be mistaken for a fraction (e.g., '3/4 days' is here printed as '3 to 4 days' where that was Tolkien's intent). I have left the following of Tolkien's abbreviations in place: 'H' for *The Hobbit*, 'L.R.' or 'LR' for *The Lord of the Rings*, 'SC' for Shire Calendar (for the month, day, and day of the week), and 'SR' for Shire Reckoning (for the year).

This text clearly postdates the 'Distances and Itinerary' document given as section (i), since it refers to it and to the rewritten version of Chapter II (New Chapter II), but it was probably written at about the same time.

The Hobbit

The times and distances of the journey from Hobbiton to Rivendell are in great confusion, and it is difficult to make sense of them. But it is important to do so, if possible, owing to the L.R., which covers same ground in more detail. The 'moons' too are out of order – but this cannot be tolerated, since Durin's Day and the incidence of New Moon is integral to the plot.

Something, of course, could be done by attributing inaccuracy to Bilbo's memory. ((This would need a note in some future edition.))

The calendar used must evidently be the Shire Calendar ((though that is not and need not be alluded to)).

Fixed points that cannot be altered are the following

1. By calculation from H p. 35 [*added*: 21 April] '100 years ago last Thursday' – since weekday-date relation did not change in SC. – The Unexpected Party occurred on Wed. 27 April SC, 1341 SR Start of journey therefore 28 April (morning) SC.[TN1]

2. By L.R. Map distance from Hobbiton to Rivendell by road was approx 412 miles. From Troll-place to Ford of Bruinen [50 >] 60 miles; ((from Ford to head of path down into Rivendell 20 miles: 80 miles from Trolls to Rivendell)).

3. Company left Rivendell on Midsummer Day (= in SC. June 30 + 2) The Moon on the previous day (Lithe: June 30 + 1) was a broad silver crescent: therefore 3 to 4 days old. NM must have been June 27/28.

NB This fits tolerably well with later narrative. For if NM occurred on June 28 it would next occur on July 23 [29, 30, Lithe, Mid Year, Lithe] = 5 days + 23 = 28.[TN2] <Next> since all months have 30 days: on Aug. 21, on Sept. 19, October 17th. There is probably time for the events after Bilbo's Birthday (Sep 22) in Lake Town before the discovery of the Key-hole – Durin's Day[TN3]

It is said (p. 62) that the Dwarves &c. stayed at least 14 days in Rivendell. As they departed on Midsummer's Day, they must therefore have arrived on June 17th <about> at earliest, say, June 15 [*added*: or late on 17].

Question is (1) how did they take April 3 days, May 30 [days], June 15/17 [days] = 48/50 days in journey of 412 miles = an average rate (on ponies mostly) of only 8 1/2 miles (or a little more or less) per diem?

At any rate on day before the Troll-adventure (it being 80 miles only from that point to Rivendell) it cannot have been only May 30th. ((Bilbo says 'tomorrow it will be June 1st')).

The itinerary worked out in 'revision' of The Hobbit[TN4] is well enough in itself but it brings the company to Rivendell in 27 days on May 24 without regard to Moons!

? Something must be said about halts etc. esp. Bree, Last Inn ((later The Forsaken Inn)).

<Ponies> very reluctant after Bree & Last Inn. <most of the time> they had to be led.

The Bridge of <?Mitheithel> is broken . . . It was here . . . Ponies had be led . . .[TN5]

As for moons: if the moon was new on June 28 it would be New on June 1st, approx. but is said to be waning p. 42 and yet get . . . <soon> after dark like a NM or early crescent.[TN6]

? Say young and thin or *wandering ((because of the <hurrying> clouds))

If, however, they arrived in Rivendell <by> June 15/17 after a journey of 80 miles (slow and wary, and in the heathland very slow) of say 6 days – not much more than 13 miles a day! – they would be at Troll-place on June 9/11: 8 to 10 days after NM. June 1 and the moon would have <appeared> full – be in the wane – but would rise late at night!

The journey from Trolls to Bruinen needs lengthening in some way.[TN7]

Here we see problems introduced in the work Tolkien had already accomplished in the Fifth Phase begin to complicate the revision process, something that no doubt helped contribute to the Fifth Phase's abandonment. Here the specific problem is that by bringing Bilbo to Rivendell two weeks earlier than had been the case in the original Hobbit, he has taken a problem already present in the text and made it worse. Specifically, if the moon is a thin crescent in the evening sky on Midsummer Eve – that is, just a few days after the New Moon – and if they spent two weeks in Rivendell (DAA.93), then it would have been a gibbous moon – that is, a moon a few days past full[TN8] but more than half – at the time of their arrival. Bilbo sees just such a moon on the night of the troll-adventure, but that takes place several days *before* their arrival, when the moon should actually have been Full or rapidly approaching Full (and hence not 'waning'). And while Tolkien had at one point considered having time pass differently or not at all within elven enclaves (cf. HME VII.353–5, 363–5, and 'Note on Time in Lórien' on HME VII.367–9), he had firmly rejected this idea by the time of the published *Lord of the Rings*. It was an important part of Tolkien's legendarium that the story took place in the imagined past of the real world – as he wrote to Forrie Ackerman, '*The Lord of the Rings* . . . takes place in the Northern hemisphere of this earth: miles are miles, days are days, and weather is weather' (JRRT to Ackerman, June 1958; *Letters* p. 272). And, one might add, moons are moons; cf. Tolkien's modest boast, in his interview with Denys Gueroult that 'I don't think the moons rise or are in the wrong place at any point in [*The Lord of the Rings*]' (1965 Radio BBC interview), a feat he only achieved during the book's revision by drawing up many-columned sheets listing where each character was on each day of the story.[TN9] No such charts exist for *The Hobbit*, since its narrative never split into multiple storylines following different sets of characters, but in the Fifth Phase Tolkien decided to treat its text with the same rigour, and the materials given below in sections (iv) and (v) probably represent the rough notes from which he could have generated such a chart correlating date, moon-phase, and action.

TEXT NOTES

1 That is, since the story is purportedly set down by Bilbo, it must use the Shire Calendar. Unfortunately, Tolkien failed to notice that *Thursday, 21st of April* is a date that cannot occur in the Shire Calendar, where the 21st always falls on a Friday (see Appendix D of *The Lord of the Rings*). It is probably for this reason that Fonstad silently shifts the Unexpected Party from Wed. 27th April and their departure on Th. 28th April to 26th April (= Wednesday) and 27th April (= Thursday), respectively in *The Atlas of Middle-earth* (page 98). Thus preservation of the 'comic precision' (see page 750) of 'a hundred years ago last Thursday' and '*Gandalf Tea Wednesday*' on the one hand and the much later decision to adapt the story to the Shire Calendar on the other set up a paradox: either Bilbo's adventure began on Thursday the 28th *or* the story was using the Shire Calendar, but both could not be true.

2 All these dates were shifted by one day, the passage having originally read:

> . . . if NM occurred on June 27/28 it would next occur on July 22/23 [28, 29, 30, Lithe, Mid Year, Lithe] July 1 = 7 days + 21 = 28.

3 Below this sentence Tolkien drew a line across the page, as if marking the beginning of a new section – i.e., shifting from the timetable after their departure from Rivendell back to their arrival and the events preceding it.

Note that the reference to a new moon on 19th October and the statement that 'There is probably time' between Bilbo's birthday (three days after the previous New Moon, which fell on 19th September just before the start of autumn) and 'the discovery of the Key-hole' suggest that Tolkien here is thinking of Durin's Day as falling on the *first* new moon of autumn, as in the original manuscript, rather than on the *last* new moon before the start of winter as in the published book. This would have solved the problem of Dain's too-rapid relief expedition and Bilbo's amazing rate of progress on the first stage of the return journey, but it would also have required the re-writing of several descriptive passages vividly conveying the rapid onset of winter; see Text Note 2 following section (iv) below.

4 This is a reference to section (i) above [Ad.Ms.H.21–4], which therefore already existed when Tolkien drafted these further notes (cf. also the

specific reference a few lines earlier to '412 miles', the exact tally given in the Distances document (page 817).

Tolkien is pointing out here that by bringing Thorin & Company to Rivendell two weeks earlier than in the published book he has replaced one anomaly in the phases of the moon with another, so that the waning moon glimpsed on the night of the troll-adventure could not be at the right time of its cycle on Midsummer Eve to be a crescent moon, as required by the scene in which Elrond reads the moon-letters. See Text Note 6 below.

5 This passage of five lines (the last three on Ad.Ms.H.20a and the first two of Ad.Ms.H.20b) is very faint, but taken with the preceding paragraph the general sense is clear. Tolkien is searching for reasons to make their journey slower and delay their arrival in Rivendell to something closer to the original book (that is, about three weeks after the date given in New Chapter II and the Itinerary), and here suggests longer stays at Bree and the Last Inn, and the distress of their ponies in the wild, which in turn would lead to a slower rate of progress on the road after leaving Bree-land.

6 Tolkien's point is that if the moon were a few days past new on Midsummer's Eve, then the time specified for the troll-encounter (whether May 19th or the day before June 1st) cannot have a waning moon – that is, one past full. In addition, such a moon would not rise until well after dark (since the full moon rises at the same time that the sun sets), and the published book specifies that 'it was *nearly* dark' (i.e., the sun had not yet set) when 'a waning moon appeared' – characteristic of a waxing, not a waning, moon. His proposed solution, given in the next line, is to convert the moon Bilbo glimpsed that night into a waxing moon ('young and thin') or else evade the problem by simply describing it as 'a *wandering* moon' and avoid specifying its phase at all. The former would require the troll encounter to take place about thirty days before Elrond's discovery of the moon-runes the night the moon had just passed the same phase at Midsummer. The latter is the solution he adopted in the 1966 Hobbit (DAA.66).

7 Actually, it is the journey from the Hoarwell to the trolls that needs lengthening, if *The Hobbit* is to agree with *The Lord of the Rings*; cf. Fonstad, *The Atlas of Middle-earth* page 97 and the tailnote to section (iv) below.

8 Technically a gibbous moon can be either waxing (between First Quarter and Full Moon) or waning (between Full Moon and Last Quarter), but the text is specific here that it was the latter, a *waning* moon.

9 These charts are now (since 1997) part of the Tolkien collection at Marquette (Additional Tolkien Manuscripts, Fourth Installment, Envelope 6, items 2, 3, & 4).

(iv)
Waxing and Waning

This single page of notes [Ad.Ms.H.17] shows Tolkien looking not backwards from Rivendell to the troll-encounter but ahead to the other crucial moon-scene, that of the new moon on Durin's Day. Once again, as with section (iii) above, Tolkien seems to be treating Durin's Day as if it fell in the first month of autumn rather than the last; whether this is inadvertence or a deliberate decision which he nowhere expressed in writing cannot now be determined.

The 'broad crescent' moon on Midsummer eve in Elrond's house fits very well with Durin's Day in Chapter XI (2nd edn p. 221) – acc. to Shire Calendar Midsummer even was the June Lithe = June 30 + 1

A broad crescent would indicate that moon was approaching First Quarter therefore New Moon would be about June 26 (say) in Shire Calendar. Five [*added*: calendar] months later it would bring New Moon about Oct 19. This fits well enough with such time indicators as there are. They had been in Lake Town a week (+ 2 or 3 days?) when Bilbo had his cold – from LR we know that <this> was his birthday = Sep 22 (SC).[TN1] They were about another week in L. Town before Thorin spoke of going. Say Sep 29. Their departure was not at once. say Oct 5. Two days rowing (Oct 7) and then their journey to the Mountain and the search for the Door could well take more than 12 days, but could be accomplished in that time.[TN2]

As for <earlier> Moon. Just before Troll adventure . . . moon was waning. It had not <?gone> (it was said not to have risen) as they arrived at Rivendell. A fortnight must be allowed from NM to FM or LQ to NM

FQ. FM. LQ.| |NM

|NM^7 FQ^7 O^7 LQ|[TN3]

The final lines of these notes just begin to explore the calculations which Tolkien developed further in section (v); see below. This little chart provided Tolkien with two months' worth of moon-phases for him to work out the problem bedeviling him, and in fact nicely demonstrates that the period between the Last Quarter moon and New Moon, during which Bilbo met the trolls almost a week's journey away from Rivendell, could not be followed three weeks later by a moon that had advanced only about a week in its cycle (that is, now being somewhere between the NM and

FQ on the second line). Tolkien's earlier solution (in New Chapter II and 'Distances and Itinerary') to move their arrival in Rivendell back from early June (circa June 7th in the original conception) to at least two weeks earlier (May 24th) also pushes 'midsummer' from around June 21st (modern calendar) to two days after June 30th (Shire Calendar).[TN4] This does give the moons in their right phases but forces the company to stay a full month in Elrond's House and fails to address the compatibility problem with *The Lord of the Rings* of why Bilbo got from the river to the trolls so quickly when Strider, the best hunter and tracker of his time, took so long. It also ignores the problem that a moon between last quarter and new cannot be seen in the early evening hours (as specified in the troll-encounter) but would only rise long after midnight.

TEXT NOTES

1 For the banquet where Bilbo had the cold (from his soaking in the Forest River while barrel-riding), see DAA.252. There is no mention in *The Hobbit* that this was Bilbo's birthday; that detail, and the date (22nd September) both come from the opening chapter of *The Lord of the Rings* (*LotR*.42). Tolkien's statement in these notes that this banquet came seven to ten days after their arrival in Lake Town (repeated from section ii above) is contradicted by Bilbo in his Farewell Speech, where Mr. Baggins is explicit that both his arrival in Esgaroth and that banquet took place on the same day, his fifty-first birthday. Even without this, circumstantial evidence from within *The Hobbit* itself would place the banquet much earlier than halfway through their stay: Bilbo was already sneezing in the early morning hours before their arrival in Esgaroth (DAA.242), so the 'three days' that his 'shocking cold' lasted are presumably the first three he spent in Lake Town (DAA.252); if these three days included his birthday then by that reckoning alone their arrival could have come no earlier than 19th September and the banquet no later than 25th September.

2 That is, Tolkien here intends for Durin's Day to fall on 19th October. This avoids the cramming together of too much incident in the last weeks of the year (see page 481) and could be achieved with the change of a single word on page 64 in the second edition (cf. DAA.96), although had he carried out a thorough revision Tolkien would also have had to deal with the various comments about the rapid approach of winter in Chapters X, XI, & XIII. I have found no explicit statement from Tolkien about any decision regarding shifting Durin's Day. As with the two competing Thror-Thrain/Thrain-Thror genealogies, Tolkien may have become confused by a single divergent passage in the text – in this case, one near the beginning of Chapter IV that still (until its post-authorial correction in the fourth edition of 1995) referred to Durin's Day as occurring in the first month of autumn. But it seems extraordinary that he

would have been guided by this passing remark, which he nowhere draws attention to in the Fifth Phase (1960) material, and not by the statement on a page he repeatedly cites from the end of Chapter III, literally divided from the other in the second edition only by a turn of the page.

3 These abbreviations stand, in proper sequence, for New Moon (NM), First Quarter (FQ), Full Moon (FM or the symbol O), and Last Quarter (LQ). The superscripts represent Tolkien's notation of the number of days to allot for each phase of the moon in its twenty-eight day monthly cycle. The significance of the vertical lines (|) seems to be to mark off the phase he wishes to highlight (i.e., the period of the waning moon between last quarter and new moon).

4 Tolkien noted that astronomically the Shire Calendar was about ten days off from our modern calendar – that is, that a date given as Mid-summer in the Shire Calendar, the actual solstice, would correspond to about 21st or 22nd June in our Gregorian calendar (*LotR*.1144).

(v)

Phases of the Moon

This single sheet of paper [Ad.Ms.H.15–16], the final piece of manuscript associated with the Fifth Phase or 1960 Hobbit, is covered with rough notes on both sides. The page has been folded in half and rotated ninety degrees so that it forms four half-pages: .15a (left), .15b (right), .16a (verso left), and .16b (verso right). The first half-page is written in red ball-point ink; the remaining three half-pages are in pencil, which unfortunately in some places has become illegible through the speed of the writing and its faintness after more than four and a half decades. As before I replace illegible words and passages by ellipses (. . .) and expand contractions where necessary to avoid confusion but have let stand the following authorial contractions: 'L.R.' or 'LR' stands for *The Lord of the Rings*, 'SR' for Shire Reckoning, and 'SC' for Shire Calendar.

<Waning> Moon June 1. sc. 4 past full
June 8. 2 before LQ.
June 15. 3 before NM[TN1]

NM June 28
LQ June 21
FM June 14
FQ June 7
NM May 30

1 <Ride> sleep in Shire . . . stay a night . . . in Bree.
. . . to F. Inn. <stay> . . . <night>

lose way in the Marshes <?Hay> ran <?low>
. . . <in> road is <?awash> . . . <least>
<Mitheithel> Bridge is broken (by Trolls.) . . .[TN2]

This marks the end of the ink text at the bottom of half-page Ad.Ms.H.15a. The top of the right-hand portion of the same page, Ad.Ms.H.15b, begins a new section or sub-section with its own header. From here on out the text is written in pencil, which is difficult to read throughout and becomes wholly illegible towards the end.

Hobbit [*added*:] Time table of journey will not work out?
• Time indications in text.
It was Wednesday when dwarves came to Bag End.

p. 35. Thrain went away 100 years last Thursday on 21st April. Since week-day relative to date did not change in Shire Calendar, 21st April was a Thursday in 2941 (= 1341 SR) the year of the Visit of the Dwarves. Therefore the U.P. occurred on 27 April (Wed.) 1341 SR. The journey to Erebor started on Thursday 28th April.[TN3]

p. 41 Bilbo says it is June 1st tomorrow at tea time on the [day >] before the adventure with the Trolls.
*It would be better to make this correct if possible (rather than assume B. was out of his reckoning). . . . that in Shire Calendar [they >] The Company had now been 32 days on the road (April 29, 30) 2; (May 1–30) 30. They had still a long way to go before Rivendell. They set out on the afternoon of June 1. After that the following time/distance <indications> occur:

p. 42 a waning moon was in the sky on the evening of May 30. On the eve of Midsummer (= Lithe June 30 + 1) and the eve of their departure from Rivendell, there was a broad silver crescent

p. 56 No singing first day = afternoon to night of June 1. nor next day June 2, nor day after June 3. 3 1/2 days journey. 'One afternoon' – gap of time <undefined> – they came to Ford of Bruinen. p. 58 that Day began to fail. it was very dim because moon had not risen.

<His> plan that they were supposed to reach the head of path down into Rivendell during early night of the day in which they had crossed the Ford (in afternoon). As they were going . . . wearily[TN4] and were in difficult country they could not have done more than 10–12 miles. In L.R. it was not made clear how far Ford was from Rivendell[TN5] (along the river course). But in the LR map 1 centimetre = 50 miles the distance from Ford to head of path down is 4 mm = 4/10 <illegible> = 20 miles.

Alter p. 56 One afternoon to One fine morning [p. 57 they rode slowly on >][TN6] and adjust narrative to . . . long day lasting on into early night. <Or> <made> a camp in the <heather> above Rivendell.

At p. 58/11 They went on until moonless twilight overtook them, and they lay that night under the bright stars. The next day was failing But <then> perhaps . . . <the journey> too . . .[TN7]

p. 62 They stay in Rivendell at least 14 days. Therefore if they left on SC Midsummer = June 30 + 2 they arrived not earlier <than> June 16 night.
How could they spend 16 days on way from Troll-shaw to Rivendell? On LR map it is 1 cm 2 mm from Troll place to Ford & 20 miles on beyond = [75 >] 60 + 20 = 80. Thus = [less than 5 miles a day >] exactly 5 miles on good days

If the Moon was waning sc. at least a day or two past full on May 30 it would be approx. same . . . on June 28. But if it were <really> waxing <for> [. . . it might be only 20/21 days from June 1 & LQ to NM. <so> New Moon. >] There <might> be no moon at all after . . .[TN8]

FQ= half moon [7 days] ◗ = <moon> before <full> [7 days] (. . .
FM O
LQ [7 days] = ◖[TN9] We must start from p. 63[TN10] which fits (by chance!) fairly well . . . the New Moon would appear about Oct 19th. (SC)

The moon is a broad silver crescent therefore about halfway to FQ, <only> 3 to 4 days from NM. It is June 30+1 therefore NM was about June 28/(27) There would therefore be a NM about June 1 but <it was> called a waning moon p. 42 [And the >] <New Moon> . . . ?

Or we must shorten the time of the journey from the Trollshaw to Rivendell. LQ on night of the Troll-adventure NM. [June 28 Therefore LQ. >] Waning moon = only just going off <full> . . . therefore say on May 28

If N.Moon was on June 27 . [LQ was on June 20. The F.M. >] FM was June 12/13
<Waning moon> must be . . . about June 15–16
They arrived Rivendell on June 16
But they <must> . . . <taken> . . . <?Say> in 4–6 days <?also> for journey from Trollshaw <?to> <?River>

<This> <is> <from> LQ <but> <?has> . . . to Waxing. <?Just> say <wandering> for waning . . . <?having> <after> <?appeared> . . .[TN11]

In this final section of the 1960 Hobbit material, we see Tolkien returning once again to the time indicators in the published text to see if setting them out would suggest a solution to the tangle. Highly significant, therefore, is the lightly pencilled message written alongside the title – *Time table of journey will not work out?* – signaling as it does his realization that the ends he wanted to achieve could only come at the cost of an even more radical revision and recasting than he had already drafted for New Chapters I and II, and that New Chapter II would itself need to be re-done. And even with this, he had still not addressed the problem of matching the dwarves' relatively swift trip from river to trolls (a matter of hours) with Strider's urgent journey over the same ground (taking the better part of a week).

TEXT NOTES

1 This line is cancelled; I retain it here because it continues and clarifies the sequence of the two preceding lines.

2 The final line on this half-page, roughly three words following '(by Trolls)', is illegible.

3 Tolkien is correct that days of the week are fixed to specific days of the month in the Shire Calendar year after year, but here he still has not noticed that since April (Astron) always begins on a Saturday, the 21st and 28th can never fall on a Thursday. U.P. = Unexpected Party.

4 This partially illegible sentence originally read 'As they were *walking (evidently <illegible> the ponies)* – that is, Tolkien seems to have fixed on the idea that Bilbo and the dwarves were walking, not riding, at this point, which could help delay their arrival in Rivendell.

5 This is because Frodo, our point of view character for this section of the story, is unconscious when he travels that distance in *The Lord of the Rings*; Book I ends with his collapse at the Ford and Book II with him awaking already safe in Rivendell some days later. He of course covers this ground again on his return journey, but compression in the denouement of a very long story prevents the inclusion of much detail of that trip other than a few vivid encounters along the way.

6 The text of the first and second editions read 'The afternoon sun shone down; but in all the silent waste there was no sign of any dwelling. *They rode on for a while*, and they soon saw that the house might be hidden almost anywhere between them and the mountains'. This passage was recast for the third edition to address the concerns raised in the 1960 Hobbit, although not in the same words: '*Morning passed, afternoon came*; but in all the silent waste there was no sign of any dwelling. They

were growing anxious, for they saw now that the house might be hidden . . .' (DAA.88 & 90).

7 Only a single short word, starting with a capital 'T', follows 'too', but I cannot make out what it might be.

8 The last word following 'after' is illegible and probably unfinished, but the gist of the sentence is clear: a new crescent would set shortly after sunset, leaving the night dark.

9 Here I think Tolkien is reminding himself of the rather confusing terminology whereby 'quarter' is applied to a half-moon (because it is a quarter of the way through its twenty-eight day cycle), and also which way the crescent faces when the moon is waxing (◗) and waning (◖), for purposes of description.

10 The allusion is to the line 'The moon was shining in a broad silver crescent' on midsummer eve – cf. DAA.95.

11 I cannot make out anything in the last two lines following this point except the words 'June 15' and the final phrase '– not . . . waning'.

See also section (iii) above for Tolkien's decision to simplify his problem by replacing 'waning' with 'wandering', a change he carried out in the 1966 third edition.

(vi)
The Wandering Moon

In all these notes and compilations on distances, dates, and moons, we see Tolkien attempting to take *The Hobbit*, a story written out of one storytelling tradition of long ago and far away, where details are only included when dramatically relevant or aesthetically effective and things work according to their own narrative logic,[1] and make it into a story like *The Lord of the Rings*, which is written in a very different tradition, where each mile of each day of each character's journey can be followed on a map and plotted on a timetable. Tolkien himself is largely responsible for creating the latter,[2] and making it the standard by which modern fantasies are judged, but he also excelled at writing the former, a traditional mode going all the way back to the Middle Ages and beyond. There is a qualitative difference between the narrator's admission that 'I don't know what river it was' (DAA.67) or 'I don't know where he came from, nor who or what he was' (DAA.118) and Gandalf's well-informed speculation about the whereabouts of the lost *palantíri* (*LotR*.621), or his partial knowledge about 'older and fouler things than Orcs in the deep places of the world' (*LotR*.327).

The Hobbit harkens back to an older tradition, where forests seem endless, a period of captivity is a *weary long time* rather than twenty-one days (August 9th–30th), dragons and goblins destroyed Gondolin 'many ages ago' (rather than exactly 6,472 years before to the very day),[3] and it is the passing of seasons rather than the counting of days that mark the passage of time. Bilbo's is a world where the moon only just past new can rise after the sun sets (an astronomical impossibility) rather than becoming visible in the west just after the sun goes down (DAA.307–8, 312),[4] because that's how Tolkien envisions the scene, and the chill moonlight falling on the now-quieting scene of devastation sets just the right note to follow the noise and flames and flashes of light and sudden violence of the immediately preceding pages.

If *The Lord of the Rings* is, as some have claimed, the 'Book of the Century', then *The Hobbit* is more than the book that made it all possible. A major contribution to the Golden Age of children's literature, it is a rare example of a work that transcends age boundaries in its readership, like Grahame's *The Golden Age*, Carroll's two *Alice* books, Twain's *Huckleberry Finn*, and very few others. It is, like Joyce's *A Portrait of the Artist as a Young Man* in relation to his *Ulysses*, or Carroll's *The Hunting of the Snark* in relation to *Alice in Wonderland*, a case of a masterpiece overshadowed by another masterpiece on a grander scale from the same author. Had Tolkien never completed *The Lord of the Rings*, he would still be remembered as one of the great fantasy authors. The achievement of the sequel has eclipsed the accomplishment of writing *The Hobbit* itself, but we should not deny the distinct appeal and charm of the original book. In the end, I think it was more than just the intractable nature of the problems facing him in recasting the book that caused Tolkien to abandon the 1960 Hobbit. Rather, he decided to trust his friend's judgment that what he was doing was 'wonderful, but not *The Hobbit*'. That is, he came to recognize that *The Hobbit* was more than *The Lord of the Rings* writ small, more than a 'charming prelude': indeed, a work deserving to stand on its own merits.

And with that realization, aside from the 'Sixth Phase' of 1965/66 forced upon him by his publishers – which he took as the opportunity for correction of some errors and the incorporation of some fixes he had settled upon during his work on the 1960 Hobbit – Tolkien's decades-long work on *The Hobbit* finally came to an end.

NOTES

1 For example, as Janice Coulter has pointed out (private communication), if Gollum's eyes glowed in the dark how did he sneak up on goblins? Or, to repeat a question Tolkien himself asked and left unanswered, why did the dwarves bring their musical instruments, some of which would have been quite bulky, to Bag-End? Overthinking such points is a hallmark of approaching a work in the first of these two traditions as if it were in the second.

2 Tolkien of course was not alone in creating this shift: Joyce's *Ulysses*, where both of the major characters' actions can be followed hour-by-hour and street-by-street through a single day on a Dublin city map, pioneered this mode in the realistic novel a decade and a half before Tolkien began work on his magnum opus. One might expect the detective novel or mystery to have pioneered this approach, but in fact Conan Doyle's Sherlock Holmes series, which defined the genre, is very much written in the old school, with a fine carelessness about dates, Holmes' fields of expertise and expert knowledge, the location of Watson's war wound (leg or shoulder), the dates (and number) of Watson's marriage(s) and bereavement(s), and even the narrator's first name (variously James or John). Before Tolkien, most fantasy novels followed the example of one of those two great masters, Dunsany and Morris, and took place in either dreamworlds à la Dunsany or deliberately unmapped and borderless medieval settings à la Morris (frameless tapestries, as it were). Post-Tolkien, world-building has become a key defining part of the genre: elaborate histories ('backstory') and chronologies, invented languages, multiple cultures and distinct humanesque races, fantasy pantheons, creation myths, and above all maps are all essential elements that make a work recognizably 'fantasy'.

3 According to the '(Later) Annals of Beleriand', the city was destroyed ninety years before the end of the First Age (HME V.142 & 144); 90 + the 3441 years of the Second Age (*LotR*.1121) + the 2941 years of the Third Age that had passed before Bilbo reached Rivendell (*LotR*.1126) = 6,472 years. The 1930 *Quenta* states that the attack came before dawn as the people were preparing to celebrate a festival known as the Gates of Summer (HME IV.144), which I take to mean greeting the dawn on midsummer's day. Appendix D of *The Lord of the Rings* states that the elven day starts at sunset (*LotR*.1141); therefore the midsummer's eve on which Elrond reads these runes is the anniversary of the day when his father's city was destroyed.

4 Note that Tolkien's friend C. S. Lewis makes the same mistake in his narrative poem *The Queen of Drum* [1927], as was pointed out to him by John Masefield, the poet laureate, to whom he sent the unpublished poem in 1938. Cf. Canto V, line 123 (page 170) and Masefield's correction on page 178 (CSL, *Narrative Poems*, ed. Walter Hooper [1969]).

If we were to pursue a mythological explanation, of course, we could do so by noting that Tilion, the Maia who steers the moon, is well-known for his wayward behavior and difficulty in keeping a regular course, being easily distracted by the beauty of the Sun-maiden (*Silm*.99–100) or overindulgence in beer or brandy (1927 Father Christmas letter, ATB poem #5, *LotR*.174–6). But while this would be a perfectly reasonable explanation in Bilbo's world, it would be special pleading in Frodo's.

APPENDICES

Appendix I

THE DENHAM TRACTS

One of the recurring questions Tolkien faced from the first publication of *The Hobbit* to the end of his life was 'where did you get the name "hobbits"?' While there seems little doubt that he was telling the truth when he said he simply made it up, the issue was confused in the mid-1970s by the discovery, in a nineteenth-century collection of North Country folklore, of the word 'hobbit' among a long list of fairies, spirits, creatures from classical mythology, and other imaginary beings. The discovery was made by Katharine Briggs, the leading expert of her time on traditional fairy folklore (and author of a superb fantasy novel, *Hobberdy Dick* [1955], incorporating many of those beliefs), who reprinted the list in her *A Dictionary of Fairies: Hobgoblins, Brownies, Bogies, and Other Supernatural Creatures* [1976], pages 93–94. Briggs herself did not comment on the appearance of hobbits in the list,[1] but her discovery was soon picked up on by an outside reader for the OED and thence reported in various newspapers (including most notably Philip Howard's piece 'Tracking the Hobbit Down to Earth', which appeared in *The Times* on 31st May 1977), but for the most part without crediting Briggs for her role in the discovery.

The list itself had appeared in a miscellany published by the Folk-Lore Society, the full title of which was *The Denham Tracts: A Collection of Folklore by Michael Aislabie Denham, and reprinted from the original tracts and pamphlets printed by Mr. Denham between 1846 and 1859*. Edited by Dr. James Hardy (with the assistance of Laurence Gomme, who also wrote the prefaces), this had been issued in two volumes in 1892 and 1895, with our list appearing as the final item in Tract VIII, 'Folklore, or Manners and Customs, of the North of England' (Vol. II pages [1]–80). Denham himself had been a mid-19th-century amateur antiquarian who collected sayings, tales, and customs from the north of England, issuing them in little self-published pamphlets or 'tracts'. These tracts went through multiple editions, expanding as he came across new material – for example, the specific tract in which our list appears went through several versions, and the word 'hobbit' did not appear in the earliest of these.[2] It thus becomes important to look at Denham's sources and the way he put these lists together.

In this particular case, the list of fantastic and folklore creatures had originally been published as an article in the 23rd December

1848 issue of *The Literary Gazette: Journal of the Belles Lettres, Arts, Sciences, &c.* (London; No. 1666, page 849). Denham's primary source was a list of 'vaine apparitions' compiled by the skeptic Reginald Scot more than two and a half centuries before in *The Discoverie of Witchcraft* [1584], an eloquent and impassioned refutation of the superstitions of his day. In Book VII of that work, after discussing the Oracle at Delphi and the Witch of Endor (1st Samuel 28. 3–25), Scot gives the following mingling of classical lore with old wives' tales:

> Chapter XV. *Of vaine apparitions, how people have beene brought to feare bugges, which is partlie reformed by preaching of the gospell, the true effect of Christes miracle.*
>
> . . . It is a common saieng [saying]; A lion feareth no bugs [bugbears, boogiemen]. But in our childhood our mothers maids have so terrified us with an ouglie [ugly] divell having hornes on this head, fier in his mouth, and a taile in his breech . . . and a voice roring like a lion, whereby we start and are afraid when we heare one crie Bough [Boo!]: and they have so fraied us with bull beggers, spirits, witches, urchens, elves, hags, fairies, satyrs, pans, faunes, sylens, kit with the cansticke, tritons, centaurs, dwarfes, giants, imps, calcars, conjurors, nymphes, changlings, *Incubus*, Robin good-fellowe, the spoorne, the mare [i.e., nightmare], the man in the oke [oak], the hell waine, the fierdrake [firedrake, dragon], the puckle [puck, pooka], Tom thome, hob gobblin, Tom tumbler, boneles, and such other bugs, that we are afraid of our owne shadowes . . . [S]ome never feare the divell, but in a darke night . . . speciallie in a churchyard, where a right hardie man heretofore scant durst passe by night, but his haire would stand upright.
>
> — 1972 Dover facsimile reproduction of the 1930 Montague Summers edition, page 86

Denham took Scot's list and expanded it from thirty-three items (thirty-four if we follow Denham in including the generic name 'bugs') to a hundred and twenty-nine, adding in new names from literary sources (e.g. the poetry of Robert Burns, from which he took *cutties*),[3] the folklore researches of others (including, for later versions of the list, Th. Keightley's *The Fairy Mythology* [1850], from which he derived *korigan*), and his own researches, which had focused on the local beliefs in Durham, Northumberland, Cumberland, and Westmoreland. His inclusion of every item from Scot's list explains the otherwise rather odd appearance of conjurors alongside (classical) nymphs and (faerie) changlings. Denham also took from Scot the deliberate jumbling of material from very different sources: his organizational principle seems not to group together related material but instead to deliberately juxtapose creatures from different traditions to stress their diversity, although small clumps of related creatures do appear here and there in the mix. Denham also seems to have deliberately padded out his list by including simple variants in spelling as separate entries, as in the case of *hobthrush* and *hobthurst* (both covered by a single footnote), *freith* and *freit*, *hobby-lanthorn* and *hob-and-lanthorn*, &c. In other cases, he takes the name of an individual (e.g., Tom Thumb, Peg Powler, Robin Goodfellow, Dick-a-Tuesday, Gyl-burnt-tail, &c.) and 'genericizes' it, so to speak, extrapolating from a proper name into a creature type.

In the following text of the final form of Denham's piece (from the 1895 posthumous collection), I have marked items deriving from Reginald Scot's 1584 list with an asterisk (*); those appearing in Denham's original 1848 list appear in normal (roman) type, while those added by the time of the final (1895) version are given in *italics*. I do not, however, record all the minor variants between Denham's earliest and latest versions – e.g. hobgoblins [1848] vs hob-goblins [1895], Pans vs. pans, pegpoulers vs. Peg-powlers, &c. Two names appearing in the 1848 list (breen, bull-bears) disappear from the final version, three (fairies, thrummy-caps, and cutties) are displaced from early in the old list to near the end of the newer one for reasons that are not apparent, and the total is increased to one hundred and ninety-seven names, four of which (fiends, hobgoblins, imps, and korreds) are duplications of names already found elsewhere in the list (as opposed to only one duplication – imps – in the original list); these repetitions are a sign that, as Tolkien wrote of Bilbo, Denham was 'not . . . an orderly narrator, and his account is involved and discursive, and sometimes confused' (Foreword to the first edition of *The Lord of the Rings*, Vol. I page [7]). To distinguish authorial comments from my own annotation, Denham's notes from the 1895 reprint are given as [D1], [D2], and so forth, while my own notes on his material are given as[1], [2].

GHOSTS NEVER APPEAR ON CHRISTMAS EVE!

'Some say that ever 'gainst that season comes
Wherein our Saviour's birth is celebrated,
The bird of dawning singeth all night long:
And then they say no spirit dares stir abroad;
The nights are wholesome; then no planet strikes,
No fairy takes, nor witch hath power to charm,
So hallowed and so gracious is the time.'
Marcellus.

'So have I heard and do in part believe it.'
Horatio.

So says the immortal Shakespeare;[4] and the truth thereof few now-a-days, I hope, will call in question. Grose observes,[5] too, that those born on Christmas Day cannot see spirits; which is another incontrovertible fact. What a happiness this must have been seventy or eighty years ago[6] and upwards, to those chosen few who had the good luck to be born on the eve of this festival of all festivals; when the whole earth was so overrun with ghosts, boggles,[D1] bloody-bones, spirits,* demons, ignis fatui,[7] brownies,[D2] bugbears, black dogs, spectres, shellycoats, scarecrows, witches,* wizards, bar-guests,[D3] Robin-Goodfellows,*[D4] hags,*[D5] night-bats, scrags, break-necks, fantasms, hob-goblins, hobhoulards, boggy-boes, dobbies,[D6] hob-thrusts,[D7] fetches,[D8] kelpies, warlocks, mock-beggars,[D9] mum-pokers, Jemmy-burties, urchins,* satyrs,* pans,* fauns,* sirens,(*)[8] tritons,* centaurs,* calcars,* nymphs,* imps,* incubusses,* spoorns,* men-in-the-oak,* hell-wains,* fire-drakes,* kit-a-can-sticks,* Tom-tumblers, melch-dicks, larrs, kitty-witches, hobby-lanthorns, Dick-a-Tuesdays, Elf-fires, Gyl-burnt-tails, knockers, elves,*[D10] raw-heads, Meg-with-the-wads, old-shocks, ouphs, pad-fooits, pixies, pic-trees,[D11] giants,* dwarfs,*[9] Tom-pokers, tutgots, snapdragons, sprets,[10] spunks, conjurers,* thurses, spurns, tantarrabobs, swai-thes,[D12] tints, tod-lowries,[11] Jack-in-the-Wads, mormos, changelings,* redcaps, yeth-hounds, colt-pixies, Tom-thumbs,* black-bugs, bog-garts, scar-bugs, shag-foals, hodge-pochers, hob-thrushes, bugs,* bull-beggars,* bygorns, bolls, caddies, bomen, brags,[12] wraithes,[D13] waffs,[D14] flay-boggarts, fiends, gallytrots, imps, gytrashes, patches, hob-and-lanthorns, gringes, boguests, bonelesses,* Peg-powlers,[D15] pucks, fays, kidnappers, gally-beggars, hudskins, nickers, madcaps, trolls, robinets, friars' lanthorns, silkies,[D16] cauld-lads,[D17] death-hearses, goblins,[D18] *hob-headlesses,*[D19] *buggaboes, kows*[D20] *or cowes, nick-ies, nacks [necks], waiths,*[D21] *miffies, buckies, gholes, sylphs, guests, swarths, freiths, freits, gy-carlins [Gyre-carling], pigmies, chittifaces, nixies,*[D22] *Jinny-burnt-tails, dudmen, hell-hounds, dopple-gangers,*[D23] *boggleboes, bogies, redmen, portunes, grants,* ***hobbits,*** *hobgoblins, brown-men,*[D24] *cowies, dunnies,*[D25] *wirrikows,*[D26] *alholdes, mannikins, follets, korreds, lub-berkins, cluricauns, kobolds, leprechauns, kors, mares,* korreds, puckles,* korigans, sylvans, succubuses, black-men, shadows, banshees, lian-hanshees, clabbernappers, Gabriel-hounds, mawkins, doubles,*[D27] *corpse lights or candles, scrats, mahounds, trows, gnomes, sprites, fates, fiends, syb-ils, nick-nevins,*[D28] *whitewomen,* fairies,*[D29] thrummy-caps,[D30] cutties,[D31] *and nisses,* and apparitions of every shape, make, form, fashion, kind, and description, that there was not a village in England that had not its own peculiar ghost. Nay, every lone tenement, castle, or mansion-house, which could boast of any antiquity had its bogle, its spectre, or its knocker. The churches, churchyards, and cross-roads, were all haunted. Every green lane had its boulder-stone on which an apparition kept watch at night. Every common had its circle of fairies belonging to it. And there was scarcely a shepherd to be met with who had not seen a spirit! [See *Lit. Gaz.* for December 1848, p. 849.]

DENHAM'S NOTES

D1 Boggle-house, parish of Sedgefield. Bellingham Boggle-Hole, Northd. [Bogle-houses in Lowick Forest, Northumberland.]

D2 There is also a river of this name in the Bishopric of Durham. Also at York is Browny Dike, a portion of the Foss.

D3 The York Barguest. See *Memoirs of R. Surtees, Esq.*; new ed., p. 80, 1852.

D4 This merry fay acted the part of fool or jester, at the court of Oberon, the fairy monarch.

D5 Hag-House. A farmstead near Brancepeth.

D6 The Mortham Dobby. A Teesdale goblin.

D7 Hob-o-t'-Hursts, *i.e.* spirits of the woods. Hobthrush Rook, Farndale, Yorkshire.

D8 The spirit or double of a dying person.

D9 Mock-beggar Hall. Of houses, rocks, etc., bearing this name we meet with many instances.

D10 Elf-Hills, parish of Hutton-in-the-Forest, Cumberland. Elf-How, parish of Kendal. Elf-Hills, near Cambo.

D11 There is a village of this name near Chester-le-Street; and singular enough a ghost story, called the 'Picktree Bragg,' is attached to it. See Keightley's *Fairy Mythology*, Bohn's ed. p. 310.[13]

D12 *The spirit or double of a dying person.*[14]

D13 *The spirit or double of a dying person.*

D14 *The spirit or double of a dying person.*

D15 This oulde ladye is the evil goddess of the Tees. I also meet with a Nanny Powler, at Darlington, who from the identity of their sirnames, is, I judge, a sister, or it may be a daughter of Peg's. Nanny Powler, aforesaid, haunts the Skerne, a tributary of the Tees.

D16 The Heddon Silky, and Silky's Brig, near Heddon. See Richardson's *Table Book*, Leg.Div., vol. ii., p. 181.

D17 Occasionally, we may hear Cowed, or rather Cowd Lad. The meaning, however, is the same; Cowd being a variation of the more refined word, cold.

D18 Goblin Field, near Mold, Flintshire.

D19 Hob-Cross-Hill. A place near Doncaster.

D20 'The Hedley Kow,' a Northumberland ghost story.

D21 *The spirit or double of a dying person.*

D22 'Know you the nixies, gay and fair?
Their eyes are black, and green their hair,
They lurk in sedgy waters.'

—*Keightley*

D23 *The spirit or double of a dying person.*

D24 See ghost story of the 'Brown Man of the Moor.' Richardson's *Table Book*.

D25 The Hazelrigg Dunny. An excellent Northumberland ghost story.

D26 'Frae gudame's mouth auld warld tale they hear,
O' warlocks louping round the wirriknow.'

—The works of Robt. Fergusson, ed. by A. B. Grossart, Edin., 1851, p. 61.

D27 *The spirit or double of a dying person.*

D28 Mother witches.

D29 Fairy Dean, two miles above Melrose. Fairy Stone, near Fourstones, in the parish of Warden, Northumberland. This stone, in which is a secret cavity, has attained a celebrity in history owing to the letters being placed therein, to and from the unfortunate Earl of Derwentwater, during the '15.[15]

D30 Thrummy Hills, near Catterick. The name of this sprite is met with in the Fairy tales of Northumberland.

D31 These are a certain class of female Boggles, not altogether peculiar to Scotland, who wore their lower robes, at least, *a-la-bloomer*. They are named by Burns, in his inimitable poem Tam-o'-Shanter. Mr. Halliwell gives the word as localized in Somersetshire.

Mr. Denham's Hobbit

Given the evidence of Denham's list, and the inclusion of 'hobbits' within it, the question then becomes threefold: what were these hobbits, where did Denham get the word, and did Tolkien know about Denham's work? So far as the first point goes, there is no doubt that hobbits were a kind of hob (also sometimes known as brownies or, more rarely, lobs), like the hob-goblins, hob-thrushes/hob-thrusts,[16] hobhoulards, hob-headless, and hob-and-lanthorns/hobby-lanthorns (a kind of Will o' the Wisp) who also appear in the list – in fact, hob names make up nine of the hundred and ninety-seven items, or roughly five percent of the whole, the largest grouping within the entire list, whereas they had been represented by a single entry (hob gobblin) in Reginald Scot's 1584 account. The traditional hob of English folklore was a solitary creature, sometimes described as a little brown man a few feet high, who attached himself to a farm or manor and, although seldom if ever seen, did chores and sometimes helped the family in times of crisis. His payment was traditionally a small cake or bannock or a bowl of milk or cream left out each night; if this was ever neglected or if he was given a gift of clothes he left forever. *Hobbit* seems to be a typical variation on the name, but one recorded nowhere else, so we cannot tell if it was a proper name of a specific hob 'genericized' by Denham (as he demonstratably does in the case of Hob Headless, another in his list, whose story is briefly retold by Briggs – *A Dictionary of Fairies* page 222) or a type of hob, like hobthrusts or hobgoblins.

As for Denham's immediate source, unfortunately the industrious folklore collector provided no note explaining where he had found the name *hobbit*. Since like several others in Denham's list the name is not recorded elsewhere, it almost certainly came through his own first-hand collection of old folklore in the Durham region or its neighboring counties – a region particularly rich in hob-stories, as Briggs notes (*ibid.*).[17] But the exact source has proved elusive and will probably remain so. As Tolkien says of his own hobbits, 'it is clear that Hobbits had, in fact, lived quietly in Middle-earth for many long years before other folk became even aware of them . . . the world being after all full of strange creatures beyond count' (Prologue to *The Lord of the Rings*, p.14), and the same is analogous of the actual folklore creature that shared the name of Tolkien's creation, which was recorded only by chance in this single instance; any associated story or stories have long since been forgotten beyond recovery.

Adding to the mystery, as we have already noted the name does not appear in the original [1848] article but was added to the list sometime between then and its posthumous appearance, long after Denham's death in 1859, in the Folk-Lore Society volumes. Given the free hand the miscellany's editor, Dr. Hardy, allowed himself for silently adding or re-arranging material (see Note 2), for a time I investigated the possibility that it had been added by Hardy himself as late as 1892–1895, but this turns out not to have been the case. According to a recent book by Peter Gilliver, Jeremy Marshall, & Edmund Weiner, who have examined some of the original tracts from which the book was compiled (the Folk-Lore Society's not-quite-complete collection of which is now at University College, London), the 1848 article was followed by an independent 1851 tract in which *hobbit* is still absent, but the word does appear in an 1853 version of that same tract, which in turn seems to have provided the base copy for the 1895 text (*The Ring of Words: Tolkien and the Oxford English Dictionary* [2006], pages 147–148). I have not been able to examine the original tracts for myself, but the evidence of Gilliver et al. pushes back the word's first recorded appearance from 1895 to 1853, beyond which its origins once again fade into obscurity.[18]

The final question of whether Tolkien knew about Denham's inclusion of the name is equally murky. Certainly he knew about Reginald Scot's list, which was reproduced and discussed by C. S. Lewis in *The Discarded Image*.[19] In addition, *The Denham Tracts* was one of the primary sources from which Joseph Wright drew for his *English Dialect Dictionary* [six volumes, 1898–1905], a work Tolkien greatly admired,[20] but this is not to say that Tolkien ever had reason to examine this specific source-volume for himself. If he had (and this is a big *if*), then he would almost certainly have discovered Denham's list, since Gomme explicitly draws attention to it in the Preface to the second volume in tantalizing terms:

> . . . the only way to study folk-lore is to treat each recorded item separately. For this purpose there will be found very interesting features here which are not to be found elsewhere. The names for the different classes of spirits (on pp. 77–78) is very full, and needs some investigation philologically and mythologically . . .
>
> —Preface, Vol. II page ix

The names in question are of course those making up Denham's list reprinted on page 846 above. And, of course, one might say that taking a single item from that list (the otherwise unknown name 'hobbit') and investigating it philologically (what might the word mean? what might a 'hobbit' be like?) and mythologically (what sort of tales might be told about such a creature?) is exactly what Tolkien does in *The Hobbit*. Such a chain of events would make Tolkien's hobbits his personal adaptation of actual folklore survivals just like the elves, dwarfs (or dwarves), wizards, goblins, giants, fire-drakes (dragons), trolls and hob-goblins, all of which occur both in *The Hobbit* and in Denham's list and all of which are given distinctly Tolkienian interpretations.[21] The possibility is tantalizing, but it remains only a possibility, with no direct evidence to back it up. Certainly if Tolkien did ever read *The Denham Tracts*, it must have been during his early years studying with Wright [1911–1915] or when himself compiling *A Middle English Glossary* [1918] or editing Middle English texts like *Sir Gawain & the Green Knight* [circa 1922–1925] at Leeds, since he had forgotten about it completely by 1930 when he actually came to write down that solitary sentence *In a hole in the ground lived a hobbit.*

Unfortunately, this attractive little scenario can hardly represent what really happened, for it runs counter to the most important evidence of all: Tolkien's own account of how he created the name, repeated over and over with great consistency over a number of years (see pages xii–xiii), and his attempts late in life (detailed in Appendix II) to find any possible earlier occurance of the name. Had Tolkien deliberately acted on the hint in Gomme's preface, it is wildly improbable that he would have completely forgotten about it and gone to such lengths, which included not just his own researches into the topic but corresponding with his old pupils Robert Burchfield, then the editor of the OED, and Roger Lancelyn Green, whom he recruited to try to track down any nineteenth century fairy-story that might have included the name (see pp. 860–62). Therefore, despite its apparent plausibility, it is highly unlikely that *The Denham Tracts* was actually Tolkien's source for *hobbit*.

How then do we explain the coincidence? For one thing, English folklore traditions about hobs obviously played a part in Tolkien's creation, including the name, and since this is the case it is not so very surprising to find that Tolkien's invention, his own personal variant, can be matched by an actual example from the historical record, albeit an obscure one. JRRT's gift for nomenclature was posited on creating words that sounded like real ones, creating matches of sound and sense that felt as if they were actual words drawn from the vast body of old lore that had somehow failed to otherwise be recorded. That his invention should match actual obscure historical words was inevitable provided he did his work well enough, as is also attested by the accidental resemblance of his place-name *Gondor* (inspired by the actual historic word *ond* ['stone'], which had once been thought to be a fragment of a lost pre-IndoEuropean language of the British isles)[22] to both the real-world Gondar (a city in northern Ethiopia, also sometimes spelled Gonder, once that country's capital; see *Letters* p. 409) and the imaginary Gondour (a utopia invented by Mark Twain in the story 'The Curious Republic of Gondour' [1870]; see my essay in the Blackwelder festschrift, p. 93 Note 24, for more detail). It is a tribute to Tolkien's skill with word-building that his invented *hobbit* should prove to have indeed had a real-world predecessor, though Tolkien himself probably never knew of it. For more on Tolkien's investigation into real-world antecedents of the hobbit, see Appendix II.

JDR NOTES

1 Although she was surely aware of it, since in her entry on Tolkien within the same book she praises his work for being 'deepened by the use of traditional folklore which gave it that sense of being rooted in the earth which is the gift of folklore to literature' – Briggs, *A Dictionary of Fairies*, page 401. In her various entries on hobs and hobmen – 'Hob, or Hobthrust' (p. 222–223), 'Lobs and Hobs' (p. 270–271) and 'Brownie' (or little brown men, p. 45–49) – she summarizes traditional beliefs and in so doing helps us see the extent to which Tolkien was influenced by them. For example, her description of the brown men (brownies) as 'small men, about three feet in height, very raggedly dressed in brown clothes, with brown faces and shaggy heads' would take very little adjustment to serve as a description of hobbits in their latter days, when they have become a shy and fugitive people who 'avoid us with dismay and are becoming hard to find' (Prologue, *LotR*.[13]). Even though Denham's groupings are somewhat erratic, it is suggestive that 'hobbit' is immediately followed by hobgoblin and brown-man (i.e., brownie) as items number one hundred and fifty-four, one hundred and fifty-five, and one hundred and fifty-six, respectively, in his final list. Elsewhere in *The Denham Tracts* he retells stories about several hobs, most notably the Cauld Lad o' Hylton ('the Cold Lad of Hilton'; Vol. I pages 55–57), Hob Thrush (Vol. II pages 355–356), and the Hazelrigg Dunnie (ibid pages 157–163).

Denham's own closeness to the material may be judged from his admission of his childhood terror of Peg Powler, a local drowning spirit,† and the precautions he took as a child to avoid attracting the attention of the fairies.††

†'the writer still perfectly recollects being dreadfully alarmed in the days of his childhood lest, more particularly when he chanced to be alone on the margin of those waters, she should issue from the stream and snatch him into her watery chambers' – Vol. II page 42.

††'I well remember that on more occasions than one, when a schoolboy, I have turned my coat inside out in passing through a wood in order to avoid the good people' – Vol. II page 88.

2 Gomme's preface to the second volume sums up the difficulties thusly: 'Mr. Denham['s] . . . peculiar practice of issuing these tracts sometimes without date or other means of identification makes it extremely difficult to ascertain whether all he published on folk-lore has been recovered. There is no complete collection . . . It often happened that a tract was issued as a simple leaflet, and that later on this would be included in another tract without any alteration of or allusion to the original publication' (Vol. II page x). Indeed, the bulk of 'Tract VIII' (ibid. pages [1]–80) in the Folk-Lore Society's compilation turns out to be from another tract (pages 21–80) titled 'Folklore; or Manners, Cus-

toms, Weather Proverbs, Popular Charms, Juvenile Rhymes, Ballads, &c. &c. in the north of England' (see the editorial footnote on the bottom of Vol. II page 21), whose title accurately reflects the miscellaneous nature of the compilation.

To compound the problem, the Folk-Lore Society volumes were carelessly edited and at several points inadvertently reprint slightly different versions of the same material – e.g., the long annotated list of items associated with fairies given as examples of 'The not yet wholly exploded belief in fairies, fays, and elves', which appears both as its own short tract (Tract XIV: 'A Few Fragments of Fairy Folklore'; Vol. II pages 110–115) and in briefer form without explanatory notes on page 30 in the same volume as a single paragraph within what the editor designated as Tract VIII. Furthermore, at a number of points the editor either rewrote passages or inserted new material. Gomme's preface (Vol. I page xi) promises that additional notes by Hardy would all be carefully identified with the latter's bracketed initials ('[J.H.]'), but in practice this is rarely the case. Contrast, for example, Denham's first-person account of the strange behavior of his mother's cat after its mistress died (Vol. II page 74) with the third-person reference to Denham on page 12 of the same volume, or quotations from letters by Denham (apparently to Hardy himself) woven into the main text on page 270 and elsewhere, not to mention many examples given in the text that are taken from works published after Denham's death (e.g. Vol. II pages 182, 226, 257, 272, 287, 356, 357, &c), the latest of these dating from 1888, when Denham had been dead almost thirty years. In short, the published text of these two volumes has undergone massive interference at the hands of its editor(s) and cannot reliably be taken as representing exactly what Denham wrote on specific points without outside confirmation from the original tracts.

3 This almost certainly involves a misapprehension on Denham's part, since in Burns' poem 'Tam O'Shanter' [1791] Cutty Sark ('short skirt/smock') is the name of a beautiful witch so called from her revealing garments, not (as he puts it in a footnote to the 1895 list) 'a certain class of female Boggles'; see note [D31].

4 Specifically, the lines that open Denham's piece† come from *Hamlet*, Act I, Scene 1, lines 158–165. Horatio and the guards are discussing the effect of the cock's crow on the ghost of King Hamlet, whose manifestation they have just witnessed.

†These lines of dialogue are absent in the 1848 article, which is simply headed 'SEASONAL INFORMATION' (a title possibly provided by the journal's editor) following by the line 'Ghosts never appear on Christmas eve!' in quotation marks; the latter was probably Denham's title, since it reappears in *The Denham Tracts* version.

5 This would presumably be the antiquarian Captain Francis Grose, author of *The Antiquities of England and Wales* [six volumes, 1773–1787], *Antiquities of Scotland* [two volumes, 1789 & 1791], and the unfinished *Antiquities of Ireland* [1791].

6 That is, seventy or eighty years before this piece's first publication in 1848, not from the time of its collection in *The Denham Tracts* – that is, in the 1770s and before.

7 Originally, in the 1848 list, *fairies* appeared here between *ignis-fatui* and *brownies*, before being moved to near the end of the 1895 list.

8 Denham prints *sirens* here instead of R. Scot's *sylens*, both in the 1848 and the 1895 lists. Some folklorists have suspected that the word should be read *sylvans* instead, meaning some woodland creature such as the satyrs, Pans, and fauns that precede it, but the point is debatable.

9 The 1895 printing actually reads *dwafs* here, but it is clear from the 1848 reading (*dwarfs*) that this is a simple misprint. Note that while Denham (and Scot) use *elves* instead of *elfs* (as indeed did Tolkien's slightly elder contemporary, Lord Dunsany), neither used the purely Tolkienesque *dwarves*.

10 Originally, in the 1848 list, *thrummy-caps* appeared here between *sprets* and *spunks*, before being moved to near the end of the 1895 list.

11 tod-lowries: In his 1848 piece, Denham glosses this as 'Phantom foxes', one of only two footnotes to the original article and the only one not picked up and repeated in the final piece.

12 Originally, in the 1848 list, *cutties* appeared here between *brags* and *wraiths*, before being moved to the penultimate position in the 1895 list.

13 A simpler version of this footnote appears in the 1848 article: 'There is a village of this name near Chester-le-street, in the county of Durham.'

14 Denham's note actually reads '12, 13, 21, 23, 27. The same with note 8.' (e.g., [D8]). That is, he interprets these six as different names for the same concept. I have repeated the text of Denham's note ([D8]) at each occurrence for the sake of clarity.

15 That is, the Jacobite Uprising of 1715; the said earl was executed for treason in 1716 for his role in supporting the Old Pretender (James Stuart, son of the deposed James II).

16 While Denham himself accepted the theory that 'hob-thrush' is a contraction of 'hob-o'-t'-hurst' (i.e., hob in the woods – see note [D7]), Briggs follows Gillian Edwards in suggesting that 'hobthrust' derives instead from hob-thyrs, *thyrs* being one of the Old English words for giant† (*A Dictionary of Fairies*, page 223); thurse (thurses) itself appears elsewhere in Denham's list. Since as Tolkien notes *hob-* is a diminutive (see page 862), the name essentially means 'little giant'.

†along with the more familiar (to the ears of Tolkien's readers, at any rate) *eoten*.

17 A secondary possibility is that the word was drawn to his attention by one of his many correspondents (one of whom was Dr. Hardy, the editor more than thirty years after Denham's death of *The Denham Tracts* themselves – see the Preface to Volume I page viii). If this is the case, the name may have come from somewhat further afield, either the northern Midlands or just over the border in southern Scotland (e.g.,

Berwickshire), both areas being similarly well-provided with hob legends.

18 Gilliver, Marshall, & Weiner state that the title page for the 1851 tract reads:

> To all and singular the Ghosts, Hobgoblins, and Phantasms, of the United Kingdom of Great Britain and Ireland, These brief Pages are Fearlessly Inscribed, In utter defiance of their Power and Influence, By their verie hvmble Seruaunte, To Com'aund, M:A:D.
>
> — *The Ring of Words*, page 147.

This is almost certainly the same tract given in a listing of Denham's works drawn up by Denham himself just before his death. The listing, published as the first item ('A List of Antiquarian Tomes, Tracts and Trifles') in an 1858 collection of Denham's work titled *Denham Tracts, or a few Pictures of the Olden Time in connection with The North of England* [1858; facsimile reprint 1974], gives as the first item of section XI ('Sundry Minor Tracts, &c.') a piece titled 'Ghosts, Hobgoblins, and Phantasms', stating that the first edition of fifty copies was printed in 1852 and ran six pages long; the second item in the same list is the second edition of the same title (eight pages, 1853). The listing may be found on page 7 of the 1858 *Denham Tracts*, which unfortunately does not include that tract among its 142 pages.

19 For Tolkien's attempt to get this book by his friend published by Allen & Unwin in 1936, see Note 23 to the commentary following Chapter IV, page 152. In the event, it was not published until 1964, the year following Lewis's death.

20 For more on Tolkien's admiration for, and usage of, Wright's book, see the commentary on Wright as a source for 'the carrock', pages 202–203.

Similarly, one might note that Tolkien had a number of connections to University College, London, where the largest single gathering of Denham's tracts is deposited; it was here that his *Songs for the Philologists* was published in 1936, and it was for many years the academic home of R. W. Chambers, a fellow medievalist with whom Tolkien sometimes shared unpublished works (and the recipient of one of Tolkien's author's copies of *The Hobbit*) and also of A. H. Smith, one of his former pupils at Leeds who became a specialist in English place-name studies. But these connections are all too late to have influenced Tolkien's invention of the word *Hobbit* in the summer of 1930.

21 Other creatures from Denham's list appearing in Tolkien's other works include wraithes (wraiths), corpse-candles, gnomes, fairies, fays, and korigans (as the Corrigan in 'The Lay of Aotrou and Itroun').

22 See *Letters* p. 410. Tolkien's probable source for this information† was John Rhys's *Celtic Britain* [1884], page 270.†† Modern scholarship has concluded that the so-called 'Ivernian' language, like the similarly once-mysterious Pictish, was in fact simply an earlier form of Celtic.

†First uncovered by Carl Hostetter and Pat Wynne in their article 'Stone Towers' (*Mythlore* #74, Autumn 1993), page 48.

††The other 'Ivernian' word to which Tolkien refers in his letter that he had forgotten was *fern*, meaning (according to Rhys) 'anything good'. Rhys also thought he detected Ivernian words underlying proper and place names such as *Bolg* (pages 268, 281) and *Nét/Nuada/Nodens* (page 263).

Appendix II

TOLKIEN'S LETTER TO *THE OBSERVER* (THE HOBYAHS)

In addition to the undoubted appearance of the word *hobbits* in Denham's list, although Tolkien probably was not aware of the fact (see Appendix I), the issue of whether or not Tolkien invented the name outright has long been confused by a vague claim that it might have come from a late nineteenth or early twentieth century fairy tale. This claim was first raised by a pseudonymous letter to the editor of the British newspaper *The Observer*, printed on 16th January 1938, just four months after *The Hobbit* had been published.

Sir: Dr. Julian Huxley, in one of his recent lectures, referred to the 'little furry men' seen in Africa by natives and, although dimly in moonlight, by at least one scientist.

What I should like to know is whether these creatures provided the inspiration for Professor Tolkien's attractive hobbit, the newest visitor to so many of our nurseries this Christmas. Naturally, I always read my children's book before giving them to them, and I noticed that the characters in the hobbit were nearly all drawn from real animal life or from real mythology. Few of them appeared to be invented.

On mentioning the hairy-footed hobbit, rather like a rabbit, to one of my contemporaries, I was amazed to see her shudder. She said she remembered an old fairy tale called 'The Hobbit' in a collection read about 1904. This creature, she said, was definitely frightening, unlike Professor Tolkien's. Would the Professor be persuaded to tell us some more about the name and inception of the intriguing hero of his book? It would save so many research students so very much trouble in the generations to come. And, by the way, is the hobbit's stealing of the dragon's cup based on the cup-stealing episode in Beowulf? I hope so, since one of the book's charms appears to be its Spenserian harmonising of the brilliant threads of so many branches of epic, mythology, and Victorian fairy literature. – Yours, etc.

'HABIT.'

This brief letter inspired a long, detailed reply which is so important as a statement of how Tolkien felt about *The Hobbit* immediately following its first publication, and so full of information about his sources and the writing of the book, that I give it here in full.

Although written within days of the publication of Habit's letter (*Letters* p. 35), Tolkien's reply was not printed until the Sunday, 20th February 1938 issue.[1]

HOBBITS

Sir. – I need no persuasion: I am as susceptible as a dragon to flattery, and would gladly show off my diamond waistcoat, and even discuss its sources, since the Habit (more inquisitive than the Hobbit) has not only professed to admire it, but has also asked where I got it from. But would not that be rather unfair to the research students? To save them trouble is to rob them of any excuse for existing.

However, with regard to the Habit's principal question, there is no danger: I do not remember anything about the name and inception of the hero. I could guess, of course, but the guesses would have no more authority than those of future researchers, and I leave the game to them.

I was born in Africa, and have read several books on African exploration. I have, since about 1896, read even more books of fairy-tales of the genuine kind. Both the facts produced by the Habit would appear, therefore, to be significant. But are they? I have no waking recollection of furry pygmies (in book or moonlight), nor of any Hobbit bogey in print by 1904. I suspect that the two hobbits are accidental homophones, and am content† that they are not (is would seem) synonyms.[2] And I protest that my hobbit did not live in Africa, and was not furry, except about the feet. Nor indeed was he like a rabbit. He was a prosperous, well-fed young bachelor of independent means. Calling him a 'nasty little rabbit' was a piece of vulgar trollery, just as 'descendant of rats' was a piece of dwarfish malice – deliberate insults to his size and feet, which he deeply resented. His feet, if conveniently clad and shod by nature, were as elegant as his long, clever fingers.

As for the rest of the tale it is, as the Habit suggests, derived from (previously digested) epic, mythology, and fairy-story – not, however, Victorian in authorship, as a rule to which George Macdonald is the chief exception. *Beowulf* is among my most valued sources, though it was not consciously present to the mind in the process of writing, in which the episode of the theft arose naturally (and almost inevitably) from the circumstances. It is difficult to think of any other way of conducting the story at that point. I fancy the author of *Beowulf* would say much the same.

My tale is not consciously based on any other book – save one, and that is unpublished: the 'Silmarillion', a history of the Elves, to which frequent allusion is made. I had not thought of the future researchers, and as there is only one manuscript there seems at the moment small chance of this reference proving useful.

But these questions are mere preliminaries. Now that I have been made to see Mr. Baggins's adventures as the subject of future enquiry I realise that a lot of work will be needed. There is the question of nomenclature. The dwarf-names, and the wizard's, are from the Elder Edda. The hobbit-names from Obvious Sources proper to their kind. The full list of their wealthier families is: Baggins, Boffin, Bolger, Bracegirdle, Brandybuck, Burrowes, Chubb, Grubb, Hornblower, Proudfoot, Sackville, and Took. The dragon bears as name – a pseudonym – the past tense of the primitive Germanic verb *Smugan**, to squeeze through a hole: a low philological jest. The rest of the names are of the Ancient and Elvish World, and have not been modernized.

And why *dwarves*? Grammar prescribes *dwarfs*; philology suggests that *dwarrows* would be the historical form. The real answer is that I knew no better. But *dwarves* goes well with *elves*; and, in any case, *elf*, *gnome*, *goblin*, *dwarf* are only approximate translations of the Old Elvish names[3] for beings of not quite the same kinds and functions.

These dwarves are not quite the dwarfs of better known lore. They have been given Scandinavian names, it is true; but that is an editorial concession. Too many names in the tongues proper to the period might have been alarming. Dwarvish was both complicated and cacophonous. Even early elvish philologists avoided it, and the dwarves were obliged to use other languages, except for entirely private conversations. The language of hobbits was remarkably like English, as one would expect: they only lived on the borders of the Wild, and were mostly unaware of it. Their family names remain for the most part well known and justly respected in this island as they were in Hobbiton and Bywater.

There is the matter of the Runes. Those used by Thorin and Co., for special purpose, were comprised in an alphabet of thirty-two letters (full list on application), similar to, but not identical, with the runes of Anglo-Saxon inscriptions. There is doubtless an historical connection between the two. The Feanorian alphabet, generally used at the time, was of Elvish origin. It appears in the curse inscribed on the pot of gold in the picture of Smaug's lair, but had otherwise been transcribed (a facsimile of the original letter left on the mantelpiece can be supplied).[4]

And what of the Riddles? There is work to be done here on the sources and analogues. I should not be at all surprised to learn that both the hobbit and Gollum will find their claim to have invented any of them disallowed.

Finally, I present the future researcher with a little problem. The tale halted in the telling for about a year at two separate points: where are they? But probably that would have been discovered anyway. And suddenly I remember that the hobbit thought 'Old fool,' when the dragon succumbed to blandishment. I fear that the Habit's comment (and yours) will already be the same. But you must admit that the temptation was strong. – Yours, etc.

J. R. R. Tolkien

20 Northmoor-road, Oxford.

†[Tolkien's note:] Not quite. I should like, if possible, to learn more about the fairy-tale connection, c. 1904.

No reply being forthcoming from 'Habit', there the matter rested for more than thirty years. It was only in the last years of Tolkien's life that he turned again to the question of possible antecedents to his invention of the word *hobbit*, as testified in letters to two of his former pupils, Robert Burchfield and Roger Lancelyn Green. The immediate impetus was the decision by Burchfield, now the senior Editor of the OED, to include 'hobbit' in the *Supplement to the OED* he was preparing. According to Gilliver, Marshall, & Weiner's *The Ring of Words: Tolkien and the Oxford English Dictionary* [2006], Burchfield sent Tolkien a proposed entry on the word in December 1969 to see if it met with his approval. Tolkien replied on 11th September 1970:

The matter of *hobbits* is not very important, but I may be forgiven for taking a personal interest in it and being anxious that the meaning intended by me should be made clear.

Unfortunately, as all lexicographers know, 'don't look into things, unless you are looking for trouble: they nearly always turn out to be less simple than you thought'. You will shortly be receiving a long letter on *hobbit* and related matters, of which, even if it is in time, only a small part may be useful or interesting to you.

For the moment this is held up, because I am having the matter of the etymology: 'invented by J. R. R. Tolkien': investigated by experts. I knew that the claim was not clear, but I had not troubled to look into it, until faced by the inclusion of *hobbit* in the Supplement.

In the meanwhile I submit for your consideration the following definition:

One of an imaginary people, a small variety of the human race, that gave themselves this name (meaning 'hole-dweller') but were called by others *halflings*, since they were half the height of normal Men.

This assumes that the etymology can stand.[5] If not it may be necessary to modify it: e.g. by substituting after 'race'

; in the tales of J. R. R. Tolkien said to have given themselves this name, though others called them . . .

If it stands, as I think it will even if an alleged older story called 'The Hobbit' can be traced, then the '(meaning "hole-dweller")' could be transferred to the etymology.

This definition, since it is more than twice as long as the one that you submitted and differs from it widely, will need some justification. I will supply it.[6]

Unfortunately, the promised 'long letter on *hobbit* and related matters' never followed, and probably was never written. It is not clear who the experts Tolkien engaged to research the matter for him were, but within a few months he consulted with Roger Lancelyn Green, another former pupil who had become the biographer of such important Victorian and Edwardian writers for children such as Lewis Carroll, James Barrie, and Andrew Lang (and later, of course, of C. S. Lewis), as well as a recognized authority on the history of children's literature in England; cf. his book *Tellers of Tales: Favourite Children's Authors and Their Books of the Last 100 Years* [1946; updated, revised, and expanded in five distinct editions between 1946 and 1969 to eventually cover the period 1800–1968], which contained short biographies of the life and works of both major (Lear, Nesbit, MacDonald) and relatively minor (Mrs. Molesworth, S. R. Crockett) figures. Accordingly, Tolkien wrote to Green on 8th January 1971 (*Letters* p. 406–407):

The Ox. E. D. has in preparation of its Second Supplement got to *Hobbit*, which it proposes to include together with its progeny: *hobbitry, -ish,* etc. I have had, therefore, to justify my claim to have invented the word. My claim rests really on my 'nude parole' or unsupported assertion that I remember the occasion of its invention (by me); and that I had not *then* any knowledge of *Hobberdy, Hobbaty, Hobberdy Dick* etc. (for 'house-sprites');† and that my 'hobbits' were in any case of wholly dissimilar sort, a diminutive branch of the human race. Also that the only E.[nglish] word that influenced the invention was 'hole'; that granted the description of *hobbits*, the trolls' use of *rabbit* was merely an obvious insult, of no more etymological significance than Thorin's insult to Bilbo 'descendant of rats!' However, doubt was cast on this as far back as 1938. A review appeared in *The Observer* 16 Jan 1938, signed *'Habit'* . . . 'Habit' asserted that a friend claimed to have read, about 20 years earlier (sc. c. 1918)[7] an old 'fairy story' (in a collection of such tales) called *The Hobbit*, though the creature was very 'frightening'. I asked for more information, but have never received any; and recent intensive research has not discovered the 'collection'. I think it is probable that the friend's memory was inaccurate (after 20 years), and the creature probably had a name of the *Hobberdy, Hobbaty* class. However, one cannot exclude the possibility that buried childhood memories might suddenly rise to the surface long after (in my case after 35–40 years), though they might be quite differently applied. I told the researchers that I used (before 1900) to be read to from an 'old collection' – tattered and without cover or title-page – of which all I can now remember was that (I think) it was by Bulwer Lytton, and contained one story I was then very fond of called *'Puss Cat Mew'*. They have not discovered it. I wonder if you, the most learned of living scholars in this region, can say anything. Esp. for my own satisfaction about *Puss Cat Mew* – I do not suppose you have found a name precisely *hobbit* or you would have mentioned it. Oh what a tangled web they weave who try a new word to conceive!

†[Tolkien's note:] I have now! Probably more than most other folk; and find myself in a v. tangled wood – the clue to which is, however, the belief in *incubi* and 'changelings'. Alas! one conclusion is that the statement that *hobgoblins* were 'a larger kind' is the reverse of the original truth.

Green was able to identify the collection from which 'Puss Cat Mew' came as Edward Knatchbull-Hugessen's *Stories for My Children* [1869] (*Letters* p. 453), the American edition of which is actually titled *Puss-Cat Mew, and other Stories for my Children* [1871]. Knatchbull-Hugessen (1829–1893) was, in addition to the author of several such books of stories for children, the son of one of Jane Austen's nieces (Fanny Knight) and a reasonably prominent politician of his day, serving in Parliament and as Under-Secretary of State under several administrations, including Gladstone's, eventually being ennobled [1880] as the first Lord Brabourne. But Green's identification did not resolve the issue, since there is no story in this collection remotely answering the description of Habit's friend and no hobbits to be found therein.[8]

In fact, the story to which Habit's friend referred was almost certainly 'The Hobyahs',[9] which appeared in Joseph Jacobs' *More English Fairy Tales* [1894]. Jacobs' work, along with its earlier companion volume *English Fairy Tales* [1891], were once almost as well known as that of his rival Andrew Lang's coloured fairy book series [1889ff] but much more sharply focused in their contents, including only stories once current in Great Britain (thus the inclusion of 'The Hobyahs' which, although collected in America, clearly harken back to the north-of-England/southern Scotland range of traditional hobs and hobgoblins, Perth being on Scotland's east coast just north of Edinburgh). And, just as Tolkien had suspected, the hobyahs of this tale are indeed goblins who in no way resemble his hobbits. Since it is quite brief, for purposes of comparison I give here the entire tale as it appeared in Jacobs' source, a piece submitted by anthropologist and archeologist S. V. Proudfit to *The Journal of American Folklore*, vol. iv no. xiii (April-June 1891), pages 173–174.[10]

THE HOBYAHS: A SCOTCH NURSERY TALE. – When a child, I used to hear the following story told in a Scotch family that came from the vicinity of Perth. Whether the story came with the family I am unable to say. I have spelled the word 'Hobyah' as it was pronounced.

The effectiveness of the story lies in a certain sepulchral monotone in rendering the cry of the Hobyah, and his terrible 'look me.'

S. V. Proudfit

WASHINGTON, D. C.

Once there was an old man and woman and a little girl, and they all lived in a house made of hempstalks. Now the old man had a little dog named Turpie; and one night the Hobyahs came and said, 'Hobyah! Hobyah! Hobyah! Tear down the hempstalks, eat up the old man and woman, and carry off the little girl!' But little dog Turpie barked so that the Hobyahs ran off; and the old man said, 'Little dog Turpie barks so that I cannot sleep nor slumber, and if I live till morning I will cut off his tail.' So in the morning the old man cut off little dog Turpie's tail.

The next night the Hobyahs came again, and said, 'Hobyah! Hobyah! Hobyah! Tear down the hempstalks, eat up the old man and woman, and carry off the little girl!' But little dog Turpie barked so that the Hobyahs ran off; and the old man said, 'Little dog Turpie barks so that I cannot sleep nor slumber, and if I live till morning I will cut off one of his legs.' So in the morning the old man cut off one of little dog Turpie's legs.

The next night the Hobyahs came again, and said, 'Hobyah! Hobyah! Hobyah! Tear down the hempstalks, eat up the old man and woman, and carry off the little girl!' But little dog Turpie barked so that the Hobyahs ran off; and the old man said, 'Little dog Turpie barks so that I cannot sleep nor slumber, and if I live till morning I will cut off another of his legs.' So in the morning the old man cut off another of little dog Turpie's legs.

The next night the Hobyahs came again, and said, 'Hobyah! Hobyah! Hobyah! Tear down the hempstalks, eat up the old man and woman, and carry off the little girl!' But little dog Turpie barked so that the Hobyahs ran off; and the old man said, 'Little dog Turpie barks so that I cannot sleep nor slumber, and if I live till morning I will cut off another of his legs.' So in the morning the old man cut off another of little dog Turpie's legs.

The next night the Hobyahs came again, and said, 'Hobyah! Hobyah! Hobyah! Tear down the hempstalks, eat up the old man and woman, and carry off the little girl!' But little dog Turpie barked so that the Hobyahs ran off; and the old man said, 'Little dog Turpie barks so that I cannot sleep nor slumber, and if I live till morning I will cut off another of his legs.' So in the morning the old man cut off another of little dog Turpie's legs.

The next night the Hobyahs came again, and said, 'Hobyah! Hobyah! Hobyah! Tear down the hempstalks, eat up the old man and woman, and carry off the little girl!' But little dog Turpie barked so that the Hobyahs ran off; and the old man said, 'Little dog Turpie barks so that I cannot sleep nor slumber, and if I live till morning I will cut off little dog Turpie's head.' So in the morning the old man cut off little dog Turpie's head.

The next night the Hobyahs came and said, 'Hobyah! Hobyah! Hobyah! Tear down the hempstalks, eat up the old man and woman, and carry off the little girl!' And when the Hobyahs found that little dog Turpie's head was off they tore down the hempstalks, ate up the old man and woman, and carried the little girl off in a bag.

And when the Hobyahs came to their home they hung up the bag with the little girl in it, and every Hobyah knocked on top of the bag and said, 'Look me! look me!' and then they went to sleep until the next night, for the Hobyahs slept in the daytime.

The little girl cried a great deal, and a man with a big dog came that way and heard her crying. When he asked her how she came there and she had told him, he put the dog in the bag and took the little girl to his home.

The next night the Hobyahs took down the bag and knocked on the top of it and said, 'Look me! look me!' and when they opened the bag the big dog jumped out and ate them all up; so there are no Hobyahs now.

Although almost forgotten in the United States and England, this gruesome little tale remained well-known in Australia, thanks to an adaptation that appeared in the *Victorian Readers Second Book*, a second-grade reader used in elementary schools in the southeast Australian state of Victoria for decades, from the mid-1920s until the early 1950s. Unsurprisingly, this version took liberties with the story, replacing little dog Turpie with yellow dog Dingo, the house made of hempstalks with a hut made of bark, and leaving out the little girl altogether; instead of simply 'the Hobyahs came' its hobyahs came 'creep, creep, creeping'. There have also been several modern versions in recent years, by far the best of which is that by Simon Stern [1977], which draws its visual imagery of what hobyahs look like from the original illustrations (by John D. Batten) to Jacobs' version but moderates the brutality of the original story towards little dog Turpie.

In the end, it is clear that neither Proudfit's folk tale nor Knatchbull-Hugessen's fairy story has a prior claim to the invention of the name 'hobbit'. Both are in fact red herrings, neither of which had any influence on our story at all, making it overwhelmingly likely that no story called 'The Hobbit' existed until Tolkien himself wrote one. It is however interesting to note that by Proudfit's account he is the first to set down a previously oral tale. Without his having done so, all trace of hobyahs would have vanished, just as whatever story originally underlay Denham's hobbit (see Appendix I) *did* vanish forever. All we can say is that it was almost certainly wholly unlike Tolkien's story; his claim to have invented hobbits as we know them stands unassailed.

NOTES

1 According to Tolkien's disclaimer to Unwin on 4th March 1938 (*Letters* p. 34), he had written 'a short and fairly sane reply for publication' and sent it in with 'this jesting reply', the latter accompanied by a stamped envelope to forward its contents to 'Habit'. The contents of the now-lost shorter version are not known, but presumably it would have covered much the same points is less detailed form (and in less entertainingly playful language).

Tolkien's letter to *The Observer* is reproduced in *Letters* pp. 30–32, but I reproduce it here as it appeared on page 9 of the original newspaper.

2 'accidental homophones . . . [and] not . . . synonyms': That is, having the same sound but not the same meaning and sharing no common origin, such as *weak* (which derives from the Old Norse *veikr*) and *week* (which derives from Old English *wicu*).

3 I.e., *quende*, *noldo*, *orc*, and *naug*, respectively.

4 This passing reference enables us to date Bilbo's contract, reproduced for the first time as the Frontispiece to this volume, as already having been in existence by mid-January 1938.

5 Etymology: that is, research into the origin of a word, tracing it as far back to its original source(s) as possible. At issue is whether Tolkien's claim to have invented the word is accepted by the OED, although apparently it was questioned by no one except Tolkien himself, solely on the basis of the 'Habit' letter thirty-two years before.

6 Slightly different excerpts from this letter appear in both *Letters* pp. 404–405 and Gilliver et al.'s *The Ring of Words* pages 143–144; the first paragraph given here appears only in *Letters* and the final paragraph only in *The Ring of Words*. The latter goes on to give the OED entry as it was actually published in 1976:

> In the tales of J. R. R. Tolkien (1892–1973): one of an imaginary people, a small variety of the human race, that gave themselves this name (meaning 'hole-dweller') but were called by others *halflings*, since they were half the height of normal men.

7 Tolkien is obviously writing from memory here without the original clipping in front of him, since 'Habit' had in fact specified a somewhat earlier date (i.e., circa 1904).

8 The story 'Puss-Cat Mew' can most readily be found in Douglas A. Anderson's collection *Tales Before Tolkien: The Roots of Modern Fantasy* [2003], pages 46–86. It is unfortunate, given Tolkien's early fondness for the tale, that Knatchbull-Hugessen did not inherit any of the writing talent of his illustrious great-aunt. Instead, *Stories for My Children* in general and 'Puss-Cat Mew' in particular exhibit all the characteristics in children's stories that Tolkien came to loathe: a facetious narrator, smug moralizing, jarring anachronisms, and prettified fairies that would have been right at home in 'Tinfang Warble' or 'Goblin Feet'. In short, Knatchbull-Hugessen's best is more or less on par with Tolkien's worst.

However, as Anderson notes (*Tales*, page 47), it is possible to see a few parallels to scenes in *The Hobbit* in its narrative; examples include the hero's fight with three dwarves in which he knocks out the tooth of one and bashes the second in the face, only to be struck down by the third (compare Thorin's fight with the three trolls, in which he knocks out Tom's fang, pokes Bert in the eye, and is then nabbed by William), the hero's acquisition of a glove of invisibility (which he uses to assassinate his various foes, just like the 'practical' burglars of whom Bilbo has heard tell – see page 92), or the hero's sitting down and turning out his pockets for crumbs when lost in the forest after escaping a deadly foe. But none of the parallels is particularly compelling, and all could be the result of simple coincidence. More interesting is that Knatchbull-Hugessen starts with a bit of nursery rhyme:

Puss-cat Mew jumped over a coal;
In her best petticoat burnt a great hole;
Puss-cat Mew shan't have any milk
Till her best petticoat's mended with silk.†

and writes his story to explain the events behind it, a very Tolkienesque enterprise.

Far more important, although not of relevance for *The Hobbit*, is that 'Puss-Cat Mew' marks the first time we know of that Tolkien was exposed to what became one of the signature motifs in his legendarium: the winning of a faerie bride by a worthy mortal (the titular cat of Knatchbull-Hugessen's story is in fact a fairy under an enchantment). This theme appears over and over again in Tolkien's work, from the story of Beren and Lúthien to that of Aragorn and Arwen, from Tuor and Idril or the story of Mithrellas of Lórien and Imrazôr the Númenórean (UT.248) to the nameless temptress of 'Ides Ælfscýne' and her equally nameless victim.

†Baring-Gould gives a somewhat different version of this same poem, which he derives from the work of James O. Halliwell (i.e., either one of the editions of *The Nursery Rhymes of England* [1842ff] or *Popular Rhymes and Nursery Tales* [1849]):

Pussy cat Mole jumped over a coal
And in her best petticoat burnt a great hole
Poor Pussy's weeping, she'll have no more milk
Until her best petticoat's mended with silk.

— *The Annotated Mother Goose* [1962],
page 171; rhyme #300

9 This identification was made as far back as 1988 in the first edition of Douglas Anderson's *The Annotated Hobbit* (page 5); more information appears in the revised edition (DAA.9).

10 Reprinted in Joseph Jacobs, *More English Fairy Tales* [1894], tale number LXIX, pages [118]–124, plus notes page 232. Despite Jacobs' carelessness – he gets both the name of the journal ('American Folk-Lore Journal') and the volume ('iii') in which the story appeared wrong – he reproduced the tale itself word-for-word as it had appeared in Proudfit's version, aside from a few minor changes in punctuation (some inadvertent).

Proudfit himself, in addition to his splendidly hobbit-like name, was a distinguished archeologist and anthropologist, with a special interest in the preColumbian settlements in the Washington DC area. A career bureaucrat, he seems to have drafted the first version of what later became the Antiquities Act when a lawyer working for the McKinley administration [1899] and later as Acting Commissioner of the Bureau of Indian Affairs under Taft intervened decisively to preserve Navaho sites in the Southwest [1909].

Briggs observes (*A Dictionary of Fairies* page 223) that although derived from Scots immigrants, the story as told by Proudfit and Jacobs retains no trace of Scots dialect.

Appendix III

THE *DVERGATAL* (THE DWARF NAMES)

As Tolkien himself noted, 'The dwarf-names, and the wizard's, are from the Elder Edda' (see page 859). In fact, they come from a list known as the *Dvergatal* ('dwarf-tally'). This list appears both in the *Völuspá* [c.1000 AD], the first poem in the collection variously known as the *Elder Edda* or *Poetic Edda*, in what is generally considered to be an interpolation to the original poem,[1] as well as in the *Gylfaginning* ('The Deluding of Gylfi') in Snorri Sturluson's *Prose Edda* (also sometimes known as the *Younger Edda* [1223]). We have it on Tolkien's own authority that he took the dwarf-names from the *Elder Edda* rather than the *Prose Edda*, but close comparison of the two reveals that in fact he consulted both. Accordingly, I give here both versions, starting with the relevant passage from the former. The Old Norse text I have taken from Finnur Jónsson's famous edition (*Sæmundar-Edda* [1905], pages 3–5), which seems to have been considered the definitive standard at the time Tolkien was writing *The Hobbit*. The translation comes from Ursula Dronke's edition (Volume II, pages 9–11) which, while still in progress,[2] sets the modern standard with its exhaustive editorial apparatus and insightful and informative commentary. In the following presentation of the *Völuspá*'s version of the *Dvergatal*, I italicize names of significance for *The Hobbit*; readers of *The Lord of the Rings* will recognize several more names used in the sequel (e.g., Nar), but for the most part I pass over these for our present purpose. I have not attempted to standardize the names, since Tolkien himself sometimes chose a variant from one source, sometime from another, and deliberately altered some of the names he took (e.g. *Dvalin* > *Dwalin* and probably also *Blain* > *Balin*).

9. Þá gengu regin öll á rökstóla, ginnheilög god, ok gættusk of Þat, hvárt skyldi dverga dróttir skepja ór Brimis blódi ok ór *Bláins* leggjum.	9. Then the powers all strode to their thrones of fate, sacrosanct gods, and gave thought to this: whether they should create companies of dwarfs from Brimer's Blood and from *Bláinn's* limbs.

10. Þar vas Módsognir	10. There did Mootsucker
	[Mótsognir]
mæztr of ordinn	become most esteemed
dverga allra,	of all dwarfs,
en *Durinn* annarr;	and Doorward [*Durinn*] next.
Þeir manlíkun	They fashioned many
mörg of gerdu,	figurines,
dverga í jördu,	these dwarfs, out of earth,
sem *Durinn* sagdi.	as Doorward [*Durinn*] told:
11. Nyi ok Nidi,	11. 'New Moon [Nyi] and No
	Moon [Nidi],
Nordri, Sudri,	North [Nordri] and South [Sudri],
Austri, Vestri,	East [Austri] and West [Vestri],
Alþjófr, *Dvalinn*,	All-thief [Althiófr], Dawdler
	[*Dvalinn*],
	<Nær, *Nain*, Nipingr, *Dain*>[3]
Bívurr, *Bávurr*,	Trembler [*Bivorr*], Trumbler
	[*Bávorr*],
Bömburr, *Nori*,	Tubby [*Bomburr*], Shipper [*Nóri*],
Ánn ok Ánarr,	Friend [Án] and Fighter [Ánarr],
Ái, Mjödvitnir.	Old Father [*Ái*], Mead Wolf
	[Miodvitnir],
12. Veigr ok *Gandalfr*,	12. Potion [Veigr] and Sprite Elf
	[*Gandálfr*],
Vindalfr, *Þráinn*,	Wind Elf [Vindálfr], Yearner
	[*Þráinn*],
Þekkr ok *Þorinn*,	Docile [Þekkr] and Darer
	[*Þorinn*],
Þrór, Vitr ok Litr,	Thrive [*Þrór*], Clever [Vitr], and
	Colour [Litr],
Nár ok Nyrádr,	Corpse [Nár] and New Counsellor
	[Nyrádr] –
nú hefk dverga,	now I have the dwarfs
Reginn ok Rádsvidr,	– Power [Reginn] and Plan-wise
	[Rádsvidr] –
rétt of talda.	correctly counted.
13. *Fíli*, *Kíli*,	13. Trunky [*Fíli*], Creeky [*Kíli*]
Fundinn, Náli,	Found [*Fundinn*], Needly [Náli]
Heptifíli,	Handle [Hepti], Drudge [Víli][4]
Hannarr, Svíurr,	Craftsman [Hannarr], Dwindler
	[Svíorr],
	<Billingr, Bruni, Billdr, Buri/Burin/
	Buin>[5]
Frár, Hornbori,	Brilliant [Frár], Horn Borer
	[Hornbori],

Frægr ok Lóni,	Famous [Frægr] and Lagooner [Lóni],
Aurvangr, Jari,	Loam Lea [Aurvangr], Earthy [Iari],
Eikinskjaldi.	*Oakenshield [Eikinskialdi].*
14. Mál es dverga	14. It is time to trace the dwarfs
í *Dvalins* lidi	in Dawdler's [*Dvalins*] troop,
ljóna kindum	for men's progeny,
til Lofars telja,	back to Praiser [Lofars] –
Þeir es sóttu	those dwarfs who sought,
frá Salarsteini	from Mansion's Stone [Salarsteini]
Aurvanga sjöt	the homes of Loam Leas [Aurvanga]
til Jöruvalla.	at Earth Plains [Iorovalla].
15. Þar vas Draupnir	15. There was Dripper [Draupnir]
ok DolgÞrasir,	And Strife Eager [DólgÞrasir],
Hár, Haugspori,	High [Hár], Grave Treader [Haugspori],
Hlévangr, *Glóinn,*	Shelter Field [Hlévangr], Gleamer [*Glói*],
	<Dori, Ori, Dvfr, Andvari>[6]
Skirfir, Virfir,	Joiner [Skirvir], Groiner [Virvir]
Skáfidr, Ái,	Crooked Finn [Skáfidr], Old Father [Ái],
16. Alfr ok Yngvi,	16. Elf [Álfr] and Yngvi [Yngvi],
Eikinskjaldi,	*Oakenshield [Eikinskialdi],*
Fjalarr ok Frosti,	Hider [Fialarr] and Frosty [Frosti],
Finnr ok Ginnarr;	Finn [Finnr] and Potent [Ginnarr].
Þat mun æ uppi	Uplifted in memory
medan öld lifir,	as long as the world lives
langnidja-tal	will be this list
til Lofars hafat.	of Praiser's [Lofars] lineage.'

It will be seen that not all of the names Tolkien took for Thorin & Company come from the *Dvergatal* as it appears in the *Elder Edda*, within the *Völuspá*. Neither Dori nor Ori occurs therein, nor Dain and Nain. Tolkien also prefers the variant *Oin* (given in two manuscripts of the *Prose Edda*) to the *Poetic Edda*'s *Ái*. It is therefore certain that he also consulted the other major source that preserved a somewhat variant text of the *Dvergatal*, Snorri's *Prose Edda*. That Snorri prized the dwarf-list is evident, since he only incorporates roughly half of *Völuspá*'s stanzas within his *Gylfaginning* (twenty-eight out of sixty-two) but takes pains to include all those telling of the creation of the dwarves and listing their names.

Snorri gives the passage as follows; I have taken Jean I. Young's translation (*The Prose Edda* [1954], pages 41–42) as my source. As before, I italicize those names used by Tolkien within *The Hobbit*.

All the gods sought then
their judgment-seats,
powers that are supreme
decided how dwarfs
should be brought into being
from bloody surf
and the legs of *Bláin*.

There many dwarfs
resembling men
they made in earth
as *Durin* said.

And the sibyl gives these as their names:

Nyi, Nidi,
Nordri [North], Sudri [South],
Austri [East], Vestri [West],
Althjóf, *Dvalin* [One-lying-in-a-trace],
Nár [Corpse], *Náin*,
Niping, *Dáin*,
Bifur, *Báfur*,
Bömbör, *Nori*,
Óri [Raging One], Ónar,
Óin, Mjödvitnir [Mead-wolf],
Vig and *Ganndálf* [Sorcerer-elf],
Vinndálf [Wind-elf], *Thorin* [Bold One],
Fili, *Kili*,
Fundin [Found One], Vali,
Thrór, *Thróin*,
Thekk [Pleasant One], Lit, Vit,
Nyr [New One], Nyrád,
Rekk, Rádsvid [Wise-in-advice].

And these too are dwarfs and they live in rocks, but the above-mentioned live in the earth:

Draupnir, Dólgthvari [Battle-stock],
Haur, Hugstari,
Hledjólf, *Glóin*,
Dóri, *Óri*,
Dúf, Andvari,
Heptifili,
Hár [Tall One], Svíar.

The following, however, came from Svarin's grave-mound to Aurvangar in Jöruvellir, and from these have sprung Lovar; their names are

Skirvir, Virvir,
Skafid, Ái,
Álf, Ingi,
Eikinskjaldi [With-oak-shield],
Fal, Frosti,
Fid, Ginnar [Enticer].

—Snorri Sturluson, *Gylfaginning* ('The Deluding of Gylfi'),
The Prose Edda, tr. Jean Young [1954], pages 41–42.

It will be seen that despite a few variations in spelling (e.g., 'Báfur' instead of Bofur and 'Thróin' instead of Thrain), all the dwarf-names appearing in *The Hobbit* appear in some form within Snorri's list.[7] Furthermore, Tolkien uses some names (Dori, Ori; Dain, Nain) and forms (Oin) that only appear in Snorri's version of the *Dvergatal*. Accordingly, we can be certain that Tolkien consulted both versions of this 'asterisk text', and continued to draw on it even after he'd completed *The Hobbit*.

NOTES

1 Cf., for example, Vigfusson & Powell's *Corpus Poeticvm Boreale* [1883] Vol. I pages 192 ('The Mnemonic Verses . . . relating to the Dwarves . . . have been removed as most certainly extraneous, though they had crept even into Snorri's text') and 79, and Dronke *The Poetic Edda, Volume II: Mythological Poems* [1997] pages 38, 92, 122, and especially 67.

2 The two volumes published so far of Dronke's edition – *Volume I: Heroic Poems* [1969] and *Volume II: Mythological Poems* [1997] – cover only nine out of the collection's twenty-nine component poems. The remaining projected two volumes are to cover the Helgi lays and the Sigurd cycle (Volume III)† and the remaining mythological and miscellaneous pieces (Volume IV).

††That is, the portions rewritten by Tolkien as *Volsungakvida En Nyja*; cf. *Letters* p. 452.

3 These four dwarf-names are missing in the Codex Regius [circa 1270], the best manuscript of the *Völuspá*, but they are present in most other manuscripts of the *Dvergatal*, including the Hauksbók [circa 1302–1310, though this material was added circa 1330–1350]; see Dronke, textual notes, page 90, and her notes on the manuscripts, page 61.

4 Dronke reads these as two names, as per the Codex Regius (Hepti, Vili) and Hauksbók (Hefti, Fili); all other manuscripts of the *Dvergatal* give them as a single name (Heptifili); see Dronke, textual notes, page 91.

5 These four names, absent from the Codex Regius, appear in the Hauksbók; see Dronke, textual notes, page 91. *Burin*, a variant of the

fourth name given in one manuscript of Snorri's version (as 'Bvrin'), would later appear in early drafts of *The Lord of the Rings* as the son of Balin, who comes to Rivendell searching for news of his father and thus attends the Council of Elrond; he was later replaced by Gimli son of Gloin (HME VI.395, 397, 400) as the dwarven member of the Fellowship.

6 These four names appear in neither the Codex Regius nor the Hauksbók versions of the *Völuspá*, but only in manuscripts of Snorri's version of the *Dvergatal* (from *Gylfaginning*). In one important manuscript of that work, *Ori* does not appear here but higher up in the list, immediately following Bömburr and Nori in stanza 11, where it replaces the name *Án*. Similarly, in two manuscripts of Snorri's version *Ái* (cf. the last line of stanza 11) is replaced by *Oin*. See Dronke, textual notes, pages 92 and 90.

7 With the possible exception of Balin, unless we accept this as Tolkien's own variant, unattested in the manuscript tradition, of *Blain*, as I have suggested on page 24.

Appendix IV

TOLKIEN'S CORRESPONDENCE WITH ARTHUR RANSOME

The following brief exchange of letters between Tolkien and fellow children's author Arthur Ransome is of interest because it marks one of the few times when Tolkien – whom C. S. Lewis claimed, not quite truthfully, nobody could influence[1] – accepted unsolicited advice on changes he might wish to make to one of his books.

At the time he wrote the letter which initiated the exchange, Ransome was already an established author, having written a book on Poe [1910] and another, controversial at the time, on Wilde [1912] and served as a foreign correspondent to Russia throughout the eventful period before, during, and after the 1917 revolution(s), and had even published a collection of Russian folktales (*Old Peter's Russian Tales* [1916]). He was also, although Tolkien probably did not know this, a childhood friend of E. R. Eddison, an author Tolkien greatly admired and one of his major precursors in the field of modern fantasy.[2] More importantly, in the 1930s Ransome was establishing himself a popular children's author in England through his 'Swallows and Amazons' series;[3] that same year he had won the first Carnegie medal for the outstanding children's book of the previous year for *Pigeon Post*, the sixth book in the series.[4]

The contact point between Tolkien and Ransome was Stanley Unwin, Tolkien's publisher, who had published at least four of Ransome's many books in the early days of George Allen & Unwin: *Six Weeks in Russia* [1919], *The Crisis in Russia* [1921], *Racundra's First Cruise* [1923], and *The Chinese Puzzle* [1927], as well as Ransome's translation of Iury Libedinsky's *A Week* [1923]. Unwin had shown considerable courage in publishing the 1919 book, which opposed the joint British-French-American invasion of Russia launched in that year in an attempt to topple the new Soviet regime and reinstate a Czarist government,[5] and even though Ransome was now being published by the firm of Jonathan Cape they had apparently remained on good terms. Accordingly, Unwin sent Ransome a copy of the newly published *Hobbit* in the fall of 1937, and soon had the following excerpt of a letter from Ransome to pass along to Tolkien:

Letter #1

I sent a copy of THE HOBBIT to Arthur Ransome, who is temporarily laid up at a nursing home in Norwich, and he writes –

> 'THE HOBBIT is my delight; great fun. Thank you
> for sending him. Do the author's new coloured
> pictures include a portrait of Bilbo Baggins?
> Or does he refrain?'

— Stanley Unwin to JRRT, letter of 15th December 1937, quoting Arthur Ransome's letter to Unwin, (unpublished; A&U Archive).

The 'coloured pictures' to which Ransome refers are the four color plates added to the second printing of the Allen & Unwin edition, which according to Hammond's *Descriptive Bibliography* (page 15) was ready for release on 19th December, although the official release date was a month later (25th January 1938). Clearly, Unwin had sent Ransome a copy of the first printing, which lacked any colour illustrations (other than the dust jacket).

As a result of Unwin's sending the book, Ransome also wrote to Tolkien himself, although it is not known whether Ransome sent the following letter to Tolkien directly (e.g., having looked up his address in *Who's Who*) or as an enclosure accompanying the preceding letter to Unwin.

Letter #2

Sir as a humble hobbit fancier (and one certain that your book will be many times reprinted) may I complain that on page 27 when Gandalf calls Bilbo an excitable hobbit the scribe (human no doubt) has written man by mistake? On page 112 Gandalf calls the goblins little boys, but he means it as an insult so that is no doubt all right. But on page 294 Thorin surely is misrepresented. Why his concern for men? Didn't he say more of us, thinking of dwarves elves goblins and dragons and not of a species which to him must have been very unimportant. The error if it is an error is a natural one due again to the humanity of the scribe to whom we must all be grateful for this chronicle. I am sir yours respectfully

Arthur Ransome

— Ransome to JRRT *Signalling from Mars: The Letters of Arthur Ransome*, ed. Hugh Brogan [1997], pages 249–250.

Aside from the complement inherent in receiving such a 'fan letter' from an established fellow author, Tolkien was clearly pleased not just by Ransome's close attention to detail but by his entering into the spirit of the book and maintaining the fiction of Bilbo's authorship and Tolkien's pose as merely the translator of the ancient text (explicitly established in the runes bordering the dust jacket), as his response in kind on 15th December shows.

Letter #3

Dear Mr. Ransome.

I'm sure Mr Baggins would agree in words such as he used to Thorin – to have been fancied by you, that is more than any hobbit could expect. The scribe too is delighted to be honoured by a note in your own hand, and by criticisms showing so close an acquaintance with the text. My reputation will go up with my children – the eldest are now rather to be classed as men, but on their shelves, winnowed of the chaff left behind in the nursery I notice that their 'Ransomes' remain.[8]

You tempt me grievously to a mythological essay; but I restrain myself, since your criticisms are good even though the offending words may be defensible. For the history of the hobbit must come before many who have not before them the exact history of the world into which Mr. Baggins strayed; and it is unwise to raise issues of such import.

I will replace man on p. 27 by the fellow of an earlier recension. On p. 112[9] I agree in feeling that Gandalf's insult was rather silly and not quite up to form – though of course he would regard the undeveloped males of all two legged species as boys. I'm afraid the blemish can hardly be got over by vocabulary, unless oaves would be an improvement? On p.294 I accept of us as a great improvement: men is there just a loose[10] rendering of Thorin's word for 'people' – the language of those days, unlike modern English, had a word that included the Two Kindreds (Elves and Men) and their likenesses and mockeries. 'Of us' exactly represents this: for Thorin certainly included 'humans' in his comment, for Elves and Dwarves were mightily concerned with them, and well aware that it was their fate to usurp the world; but he was not at that moment thinking chiefly of *Men* (with a capital). The ancient English, of course, would have felt no hesitation in using 'man' of elf, dwarf, goblin, troll, wizard or what not, since they were inclined to make Adam the father of them all . . .

I must apologize for writing at such length. I hope you are well enough to endure it or forgive it, trusting that your address does not indicate a serious illness. I hope the enclosed list of other minor errors will serve to correct your copy – but, *if* there is a reprint (sales are not very great) I hope you will allow me to send you a corrected copy.

Yours very respectfully . . .

Ransome replied at once, making clear that whatever mythological premise underlay the word-choice it was for him a matter of decorum, what Tolkien himself would have called a slight flaw in the sub-creation that sparked a momentary loss of secondary belief, that had motivated him to voice the objection.

Letter #4

To J. R. R. Tolkien

Dec. 17 1937 Norwich

Dear Professor Tolkien,

Thank you for your most interesting letter.

BUT: I did not intend any criticism whatever of the 'boys' of p. 112. I mentioned it only to illustrate (by contrast) my slight discomfort due to 'man' on p. 27. And that discomfort had no relation to mythology. I had very much admired the delicate skill with which you had made Mr. Baggins so Hobbitty (forgive the word) and the word 'man' on p. 27 seemed a leak or a tear in the veil, undoing just a little of what you had done. That was all. I thought the word had slipped from the scribe's pen by accident. The Hobbitness of Mr. Baggins seems to me one of the most difficult and triumphant achievements of the book . . . And so valuable that, regardless of mythology, it seemed worth while to complain about the one word which in one place, just for a moment, raised a faint doubt.

I have copied your corrections into the book. Thank you for letting me have them.

I had an operation nearly a month ago[11] and hope to get out quite soon now. *The Hobbit* has done a great deal to turn these weeks into a pleasure. And as for new editions . . . there will be dozens of them: of that I have no doubt whatever.

Yours sincerely,

Arthur Ransome

— *Signalling from Mars*, page 251.

With that, the brief correspondence between the two men seems to have ceased – not, however, without having left its mark upon *The Hobbit*. The points Ransome had raised Tolkien at once passed along to Allen & Unwin, along with his proposed solutions:

Letter #5

P.S. . . . Mr Arthur Ransome objects to *man* on p. 27 (line 7 from end). Read *fellow* as in earlier recension? He also objects to *more men* on p. 294 l[ine] 11. Read *more of us*? *Men* with a capital is, I think, used in text when 'human kind' are specifically intended; and *man*, *men* with a minuscule are occasionally and loosely used as 'adult male' and 'people'. But perhaps, although this can be mythologically defended (and is according to Anglo-Saxon usage!), it may be as well to avoid raising mythological issues outside the story. Mr Ransome also seems not to like Gandalf's use of *boys* on p. 112 (lines 11, 13). But, though I agree that his insult was rather silly and not quite up to form, I do not think anything can be done about it now. Unless *oaves* would do? JRRT.

—JRRT to A & U, 19th December 1937; *Letters* p. 28.

Of the three specific 'cruxes' raised by Ransome, it is interesting to note that Tolkien responded differently to each. The first, 'excitable little man', was indeed changed, not to Ransome's proposed 'excitable little *hobbit*', but rather to 'excitable little *fellow*' (DAA.47–48). That is, he agrees with Ransome's criticism that the phrasing of the text needs changing but comes up with his own solution; the 'earlier recension' is of course a fiction referring to the framing device and Tolkien's pose as translator, as comparison to the actual manuscript text (pp. 8 & 39) of this passage shows. The second, 'naughty little boys' (DAA.151–152), was ultimately allowed to stand, since neither Ransome nor Tolkien could find a satisfactory replacement. Tolkien's proposed change of 'boys' to *oaves* (i.e., the plural of *oaf*) would have been extremely problematic, as he would have discovered when he investigated the etymology of the word, because *oaves* (more usually spelled *oafs*; earlier *ouphes, aufs*) in fact derives from *elves* and ties in with the old belief that a physically or mentally disabled child (e.g., one with Down's Syndrome) was a changeling or 'elf' (oaf). Finally, for the third 'crux', the suggested replacement of 'If more men . . . it would be a merrier world' with 'If more *of us* . . .', Tolkien adopted Ransome's correction directly (DAA.348), noting that it was 'a great improvement'.

Beyond these specific corrections, Ransome's objection seems to have led Tolkien to refine his subsequent usage. Even though he had explained some of the concepts underlying his use of the generic *men* (more or less human-shaped creature) as opposed to the specific *Men* (human), Ransome had remained dubious, and Tolkien clearly came to agree with him and henceforth tended to avoid that generic usage, especially in the new book he was just starting, *The Lord of the Rings*. It is interesting to note that in his letter to Ransome, written just days before he began writing *The Lord of the Rings*, Tolkien already lists wizards as a separate race distinct from human men. As for the 'ancient English' belief that all such beings were descendents of Adam, one of his primary sources here was no doubt the Beowulf-poet, who describes Grendel as a descendent of Cain (line 107a). Finally, the term 'the Two Kindreds' for the elder and younger children of Ilúvatar, Elves and Men, seems to have arisen in a revision to the 1930 *Quenta* (see HME IV.154 & 156); it was soon adopted into the 'Earliest Annals of Beleriand' (HME IV.306), 'The Fall of Númenor' (HME V.18), and the 1937 *Quenta Silmarillion* (e.g. HME V.302). Its presence here, in the context of *The Hobbit*, shows that already in the months immediately following the latter's publication he was explicating details from it in terms of his legendarium and was concerned to show that they were in harmony, a process that reached its culmination with *The Lord of the Rings*.

Finally, the list of 'other minor errors' Tolkien sent Ransome was probably the same ones he submitted to Allen & Unwin the following day (16th December 1937), too late for inclusion in the second printing; cf. Hammond's *Descriptive Bibliography* pages 4, 7, & 15. However, researcher Lyn Mellone has discovered that Ransome's copy of *The Hobbit*, now in the Ransome Room of the Museum of Lakeland Life in Kendal, Cumbria in the northwest corner of England, does indeed have the corrections he received from Tolkien carefully marked in the appropriate places in ink, with those proposed by Ransome (e.g. 'excitable little hobbit') in pencil.[8] Some of these typographical corrections were fixed in the third and fourth printings (*Descriptive Bibliography*, page 16), but most had to wait until the fifth printing (the second edition) of 1951. Although Ransome was still alive (and in fact did not die until 1967, at the age of eighty-two), by this time Tolkien's promise to send him 'a corrected copy' seems to have been forgotten. However, in their entry on Ransome in *The J.R.R. Tolkien Companion and Guide* (Vol. II, pages 813–814), Scull & Hammond note that Tolkien did arrange to have Ransome sent an advance copy of *The Lord of the Rings* and that the recipient 'read it enthusiastically'.

NOTES

1 'No one ever influenced Tolkien – you might as well try to influence a bandersnatch' (CSL to Charles Moorman, 15th May 1959; *Letters of C. S. Lewis*, ed. Walter Hooper [1988], page 481). However, not only did Tolkien change the wording in *The Lord of the Rings* at one point when Rhona Beare questioned the implications of one phrase (see *Letters* pp. 277 & 279), but Lewis himself had a significant impact on 'The Lay of Leithian' (see HME III.315–329). Perhaps significantly, Tolkien tended not to adopt Lewis's suggestions but instead recast passages that Lewis had criticized. It seems fair to conclude, therefore, that he gladly corrected errors brought to his attention but often changed things in his own way rather than directly accepting others' suggestions.

2 For more on Ransome and 'Ric' (Eric Rucker) Eddison, see Ransome's autobiography (*The Autobiography of Arthur Ransome*, ed. Rupert Hart-Davis [1976], pages 37–40) and also the biography by Hugh Brogan† (*The Life of Arthur Ransome* [1984], pages 10–11). Tolkien admired Eddison's *The Worm Ouroboros* [1922] (except for the nomenclature, which is markedly eccentric), but strongly objected to the philosophy behind Eddison's later 'Zimiamvian' books (*Mistress of Mistresses* [1935], *A Fish Dinner in Memison* [1941], and the unfinished *The Mezentian Gate* [1958]) – cf. JRRT to Caroline Whitman Everett, letter of 24th June 1957; *Letters* p. 258. Tolkien and Eddison actually met at least twice when ERE attended Inklings meetings at Lewis's invitation in 1943 and 1944, at which he read from his later works.

†Brogan himself was a correspondent of JRRT when young; see *Letters* pp. 129, 131, 132, 185–186, 224, 225–226, & 230.

3 The books in the 'Swallows and Amazons' series are as follows: #1. *Swallows and Amazons* [1930], #2. *Swallowdale* [1931], #3. *Peter Duck* [1932], #4. *Winter Holiday* [1933], #5. *Coot Club* [1934], #6. *Pigeon Post* [1936], #7. *We Didn't Mean to Go to Sea* [1937], #8. *Secret Water* [1939], #9. *The Big Six* [1940], #10. *Missee Lee* [1941], #11. *The Picts and the Martyrs* [1943], #12. *Great Northern?* [1947], #13. *Coots in the North* [unfinished; posthumously publ. 1988].

4 Subsequent Carnegie medal winners include such famous books as Mary Norton's *The Borrowers* [1952], C. S. Lewis's *The Last Battle* [1956], Richard Adams' *Watership Down* [1972], and Philip Pullman's *His Dark Materials*, Book I [1995].†

†This last is better known in the United States as *The Golden Compass*.

5 See Ransome's autobiography, pages 268–269, and also Unwin's autobiography, *The Truth About a Publisher* [1960], pages 165–166, for the two men's perspectives.

6 Men rather than children: John Tolkien was now twenty years old, and Michael seventeen. Confirmation of Tolkien's statement that

the 'Swallows and Amazons' books were popular in the Tolkien household and that his sons retained their Ransomes even after they were grown was discovered by researcher Lyn Mellone in the summer of 2006. According to her posting on TarBoard, the online Arthur Ransome discussion board (http://cres1.lancs.ac.uk/%7eesarie/tarboard/messages/23986.htm), Adam Tolkien, Christopher's younger son, responded to her queries by affirming the popularity of the books among Tolkien's children, stating that not only did 'Christopher [recall] specifically *Swallows and Amazons* and *Missee Lee*' – which, as Mellone notes, was published four years after *The Hobbit* and thus testifies to continued interest on their part – but that he had in turn passed them along to his own son, Adam, who had enjoyed them very much in his turn.

7 Ransome's operation: he had undergone surgery for a hernia (Brogan, *Signalling from Mars*, page 249). The 'nursing home' in which he was staying, by the way, was not a euphemism for an old folks' home but rather a convalescent home for those recovering from long-term illness or major surgery.

8 See Mellone's account, detailing each annotation, at the online Ransome discussion list TarBoard, specifically http://cres1.lancs.ac.uk/%7eesarie/tarboard/messages/23986.ht.

INDEX

This index does not attempt to list every appearance of every name – something which would extend it to interminable length – but rather to enable readers to find specific passages within this work, supplementing the many cross-references within the text itself. An asterisk by a name indicates a member of Thorin & Company.